MW00852296

HOW PRIME MINISTERS DECIDE

HOW
PRIME MINISTERS
DECIDE

Neerja Chowdhury

ALEPH

ALEPH BOOK COMPANY
An independent publishing firm
promoted by *Rupa Publications India*

First published in India in 2023
by Aleph Book Company
7/16 Ansari Road, Daryaganj
New Delhi 110 002

ISBN: 978-93-90652-45-7

5 7 9 10 8 6 4

Printed in India.

To the two men in my life
Arun
and
Nakul

ʃ

CONTENTS

INTRODUCTION

The top is always lonely. It is lonely for the CEO of a company. It is lonelier for the head of any government, the effect of one misstep lingering for generations. But lonelier still is the person at the top in India, for all the power prime ministers wield and the swarms of adulating hangers-on who surround them. The culture of 'ji huzoori' (compliance from below and deference to those above) isolates the prime minister even more.

As I looked at how prime ministers take decisions, I found different prime ministers expressing this sense of loneliness in their own way. 'The final responsibility is yours...that can be awesome,' India's controversial prime minister V. P. Singh said to me while undergoing dialysis at Apollo Hospital in 1999. 'The higher the responsibility, the lesser the freedom. You cannot say I am going for golf, for a party, or going away for a week to see my family. At the top, the leaders are denied these human things. It is a loneliness in a very emotional and personal sense.' The indomitable Chandra Shekhar, prime minister for five months in 1990–91, and constantly surrounded by courtiers, echoed what VP had said. 'Yes, the top is lonely...in the sense you have to be there when nobody else is there, particularly when "crucial decisions" have to be taken.'

'The space to yourself is just not there, milne walon ka taanta laga rehta hai (there is a constant stream of people wanting to meet you),' said I. K. Gujral, prime minister from 1997–98, 'our feudal attitude to darshan being what it is.'

The loneliness increases as a politician nears the summit and this was also expressed by more than one prime minister. In one of the many poems he had penned, Atal Bihari Vajpayee wrote poignantly, 'The higher you go, the more lonely you are.' 'My biggest mistake was joining politics,' he added, expressing the pain of being at the pinnacle. 'It has brought a strange kind of void to my life.'

The lack of friends at the top becomes more noticeable when things go wrong. When the scams tumbled out against Manmohan Singh's government in his second term in office, even his friends and followers turned their faces away from him. He would be seen in parliament, his eyes expressionless, walking from one house to the other. Rajiv Gandhi, who had enjoyed an unprecedented majority of 414 members of parliament (MPs) in the eighth Lok Sabha, had few he could turn to as he tried to save his beleaguered government in 1988–89.

A prime minister can trust only a minuscule number of people, if any. All who come to see her or him mostly come with a motive. Even the best of them come to ask for something. 'The moment someone enters my room,' Indira Gandhi had once said, 'I know exactly what they will ask for.' She had learnt this instinctively over the years.

India's first prime minister Jawaharlal Nehru was one of those who put to good use the solitude that high office brought. During the freedom movement, he turned to reading and writing in his prison cell. During long stints he spent there, he wrote prolifically; his writings included his autobiography and the monumental *The Discovery of India*. But Nehru's loneliness was palpable in the last days he spent in Dehradun in May 1964. He sat under a camphor tree, mostly silent. He returned to Delhi on 26 May. In less than twenty-four hours, Nehru had moved on—into a universe unknown. By his bedside lay a book of poems by Robert Frost with its famous lines: 'The woods are lovely, dark and deep,/ But I have promises to keep,/ And miles to go before I sleep....'

Whether they want it or not, the highest office distances the leader from people. Some prime ministers have cultivated aloofness to create an aura of invincibility. Indira Gandhi was naturally reserved, but she could become unapproachable; it put her on a pedestal, and had people guessing what she was about. Narendra Modi pitched the prime minister's 'lonely' position as an asset to create political capital. It helped him portray himself as a strong leader, able to stand aloof, dedicated to the nation, reinforcing a 'main hoon na' (I am there for you) image. His PR machinery constantly put out photos which emphasized this image of being alone. There was Modi alone at Rudra Cave in Kedarnath, draped in a saffron shawl, meditating for seventeen hours, at the end of campaigning in the 2019 election. There was Modi standing alone in front of the 182-metre-high statue of Sardar Patel, or seated alone in an empty railway coach in South Africa looking into the future. Or Modi coming down the steps from Air India One, with no officials, or ministers seen behind him. Even walking alone in an underpass he had inaugurated.

■

There is no dearth of people to take care of the prime minister's slightest need, officials to spell out the pros and cons of a decision, intelligence agencies to provide the inputs needed. The prime minister can tap experts for background information to help with policy decisions. And now there is the latest communication technology to transmit the prime minister's word to all corners of the world within seconds. There is the cabinet to take decisions in a system where the prime minister is supposed to be the first amongst equals—but in practice it is much more than that.

Over the years, I asked myself why the final responsibility seemed to rest even more with an Indian prime minister. Is it because we are still a largely feudal society? Or because a democratic set-up was superimposed on a feudal order and the prime minister is expected to be the mai–baap (mother–father)? Or because our democracy has not yet developed a strong institutional framework to make the responsibility truly collective? Or is it also because we are an entrenched patriarchy, ultimately turning to a father figure to take the decisions for us? It compelled Indira Gandhi to become 'the only man in the cabinet', tougher than her male colleagues—provoking US Secretary of State Henry Kissinger to wish that the American establishment had a man who was as strong as Indira Gandhi!

There are no simple answers to these questions.

I chose to start the book with the prime ministers' loneliness because they are as human as anyone else, and do not function in the abstract. But history captures mostly events, rarely the processes, the dilemmas, the emotional upheavals in the midst of which a prime minister has to make decisions.

■

While the top is a lonely place, it is crowded with competing pressures. One of the things that fascinated me as I covered national politics, writing about prime ministers (PMs), prime ministers' offices (PMOs), political parties, and parliament for over forty years as a journalist, was how seemingly straightforward decisions by prime ministers were not so simple. To an ordinary person, it appears that the head of government can do whatever s/he wants. But the real story is usually very different—enmeshed as it is in manoeuvrings, intrigues, agendas—even with powerful PMs like Indira Gandhi and Narendra Modi.

There was sometimes hubris, always craftiness, occasionally prejudice, but also flashes of wisdom at play. Above all, there was the prime minister's compelling need to survive—and triumph politically.

The erudite ninth prime minister of India, P. V. Narasimha Rao, summed up decision-making at the top as a 'web of larger interests, petty approaches and genuine views'. This 'web' of vested interests Rao talked about included powerful lobbies at work, at home and abroad. There was caste and community to placate in a highly diverse and multi-faith nation like India; the machinations of opponents to pre-empt; and pressure from foreign capitals to deflect.

It takes skill and experience and ruthlessness—and above all sheer luck—for individuals to succeed in Indian politics. The survival instinct was very strong in all those who reached the top.

Decision-making, it goes without saying, is not divorced from the historical context in which it takes place. Nor does the PM inherit a clean slate when s/he takes over.

In the following pages, I have tried to capture some of the pulls and pressures prime ministers were subjected to, and the behind-the-scenes, turbulent, often suspenseful drama which accompanied the most significant decisions taken by some of India's prime ministers.

I focus on major decisions made by six prime ministers—Indira Gandhi, Rajiv Gandhi, V. P. Singh, P. V. Narasimha Rao, Atal Bihari Vajpayee, and Manmohan Singh. I decided to write on prime ministers who were able to rule for a full five-year term—with some exceptions. I left out Jawaharlal Nehru, though he ruled India for seventeen of its most formative and challenging years. Though a colossus who created the edifice of modern India, I decided to omit Nehru not because it has become fashionable to rubbish him, but because my own consciousness of Indian politics started after his reign was over.

V. P. Singh I have included, even though his government lasted only eleven months. He features because his premiership changed the politics of North India for all time to come; and he dealt a body blow to the Indian National Congress—which won India its freedom—from which the party has yet to recover.

The prime minister difficult to leave out was Narendra Modi—he loomed so large in the country's consciousness. After a great deal of deliberation, I decided not to scrutinize a specific decision made by him, as I have done with six other prime ministers, though more than one major decision Modi took, including the demonetization of much of the nation's currency, and the dismantling of Article 370, deserved to be put under the microscope. However, when I began researching the way Modi took his controversial decisions as prime minister, I soon realized the difficulties I would run into. For a start, as the incumbent prime minister at the time the book was being written, his premiership was still a work in progress. (At the time of writing he was getting ready to make a bid for a third term in office.) I did not have the advantage of hindsight to assist me, as in the case of the other prime ministers. More important, in India, few with proximity to the PM, privy to the goings-on at the highest level of government, talk openly and candidly about what really went on behind the scenes, while the prime minister is still in office. Those who had talked to me about the other prime ministers did so after the PM they were close to had demitted office. In the case of an incumbent PM, there was also the risk of being overtaken by events and becoming dated.

I refer to Modi's decision-making style, totally different from that of any other prime minister, in the epilogue of the book, in the hope that I will be able to do a more detailed study on him at a future date. For the Modi phenomenon represents a complete break from the past, and a paradigm shift in Indian politics.

■

I cut my teeth in journalism working for the Bombay-based newsweekly *Himmat*, which resisted the Emergency (1975–77), when Indira Gandhi was all powerful. In the years that followed, working at *The Statesman* as its civil rights correspondent, as political editor of the *Economic Times*, then in the *Indian Express* as political editor for ten years, and later as a freelance journalist writing on politics, I got a ringside view of all the country's prime ministers—and the men and women who ran India—from Indira Gandhi to Narendra Modi.

Before I get to the prime ministerial decisions I have looked at, a quick review of all the prime ministers who ruled India, and the powers they wielded, would help to provide some context to the reader. In the seventy-five years since Independence, India has had fourteen* prime ministers. Their number would be fifteen, if Gulzari Lal Nanda was included in the list. A Punjabi Khatri from Sialkot (now in Pakistan) he took over as interim PM twice, once after the death of Jawaharlal Nehru in 1964, and then again after Lal Bahadur Shastri died in 1966. On both occasions, he ruled the country for thirteen days, establishing the convention of an interim PM taking charge if the incumbent died in harness. It is this norm which Pranab Mukherjee cited when Indira Gandhi was assassinated in 1984, for which he was penalized politically. Nanda is also remembered for converting the 27.5-hectare mansion, Teen Murti House, where Nehru had lived, into a memorial for him. He took the decision before Shastri could move in; otherwise, it would have become the official residence of the prime minister.

The story of India's prime ministers starts with the aristocratic and refined Jawaharlal Nehru, with his trademark red rose in the achkan, adored by the Indian masses. As the country's first and longest serving prime minister who steered the country from 1947 to 1964, he built the institutions which laid the foundations for modern India—the Election Commission, Planning Commission, Indian Institutes of Technology (IIT), Indian Institutes of Management (IIM), All India Institutes of Medical Sciences (AIIMS), premier institutes of scientific learning like the Department of Atomic Energy (DAE), Bhabha Atomic Research Centre (BARC), Indian Space Research Organisation (ISRO), Council of Scientific and Industrial Research (CSIR), and so many more.

Nehru was chosen by Mahatma Gandhi—not by the Congress Party—to become the Congress president in 1946, and then naturally go on to become the prime minister in 1947. He was chosen, given his dynamism and hold over the masses, his appeal to the youth, his acceptance amongst the minorities and his ability to negotiate with the British. He wanted

---

*Various sources count the number of prime ministers differently. The PM India website lists fifteen, including Gulzari Lal Nanda, but this book follows the more popular convention of counting only duly elected prime ministers—fourteen individuals have held that office to date. Of these, five—Jawaharlal Nehru, Indira Gandhi, Manmohan Singh, and Narendra Modi—have held office for more than one term. There are also several individuals who did not complete a full term.

Indians to be secular and acquire a scientific temper.

Lal Bahadur Shastri, who succeeded Nehru as prime minister in 1964, was not a 'Shastri' to begin with. His name was Lal Bahadur Verma and he was from a Kayastha family. He added Shastri to his name when the degree of 'Shastri' was conferred on him following his graduation from the Mahatma Gandhi Kashi Vidyapith in Varanasi. As a class ten student, Lal Bahadur had gone to hear Mahatma Gandhi and Madan Mohan Malaviya speak in Varanasi. The next day he walked across to the local Congress office and announced he was now going to work full-time for the country's freedom. His family—he was the son of a poor schoolteacher who had died when Lal Bahadur was eighteen months old—was livid. But it was his mother's words that were to stay with him all his life: 'Think deeply about the right course,' she told him, and '...hold firmly to your decision.'

Nehru had given enough indications during his lifetime that he viewed the diminutive and low-profile Shastri as his successor. Thinking he would be an effete PM—he was often called the 'little sparrow'. When Pakistan attacked India in 1965, he turned the tables on them and attacked Sialkot and Lahore—and won the war. The 'homespun' prime minister became a national hero, coining the popular slogan 'Jai Jawan, Jai Kisan'. He signed a peace agreement with Pakistan in Tashkent, and within hours of it, he had died, his premiership lasting only nineteen months.

Indira Gandhi, who took over as prime minister after Shastri's death in 1966, was the first and only woman prime minister to rule the country. Called a 'goongi gudiya' (dumb doll) by socialist ideologue Ram Manohar Lohia, 'this chokri' (chit of a girl) by her rival Morarji Desai, and 'the old witch' by US president Richard Nixon, Indira Gandhi came to be hailed as 'Durga'. She helped hive off a new nation of Bangladesh from Pakistan in 1971, changing geopolitical realities, displaying phenomenal courage, a sense of political timing, and an ability to take risks. But she also imposed the Emergency in 1975 abridging citizens' fundamental rights—only to call for elections herself in 1977. She was killed by her own security guards in 1984 for ordering the army inside the Golden Temple in Amritsar, to flush out Sikh militants.

Morarji Desai became prime minister in March 1977 when he was eighty-one. Also the son of a schoolteacher, Desai came from an Anavil Brahmin family of Gujarat. The upright but inflexible Desai, an avowed Gandhian, headed the Janata Party government in 1977, the first non-Congress government to come to power at the centre. Its significance lay in its dismantling the authoritarian regime of Indira Gandhi. His government lasted for two and half years but fell under the weight of its contradictions and the mega-sized egos of its leaders.

Charan Singh was the first peasant prime minister, representing the rise of the middle castes in India; this surge had led to the formation of nine state governments from Patna to Amritsar in 1967. Though from Uttar Pradesh, Singh had a mass following in the northern plains. But paradoxically he was the only prime minister who could not prove his majority on the floor of the house. Indira Gandhi had propped him up as prime minister on 28 July 1979 to bring down the government of Morarji Desai, only to withdraw support within twenty-three days. She came back to power in January 1980.

The charming, tech-savvy, forty-year-old Rajiv Gandhi was the youngest prime minister India has had—and represented a break from the past. He heralded the arrival of a new generation of leaders on the Indian scene. The easy-going older son of Indira Gandhi was a pilot in Indian Airlines when his younger brother, Sanjay—who was being groomed by Indira Gandhi as her successor—died in an air crash. A reluctant Rajiv was quoted saying he had entered politics because 'Mummy has to be helped somehow.' He wanted to fashion a new and modern India and prepare the country for the twenty-first century. He lowered the voting age to eighteen, brought about a telecom revolution in India, encouraged computerization, took public call offices (PCOs) down to the villages, and set up technology missions. But it was the old India, dominated by caste and community which he did not fully comprehend, that proved to be his undoing.

Vishwanath Pratap Singh was the raja of a small princely state near Allahabad (Prayagraj), but turned out to be a royal and a subaltern rolled into one. Finance minister in Rajiv Gandhi's government, he broke with Rajiv on the issue of corruption—specifically the alleged payment of illegal kickbacks to facilitate the purchase of 155 mm howitzer guns from the Swedish armaments company, Bofors. VP went on to fashion an alternative to the dominant Congress. He brought together virtually the entire phalanx of anti-Congress forces in the country, of the Right, Left, and Centre, as well as the regional parties, all within two and a half years—and defeated Rajiv at the hustings in 1989. He replaced Rajiv as prime minister.

The 'PM India remained deprived of'—that was the way Chandra Shekhar was often described. After V. P. Singh, he headed a government led by a breakaway rump of the Janata Dal, supported by the more dominant Congress led by Rajiv Gandhi.

A leading figure of the Praja Socialist Party in the 1950s and 60s, Chandra Shekhar joined the Congress and was hailed as a 'Young Turk' during Indira Gandhi's premiership for espousing the socialist cause. But he parted company with her during the Emergency and was put in jail. Though a pragmatist, he remained consistently opposed to the liberalization of the economy. He led a yatra from Kanyakumari to Delhi in 1983, walking 4,260 kilometres in his chappals to galvanize the Opposition against the Congress. Women would wait for him by the wayside with their infants, asking him to name them after one of the heroes of the freedom struggle.

As PM, he came close to resolving the Ayodhya tangle through negotiations between the Hindus and Muslims. But before the agreement could be finalized, the Congress pulled the plug on his government, which lasted only seven months—and general elections were announced for May 1991.

With P. V. Narasimha Rao taking over in June 1991, power devolved south of the Vindhyas for the first time in the history of the Indian republic. Rao was all set to be a priest when destiny willed otherwise. After Rajiv Gandhi's assassination in May 1991, he became prime minister. An underrated PM, the scholarly Rao liberalized the economy, opening it to foreign capital, and calmed the situations inflamed by caste and religious conflict in Punjab and Jammu and Kashmir. Experienced and far-sighted, but with the 'charisma of a dead fish'—he was not what mass leaders are made of. Yet he was the only non-Nehru–Gandhi Congress PM to last his full term till 1996.

The importance of Atal Bihari Vajpayee, who succeeded Narasimha Rao in May 1996, lay in who he was—a moderate who managed to survive in the ecosystem of the right-wing, pro-Hindu Rashtriya Swayamsevak Sangh (RSS). Vajpayee came from a poor Kanyakubja Brahmin family in the princely state of Gwalior. His grandfather had migrated from Bateshwar in UP to Gwalior in Madhya Pradesh. His father was a schoolteacher, and also a poet—an environment that gave birth to the poet in Vajpayee. Over the years, he acquired a felicity with words, with legendary pauses punctuating his speeches. This was to be his passport to success in politics. His first government lasted only thirteen days in 1996. In 1998, Vajpayee formed a government at the head of a twenty-four-party coalition called the National Democratic Alliance (NDA). This time, his government lasted thirteen months. It fell again in April 1999, when Vajpayee lost a no-confidence motion by one vote. But he came back to power for a third time in the general elections in 1999, and remained prime minister till 2004.

Haradanahalli Doddegowda Deve Gowda was the first Shudra to become prime minister of India in 1996. As a schoolboy, Deve Gowda used to deliver milk to Brahmin families in the village, and they would sprinkle water on it before taking it inside. His caste, the Vokkaligas, an agrarian community, are categorized as a 'backward class'. His father could afford to send only one child to school out of the four he had, and chose Deve Gowda, who became a first-generation literate in his family—and became a civil engineer. Even today, people in his home district of Hassan remember the culverts he built. In 1996, Deve Gowda headed the United Front (UF) government, a coalition of the Janata Dal and regional parties, propped up in power by the Congress (just as it had supported Chandra Shekhar for a few months in 1990). It was popularly known as a 'government of chief ministers'—these were chief ministers (CMs) who headed regional parties and called the shots in the UF government. With Deve Gowda's elevation, power had moved yet again to the South.

One of Inder Kumar Gujral's early memories as a boy of ten was seeing Jawaharlal Nehru 'riding a white stallion through the crowded streets of Lahore'. His parents had taken him to the historic session of the Congress in Lahore in 1929, where Nehru took over as Congress president and declared purna swaraj (complete independence) as the party's goal. It deeply affected Gujral and his parents who were Punjabi Khatris from Jhelum. Gujral became a communist during his college years. After the family came across to the Indian side during the country's partition, he joined the Congress. He became a prominent member of Indira Gandhi's 'kitchen cabinet' in 1966, then a diplomat, who rose to become foreign minister in the V. P. Singh government and under Deve Gowda—and finally the prime minister of India in 1997 replacing Deve Gowda. The 'Gujral doctrine' he espoused envisaged improved relations with India's neighbours.

The super-cautious, technocrat prime minister, Manmohan Singh, succeeded Vajpayee in 2004, in an unexpected turn of events. Sonia Gandhi was poised to take over as PM, and then decided to step back. She anointed Manmohan Singh instead. A Sikh, he was the first from a minority community to head the national government. Singh also rose from humble beginnings. As a child, he had to walk a long distance to school. He used to study under the dim light of a kerosene lamp—but went on to become an internationally recognized economist. 'I am what I am,' he used to say, 'because of education.' He remained prime minister for ten years at the head of the United Progressive Alliance (UPA), a coalition led by the Congress.

The rise of Narendra Modi in 2014 ended the coalition era in India that had spanned the premierships of V. P. Singh, Chandra Shekhar, Deve Gowda, I. K. Gujral, Atal Bihari Vajpayee, and Manmohan Singh. Even P. V. Narasimha Rao led a minority government, to begin with, and had to rely on the support of smaller parties. The coalition era lasted for a quarter of a century, from 1989 to 2014. These governments represented the transition that was taking place in Indian politics. The Congress, which till 1989 had ruled the country for thirty-nine years out of the forty-two years since Independence, was in decline. Other political forces were moving into the space vacated by it. The BJP was on the rise, but was unable to replace the Congress on its own. Between 1998 and 2014, a fragmented polity firmed up around a two-coalition (not two-party) arrangement. The Congress led one grouping, the United Progressive Alliance (UPA) and the BJP, the National Democratic Alliance (NDA). Until Narendra Modi came to power.

Modi took over as prime minister in May 2014 with the BJP winning a majority on its own for the first time in the country's history. He was re-elected to power with an increased tally (303 seats, up from 282) in 2019. A polarizing PM, Narendra Modi shaped a 'new BJP', different from the party under Vajpayee and L. K. Advani. He pursued the BJP's core, pro-Hindu agenda and widened the social base of the party. With Modi's rise, power was devolving to groups which had been on the periphery of the country's power structure. A chaiwallah in his youth, a Ghanchi (oil miller) by caste, Modi was the second OBC (Other Backward Classes), after Deve Gowda, to become prime minister of India. But he was different from all his predecessors.

■

Once they occupy the hot seat, prime ministers are supposed to represent the whole country, irrespective of the region, caste, or community they come from. It is, however, instructive to look at the social background of India's prime ministers to see if this tells us anything about the deepening, or otherwise, of India's democracy. Representing different backgrounds— elite and rustic, North and South, minority and majority, Brahmin and backward, man and woman—India's prime ministers have symbolized India's incredible diversity.

Six of the fifteen prime ministers were Brahmins, at the top of the social ladder (Jawaharlal Nehru, Indira Gandhi, Morarji Desai, Rajiv Gandhi, though he was a half Brahmin from the mother's side, Narasimha Rao, and Atal Bihari Vajpayee). V. P. Singh and Chandra Shekhar were Rajputs, Shastri a Kayastha, and Gulzari Lal Nanda and I. K. Gujral were Punjabi Khatris—all upper castes.

Two were from politically powerful peasant castes (and Shudras)— Charan Singh, a Jat, and H. D. Deve Gowda, a Vokkaliga. Though a powerful and prosperous farmers' leader, Charan Singh's angst about what it meant not to belong to an upper caste was unconcealed. 'I am...born in a Jat family. A Muslim I can become.... But I cannot become a Brahmin...a Rajput...nor...a Vaishya,' he had said in 1977. 'And if I want to become a Harijan, even that is impossible, because the Constitution does not permit it.'

There has been no Dalit, or Muslim, or tribal, or Christian—as yet—to sit in the PM's chair. But clearly, communities which were on the margins of society have been moving centre stage and ascending the power structure.

While three of the Indian PMs were from Punjab (Gulzari Lal Nanda, Inder Kumar Gujral, and Manmohan Singh) in the North, two from Gujarat (Morarji Desai and Narendra Modi) in the West, two from the South (H. D. Deve Gowda and P. V. Narasimha Rao), there has been none from eastern or Northeast India so far. As many as eight out of the fourteen PMs were from Uttar Pradesh—Nehru, Shastri, Indira Gandhi, Charan Singh, Rajiv Gandhi, V. P. Singh, Chandra Shekhar, and Atal Bihari Vajpayee (whose family was originally from UP, settled in Madhya Pradesh, but he contested several elections from Lucknow).

Being the largest state, Uttar Pradesh (UP) has played a dominant role in Indian politics. The decline of the Congress became irreversible because of its inability to revive in UP. The BJP became a national player under Modi, winning a clear majority in 2014 and 2019, because it won the support of UP. In 2014, Modi himself shifted his constituency from Vadodara in Gujarat to Varanasi in UP.

This may sound incredible, but five out of fourteen of the PMs were from Allahabad—Nehru, Shastri, Indira, Rajiv, and VP, whose zamindari estate of Manda was very close to Allahabad. This was partly because Allahabad was a hub of the freedom struggle but also because it was home to the Nehrus who influenced the country's politics for half a century and more after Independence.

•

J. R. Jayewardene, a former president of Sri Lanka, had once said that (as chief executive of his country) he had the power to do anything except change the sex of an individual! Although India is a parliamentary democracy based on Britain's Westminster model, the head of government, the prime minister, is all powerful. The power of the position has been growing. Some have even called it a prime ministerial dictatorship within a parliamentary democracy. In practice, the prime minister's powers go beyond those bestowed on him or her by the Constitution. This is particularly so with a PM whose party enjoys a majority and who is popular.

While the council of ministers is collectively responsible to the Lok Sabha for its actions, in reality, under a strong PM, the cabinet follows the prime minister's wishes. It is the prime ministers who pick their ministers. And remove them. When the PM is a popular figure who is able to win elections for the party, cabinet ministers cede even more of their power to the PM. They become dependent on the PM to win elections for them—as was the case with Indira Gandhi and Narendra Modi. They managed to go beyond their parties by establishing a direct connect with the masses.

•

The PM can control the entire system of governance through the appointments s/he makes—among others to the Central Bureau of Investigation (CBI), Central Vigilance Commission (CVC), Union Public Service Commission (UPSC), Comptroller and Auditor General of India (CAG), Election Commission of India (ECI), and Finance Commission.

The Constitution lays down, for instance, that the appointment of the Comptroller and Auditor General of India (under Article 148), the official auditor of the central government, shall be made by the president. But it does not say anything more about it. The president, who is bound by the advice of the cabinet, has to ultimately go by what the PM wants. This is also the case with appointments to other constitutional bodies like the UPSC which takes care of recruitment to the bureaucracy, and the ECI which ensures the conduct of free and fair elections.

The Appointments Committee of the Cabinet (ACC) is supposed to decide on all important appointments for constitutionally mandated statutory bodies like the governor of the Reserve Bank of India (RBI). 'Actually it is the PM who makes the appointments,' Bhuvnesh Chaturvedi, who was minister of state (MoS) in Narasimha Rao's PMO used to say with his typical candour, '....the ACC gives retrospective effect to it.' For much of its existence, the ACC comprised the PM, home minister, and the minister of the relevant department. But after the Modi government came to power, only the prime minister and home minister remain on it.

The selection of the heads of the CVC and CBI is supposed to be a little different, thanks to guidelines framed at the instance of the Supreme Court in 1997. The CVC and CBI directors are supposed to be selected by a committee comprising the PM, the leader of the single largest Opposition party, and the chief justice of India (CJI). A panel of three names is put up to the committee. However, here too there are ways to ensure that the shortlisted names are all cleared by the PM first. Or the leader of the Opposition (LOP) and CJI are informally persuaded to go along with who the PM wants. Again, as Chaturvedi used to say, 'At the informal level a lot of things are made possible.'

It is, however, the dull-sounding Ministry of Personnel, Public Grievances and Pensions that has been really crucial for every PM. Virtually every prime minister has chosen to retain control of this ministry. For it supervises the CBI, which is increasingly probing politically sensitive cases involving Opposition leaders—a sword that a PM can keep hanging over the heads of opponents. In May 2013, the Supreme Court had sharply indicted the UPA government by calling the CBI a 'caged parrot' and 'its master's voice', for misusing the top investigating agency in the allocation of coal-field licences. While every government has tried to use the CBI against its opponents, the Modi government added the Enforcement Directorate (ED) as an additional instrument to use against its adversaries.

An important part of the Ministry of Personnel, Public Grievances and Pensions is the Department of Personnel and Training (DOPT) which is responsible for All India Services like the Indian Administrative Service (IAS). The PM, as the minister in charge, can control the functioning of the entire bureaucracy, through transfers and postings. In the early years after Independence, the Home Ministry used to oversee the DOPT. After her sharp differences with her home minister, Y. B. Chavan, Indira Gandhi brought it under the PM's control in 1970. This is when the PMO became all powerful. When Charan Singh became home minister in 1977, the department went back to the Home Ministry. It was Rajiv Gandhi who brought it back directly under the PM's charge by putting it under a new ministry he created—Personnel, Public Grievances and Pensions. When Atal Bihari Vajpayee ceded power to his deputy prime minister, L. K. Advani, he allowed him to take charge of the DOPT. It made Advani a powerful figure in government.

Though a chief minister is not answerable to the prime minister, there are provisions in the Constitution which enable the centre, if it so decides, to curb the powers of states. The central government can work through the Finance Commission (under Articles 280–282) to informally influence the proportion of the centre–state share in the financial pie—a way to control chief ministers. The Constitution also provides for the invocation of a state of emergency (under Article 352) in the country or in any part of it (i.e., a state), which would allow the centre to give directions to a state on what it should do.

Then there is the much-misused Article 356 which provides for President's Rule in a state, if the governor (who is appointed by the central government) makes a case for the 'failure of the constitutional machinery'. This can pave the way for the sacking of the state government, bringing it directly under central control. The Janata government, when it came to power in 1977, dismissed nine state governments run by the Congress. Indira Gandhi paid them back in the same coin when she came to power in 1980.

∎

Article 217 of the Constitution provided for the appointment of judges by the president (meaning government) in 'consultation' with the chief justice of India. But in the early years, governments would only inform the chief justice of their decision. This changed in 1993, during P. V. Narasimha Rao's premiership. A nine-judge bench of the Supreme Court interpreted 'consultation' to mean 'concurrence'.

Over the years, the judiciary managed to build safeguards in the appointment of judges through what came to be known as the collegium system which selects judges for the high courts and the Supreme Court. In 1999, the collegium, consisting of the chief justice of India and the two most senior judges of the Supreme Court was enlarged, providing for five judges, who were expected to make their decisions collectively. With judges deciding on the appointment of fellow judges, the judiciary came in for criticism for a lack of transparency in the process.

In 2014, the central government set up the National Judicial Appointments Commission to appoint judges through legislation. This was struck down in 2015, with the Supreme Court ordering the restoration of the collegium system.

The government can always delay the judges' appointments by sitting on the names proposed by the chief justice, sometimes for years, taking cover behind what is called the '360 degree' process of doing 'due diligence', as the government agencies go into the antecedents of the candidate to determine suitability before the selection of the judge is finalized. As this book was being completed, a battle raged on between the government and the judiciary, with the government seeking a direct role in the appointment of judges.

•

Powerful PMs, like Indira Gandhi and Narendra Modi, have chosen to rule through the Prime Minister's Office (PMO). The PMO is as powerful as the prime minister wants it to be. For all the challenges he faced to get a new nation up and running, Jawaharlal Nehru had a low-profile Prime Minister's Secretariat (PMS) now known as the PMO. Nehru's PMS had only a joint secretary level officer heading it—M. O. Mathai, who was private secretary to Nehru. Mathai became famous later when he fell out with the Nehrus and wrote a sensational tell-all book about the family. Though Nehru had little challenge to his authority after the death of Sardar Patel in 1950, he preferred to work through his cabinet ministers. Leaders in their own right during the freedom movement, they could act relatively more independently than was the case in later years.

It was the more diffident Lal Bahadur Shastri who felt the need for a senior officer to take care of his office, and brought in L. K. Jha as secretary in the PMS. Jha, an ICS officer, looked after all aspects of the prime minister's functioning and came to wield more power than the cabinet secretary, who is the head of the bureaucracy. It was Jha who convinced Shastri to go to Tashkent to engage with Pakistan after the 1965 war between the two countries.

Indira Gandhi was the first leader to make the PMS all powerful. She first deputed a deputy minister, Dinesh Singh to take charge of it. In 1967, she appointed the powerful P. N. Haksar as secretary in the PMS; in 1971, he became her principal secretary. The left-leaning Haksar was not just the implementer of her instructions, he also influenced all her major policy decisions between 1967–72 from bank nationalization to helping create the new nation of Bangladesh. Haksar, who knew Indira since their days in Allahabad, would call her Indu in private. But in public she was prime minister.

The PMS became the PMO during Morarji Desai's premiership. The self-sufficient Desai did not feel the need for it; he downgraded it and it dealt mostly with problems of coalition management.

The wily P. V. Narasimha Rao did not feel the need to rely on a single official or a coterie. Though Amar Nath Verma was his principal secretary, Rao used Naresh Chandra for unorthodox tasks—as the head of the Ayodhya Cell to find a way out of the temple tangle, and then as his point person with the scientists to ready for a nuclear test in 1995.

Since Independence, there have been two really powerful principal secretaries who indisputably influenced the decision-making of prime ministers. They were P. N. Haksar and Brajesh Mishra, Vajpayee's principal secretary. Mishra, also the national security advisor, was often called the de facto head of the government. Vajpayee did not involve himself in the nuts and bolts of decision-making. He left these to Mishra.

Manmohan Singh's PMO was 'unpretentious' and 'subdued', in sync with his own personality. Singh would hardly speak even in cabinet meetings, and ran his government through Groups of Ministers (GoMs) and Empowered Groups of Ministers (EGoMs), many of them were headed by the experienced Pranab Mukherjee. But it was Sonia Gandhi who was the real centre of power in the UPA government Singh led; she worked through her political secretary, Ahmed Patel.

Narendra Modi governs through his PMO, which oversees the functioning of every ministry. The PMO sets the agenda for the ministries—ministers implement programmes that they are instructed to carry out. The exception is the home minister, Amit Shah, who plays a significant role in decision-making at the top. Modi's principal secretary, Nripendra Mishra, Nippy to friends, who held office for the first five years of Modi's first term as PM (from 2014–19), and then P. K. Mishra who replaced him, were neither as powerful as P. N. Haksar or Brajesh Mishra nor as visible—and they preferred to keep a low profile. A powerful figure in Modi's PMO, and a man who had the prime minister's confidence, was his national security advisor, Ajit Doval. But Doval too chooses to remain under the radar.

■

Beyond the official powers conferred on prime ministers by the Constitution, there are many informal ways in which they can checkmate those who oppose them.

Prime ministers are known to keep dossiers on their opponents, rivals, and potential challengers. Some PMs accepted that these dossiers exist. But they were quick to add that they themselves never used the information against their opponents. 'Yes, there are dossiers,' Chandra Shekhar had told me. 'I never used them. I only got information from the IB. I was told that even in Indira Gandhi's time, they were not used. Their mere presence was enough.'

'There are...files in the PMO on politicians and leading bureaucrats and many other important people. They are kept under lock and key with the PMO,' revealed Bhuvnesh Chaturvedi, minister of state in P. V. Narasimha Rao's PMO. 'They contain information about corruption, women, and all kinds of misdoings.' He added: 'The practice was started during Indira Gandhi's time. And it was the Research and Analysis Wing (R&AW)—though it was meant to collect external intelligence—(which) helped put it together.... She was apprehensive about her position.' Most prime ministers would have wanted to keep their adversaries on a leash.

•

I remember a minister who would call me within minutes after an interview with a PM had ended. 'So how did the meeting go?' he would ask. I would wonder how he had come to know about it so soon. He was obviously trying to tell me how much of an insider he was. The late chief minister of Haryana, Bhajan Lal—the name is only illustrative—had perfected this art. Whenever he visited Indira Gandhi's house, he would tip the peons, guards, gardeners, and sundry others handsomely. They would keep him posted on the daily comings and goings in the prime minister's residence.

The power enjoyed by Indira Gandhi's aides R. K. Dhawan, who had started off with her as a stenotypist, and Makhan Lal Fotedar, who manned her office at the PM House (PMH) was legion. They had proximity to her on an hourly basis. Such was the clout Dhawan came to wield that when his father died, virtually the who's who of India came to condole his death.

Prime ministers can meet anyone they wish to meet. But a powerful aide can control access to the PM; s/he can choose to give appointments to people who will give the PM the information s/he wants the PM to get. That's why leaders build their own network, independent of the intelligence agencies and official channels, for getting feedback. They cultivate mediapersons, friends, bureaucrats, and party colleagues who give them information about what is really going on.

•

Now, to the prime ministerial decisions I have looked at, which cover fifty years of Indian politics. I chose decisions which influenced politics and society long after they were made.

In the case of Indira Gandhi, I look at why she decided to call for elections in January 1977—which took both friends and foes by surprise— and continues to tantalize analysts more than forty years later. I go on to look at the moves she made between 1977–80 which brought her back to power. How, for instance, did she win over her arch opponent, the maverick Janata Party leader Raj Narain who had damaged her the most? It was he who had got her disqualified from parliament in 1975, and defeated her in 1977 but she used him to implode the Janata government. How did she neutralize Jayaprakash Narayan (JP)—who had led the movement for her ouster as PM, provoking her to impose the Emergency in 1975? How did she damage Dalit leader Jagjivan Ram, who was the only one who could have prevented her return to power in 1980? And having lost the support of the Muslims during the Emergency, how did she go on to Hinduize her politics, managing to consolidate the Hindus behind her in 1980—a move that was to have a long-term impact on Indian politics?

These were elements in her comeback story: Indira Gandhi used saam, daam, dand, bhed (persuasion, bribery, punishment, and division), in the words of Chanakya's political manual, *Arthashastra*, as her tools of statecraft to manoeuvre her way back to power—within thirty-three months of the Congress being wiped out all over North India. It was during this period that she really emerged as a maestro of realpolitik. 'Power at any cost' gained political currency, and she was to become a role model for generations of politicians across parties who came after her. They tried to emulate how she had vanquished her opponents, become larger than her party, and managed political contradictions to regain power.

Naiveté marked the early prime-ministerial actions of Rajiv Gandhi. Earnest and well-meaning, his response to the Shah Bano judgment by the Supreme Court of India in April 1985, giving alimony to an aggrieved Muslim woman, proved to be his undoing. The choices he made unleashed forces that overwhelmed him despite his brute majority in parliament.

If there was a set of decisions which gave an impetus to the BJP's growth nationally, it was the two decisions that Rajiv took after the Shah Bano verdict. He first decided to enact the Muslim Women (Protection of Rights on Divorce) Act, 1986, to undo the Shah Bano judgment to placate an agitated Muslim community. Then, in haste, he tried to assuage the sentiments of the Hindus when they came out in protest. He enabled the opening of the locks at the disputed Babri Masjid allowing Hindus to offer prayers at the site. Though the structure was unlocked by judicial fiat, Rajiv's hand was seen behind it.

The debate still continues on who was ultimately responsible for the decision to open the locks. Was it Rajiv Gandhi's own decision? Or did his cousin, Arun Nehru, then the second-most powerful man in his government, keep him in the dark and present him with a fait accompli? Did the RSS influence the prime minister's decision to unlock the structure on 1 February 1986 so that he could become a 'king of Hindu hearts'?

Rajiv Gandhi's twin decisions set off forces which were to fashion the politics of the next three decades. It finally led to the installation of the BJP on the Delhi throne in 2014 with a clear majority.

Prime minister for less than a year, V. P. Singh changed the political history of India with his decision to implement the Mandal Commission Report. The report, prepared by B. P. Mandal, had made a case for reserving 27 per cent of jobs in government for the socially and educationally backward classes, popularly known as the Other Backward Classes. The OBCs comprised 52 per cent of India's population as per the 1931 census. Thereafter, Mandal was a term used for affirmative action

for the OBCs. VP's decision escalated the BJP's agitation for 'Mandir'—
shorthand to describe the demand made by the Vishwa Hindu Parishad
(VHP) and the BJP to raise a Ram temple on the spot where the Babri
Masjid stood.

Was 'Mandir' a response to 'Mandal', as is widely held? Or was Mandal
a counter to the temple politics of the BJP—as V. P. Singh tried to craft a
new constituency to beat back an assertive BJP and save his beleaguered
government?

The decision, and the backlash to it, spawned a new OBC leadership
which ruled India and its states for a quarter century afterwards. They
included Lalu Prasad Yadav, Mulayam Singh Yadav, Nitish Kumar, Kalyan
Singh, Uma Bharati, Akhilesh Yadav, Shivraj Chouhan, Ashok Gehlot, and
so many others. Narendra Modi was to emerge as a powerful OBC prime
minister of India in 2014.

In the conflict between caste and religion that Mandal and Mandir
spawned, it was the Indian National Congress that lost out—and has yet
to recover thirty-three years later. The V. P. Singh government was short-
lived, but reservations for the backward classes became an irreversible
reality which no government after VP could undo. The Mandalization
of Indian politics continues apace, as marginalized groups, wooed by all
parties, realize the importance of their vote.

The demolition of the Babri Masjid on 6 December 1992 was a defining
moment in India's history. The failure of P. V. Narasimha Rao to protect
the structure was the ultimate non-decision by a sitting prime minister.
The mighty agencies of the Government of India and the state government
in Uttar Pradesh watched helplessly as violent mobs climbed atop the Babri
Masjid and razed it to the ground with ropes, shovels, and pickaxes.

Many questions remain unanswered decades after the demolition took
place. Did Narasimha Rao collude with the BJP to bring down the Babri
Masjid, as some believe? Or did he just allow the structure to come down
once the demolition had started, hoping it would remove a festering sore
from India's body politic, and thereby thwart the BJP's ambitions? Could
Rao have done more to stop the demolition—which represented the failure of
the Indian state to protect a place of worship, even though it was disputed.

Before he became prime minister, Atal Bihari Vajpayee used to joke
that he was the longest prime minister-in-waiting in India. Vajpayee will
be remembered for the nuclear tests of 11 and 13 May 1998 that put
India in the big league of nuclear-weapon states (NWS). A nuclear hawk
in 1964, he turned a dove in 1979 when as foreign minister under Morarji
Desai, he opposed a nuclear test. But, in 1998, he acted swiftly. What
brought about these flip-flops which ultimately set India on the road to
the global high table? What made Vajpayee take a step which other prime
ministers had decided against, except Indira Gandhi who had gone in for

a nuclear test in 1974? While Vajpayee successfully managed the aftermath of the decision internationally, he could not contain its fallout within his party—and he walked into the sunset.

A unique chemistry between US president George W. Bush and Indian prime minister Manmohan Singh made possible the Indo–US Civil Nuclear Deal signed in 2008. It was the one decision on which Singh staked his prestige and premiership, displaying an unexpected resolve to get what he wanted. The US saw India as an 'anchor of stability in Asia' and a counter to China. For India, the deal ended the nuclear apartheid it had faced since its nuclear tests in 1974 and 1998—and opened the way for nuclear commerce.

How did the mild mannered 'Doctor sahib' manage the opposition from the powerful Sonia Gandhi, who was 'half prime minister' in his tenure? How did he upstage the Left parties, which had propped up his government, but finally withdrew their support to it? Who were the fixers, national and international the avowedly apolitical Manmohan Singh mobilized in Delhi and in Washington DC to garner support? Manmohan Singh used every trick in the book to ensure that the deal went through, displaying a killer instinct few thought he possessed. His victory paved the way for a new and strategic partnership with the US.

■

If an institution is an individual's long shadow, as has often been said, the prime minister's decision-making casts a rare light on how governments work in our multi-party, fractious democracy. For they not only sit at the top of the pyramid of power, they are at the centre of ideas, navigating pressures, balancing competing claims, and grappling with the upsurge of ground-level forces knocking at their door. Each prime minister responded to these challenges in their own distinct style—to shape and reshape India's democracy.

This book is about power and its exercise by those who held the highest public office. Even a PM at the head of a coalition government is very powerful—I. K. Gujral, considered among the weakest of PMs, would often say this. These chapters will illustrate how the PM's power played out under majority rule as well as in a coalition government—and the extent to which checks and balances were able to curb the excesses of this power.

This couldn't be more relevant than today. Despite instant communication and 24x7 streaming, unprecedented access to the news cycle by an unprecedented number, what still remains behind the veil is how prime ministers decide at the highest level. The chapters that follow lift the veil, one prime minister at a time, and reveal how the moving parts work.

■

A personal postscript: barring Nehru, Shastri, and Gulzari Lal Nanda, I have had the opportunity and the privilege to meet all the prime ministers and my interviews with several of them inform this book. When I was nine, I heard Nehru at my school's annual day function speak about his trips to various countries—the details are dim, the mere fact that Chacha Nehru was with us was enough.

This book, in a way, builds on my four decades of daily reporting, and column writing, analysing events—in those earlier years knocking on doors, sitting in waiting rooms, waiting for players in government and political parties. More importantly, it was my 'sources'—the unseen, the unsung, and unheard, many of whom at great risk—helped me lift the veil. These included women and men who enjoyed the PM's confidence, ministers, MPs, party leaders, my fellow travellers in the media, bureaucrats, industrialists, and countless others who revolved in ever-increasing orbits around the prime ministers.

Many a time I had a ringside view of events, at other times it was a look from a back bench. Sometimes the prime ministers struck high notes, at other times their actions exposed the ugly underbelly of Indian politics. But almost as an article of faith, I jotted down conversations, formal or informal, to be used for the day's story—or to be kept for a later date, in the hope that I would write a book. Countless notebooks stacked away in forgotten almirahs; thousands of pages of documents, studies, news reports and books; freed from the tyranny of the journalistic deadlines, I dived deep and resurfaced with treasures I was not even aware I had. To these, I added more interviews, and further study, to write this book.

During the Covid years, all the characters I have written about came to life and crowded my study. As I revisited my conversations, I rediscovered the excitement of a high decibel drama—vibrant, constantly changing, always surprising. In the end, it helped me write a story that hasn't been told. A story of how India's prime ministers think and make decisions—a story that marks the coming of age, and, for all its fault lines, the maturing of India's incredible democracy.

CHAPTER 1

THE PRIME MINISTER
WHO ROSE FROM THE ASHES
Indira Gandhi Stages a Comeback

I

'I think I will just go to the hills and retire there,' mused Indira Gandhi to a couple of visitors at her Safdarjung Road home. 'Maybe I will take a small cottage somewhere in Himachal Pradesh, and write my memoirs.'

'After all, what are my needs?' she went on reflectively. 'Mera kharcha hee kya hai (I don't need much money to live)? I can live very simply.'

She was talking to Kapil Mohan and Anil Bali, who were from the well-known Mohan Meakin liquor manufacturing company, famous for its Old Monk rum. In the 1970s, they were known for their proximity to the prime minister. The Mohan family, networked across the political spectrum, had supported Mrs Gandhi since the late 1960s.

She sat with them under the jamun tree on the back lawn of the sprawling bungalow. The garden was green and full of vibrant colour in Delhi's brief spring. But her mood was far from upbeat. She looked at the trees around the garden—she loved trees—the tall, sentinel-like kadams on the right and the solitary chir pine, arresting because of an unusual clump of foliage at the top. But they seemed to bring her no solace. This morning in April 1977, it seemed that little would.

Until two weeks ago, Indira Gandhi had been prime minister of India. Today, she was not even a member of parliament. The Congress Party she led had lost the general election in March 1977. The defeat had come as a real shock. She had even lost in her own constituency of Raebareli—a stunning setback for a leader who had been hailed as 'Durga' after she helped create the new nation of Bangladesh in 1971. The international press had called her the 'empress of India'.

The Indian National Congress, which had won the country its freedom and ruled it uninterruptedly for thirty years since Independence, was virtually wiped out all over North India. The Janata Party and its allies had swept the polls, winning all 345 seats in the northern states. On 22 March 1977, Indira Gandhi had resigned as prime minister, a position she had held for eleven years.

Dispirited by her monumental defeat, she was now seriously toying with the idea of disappearing into the hills, and retiring from politics. 'I will take a place somewhere, maybe where there are trees (all) around and a spring. I can spend the rest of my life there. And I can read books.'

'Madam, will you write a book?' the twenty-nine-year-old Bali asked her excitedly.

'Maybe, but then who will want to read my memoirs?' she said morosely. She knew she had become a hate figure. The country had turned against her.

'Please look for a cottage for me,' she told Mohan and Bali. 'I am very tired now. And I am fed up of this politics.'

Suddenly she said, 'I had an inkling that I might lose.' They looked surprised. For they knew she had received feedback that she would win. In fact, the intelligence agencies had told her she would win 340 seats. Congress leaders had briefed her that she would come back to power. In Lucknow, two days before the results, the chief minister of Uttar Pradesh, N. D. Tiwari, had assured her confidently, 'We are winning 70 seats (out of 85) here.'

'You know, when I came out of that office after filing my nomination papers (in Raebareli) and started speaking to the people who were gathered there, I knew there was something wrong,' she told Mohan and Bali. 'I couldn't sense the enthusiasm that used to be there earlier.' She had also sensed that things were amiss during the campaign. On one occasion, when the Bollywood actor Dilip Kumar had come to campaign for her in western UP, people started to walk out after he finished speaking, not waiting for the prime minister to begin her address.

Earlier that morning, when Mohan and Bali had walked into 1, Safdarjung Road, they were surprised to be taken straight to the garden at the back where easy chairs had been placed. It was 11 a.m. in early April, and the days were getting warm. Usually, they would meet her in the tastefully furnished sitting room where she received foreign dignitaries, politicians, and other important visitors. Upon enquiring, they discovered that, since her defeat, she had taken to seeing visitors in the garden. She suspected that the ruling Janata Party government, led by Morarji Desai had bugged the house. She was also not sure what the Americans were up to. She had become 'paranoid' since she had heard about the bugging of Egyptian President Anwar Sadat's premises by the Americans. Like other politicians, she too had got some 'contraption installed on the roof to prevent satellite surveillance of the house'. Despite these precautionary measures, she remained on her guard.

Unlike Indira, who was seeing the end of the road for herself politically, this was not how Kapil Mohan saw it. The Mohan Meakin family had a longstanding relationship with Indira. Mohan had been close to her younger son Sanjay all through the Emergency. Industrialists like him had seen too many twists and turns in politics to believe in permanent victory or defeat. But he did not say anything to contradict her; there would be time enough for that later on.

She asked for tea and chicken sandwiches to be brought for her visitors. 'I don't know what to do about these carpets of mine,' she then said, her voice tinged with frustration. Handicrafts and handlooms were a known love of hers. Her beautiful Kashmiri carpets were prized possessions and adorned every room in her house. The one in the dining room was exotic and almost as large as the room itself. She said, 'They were mostly given by my parents, I don't know where I can keep them.... This government,' she said with a touch of bitterness, 'won't even allocate me a house now.... It is not a courtesy they will extend to a former PM.' As things turned out, a few days later—on 11 April 1977—she moved into 12, Willingdon Crescent, a government property. It was vacated for her by family friend Mohammed Yunus. The Janata government did not object.

'Madam, please don't worry,' Mohan assured her immediately. 'I will send carpenters and packers from Mohan Nagar to pack them properly. We will make sure they don't get damaged.' He added, 'We will keep them safely for you in Mohan Nagar till you want them back.' Indira looked relieved. She then brought up what had really been weighing on her mind. 'I am not worried about myself,' she told Mohan. 'I am worried about Sanjay and his safety. I don't know what they will do to him.... What can I do about his security?' She sounded edgy, as she talked about her political heir apparent.

Only a few days earlier, she was feared—as a dictator, she had abridged citizens' fundamental rights, jailed political opponents, and imposed press censorship during the Emergency she had imposed for nineteen months from 1975 to 1977. Suddenly she looked vulnerable.

'I am really worried about Sanjay's life,' she kept repeating. 'They will not allow him to live.' She was afraid that the Janata Party regime would 'harm him' and put him 'behind bars'.

'She had told me this more than once,' Bali was to say later.

Again, Mohan tried to reassure her. 'Don't worry, madam, we will take care of that.'

She looked at him enquiringly.

'We have a guest house in Solan. It's on top of (a) hill in a secluded spot. It also has a beautiful view. He can go and stay there. I will make all the arrangements. Nobody will know anything about it.'

'You let me know,' he added, 'when you would like to him to go.'

'Anil here,' Mohan said, pointing to Bali, 'can go with him and take care of everything.'

She looked uncertain, but did not say anything. Sitting in the garden that day, she talked about how strange everything felt. She found herself at a complete loss as to what to do with herself. Suddenly, there was no office to go to. There was no office car, no staff car. They had been withdrawn. She didn't even have a car of her own. She had no telephone operator to help her get through to people she wanted to talk to. She could not even remember the phone numbers of her friends. All this had been taken care of for her by others for so many years. Overnight, no files were being sent to her. At least that would have occupied her.

II

On 20 March 1977, as night fell, Delhi was agog with the poll results that were pouring in. It was clear that the Congress was losing. Indira Gandhi's personal assistant R. K. Dhawan rushed in and told her that she was trailing in her constituency. Then he paused uncomfortably and said the margin of defeat had been increasing. When her friend and biographer Pupul Jayakar walked in around 8 p.m., Indira was sitting all alone. 'Pupul, I have lost,' she told her friend forlornly. They sat together without saying anything more.

Indira Gandhi called an emergency meeting of the cabinet late that night. Sounds of celebrations could be heard in the streets outside. It was to be 'a night of wild rejoicing'. There were drumbeats, dancing, distribution of sweets to celebrate Indira's defeat. The cabinet meeting was held this time at her residence at 1, Safdarjung Road, in one of the small rooms where she would receive visitors—and was brief. Like Indira, many of her ministerial colleagues present knew they had lost. She told her colleagues that she would be sending her resignation, and that of the council of ministers, to the president. The main agenda of the meeting was to decide whether to lift the Emergency. A majority of the cabinet ministers felt it should be revoked immediately. They feared the Janata government might use it against them. On 25 June 1975, when she had imposed the Emergency, she had not consulted the cabinet; it was only informed afterwards. This time, a defeated Indira chose to get the cabinet's clearance—before she took the decision to revoke the Emergency.

Very quickly, Cabinet Secretary B. D. Pande and Home Secretary S. L. Khurana moved to an adjoining room. They sat down to ready the notification for the acting president, Vice President B. D. Jatti, to sign. He had been officiating as president after the death of President Fakhruddin Ali Ahmed on 11 February that year. Pande got the note approved by Indira after 1 a.m. on 21 March. He then rushed to the vice president's house at 6, Maulana Azad Road. It was 2 a.m. by the time he was done.

At 1, Safdarjung Road, an exhausted Indira Gandhi called her son Rajiv and daughter-in-law Sonia. She told them to leave immediately and go and stay with friends for a few days; she feared for their safety. They picked up their two sleepy children, Rahul and Priyanka, and left. Her younger son Sanjay and his wife Maneka had been in Amethi that day. They returned to Delhi late at night. B. D. Pande heard them talking to

Indira Gandhi in the corridor when he went to get the Emergency papers signed by her. They looked 'visibly upset'.

She remarked dejectedly to Sanjay, 'I have done what I could. Now I want to live in peace,' recalled Kamal Nath, a close associate of Sanjay who had also returned with him.

On 22 March 1977, all the results were officially in. Indira Gandhi drove to 6, Maulana Azad Road, to submit her resignation to B. D. Jatti. Sangamma (Jatti's wife), who was also there, kept sobbing through the meeting. Jatti took the envelope containing Indira's resignation letter absentmindedly. But he did not open it. It was when Indira got up to leave that P. N. Dhar—her principal secretary—whispered to the acting president that he had forgotten what was constitutionally required—to ask the prime minister to continue till alternative arrangements had been made. 'Yes, yes, yes,' Jatti said, and hastily did what was required.

Indira Gandhi went on the air on All India Radio soon thereafter. 'My colleagues and I accept the people's verdict unreservedly and in a spirit of humility,' she told the country.

Sanjay Gandhi, the enfant terrible of the Emergency, who had also lost his parliamentary seat in Amethi, was being dubbed the villain behind her defeat. People said the bachada (calf) had devoured the gai (cow). (The Congress Party symbol at the time was the cow and calf.)

'Sanjay to quit active politics' the newspaper headlines announced the next day. An uncharacteristically subdued Sanjay told reporters he was 'sorry if what I did in my personal capacity had recoiled on my mother whose life has been spent in selfless service'.

Initially, Indira Gandhi had been shell-shocked by her defeat. But, as in the past, she was stoic in a crisis. But, after that, depression set in. For days, lonely and isolated, she refused to meet people. It was painful to be suddenly viewed as a villain. She knew that people were writing her off; this hurt her the most.

In the days after her defeat, an apprehensive Indira Gandhi sent her daughters-in-law, Sonia and Maneka, and her grandchildren, Rahul and Priyanka, to the hills, to keep them out of harm's way. They stayed at the home of a friend, Suman Dubey. She sent her older son, Rajiv, to Mumbai to see if a private plane could be hired to fly the family out of India. While Rajiv was in Mumbai, V. V. Nagarkar, a joint director in the Intelligence Bureau in Delhi, was tipped off by his IB colleagues about Rajiv's Mumbai visit. Being from Mumbai, Nagarkar was well connected with the intelligence network in the metropolis. 'I heard this from Nagarkar himself,' recalled Ravi Nair, who was at the time political secretary to George Fernandes. (A hero of the Emergency, Fernandes had just become communications minister in the Janata Party government—though soon thereafter he was shifted to the Industry Ministry.) Nagarkar immediately passed on the information to Prime Minister Morarji Desai. A worried Desai rang up Jayaprakash Narayan, a socialist-turned-Gandhian who had helped to create the Janata Party. They met at the Gandhi Peace Foundation in Delhi, where JP was staying. Both leaders decided that 'this had to be handled with care'. The government could not risk being charged of ill-treating a defeated prime minister and her family.

'JP and the PM met Indira Gandhi,' revealed Ravi Nair. 'They assured her that no harm would come to her family. And that she need not worry about their physical safety.'

'I want to retire to the Himalayas,' she told Morarji Desai. 'I want only one guarantee, and that is the safety of Sanjay.' There were rumours that Rajiv and Sonia, along with their children, Rahul and Priyanka, might leave India and head to Italy.

Nagarkar had also learnt that within hours of Indira Gandhi's defeat, two 'trunks full of documents' had been spirited away from 1, Safdarjung Road, to her farmhouse in Chhatarpur and buried there. Nagarkar prepared a note on this for the government. He gave a copy of it to George Fernandes, who asked Ravi Nair to do a recce. Nair and a deputy superintendent (DSP) of the IB made their way to the farmhouse. 'I remember the DSP was supposed to come with a gadget which had to come from Hyderabad,' said Nair. The handheld device could detect metal underground. But the DSP came without it. They found nothing at the farmhouse. About a month later, the device arrived. This time Nair accompanied another officer to Indira Gandhi's farmhouse at Chhatarpur. Again, the effort yielded nothing. 'A gardener told us that the sandooks [trunks] had been dug up and taken away in the meantime,' Nair said. Just as Indira was paranoid about what the Janata government might do to Sanjay, the Janata leaders were highly suspicious of what she might get up to, to undo the new government.

■

Not long after the Janata government took over, the cabinet—prodded by Home Minister Charan Singh—decided to dismiss the Congress governments in nine states. It decided that these states too had lost their mandate to rule after Indira Gandhi's defeat in the national election. The cabinet sent its recommendation to dissolve the state assemblies to acting president Jatti. Jatti decided to withhold his consent, not once but twice. He let it be known to the government—on 29 April 1977—that he needed more time to consider the matter. This sent the government into a tizzy. Jatti was, after all, only a ceremonial head. He was obviously delaying the decision deliberately. His refusal to sign could have brought on a constitutional crisis, preventing the elected government's writ to run.

An anxious PM Desai summoned an urgent meeting of the cabinet on 30 April 1977. The consternation of the ministers was palpable; they were worried about what the acting president might do. They knew that Jatti was an Indira loyalist and owed his rise to her. Though no minister stated it explicitly, the question hung there, unasked, 'Could Jatti, as the supreme commander of the armed forces, call in the army and overthrow the new government?' There had been whispers in the corridors of power a few days before the elections, that the chief of army staff had made an offer to Indira Gandhi—that he would 'bring troops to New Delhi to protect her in case she lost the elections and the Opposition decided to organize a march against her home'. The crowd might get out of control and attack her residence, he had reportedly told her.

'Don't worry about me,' Indira Gandhi had replied. 'What I do ask is that you look after my children.'

R. N. Kao, chief of R&AW looking after the country's external intelligence, had made a similar offer to her. 'I have many armed paramilitary forces (under me) and I would like to bring them to Delhi, just in case there is violence.'

But, on 30 April 1977, Defence Minister Jagjivan Ram tried to allay the fears of his cabinet colleagues. Any move by the army, he said, was unlikely. He did reveal, however, that during the Emergency, Defence Minister Bansi Lal had met the army chief, and asked him to endorse the Emergency. But the chief of army staff, General Tapishwar Narain Raina, had refused. General Raina was a professional officer, Ram told his colleagues. And the army was a force whose professionalism should not be doubted. Despite Ram's reassuring words, several ministers were left with a 'spooky' feeling that day.

Late that night, George Fernandes got a call from the intelligence officer Nagarkar again. Like Fernandes, Nagarkar had a socialist background and had been opposed to the Emergency. 'Something is afoot,' he warned Fernandes. His colleagues in the IB had been monitoring the calls of Congress leaders. He did not know what was being planned but he asked George 'to be careful'. He did not say so, but the allusion was to the possibility of a coup. As Fernandes put down the receiver, the phone rang again. It was his socialist colleague Madhu Limaye on the line. He too had been alerted.

After the calls from Nagarkar and Limaye, George Fernandes sent Ravi Nair to take a 'chakkar' (round) of the high 'security' areas of New Delhi. Fernandes's official vehicle had left for the day. So, Nair did his rounds on a borrowed two-wheeler. As he drove around Lutyens' Delhi that night, his mind went over the Kapp Putsch he had read about, the attempted coup in Germany to overthrow the national government in 1920, which was to unravel the fledgling Weimar Republic, and establish an autocratic government in its place. But Nair found no unusual activity around Army Headquarters or the Central Telegraph office or All India

Radio or Parliament House. He came back and reported the 'all clear' to Fernandes.

The next day, on 1 May 1977, 'George led 200–300 of us socialist youth', to hit the streets, recalled Ravi Nair. 'We marched to Rashtrapati Bhavan, and demanded Jatti's resignation.' Behind the scenes, the Janata government read the riot act to Jatti. It invoked the dreaded 42nd Constitutional Amendment passed during the Emergency, which stipulated that the president had to abide by the advice of the council of ministers. Finally, Jatti fell in line. That night, he signed the dismissal order of the nine state assemblies. The Desai government announced fresh elections in these states on 11 June 1977. The Janata Party came to power in seven of them—UP, Madhya Pradesh, Rajasthan, Himachal Pradesh, Haryana, Bihar, and Orissa. Two non-Congress parties, the CPI (M), and Akali Dal, were victorious in West Bengal and Punjab. The Congress was trounced everywhere.

■

There was no love lost between Indira Gandhi and the inflexible Morarji Desai, who had been deputy prime minister under her in 1967. For all their rivalry over the years, Desai was reluctant to prosecute her for the Emergency and its excesses. But he was under immense pressure to do so from his home minister, Charan Singh, George Fernandes, and other ministerial colleagues.

Charan Singh demanded a Nuremberg type of trial against her. The Janata Party leaders were not in a mood to forgive or forget. The prime minister had promised Indira Gandhi that her family would be physically safe, they argued, not that Sanjay Gandhi would be let off the hook for his crimes during the Emergency.

By April 1977, the Janata government decided to set up eight commissions of enquiry headed by retired judges to investigate the alleged misdeeds of Indira Gandhi, Sanjay Gandhi, and senior Congress leaders like Bansi Lal, V. C. Shukla, and Pranab Mukherjee. Justice H. R. Khanna was to look into the misuse of resources and government agencies by Sanjay in the Maruti company he had floated to produce a people's car. Another commission was to probe how JP had been treated in prison during the Emergency, which led to the failure of his kidneys. The government even decided to investigate the death of socialist leader Ram Manohar Lohia in 1967! (Over the years, this had troubled socialists who suspected foul play.) But the mother of all the enquiries was headed by a former chief justice of India, J. C. Shah. He was to investigate the 'excesses, malpractices and abuse of authority' during the Emergency, even by 'the highest political authority'. Indira, who dubbed the commission as nothing but 'political vendetta', did not appear before it when asked to do so twice. Finally, when she did so in January 1978, she said it was the collective responsibility of the cabinet and denied any knowledge about its excesses.

■

In June 1977, an anxious Indira Gandhi decided to take Kapil Mohan up on his offer. She decided to send Sanjay to Solan to keep him out of the public gaze. He went there incognito and stayed at the Mohan Meakin company guest house. Anil Bali accompanied him. Bali had become a staunch Indira loyalist ever since his uncle V. R. Mohan, who was the elder brother of Kapil Mohan and head of Mohan Meakin until he died, had taken him to meet the prime minister in 1969. She had told a nervous twenty-one-year-old Bali never to forget that 'information is power'.

Thereafter, he would get information about what Indira Gandhi's opponents were up to.

The caretaker of the Solan guest house, Kinu Ram, took care of Sanjay who had also taken a personal attendant with him from Delhi. The thirty-one-year-old Sanjay liked vegetarian food. In Solan, his diet was made up of mushrooms, vegetables, fruits, milk. He was not given to having carbonated drinks. It was a different Sanjay from the teenager who had been known for his wild and wayward ways.

Sometimes he would read. Or try to play the old piano in the sitting room on the first floor of the guest house.

'Do you know how to play the piano?' Anil Bali had asked him the first day by way of making conversation. 'No,' was Sanjay's one-word reply. Sanjay was not given to talking much. His replies were either monosyllabic or, at best, one-liners. They had just arrived at the guest house. The rooms inside the green and white cottage—near which the hill train from Kalka to Shimla passed—had many photographs on its walls—there was one of the formidable-looking family patriarch Narendra Mohan looking at a tiger skin mounted on a wall. In an adjoining room there was a billiards table of 1820s vintage made from the famous Burma teak.

Solan was known for its salubrious surroundings. Occasionally, Sanjay would step out for a walk. But this would make Bali nervous. 'I got him a monkey cap, so people would not recognize him.'

Finally, Sanjay Gandhi grew impatient with his captive existence. Sixteen days after arriving in Solan, he decided to return to Delhi. He drove back in his own car, with Bali following him in another vehicle. At Kalka, Sanjay's car broke down. He got out to examine what had gone wrong. People gathered around the vehicle and he was recognized immediately. The crowd became aggressive. 'Log maarne ke liye taiyyar thae (People were ready to beat him up). It showed the extent of hostility towards him at the time,' Bali said.

'I had to quickly put him in my car and move away fast.'

During his sojourn in Solan, the reclusive Sanjay was quietly getting ready for battle. He had been his mother's closest political confidante during the Emergency years. He now began to plan her comeback.

'If the Janata Party had left Sanjay alone, Indira Gandhi might have been finished politically,' Kamal Nath, who was close to Sanjay and Indira Gandhi, said years later.

But the Janata men decided to go after Sanjay. And Indira Gandhi made up her mind to fight back. It was then that her mood underwent a sea change. Her first instinct had been to retire. Now she decided to mount a counteroffensive.

She first called on her spiritual guru Sri Ma Anandamayi in Haridwar to recharge her spiritual batteries. With the state elections announced for June 1977, she threw herself into the poll campaign. Her party colleagues could not get over the energy she displayed. She could take a short nap in the car or the plane and look absolutely fresh for the next round of battle.

'Take that crying look off your face,' she admonished a youthful Ambika Soni, who had been made Youth Congress president during the Emergency by Sanjay. 'You must show your thirty-two teeth and look happy all the time. You have to develop a thick skin, flip the page, and move on.'

'Or,' she added quite seriously, 'you should quit politics.'

On 24 July 1977, she took off for Sarvodaya leader Vinoba Bhave's ashram at Paunar in Maharashtra. During the course of her three-day stay there, she had seven sittings with Vinoba Bhave the 'sarkari sant' as he was called by the media after his support for the Emergency. He had called the Emergency an 'anushasan parva' (era of discipline) which had given legitimacy to her action.

When Indira Gandhi left Paunar, Bhave told newspersons that they had not talked about politics. 'I never came for talks,' Indira said on her part, 'I just came to meet him (Vinobaji).'

At one of her meetings with Anil Bali in July 1977, she told him, and this was said almost by way of an order, 'Morarji Desai, Charan Singh, and Jagjivan Ram are big egoists, play on their egos.' She instructed Kapil Mohan to widen the differences between the Janata's top three leaders; he had across the board links with all of them. Indira knew she had to exploit the insecurities of the troika and exacerbate their differences. She did not have to work very hard. Soon they were squabbling openly. She wanted to demonstrate that, unlike her, the Janata government was incapable of governing the country. Her mind had started to tick. Her old spirit was coming back.

∎

The biggest decision she took in 1977 was to reach out to the very man responsible for her downfall—the maverick socialist leader, Raj Narain. He had contested against her from Raebareli in the 1971 parliamentary elections. She defeated him. He challenged her victory in the Allahabad High Court, accusing her of electoral malpractices. In June 1975, the court set aside the election result, setting in motion a train of events that culminated in the Emergency on 25 June 1975. In the 1977 elections, Narain defeated her in Raebareli—and was hailed as a giant killer.

Initially, Indira Gandhi was very reluctant to engage with him. It was Sanjay who persuaded her to overcome her reservations. 'Sanjay had matured after Mrs Gandhi went out of power,' remarked Jagmohan Malhotra in a private conversation. A powerful bureaucrat—popularly known by his first name—he was a member of Sanjay's coterie, responsible for several controversial actions during the Emergency.

Kapil Mohan acted as the bridge between Indira Gandhi and Raj Narain. Two men in the Intelligence Bureau also played a part in facilitating the meetings between Raj Narain and Sanjay Gandhi; so did a couple of Mumbai industrialists. In the months that followed, Narain was to become her one-man demolition squad, leading to the implosion of the Janata Party.

In this, as with other moves Indira Gandhi made, Sanjay was the key architect. He had convinced his mother that they should take the battle into enemy territory, and divide the ranks of their opponents. Earlier, she used to counsel patience and courtesy to him. She believed they yielded better results than impatience or abrasiveness. But, by mid-1977, it was Sanjay who convinced Indira that she should stoop to conquer.

Perhaps Jagjivan Ram, if he had become prime minister instead of Morarji Desai, might have been a match for Sanjay Gandhi. But it was to remain one of those untested ifs of history. Indira Gandhi knew that being a Dalit and a shrewd administrator, Ram could block her comeback if he emerged as an alternative pole in the Janata grouping—a possibility that could not be ruled out. She could not forget that his exit from the Congress on 2 February 1977, along with H. N. Bahuguna and Nandini Satpathy, had electrified the country—and catalysed the situation in favour of the Janata Party.

Jagjivan Ram had formed the Congress for Democracy (CFD), later to merge with the Janata Party. He had hoped to become prime minister, at the head of the Janata government, but the coveted position went to Morarji Desai. But he waited in the wings for the right moment to make his bid for the top job. She knew she would have to blunt the threat he posed. And wait for the propitious time to strike.

She also knew that she would have to placate Jayaprakash Narayan who had called her a 'dictator' only two years earlier. This was the man she had thrown into prison on 25 June 1975 for wanting to overthrow her government. He had led the Bihar movement of youth against corruption and rising prices in 1974; it had snowballed into the force that had eventually swept her away as prime minister.

By mid-1977, JP was ailing. Tired and spent, he was now on dialysis for life. But he continued to wield moral authority. She knew he was already disappointed with the Janata government he had fathered; this was something she could use to her advantage.

She also knew she had to Hinduize her politics. She was aware the Muslims had deserted her in the 1977 elections. Sanjay's programme of forcible nasbandi (sterilizations) had angered the community. She would have to fashion an alternative base to offset the loss of Muslim support. The Rashtriya Swayamsevak Sangh (RSS) had made overtures to her all through the Emergency. RSS chief Balasaheb Deoras had written to her several times. Some RSS leaders had reached out to Sanjay through Kapil Mohan. Now, in 1977, she would have to see how to respond. But she would have to play this one very carefully.

She laid out her pieces on the political chessboard carefully—now she would wait for her opponents to give her the openings she could seize. She would show them what Indira Gandhi was capable of.

III

Before I go into why Indira Gandhi decided to order elections in 1977 which led to her defeat, and how she crafted a strategy to bounce back to power in only thirty-three months, it would help to go back to understand what shaped her political persona. There were five men who influenced Indira Gandhi's life and decision-making, according to the historian Ramachandra Guha: her father and India's first prime minister, Jawaharlal Nehru; her husband, Feroze Gandhi; and her principal secretary cum political advisor, P. N. Haksar, who guided her between 1967–73, considered her best years in politics. Then there was Jayaprakash Narayan, who opposed her rule, leading her to impose the Emergency. But it was her son, Sanjay, who wielded the maximum power over her. He was her 'blind spot', and she had 'very little control over him'.

These were men who influenced her ideologically at different times in her life. As a girl, and later as a student in England in the 1930s, under the influence of her father and husband, her sensibility was decidedly liberal and left-leaning. In the late 1950s, she tilted rightwards under the influence of Congress heavyweights like U. N. Dhebar and G. B. Pant, who were unhappy with Nehru's socialist and pro-communist policies, and saw her as the way to influence him. In the late 1960s and early 1970s, she took a leftward turn again with P. N. Haksar and his Marxist colleagues guiding her government. From 1973–74 onwards, her rightward shift was visible again when the rabidly anti-communist Sanjay began to play a dominant role in the affairs of the Congress Party and the government. In the early 1980s, she was moving away from the statist path of development—even though she continued to use socialist rhetoric—and told the Lok Sabha on 1 March 1982: 'Regulations, whose only virtue is restriction on production, do not make us more socialist.'

As she grew into her political persona, Indira demonstrated that, unlike her father, she was a master of realpolitik. She did not really have an ideological compass to guide her actions. She had admitted in 1963, in a moment of candour, 'I don't really have a political philosophy. I can't say I believe in any ism.' She added, 'I wouldn't say I am interested in socialism as socialism. For me, it's just a tool.'

But, interestingly enough, 'religiosity and nationalism' were to become 'guiding tenets' of her premiership. When asked by a *Washington Post* correspondent on what had helped her withstand pressures during the 1971 India–Pakistan war, she said it was her belief in 'Hindu philosophy and a deep commitment to India'. Though a 'de-ideologized' leader, at key moments, she was to demonstrate the traits of a brilliant tactician, with an unerring sense of timing, immense courage, and an ability to take risks—and, above all, an understanding of power politics, which she used to her advantage. Time and again she was to outwit opponents who were far more experienced and powerful than she was.

■

Not unexpectedly, it was her father, Jawaharlal Nehru, who was the first person to have a profound influence on her life. He expected her to be strong always. It was Nehru who initially taught her how to cope in a crisis. In April 1931, while Nehru, his wife, Kamala, and fourteen-year-old Indira were on a visit to Ceylon (Sri Lanka), an incident occurred which was to impact her deeply. While on a ride up a steep mountainside, their car skidded to the edge of a precipice. Indira hurled herself out of the front passenger seat, leaving her father and mother inside. But for the sharp reflexes of the driver, all the other occupants of the car would have plummeted to their deaths. Nehru told her what she had done was wrong. 'Deeply ashamed, Indira never again panicked in the face of danger. Later in life, her father's counsel would help her take charge in a crisis. It was in these situations that she learnt to manage adversity.'

Born in Allahabad, on 19 November 1917, and brought up in the sprawling Anand Bhavan, the mansion that was home to the Nehrus, Indira's entire childhood was intertwined with the national movement. Anand Bhavan was galvanized by Mahatma Gandhi's satyagraha. She was just two when her father was first sent to jail. When the Prince of Wales visited Allahabad in 1921 during a tour of India, and Indira's grandfather,

Motilal Nehru, organized a hartal in protest, for which he was arrested, the three-year-old Indira sat on his lap as he refused to defend himself in court.

In 1929, Jawaharlal Nehru took over as the president of the Congress Party from his father, Motilal. In his presidential address, Nehru was to declare purna swaraj as the party's goal. He spent hours drafting the resolution. He then called his twelve-year-old daughter into the room and asked her to read it out. He wanted to hear how it would sound.

As she read it, she emphasized every word: 'We believe that it is the inalienable right of the Indian people, as of any other people, to have freedom and to enjoy the fruits of their toil and have the necessities of life, so that they may have full opportunities of growth.'

She continued, 'The British Government in India has not only deprived the Indian people of their freedom but has based itself on the exploitation of the masses, and has ruined India economically, culturally, and spiritually.'

Here she paused. And then she continued with deliberation, 'We believe, therefore, that India must sever the British connection and attain Purna Swaraj or complete independence.'

By reading out the resolution, Indira Gandhi became the first Indian to take the vow for India's independence.

Although Indira went to many schools, and had various tutors, Nehru continued to be her real teacher. He wrote voluminous letters, on all manner of subjects, to his daughter over the many years he spent in jail. If his life had not been overtaken by the freedom struggle, he would have made a brilliant educator. He tried to assuage the guilt he felt at not being able to be around for her by giving her the best of his mind.

Indira's father expanded her mind and taught her fortitude and leadership; her mother, Kamala, with whom Indira spent much of her lonely childhood, fashioned her spiritual beliefs—like the faith she came to have in the Bengali spiritual guide, Ma Anandamayi. Taking care of her frequently ill mother, Indira grew conscious of the many slights her mother had to suffer in the Nehru household, particularly from her aunts, Nehru's sisters, Vijaya Lakshmi Pandit and Krishna Nehru Hutheesing.

Independence, the ability to respond in a crisis, and to keep her feelings under wraps led to her becoming reserved, even aloof. When she was older, Indira described how she created an inner psychological space into which she would retreat, enabling her to shore up her energy and stamina. 'It was an extremely insecure childhood,' Indira was to say later, 'because we did not know from day to day who would be alive, who would be in the house and what would happen next.'

One of the greatest teachers of her childhood was the freedom movement through which she lived. 'I was part of the processions and meetings and everything that took place.' The 1930 Dandi Salt March, in the course of which Mahatma Gandhi raised a fistful of salt in defiance of the salt tax imposed by the British, had electrified the country. Women joined the mass civil disobedience movement in large numbers. So did the women of the Nehru household. With one stroke, Gandhi had liberated women, and 'made possible a woman prime minister thirty-six years later'.

Kamala Nehru astounded her family by the way she threw herself into the struggle. She began to make powerful speeches, becoming more than a 'shadow of her husband'. One day, a young man, leaning against the wall of his college in Lucknow, watched Kamala give a speech. She had not been keeping well and fainted. He ran to help her. Soon thereafter he dropped out of Ewing Christian College and became devoted to her. His name was Feroze Gandhi.

Feroze became committed to the cause of India's freedom. In 1932, he proposed to Indira one month short of her sixteenth birthday. The proposal jolted her. Kamala told her husband that she did not want Indira to marry him because 'he was unstable'.

However, Indira and Feroze grew closer after Kamala's death in 1936. He was with the Nehrus when Kamala died. And later, as Indira grieved for her mother, and fell ill with TB in the months that followed, Feroze, as she put it years later, 'was always there for me'.

While in the UK in the 1930s, Feroze at the London School of Economics, and Indira at Oxford, both became part of a circle of leftists around the maverick politician, V. K. Krishna Menon, the face of the India League lobbying for India's independence in British political circles. Feroze and Indira inhabited an exciting world of ideas and revolutionary fervour.

In 1941, they returned to India. She told her father she had decided to marry Feroze. This greatly troubled Nehru; he saw huge differences in their backgrounds. He found Feroze 'loud, boisterous and a great user of expletives. Nehru was soft-spoken, subtle, and did not swear even when enraged.'

While he urged Indira to consult relatives and friends before taking a decision, Nehru shot off a letter to Gandhi seeking his guidance. Interestingly enough, and this is one of those unknown little titbits of history, Nehru's letter to Gandhi remained with Gandhi's secretary Mahadev Desai for years. He had written on it 'Only for my or Nehru's eyes'. After Mahadev Desai's death, his son Narayan Desai discovered the letter at home—it hadn't been among the papers handed over to the Government of India for the compilation of the Collected Works of Gandhi. Narayan Desai wrote to Nehru immediately, asking to see him. Nehru—he had been fond of a younger Narayan years ago and sent him a copy of Glimpses of World History and some of Indira's books of class four and five—wrote back in his own hand, 'Meet me at Baroda station' where he was going to stop over on one of his tours.

Narayan Desai handed over the envelope to Nehru. 'It was my moral responsibility to reach this to you,' he told the prime minister. The subject of the letter—Indira Gandhi—sat by Nehru's side in the compartment, silently listening to the exchange between the two men. By now she was the prime minister's official hostess, the mother of two sons—and estranged from her husband.

But back in November 1941, after receiving Nehru's letter, Gandhi had tried to talk Indira out of her decision to marry Feroze. She should not rush into marriage. In the end, he gave in but on the condition that she and Feroze would not do anything without Nehru's consent. Finally, Nehru, too, gave in.

To her utter surprise, Gandhi advised her against a simple ceremony. If it was a small ceremony, people would suspect that the family did not approve. So, the wedding took place in full public gaze.

Indira and Feroze were married on Ram Navami on 26 March 1942. The ceremony was held under a canopy on the veranda of Anand Bhavan. Indira came down at 9 a.m. from her room, dressed in a pale pink khadi sari. It had been woven with thread spun by Nehru while he was in jail. She wore no gold jewellery, only a garland of flowers and glass bangles.

Gandhi could not attend Indira's wedding. He was travelling to Delhi to meet Sir Stafford Cripps to discuss the transfer of power from Britain to India. Cripps sought India's support for the British World War II effort in exchange for the promise of elections and full dominion status after the war. The Congress rejected the proposal, seeking full independence; Gandhi called the proposal 'a post-dated cheque on a failing bank'. It led to the Quit India Movement in 1942.

Like the turbulence of the period, the Feroze–Indira marriage was also turbulent; it did not last. Nehru's fears—and Kamala's apprehensions—came true. Feroze allegedly began to have flings with other women. Indira decided to move in with her father. He had decided to shift from the more modest house at 17, York Road (now Motilal Nehru Marg), where he had initially lived as prime minister, to the grander Teen Murti House where the commander-in-chief of the British Indian army had lived. Her sons, Rajiv and Sanjay, moved with her.

After Feroze became an MP in 1952, he was often critical of his prime minister father-in-law. He would usually come and see his boys at breakfast at Teen Murti House. Sometimes he would take them to his house, and 'show them his garden, his hunting trophies, his fishing tackle'; he taught them to saw wood. Sanjay was 'especially close' to his father and Feroze was probably fonder of his younger son, 'presumably because both liked doing things with their hands'. Once, when the boys were in Delhi on a visit from Doon School, where they were studying, Feroze asked them to come to parliament to meet him. From the visitors' gallery Sanjay heard his father make a stirring speech. As soon as Feroze saw them, he rushed to them and hugged them simultaneously, one under each arm.

Nehru too was very fond of his grandsons. He once spent two hours on the phone at night to try and procure an electric toy train that Sanjay had seen at a friend's house and insisted on acquiring right away. Even though the shops had all closed by then, Nehru managed to get it for him by midnight. But in their later years, 'Sanjay and Rajiv...counted their grandfather among the major factors in the break-up of their family life....'

In 1960, Feroze had a heart attack and died. He was only forty-eight. Feroze's death made Sanjay resentful; he blamed his mother for the 'neglect and death of his father'. Increasingly, she could not control him. 'Wayward' and 'wild', and frequently getting into trouble, he was a handful for his mother according to Pupul Jayakar. But Indira remained an indulgent mother.

■

As her father's official hostess, Indira Gandhi's involvement in politics in the 1950s was much greater than any formal designation may have suggested. She was a key advisor to Nehru. 'People do not realize how much Papu depended on me,' she once said, referring to the role she had played during his premiership. In 1955, she became a member of the Congress Working Committee (CWC), the party's top decision-making body—and her springboard to active politics.

Many saw Indira as a convenient conduit to her father—like G. B. Pant and U. N. Dhebar, who, as already mentioned, were opposed to Nehru's left-leaning politics. They felt Indira would be able to check his proximity to the socialists and communists. Pant was union home minister and Dhebar had been Congress president from 1955–59. Both prevailed on her to become Congress president. She took over from Dhebar in 1959.

She convinced Nehru to dismiss the communist government in Kerala in July 1959, when there was unrest in the state. This was the first time that the central government had dissolved a state government. It was also the first display of Indira's 'ruthlessness' and her indifference to democratic norms. 'The unrest in Kerala...touched a raw nerve in her,' her biographer, Katherine Frank, wrote perceptively. 'Indira did not share Nehru's faith that democratic institutions would survive unstable circumstances. In the face of conflict and instability, her instinct was to choose order above democracy.'

She did not always agree with her father. Indira had clashed with him over the bifurcation of the state of Bombay into Gujarat and Maharashtra. Nehru was against it. She was more hard-headed. As Congress president, she appointed a committee to look into the matter. On 4 December 1959, it recommended that the state be split and Bombay be given to Maharashtra. She had her way.

Indira considered her father too 'soft'. She said he was 'a saint who had strayed into politics'. She saw herself as a 'tough politician'. 'Mera baap sant thaa, main nahin hoon (My father was a saint, but I am not),' she told UP Congress leader Banarasi Das in 1969, keeping him standing, not even looking up at him. The message was for Chandra Bhanu Gupta, the powerful chief minister of UP, who had turned against her and joined hands with the 'Syndicate' of leaders opposed to her.

■

When Nehru died on 27 May 1964, the Syndicate chose Lal Bahadur Shastri as his successor. When Shastri had resigned as part of the Kamaraj Plan in 1963, there had been speculation that Nehru looked upon him as his successor. In 1963, Tamil Nadu chief minister K. Kamaraj had scripted the purge of six cabinet ministers, including Shastri, and six chief ministers, including himself, to move to the party organization. But Shastri was all along convinced that Nehru wanted his daughter to succeed him, although Nehru remained equivocal on the issue. When Indira became Congress president, Nehru was mildly 'disapproving'; he did not want to invite the charge of nepotism or encouraging a dynastic arrangement.

When Shastri invited Indira to join his cabinet, initially she was reluctant. But she agreed when she heard he might induct her aunt, Vijaya Lakshmi Pandit instead. She wanted to be foreign minister; he offered her the Information and Broadcasting ministry. He made her number four in the cabinet—showing a steely side to him. This did not please her, and she crossed swords with him on several occasions, often referring to him in derisive terms. 'Do you think this government can survive,' she once said contemptuously, 'if I resign today?'

IV

On 11 January 1966, the phone rang in Inder Kumar Gujral's bedroom. It was 3 a.m. Yashpal Kapoor, Indira Gandhi's aide, was on the line. 'Lal Bahadur Shastri has died of a massive heart attack,' Kapoor told a stunned Gujral. The prime minister had been in Tashkent when the end came. He had just signed a peace accord with Pakistan president Yahya Khan.

'Mrs Gandhi wants you to come over immediately,' Kapoor said urgently. Gujral was a member of the 'backbencher's club' of left-leaning parliamentarians who advised Indira politically during her tenure as I&B minister—they would later become her 'kitchen cabinet'.

When Gujral arrived at Indira Gandhi's residence, she was waiting for him impatiently. Soon, they were joined by the publisher of *Seminar*,

Romesh Thapar. Like Gujral, he too was a close friend of Indira's. 'Mrs Gandhi was quite excited.' She thought she could now become the 'foreign minister'. Gujral and Thapar looked at each other 'nonplussed'. They told her she could be 'elected the prime minister'.

Indira's coterie met again the next morning. This time others—UP Congress leader Uma Shankar Dikshit, whom she trusted, and Dinesh Singh, the suave former raja of Kalakankar who was to become minister of state in her first cabinet—were also present. They decided she should not push her candidature. She should, instead, be seen as a reluctant player—non-committal and self-effacing. These men were enunciating a well-tested principle of politics—that those who threw their hat in the ring early were the first to get eliminated from the race. Invariably, their opponents would get the opportunity to marshal forces against them.

The strategy paid off.

The next day, on 12 January 1966, dressed in a black sari and dark glasses, a grieving Indira Gandhi sat at Palam airport waiting for Shastri's body to arrive from Tashkent. A political wag present there pointed to Indira Gandhi, and remarked to journalist Nikhil Chakravartty that there sat 'the hat-trick' from Allahabad. He was predicting that she would be the next prime minister—like Nehru and Shastri, she was also from Allahabad.

On 19 January 1966, the Congress Parliamentary Party (CPP) elected Indira Gandhi as its leader—she went on to become prime minister at the age of forty-seven. She defeated Morarji Desai who had stridently pushed his candidature. The self-righteous Desai was anyway not popular with the MPs. The Congress Party president K. Kamaraj successfully built a consensus in Indira's favour. She won 355 votes against Desai's 169 votes. Soon after the victory, she called on Desai to seek his blessings.

'It was a brilliant public relations exercise,' recalled Natwar Singh, who was part of her secretariat from 1966 to 1971 and later became foreign minister.

Initially, her political opponents made the mistake of underestimating her. Morarji Desai had called her 'this chokri' soon after she was elected as the prime minister designate by the CPP in January 1966. A few months later, after she had taken over as prime minister, and would find herself tongue-tied in parliament, socialist leader Ram Manohar Lohia dubbed her a 'goongi gudiya'. Others were equally dismissive. A Delhi magazine had described her as 'an innocuous person', taking over as India's prime minister. She would not say much when people went to see her. A good listener, she would often doodle on the writing pad before her. Over the years, she had learnt to use silence as a tool she could put to good use. It gave her time to get a measure of her visitors and to keep them guessing about what she would do.

Her prime ministership got off to a rocky start. The country was in the grip of a severe drought with the monsoons failing for two seasons in a row in 1965 and 1966. Food production had dropped sharply. Pictures of skeletal children with spindly legs, matted hair, and vacant eyes, victims of the 1966–67 famine in the eastern part of the country, appeared frequently in the media. Exacerbating the crisis was the suspension of US aid to India and Pakistan after the 1965 war between the two countries.

She decided to visit the US and confided in journalist Inder Malhotra that her purpose was to 'get both food and foreign exchange without appearing to ask for them'. In late March 1966, she landed in Washington DC on a windy morning. She was given a red-carpet welcome by President Lyndon Johnson and his wife Lady Bird. During her visits abroad, Indira Gandhi made it a point to be dressed elegantly, even glamorously, with her 'new, bouffant hairstyle, full make-up and jewellery'. Johnson found her 'irresistible'.

She felt the visit had been a great success. Johnson had said he wanted to ensure that 'no harm comes to this girl' and promised 'three million tons of food' and '$9 million in aid'. Indira Gandhi on her part did not attack the US on its intervention in Vietnam. The only thing she refused to do was to 'whirl around the dance floor with the American president at a White House banquet'. She told Johnson that it would make her unpopular back home.

Although aid would be forthcoming to help the country tide over the crisis it faced, the World Bank and IMF conditions that were imposed were harsh. They included the devaluation of the rupee—and she went ahead and devalued the rupee by a whopping 36.5 per cent. The official announcement was made on 6 June 1966 with 6/6/66 becoming a defining moment.

'It was L. K. Jha, her principal secretary, who...influenced her decision on devaluation,' Natwar Singh was to say years later.

She was criticized both by the Left and the Right for her sellout to America. Her own party—the Congress Working Committee—denounced her action. An upset Kamaraj bemoaned his decision to install her on the throne: 'A big man's daughter, a small man's mistake.' Her problems with Kamaraj—and the old guard leaders—started with the devaluation. So did her leftward tilt, which was to last till 1973. Members of her 'kitchen cabinet'—I. K. Gujral, Uma Shankar Dikshit, Dinesh Singh, and Nandini Satpathy among others—urged her to give an ideological spin to her decisions to counter the impression that she was coming under pressure from the US. She started to attack the US's Vietnam policy as 'imperialist aggression'. Johnson was livid. He put the wheat supply to India under the PL 480 programme—it was paid for in rupees—on a tight leash. While devaluation influenced her political trajectory for close to a decade, her 1966 US visit made her think hard.

An Alabama paper had headlined her visit 'New Indian leader comes begging'. She realized that India had to become self-reliant in its food needs to maintain its independence. She began to encourage policies and research which would improve the country's food production. This eventually led to the Green Revolution, which was to make India self-sufficient in food—but was later to throw up other problems, with the use of chemical fertilizers and pesticides.

•

It was while campaigning in Raebareli in February 1967 for the general elections, that Indira Gandhi reached out to Parameshwar Narayan Haksar, a professed Marxist; he was India's deputy high commissioner in London at the time. She wrote him, asking him to come to Delhi to work with her. She admitted her invitation was premature for she did not know the outcome of the ongoing elections.

'Yes, of course, yes,' P. N. Haksar replied immediately.

In Haksar, she was looking at someone who would be personally loyal to her, generate ideas, and be her sounding board. Haksar had known Indira since she was two years old and he a boy of ten, and he remembered the little girl with big eyes. The connection had endured—he was a local guardian to her sons, Rajiv and Sanjay, when they were in London in the mid-1960s. Haksar joined the Prime Minister's Secretariat as secretary in 1967. In 1971, he became Indira's principal secretary. He was seen as the 'most powerful bureaucrat in the country post-independence' and considered the 'father of the prime minister's office'. Haksar was credited with many of the major decisions made by Indira between 1967–72, though he never let this be known. Nor did he ever take the credit for them. There was no decision, political, economic or related to foreign policy which did not carry Haksar's stamp.

Indira Gandhi made her first move against the Syndicate on 9 July 1969. She circulated a note at the All India Congress Committee (AICC) meeting in Bangalore, which advocated a state-led economic transformation, including 'social control' of banks. Because she ended the note with, 'these are just some stray thoughts rather hurriedly dictated', the note came to be called her 'stray thoughts'.

Ten days later, on 19 July 1969, she converted one of her 'stray thoughts' into reality—and in a stunning move she nationalized fourteen private banks. But just before that, in another swift move, characteristic of her decision-making, she stripped Morarji Desai of the finance portfolio. Her decision to nationalize private banks was 'one of the best kept secrets of the Government of India', which nobody knew about 'except for four or five people' including Haksar.

She now decided to take the battle into enemy territory. The Syndicate had managed to have its way in selecting Neelam Sanjiva Reddy as the official candidate of the Congress for the post of the president of the republic. But Indira, who feared she would be replaced as prime minister if Reddy was elected, asked for 'a vote of conscience' by party leaders. She threw her weight behind V. V. Giri, who was vice president and was contesting as an independent candidate with her tacit support. On 20 August, Giri narrowly won the election, and became the president of India.

Finally, Congress chief S. Nijalingappa expelled her from the party on 12 November 1969 for 'indiscipline'. She formed her own Indian National Congress (Requisition), or Congress (R) as it came to be known, while the original party was renamed the Congress (Organization) or Congress (O). The old guard had thought she would be pliable when they chose her as prime minister in 1966. But she turned the tables on them. It was a significant milestone in Indira Gandhi's political journey; it was only after the split in the party in 1969 that she came into her own.

Continuing with her progressive measures, in September 1970, she took another step which brought her popular acclaim—the abolition of privy purses and privileges of the erstwhile princes. These were tax free privileges and allowances made to 278 princes (at the time) by the central government—through a constitutional guarantee when they agreed to integrate their princely states with free India at Independence. With the passage of the 26th Constitutional Amendment Act, they ceased to exist—though her decision could be enforced only after a two-year legal battle.

In the elections that followed in 1971, she electrified the country with her 'garibi hatao' (remove poverty) slogan and led the Congress (R) to a massive victory, winning 352 seats in the Lok Sabha, the lower house of parliament. In time to come, she would become the main Congress Party. (But the Congress (O), which had been drastically reduced in stature after 1971, had one last hurrah, though it was short-lived, when it merged with the Janata Party in 1977, and wrested power from Indira after the Emergency.)

The high point of Indira Gandhi's political career, however, came in 1971 when she made geopolitical history. After her stupendous victory in the general election in March 1971, she scored an even bigger triumph later in the year when she vanquished Pakistan in a war, and displayed an audaciousness in the creation of the independent nation of Bangladesh in December 1971. It was Haksar who devised the nuts and bolts of the strategy—and advised her that she should not be in a hurry to move in militarily into East Pakistan. No military intervention would work unless there was an insurrection in East Pakistan which India could then support—if needed. India trained and supported the Mukti Bahini (freedom fighters)—before sending in its troops.

Even before the formation of Bangladesh, it was Haksar, along with diplomat D. P. Dhar—they were part of what was called the 'Kashmir mafia' around her—who advised her to go in for the Indo-USSR Treaty of Peace, Friendship and Cooperation to safeguard India's strategic interests in view of the growing nexus between Pakistan, China, and the US. The moment US secretary of state Henry Kissinger went to China from Pakistan on a secret and surprise visit, Indira moved swiftly and signed the Indo-USSR Treaty of Peace, Friendship and Cooperation on 9 August 1971.

The US was furious with India and its prime minister. President Richard Nixon called her an 'old witch'. She met him on 4 November 1971 as he tried unsuccessfully to persuade her to withdraw the troops on the Indo-Pak border. She was at her 'combative...best' and 'did all the talking with Nixon'. She took on the US during the Bangladesh conflict, not flinching when the US Navy's 7th Fleet steamed into the Bay of Bengal in a show of intimidation.

Pakistan attacked India on 3 December 1971. Three days later, Indira Gandhi recognized the new nation of Bangladesh. Her opponent, the right-wing Bharatiya Jan Sangh leader, Atal Bihari Vajpayee, hailed her as 'Durga'.

However, after her phenomenal Bangladesh victory, the equation between 'Induji' and 'Babooji', as Haksar's friends addressed him, began to change. She had now taken wing and could fly on her own. Seen as a mass leader in her own right, she had left behind the tag of being Nehru's daughter. She no longer needed an assertive Haksar at her elbow with an opinion on every subject. The decisive break between the two came in December 1972 over Haksar's sharp criticism of Sanjay Gandhi. He told her the prime minister's son should not be doing business— he headed Maruti, a project to build a small 'people's car'—from the PM House. 'You will have to make up your mind,' Haksar said in his inimitable direct style, 'you can either be a mother (to Sanjay) or the prime minister. You can't be both.'

'Haksar told me this himself,' revealed Natwar Singh, who had access to Haksar on a daily basis, being in the PM Secretariat from 1966–71.

Sanjay never forgave Haksar for criticizing him. The rift had been in the making for a while. Sanjay did not like the enormous influence Haksar, and his left-leaning friends, exercised over his mother. He took pride in calling himself an anti-communist. 'He used to say that the communists should be thrown in the sea,' recalled Anil Bali. Indira tried to defuse the conflict by making Haksar, by now a 'silent critic', deputy chairman of the Planning Commission in 1973. He continued to advise her informally, and even undertook sensitive assignments on her behalf.

Haksar had imbued Indira Gandhi's decision-making with the vision of a forward-looking, scientifically tempered, and secular India. Called Indira Gandhi's 'ideological compass' from 1967–73, he saw her taking forward her father's progressive policies. But after 1973, Indira had moved in a direction different from the one Haksar had hoped she would walk.

When she was re-elected in 1980, Haksar was to write her a warm personal letter of congratulations, enunciating a truism which made for success in politics: 'As in war, so in peace, the art always lies in either winning over the enemy or destroying him completely.' But, he added, 'Historical experience shows that there are greater rewards for the art of reconciliation than of annihilation'. He signed the letter using his nickname (Babooji). She acknowledged his note. But she addressed him formally as Mr Haksar. And she signed the letter 'Indira Gandhi', not Indu, or Indira as she used to do in the earlier years, addressing him as PN, or PNH, or Babooji. Once Haksar was forced out, Sanjay stepped in as his mother's main advisor. Coincidentally or consequentially, Indira's troubles were exacerbated with the exit of Haksar and the rise of Sanjay.

V

There were three critical phases in the sixteen years that Indira Gandhi was prime minister. Two of these phases, from 1966–73, and from mid-1980–84—when she sent the army into the Golden Temple in Punjab, which culminated in her assassination—were without Sanjay's influence. He was really not on the scene politically until 1972–73, though he had come back to India from the UK in 1967. It was during the middle period, from 1973–80, that Sanjay played a dominant role, and was seen as the power behind the throne. He grew increasingly powerful until, at the height of the Emergency, Indira claimed not to know any more some of the things he was doing.

Being anaemic from an early age, Indira Gandhi had a very difficult pregnancy with Sanjay, almost dying while giving birth to him. She had actually wanted a girl when she was pregnant with Sanjay, and had even chosen a name for her. Her kuldevi (family goddess) was called Sharika and this was the name she wanted to give her daughter, if a girl was born to her. Sarika was the name subsequently given to family friend and Congress leader Captain Satish Sharma's daughter.

Known as a rebel without a cause, Sanjay's life had followed a turbulent trajectory. As a boy, he used to break flower pots in his grandfather's house at Teen Murti Bhavan, and pull the ears of the dogs. He was a difficult child, not given to study, and would frequently get into scrapes. Indira first sent him to Modern School in Delhi to study and then shifted him to the elite residential Doon School in Dehradun. But he hated school and had to be moved from there as well, and completed his schooling from St. Columbus School in Delhi.

In a rare moment of candour, Indira Gandhi had once confided to her friend, Pupul Jayakar: 'Rajiv was courteous, well behaved, a fair student; Sanjay was rebellious, destructive, uninterested in all school activities, rude to his teachers and altogether unmanageable. He grew up a wild, wayward youth, often in scrapes, fiddling with cars, attracting questionable friends.'

From an early age, Sanjay had been interested in meccano sets, cars, and aeroplanes. That is why she sent him for an internship to the Rolls-Royce company in Crewe in England. However, he did not complete the three-year training programme and returned in two years.

After his return, he showed an interest in manufacturing a small, cheap, indigenously produced car. Indira Gandhi encouraged the project; she hoped her son would make something of his life through manufacturing the vehicle he was so set upon. The government gave him a licence to manufacture it in 1971. It extended him many favours to help get the project off the ground. A company, Maruti Motors Ltd, was incorporated in June 1971 with Sanjay Gandhi as its first managing director. The chief minister of Haryana, Bansi Lal, helped with 297 acres of land which were given for the factory at a throwaway price. In his eagerness to oblige Sanjay and his mother, Lal ruthlessly evicted farmers from their land. Since he was the prime minister's son, there were car dealers who vied with each other to give huge sums of money as advances for the vehicles he was going to deliver to them. Fifty thousand cars were to be produced—10,000 by October 1973, 25,000 by 1974, and the rest later. However, not a single car was manufactured. It was only after Sanjay's death that Indira tied up with Suzuki in Japan for the production of the Maruti cars seen today on Indian roads. On 14 December 1983, when a little white Maruti 800 rolled out of a factory in Gurgaon, she addressed executives of the new venture in a voice that cracked with emotion.

When the small car project did not take off, Sanjay turned his attention to politics. At twenty-eight, he said he wanted to change the country. Indira Gandhi encouraged him. She virtually gave him the run of the Congress organization from 1975 onwards. But it was only with the declaration of the Emergency in June 1975 that Sanjay's involvement in national politics really became visible.

■

12 June 1975 was a day Indira Gandhi—and the country—would remember for long afterwards. All day on 11 June, she had been restless—and looked tired. She knew the Allahabad High Court judgment challenging her election as member of parliament was due the next day. It could spell trouble.

The day had started on an ominous note. A little after 6 a.m., she got word that D. P. Dhar had died. She rushed to Govind Ballabh Pant Hospital where he had had been admitted. He had been part of Indira's core team, was posted as India's ambassador to Moscow, and was on a visit to Delhi when the end came. At the hospital she took charge herself, and gave instructions about the funeral. At 10.05 a.m. came the news they had all been waiting for. Indira's information advisor H. Y. Sharada Prasad barged into Principal Secretary P. N. Dhar's room in South Block. 'The Allahabad judgment has come and the Prime Minister has been unseated,' he said agitatedly. Dhar dashed off to the PM House. Word had already got around; Congress leaders had begun to gather at 1, Safdarjung Road. Those already there had divided themselves into two groups. One was discussing the legal implications of the verdict. The other group was discussing the political fallout in hushed tones.

The legal group, led by Law Minister H. R. Gokhale, was poring over the different aspects of the judgment—with eminent lawyer Nani Palkhivala and West Bengal chief minister Siddhartha Shankar Ray, whom Indira had called to Delhi a day earlier. The Allahabad High Court had held her guilty of electoral malpractices in her win in the Raebareli Lok Sabha seat in the 1971 election; her defeated opponent, the veteran socialist politician Raj Narain, had challenged her victory. The court held her guilty under the Representation of the People Act, 1951. She had used a government servant, Yashpal Kapoor, an officer on special duty (OSD) in the Prime Minister's Secretariat, as her election agent. Justice Jaganmohan Sinha, who delivered the judgment, had also disqualified her from parliament, and from running for office for six years. Indira would now have to appeal against the verdict in the Supreme Court.

Congress President D. K. Barooah held forth on how to manage the political fallout. Indira Gandhi moved between the two groups, looking 'uncommunicative and withdrawn'. Around 10.30 a.m., she went into a huddle with Sanjay and R. K. Dhawan. Dhawan then came out of the meeting and went into overdrive. He worked the phones—and instructed party leaders to organize demonstrations in her favour. Soon Bansi Lal joined them. He too started phoning, ordering deputy commissioners to mobilize crowds in Haryana.

Some party leaders counselled her to resign. 'The day the Allahabad judgment came.... I told her that perhaps it would be a good idea for her to resign and send her resignation to president Fakhruddin Ali Ahmed,' the veteran parliamentarian Karan Singh told me. The president, he suggested, could always turn down her offer—and ask her to continue in office 'till the Supreme Court gave its judgment'. It would make the situation better for her. 'She did not say a word (in response),' Singh recalled. 'But (clearly) she did not like it very much.

'If, at all, she toyed with the idea of resigning till the Supreme Court gave its verdict, she ruled it out quickly. There were two groups who did not want her to resign. One was led by Monuda (Siddhartha Shankar Ray), and included D. K. Barooah and H. R. Gokhale,' Karan Singh said.

'The other was Sanjay's group made up of Sanjay himself, V. C. Shukla, Om Mehta, and Bansi Lal.'

Janata Party leader Shanti Bhushan, who was also Raj Narain's lawyer, alleged later that Indira Gandhi had tried to influence Justice Sinha. A few days before the judgment, the chief justice of the Allahabad High Court, Justice D. S. Mathur, had gone with his wife to meet Justice Sinha. He told Sinha that Indira had decided to elevate him to the Supreme Court—after he decided the case. Chief Justice Mathur had been given this message by his relative, Dr K. P. Mathur, who was Indira's personal physician. 'However, Justice Sinha's strong conscience did not permit him to take the bait,' Bhushan was to reveal. Bhushan said he was told this by Justice Sinha himself, when they were both playing golf in Allahabad years later.

There was a third blow yet to come before 12 June 1975 came to a close. In the evening, the results of the just held elections to the state assembly in Gujarat started to pour in. The Congress was trounced by the Janata Morcha, a loosely united front of Opposition parties. This came as a shock to Indira Gandhi. It showed she was losing ground.

•

It is unusual, and rare, for a court verdict to change the history of a country. That's what the Allahabad High Court judgment did. Indira quickly filed an appeal in the Supreme Court. The vacation judge, Justice V. R. Krishna Iyer, granted a conditional stay on Justice Sinha's order. It allowed her to continue as prime minister. But she was debarred from taking part in parliamentary proceedings or drawing the salary of a member of parliament.

The Supreme Court stayed the verdict on 24 June 1975. A day later, on 25 June 1975, Indira Gandhi declared a state of emergency in the country under Article 352 of the Constitution on the ground that internal disturbances threatened the country's security—and she assumed a set of powers to deal with the situation. Late that night, she rushed her aide, R. K. Dhawan, to Rashtrapati Bhavan with a draft of the document for President Fakhruddin Ali Ahmed to sign. The president signed the Emergency decree at 11.45 p.m. The prime minister dispensed with the need to get it cleared by the cabinet; it came into effect immediately. The cabinet ratified it the next morning.

Neither her cabinet colleagues nor the cabinet secretary, B. D. Pande, nor her principal secretary, P. N. Dhar, had even a whiff of what she was planning to do. They were summoned in the early hours of the morning to a meeting of the cabinet which was held on 26 June 1975. The meeting was held at '5 or 6 a.m.', Pande was to recall years later, where they were told about the Emergency.

Of all those advising her to opt for Emergency, the most important voice was that of Sanjay Gandhi. 'Sanjay was an important influence in her decision to opt for the Emergency,' affirmed Karan Singh.

On the night of 25–26 June, Indira Gandhi arrested most of the country's leading Opposition leaders. They included Jayaprakash Narayan, Morarji Desai, Charan Singh, Atal Bihari Vajpayee, L. K. Advani, Chandra Shekhar, and many others. Many of them had addressed a rally at Delhi's Ram Lila grounds earlier in the evening on 25 June. Calling for her resignation, JP had thundered, 'Simhasan khali karo ki janata aati hai (Vacate the throne, the people are now here)'—quoting the words of the famous Hindi poet Ramdhari Singh Dinkar.

JP had appealed to the police and the armed forces not to obey the 'illegal and immoral' orders of the government. The police came for JP at 3 a.m. He was staying at the Gandhi Peace Foundation, and had gone to bed very late. He was woken up and told that policemen were waiting to take him away. In response, he uttered just four words—quoting the Chanakya niti: 'Vinash kale vipreet buddhi (When the time for destruction comes, the mind starts to work in the wrong direction).'

Indira Gandhi went on to impose press censorship and suspend civil liberties. She brought in a plethora of laws and constitutional amendments to abridge fundamental rights. These included the order under the draconian Maintenance of Internal Security Act, 1971, (MISA) under which grounds for detaining a person need not be given. There was also the Constitution (Thirty-eighth Amendment) Act, 1975, which placed the Emergency beyond judicial review and kept anything related to the prime minister out of the purview of the courts. A presidential order suspending fundamental rights under Article 19 was passed, and the right to habeas corpus was suspended through a judgment of the Supreme Court. The term of the Lok Sabha was extended by a year twice, first in February 1976, and then again in November 1976 (till March 1978).

The actions taken by Indira Gandhi were harsh and authoritarian. 'You have been calling me a dictator when I was not. Now, yes, I am,' she said in parliament on 22 July 1975. Her statement was sent out to the news agency, the Press Trust of India (PTI). But it was killed five minutes later by the censor.

Sanjay Gandhi ran the show for her during the Emergency. Fawning chief ministers and aspiring Congress leaders competed with each other to pay court to him. He called the shots and was abrasive to boot. But most Congressmen meekly put up with being humiliated and pushed around.

Sanjay used members of the Youth Congress as his shock troops. His core team included Kamal Nath, Jagmohan, V. C. Shukla, Bansi Lal, Om Mehta, Jagdish Tytler, and Navin Chawla; Akbar Dumpy Ahmad was to join him later. Sanjay's high-handedness did not leave senior leaders untouched. He downgraded Finance Minister C. Subramaniam who had stayed by Indira Gandhi's side during the 1969 split. He gave a leg-up instead to his junior, Pranab Mukherjee, who supported the Emergency. (Mukherjee, however, was to say later that the Emergency 'could have been avoided'.)

His treatment of long-time Indira loyalist I. K. Gujral was meant to be a message to other party leaders. Soon after the Allahabad judgment, Sanjay summoned Gujral, who was Information and Broadcasting minister at the time. 'The All India Radio is not projecting Indira Gandhi enough,' he told Gujral dismissively. 'You are not handling All India Radio properly. All the (AIR) news bulletins should be sent to me first,' Sanjay instructed Gujral.

'I will not send them to you, I will send them to your mother,' Gujral retorted. 'You are my son's age,' he went on, 'if you want to speak to me, then you have to speak with respect.'

But Indira backed her son. She told Gujral. 'The I&B is no more your cup of tea. The press needs firm handling.' The day the Emergency was imposed, Gujral was sacked as Information and Broadcasting minister. V. C. Shukla took over; he was later to be indicted as a 'medieval despot' by the Shah Commission. Gujral was banished to the less important Planning Ministry and later sent as ambassador to Moscow.

Sanjay then sent Congress leader K. D. Malviya—Bhaiji as he was universally called—to Lucknow to speak to H. N. Bahuguna, known for his grip over the Congress in UP. 'Sanjay wants to send you as ambassador to Australia,' Bhaiji told Bahuguna. Bahuguna was incensed. 'When I left my village in Kumaon, I came away to do politics, not to do somebody's "naukri",' Bahuguna shot back. The next day Sanjay sent him another emissary, this time the owner of a hotel. The irate Bahuguna's reply was the same. 'Tell them I am not a Gujral.' After that, Bahuguna was sidelined in the party.

Sanjay's style was peremptory. He had summoned Tariq Anwar to Delhi from Bihar where he edited a youth magazine. 'Youth Congress chala sakoge kya (Can you run the Youth Congress)?' he asked Anwar abruptly when he arrived.

Tariq nodded.

'I want to make you the state secretary of the Youth Congress in Bihar.'

'The meeting lasted two minutes,' Anwar recalled. 'He did not even ask me to sit down.'

Anwar returned to Bihar to get on with his new responsibilities.

Sanjay was also short-tempered—it did not matter whether he was dealing with a senior minister or a junior functionary. Once, he and Vir Bahadur Singh, a Sanjay loyalist, later to become the chief minister of UP, were driving through the UP countryside. Sanjay was at the wheel. After taking several wrong turns, they were hopelessly lost.

'Which way do we go now?' asked an irritable Sanjay.

'I don't know,' replied an uncertain Vir Bahadur.

Sanjay stopped the vehicle. He asked Vir Bahadur to get out. Shutting the door, he drove off, leaving a shocked Vir Bahadur in the wilderness with no human habitation in sight.

His name provoked fear, as he wielded the brute power of the state. Sanjay Gandhi came up with a five-point programme to 'improve' the country—family planning, abolition of dowry, tree planting, adult education, and the eradication of the caste system. Everywhere hoardings were installed commanding the people: 'Talk less and work more'. He embarked on pitiless 'beautification drives' in the capital, the most infamous being the one in April 1976 at Turkman Gate near the iconic Jama Masjid. Bulldozers razed 150 pukka houses, displacing families, with women shrieking and children crying. They were relocated 24 kilometres away from what had been their homes all their lives. People were terrified even to talk about what had happened. As the press was censored, hardly anything appeared in the media.

There was huge resentment over Sanjay Gandhi's family planning programme—a euphemism for forcible sterilizations. According to government figures, more than 7 million men were sterilized in 1976. There were cases of farmers being sterilized under duress; they were threatened that their water and electricity would be cut off if they did not submit to it. Fathers were told their children would not gain admission to school if they refused to be sterilized. Tubectomies were also performed on women.

Soon, the despair and fear of the people began to change to anger. By the end of 1976, when I visited Delhi's Turkman Gate area and the 'resettlement colonies', people had begun to say in undertones, 'Let the elections be held and we will teach them a lesson.' But even those opposed to Emergency rule were stunned when Indira Gandhi suddenly announced elections on 18 January 1977—the country would go to the polls in the third week of March.

VI

Indira Gandhi's unexpected decision to announce elections in January 1977, which led to her disastrous defeat, continues to tantalize observers more than four decades later. It is the subject of a debate that has not died down. On the face of it, there was no compelling reason for her to opt for elections when she did. She was firmly in the saddle. Legally, too, the Lok Sabha had another fifteen months to go before its term ended.

Sanjay Gandhi was dead against his mother's decision to call elections. Five days after the Janata Party won a sweeping victory, with 298 seats and 43.4 per cent of the popular vote, Sanjay told his friend and confidant Dumpy Ahmad, 'What a mistake it has been to go in for elections.' Not only had it been a mistake to hold elections, it had been an even bigger mistake to hold them in March 1977.

'Sanjay was driving a Matador and I was sitting in the front with him,' Dumpy recalled. 'We were coming from the Maruti factory in Haryana.'

'I had told Mummy,' Sanjay told Dumpy, 'to release these guys (from jail) in February and then have elections after the monsoons, either in October or November. I said by then they would be fighting like cats and dogs.... But Mummy didn't listen to me.'

'These guys' that Sanjay was referring to were the Opposition leaders whom Indira Gandhi had imprisoned during the Emergency—and released after announcing the elections.

Sanjay and Dumpy had been together at Doon School. They met by chance in Lucknow in February 1977. Within days, Dumpy had landed in Amethi, from where Sanjay was contesting for the Lok Sabha. He went to the Khadi Bhandar in Hazratgunj in Lucknow, and bought three white pyjamas and three white kurtas.

'The pyjamas were for eleven rupees each and the kurtas for thirteen rupees each.'

'Do you also need a Gandhi topi (cap)?' asked the salesboy helpfully. 'That is for two rupees.' Dumpy decided the topi didn't quite suit his style. When Dumpy decided to join politics to help Sanjay, his father warned him, 'If you go, be prepared to spend the next five years in jail.' Dumpy stayed by Sanjay's side until his death in June 1980—and came to have free access to the Gandhi household.

Like Sanjay, most of his other buddies were also opposed to elections. They included Bansi Lal, and Indira's personal aide, R. K. Dhawan. 'But Indira Gandhi was adamant.'

Three days after Morarji Desai was sworn in as prime minister, Sanjay predicted the government would not last long. 'I don't give the Janata government three years,' he told Dumpy the day they were driving back from the Maruti office. The Janata leaders proved him wrong. They collapsed in just twenty-eight months.

∎

Political analysts, academics, and the media continue to put out hypotheses on the real reason why Indira Gandhi chose to hold elections.

The liberals like to believe that Nehru's daughter had triumphed over Sanjay's mother. She had opted for the polls because she wanted to undo the Emergency. It had damaged her image as a democrat, and she did not like to be seen as a dictator. And that, as a child of the freedom movement, somewhere the remnants of Nehru's legacy had lingered on in her. Her personal friends in Western democracies, like American photographer Dorothy Norman whom she was particularly close to, had distanced themselves from her; this rankled with her. She had got to know many of them while travelling the world with her father Jawaharlal Nehru, an avowed democrat.

She had apparently told several people from November 1976 onwards—they included her information advisor, H. Y. Sharada Prasad, and principal secretary, P. N. Dhar—that despite being told by the IB that she would win 340 seats, she knew she would lose. But she was nevertheless going to go ahead with elections. Michael Foot, the British politician and the leader of the House of Commons, for whom she had deep regard, 'obliquely hinted to my father (H. Y. Sharada Prasad),' Ravi Visvesvarya Sharada Prasada was to reveal, that 'Indira Gandhi would call for elections even though she knew she would lose.' Apparently, she also told her good friend US Senator Charles Percy that she would 'lose the elections badly, and that she was worried about her son Sanjay Gandhi.'

Janata Party leader Chandra Shekhar used to tell his supporters that if they wanted Indira Gandhi's attention, 'Yeh gore logon se likhwao (Get this written by foreign correspondents).' An article in the *New York Times* would bestir her more than a piece in a national daily or a speech by an Opposition leader. And yet, while the critical opinion of her friends in Western democracies would have affected her, it is not as if she had to face sanctions against India. Several foreign leaders had defended her Emergency action. The economic situation in the country had also improved. The World Bank was impressed by her handling of industrial relations; six donor nations sent India ₹9.39 billion in foreign aid, which it had not received since 1967–68. India's foreign exchange reserves nearly doubled from ₹9.69 billion in 1974–75 to ₹18.69 billion in 1975–76.

The second hypothesis was put out by Pupul Jayakar. Jayakar offered a spiritual explanation for why Indira Gandhi decided to hold elections. She maintained that spiritual guru Jiddu Krishnamurti, whom Indira used to see, and whom Jayakar had faith in, had influenced her. Indira had met Krishnamurti in Jayakar's house on 28 October 1976. A disturbed Indira had told Krishnamurti that she did not know how to dismount the tiger she had mounted.

'Right action is necessary,' Krishnamurti advised her, 'it does not matter what the result will be.' And, as she was leaving, he told her, 'Do you realize that if you act rightly, you will have to face the consequences?' Jayakar later wrote: 'It was on October 28 (1976) that a frail movement arose in Indira to end the Emergency and call for elections whatever the consequences.'

The third reason—she was concerned about the mounting pressure from those who had been her staunch supporters like Vinoba Bhave and the CPI (M). By October 1976, the CPI had also stepped up its criticism of Sanjay's family planning measures and beautification drives—and called for elections as the only way out.

As we have seen earlier, Bhave had supported the Emergency as an era of discipline. According to Gautam Bajaj, an associate of Bhave who had lived at his ashram for fifty-eight years, Bhave had started to urge her as early as September 1975 to release JP and to hold elections.

'Will you hold the elections ultimately by February 1977?' Bhave asked her, when Indira Gandhi went to call on him on 24 February 1976.

'It is difficult to say,' she prevaricated. 'We have put off the elections by a year.... But the threat before the nation has not (yet) gone away.'

'Why don't you decide to hold elections in February next year (1977),' Bhave insistently tried to pin her down to a definite timetable. She could start the process of normalization by 'releasing people in October (1976)...' itself.

'Since you imposed the Emergency on June 25–26 last year, you could lift it on June 25 this year (1976),' he suggested helpfully.

She had contemplated such a step, she told him. But the assassination of Bangladesh president Sheikh Mujibur Rahman on 15 August 1975 stopped her in her tracks. She feared she too might be killed.

'Indira Gandhi had respect and affection for Vinobaji,' recalled Bajaj, 'but no real commitment to his ideas.'

The fourth factor—and some believe the real reason for her action—was Sanjay himself. Her younger son was becoming uncontrollable and a law unto himself. On 27 July 1976 Sanjay did something which hit her hard. A year into the Emergency, he criticized the CPI which was supporting her government, and spoke openly against the Soviet Union, which had backed the Emergency. He gave an interview to *Surge* magazine which was intended to please the Americans. Sanjay had rubbished the socialist economy, praised big business, and called for the demise of the public sector. Fearing an adverse reaction from the CPI and the Russians, Indira was so agitated that she pulled out her principal secretary P. N. Dhar from an important family function to do damage control. As she waited restlessly for Dhar to arrive, she put down in writing a two-page note, in her own hand, briefing him on what he should do. Dhar was to write later, 'It was a daring attempt (by Sanjay) to bypass the Prime Minister.' It showed that Sanjay had become 'impatient for the driver's seat'.

Having brought about the Emergency 'with ease', and with a political organization like the Youth Congress directly under his control, Sanjay had begun to establish contact with chief ministers—and with other countries without referring to his mother. He thought his mother was 'a ditherer' and would act only when 'pushed by a person with stronger convictions'—him. 'It was apparent to me...that Indira was...afraid of her son,' P. N. Dhar was to write. Sanjay was becoming a law unto himself. But whatever her own problems with him, Indira Gandhi would not 'hear a single word critical of him' from others.

Towards the end of 1976, Sanjay decided that the Constitution should be changed and there should be a presidential form of government. Though Indira Gandhi had toyed with the idea of revisiting the Constitution, publicly she had remained ambivalent about it. In mid-1976, she had asked Congress leaders D. K. Barooah, Rajni Patel, and Siddhartha Shankar Ray—the triumvirate who advised her on legal and constitutional affairs—to examine the issue. They sent her a paper, recommending the constitution of a new constituent assembly to move towards a presidential form of government. The paper was actually—and anonymously—authored by A. R. Antulay. Barooah leaked the paper; Sanjay and his team picked it up and some of them called for the existing parliament to be converted into a constituent assembly. The proposal was to have a directly elected president, with more powers than those enjoyed by the US president—but without the checks and balances which existed in the US system.

To step up pressure on his mother, Sanjay and his coterie got the state assemblies in UP, Punjab, Haryana, and Bihar to pass resolutions to set up a constituent assembly—making Indira Gandhi very unhappy.

Some believed that Sanjay would have changed the Constitution and ultimately taken over as the president of the republic. Others suspected he wanted to dispense with elections altogether. Bansi Lal, closest to Sanjay at the time, had told Indira Gandhi's cousin, B. K. Nehru, 'Get rid of this election nonsense...just make our sister (Indira) president for life and there's no need to do anything else.'

Sanjay had, with his cabal, tightened his hold over the government's decision-making processes. Many analysts believed that elections were the only way she could have regained her grip over the government.

P. N. Dhar, Indira Gandhi's principal secretary, maintained all along that she was opposed to a presidential form of government. In that case, why did she encourage the triumvirate—these were men trusted by her—to re-examine the Constitution? Did she want to use the exercise to strengthen the prime minister's powers and clip the wings of the judiciary, but without going in for a change in the parliamentary system of governance? And was it also a ploy to fob off criticism of her in the Western capitals? For Dhar had told the US ambassador in India that Indira Gandhi had declared the Emergency because she wanted to move away from the Westminster type multiparty democracy to a presidential form of government as existed in the US.

As late as November 1976, which is only two months before she announced the polls, she had, in fact, postponed elections by a year—and done it for the second time. This was on 5 November 1976. In the same month, she got the Constitutional (42nd) Amendment, 1976, passed in the Lok Sabha. Far from undoing the Emergency provisions, this amendment gave sweeping powers to the Prime Minister's Office, reduced the power of the courts to scrutinize the constitutional validity of laws, made fundamental rights non-justiciable, and added fundamental duties to the Constitution. This was seen by the Opposition as a move towards a 'one party dictatorship under the cover of Constitution'—rather than a move towards elections to restore democratic functioning.

By the end of 1976, and this could have made her take the plunge, she was making headway in softening up the Opposition leaders. She had made overtures to several of them in early 1976. Slowly they were coming around—provided she held elections. She did not think they would pose a challenge to her at the polls.

'That is when she started thinking of elections,' Inder Malhotra wrote, 'as the only way to stop things from getting out of hand.' Polls might help her re-establish her eroding authority, and nip in the bud the growing demand for a presidential form of government by Sanjay and his coterie.

■

In early 1976 itself, Indira Gandhi had started to reach out to Charan Singh, Atal Bihari Vajpayee, and Chandra Shekhar who were either in jail or under house arrest. By the end of 1976, some of them were in a conciliatory mood.

Satyapal Malik, who was then a young associate of Charan Singh (later in his career, he would become governor of Jammu and Kashmir, Goa, and Meghalaya) revealed how Indira Gandhi had arrived at an understanding with Charan Singh in March 1976 that led to the kisan leader's release on 7 March 1976.

She used Malik's services to bring around the difficult Charan Singh, who had been her most bitter critic. In February 1976, she transferred Malik from Fatehgarh jail, where he was imprisoned during the Emergency, to Tihar jail. According to Malik, when he arrived at Tihar, he was taken straight to the jail superintendent's room. To his surprise, he found Congress leader H. K. L. Bhagat waiting for him. Bhagat came straight to the point, 'You are going to be put in the cell next to Charan Singh. Aap baatcheet kar laen un se (You talk to him).'

'The Prime Minister wants to hold elections and release Opposition leaders,' Bhagat told Malik. 'Par woh bahar aakar upadrav na karaen (But they should not create disruptions once they are out).'

'He was not averse to the idea,' Malik said of Charan Singh.

'But Satyapal,' Charan Singh warned his younger colleague, 'I don't trust Bhagat.... You get these fellows to release you (first) and then go and talk to Mrs Gandhi yourself.'

Malik was released. He met Indira Gandhi.

'Hum toh haath barhate hain unki taraf (I offer my hand of friendship to him),' she told Malik, referring to Charan Singh, 'par woh haath peeche kar laete hain (but he is the one who pulls back).'

Malik reported back to Charan Singh. 'But I should not be released alone,' Charan Singh told Malik. 'It should be done with 4–5 others.'

'So, others like Biju Patnaik, Piloo Mody, Radhakrishnan of the Gandhi Peace Foundation were also released around the same time as Charan Singh.'

After his release, Charan Singh stuck to what he had promised—that he would not attack Indira Gandhi in public, according to Malik. Only on one occasion, did he get carried away and gave a 'teevra bhashan' (strong speech) in the UP assembly. That was on 23 March 1976, a couple of weeks after he was released, when he spoke for four hours on the Emergency and how Indira had thrown 100,000 people behind bars.

It was several months later, on 4 December 1976, that Biju Patnaik, Charan Singh's colleague in the Bharatiya Lok Dal, hosted a high-powered, exclusive lunch at his 3, Aurangzeb Road residence. Besides Charan Singh and him, there were Om Mehta and Mohammed Yunus, a confidant of the prime minister's, on the government side. Though Brahmanand Reddy was the home minister, it was Om Mehta, minister of state for Home, who used to call the shots, given his proximity to Sanjay.

'I sat in the room outside,' Malik recalled. 'Documents were exchanged inside.'

Biju Patnaik had gone armed with an 'approach paper'—to provide the basis for an understanding between Indira Gandhi and the Opposition leaders. But when many of the Opposition leaders met a few days later at H. M. Patel's House, on 16–17 December, they put forth their conditions. They agreed to 'behave responsibly', but in turn the government would have to restore civil rights, lift curbs on the press, and let the judiciary function independently. On 1 January 1977, Patnaik conveyed their demands to Om Mehta—and suggested that Indira carry forward the dialogue.

Indira Gandhi was also at work on Jan Sangh leader Atal Bihari Vajpayee. Om Mehta met Vajpayee in December 1976; he complained that the Akhil Bharatiya Vidyarthi Parishad (ABVP) boys had indulged in violence and uprooted rail tracks. By this time, Vajpayee was staying at 1, Ferozeshah Road, under house arrest. He had been transferred from Bangalore jail to Delhi for slip disc surgery at AIIMS. He was able to move out occasionally under watch. Hearing about the government's overtures to Vajpayee, Ram Bahadur Rai, then national secretary of the ABVP, rushed to see him. He had just been released from Shivpur jail in Madhya Pradesh. Vajpayee suggested an apology by the ABVP. He counselled Rai, 'Chunav karane ke liye agar khed prakat karne se madad miltee hai, toh ABVP ko taiyaar rehna chahiye. (In order to hold elections, if it becomes necessary for the ABVP to express regret for the violence it had indulged in, it should be prepared to do so.)'

Rai was furious; he denied that the ABVP had indulged in any violence. 'There is no question of expressing regret,' he told Vajpayee. 'We would prefer to do hinsa (violence) than express regret.'

The mood amongst the Opposition leaders was now changing. Many felt they had to somehow get Indira Gandhi to declare elections.

The RSS backed this view. This became clear at a meeting of the RSS and ABVP in Delhi on 28–29 December 1976. Present at it were Ram Bahadur Rai, Bhanu Pratap Shukla, Ashok Singhal, Madhav Rao Muley, and Bapu Rao Moghe. They endorsed JP's call—that an effort be made for early elections and for the four Opposition parties to merge. From the time he was released in 1975, JP had repeatedly called upon Opposition leaders to form a unified party. By this time, the RSS had offered to cooperate with the government—provided its jailed workers were set free.

Besides reaching out to Charan Singh and Vajpayee, Indira Gandhi also sent her emissaries to Chandra Shekhar. He had been put under house arrest on Delhi's Rouse Avenue. The only leader who held out was Morarji Desai.

Sensing a climbdown by several Opposition leaders, Indira Gandhi was now confident that she would win the election. Most of those who had opposed her were now tired men. By the end of 1976, she had managed to bring them around sufficiently.

Decisions at the top are influenced by complex and layered considerations. Indira Gandhi would have weighed up all the pros and cons—Sanjay's growing power and unpopularity, her eroding authority, international opinion, domestic pressure, her own inner turmoil, and the feedback on her chances of winning. She decided that the balance of advantage lay in opting for elections at that particular juncture.

She may not have fully believed the IB's feedback of an easy win. Or the projection by a think tank in Delhi—that she was all set to come back to power. While no politician is 100 per cent certain of winning an election, she was reasonably sure of winning.

'Let's be clear, Indira Gandhi opted for elections,' Natwar Singh said to me, 'because she was sure she would win.'

She called P. N. Dhar and told him to meet the chief election commissioner, T. Swaminathan. On 1 January 1977, Dhar invited Swaminathan home for tea and told him to get ready for elections. A pleased Swaminathan quipped that the occasion called for more than just tea to celebrate. That evening he sent Dhar a bottle of whisky.

On 18 January 1977, Indira Gandhi announced elections to a surprised nation. The date for the election, however, was decided 'by the Prime Minister's astrologers'.

Indira Gandhi was too much of a hard-headed politician to be suddenly conscience stricken about her democratic and liberal heritage, and opt for elections for that reason. Nor was she a leader who would advance the polls knowing she was going to be defeated. This did not square with her political persona. 'Om Mehta told me that Indira Gandhi wanted to legitimize the Emergency through elections,' Satyapal Malik told me. 'Mrs Gandhi also wanted to legitimize her succession plan through the polls.'

While many reasons have been given for Indira Gandhi's decision to call for elections, one of the most compelling ones, I feel, was to put in place a succession plan for Sanjay. All along, she had been grooming Sanjay as her successor. For all practical purposes, he was running the government—and the party—during the nineteen months of the Emergency. And she had done nothing to stop him. She wanted her son to succeed her. But she wanted to curb his adventurism, to delink him from some of his unsavoury colleagues who had developed a vested interest in the Emergency. She also wanted him to 'serve a period of apprenticeship', before he took over from her. Indira would have calculated that elections might steady Sanjay. Most important, they would endorse Sanjay's role— and make him acceptable nationally and internationally. She wanted to project him as 'the rising son of India'.

Through elections, she also wanted to put in place Sanjay's team, a new group of people who would owe their loyalty to him. The established leadership of the Congress was unhappy with his style of functioning. They had to make way, or be removed. Indira Gandhi had planned to give tickets to 200 members of the Youth Congress, which was taking shape under Sanjay, having grown into a six-million-member outfit by early 1977. Mrs Gandhi had been impressed with them at the Gauhati session of the Congress in November 1976, and remarked with satisfaction, 'Our thunder has been stolen.'

But neither she nor the IB had anticipated the speed with which the Opposition parties would unite. She could not have imagined that five days after the announcement of elections, the Opposition groups would merge their parties into a single entity. Leaders of the four largest outfits of the Opposition, the Congress (O), Bharatiya Lok Dal, Bharatiya Jan Sangh, Socialist Party, and Young Turks led by Chandra Shekhar met at Morarji Desai's house at 5, Dupleix Road, in New Delhi on 23 January 1977. Many of them had been together in jail for nineteen months; this had created a new bonhomie among them—something she had not taken into account when she released them.

Contrary to her and Sanjay's expectations, they did not waste time in forming a new entity called the Janata Party. This was not the only surprise in store for her. A few days later, she was shocked when Jagjivan Ram suddenly quit the Congress. He floated a new party, the CFD, which went on to align with the Janata Party. She then decided to play it safe and gave more tickets to established Congress leaders to prevent them from joining Babuji. She ended up giving only twenty tickets to Sanjay's loyalists.

Very soon into the campaign, Indira Gandhi realized things were not going according to plan. As she told journalist Pran Sabharwal, a few days after she announced elections, 'Jab se election announce hua hai, chaprasi theek se paani tak nahin pila rahe hain (From the moment I have announced the election, even the peons are cold-shouldering me).'

She had not been able to gauge the fear and opprobrium Sanjay had evoked—or chosen to ignore it. There were rumours that if the Congress won, Sanjay would become the home minister. Many were petrified. The Emergency had insulated her from the ground; people told her what she wanted to hear. 'When you stifle the flow of information to the people,' Krishan Kant, the Congress's one-time young Turk, had warned in parliament, 'you are blocking the channel of information to yourself.'

Wherever she campaigned, she sensed the people's hostility. At a poll rally at Delhi's Boat Club in February, 1977, the assembled government servants shouted at her, 'No DA, no vote.' Some of them started to wave their fists at Indira Gandhi. She sat there stone-faced. 'Where is your son? Where are you hiding him? Give us two sterilization cases and we will give you our vote.'

Indira Gandhi was trounced at the polls.

Though several Opposition leaders had been apprehensive that she might rig the polls, the results showed the elections had been free and fair. The Janata Party, as already noted, won 298 Lok Sabha seats, and 43.4 per cent of the popular vote. But with its allies—the Shiromani Akali Dal (9), Dravida Munnetra Kazhagam (DMK) (2), Communist Party of India (Marxist) (CPI (M)) (22), Revolutionary Socialist Party (4), All India Forward Bloc (AIFB) (3), Peasants and Workers Party (5), Republican Party of India (Khobargade) (2)—the number added up to an impressive 345. Jagjivan Ram's CFD, which notched up 28 seats, had fought the election with the Janata Party, though it maintained its separate identity during polls. It formally merged with the Janata Party only after the elections. The Indira Congress won 154 seats.

Such was the euphoria that greeted the Janata Party victory—and Indira Gandhi's defeat—that elated shopkeepers opened their doors at midnight to distribute mithai to all till the early hours of the morning. I remember standing by the roadside in Colaba in Mumbai on 21 March 1977, waiting for the arrival of newly elected Bombay members of parliament Ram Jethmalani and Mrinal Gore; when they turned up, the crowd erupted with joy. A drummer banged away with gusto, people danced to words coined spontaneously, 'Zor se bolo Janata Party, pyar se bolo Janata Party, upar dekho Janata Party, neeche dekho Janata Party (Say it with fervour,

Janata Party, say it with love, Janata Party, look up and it is Janata Party, look down and it is Janata Party).'

For them, and for millions of Indians, the dictator Indira Gandhi was finally gone.

VII

Within four months of losing power, Indira Gandhi's mood underwent a change. So did the mood of the country. Unmindful of the unprecedented opportunity given them, Morarji Desai, Charan Singh, and Jagjivan Ram started to pull in different directions. Indira was now looking for ways to bounce back.

The first opportunity came with the mass killings of Dalits by upper-caste landowners in Belchi, a small village in Patna district in Bihar, in May 1977. It had shocked the country. When the incident occurred, she did not take much notice of it. But in July, she decided it would be a good issue to flag. She went to Belchi. With heavy rains lashing the Bihar countryside, her journey was impeded by mud and slush. She had to abandon her vehicle halfway. Undeterred, she got on top of an elephant for the last lap of her journey to the marooned village. The picture of her on the elephant was to become the symbol of her turnaround.

The Dalits, who had been terrorized by local upper-caste landlords, welcomed her with open arms. 'Main hoon na (I am there for you),' she signalled to them. She sat there, the quintessential amma, listening to their woes. This was a role she knew how to play. Belchi sent the adrenaline flowing through Indira Gandhi's veins again. It also sent a signal to her partymen, which she had intended—that, despite her defeat, there was no challenger to her in the Congress. And that people viewed her, and only her, as the leader. And that the party's comeback could take place only under her leadership. Indira was conscious that communities that had formed the backbone of the Congress were deserting her. The Muslims had been incensed by the forced sterilizations. The more powerful among the Dalits were gravitating towards Jagjivan Ram, who was in a position to dole out patronage as defence minister in the Janata government. She had to reach out to the Dalits and regain their trust.

But Indira Gandhi had chosen Belchi for another reason as well—JP. She had decided she would call on him in Patna, after going to Belchi. He had been instrumental in welding the Janata together, and ensuring her defeat. The time had come to mend the estrangement—it would pay her rich political dividends.

14 August 1977 was a cloudy day in Patna. Indira Gandhi drove to Kadam Kuan, a two-storey building in the heart of the city that housed the Mahila Charkha Samiti, an organization that JP's wife, Prabhavati,

used to run before her death in April 1973. JP used the first floor as his residence. By this time, he was on regular dialysis, his kidneys damaged during the 130 days he had spent in solitary confinement in Chandigarh during the Emergency.

He had been released almost five months after being arrested, in November 1975, when his brother, Rajeshwar Prasad, wrote to Indira Gandhi—that JP might not 'survive for more than two months'. 'It is for you to decide,' he wrote, 'whether it would be in the interest of the government if JP dies in jail.' Three days later, JP was released on parole. When his health continued to worsen, his detention order was revoked.

JP himself suspected that he had been slowly poisoned while in detention. 'A number of my friends have expressed a doubt, which I share,' he wrote in an open letter to his supporters in February 1977, 'that my kidneys may have been deliberately damaged.' When the Janata government came to power, an enquiry was instituted into JP's detention but nothing came of it, mired as it was in controversies and delays; however, an interim report found that JP's detention had been characterized by inexplicable neglect—this created a ruckus in parliament.

■

JP's relationship with Indira was a complex one. During 1973–74, he had spearheaded the stir for a 'total revolution'. It had started as the Nav Nirman Andolan by students in Gujarat, which had devoured the Congress government of Chimanbhai Patel. Like their counterparts in Gujarat, the youth in Bihar also took up the cry against rampant corruption and rising prices, and called for electoral reforms; they asked JP to head the movement. It led to the demand for the exit of the Congress government of Abdul Ghafoor in Patna—and escalated into a cry for the resignation of Indira Gandhi.

The anthem of the Bihar movement, sung by one of JP's associates, Janaki—'*Jayaprakash ka bigul baja toh jaag uthi tarunai hai, tilak lagane tumhe jawano, kranti dwar par aayi hai* (Jayaprakash's bugle has awoken the youth, for revolution now stands at your doorstep and beckons you)' would reverberate through the Bihar countryside in 1974–75, as JP criss-crossed the length and breadth of the state. He urged the youth to create a casteless society, to break their janeus for social transformation to take place.

'What, now?' a youth sitting atop a tree at one of his meetings had asked.
'Yes.'
And scores of them threw their janeus at him.
'This is the beginning of sampurna kranti (total revolution),' an elated JP said.
Many associated with the Bihar movement would go on to govern

their states or play an influential role in the years that followed. They included Lalu Yadav, Nitish Kumar, Ravi Shankar Prasad, Sushil Modi, Govindacharya, Shivanand Tiwari, and Lalmuni Chaubey.

JP helped bring the Opposition parties together to take on Indira Gandhi when she declared elections in January 1977. During the poll campaign, his presence electrified people wherever he went. I remember a rally he addressed in January 1977 at Mumbai's Shivaji Park. The park was jam-packed. Bright lights played over the hunched figure seated in a chair on the dais. He could not stand and speak, given the battering his health had taken while in prison. It felt as if he was whispering. But there seemed to be pin-drop silence in that large park. Over a lakh of people gathered there strained to catch every word he was speaking. Very simply, he urged them to defeat the dictatorial government of Indira Gandhi.

They did.

■

JP believed his fight with Indira Gandhi was not personal—some of his colleagues had to learn to accept this. One day, his associates, Kumar Prashant and Janaki, found a bunch of letters while cleaning up at Kadam Kuan. 'Suddenly we came across this potli (bundle),' Kumar Prashant recalled. 'There were about 20–25 letters wrapped up in a piece of cloth. We showed them to JP.'

'Ah,' he said in a tone of satisfaction. 'Good, they have been found.'

These were letters that Kamala Nehru, Indira's mother, had written to Prabhavati, JP's wife. Prabhavati and Kamala had become friends over the years—their friendship had begun when JP and Prabhavati had stayed at Anand Bhavan in the 1930s. This was after JP, then a Marxist, had returned from the US after seven years of study there, and decided to throw himself into the freedom movement.

Kamala started to confide in Prabhavati, and would unburden herself in the letters she wrote to her over the years.

'We read 2–3 letters to JP,' recalled Kumar Prashant.

'I remember lines like "kuchh log apne aapko bahut superior samajhte hain (Some people think they are superior to others)". It was an obvious allusion to Nehru's sister Vijaya Lakshmi Pandit.

There were references to other members of the (Nehru) family also, including Nehru, about whom Kamala Nehru was unhappy, as happens in any family.... She wrote about how difficult it was for those who entered the Nehru family, she said it was an elite family, that Jawaharlal was not able to stand up to the family (for her).'

She also told Prabhavati how fortunate she was to have JP who gave her (Prabhavati) her due. There were words to the effect, Prashant said, 'Tum bhagyashali ho ki tum se barabari se baat karte hain (You are really fortunate that JP talks to you like an equal).'

The next day JP told Kumar Prashant, 'I don't want these letters to fall into the wrong hands. They can be misused. Indu ko hee dae daen (We can give them to Indu),' he said. 'Jo theek samjhe woh kare (She can do what she thinks fit).'

'Why don't we make a copy of them?' Prashant suggested. 'They will then be safe.'

'Woh bhi safe rakhegi (She will also keep them safe),' JP said irritably.

Prashant pressed again. 'Kisi sanghralaya ko dae sakte hain surakshhit rakhne ke liye (We can give it to some library for safe keeping).'

'Isko copy karna chahta (If I had wanted to keep a copy),' JP retorted sharply, 'toh daene ki baat hee na karta (why would I be talking of handing them over)?'

'Is mahaul maen mein nahin chahta ki koi personal attacks ho (In the present climate, I don't want things to degenerate into personal attacks),' JP said. 'Vishwas karke chalte hain (We should have trust in her).'

He was apprehensive that somebody from the Opposition might lay their hands on the letters. He did not want anyone to mount 'personal' attacks on Indira Gandhi and the Nehru–Gandhi family.

JP called up Indira. He told her he wanted to see her. K. S. Radhakrishna, who was the secretary of the Gandhi Peace Foundation where JP used to stay when he was in Delhi, drove him to the PM House at 1, Safdarjung Road. He waited outside while JP went in.

JP handed the packet to Indira. 'These are letters Kamala had written to Prabhavati,' he told her. 'I didn't want (them) to fall in the wrong hands.'

'Thanks,' she said. She neither looked at the packet nor asked any question about the letters. She was trying to show her complete unconcern about the matter, JP told Prashant later.

At this meeting, Indira Gandhi asked JP to 'help (her)'. She wanted him to tone down his criticism of her.

He told her he was waging a fight against corruption.

'Are you saying that I am the one who is corrupt?' Indira asked him indignantly.

The person at the top had to take responsibility, JP told her sagely. He was working for a movement for change. There was nothing personal against her.

Many of the Gandhians were unhappy with JP for his decision to hand over the letters to Indira Gandhi. They criticized Kumar Prashant for not managing to dissuade JP. Narayan Desai and Harideo Sharma, deputy director of the Nehru Memorial Museum and Library, called it a big 'mistake'. For these were documents which had immense historical value.

■

Now, a couple of years later, in circumstances which had changed, JP waited on the spacious first floor veranda of his house for Indira Gandhi to arrive. He sat in an easy chair, with a silver box beside him. It contained cloves which he would pop into his mouth from time to time to refresh his breath, which regular dialysis had turned sour.

Indira, dressed in a sombre, white bordered sari, accompanied by Sarvodayite leader Nirmala Deshpande, arrived punctually at 10 a.m., the time they had arranged to meet.

JP took Indira to his small, austerely furnished room. It had a narrow cot, and a couple of upright chairs, on which both of them sat. That day, the daring and handsome hero of the Quit India movement who had given British jailers the slip in 1942 when he was in Hazaribagh Jail, looked unusually frail.

'Kaise aana hua (What brings you here?)' JP asked her. 'Koi takleef toh nahin hui (I hope you had no difficulty coming here').

Indira talked about her visit to Belchi. She had come to Patna straight from there. 'Bahut dukhad thaa (It was very painful).'

JP said. 'When I was well, I was able to go to these places myself.'

'How are the children?' he then asked. They talked about what her boys were doing.

'What arrangements have you made in Anand Bhavan?' JP asked conversationally. Indira Gandhi reminded him that she had donated the property to the government in 1970. He recalled his stay there when as a Marxist he came back to India in 1929 after his studies in the US. And how, at the instance of Bhai [Nehru], he had thrown himself into the freedom movement, and then gone on to form the Congress Socialist party within the Congress (in 1934), along with other socialists like Acharya Narendra Dev, Asoka Mehta, and Ram Manohar Lohia.

Indira Gandhi had always viewed JP's politics with suspicion. She was convinced that JP wanted high public office. 'It's nonsense to say that he did not want office. One part of him did....' she wrote to Hungarian-born Fori Nehru, who was married to Indira's relative, diplomat B. K. Nehru. Somewhere it rankled with her that her father had at one time seen JP as his successor. In 1953, Nehru had invited JP to join his cabinet. He wanted JP to be the deputy prime minister. B. K. Nehru, who was an ICS officer at the time, had written an aide-memoire about Nehru's invitation to JP. 'The PM told Mr Narayan...that he needed somebody to point out where he was going wrong...The Prime Minister invited Mr Narayan to form such an opposition within his cabinet....'

'The Prime Minister asked Mr Narayan, cajoled him, then begged him...but Mr Narayan's answer was steadfastly "no".'

Nehru told JP he needed the socialists to return to the Congress fold to counter the pressure from the more conservative right-wing elements in the party. The Praja Socialist Party (PSP) discussed the proposal for the Congress–PSP merger. Asoka Mehta was for JP joining the government. Ram Manohar Lohia and some others opposed it. At a meeting of the PSP at Betul in June 1953—where he was accused of being power hungry—JP broke down. After that, he decided to move away from power politics.

JP may have seen himself more as the Mahatma's successor than Jawaharlal's deputy. Gandhi had once told him that he was his true follower, as he wanted to destroy the legacy of the British, whereas Nehru only wanted to remove the British. JP was constantly waging a 'moral struggle' to find both the 'right aims and the right means to achieve them'. But Indira Gandhi found the causes he took up—working with Vinoba Bhave in the Bhoodan movement to voluntarily donate land to the landless, or getting the dacoits to surrender in the Chambal Valley, or effecting a truce in insurgency-torn Nagaland—'confused'. Yet, she was aware that he wielded enormous moral authority. That is why she was in Patna that August day.

On this visit Indira did not talk to JP about politics. Nor about any of the problems she was facing at the hands of the Janata government. Maneka, Sanjay's wife, had already met JP about the difficulties the family was facing. Their phones were being tapped and mail opened. JP was furious. After Maneka left, one of his associates couldn't resist asking, 'But Indira Gandhi had also tapped the phones of all the Opposition leaders....?'

'But now democracy has been restored,' JP retorted.

The meeting lasted fifty minutes. When it ended, a frail JP walked to the head of the stairs to see Indira off. When presspersons waiting downstairs at Kadam Kuan mobbed her, she told them it was a 'personal' visit. She smiled widely, waved, and drove off.

The journalists came up to get JP's reaction. He said he had told her, 'Jitna tumhara bhootkaal ujjwal raha hai, utna hee tumhara bhavishya bhee ujjwal ho (I told her that may she have as bright a future as her past had been).'

When word got around of what he had said to her, editor Kuldip Nayar rang the house. 'How could JP say this about her?' he asked Kumar Prashant angrily. 'Her past has been a dark chapter, not a bright one,' he fumed, referring to the Emergency. The Janata Party leaders were equally incensed. Prashant passed on their messages to JP.

'Ghar aye ko dua dee jaati hai ya bad-dua deni chahiye (Do you bless a guest who has come to your home or do you curse them)?' JP replied.

Apart from his natural courteousness, JP was also becoming increasingly disillusioned with the Janata leaders—and possibly more angry with them than with Indira Gandhi. He had given the Janata government one year to perform, and was deeply dissatisfied with the progress they had made. In October 1978, the Janata leaders would urge him to issue a statement asking people not to vote for Indira Gandhi; she had decided to contest for the Lok Sabha from Chikmagalur in Karnataka. George Fernandes, now minister of Industry, entreated JP to put out such an appeal. JP refused. 'I am now not fighting a political battle,' he told Fernandes. 'That phase is over. You people are fighting the political battle (now).'

The political battle he had waged against Indira Gandhi to end her authoritarian rule was over. It had come to an end the day he selected Morarji Desai as the PM designate. He did not even participate in the victory celebrations of the Janata Party. Madhu Limaye came personally to escort him to the victory rally at the Ram Lila Grounds. He sat unmoved. After Limaye left, he asked to be driven to Indira's house. She came out on the porch to receive him. 'I saw him put his hand on her shoulder,' recalled Kumar Prashant, who had accompanied him, 'I heard him say, "Khel maen haar jeet toh hoti rehti hai. Isko khel ki tareh hee lena chahiye" (There is victory and defeat in the game, one should treat this only as a game).'

Then both of them went inside.

For all his political differences with her, JP held Indira in affection. She was Indu, the daughter of his friend Nehru, whom he would address as 'Mere pyare bhai (My dear brother)' whenever he wrote to him. On 14 August 1977, Indira Gandhi had made the trip to Patna to neutralize JP. But JP being JP did not have to be neutralized. He lived by values very different from hers; in prison he had penned a poem with the lines, 'Safalta aur vifalta ki paribhashayen bhinn hain meri (My definition of success and failure is different).' He made a distinction between the personal and the political. She used the personal for the political. After this meeting, until his death two years later on 8 October 1979, he did not make a single statement attacking her. Indira Gandhi had achieved what she had set out to do.

VIII

The next turning point in Indira Gandhi's comeback story came on 3 October 1977. The CBI came to arrest her that day, and she quickly turned the situation to her advantage.

'Sanjay, I, and Surendra Singh were playing badminton at 12, Willingdon Crescent, when the police came to arrest Mrs Gandhi,' recalled Dumpy Ahmad. 'But they had no warrant (of arrest) for her.' Sanjay quickly took Dumpy into the house and gave him a list of MPs and press people. 'Ask them to get here as soon as possible,' Sanjay directed Dumpy. He then started calling up members of the Youth Congress, asking them to hit the streets in protest.

Indira Gandhi's personal aide, R. K. Dhawan, was also working the telephone lines. He was calling up the newspaper offices. 'If you want a big story, come quickly to 12, Willingdon Crescent,' Dhawan told reporters.

Indira Gandhi's plan had been set in motion.

She had been tipped off that she was going to be arrested. There were people in the CBI and the IB, especially at the top levels, still loyal to her. T. V. Rajeswar, who had been director, Intelligence Bureau (DIB), during the Emergency, had been sent back to his home state, Andhra Pradesh. But Indira Gandhi had got Chenna Reddy, the Congress chief minister there, to post him as resident commissioner of Andhra Bhavan in Delhi. Rajeswar kept in close touch with the IB in Delhi and was suspected of being one of those who had alerted her to her impending arrest.

The Janata Party leaders had held several meetings to discuss whether they should arrest Indira Gandhi. Charan Singh, as we have seen, called for a 'Nuremberg-style trial'. George Fernandes, whose two brothers had been tortured while in jail to extract information from them about Fernandes's whereabouts, called for her arrest. So did the Jan Sangh leaders—Vajpayee, Advani, and Nanaji Deshmukh. However, and this was surprising, given his long-standing rivalry with Indira Gandhi, it was the prime minister, Morarji Desai, who advised caution: 'We must take action only according to the law.' Another dissenting voice was that of Chandra Shekhar, president of the Janata Party, who felt that the people had already punished her by defeating her at the hustings.

But, as the days went by, Charan Singh's desire to put her behind bars intensified. Finally, Morarji Desai urged Singh to ensure that the operation was foolproof and did not misfire.

When the CBI came for her, she was ready for them. She had even prepared her press statement in advance. 'Handcuff me,' she shouted at Superintendent of Police N. K. Singh, who was leading the CBI team, as she came out of the house. 'I will not go till you handcuff me,' she told him. The police wireless crackled, 'King five to queen four, king five to queen four...'; back in the Home Ministry, an anxious Charan Singh paced up and down the room keeping a minute-by-minute track of the drama that was unfolding at 12, Willingdon Crescent. Indira Gandhi then sat down on a cane chair on the veranda. And she demanded an arrest warrant. The CBI did not have one. 'Madam...it is not necessary for the CBI to serve a copy of the warrant of arrest or an FIR,' N. K. Singh said, not knowing how to handle the situation. N. K. Singh had been chosen personally by Charan Singh to lead the operation.

She was playing for time. She knew that Sanjay was mobilizing the media. The crowd around the house was growing by the minute. By now one of her lawyers, A. N. Mulla, who was a former judge, had arrived. So had Congress leaders like H. K. L. Bhagat and Bansi Lal. Finally, one of the officers gave her a piece of paper which was described as the First Information Report (FIR). He told her she could be released then and there, if she would furnish a personal bond.

'Why should I?' she countered.

It was only at 8 p.m. that she was ready to move. By then, press people had gathered in large numbers at 12, Willingdon Crescent.

She emerged from the bungalow to the flash of cameras. She answered every question journalists put to her. And, uncharacteristically, for she was not given to face the media too often, she waited in case more questions were forthcoming. The press statement she had prepared was distributed to the reporters.

Then suddenly, her muscular, moustachioed bodyguard lay down in front of the jeep which was to take her away. He shouted that it would have to move over his dead body. By now a row of cars, jeeps, and buses was lined up outside the house. They were all set to follow her. Sanjay's boys had gathered in full force. She had ensured that when she left Willingdon Crescent, it would be with great fanfare, and with a cavalcade of vehicles following her.

'The CBI were taking her towards Bhatkal (Lake) in Haryana,' recalled Dumpy Ahmad. They had to stop at a railway crossing, which had just been closed. Indira got out of the car and sat on a nearby culvert, refusing to budge. No way would she go out of the territory of Delhi, she asserted. The CBI officers were nervous. They had been told not to handcuff her or ill-treat her in any way. Finally, the CBI had to turn around and bring her back to Delhi. She was taken to the Police Lines in North Delhi. She spent the night there in the company of Nirmala Deshpande, who had accompanied her.

The next day she was produced before the magistrate at Parliament Street. Outside, the riot police were trying to control the crowds. Some shouted, 'Indira Gandhi zindabad', others raised murdabad slogans. The police had to lob tear gas shells to disperse the mob, some of it entering the courtroom.

Inside the court, Indira Gandhi stood in the dock, and asked for water. Sanjay went out to get a glass for her. She dipped her handkerchief in it, and gently dabbed her eyes to remove the effect of the tear gas. Indira was known for her sense of timing. But she also possessed an incredible sense of optics—and she displayed her histrionic skills that day—which would gain her public sympathy.

The magistrate released Indira unconditionally.

From the 'villain' of the Emergency, overnight she became a martyr at the hands of vengeful old men. Charan Singh's popularity slumped. All he could do was to complain angrily that 'they have sabotaged me once again'. It was clear that the operation had been badly botched from the outset. On the day of her arrest, when he had been shown the warrants, Singh had been livid. 'These are not the cases on which we should have taken action now,' he shouted at the officers. But by that time it was too late. The CBI team was already at her house.

Indira Gandhi had not only got the better of Charan Singh, she had managed to highlight the ineptitude of the Janata government, and deepen the cracks between its leaders. Even Janata Party President Chandra Shekhar criticized Singh for his incompetence.

By arresting her, Charan Singh thought he would become the hero. Instead, it was she who emerged as the heroine of the plot.

IX

'Ab aap Raj Narain se mil lo (The time has come for you to meet Raj Narain),' Kapil Mohan sent word to Indira Gandhi in July 1978.

By the middle of 1978, the top leaders of the Janata government were openly at war. Prime Minister Morarji Desai had sacked Home Minister Charan Singh and Health Minister Raj Narain on 30 June 1978; they were now in revolt. The moment had come for Indira to emerge from the shadows and strike.

'Main nahin miloongi, Sanjay mil laenge (I will not meet him, but Sanjay will meet him),' she told him.

'Sanjay had become very close to Kapil Mohan,' said Congress leader Kamal Nath.

By now, Sanjay had managed to convince his initially reluctant mother that Raj Narain was critical to their plans to overthrow the Janata government. He was close to Charan Singh—he often called himself Hanuman to Charan Singh's Ram. Jailed no less than 100 times for participating in agitations, 'he was seen as a terror by the British in the 1942 Quit India movement'. With the toppling game coming as second nature to him—he could have been a champion wrestler if he had not entered politics—he had helped to install Singh as the chief minister of UP in 1967, helped to dethrone him in 1968, and then joined the Bharatiya Lok Dal when Singh floated it in 1974. He now wanted to make him prime minister in place of Morarji Desai. His mantra was clear: 'Follow Chaudhary sahib'.

■

Sanjay had been getting detailed—and regular—feedback from Kapil Mohan about the growing tensions inside the Janata government. In March 1978, Bihar chief minister Karpoori Thakur, who was a powerful leader of the socialist movement, decided to reserve 26 per cent of government jobs for backward classes in the state, implementing the recommendations of the state-appointed Mungeri Lal Commission. The move unleashed widespread protests and violence. The upper castes—who formed the backbone of the Jan Sangh—were highly agitated.

The understanding between the Charan Singh-led Bharatiya Lok Dal (BLD) and the Jan Sangh, forged in June 1977, started to come apart. Under this tactical alliance (all within the Janata Party), the two parties had managed to install six chief ministers between them, following the state polls in June 1977. The BLD had managed to enthrone Karpoori Thakur as chief minister in Bihar, Ram Naresh Yadav in UP, and Devi Lal in Haryana, while the Jan Sangh placed Bhairon Singh Shekhawat in Rajasthan, Shanta Kumar in Himachal Pradesh, and Kailash Joshi in Madhya Pradesh. Fearing the loss of upper-caste support, the Jan Sangh moved away from Charan Singh, aligning itself with Morarji Desai's Congress (O) instead. (See Chapter 3 for more details.)

Charan Singh now upped the ante against the Jan Sangh. And he started to condemn the misdoings of the prime minister's son, Kanti Desai.

In June 1978, Charan Singh wrote a letter to Morarji Desai describing the cabinet, of which he was still a part, as 'a collection of impotent men' not capable of bringing Indira Gandhi to justice. Morarji Desai retaliated by showing both Singh and Raj Narain the door. Their resignations were accepted by the president on 1 July 1978. The countdown for the fall of the Janata government—to take place a year later—had begun.

•

It was through Ram Manohar Lohia that the Mohan Meakin family had first got to know Raj Narain. Lohia and RSS leader Nanaji Deshmukh were good friends of V. R. Mohan, Kapil Mohan's older brother. V. R. Mohan's wife, Comilla, considered herself a Rakhi sister of both Lohia and Deshmukh.

Kapil Mohan would take care of Raj Narain's needs for cars, money, and travel. Years later the company was to get a film made on him called *Great Hanuman* in which he himself had acted. 'They were like brothers,' Kapil Mohan's wife, Pushpa Mohan, recalled. 'Raj Narain would sit on Kapilji's bed and they would talk.'

'Raj Narain was a vegetarian and liked dal, sabzi, kheer...and would always praise the food that was cooked,' Pushpa said. 'Raj Narain used to often phone me and say, "Bahurani, aaj dus logon ka khana bhej do.... (Daughter-in-law, please send food over for ten people)"' Or he would call Anil Bali, mostly at '5.30 a.m.' and ask him to send breakfast for '15–20 people' who were coming to see him. The Mohan Meakin canteen would deliver the 'nashta' at his residence.

A socialist from 1934 to 1974, Narain had become quite religious while in jail during the Emergency. He had started doing puja and believing in astrology. After the announcement of elections in 1977, when he was released from jail, he had gone to Lucknow to meet his astrologer, P. D. Kapur.

'What does the future hold for me?' he asked.

'You are going to win,' the astrologer told him.

The Janata leaders had wanted a weighty leader to take on Indira Gandhi in the 1977 elections. They had sounded out both Chandra Shekhar and A. B. Vajpayee. Neither was willing to stand against her. Raj Narain accepted the challenge—and he won.

Narain liked to think of himself as a 'giant killer'. After all, he had bested Indira in the magistrate's court in 1975 and in the people's court in 1977. Although he was often referred to as a court jester and maverick by the media, he was no pushover. He deliberately cultivated a rustic image to 'declass' himself—one of the goals of the socialists of the time—and to seek attention. And his clownish demeanour hid a will of steel and a fierce determination to bring down anyone who crossed him. If he was for somebody, he was totally for that person, but if he was against somebody, he would mount a no-holds-barred opposition.

An MA and LLB, he also had an impressive lineage, which he would sometimes refer to when riled. Once he had shouted in anger, 'Bol dena hum Raja Balwant Singh ke khaandan se hain, ma ka doodh piya hai, eent se eent baja daenge (Tell them I belong to Raja Balwant Singh's family, I have had my mother's milk, I will take you on).'

Though he had brought Indira Gandhi to her knees, he felt he had not got his due from the Janata regime. And he did not forgive Morarji Desai for sacking him. Nor was Desai willing to forgive him for his opposition. Once when he was still a cabinet minister, he had gone to receive the prime minister at the airport and dabbed his jacket with ittar (perfume). Desai smiled sarcastically and remarked, 'You put ittar but spread bad odour about me.'

•

When Raj Narain came to meet Sanjay Gandhi in July 1978 at the 46, Pusa Road home of Kapil Mohan, he had decided to forgive and forget memories of the 'namak wali patali dal' (heavily salted watery lentils) that he had to eat day after day, and the stinking bathrooms he was compelled to use in Tihar Jail during the Emergency—courtesy Indira Gandhi and Sanjay.

At their first meeting, Sanjay and Narain began by expressing their 'gilae-shikwae' (complaints and grievances). This led to a series of meetings between the two. Either Dumpy Ahmad or Kamal Nath would drive Sanjay to Kapil Mohan's house. Sometimes, they would sit in the car outside 46, Pusa Road, while Sanjay conferred with 'Netaji' inside. At other times, they would wait in a room outside the study where the meeting usually took place.

'I would often sit outside the room along with Kapil Mohan when the two talked inside,' Dumpy Ahmad recalled.

'Kapilji would meet his guests and leave them alone to talk in his study room,' recounted Pushpa. 'The room was soundproof.'

Sometimes, they would meet under the guise of a social function. 'Once we had the annaparashan (first food given a child) ceremony of our nephew. "Netaji" came. Sanjay also came.'

From their first meeting onwards, they decided that Morarji Desai had to go and Charan Singh made prime minister. In the months that followed, the plan, as it slowly took shape, was scripted by Sanjay Gandhi and Raj Narain, monitored by Indira Gandhi, and facilitated by Kapil Mohan. Both Sanjay and Narain also came to the view that Jagjivan Ram would have to be marginalized first. Babuji was emerging as a serious challenger to Morarjibhai inside the Janata Party and could queer the pitch for them; even the erstwhile Jan Sangh group had begun to look at Babuji as someone who would better manage a faction-ridden government.

While Indira Gandhi did not trust Jagjivan Ram, there was no love lost between her and Charan Singh either. He had flayed Nehru and his policies, contemptuously dubbing cooperative farming as 'a Bolshevik move', and had maintained that Mahatma Gandhi should have chosen Sardar Patel as prime minister and not Nehru, who did not understand India.

A bitter critic of Indira for long, he had called her a liar, and as 'wicked as Cleopatra' to British author David Selbourne. But, all along, he had vacillated between his desire to cooperate with her, as we saw, when he had come to an understanding with her in March 1976, to putting her in jail. 'He used to hate her,' Satyapal Malik revealed, 'really because she was PM and he wanted to be PM. And because she had put him in jail, he wanted to put her in jail.' But, in 1978–79, his need to become prime minister was more compelling than his desire to punish her.

■

Apart from obliging politicians, like many industrialists do, with an eye on long-term gains, the top brass of Mohan Meakin had their own reasons for being interested in the ouster of Morarji Desai—and for helping Indira Gandhi. Desai, a passionate advocate of the policy of prohibition, wanted to shut down their liquor manufacturing plants. Desai was suspicious of what they were upto, knowing their proximity to Indira.

The origins of Mohan Meakin went back to the infamous Brigadier General Reginald Edward Harry Dyer, who had ordered his troops to open fire on unarmed protesters gathered inside Jallianwala Bagh in Amritsar in 1919, killing hundreds of unsuspecting people. His father, Edward Abraham Dyer, had moved from England in the 1820s to set up the first brewery in India. Years later, it was acquired by an Indian, Narendra Nath Mohan, and came to be called Mohan Meakin Breweries. Kapil Mohan dropped Breweries from the name.

Indira Gandhi held V. R. Mohan, Kapil Mohan's older brother, who headed the company before his death, in high regard. She had conferred the Padma Bhushan, the country's third highest civilian award, on him. She had also given him the Lok Sabha ticket to contest from Lucknow in the 1971 general elections. When he lost, she brought him into the Rajya Sabha.

At one time, before Maneka came into Sanjay's life, Indira had toyed with the idea of marrying Sanjay to Manjula, V. R. Mohan's daughter. Manjula, however, had someone else in mind. 'Colonel (V. R. Mohan) bahut pareshan thae (Col V. R. Mohan was very agitated),' Pushpa Mohan recalled, 'they worried about how they would break this to the Prime Minister.' V. R. Mohan and his wife went to see Indira. They told her about their daughter's decision. She laughed. 'Don't worry,' she assured them. 'I did the same thing.' She told them the story of how she had married Feroze Gandhi against the wishes of her father. When Manjula got married to the boy of her choice, Indira Gandhi invited her and her in-laws for tea and gave her 'a sari and ₹1,100'. 'Indiraji treated us as family,' Pushpa Mohan said. 'She would ask me to make nimbu ka achar. She liked it the way we made it.'

After V. R. Mohan died in 1973—he was only forty-six—the more pragmatic Kapil Mohan took over the company. While Indira had an affinity with V. R. Mohan, Kapil was closer to Sanjay. The 'all powerful Sanjay' had helped Kapil in 'so many ways' with his business during the Emergency years. 'I don't want to spell this out,' recalled Subhash Arya, the BJP politician, and shied away from giving any details. Sanjay had gifted the first Maruti car produced by his Maruti Udyog to Kapil Mohan. 'I brought the car to Kapil myself,' Anil Bali recalled.

∎

Though Indira Gandhi was collaborating with Raj Narain, she remained constantly vigilant about what he was up to. 'One morning I arrived at her residence to find four water tankers standing there—they had been washing the entire area around the house,' recalled Anil Bali. 'I asked what had happened.' The guards had found a man outside the house, scattering jau (grain) and chanting a mantra under his breath. He told his interrogators that he had been sent there by Narain. Indira suspected that Narain must have been doing some jadoo tona (black magic) outside her home.

'Talk to Raj Narain and find out what's he been up to?' Indira's political aide M. L. Fotedar told Bali.

'Netaji yeh sab kya hai (Netaji, what is all this),' Bali asked Raj Narain.

'Bol dae us budhiya ko ki chinta mat kare (Tell that old hag not to worry),' he said. He had wanted to pray for her protection. 'Shri Indira Gandhi maen mati nahin hai (Mr Indira Gandhi does not have good sense),' he said. He would call her shri for effect. She would refer to him as Banarsi babu.

■

During his many meetings with Raj Narain, Sanjay Gandhi continued to refine their strategy to make Charan Singh prime minister. 'He will have the support of the Congress (I),' Sanjay assured Narain. They pored over the arithmetic of the 6th Lok Sabha. The Janata Party by then had 302 seats, and 345 with allies. Indira Gandhi's Congress had 72, the Congress (S) led by Y. B. Chavan, after the Congress had split in January 1978, had 75. In the Janata Party, Charan Singh's BLD had 71, the Socialists and CFD had 28 each, the Jan Sangh had 93, the Congress (O) of Morarji 51, Chandra Shekhar's group of Young Turks 6, and 25 were unattached.

Both Sanjay Gandhi and Raj Narain knew that they would have to break the Janata Party for Charan Singh to make it to the top. And the way to do it would be to wean away the BLD and Socialist MPs from the parent body. For that to happen, Narain would have to step up the attack against the Jan Sangh and RSS they opposed. Narain also planned to woo all the ex-socialists present in the Janata factions; they numbered 60 in all (they included 28 of the Socialist Party led by George Fernandes, 26 of the Raj Narain group in the BLD and 2 from the Chandra Shekhar group of Young Turks).

One day, to please him, Sanjay told Narain, 'Aap bhi ban sakte ho PM (You too could become PM).' Narain nodded sagely. But he was too shrewd to fall for the lure. 'Yes, my son, it is true,' he told Sanjay, '...but for the moment let Chaudhary sahib (Charan Singh) become the prime minister.'

Raj Narain's softening towards Indira Gandhi became publicly visible by the end of 1978. Only six weeks after she had won the by-election to the Lok Sabha from Chikmagalur in Karnataka in November 1978, the Committee of Privileges of parliament cancelled her Lok Sabha membership. It held her guilty of contempt of parliament for an offence she had committed when she was prime minister—she had prevented officials from collecting information to answer a parliamentary question on Sanjay Gandhi's Maruti project. When she refused to apologize, parliament sent her to jail on 20 December 1978. She remained there for ten days—till the house was adjourned. When Prime Minister Morarji Desai thundered in parliament, 'No one is above the law,' Narain defended her vociferously. She had got the people's mandate, he argued. Parliament had no right to undo it.

■

By the end of 1978, Raj Narain was riding high, as his strategy to undo the Morarji Desai government began to take shape. An incident from that time shows how keenly Sanjay was courting Narain.

'I had just come back from the US and had gone to call on Raj Narain,' recalled the sociologist Anand Kumar. 'This must have been on 2 January 1979.'

On that day, they sat together after dinner at 8, Race Course Road, the ministerial bungalow which had been allotted to Raj Narain as health minister. He had changed the number of the bungalow from 9 to 8, eight being more auspicious for him. It was well past 10 p.m.

Narain was holding forth on the Quami Ekta Manch he had just floated to create 'communal harmony'. It was part of his plan to mount an offensive against the RSS and erstwhile Jan Sangh's communal agenda.

'I want you to give your time to it, now that you are back,' he told Anand Kumar. Till he became an MLA in 1952, Narain was nurtured by Kumar's grandfather, Vishwanath Sharma. Later, in the 1960s, he relied upon his uncle Krishna Nath, a close associate of Ram Manohar Lohia. Anand Kumar would call Narain chacha.

At this point Narain's PA walked into the room.

'Sahib, woh log aa gaye hain (Sir, those people have come),' he said to his boss.

'Kaun log (Which people)?' Raj Narain asked.

'Wahi,' the PA emphasized the word, in obvious awe of the visitors.

'Acha, bhej do andar (OK send them in),' Raj Narain said as he twigged to what his PA was hinting at.

The PA escorted two people inside.

'One was a young man, fair and tall, and the other I recognized as R. K. Dhawan,' Anand Kumar recalled.

Kumar noticed, and he made a mental note of it, that Raj Narain did not get up to greet his visitors. By this time Kumar had figured out the identity of the fair, young man. It was Sanjay Gandhi.

'Aaiye baithiye (Please take a seat),' Raj Narain welcomed his visitors. 'Aap ke liye kya mangwayain (What can I offer you)?'

Then he introduced Anand Kumar to them as having just 'returned from America'. Kumar had come back after four years of study in the US, and helped to mobilize support against the Emergency abroad. 'For us Sanjay Gandhi was the super villain.' He quickly made his getaway.

This incident showed that by then Narain and Sanjay were meeting frequently, although Narain had kept his meetings with Sanjay a closely guarded secret known only to very few. Fellow socialist leader Madhu Limaye—the two worked closely against the Jan Sangh and RSS in 1978–79—was to ask him six months later whether he had met Sanjay Gandhi secretly so as to form a government with Indira Gandhi's help. With a straight face, Narain replied, 'He called on me twice.... But I did not discuss politics with him.'

∎

All through the period of her comeback, Gandhi's foremost concern was how to keep Sanjay safe. And the best way to do that was to get rid of the Janata government as soon as possible; they were unrelenting in their efforts to bring Sanjay to book. Denied bail by the Supreme Court, Sanjay had already spent a month in jail in May 1978 in the *Kissa Kursi Ka* case, which was moving towards a final verdict. *KKK* was a political spoof, which had been filmed by the three-term MP from Rajasthan, Amrit Nahata, a Congressman who had joined the Janata Party in 1977. The prints of the parody on Sanjay and his Maruti project, starring Shabana Azmi and Utpal Dutt, had derisive lines like, 'Sir, give this man a licence to manufacture small cars because he learnt it in his mother's womb.' They were first submitted for the censor's clearance in April 1975, before the Emergency. But during the Emergency, these prints were destroyed. When the Janata government came to power, it charged Sanjay and Information and Broadcasting minister V. C. Shukla of destroying them and for influencing witnesses.

Indira Gandhi was very tense before the final verdict in the *KKK* case. But she was relieved when Sanjay and Shukla, though given two years of imprisonment in February 1979, were given bail and could appeal in a higher court. The Supreme Court was to acquit Sanjay and Shukla of the charges in April 1980, after she came back to power.

On 31 May 1979, Sanjay would also be indicted for the misuse of power in his business dealings in the Maruti case. Indira knew that with the Shah Commission having indicted her, Sanjay, and other senior Congress leaders, the government was getting ready to set up special courts to try her. She was clear she had to strike before they got Sanjay—and her.

X

Luck favoured Indira Gandhi in the second half of 1978. The first windfall was a sex scam involving Suresh Ram, Jagjivan Ram's son.

On 21 August 1978, there was a car accident in front of the gates of the Mohan Meakin plant in Mohan Nagar on the outskirts of Delhi. The car, a Mercedes, hit a man who died on the spot. Inside the car were a man and a young woman. Fearful that they would be attacked by witnesses, they rushed towards the gates of the plant. The watchman, who had seen the accident, called up the office on the intercom. Anil Bali, then the manager, came out. He recognized Suresh Ram, son of Defence Minister Jagjivan Ram, and took him inside.

Suresh Ram told Bali that he was being followed and was trying to shake off his pursuers, when the accident took place. His car had been tailed by two Janata Party workers, K. C. Tyagi and Om Pal Singh, who had been protégés of Raj Narain, and had been keeping Ram under surveillance for several days.

'Babuji dekh laenge garhi ko (My father will take care of the car),' Suresh Ram told Bali about the damaged car. Bali sent the couple home in one of the company's cars.

The FIR Suresh Ram filed that day in the Kashmere Gate police station, told a somewhat different story from the one he had narrated to Bali. He alleged that he had been kidnapped the night before (20 August 1978) by a dozen hefty men. Apparently, his Mercedes Benz had been followed by two taxis in New Delhi. When they reached a lonely spot near Nigambodh Ghat, his pursuers overtook him, forced him to stop the car, jumped out and whipped out their revolvers. They opened the door of the car, and made the young woman sit at the back. They forced Ram to drive to Modinagar; and he and the woman were taken to a room inside a school. They asked Ram to sign blank papers. When he refused, they beat him up until he lost consciousness. They were told they had both been photographed in compromising positions.

Raj Narain's associate Om Pal Singh said that they had been tailing Suresh Ram because he was involved in all kinds of 'nefarious activities'. They knew he used to take photographs with a 'Polaroid camera', to keep his girlfriend, Sushma Chaudhary, a student at a Delhi college, who was from the Jat community, in check and get vicarious pleasure from the exercise. They wanted to lay their hands on the photos and found them in the glove compartment of the car Suresh Ram was driving. As soon as Narain's boys managed to lay their hands on photographs of Suresh Ram and his girlfriend, they rushed the pictures to their boss.

That night, Jagjivan Ram met Narain. The meeting was arranged by Kapil Mohan at his house. Though Kapil was close to Indira Gandhi, he had equally good relations with Ram, and others across the political spectrum. Suresh Ram would visit him, as would Kanti Desai, Morarji Desai's son.

That night, 'Babuji Raj Narain ko manane aaye thae (Jagjivan Ram arrived to try and bring Raj Narain around),' Bali recalled.

Jagjivan Ram obviously 'wanted to strike a bargain' with Narain.

Kapil Mohan welcomed his high-powered guest, and called for tea and refreshments. But Babuji was in no mood for them. Jagjivan Ram and Narain were inside for 'about twenty minutes'. When Ram emerged from the meeting, Kapil saw him off to his car. This must have been around '11.45 p.m.'.

When Kapil Mohan came back into the house, Narain quipped gleefully, 'Aaj yeh kaboo maen ayae (Today he has been caught out).' He said: 'Babu Jagjivan Ram offered me anything I want—money, CMship of a state, anything at all in return for the photographs.' Apparently Jagjivan Ram also told him, 'Main PM banane wala hoon, kisi ko mantri banana ho toh batana (I am going to become PM soon, let me know if you want anyone made minister),' Despite all the blandishments offered by Ram, no deal was struck between him and Narain.

Then Raj Narain handed over some of the photographs to Kapil Mohan, 'around fifteen of them', and kept the rest. 'There must have been forty to fifty of them,' recalled Bali.

As soon as Narain left, Kapil Mohan turned to Bali with an urgency, 'Take these photographs to Sanjay. Now. Immediately.'

A surprised Bali drove to Indira Gandhi's house in the dead of night. 'I must have reached there around 1 a.m. I asked to see Sanjay Gandhi and said it was most urgent.'

Sanjay was woken up.

'Yeh koi aane ka waqt hai (Is this a time to come)?' he fumed.

'I told him about the accident and handed him the photographs.'

He looked at them, 'Tu kya mujhe pornography dikhane aaya hai (Have you come to show me pornography)?'

'Yeh pornography nahin hai, yeh Suresh Ram hai (This is not pornography; this is Suresh Ram).'

Without saying anything more, Sanjay went inside the house. 'He woke up Madam.'

Indira Gandhi came out. 'She was wearing a cap on her head.'

She asked, 'Who else knows about this?'

Bali told them about K. C. Tyagi and Om Pal Singh.

'You keep them both safe somewhere,' Sanjay told Anil Bali. (Jagjivan Ram was after all the defence minister and could have got Indira Gandhi's house raided to seize the photographs.)

Indira instructed Bali, 'And you tell Kapil Mohan to keep Raj Narain under control.'

■

The next morning (on 22 August) the phone rang at 2, Telegraph Lane, the home of Krishan Kant, who was then a Janata Party MP. It was 9 a.m. The family was sitting at the dining table having breakfast. The phone was in Kant's bedroom and he went there to answer it. The call was from the defence minister's residence. When he returned to the dining room he remarked, 'Ek aur bete nae apne baap ko duba diya (One more son is the undoing of his father).' Those cryptic words were the only ones he uttered that morning to his family.

Ten minutes later, an official car came from the defence minister's residence to pick him up. When he arrived at 6, Krishna Menon Marg, where Jagjivan Ram lived, he asked all those seated with him to leave the room. When they were alone, Ram stood up, took off his Gandhi cap and placed it at Kant's feet. 'Ab meri izzat apke haathon maen hai (My self-respect now is in your hands),' he said to Kant. He told Kant that his son, Suresh Ram, had got into trouble. Although he was widely seen as a spoilt brat in Delhi circles, and had got into several scrapes, this time it was serious. He had been using a room at Western Court, a building meant for MPs not far from the Parliament House, to meet his girlfriend. Two nights earlier (20 August), he was going to drop her back home when he was tailed by two henchmen of Raj Narain, K. C. Tyagi and Om Pal Singh. He told Kant what Suresh Ram had filed in his FIR. Babuji then requested his old friend Kant to manage things. He did not want adverse publicity. As they had been together in the Congress for years, the two men held each other in high regard. Kant had been expelled from the party in mid-1975, and Ram had quit the party on 2 February 1977.

Krishan Kant was the only one outside Jagjivan Ram's core group whom Babuji had taken into confidence about his intention to leave the Congress, weeks in advance. This was as early as December 1976.

'They used to hold secret meetings at 6, Krishna Menon Marg, to discuss when Babuji should walk out of the party,' recalled Krishan Kant's son, Rashmi Kant.

During those winter weeks in December 1976, Kant would slip out of the house at 11 p.m., his head covered, his face half hidden with a dark kambal (blanket).

Even though the Emergency was in place, there would be no policemen around, as he made his way out of the house. Suresh Ram would pick him up in his car at the corner and they would drive over to Jagjivan Ram's house. Jagjivan Ram would ensure the guards at the gate of his official bungalow took a 'tea break' at the time Krishan Kant was being driven in. He would ensure that a couple of his personal staff manned the gate at the time. Babuji knew that Indira Gandhi kept him under surveillance, monitoring all those who visited him.

'They would decide the time of the rendezvous at their previous meeting,' recounted Rashmi Kant. They knew they could not fix it on the phone, for they suspected that their phones may be tapped. It was the stuff thrillers are made of.

'I knew my father was going out to meet some important person, and they met quite regularly. He would leave the back door of our house open, so that he could quietly slip in in the early hours without having to ring the front door bell. It was later that he told me the whole story.'

Sometimes H. N. Bahuguna would also be present at these late-night meetings. They talked about when—and how—Babuji should leave the party. This was two months before Jagjivan Ram actually left the party on 2 February 1977. It was also more than a month before Indira Gandhi announced elections on 18 January 1977. 'My father had the sense that Babuji knew that Mrs Gandhi was planning to go for elections soon,' Rashmi Kant added.

Jagjivan Ram was very keen that the Young Turks team up with him when he quit the Congress. 'My father told him he would have to talk to

Chandra Shekhar, who was the leader of the group.' Chandra Shekhar was in jail. He had been picked up on 25 June 1975, the day the Emergency was imposed, along with other Young Turks Mohan Dharia and Ram Dhan. Indira Gandhi had not arrested Krishan Kant, even though the Young Turks would meet with JP at his house during 1974–75. Whenever they would meet, two Local Intelligence Unit (LIU) fellows would come and sit uncomfortably on a parapet running along a drain opposite the house to keep surveillance on them. Once in a while, Chandra Shekhar would walk across to them and say, 'I know you are doing your job, I will tell you what we discussed' and they would move away sheepishly.

Eventually, Chandra Shekhar decided against going with Jagjivan Ram's CFD.

Krishan Kant helped Jagjivan Ram deal with the media. Jagjivan Ram was worried because Suresh Ram's photographs had made their way to newspaper offices. A front-page item appeared in the *Indian Express*. It was written by Saeed Naqvi—and it was a piece not unsympathetic to Suresh Ram.

'RNG (*Indian Express* proprietor Ram Nath Goenka) called me,' Naqvi was to recall years later, 'and asked me to accompany him in the car. We sat in his Studebaker. When he used to go to meet important people, he would travel in his Studebaker. On the way, using four letter words against Raj Narain, he said, "We have to help Babuji".' When they arrived at Jagjivan Ram's house and went inside, 'Ram was crying copiously.' He told them what had happened to Suresh. Naqvi wrote his piece. 'It was a command performance (by me),' he admitted ruefully.

Otherwise, the mainstream media remained silent on the sordid affair. Later, though, the matter rocked Lutyens' Delhi—and the country. *Surya* magazine, edited by Sanjay's wife, Maneka, published a two-page spread of photographs showing forty-six-year-old Suresh Ram and Sushma Chaudhary, 'indulging in sexual acrobatics'. The article was headlined, 'The Real Story'. Though the evidence uncovered by its 'investigative team' would hardly stand up in a court of law, *Surya* ran headlines like 'Sushma pawn in international spy ring', and 'Defence secrets leaked to Chinese Embassy'. The magazine's sales, which had slumped after the Emergency, soared. And Jagjivan Ram's reputation nose-dived.

The court was finally to acquit Om Pal Singh and Tyagi. Whatever the truth of the matter, it was clear that the photos were part of a plan by 'Charan Singh and his henchman (Raj Narain)' to entrap Jagjivan Ram's only son, Suresh Ram in a 'sordid sex scandal'. The idea was to damage Jagjivan Ram. Both Charan Singh and Indira Gandhi knew he was the only other serious contender for the top job—and would need to be marginalized if their plan were to succeed.

Besides Jagjivan Ram's Dalit credentials, Indira Gandhi feared his administrative abilities. He had been part of the union cabinet for an uninterrupted thirty-one years, since the interim government headed by Nehru in 1946. He had led many ministries like communications, food, agriculture, defence. His name had surfaced briefly for the top job when the Allahabad High Court disqualified Indira on 12 June 1975. For six days her position had looked 'precarious'. Even as street protests broke out and the Janata leaders demanded her resignation, restiveness grew in the Congress. Many in the party expected Jagjivan Ram, as the most senior minister in the cabinet, to take over. The IB had told her that she enjoyed the support of only 191 of the 350 Congress members of parliament. She could be replaced as leader. But she refused to resign.

She knew she could not risk Babuji as PM, even as a stopgap. For there was nothing like an interim arrangement in politics. It would be difficult to dislodge a Dalit, without antagonizing the Dalits who were an important vote bank of the Congress. Moreover, as defence minister from 1970–74, in charge of the armed forces, he had strengthened his hold on key links in the system. While she, with the court judgment against her, had now become vulnerable. But by 18 June 1975, she had managed the situation in her favour, compelling Jagjivan Ram also to fall in line and support her.

Again, in March 1977, Jagjivan Ram almost made it to the top when the Janata Party came to power. There were three claimants to the throne—Morarji Desai, Charan Singh, and Jagjivan Ram. A majority of the Janata Party MPs had spoken in Ram's favour. However, the final decision had been left to JP and J. B. Kripalani, a respected Congress leader who broke away from the party to form the Kisan Mazdoor Praja Party (KMPP)—and had opposed the Emergency. 'The idea was to prevent a split in the Janata Party,' Rajmohan Gandhi was to say years later. The duo opted for Morarji Desai. He was the most senior contender, a proclaimed Gandhian and had been in jail throughout the Emergency.

Two things went against Jagjivan Ram for PM—he had been with Indira Gandhi till recently and he had moved the resolution on the Emergency in parliament in 1975. But he didn't see it that way, he told his supporters bitterly, 'A Chamar can never be the prime minister of this country.' It was JP who persuaded an irate Ram to join the government as defence minister.

Again in 1978, a year into the Janata government, Jagjivan Ram began to see a glimmer of hope, as Morarji Desai began to lose ground, and many MPs started to view Ram as a possible alternative. But the sexcapade of his son Suresh Ram proved to be a setback to his ambition once again.

Morarji Desai was not unhappy to see his rival cut to size. Charan Singh was elated. For Indira Gandhi it came as a windfall. 'Kissi bhi keemat par Jagjivan Ram pradhan mantri nahin banane chahiye', she would tell her confidantes. 'Hatenge nahin zindagi bhar (Jagjivan Ram should not become prime minister at any cost. He will not step down all his life).'

As for Jagjivan Ram, Suresh had always been his weak spot. When some years later, Suresh died in mysterious circumstances, Jagjivan Ram said brokenly to Krishan Kant, 'Maain toot gaya hoon (I am a broken man).'

While Charan Singh and Raj Narain were the executors of 'Operation Suresh Ram', Indira Gandhi's more than usual interest in the affair made many wonder about her role from deep in the shadows. Why else would Kapil Mohan rush Suresh Ram's photos to Sanjay Gandhi in the middle of the night? It might have just been a happy coincidence that one of her main rivals was delivered into her hands. For coincidences do happen when the gods turn benign. And they were turning benevolent towards Indira.

XI

'My sense was that Indira Gandhi turned to this dharamkaram (religious rituals) really for Sanjay,' said Anil Bali, who had come to have easy access to her in the years she was out of power. An astrologer had warned her that Sanjay's horoscope showed 'a lifeline cut short'—this had contributed to her increased temple going after 1977, when she had become overtly religious and paranoid about Sanjay's safety.

She had not always been so explicitly religious. In 1966, she took the PM's oath on the Constitution of India. In 1980, she did it in the name of God. Nehru had been an agnostic; her mother Kamala was a deeply religious woman. She was influenced by both, at various times in her life. When Nehru died in 1964, she decided to cremate him with Hindu rites. She did this despite Nehru's explicit instructions in his will, not to give him a religious funeral. But Indira decided otherwise. She knew she was defying her father's wishes. But politicians and religious leaders convinced her that the people of India would not accept a non-religious funeral for Nehru. The pragmatist in her won. She had taken to consulting astrologers during the Emergency. But it was during her years in the wilderness, from 1977–80 that she really came to be 'seen as a Hindu first and a Hindu last'.

After she lost power, she visited temples, big and small, obsessively. In October 1977, she went to the Ambaji temple in Gujarat, considered one of the fifty-one Shakti Peeths; she prostrated herself there. She went to Vaishno Devi, she took part in the Kumbh Mela in 1977. She visited the parmacharya, the most senior shankaracharya of Kanchi, in November 1977, under heavy police escort, especially as she had been greeted by 'Indira go back' slogans everywhere in Tamil Nadu. When she arrived at the retreat of the Parmacharya, he came out of his room. Indira stood on the other side of the well which was between them. The spiritual leader did not say anything but continued to stand where he was. He then looked down.

'My family is in distress,' Indira Gandhi said. 'I need your blessings.'
The Parmacharya stood there for a few more minutes. Then, without saying anything, he turned around and went back into his room. Indira was very upset. But she did not leave. She asked for another audience with him. He came out again. This time she said, 'The country is passing through a difficult phase. Your blessings are needed.' This time he raised his right hand and blessed her. Later, her associates tried to explain away his perceived displeasure. He did not talk to her, they said, because he was observing maun (silence). She had called on him several times as prime minister—and sought his blessings when Sanjay got married in September 1974. Those in Kanchipuram believed that Indira decided on the hand as the Congress symbol because the parmacharya had raised his right hand in blessing.

Others felt she changed her party's symbol from the cow and calf to the hand because of Baba Devraha. He was a siddha yogi who lived on a 12-foot-tall wooden platform on the banks of the Sarayu River in eastern UP; he would descend from his perch only for a dip in the river. When she made her way to see him in 1978, the baba came down specially to meet her. He raised both his hands to bless her.

Anandamayi Ma gave her a rare ekmukhi rudraksh, a necklace of 108 brown beads she habitually wore as a kind of talisman to protect her in critical situations. Another spiritual figure she reached out to was Jiddu Krishnamurti. Rajneesh flourished in her time. The Chhattarpur temple in Delhi was built during her tenure. Dhirendra Brahmachari found patronage in her court and taught her yoga. A constant presence in the Gandhi house, her family and friends worried about the influence he had over her. She patronized the Sri Aurobindo Ashram. The list of religious institutions she reached out to was long.

At home, she had a small puja room. Every day, 'there would be an offering of 108 flowers'. When she won in the January 1980 elections, and returned to her old home at 1, Safdarjung Road, she conducted elaborate prayers to purify the place. She wanted to remove all traces of the previous occupant, Morarji Desai. That same year (1980), on 16 February, there was a solar eclipse. Indira asked a pregnant Maneka to retire to her room. An eclipse was considered inauspicious to the unborn child. Her friend Pupul Jayakar was disturbed to see her become more and more superstitious. Years later, after the June 1984 Operation Bluestar, when she had sent the army into the Golden Temple to flush out the Punjab militants seeking Khalistan, 'Mrs Gandhi conducted a mahamrityunjay paath at her home for a month,' said Satyapal Malik. 'Arun Nehru had personally told me this.' She was apprehensive that she might be killed.

'Mrs Gandhi was very religious,' Karan Singh affirmed. 'She wore different colours of saris on different days (because of religious reasons).'

What started off as a matter of personal faith was also to become a political strategy to return to power in 1980.

∎

Indira Gandhi's increased temple going was not lost on the RSS leadership. RSS chief Balasaheb Deoras had once remarked during the course of a conversation, 'Indira Gandhi bahut badi Hindu hai (Indira Gandhi is a staunch Hindu).'

'Balasaheb Deoras and his brother saw in Indira Gandhi a potential leader of the Hindus,' said Anil Bali, who would see the RSS chief and his brother Murlidhar Deoras (popularly known as Bhaurao) on behalf of Kapil Mohan.

In 1971, the RSS praised her for hiving off Bangladesh, and weakening Pakistan. The then RSS chief Madhav Sadashiv Golwalkar, popularly known as Guruji, wrote to her, 'The biggest measure of credit for this achievement goes to you.' In 1974, she won the RSS's admiration again for exploding the nuclear device—the RSS had always advocated a militarily strong India.

Indira Gandhi's rightward shift coincided with Balasaheb's rise as the RSS's sarsanghchalak in June 1973. By then, she was moving away from her leftist policies. P. N. Haksar was out. Sanjay was in.

The politically savvy Balasaheb wanted to mainstream both the RSS and the Jan Sangh. He used to openly proclaim that he was an agnostic; he would often refer to himself as 'a communist within the RSS'. After him, it was Mohan Bhagwat who was to display a similar political acumen. While RSS founder Keshav Baliram Hedgewar's focus had been to consolidate the Hindus, and his successor Golwalkar tried to give a spiritual direction to the organization, Balasaheb encouraged both the Jan Sangh and the ABVP to support the students' Nav Nirman movement in Gujarat and the Bihar movement led by JP in 1974 against the Congress government. Sensing the growing unhappiness in the country with the sudden spurt in oil prices and the economic hardships that followed the 1973 Yom Kippur War in West Asia, Balasaheb had advised L. K. Advani, then a rising figure in the Jan Sangh, to sharpen his attacks on Indira Gandhi. But when the Emergency was declared on 25 June 1975, Balasaheb was impressed, initially, with the 'discipline' it sought to inculcate, the safai (cleanliness) it tried to bring on the streets, and the order Indira Gandhi said she wanted to enforce in the country.

∎

Five days after the Emergency, Indira Gandhi jailed Balasaheb Deoras—she banned the RSS and twenty-five other organizations on 4 July 1975. The RSS leadership decided to support the underground activities of the Lok Sangharsh Samiti (LSS) set up by JP—and helped establish an underground press and mobilize overseas support to resist the Emergency. But soon the RSS leaders decided that, even as its leaders remained in jail, it would try and effect 'a compromise' with Indira.

Balasaheb Deoras wrote his first letter to Indira Gandhi from Yervada Jail on 22 August 1975. He began by praising Indira Gandhi. 'Your address (on 15 August 1975 from Red Fort) was timely and balanced.' Indira ignored the letter. Balasaheb wrote her again on 10 November 1975. This time, he congratulated her on the Supreme Court setting aside her disqualification from parliament, ordered by the Allahabad High Court on 12 June 1975.

He also tried to distance the RSS from JP's movement, which had demanded her resignation. '(The) Sangh has no relation with these (Bihar and Gujarat) movements....'

Yet again, Indira did not respond. Balasaheb now appealed to Vinoba Bhave, who had her ear. Balasaheb had learnt that Indira was going to Bhave's Paunar Ashram on 24 January 1976. He wrote Bhave on 12 January: 'I beg you to try to remove the wrong assumptions of the PM about RSS so that (the) ban on (the) RSS is lifted and RSS members are released from jails...and...are able to contribute to the progress...under the leadership of the PM.'

Around this time, many jailed RSS workers gave unconditional undertakings to get out of prison, signing standard forms the government had prepared that they would not do anything 'detrimental to internal security and public peace'. Though Bhave did not respond immediately, he was to play a major role in softening Indira Gandhi's stance towards the RSS. Besides Bhave, 'it was also Bal Thackeray who persuaded the RSS to support the Emergency,' revealed Kamal Nath. Sanjay Gandhi used Nath, then his ace lieutenant, to start 'back channel' talks with Bal Thackeray. Founder of the Shiv Sena and known as the Strongman of Maharashtra, Thackeray had been a strong critic of the Congress. After the Emergency in 1975, Sanjay spoke to him on the phone and sent Nath to Mumbai to meet him. Nath thought he would be meeting a stern and unyielding figure. 'But I found him to be cordial, warm, and affable,' he said.

Thackeray agreed to support the Emergency. 'It's good for the country,' he told Nath. Then he added, 'Once the law and order situation improves, the Emergency can be lifted.' He played a stellar role in convincing the RSS brass also to support the Emergency, Kamal Nath told me. Forty-four years later, in 2019, when Sonia Gandhi was faced with the decision—whether or not to support a Shiv Sena-led Maha Vikas Aghadi government in Maharashtra, she was reminded of the support Bal Thackeray had given Indira Gandhi in 1975.

In the years that followed, the RSS maintained that it had opposed the Emergency, underplaying the support it gave Indira Gandhi. The controversy continues to resurface from time to time.

■

Balasaheb Deoras tried hard to meet Sanjay and Indira during the Emergency years. 'But Mrs Gandhi refused,' revealed T. V. Rajeswar, who as deputy director of the Intelligence Bureau had a ringside view of events of the period.

Knowing the influence Sanjay exercised on his mother, the RSS was also drawn to him because of his anti-communist and pro-America views. *Panchjanya*, the RSS mouthpiece, praised him. A Pune Marathi daily, *Tarun Bharat*, also associated with the RSS, even brought out a 'Sanjay Gandhi Special Number'.

Balasaheb eventually managed to 'quietly establish a link with the PM House'—according to Rajeswar. Kapil Mohan was a go-between Sanjay and the RSS. Later, after Sanjay's death, Mohan was to facilitate meetings between Rajiv Gandhi and Bhaurao Deoras, at the instance of Indira Gandhi. (See Chapter 2 for more details.) When the diabetic, and insulin-dependent Balasaheb's health took a turn for the worse, it was Bhaurao who became his pointsperson. He was a frequent visitor to Kapil Mohan's house at 46, Pusa Road.

Indira Gandhi decided to respond to Balasaheb's overtures just before the 1977 elections. She sent a message to him with the request 'Chunav se Sangh alag ho jaye (The RSS should stay away from the elections)', according to BJP leader K. N. Govindacharya who was a protégé of Bhaurao's and worked closely with him. She urged Balasaheb not to support the Opposition parties, and to prevent the Jan Sangh from casting its lot with the Janata Party.

Balasaheb sent word back that it was too late for them to pull back. Elections were underway. It was not possible to do a turnaround. 'We cannot leave them (Janata Party) midstream. But we will talk after elections,' he said, keeping the door ajar for future communication.

Since Balasaheb had not agreed to her proposal he was kept in jail till 21 March 1977, unlike others who had been released after the announcement of elections on 18 January 1977.

'Indira Gandhi was in touch with RSS leader Eknath Ranade, with whom she had a good relationship,' Govindacharya said. 'The line of communication was from Eknath Ranade to Moropant Pingle to Balasaheb Deoras.' She had got to know Ranade on one of her trips to the South when she visited the Vivekananda Rock Memorial in Kanyakumari which he had set up. She was very impressed with what she saw. After that she kept in touch with Ranade, a pracharak in the Sangh since 1938. She was constantly looking for independent channels to give her feedback about the RSS—its thinking and the moves it proposed to make. Even when Golwalkar was sarsanghchalak of the RSS, 'she used to keep in touch with Ramakant Patil of the Sarvodaya, who had close connections with the RSS', according to Govindacharya.

On his part, Ranade opposed political agitations by the ABVP during the Emergency. So, when Congress leaders P. C. Sethi and V. C. Shukla began to target Ranade, alleging the Vivekananda Kendra he led was funded by the RSS, Indira Gandhi got them to back off. Instead, she made Ranade a member of the Indian Council of Cultural Relations (ICCR). This made some in the RSS suspicious; they feared she might split the RSS as she had split the Congress.

Just as the RSS brass had reached out to her for help, she too used the RSS for her purposes—but carefully kept a distance between the organization and herself. For all her opposition to the RSS, she had managed to get it to support the Emergency. Sensing the unhappiness amongst the Muslims about the Congress, she wanted to Hinduize her politics, aware that a silent nudge from the RSS or even a neutral stand by them towards her might help.

■

'The RSS helped Indira Gandhi come to power in 1980,' maintained Anil Bali. 'She knew the RSS had supported her,' Bali claimed, 'but she never acknowledged it publicly. She used to admit privately that had it not been for the support by the RSS, she could not have won 353 seats, one more than she had won in her heyday in 1971.'

Karan Singh also hinted that 'maybe she was in touch with the RSS.... She had her own calculations.' He added, in her defence, '(However), she was neither anti-Hindu, nor anti-Muslim.' T. V. Rajeswar was categorical in his assertion that the RSS had supported her in the 1980 elections. '(The) RSS,' Rajeswar said, 'had specifically conveyed its support to the Congress in the post Emergency elections.'

Though he did not subscribe to this view, Govindacharya admitted that many Congress leaders 'believed it to be true'. What was however true, he said, was that the Congress had sought the RSS's help in several elections. 'Even before the 1989 elections...R. K. Dhawan had sent word, seeking our (RSS) help to support the Congress,' Govindacharya recalled. 'I went to see him. I remember he fed me samosas and kaju.' 'After all,' Dhawan told him, 'you had supported us in the earlier elections also (referring to 1980 and 1984).' Before the 1984 elections, RSS leader Nanaji Deshmukh had exhorted people to vote for the Congress: 'Naa jaat par naa paat par, mohar lagegi haath par (Go neither for caste or creed, only stamp the hand symbol [of the Congress party]).'

In 1980, the RSS might have viewed Indira Gandhi with favour for another reason—the Janata Party's decision to project Jagjivan Ram, a Dalit, as its prime ministerial candidate did not go down well with the

RSS's upper-caste supporters. Its leadership was also unhappy with Atal Bihari Vajpayee who had publicly criticized the organization in a signed article in the *Indian Express* in August 1979. 'Why does it (RSS) not open its doors to non-Hindus?' he had asked. He had asked the Sangh leadership to clarify 'that by Hindu Rashtra (it meant) the Indian nation which includes non-Hindus as equal members.'

In 1980, Vajpayee was trying to secularize his image while Indira Gandhi was trying to Hinduize the face of the Congress.

XII

23 December 1978 was a cold winter day in Delhi. It was Chaudhary Charan Singh's seventy-seventh birthday. Around 800,000 farmers had gathered at Delhi's Boat Club to celebrate. An event of this size was something Delhi had not seen for a long time—there was a sea of humanity as far as the eye could see. Singh was making a power statement that day—signalling that he could not be ignored. He had been preparing for this day since he had been sacked from the cabinet six months earlier. His compatriot and Bihar chief minister Karpoori Thakur thundered from the dais: 'The kisan will demand no more, he will (now) take.' When Singh spoke, he announced the birth of a new power structure. The farmers had awakened and so had the middle peasant castes. They had been subdued for long. Everything he said was directed against Morarji Desai, the prime minister.

But the farmers present at the rally discussed not so much what Charan Singh said that day. They were excited about Indira Gandhi's birthday greetings to Singh—and what it could mean for Chaudhary sahib's politics. The farmers sniffed new alignments in the air. Indira was in prison that day, having been found guilty of contempt of parliament. The brilliant tactician that she was, from prison she had ordered a bouquet of flowers to be sent to Singh on his birthday. The gesture became the subject of animated conversations that day.

When parliament adjourned on 26 December, she was released from Tihar Jail. When she stepped out of prison, she was greeted by the beating of drums and distribution of sweets. 'Indira Gandhi amar rahe' slogans rent the air. She looked at the crowds gathered outside, smiled coolly, and said, 'I had a good rest.' The mood in the country was changing; she had sensed it even inside the prison. Guards and officials inside had saluted her respectfully.

27 December 1978 was another big day for Chaudhary sahib. He had become a grandfather that day. Using the occasion, he decided to invite Indira Gandhi home for tea. The child, Jayant, had been born in America and was there with his parents, Ajit Singh and his wife. 'Mrs Gandhi chai pee laengi, toh Morarji theek ho jayenge (If Mrs Gandhi

has a cup of tea with me, Morarji Desai will be set right),' Charan Singh remarked to Satyapal Malik. When Indira arrived for tea, Charan Singh was at the gate to receive her. 'Gupp shupp hui (They chit-chatted),' Malik said. 'Both sides were happy (with each other that day).' While the wily Singh was sending a message to Morarji Desai that if needed he could join hands with Indira Gandhi, she was signalling her political relevance to Desai—that she too could fish in troubled waters and create problems for the Janata government.

The tea party had its desired impact. Morarji Desai went into damage control mode—he decided to bring back Charan Singh to the cabinet. On 24 January 1979, he made him deputy prime minister, and gave him the finance portfolio—it enabled him to announce sops for the farmers in the union budget that year. But, to strike a balance, and under pressure from the Jan Sangh leaders in the party, Desai also inducted Jagjivan Ram as a second deputy prime minister. But he refused to take back Raj Narain. Narain's resolve to topple Desai increased manifold. He was by now working in tandem with Madhu Limaye. Limaye was convinced that the 'communal' Jan Sangh group inside the Janata government had to be marginalized at all costs.

They raised the issue of the 'dual membership' of the erstwhile Jan Sangh members (wherein they owed their loyalty both to the Janata Party as well as to the RSS)—and reached out to the socialists in the party and members of Charan Singh's BLD to raise their voices against it. They feared the first non-Congress government at the centre was helping the thrice-banned RSS become more of a mainline force—accepted by those very forces which had rejected it earlier. Even before the Emergency, the RSS had started to engage with JP, whom Balasaheb compared to Gandhi and Bhave, and Savarkar. JP had said in March 1975: 'If the RSS is fascist, so am I'—giving the organization legitimacy, a statement which continued to generate controversy for years afterwards. The vexed issue of the 'dual membership' of the Jan Sangh members was to lead to the destruction of the Janata government, as we will soon see. But before we come to that, the story took many a dramatic turn.

As deputy prime minister, Charan Singh was settling into his new role, when trouble erupted in Uttar Pradesh. The UP chief minister, Ram Naresh Yadav, one of his protégés, was removed as chief minister in February 1979. A few months later, two other protégés of Charan Singh's, Karpoori Thakur and Devi Lal, were shown the door—Thakur on 20 April 1979 as CM of Bihar, and Devi Lal on 28 June 1979 as CM of Haryana. The Jan Sangh–Congress (O) backed Bhajan Lal replaced Devi Lal. A new line-up was becoming visible inside the Janata Party—the coming together of a beleaguered Morarji Desai and the erstwhile Jan Sangh wanting to expand its footprint.

Raj Narain, who was in touch with Sanjay Gandhi, kept dangling the possibility of the prime ministership before Charan Singh. Singh decided to join hands with the socialists to demand that the Jan Sangh members sever their ties with the RSS. Singh hoped to keep the Muslims on his side with his attack on the pro-Hindu Jan Sangh and the RSS.

It was not just the egos of the top leaders creating problems for the Janata government. It was also the contending interest groups they represented, pulling in different directions. The Jan Sangh had the advantage of having a strong organization, which none of the other factions in the Janata Party did. The Jan Sangh and Morarji Desai's Congress (O) were supported by the upper castes, and the middle classes. Charan Singh, who had a mass following from Amritsar to Patna, represented the Jats and the OBCs; the powerful CMs who were with him—Karpoori Thakur and Ram Naresh Yadav were both OBCs and Devi Lal was a Jat. A veteran Janata politician like Jaipal Reddy used to say, 'North India has seen two powerful mass leaders in the post Nehru era—Indira Gandhi and Charan Singh.'

As the various groups within the Janata coalition jockeyed for power, JP tried to persuade the RSS to become more inclusive and to open its doors to non-Hindus—to stave off the crisis in the Janata government.

By now, the man at the top, the usually inflexible Morarji Desai, was making desperate attempts to prevent his government from coming apart. In an effort to keep the situation under control, he summoned an urgent meeting of the Janata Parliamentary Board on 9 May 1979. He had managed to placate Charan Singh by setting up special courts to try Indira Gandhi. Much to the relief of the PM, Singh told his colleagues at the meeting, 'I want this government and the party to stay.' To the surprise of many present, Charan Singh virtually disowned his Hanuman, Raj Narain. He accused Narain of pushing the party towards a split. And in one of his rare moments of humility, Singh turned to Desai and said, 'Maybe if you advised him, he would tone down his statements.' Some others suggested that the PM should take back Narain into the cabinet. 'He will create problems for only one ministry (if reinducted in government)...otherwise he will continue making problems for the entire party.'

Charan Singh's flip-flop worried Indira Gandhi who got word of it from her still loyal sources in the IB. Till then, everything was going according to Sanjay Gandhi's plan. Sanjay immediately sent Kamal Nath to Singh. 'This is not the time (to strike),' Singh told Nath evasively. 'The Special Courts are soon going to be set up,' he said, expressing satisfaction. 'Indira Gandhi is going to face trial.'

Ready for a fight, Indira Gandhi led a procession against the Special Courts on 16 May 1979, culminating in a rally. But the response she got was lukewarm. The next day, President Sanjiva Reddy gave his assent to the Special Courts Bill. On 17 May 1979, it came into force.

■

The decks had now been cleared for the Special Courts to try Indira Gandhi—for the crimes and excesses committed by her government during the Emergency for which the Shah Commission had indicted her, Sanjay, and some of her colleagues. A couple of the special courts were going to be set up immediately, in May itself.

An alarmed Sanjay summoned a meeting of his war council. The group comprised Kamal Nath, Akbar Dumpy Ahmad, Bansi Lal, H. K. L. Bhagat, and others. They decided to challenge the Special Courts Act. Kamal Nath suggested that they challenge the Act in Calcutta, not Delhi. Sanjay rushed Indira Gandhi off to Darjeeling. Maneka accompanied her mother-in-law. Sanjay joined them three days later. The Special Court's summons was served on Indira on 20 June 1979 in Darjeeling—not Delhi. As a result, the petition got posted for hearing in Calcutta.

Meanwhile, Kamal Nath had been meeting the legal fraternity in Calcutta, where he knew many more people, having lived there for many years.

Nath also met people in the Judiciary informally to ascertain their views on the Act. One of the judges said to him, 'This should be used in special situations, not against special people.'

Kamal Nath was elated by this 'lucky break'. He went back to brief Sanjay about his conversation with the judge, and the opening it provided. This was in June 1979.

Indira Gandhi immediately flew down to Calcutta and filed an appeal in the Calcutta High Court. She sought a stay order against the summons which had been served on her. The judge admitted her appeal—and stayed the summons. Indira and Sanjay flew back to Delhi the next morning. They went to the Supreme Court with the stay order. Though the apex court had already upheld the constitutional validity of the Special Courts Bill, Indira had ensured that no further proceedings could take place in the Special Courts till the stay order was vacated by the Calcutta High Court. She had managed to buy time—and win another round.

■

In the middle of 1979, to an outsider, it would seem that Morarji Desai was firmly ensconced in the saddle. But the surface calm hid the storm which was brewing inside. Raj Narain now stepped up pressure on Desai— and on his own dithering leader Charan Singh. The Janata Party removed Narain from its national executive in June 1979, and he resigned from its primary membership. Now, neither Narain nor the three powerful chief ministers divested of office—Devi Lal, Karpoori Thakur, and Ram Naresh Yadav—had any stake left in the Janata Party. They joined hands to bring down the Morarji Desai government. On 6 June 1979, Narain asked the Lok Sabha speaker to allot him a separate seat. Three days later, he formed a new party. He called it Janata Party (Secular). Ten MPs shifted to his side immediately. The next day nine more joined him. Their numbers grew— and continued to swell in the hours that followed.

Monsoon sessions of parliament were known to be usually turbulent. The session in 1979 was no different. On 11 July, when parliament opened, the Congress (S) leader, Y. B. Chavan, moved a no-confidence motion against the Morarji Desai government. Only a few days earlier he had been declared leader of the Opposition, replacing the Congress (Indira)'s C. M. Stephen. As LOP, Chavan was naturally raring to establish his anti-government credentials. One of Indira's staunchest supporters, Devraj Urs, the smart pipe-smoking chief minister of Karnataka, had broken ranks with her—and joined hands with the Y. B. Chavan group. This upset her no end. For it was Urs who had enabled her victory in 1978 from Chikmagalur, when slogans would rend the air, 'Ek sherni, sau langur, Chikamagalur, Chikamagalur (One lioness versus a hundred monkeys that's the story of Chikamagalur).' That evening when a Dalit Congress leader B. P. Maurya called on her, he found her almost in tears. 'Urs...has left...and...I'll be convicted by the end of October...'

But soon, she was back to tracking every move made by the MPs— and knew not just the arithmetic of the Lok Sabha backwards but also the composition of the Janata Party. Of the 302 MPs of the Janata Party, 93 belonged to the Jan Sangh, 71 to the Bharatiya Lok Dal (of these, 31 belonged to the Charan Singh group, 26 to the Raj Narain group, and 14 to the Biju Patnaik group). Then there were 51 from the Congress (O) faction, headed by Morarji Desai, and 6 were Young Turks led by Chandra Shekhar. Both the Socialist group and the CFD led by Jagjivan Ram had 28 each and the rest were members not attached to any party.

Even though her Congress faction in parliament had diminished, Indira Gandhi and Sanjay now stepped up their efforts to bring down Morarji Desai as PM—and install Charan Singh in his place. But, suddenly Singh had become their biggest problem. He was blowing hot and cold—and politics was in a state of 'restless motion'.

Again Sanjay Gandhi rushed Kamal Nath back to the vacillating Charan Singh. 'Mauka kho jayega (You will lose the opportunity if you don't move now),' Nath reasoned with Singh.

'I will let you know tomorrow,' Charan Singh prevaricated.

Kamal Nath guessed why Charan Singh was hesitating. He decided to act on his hunch.

'I found out who was his astrologer,' said Kamal Nath. 'I went to see him. He lived in Daryaganj.'

'These are not good times,' the astrologer moaned.

'Then make them good,' Nath directed him. 'I managed to persuade him.'

'It was during those critical days,' Pupul Jayakar was to write later, 'that Charan Singh's favourite astrologer informed him that the stars were propitious for his achieving the highest position in the country. It was with this assurance that he (Charan Singh) finally resigned.'

■

Even as most of the 71 Bharatiya Lok Dal MPs were gravitating towards Raj Narain in those hours, all eyes were now on the socialist bloc of 28 MPs inside the Janata Party. Indira Gandhi was shown the names of these MPs who were ready to 'defect'. She went down the list with her forefinger. It paused against only one name—George Fernandes. She did not believe he would defect. He did. He had put up a spirited defence of the government during a debate in parliament on Thursday, 12 July 1979. But he had made a 180-degree turn by Saturday, 14 July. That evening, the socialists, including Fernandes, decided to break away from the Janata Party. The Janata leaders were shocked. Even Fernandes's family could not comprehend this turnaround. It was Fernandes's socialist colleague, Madhu Limaye, who had persuaded him to change sides.

On 15 July, Limaye addressed a brief press conference in one of the bungalows on Pandara Road normally allotted to MPs. 'If the creation of the Janata Party was a historic necessity for the purposes of defeating the Emergency and Indira dictatorship,' Limaye told us astonished journalists, '(the) total break-up of the Janata Party is the historic necessity (today)…. Without doing this,' he went on, 'it would not be possible to fight the communal virus or provide an alternative government.'

Limaye had initially failed to convince Fernandes with his ideological arguments. Then he made an appeal to Fernandes at the emotional level, Fernandes's colleague, Jaya Jaitly, was to reveal years later. Apparently, Limaye said: 'Do all our years of friendship mean nothing to you?' Fernandes replied, 'Madhu, if it all comes to just that, I will submit my resignation tomorrow morning.'

'George knew he was committing hara-kiri,' said his associate Ravi Nair years later, 'when he changed his mind that Saturday evening (14 July 1979) when the socialists had met.'

On Sunday, 15 July 1979, Fernandes and the socialist group of MPs in the party quit the Janata Party and joined hands with the breakaway Janata (S), which Raj Narain had floated, and was leading the revolt. Charan Singh was to assume its leadership on 16 July. H. N. Bahuguna had also left Jagjivan Ram's side after Indira Gandhi had reached out to him and convinced him to defect.

Ninety-three MPs walked out of the government that day—they belonged to the BLD, Socialists, and CFD (which left with H. N. Bahuguna); some were independent. Morarji Desai was left with only 214 MPs supporting him; he needed at least 270 for his government to survive.

Seeing the numbers stacked against him, Morarji Desai drove to Rashtrapati Bhavan on 15 July 1979. He had decided not to face the no-confidence motion slated for the next day. He handed in his resignation to President Neelam Sanjiva Reddy. In less than a week, the Janata government had unravelled with a speed that was breathtaking.

■

The situation became even more bizarre after Morarji Desai's exit—but Indira Gandhi did not let down her guard. In the hours before Desai's resignation, Jagjivan Ram tried to mobilize support for himself and was promised the backing of the Vajpayee-led Jan Sangh group; he had promised the deputy prime ministership to Vajpayee. His bid for the prime ministership might have succeeded had Desai resigned as leader of the Janata Parliamentary Party (JPP), and made way for Ram. For Desai had resigned only as PM, not as leader of the JPP. But Desai refused. Even a day after he resigned, on 16 July, JP beseeched Desai: 'Step down from the leadership of the Janata Parliamentary Party.' He remained adamant; he was not going to make way for Ram.

The president now called upon the second largest party in the Lok Sabha, the Congress (S), to form the government. Y. B. Chavan declined. Instead, Chavan, with his 75 MPs, offered to support the group led by Charan Singh. It was then that Indira Gandhi made her grand gesture—to lend Singh the support of her 72 MPs. Singh wrote to Indira Gandhi and thanked her for her 'unconditional support'. This was meant to provide a fig leaf to the socialists to accept the support of 'dictator' Indira Gandhi whom they had so vehemently opposed. The socialists' dilemma—whether to back the Congress they had fought all their life or support the BJP they held to be communal—was to dog their steps for the next four decades.

Charan Singh had managed to rustle up the support of 269 MPs— Janata Party (S) (93), Congress (S) (75), Congress (I) (72), AIADMK (18), RPI (6), PWP (5). It was a close call. But Madhu Limaye was confident of the support of the 22-member CPI (M) for Singh.

Like Indira Gandhi, the Janata men who had dismantled her authoritarian regime had also 'buried aeons deep ideology and principles'. They now believed that everything was 'fair in love and war'. The president now invited Charan Singh to form the government—and to prove his majority within a month.

Charan Singh was sworn in as PM on 28 July 1979. Y. B. Chavan took over as deputy PM. Raj Narain did not join the cabinet. He had fulfilled his vow to topple Morarji Desai and install Charan Singh as PM. 'My life's ambition is fulfilled,' a euphoric Singh told his supporters.

Soon after he was sworn in, he called up Indira Gandhi. He said he would come and call on her at 12, Willingdon Crescent. He was going to visit an ailing Biju Patnaik in the Willingdon Hospital (now renamed Dr Ram Manohar Lohia Hospital). He would stop at Indira's residence on his way back. However, as Satyapal Malik recalled, one of his relatives dissuaded him at the last moment. 'Why should you go to her, you are PM now. She should come calling on you.'

Charan Singh decided to skip the visit.

Indira Gandhi was waiting in her portico for the PM, a bouquet of flowers in her hand. There were around 25 senior Congress leaders standing there with her. 'I was there at her house at the time,' Malik said, 'waiting for the PM to arrive.' Indira saw the prime minister's cavalcade of cars drive past her house instead of turning into her gate. 'I saw her face turn red,' recalled Malik. 'She threw away the bouquet and went inside the house. I knew then that the Charan Singh government was not going to last very long.' Malik said.

Indira Gandhi felt humiliated as word went around that she had waited with a garland and the new PM did not show up. Later, Charan Singh tried to make amends. But she sent word back to him, 'Ab nahin (Not now).'

After this, Charan Singh's problems kept mounting. A condition implicit in Indira Gandhi's support to Singh—though it was supposed to be 'unconditional'—was that the new prime minister would scrap the Special Courts which were trying her and Sanjay. But, Singh continued to harp on the need to bring Indira to trial. 'If Indiraji wants to support me, there can be no bargain,' he said, ruling out the withdrawal of Special Courts. She worried only about one thing—that he did not team up with Jagjivan Ram again and get the support of the Janata Party he had quit. If he had got Ram's backing, even at that stage (the Janata Party still had 211 MPs), Singh's government could have survived, even without her help. For all Singh's dislike of Ram, both men were capable of doing a deal. That is why she had decided to support Singh as prime minister; it had made the split in the Janata Party irrevocable.

Indira Gandhi now reached out to Jagjivan Ram. Kamal Nath first set up a meeting with Suresh Ram, and Indira Gandhi followed it up by sending her troubleshooter, Bhishma Narain Singh, to meet Ram. Jagjivan Ram also wanted to explore if he could become PM with her support. But she offered to make him only a caretaker prime minister. Ram saw through her ploy. He used her offer, which he turned down, to strike a bargain with the Janata leadership. The Janata Party declared him its prime ministerial candidate in the 1980 general elections.

In 1979, Indira Gandhi was not really interested in the continuation of Charan Singh's government in power. If it were not twenty-three days, it might have lasted for forty-six days. Or at best, for ninety-two days. From the beginning her plan was to discredit and remove the Janata trimurti one by one. And then to go for a mid-term poll.

'Do you think we can tolerate a man who called Indiraji a liar?' Sanjay Gandhi told a crony, 'We will...make mincemeat out of the man.'

'Sanjay Gandhi had a Machiavellian mind nobody on the Janata side could match,' said Ravi Nair.

Twenty-three days after she had propped up Charan Singh as PM, Indira Gandhi withdrew her support to him. He resigned on 20 August 1979, and recommended the dissolution of the Lok Sabha. The president did not give Jagjivan Ram a chance to form the government, a grievance he nursed till the end of his life. Instead, President Reddy chose to accept the recommendation to dissolve parliament by a government which had not yet proved its majority. Singh was the only prime minister in the history of independent India who could not prove his majority on the floor of parliament. The president asked him to continue as caretaker PM—and called for elections in January 1980.

The Janata Party went to the polls with Jagjivan Ram at the helm. Leaders from the Y. B. Chavan-led Congress (S) started to gravitate to Indira Gandhi again. H. N. Bahuguna returned to the Congress (I) fold, and was made secretary general of the party; he brought Indira the support of the Muslims led by the Shahi Imam of Jama Masjid in 1980. She used him but did not take him into her cabinet after she came back to power in 1980.

The erstwhile Jan Sangh leaders, Vajpayee and Advani, launched a new party in April 1980, and called it the Bharatiya Janata Party (BJP). The Janata Party (Secular) renamed itself the Lok Dal before the 1980 elections. Its president, Charan Singh, expelled his vice president and his Hanuman Raj Narain for anti-party activities on 1 April 1980. Narain was to contest against Singh the man he had installed as PM in the 1979 in the 1984 polls. Though he lost that election, his relationship with Singh was at an end; surprisingly, his relationship with the Gandhi family endured till the end of his life.

When Rajiv Gandhi came to power in 1984, he allotted Raj Narain a house in Laxmi Bai Nagar, as part of the freedom fighter's quota he especially constituted. Narain had told him, 'Your mataji (mother) came in my dreams. She said she was pained that I did not even have a house of my own to live in.'

The scattered and defeated non-Congress forces were to regroup again ten years later under the leadership of V. P. Singh—and trounce the Congress again in 1989, as we shall see in Chapter 3. But, in August 1979, their fragmentation was complete—as the Janata experiment passed into history. Indira Gandhi had succeeded in her mission.

XIII

In 1971, a correspondent of *Newsweek* had asked Indira Gandhi during the campaign: 'What is the issue in this election?' 'I am the issue,' she had replied quite unabashedly. She knew that, as in 1971, so also in 1980, the elections revolved around the pronoun 'she'. She—Indira Gandhi—had become the central issue of the elections again.

Indira Gandhi hit the road in September 1979, even as the stunned Janata leaders were gathering their wits together—or blaming each other for the fall of their government. She left her house with two suitcases which contained eight elegant saris, eight full-sleeved blouses; two flasks, one for boiled water, the other for cold milk; dry fruits; and an orange-coloured, Japanese-made, portable tubelight. She covered over 40,000 kilometres by car, plane, and helicopter in the first ten weeks alone as she criss-crossed the country to pursue victory at the polls.

She spoke about the infighting amongst the Janata leaders, labour unrest, and soaring prices. Slogans like 'Janata ho gayi fail, kha gaya chini aur mithi ka tel (The Janata government has failed, it's been devoured by the kerosene and sugar shortages)' abounded. The media called it a 'kerosene and sugar election'. But Indira Gandhi kept the focus firmly on herself—on the decisive leadership that only she could provide. She did not talk much about socialism, secularism, or about removing poverty. She only asked people to elect a 'government that works'.

In November 1979, S. Venkat Narayan, the executive editor of *India Today*, who had covered Indira Gandhi's election campaigns in the past, accompanied her on the campaign trail. He and a German photographer travelled with her for a few days in a Fokker Friendship aircraft provided by an Andhra industrialist. They flew to towns and cities in Madhya Pradesh, Maharashtra, Andhra Pradesh, and Tamil Nadu. In Chennai, she arrived in the middle of the night and addressed enthusiastic supporters on Mount Road, along with M. Karunanidhi. Wherever she went, crowds awaited her. She was contesting from two constituencies, Raebareli in UP and Medak in Andhra Pradesh. In Medak, the top leaders of Andhra Pradesh from her party, P. V. Narasimha Rao, Marri Chenna Reddy, and N. Janardhana Reddy, accompanied her to the collector's office where she filed her nomination.

She would freshen up just before the plane landed at the next stop on the campaign trail. Her speeches everywhere were brief. She would speak for only ten to fifteen minutes. 'Vote for the hand', was her simple message at the end. But she would make a point of saying it in the local language. At night, driving through the countryside, she would fix the portable tubelight at an angle in the car so that her face would be lit up for the crowds lined up to see her. Darshan was all they wanted. She knew this.

Based on what he had seen, S. Venkat Narayan predicted that Indira Gandhi was coming back with a massive majority. 'Churchill had to wait for six years to return to power, Napoleon for seven and De Gaulle for 12 years,' he wrote. 'If Mrs Gandhi returns to power next month, it will certainly be the quickest comeback in recent political history.'

The issue hit the stands the next day. Her office called him.

'Venkatji, namaskar. Main Yashpal Kapoor bol raha hoon. Aap jante hi honge (This is Yashpal Kapoor speaking, you must have heard of me).' It was the voice of Indira Gandhi's longest serving aide, Yashpal Kapoor. 'Madam asked me to ring you up and thank you.'

'Why?'

'You have written saying she is winning.'

'Please convey my thanks to her. But please tell her if people had thrown shoes at her, I would have written that also.'

'Would you like to meet her?' Kapoor asked.

'Is there any journalist who would say no to an interview with Indira Gandhi?'

'We are going to Kanpur from the technical area at 3 p.m. You can come there.'

It was twelve noon already. Narayan, who had been on the road for days, unshaven and dishevelled, tried to get his wife to rush his shaving kit and a hairbrush to the office. She could find neither. 'But she sent me a suit I had bought in London.'

The next day he got to interview Indira Gandhi in the Fokker Friendship, in which a little area was cordoned off near the cockpit. Sitting in that corner, she would dictate letters. Her steno would type them on a Remington typewriter, 'of World War II vintage'. She would then correct them before the final copy was typed up for her to sign.

Indira looked at Narayan's unshaven face and then at the object in his hand. 'What is this?' she asked suspiciously. It was a tape recorder. It was the only portable one the *India Today* used to have in those days.

'I don't think this will work,' she said, looking at it with contempt.

'I will be taking notes and you will not be misquoted.'

The interview started.

'If you come to power, what will be the role of V. C. Shukla and Sanjay Gandhi?' Narayan asked her.

Her brow wrinkled at the mention of Sanjay Gandhi.

'I am not an astrologer,' she said. 'If we come to power, we will take it from there.'

They landed back in Delhi at 10 p.m. But there was no sign of a ladder to help them alight. Fifteen minutes passed. She was getting restless.

'Yashpal?' she called out to her aide.

'Yes, ma'am.'

'What is the height between the plane and the ground?' she asked.

'About ten feet,' he replied.

'I am going to jump, you people come when the ladder arrives,' she told him.

She jumped from the plane and walked away briskly towards the terminal building. Everyone else waited for the stepladder to arrive to disembark.

The next morning, when the issue of *India Today* hit the stands, it carried Narayan's interview with Indira. But the cover carried even more startling news put out by two psephologists—Prannoy Roy and Ashok Lahiri from the Delhi School of Economics—based on an opinion poll with 25,000 people. They predicted a landslide win for Indira Gandhi. That is what it turned out to be. She won 353 Lok Sabha seats, one more than what she had got in her heyday in 1971.

There were many reasons for Indira's victory in 1980. People were tired of the warring and inept Janata leaders who had lost sight of why people had put them in power. In contrast, Indira projected herself as a strong and decisive leader. People were weighed down by the prices which had gone up by over 20 per cent from February 1979 to the end of year. She made full use of the people's economic hardships to drive home the point that only she could give them relief.

There was also a backlash by the upper castes. They reacted to the assertiveness displayed by the rise of the middle peasant castes represented by Charan Singh—and went back to the Congress (I) fold. Many Dalits who had looked to Babu Jagjivan Ram as an alternative in 1977 also returned to Indira Gandhi's side. Against expectation, she also received support from some Muslims, even though Sanjay's forcible sterilization campaign had alienated many; this helped her partially recreate the Congress's old Brahmin–Dalit–Muslim vote base. Sanjay had deliberately kept a low profile throughout the poll campaign. Indira's temple going and her 'pro-Hindu' turn during 1977–80 made up for the loss of Muslim support. And it helped her take the 'Hindu-first' card away from the BJP.

The carefully calibrated campaign by Indira and Sanjay to discredit the Janata government over thirty-three months had paid off. As Indira Gandhi basked in her victory, a young colleague remembered what she had told her back in 1977. 'Don't you know, you cannot go off centre-stage?' Indira had said to Ambika Soni. 'For in the wings, it is very cold.'

■

Indira Gandhi was sworn in, once more, as India's prime minister on 14 January 1980. She had well and truly bounced back. She rejoiced, less for herself and more for Sanjay. Sanjay won from Amethi handsomely. It was he who had selected the Congress candidates. This time, unlike in 1977, of the 353 who won, 234 were not only first-timers but were new to politics. And 150 of them were 'staunch Sanjay supporters'. They were personally chosen by him to consolidate his power base. The victory had given him legitimacy as the country's 'crown prince'. He was also quick to rehabilitate old loyalists like Jagmohan Malhotra. Removed by the Janata government as the controversial vice chairman of the Delhi Development Authority for the bulldozers he had deployed in the Turkman Gate demolitions, he was now made lieutenant governor of Delhi.

Six months after the Lok Sabha elections, Indira dismissed nine state governments on the ground that they too had lost the mandate to rule— just as the Janata government had done in mid-1977. The Congress swept back to power in eight of them, except in Tamil Nadu. Sanjay installed 'his men' as CMs of most states—Madhav Sinh Solanki in Gujarat, Arjun Singh in Madhya Pradesh, Jagannath Pahadia in Rajasthan, A. R. Antulay in Maharashtra. They took charge in the second week of June 1980.

Sanjay wanted to become the chief minister of Uttar Pradesh, the country's largest state. The party had won handsomely in UP, getting 309 out of 425 seats in the assembly. It had notched up 51 out of the 85 seats in the Lok Sabha elections six months earlier.

On 31 May 1980, Sanjay sent Dumpy Ahmad to Lucknow to prepare the ground for his installation as chief minister. Within three years, Dumpy had become one of Sanjay's closest aides. Unlike those who left Indira Gandhi's side when she went out of power, he had decided to work with Sanjay just when he was out of power.

Dumpy Ahmad's Lucknow mission was to create a consensus around Sanjay's name as the CM-designate and leader of the UP legislature party.

On 4 June 1980, the UP legislature party met in Lucknow. Shiv Shankar was the party observer. Everything was in place. The Congress legislature party passed a resolution electing Sanjay Gandhi as the leader. Other than that, they left the decision to Indira Gandhi.

The meeting called at 11 a.m. was over by noon. Dumpy Ahmad flew back to Delhi in the defence minister's plane. C. P. N. Singh, who was minister of state for Defence and trusted by the Gandhis, had arranged it. By 2 p.m., Dumpy Ahmad was back at 1, Safdarjung Road, waiting restlessly to see Indira Gandhi. He could meet her only at 4 p.m.

'I handed the resolution to her.'

'The MLAs want Sanjay to be the CM,' Dumpy Ahmad told her.

'No,' Indira Gandhi told him flatly. 'I can't spare him.'

'He has to have experience (of administration),' Dumpy Ahmad protested. 'What better place than UP to acquire it?'

'Don't get on my nerves,' she told him irritably. 'He can't be made CM.'

Dumpy Ahmad stayed on at the house till dinner time. 'I used to be there 24/7 in those days.' He raised the issue again at dinner, this time in front of Sanjay.

Indira Gandhi put her foot down again.

'I have made up my mind,' she told them flatly. They could choose whoever else they wanted, she offered, and she would appoint that person.

Indira who could not say 'no' to Sanjay throughout her life, said a firm and repeated 'no' to him now.

'From the dinner Sanjay sent for R. K. Dhawan,' recalled Dumpy. Ahmad Dhawan was asked to call up V. P. Singh. Initially, VP was reluctant to take over as chief minister—but eventually he agreed.

In June 1980, Indira Gandhi did not want to rock the boat by appointing Sanjay as the chief minister. She knew he would arouse the ire of the Opposition; his appointment would kick up a controversy around him once again. She wanted the dust to settle on the odium around the Emergency— and his role in it—before making her next moves. She had a larger role in mind for him, as her successor. But she wanted him to grow into it gradually. In any case, she wanted him by her side in Delhi. She had come to depend on him during her lean years—and gave him full credit for the Congress's victory in 1980.

'Tell your friend (Sanjay), he cannot become CM,' Indira also told Congress leader H. R. Bhardwaj. 'Tell him that if he insists, I will resign.'

Sanjay, otherwise used to getting his way, did not insist this time. Two weeks later, he was no more.

XIV

On 13 December 1980, a helicopter carrying Indira Gandhi landed at Yol Camp in Kangra. The chief minister of Himachal Pradesh, Ram Lal, was there with his ministerial entourage to receive the prime minister. Indira had arrived to pray at the temple of Chamunda Devi in Palampur, considered an incarnation of Goddess Durga. Interestingly, Indira herself had been hailed as 'Durga' nine years earlier, after the liberation of Bangladesh.

The sixteenth-century temple drew thousands of devotees every year. Indira Gandhi was a great believer in the goddess. Until she died in 1984, prayers were offered regularly in her name at the temple, and prasad would be taken back to her in Delhi. 'She would put money in a lifafa (envelope) and give it to me,' Anil Bali recounted. 'Every two months, I would take ₹101 from her for the temple.'

This time, though, she was on a sombre mission. She had arrived to offer prayers in the memory of Sanjay who had died in an air crash on 23 June that year. He had been flying a small plane, a Pitts S2-A, and lost control of the aircraft. Indira had been slated to come to Chamunda with him a day before he died.

When she won in January 1980, Anil Bali had suggested to her that she should personally visit Chamunda Devi after taking the oath of office, and get the goddess's blessings. The day she took the oath on 14 January 1980, she had organized a kirtan at her residence at 12, Willingdon Crescent. She had rushed back home to take part in it, soon after the swearing-in ceremony at Rashtrapati Bhavan.

'Madam, you have to go to Chamunda Devi,' Anil Bali reminded her at the kirtan.

'Yes,' she agreed 'Give me four to five months.'

In the first week of May 1980, Bali received a letter from R. K. Dhawan. It said the prime minister wanted to visit Chamunda on 22 June (1980). She would land there at 4:45 p.m., Dhawan wrote. He asked Bali to organize her programme. Bali went to Chamunda and made arrangements for a puja to be done by her when she came. This was to be followed by a havan and a langar to feed the local people and worshippers at the temple.

On the evening of 20 June, a message arrived in Chamunda that the prime minister's programme had been cancelled. The entire government of Himachal Pradesh, including Chief Minister Ram Lal, had been camping there, awaiting her arrival. When the priest heard she was not coming, he reacted sharply. 'You tell Indira Gandhi, this is Chamunda. Ma will forgive if an ordinary mortal is not able to come. But the Devi (goddess) will not forgive if the ruler shows disrespect. Devi ki avamanana nahin kar sakte (The ruler cannot insult the goddess.)'

'Panditji,' Bali tried to pacify him, 'there must be a good reason why she could not come.' They went ahead with the kirtan and prayers on the 22nd as planned. On the 23rd morning, the group left town. 'We had reached the Jwala Mukhi temple, 50 kilometres on, when my secretary came running (to me),' Bali remembered.

'Sanjay Gandhi's plane has crashed,' he said, 'and Pakistan radio is broadcasting it.'

Thirty-three-year-old Sanjay had lost control of the aircraft while doing an aerobatic manoeuvre. Sanjay was known for performing dangerous stunts while at the controls of the small aircraft he flew—a reflection of his devil-may-care attitude to life. Maneka, his wife, had gone for a 'joyride' the previous evening when he wanted to show her his latest toy. 'In the plane I screamed and screamed for, I think, two hours,' she said later. 'When we came down, I ran home and told my mother-in-law, "I have never asked you for anything in my life. I need you now to tell Sanjay not to fly 'this' plane again".'

The news of Sanjay's death shocked the country.

Anil Bali and Kapil Mohan's family (who had been at the Chamunda temple) rushed back to Delhi. Bali headed straight for Indira Gandhi's residence. It was 2.30 a.m. when he arrived. Indira sat with the body. She saw him and got up to have a word with him.

'Does this have something to do with my not going to Chamunda?' she asked Bali.

'Madam,' Bali tried to calm her, 'this is not the time (to talk about it). I will tell you later.'

At the chautha (fourth day) ceremony, Bali arrived at 1, Akbar Road. Flanking Indira Gandhi were Sunil Dutt and his actor wife, Nargis. But Indira beckoned to Bali and took him aside, 'Now tell me what happened.' Bali told her what had happened the day she was expected at the Chamunda temple.

'I don't know who cancelled my programme,' she said thoughtfully. They were to come to Chamunda from Jammu, she said. Sanjay had accompanied her and was to come with her to visit the temple. She'd been told that the weather had deteriorated and that it was raining very hard at Chamunda. The helicopter would not be able to land there in the coming hours. So, they decided to return to Delhi a day earlier. A mystified Bali told her that the weather had not been bad in Chamunda. Nor had it been raining. Somebody had decided on her behalf to give Chamunda a miss. Later, Indira confided to Pupul Jayakar that Sanjay's death was her fault. She had not performed the rituals and prayers she had wanted to.

Several months after Sanjay's death, Indira Gandhi's political aide, M. L. Fotedar, phoned Bali.

'The prime minister wants to see you,' Fotedar said. 'Be sure to be there at 7.30 in the morning.'

She had instructed her attendant, Nathu Ram, to let Bali inside the residence.

She had a cap on her head. 'She had obviously dyed her hair,' Bali recalled. She came to the point immediately. 'I want to go to Chamunda,' she told Bali. She asked him to make the necessary arrangements.

On 13 December 1980, she went to Chamunda.

'As she performed the puja, the pandit's hands shook.'

'I am a diehard Hindu.... And the way she read the mantras for Purnahooti, and when she went to do her mathathekna (bowing the head) in the sanctum sanctorum, or (when) she was performing the mudras for kali ki puja, she did it to perfection.

'And she wept. She just wept and wept and wept. I recalled that the pandit had said that she would come (there) weeping.'

'You now have 60 crore beti betiyan (sons and daughters),' the priest said as he tried to comfort her. 'Aap inko dekhiye.' And he added, 'Aaj ke baad rona nahi (You look after them. You are not to cry after today).'

She took the prasad, did a parikrama (round) of the temple, and left. Accompanying her were Home Minister Buta Singh and Himachal

Pradesh chief minister Ram Lal. Outside, she planted trees—one of the key elements of Sanjay's five-point programme during the Emergency. She had taken with her Jagannath Sharma who at one time had worked as a mali for her husband, Feroze. She ensured that a ghat was constructed in Chamunda in Sanjay's name. 'It cost ₹80 lakhs which was borne by Congress leader Sukhram, later to become the chief minister of Himachal Pradesh,' Bali said.

After Sanjay's death, many had wondered if Indira Gandhi would quit politics. She did not. But his death affected her deeply.

In 1977, Sanjay had brought about Indira Gandhi's downfall. In 1980, it was Sanjay who had helped her stage a comeback. Within thirty-three months of her being dethroned, she was once again enthroned as the prime minister of India. In all the decisions she had taken after her defeat, her younger son had been her crutch, her co-conspirator, her comrade-in-arms. And now he was gone. In some way, the prayers she had offered to the goddess on that cold December day in 1980 helped her come to terms with Sanjay's death. Before leaving the temple premises, she said quietly, 'I have never seen such a beautiful place.'

When Indira Gandhi flew back to Delhi from the Chamunda Devi temple, she headed straight for a function she was scheduled to address. The event had been organized by *Quami Awaz*, the sister paper in Urdu of the *National Herald*. She walked into the venue in her usual brisk way, but there was a look of fragility about her. Before the function ended, she called her older son, Rajiv Gandhi, to the dais and introduced him to the gathering. Those present made a mental note of it. For, that evening, without saying so openly, Indira Gandhi was launching her new political heir apparent.

CHAPTER 2

THE SECULAR PRIME MINISTER
WHO UNDERMINED SECULARISM

Rajiv Gandhi's Waffling over Shah Bano

I

'Rajiv, if you can't convince me about this Muslim Women's Bill, how are you going to convince the country?' Sonia said to her husband, Rajiv.

Rajiv was at the time prime minister of India, and she was only half teasing him. 'You must stand by the Supreme Court judgment,' she told him seriously.

'This Sonia said in my presence,' D. P. Tripathi told me. 'Nobody has reported (this so far).' Tripathi, the veteran politician, was at the time a member of Rajiv Gandhi's inner circle—later he would become a member of parliament from the Nationalist Congress Party.

The conversation took place sometime towards the end of 1985 at the PM's official residence at Race Course Road. The left-leaning Tripathi used to be a frequent visitor there in those days and was seen as one of the PM's advisors.

The law Sonia Gandhi was referring to was popularly called the Muslim Women's Bill—an abbreviation of the Muslim Women (Protection of Rights on Divorce) Bill, 1986. Sonia knew Rajiv was seriously contemplating enacting the bill. Little did she know then that it would set off a political firestorm—and permanently alter the contours of Indian politics.

Rajiv Gandhi was considering the bill in order to undo a judgment which had been delivered by the Supreme Court on 23 April 1985. It came to be known famously as the Shah Bano case. The court had ordered that maintenance be paid to Shah Bano, an aggrieved Muslim woman who had been divorced.

Concerned that the bill should not deprive a poor, aggrieved, divorced Muslim woman of maintenance that was her due, that day Sonia Gandhi was asking her husband not to go in for the Muslim Women's Bill.

'This is a disastrous path,' Tripathi warned Rajiv Gandhi. 'You will lose your credibility.'

The politically-savvy Tripathi was worried about the consequences the proposed legislation could have. In the days that followed, he repeatedly urged Rajiv Gandhi not to be swayed by the fundamentalists in the Muslim community. 'It will give an impetus to the RSS and other Hindu organizations,' he warned Rajiv.

Unable to persuade Rajiv, an agitated Tripathi called up Jyoti Basu and Harkishan Singh Surjeet, asking them to intercede with Rajiv. He thought Rajiv might listen to them. Both were senior leaders of the CPI (M). If Rajiv went ahead, it would become 'very difficult' to stop the march of the 'Hindu fanatical forces', he told the PM.

'That is exactly what happened.' For the bill was followed by the 'equally disastrous...decision' to open the locks of the disputed Babri Masjid which was being claimed by Hindus as the Ram Janmabhoomi, the birthplace of Lord Ram.

In 1985, Rajiv Gandhi was being seen as a new star on the country's horizon. The media had dubbed 1985 as the 'Year of Hope' in India. Rajiv had managed to calm down the country after the brutal assassination of his mother Indira Gandhi in October 1984 and its violent aftermath. Tripathi did not want Rajiv to do anything which would take away from the initiative he had seized. For, he knew, the surface calm hid a turbulence— this went unnoticed except by those close to the seat of power. But the turmoil would soon spill over into the political arena over the Muslim Women's Bill.

■

On 23 April 1985, when the Supreme Court of India delivered its judgment in the case—*Mohammed Ahmed Khan vs Shah Bano Begum and others*— few could have imagined the Pandora's box it would open. Or that its ripple effect would fashion the country's politics for the next three decades.

Shah Bano, a sixty-two-year-old Muslim woman, had been divorced by her husband, Mohammed Ahmed Khan, after forty-five years of marriage and was seeking maintenance from him. The court, in its judgment, had granted her request.

Khan was a lawyer in Indore, in Madhya Pradesh. Shah Bano had married him in 1932. They had five children. After fourteen years of marriage, Khan decided to take another woman as his second wife. In 1975, he threw Shah Bano and his children out of the house. Three years later, in April 1978, she filed a petition in court asking that her husband pay her maintenance under Section 125 of the Criminal Procedure Code (CrPC). Section 125 CrPC was enacted to provide succour to any destitute person, irrespective of religion, and this included divorced women; it made the husband responsible for his wife's welfare, during marriage and even after divorce, if she could not fend for herself. Shah Bano said her husband had assured her a sum of ₹200 every month when he asked her to leave his house—but had reneged on his promise.

Six months after she had approached the court, Khan pronounced talaq three times and divorced her. The divorce was irrevocable, he said.

THE SECULAR PRIME MINISTER WHO UNDERMINED SECULARISM 87

So it was not his responsibility to take care of her. Or to pay her any maintenance. For, he argued, the Muslim Personal Law in India required the husband to provide her maintenance only for the iddat period after the divorce. Iddat is the customary three-month waiting period after divorce, prescribed by the Muslim Personal Law.

The case went on for seven years. The magistrate's court in Indore ruled in August 1979 that Shah Bano and her children should be paid ₹25 per month. A higher court—the Jabalpur bench of the Madhya Pradesh High Court—increased the amount to ₹179.20 per month. The Supreme Court, the country's highest court, did not think of enhancing the amount; it left it unchanged. But it argued—and it is this which led to an outcry—that a husband was bound to maintain his wife even after the lapse of iddat, if she could not take care of herself. The court gave its ruling under Section 125(3) of the CrPC, the civil law of the land, that had nothing to do with personal law.

Rajiv Gandhi, who had burst on to the Indian political scene as a modern, forward-looking prime minister, initially welcomed the judgment. The Congress Party defended it on the floor of parliament. Rajiv fielded one of his young Muslim ministers, Arif Mohammed Khan, to defend the court's verdict. But then pressure started to build on him. The judgment created an uproar in the Muslim community. Conservative Muslim leaders saw the court's verdict as interference with their personal law. They met the prime minister and beseeched him to undo the verdict by enacting a new law. Under pressure from them, and from leaders within his own party who feared the loss of Muslim support, Rajiv made an about-turn. He instructed his law minister, Ashoke Kumar Sen, to draft a bill which would undo the Shah Bano judgment.

The Muslim Women's Bill called for a reasonable and fair sum to be paid to a divorced Muslim woman, but it had to be paid for the three months which constituted the period of iddat. After that period, no further payment needed to be made. (But herein lay a catch which we will come to later in the chapter.)

Many Hindus reacted sharply to the proposed bill. More than its provisions, they objected to Rajiv Gandhi caving in to Muslim pressure—what came to be flayed as 'appeasement' of the community.

To assuage irate Hindu sentiment, Rajiv Gandhi went in for what was a typical 'management solution' according to D. P. Tripathi. The solution was suggested to Rajiv by his cousin and advisor, Arun Nehru. And that was to open an enclosure within the Babri Masjid to allow Hindus unfettered worship of their deity.

The masjid was a sixteenth-century mosque built by Mughal emperor Babur's general, Mir Baqi, in Ayodhya, UP, which had been locked up since 1949 to prevent the dispute over the structure from escalating. The VHP claimed the mosque had been built on the site of the birthplace of Lord Ram by demolishing a temple there. They called it Ram Janmabhoomi. The Babri Masjid–Ram Janmabhoomi dispute had continued to boil over from time to time, since the nineteenth century. Neither the British during the Raj, nor successive governments in independent India, had managed to unravel the tangle.

In December 1949, a group of Hindus surreptitiously placed an idol of the deity Ram Lalla (child Ram) inside the mosque in the dead of night—to strengthen their claim to the place of worship. The administration locked up the building. But a court judgment allowed Hindus to worship the idol from behind a locked grille. The VHP had been demanding that the Babri Masjid be unlocked to allow Hindus unfettered worship of their deity.

Rajiv Gandhi had thought that the Muslim Women's Bill would satisfy the Muslims, and the opening of the locks on the grille would make the Hindus happy.

'This was the sum total of Rajiv Gandhi's thinking,' said Tripathi. But instead of pleasing the Muslims and the Hindus, Rajiv ended up alienating both communities. The communal temperature flared up in UP.

Rajiv's response to the Shah Bano case was to give a fillip to the Hinduization of politics—and lead to the rise of the BJP.

Three years later, in the 1989 general elections that took place, the Congress was to fall between two stools. Rajiv Gandhi's impressive majority in parliament slumped from 414 to 197. His own finance minister, V. P. Singh, who had parted ways with Rajiv on issues of corruption, would go on to form the next government and take charge as prime minister (as we shall see in the next chapter). The Congress never really recovered from that shock. It failed to get a clear majority in any national election after that. The Shah Bano judgment turned out to be the small pivot on which the big door of Indian politics swung for three decades afterwards.

II

The day started early for Rajiv Gandhi on 31 October 1984. It was a day which was to change his life. He was on the campaign trail in West Bengal. A faction-ridden Congress had swung into poll mode early, though general elections were still many weeks away. By 9 a.m., he was already addressing his second meeting at Contai. Pranab Mukherjee was sitting beside him on the dais; he was from West Bengal and finance minister in Indira Gandhi's government. Suddenly, in the midst of Rajiv's speech, Mukherjee passed him a chit. It asked him to cut short his speech. Realizing something was amiss, Rajiv ended his speech quickly. Mukherjee showed him the message that had come from Delhi over the police wireless, 'Indira Gandhi assaulted, return to Delhi immediately.' Two of her security guards, both Sikhs, had shot her at point blank range at 9.10 a.m. that morning. She had been walking across to her office from her residence next door.

Within ten minutes Rajiv and Mukherjee left Contai. Rajiv shifted from his Ambassador car to the Mercedes of Ghani Khan Choudhury. The bigger car would enable them to move faster. Rajiv wanted to drive himself, but was dissuaded from taking the wheel. Like Mukherjee, Railway Minister Choudhury had also accompanied Rajiv on the trip. Rajiv sat in the front, with a transistor glued to his ear for the latest information. Sixteen bullets had been pumped into Indira Gandhi's body, the BBC said. 'How potent are the bullets used by VIP security?' an anxious Rajiv asked his personal security officer (PSO) sitting at the back of the car with the two ministers. They were powerful, the PSO replied. 'Did she deserve all these bullets?' Rajiv said, directing the question to no one.

None of them spoke much on the journey. But they guessed the assassination was payback for Indira Gandhi's decision to send the army into the Golden Temple on 1 June 1984 to finish off Jarnail Singh Bhindranwale. The Sikh militant had holed up in the revered Sikh shrine, preaching the creation of a separate Sikh nation.

Given the bad state of the roads, it took Rajiv two hours to reach Kolaghat helipad. A helicopter was waiting to take them onwards. They landed in Calcutta and were rushed straight into a special Indian Airlines flight. It took off immediately.

On board they found others who had also got word from Delhi; they included Uma Shankar Dikshit, then governor of West Bengal, his daughter-in-law, Sheila Dikshit, and Lok Sabha speaker, Balram Jakhar.

Soon after take-off, Rajiv went into the cockpit. A few minutes later, he came out, and declared flatly, 'She is dead.'

There was a stunned silence in the aircraft. Rajiv remained outwardly composed. He went back into the cockpit and spent most of the time there so as to get the latest news.

Once the shock began to wear off, those on the flight started to discuss the arrangements that would now have to be made. 'I cited precedents,' Mukherjee was to write later, 'from the time when Prime Minister Nehru, and later, Shastri passed away while in office ...In both the instances, an interim government was formed with Gulzari Lal Nanda, the senior most minister, as the interim prime minister.'

These words by Mukherjee were seen as a bid by him to take over as interim PM. But Mukherjee said he had also added that while Nehru and Shastri had died a natural death, Indira Gandhi's assassination had created an 'extraordinary situation'. So those present decided that Rajiv should take over his mother's mantle. Pranab Mukherjee said he took Rajiv to the back of the aircraft and urged him to take over as prime minister.

'Do you think I can manage?' Rajiv had asked him uncertainly.

'Yes...we are all there to help you,' Mukherjee reassured him.

Rajiv Gandhi however had a different take on what had transpired in those hours.

In an interview in 1986, he was asked what had happened in the plane that day—whether Mukherjee had staked his claim to be PM.

'We couldn't really talk about it,' Rajiv had replied. 'I don't know what he talked (about) with the others.'

The plane landed in Delhi around 3 p.m. Along with the officials led by Cabinet Secretary Krishnaswamy Rao Sahib who had come to receive Rajiv, an edgy Arun Nehru waited impatiently for his cousin. He quickly whisked Rajiv into his car, and raced to the All India Institute of Medical Sciences (AIIMS), where Indira Gandhi's bullet-riddled body lay.

After Indira Gandhi was shot, she had been rushed to AIIMS by her daughter-in-law, Sonia Gandhi, and R. K. Dhawan, her personal assistant. Arun Nehru had swung into action soon after she was brought to the operation theatre in the morning. As shocked Congress ministers, chief ministers, and party leaders arrived at the hospital, he spoke to each of them individually—and in small groups—as they waited in the corridor on the eighth floor outside the operation theatre.

He mooted Rajiv's name as his mother's successor. Rajiv seemed to be the natural—and non-controversial—choice. The Congress leaders agreed readily enough. Arun Nehru was only a party MP, though a third cousin of Rajiv. But senior leaders had seen him exercise enormous authority in the years that Indira Gandhi had been prime minister after 1980.

In his inimitably pushy style, Arun Nehru took charge on 31 October 1984. He wanted to ensure that it was Rajiv, not Pranab Mukherjee, who was sworn in as prime minister. An interim PM, he knew, would be difficult to dislodge, particularly if it was someone as savvy as Mukherjee and that too when Indira Gandhi was no longer around to keep an eye on him. He knew his cousin would find it difficult to navigate the new terrain and would need help. No one questioned Nehru's role that afternoon.

During the course of these conversations, Arun Nehru had convinced many Congress leaders that the vice president, R. Venkataraman, should swear in Rajiv Gandhi immediately; they did not have to wait for President Zail Singh to return to the capital. He was abroad and was rushing back to Delhi. Arun Nehru was apprehensive that Giani Zail Singh, with whom Indira Gandhi had had a difficult relationship might insist on swearing in Pranab Mukherjee as PM. He was after all the number two in Mrs Gandhi's cabinet. And, as Mukherjee had pointed out, there were precedents of the number two being sworn in—after the death of Jawaharlal Nehru and of Lal Bahadur Shastri. The CPP had not met to elect Rajiv as leader. Nor was it possible for it to meet at such a short notice. Nehru suspected that Mukherjee had a plan up his sleeve to upstage Rajiv.

Arun Nehru knew Giani Zail Singh well. Soon after he joined politics in 1980, he had collaborated with Zail Singh, then the home minister, in the early months of the political unrest in Punjab. Both wanted to replace the Punjab chief minister Darbara Singh, and upstage the Akali Dal, an influential Sikh-dominated party in Punjab.

Though Indira Gandhi had made Zail Singh the president in 1982, preferring him to P. V. Narasimha Rao whom she had also considered for Rashtrapati Bhavan, her relations with Zail Singh had soured with the escalation of the crisis in Punjab. He would resort to pinpricks, like deliberately keep her waiting at the airport during ceremonial 'see-offs'—when the prime minister was expected to be present when the president left town or when he returned to Delhi after an official visit.

With Indira Gandhi now gone, there was no telling what the president might do. Nehru did not want to risk any slip at this stage.

Leaving his cousin in the room where Indira Gandhi's body lay, Arun Nehru came out to have a quiet word with P. C. Alexander, Indira's powerful principal secretary.

Alexander heard out an impatient Nehru make a case for the need to swear in Rajiv as PM immediately. 'No risk can be taken,' Nehru told him. Who would take the responsibility if the president refused to swear in Rajiv, he asked an uncertain Alexander.

As a bureaucrat, Alexander was not so sure about the action Nehru was proposing. As it is, he found himself in an extraordinary situation. Technically speaking, with Indira Gandhi's death, Alexander had also ceased to be principal secretary who could take decisions on her behalf. He was also worried about the legality of the move. Zail Singh had after all not delegated his authority to the vice president. The president could, if he wanted, challenge the move as unconstitutional.

Alexander told Nehru he would consult Rajiv.

Nehru started to move towards the anteroom, where Rajiv had gone to talk to Sonia. He would go and speak to his cousin, he said. But before the portly Nehru could move, the tall and sprightly Alexander had beaten him to it. He entered the room where Rajiv stood with Sonia. He heard Sonia pleading with her husband not to take up the prime ministership.

She feared he would be killed. Rajiv kissed her on the forehead and said he had 'no choice...he would be killed anyway'.

Alexander tapped Rajiv on the shoulder. Rajiv disengaged himself from Sonia's arms. He followed Alexander into the bathroom. It is there that the principal secretary had a quiet word with Rajiv. Rajiv listened intently to what Alexander had to say. He agreed that they should wait for the president to return.

By now it was 4 p.m. Already, the country had been leaderless for six hours. There were reports of anger building up at Indira Gandhi's assassination; the situation was fraught with danger. After Jawaharlal

Nehru's death on 27 May 1964, an interim PM had been sworn in within two hours. Nehru had died at 2 p.m. and Gulzari Lal Nanda was in place by 4 p.m. When Shastri died on 11 January 1966, in Tashkent at 1.32 a.m. (2.02 a.m. IST), by 3.15 a.m. Gulzari Lal Nanda had taken his oath as PM.

While in the plane from Calcutta, and realizing the complexity of the situation that now confronted them, Pranab Mukherjee had persuaded Rajiv Gandhi to convey the message to Delhi—that Mrs Indira Gandhi's death should not be officially announced until the new government had taken over. At the Delhi end, Vice President Venkataraman had also expressed the same view to the Congress leaders present at the hospital. Both Venkataraman and Mukherjee were seasoned politicians who could look ahead and pre-empt trouble.

■

Pranab Mukherjee reached the hospital ten minutes after Rajiv Gandhi. Within minutes he realized that most of the Congress leaders there were against him taking over as interim PM. When Alexander asked him about Arun Nehru's idea of the vice president administering the oath of office to Rajiv, Mukherjee suggested that instead the Congress Parliamentary Board (CPB) should be called immediately. The CPB, a subgroup of CWC, the party's highest policy making body, could take a view, since there was no time to call the CPP to elect the leader. The CPP could ratify the CPB's decision later.

The CPB met at 5 p.m. that day. From AIIMS, Mukherjee and Narasimha Rao—who had also by now arrived at the hospital—left for 1, Akbar Road, Indira Gandhi's office adjacent to her residence at 1, Safdarjung Road.

Mukherjee could not locate his car in the melee of vehicles at AIIMS. Arun Nehru drove him to 1, Akbar Road, and then rushed off to the airport to receive the president.

Whatever the mantra Nehru whispered in President Zail Singh's ear while escorting him to AIIMS that fateful evening, he would have calculated—and Zail Singh would have agreed—that it would be easier to control a trusting Rajiv than any other incumbent.

There were two vacancies in the eight-member CPB. Of the six, Indira Gandhi, ex officio member of the committee as leader of the party in the Lok Sabha and as Congress president, was now dead. Two members, Maragatham Chandrasekar and Kamlapati Tripathi were out of town. It was left to the remaining two members, Narasimha Rao, who was home minister, and Finance Minister Pranab Mukherjee to take a decision.

They went through the formality of passing a resolution—that Rajiv Gandhi was elected leader of the CPP. G. K. Moopanar, who was secretary of the CWC, wrote a formal letter to the president that Rajiv Gandhi be invited to form the government. The decision taken, all of them left for Rashtrapati Bhavan.

Mukherjee's role that day was to become the subject of an intense controversy in the months that followed; it was held against him till the end. Later, Mukherjee told a Bengali journalist in confidence—who told me—that he suspected P. V. Narasimha Rao of spreading the canard that Mukherjee wanted to become the interim PM.

■

Soon after noon on 31 October 1984, it had become clear to us in the media at the scene that Indira Gandhi was no more. I had bumped into a doctor I knew, Dr Urmil Sharma, who offered to go to the eighth floor and find out for me what was happening. When she came down, she motioned to me to follow her. We walked silently across to her residence on the campus. As soon as we were inside, she said in a hushed voice, 'It's all over.' Later, I heard in the hospital that the BBC had announced her death just after 2 p.m. The government had put out no statement on the attack on the prime minister.

At 5 p.m., the assembled media had seen Arun Nehru arrive at AIIMS with Zail Singh. Before the president's car turned into the gates, there was a commotion outside. By then, large crowds had gathered there. We found out later that Singh's car had been stoned by angry protestors who had started targeting Sikhs. Word had got out that Indira Gandhi had been shot by her Sikh bodyguards—a precursor to the violent anti-Sikh riots that would soon engulf the city. Singh's driver managed to speed into the hospital precincts. But the president's secretary, Tarlochan Singh, whose car had followed the president's vehicle, was not so fortunate; the windshield of his vehicle had been smashed. He had to change course and flee towards Rashtrapati Bhavan.

On the eighth floor of the hospital, the president commiserated with Rajiv Gandhi. Putting his hand on Rajiv's shoulder, he asked, 'Chalaen (Shall we go)?'

'Where?' asked Rajiv.

'For oath taking,' said Zail Singh.

'I will go home, change, and join you,' Rajiv replied.

Later, Zail Singh told a group of politicians from Punjab, 'That day, when I administered the oath to Rajiv as PM, I paid back all the ehsaans (favours) Indira Gandhi had done me.'

■

It was a tired, jet-lagged president who swore in Rajiv Gandhi as the sixth prime minister of India. The oath took place at 6.45 p.m. on 31 October 1984. An 'eerie silence' hung over the ceremony held in the chandeliered Ashoka Hall at Rashtrapati Bhavan.

On one side stood the officials—Principal Secretary P. C. Alexander, Cabinet Secretary Krishnaswamy Rao Sahib, Home Secretary M. M. K. Wali, and Secretary to the President A. C. Bandyopadhyay—their heads bowed. On the other side sat the four grim-looking leaders who were to be sworn in along with Rajiv Gandhi—Pranab Mukherjee, P. V. Narasimha Rao, Shiv Shankar, and Buta Singh. Rajiv had added Buta Singh's name to the list of ministers at the last minute, after arriving in Rashtrapati Bhavan. Mukherjee had counselled the PM-designate to include Buta Singh, a Dalit Sikh, keeping in mind the sensibilities of the Sikhs, after Mrs Gandhi's assasination by her Sikh bodyguards. The president began by observing a two-minute silence in the memory of the slain leader.

Rajiv's voice trembled as he read the oath of office and secrecy, 'I, Rajiv Gandhi, do solemnly affirm...'

Minutes after the oath-taking ceremony, Rajiv Gandhi's cabinet held its first meeting presided over by the new prime minister. It took place in Rashtrapati Bhavan. After a condolence resolution, calling for 'peace, communal harmony and unity', the cabinet finalized the funeral arrangements for Indira Gandhi. It decided that her body would lie in state at Teen Murti House for three days and the funeral would take place on 3 November 1984.

It was only after all these formalities were over that Rashtrapati Bhavan put out a press release. It formally announced Indira Gandhi's death. Vice President Venkataraman told public telecaster Doordarshan that a new government headed by Rajiv Gandhi had taken over.

Rajiv now rushed back to AIIMS to take his mother's body to 1, Safdarjung Road for the night, for the family to bid her a quiet farewell. It was shifted to Teen Murti House the next morning where her father had lived as India's first prime minister and she had been his official hostess.

In the hours that followed, Rajiv decided to retain the team of Indira Gandhi's ministers and officials. Pranab Mukherjee remained finance minister and Narasimha Rao retained the home portfolio.

■

P. V. Narasimha Rao had headed to his office in North Block, from 1, Akbar Road, after passing the CPB resolution electing Rajiv as the leader of the parliamentary party. At about 6 p.m., his phone rang. It was Arun Nehru on the line. 'We have received intelligence reports that there will be widespread violence in the city tomorrow,' Arun Nehru told Rao, according to Rao's biographer, Vinay Sitapati.

'We will need to ensure a coordinated response,' he told the home minister. 'It will be better if a single nodal authority deals with the situation.' As home minister, the Delhi Police came directly under Rao. So did law and order in Delhi which was a union territory. Not knowing what was coming next, Rao listened to what Nehru was saying. He did not say anything himself. Nehru told Rao that the PMO would now handle the situation in Delhi—in other words for Rao to stand down as home minister as far as dealing with the aftermath of Indira Gandhi's assassination was concerned. He asked Rao to forward to the PMO all the information coming into the Home Ministry about the anti-Sikh violence that had begun in the city. 'The PMO will coordinate a single response to the violence', he instructed Rao. His message was clear—the PMO, and not the Home Ministry, would now be in charge.

There was an official present in the room when Rao spoke to Nehru. He was Rao's trusted aide. Rao told the aide afterwards what Nehru had said to him on the phone, a conversation the official later related to Sitapati. 'I checked this out (also) with one other official who was in the know, and had worked with Rao in those days,' recalled Sitapati.

In the hours that followed, violence against the Sikhs engulfed large parts of Delhi and North India; it was to spiral out of control in the following three days.

Groups of agitated citizens called on Rao in those hours—among them I. K. Gujral, then a Congress leader later to become prime minister, General J. S. Aurora, who had been the general officer commanding-in-chief of Eastern Command during the 1971 war with Pakistan, and Arjan Singh, who had led the Air Force in the 1965 war against Pakistan. They beseeched the home minister to deploy the army immediately.

The day after the assassination, an agitated Pupul Jayakar, Indira's close friend, called up Rao. She was told he was with the PM. She drove straight to 1, Safdarjung Road, and found Rao sitting with Rajiv. She told the PM about the phone calls she had been getting about the gruesome killings and rape of Sikh women that were taking place.

Rajiv looked bewildered, uncertain about what to do next. Jayakar urged Rajiv to get the army out to restore order immediately. Rajiv turned to Rao and asked him if the army should be deployed. Rao remained silent. Rajiv then asked Jayakar to put in writing what she had told him and send it to him urgently—which she did. But the army was not deployed and the killings continued.

When Arun Nehru had called Narasimha Rao at 6 p.m. on 31 October, the country did not have a prime minister, even as violence had begun to engulf the capital. Even if Nehru was giving directions to Rao at the behest of Rajiv Gandhi, it was forty-five minutes before Rajiv had taken over as PM. Till then, Rao as home minister of India was responsible for maintaining law and order in Delhi, more so in the absence of a prime minister. He could have called in the army. Rao chose not to act.

While Rao had a sense of how Indira Gandhi would have responded to a situation, Sitapati said, Rajiv as prime minister 'was an unknown quantity to him'. Rao was not sure how he would react. Nor did he know whether Nehru's directive to him had Rajiv's backing. What he did know was that Nehru was powerful. He had seen the influence he had wielded when Indira was alive. Hours earlier, he had watched him in action at AIIMS, taking charge of the situation to get his cousin Rajiv sworn in as PM.

'Rao's concern at the time would have been what will happen to him as a minister than what would happen to the Sikhs under attack,' said Sitapati. The canny Rao may well have been relieved that Nehru's phone call to him had let him off the hook as home minister in the midst of an escalating crisis. Hardened by the laws of the jungle that operated in politics, Rao had learnt early that when the storm struck, the blade of grass which swayed survived. But a tree which stood erect crashed.

'It was his vilest hour,' said Sitapati.

As things would turn out, commission after commission probing the anti-Sikh killings following Indira Gandhi's assassination, absolved Rao of any role in the violence. It was Rajiv Gandhi who was blamed for the brutal massacre of the Sikhs in 1984. Nobody even remembered who the home minister of India was at the time.

■

As Arun Nehru's car moved out of AIIMS on the evening of 31 October 1984, he spotted local Congress leader Arjun Dass in the crowd. He put out his head and yelled at him, 'Choorhiya pehen rakhi hain kya? Maa ko maara hai (Are you wearing bangles? Your mother is being killed).' Dass, a member of the Delhi Metropolitan Council had been a close associate of Sanjay Gandhi. He was later named by a report of a civil liberties group (People's Union for Civil Liberties) as an instigator of violence against the Sikhs—and was mysteriously assassinated in 1985 by two gunmen carrying automatic weapons while he was in his auto parts shop.

As night enveloped Delhi, and Indira Gandhi's body was taken to her residence, meetings were held in different parts of the city by senior Congressmen. They reportedly mobilized their supporters and asked them to spread out all over the city; the murderous mobs were armed with kerosene, knives, and tyres. They were also given voter lists to indicate the localities where Sikhs lived. Later, several prominent Congressmen would be accused of leading mobs—Lalit Maken, H. K. L. Bhagat, Sajjan Kumar, Jagdish Tytler, Kamal Nath. Most of them had been closely associated with Sanjay Gandhi when he was alive and many had transferred their loyalty to Arun Nehru after Sanjay's death.

H. S. Phoolka, who was to legally represent scores of Sikh families who had been affected by the violence, confirmed that there were 'readily available lists' of Sikhs to be targeted in the capital after Indira Gandhi's assassination. They could not have been prepared at short notice. 'When we were collating material to present before the (Ranganath) Misra Commission (probing the anti-Sikh violence),' Phoolka said, 'we were told by some people in the intelligence community that shortly before Operation Bluestar (in June 1984), fearing (a) reaction from the Sikhs of Delhi, detailed information about the community had been gathered by the Government.'

The government estimated that 2,733 Sikhs were killed in Delhi over the next three days and 3,350 nationwide. But, according to independent sources, 8,000 to 17,000 were killed across forty cities in the country in the mass violence that followed Indira Gandhi's assassination.

Going back to Statesman House (where I worked), the evening of 31 October 1984, I found the cobbler who used to sit outside the gate sobbing, 'She was our Amma, she has gone.' Fires could be seen billowing from several parts of the iconic Connaught Place (CP), as buildings were set alight. Walking around CP, I met a fellow journalist who said, his voice choked with emotion, 'See, our Delhi is going up in flames.' In the days that followed, a visit to Trilokpuri—the worst hit of the various Delhi neighbourhoods heavily populated by Sikhs—showed just how gruesome the killings had been. My own family had migrated to Delhi from Pakistan after the country's Partition, and I thought to myself that this is what it must have been like in 1947. Sikh women wailed about how their menfolk had been burnt alive, 'necklaced' by burning car tyres. They spoke about Congressmen leading the mobs that had come to attack them.

I discovered, as I visited other colonies, that many Hindus had given shelter to their Sikh neighbours or friends. But some of those very Hindus had gone to other parts of the city to take part in the violence against Sikhs. The first impulse stemmed from the need to maintain social relations, the second was about venting communal hatred. The two could coexist, I learnt during those days.

The killings went on for three days. Between 31 October and 3 November, Rajiv Gandhi stayed by his mother's body at Teen Murti House, his face reflecting gravitas and poise.

It was only after Indira Gandhi's last rites were performed by Rajiv on 3 November on the banks of the river Yamuna that peace returned to the city. Only after that did Prime Minister Rajiv Gandhi finally call out the army in Delhi. It was three days too late. There is still no clear answer to why he did not act decisively to stop the killings.

Maybe Rajiv Gandhi was in a daze. Maybe he was confused about what he should do, leaving everything to Arun Nehru and others. His inaction led to one of the worst tragedies in the history of modern India.

III

Arun Nehru's tryst with politics began in 1980. It was a few months before Rajiv Gandhi took the leap into politics to 'help Mummy' after his brother Sanjay died.

In January 1980, Indira Gandhi had won both the seats she had contested in the general elections. She decided to retain Medak in Andhra Pradesh and give up Raebareli in Uttar Pradesh.

'We were sitting at the lunch table at 12, Willingdon Crescent,' recalled Akbar Dumpy Ahmad. 'There was Sanjay, Maneka, and me. Mrs Gandhi joined us. We were discussing who should be fielded from Raebareli (in the by-election that was to take place there). The name of Mohammed Yunus surfaced.'

Yunus was a known family loyalist, trusted by both Indira Gandhi and Sanjay. He had retired from the foreign service in 1974, and headed the Trade Fair Authority of India, which established the exhibition complex at Pragati Maidan in Delhi. Sanjay was a close friend of Mohammed Yunus's son, Adil Shahryar. When Indira had lost the election in 1977, Yunus had vacated his house at 12, Willingdon Crescent, for her and moved to a small MP's first floor apartment at 12, South Avenue, which had been allotted to Hamida Habibullah (Wajahat Habibullah's mother). In 1982, Shahryar was convicted of a serious crime in the US, after a full trial before a jury. But US president Ronald Reagan had personally signed an order for his release on 11 June 1985, the day Rajiv, who was by then prime minister, arrived in Washington DC on a state visit. It was meant to be a goodwill gesture to the Indian PM.

All their lives, Mohammed Yunus had been Yunus chacha to Sanjay and Rajiv—like family. But, for some reason, Indira Gandhi was not for fielding Yunus from Raebareli; she was 'absolutely clear' that it had to be someone from the family.

Suddenly, Maneka said, 'Why don't we give the ticket to Fatty?'

Fatty was Arun Nehru. Everyone thought it was a good idea. Sanjay's great-grandfather, Motilal Nehru, and Arun Nehru's great-grandfather, Nand Lal Nehru, were brothers. There could be no doubting Arun's impeccable political lineage as a member of the Nehru clan. 'Sanjay immediately asked R. K. Dhawan to get in touch with Arun Nehru.'

Nehru landed in Delhi a day later. When he walked into 12, Willingdon Crescent, Sanjay was in the sitting room. 'Motu, chunav larhega (Fatty, will you fight the election)?' he teased his cousin.

'I remember he was wearing a grey flannel blazer and a tie when he arrived,' said Dumpy Ahmad. He told Arun Nehru to go to Khadi Bhandar in Connaught Place, and get outfitted with kurta pyjamas for his new role.

'On second thoughts, it will be better to buy material and get your kurtas stitched, given your size,' he told Nehru.

Nehru's political journey began amidst banter about his corpulence. But the portly Nehru turned out to be no pushover. He had already made his mark in the corporate world. By thirty-seven, he had become president of the Indian branch of the multinational company, Jenson & Nicholson, remembered for its popular slogan 'Whenever you see colour, think of us'.

He got off to a blazing start by winning the Raebareli seat in April 1980. He was indefatigable in his campaigning, and won by a handsome margin. With Indira Gandhi's support, the outcome was never in doubt.

■

Until Sanjay died, Rajiv and Sonia had stayed away from politics, although they lived in the PM House. They had their own circle of friends among the elite of Lutyens' Delhi. Sometimes, one or two of their close friends would drop in on Sunday. They would then take off to their farmhouse on the outskirts of Delhi to do target shooting and spend leisurely time together as a family. In the evenings, they would often go to dinner parties at the homes of their friends.

Both Rajiv and Sonia were critical of the Emergency, and the role Sanjay had played during its darkest days. The day Indira Gandhi was defeated in the 1977 elections, an upset Rajiv had told Pupul Jayakar, 'I will never forgive Sanjay for having brought Mummy to this position.'

Indira Gandhi, who had faced flak on Sanjay's role in government, decided to tread cautiously when it came to Rajiv's entry into politics. Three months after Sanjay's death, she suddenly decided she should hold consultations on who should succeed her. She asked her aide M. L. Fotedar to assess who should take over, were something to happen to her. She gave him two names—Pranab Mukherjee and P. V. Narasimha Rao. Fotedar added a third name—that of R. Venkataraman. She gave him one month to 'complete the exercise'. She wanted to ascertain how the party would react to the question of a successor. Congressmen are quick to read the mind of the leader. Fotedar came back to her and said he had found the reaction to all three names 'unsuitable'. Instead, he made a case for Rajiv to be her successor. 'In those months, while walking from 1, Safdarjung Road, to the adjacent bungalow at 1, Akbar Road, 'she used to discuss with me the pros and cons of Rajivji entering politics.' Word spread that Mrs Gandhi wanted Rajiv as her successor. Party leaders vied with each other to let it be known that they wanted Rajiv anointed as the crown prince. Arun Nehru organized a group of around fifty MPs who called on Mrs Gandhi; they urged her to ensure it was Rajiv who took Sanjay's place.

The chief minister of Madhya Pradesh Arjun Singh despatched 100 MLAs to Indira Gandhi to plead with her to bring Rajiv into the party. H. K. L. Bhagat and Buta Singh were not to be left behind.

By this time Maneka Gandhi, Sanjay's widow, was beginning to work on 'an independent line in her effort to enter politics'. She was holding political meetings, against the wishes of her mother-in-law. Soon enough, there was an ugly break between the two. Maneka left the PM House in the middle of the night on 29 March 1982, with her two-year-old son, Feroze Varun Gandhi, in the pitiless glare of media publicity. Though it was a wrench to see Varun leave with his mother—Mrs Gandhi was very attached to him and he would sleep with her at night—Indira needed to ensure there was no ambiguity about her heir apparent and number two in the Congress hierarchy. And she wanted to lose no time in making this known in party circles.

■

'She (Sonia) is dead against the idea of (my) getting into politics,' Rajiv had told an interviewer candidly.

When Sanjay died in June 1980, Rajiv had been reluctant to take on his brother's mantle. He had never been interested in politics. In fact, it bored him. He had left politics to his mother and to Sanjay. And Sonia, as he had said, was totally opposed to the idea. It took Rajiv several months to arrive at a decision.

'One afternoon, in late 1980, Rajiv told me quietly on the lawns of 1, Akbar Road, his decision to step into active politics, and come into the Lok Sabha from Amethi,' recalled journalist Suman Dubey who was to become Rajiv's press advisor when he took over as PM, and a loyal friend of the Nehru–Gandhi family.

'The way I look at it,' Rajiv had said, 'is that Mummy has to be helped somehow.'

Finally, on 5 May 1981, he decided to give up his job as a pilot with Indian Airlines and join the Indian National Congress (I). He decided to contest elections from Amethi, the family pocket borough, from where Sanjay had won in January 1980.

'Rajiv makes debut'—banner headlines announced on 12 May 1981. He was in Amethi to file his nomination papers for the Lok Sabha by-election, ending weeks of suspense. Rajiv was accompanied by the chief minister of Uttar Pradesh V. P. Singh, members of the Youth Congress, his cousin, Arun Nehru and Sonia. When Sonia had expressed a desire to accompany her husband to Sultanpur where he was to file his nomination papers, Indira Gandhi had advised her daughter-in-law, 'Sari pehenna, teeka lagana (Wear a sari and put on a bindi).'

Rajiv's principal opponent would be the Lok Dal's candidate Sharad

Yadav, who had been the united Opposition's candidate in Jabalpur in 1974 and had defeated the Congress candidate.

Knowing his organizational prowess, Mrs Gandhi had asked Arun Nehru to organize Rajiv's election campaign. Arun Nehru left nothing to chance. He camped there all through the campaign; he planned it down to its last detail as he would have done the launch of a consumer product in his previous avatar as a corporate executive. He knew a handsome victory for Rajiv would earn him brownie points with Indira.

As prime minister, Indira Gandhi did not campaign in by-elections as a rule. But she especially went to Amethi to give a leg up to Rajiv. The Mohan Meakin team of Kapil Mohan was there in full force, taking care of every last detail, providing even the food that Indira and Rajiv liked. Anil Bali personally supervised the arrangements. The day Indira came, Bali recalled, 'I had arranged for lunch Dussehri mangoes, lemon chicken and arhar dal without any masala that I knew Mrs Gandhi liked.' It was after all a high profile battle to launch Indira Gandhi's heir apparent.

Rajiv Ratna Birjees Gandhi, 37, defeated Sharad Yadav by a whopping 237,000 votes in June 1981. With the win in Amethi, Rajiv had taken the first step which would take him to the pinnacle of power. When they were at the Lucknow airport after the victory to return to Delhi, Anil Bali turned to Rajiv and remarked effusively, 'I am having the privilege of travelling with the next prime minister of India.' Rajiv just smiled—but did not say anything.

Rajiv took oath as MP on 17 August 1981 and was drawn into the gargantuan machinery called the Indian National Congress (I). His first assignment, even before he had taken oath as an MP, was to attend the wedding of Prince Charles and Lady Diana Spencer in London on 27 July 1981.

Indira Gandhi ensured that Rajiv's entry into politics was made as smooth as possible—she made him responsible for organizing the ninth Asian Games which India was to host in November 1982. He headed the organizing committee. Given his proximity to the prime minister, he could iron out the glitches and get even last moment allocations of funds cleared. Sanjay supporter Jagmohan, who had carried out the unpopular demolitions in Delhi during the Emergency and was instantly rehabilitated when Indira Gandhi came back to power in 1980, had been made the lieutenant governor of Delhi. With him by Rajiv's side, they laid out brand new roads, widened existing ones, constructed flyovers and new infrastructure, and built the 60,000-seater Jawaharlal Nehru Stadium. The Siri Fort Auditorium and the Asian Games Village were put up, not far from the forgotten ruins of an old fort erected by the Mughal ruler Alauddin Khalji in the fourteenth century.

The inaugural on 19 November 1982—it happened to be Indira

Gandhi's birthday—was a gala affair. 3,411 athletes participated in the event. Rajiv won accolades for the games—but also for the transformation of Delhi into a modern city. He was hailed as a forward-looking, tech-savvy leader, who believed in professional management and could meet deadlines.

The era of colour television that the Asian Games heralded in India was the cherry on the cake. Indian families excitedly watched the games in vibrant colour on their TV sets, telecast by public broadcaster Doordarshan. Rajiv was given the credit for it, and for managing to convince his one-time-socialist mother to go in for colour TV. It was a move designed to go down well with India's middle class whose darling he was to become.

■

Rajiv Gandhi's style of functioning was very different from Sanjay's. Once he became general secretary of the party on 3 February 1983, he set about organizing his office at 2A, Motilal Nehru Marg. Unlike other party offices at the time, Rajiv's office had a computer, files of newspaper clippings, other data banks, books and documents under subject heads and a Xerox machine. And there were pictures and carpets—a Sonia touch—to create an ambience of warmth and welcome. Manning his office was Vincent George who was to emerge as a powerful aide and was to stay with him till the end. After Rajiv, George—he had a sharp institutional memory—worked with Sonia when she became president of the party until he was shunted out.

Just as Indira Gandhi had wanted to create a team around Sanjay in 1977, and then again in 1980, she wanted to put together a team for Rajiv. She asked Arun Nehru to recruit people who would be loyal to Rajiv and would not betray him.

Unlike Sanjay, who had become a figure of hate, Rajiv had the advantage of starting on a clean slate. She had not forgotten the problems she herself had faced when she had taken over as PM in 1966.

Though Rajiv had inherited Sanjay's group of Youth Congress boys, very quickly he started to build his own team. He showed a preference for 'English-speaking, Doon School-educated Indians' he had grown up with. They were the business executive types who relied on modern technology, data, and computers to do their jobs rather than depend on sycophantic hangers-on. But they were mostly wealthy men and women, from the 'drawing room' set, who, like him, had little exposure to India's ground realities. He persuaded his old friend Arun Singh to quit Reckitt & Colman, the company he was working for in Calcutta, and join him. In 1984, he was brought into the Rajya Sabha from Uttar Pradesh and was MP till 1988. While Arun Singh's company sold shoe polish, Arun Nehru had sold paint before becoming a Lok Sabha MP. Rajiv also brought in Vijay Dhar, a Kashmiri Pandit whose leftist father D. P. Dhar had been India's ambassador in Moscow and had helped craft the Indo-Soviet Friendship Treaty just before the formation of Bangladesh in 1971. It was Vijay Dhar who was to introduce telecom guru Satyan Gangaram Pitroda or Sam Pitroda to Rajiv. Later Rajiv inducted Satish Sharma, a fellow pilot with him in the Indian Airlines, another 'Dosco' (Doon School alumnus) Mani Shankar Aiyar, journalist Suman Dubey, and actor Amitabh Bachchan—both were close friends—into his team, in different roles.

But during 1982–84, it was the three musketeers—Arun Nehru, Arun Singh, and Vijay Dhar—who worked closely with Rajiv.

■

It soon became clear that while Rajiv Gandhi was well meaning, he was also naive. His naiveté was to be his undoing time and again in his political career—whether it was in Andhra Pradesh, Jammu and Kashmir, Punjab, or in the way he handled the Shah Bano affair.

On 3 February 1982, six months after he became an MP, Rajiv landed at Begumpet airport in Hyderabad. He was on a visit to Andhra Pradesh. As he came down the steps of the plane, he was astonished to see 200 people gathered on the tarmac to receive him. Leading them was the portly Andhra Pradesh chief minister, T. Anjaiah, who had come to receive Rajiv with great fanfare. Though Rajiv was only a party MP, he was now seen as Indira Gandhi's successor. Suddenly, the sound of drums rent the air and Congress workers started to dance to their beat at the airport. Rajiv was furious. To him, a former Indian Airlines pilot, airport security was being violated. Nor did he like the pomp and pageantry that was put on for him.

A livid Rajiv shouted at Chief Minister Anjaiah in full view of those gathered there. 'If there is no order and the whole thing is not over in fifteen minutes, I will go back.'

A crestfallen Anjaiah was on the verge of tears. He apologized profusely. After his advisors had calmed Rajiv down, he left the airport and headed to Tirupati leaving a miserable Anjaiah at the airport. The chief minister quickly sent word to groups who had lined the route to take down the hundreds of welcome arches they had put up for Rajiv.

New into politics, Rajiv wanted to check sycophancy, introduce a new political culture in the Congress. But he was dealing with a feudal India and entrenched practices in the Congress of which he was now a part. His peremptory behaviour drew 'howls of protest'.

The media—and the Opposition leaders—went to town criticizing his treatment of an elected chief minister. That Anjaiah was a Dalit made things worse.

For some time, resentment had been brewing in the state against the high-handed manner in which Delhi had treated chief ministers. The chief ministers in Andhra Pradesh had been changed frequently, and not allowed to function independently. Anjaiah had replaced M. Chenna Reddy fifteen months earlier. Three weeks later, Anjaiah was sent packing. Bhavanam Venkatarami Reddy took over and lasted only seven months. He was replaced by Vijaya Bhaskar Reddy in September 1982.

Rajiv Gandhi's faux pas turned out to be very costly. Six weeks after this incident, popular Telugu actor N. T. Rama Rao, with 300 films to his credit—in many of them he played the role of one god or another—launched a new political outfit to restore the injured pride and self-respect of Telugus. In only nine months' time, the Telugu Desam Party (TDP) he headed had swept the polls in Andhra Pradesh. He won 201 out of 294 seats in elections that were held in January 1983. The Congress, which had never lost the state, was virtually wiped out. The TDP was to stay in the politics of Andhra Pradesh in the years that followed.

∎

While Rajiv Gandhi was artless, Arun Nehru easily slipped into the world of politics. He had been quick to read Indira Gandhi's mind; she wanted to groom Rajiv to succeed her. She would repeatedly tell Arun to ensure that people did not take advantage of Rajiv. That was one reason why she had wanted a family member to come into parliament from Raebareli. She knew that Rajiv was both gullible and trusting, and would need help.

With Indira Gandhi's support, Arun Nehru became very powerful in the early 1980s. Chief ministers and party leaders started to pay court to him to get things done. Industrialists called him a 'one window clearance' in those days of the license-permit-quota raj and crony capitalism. Used to running a company at an early age, he exuded authority, took decisions quickly, and threw his weight around to get his way.

Senior journalists who did not do his bidding had to face his ire. Editor of the Urdu paper *Nai Duniya*, Shahid Siddiqui, had been taken to meet Nehru by a group of young Congress MPs. The Congress had just lost the Jammu and Kashmir elections in June 1983; a government headed by Farooq Abdullah was in place and he had won handsomely. But this was a government that Nehru had eyed.

'Arun Nehru was sitting on a chair, with legs stretched (out),' Siddiqui recalled. 'There were no chairs in front of him. People stood around. He exuded arrogance,' Siddiqui said.

'I want you to write against Farooq Abdullah,' he ordered Siddiqui. Farooq Abdullah had taken to riding a two-wheeler and had taken Bollywood actor Shabana Azmi riding pillion around the Dal Lake. It had shocked people and reinforced his playboy image.

Nehru turned to Siddiqui and said, 'Aur tum jao Kashmir. Aur Farooq ki photo kheecho, Shabana ke saath (Go to Kashmir and take a photo of Farooq with Shabana).'

Siddiqui protested. 'This will not be in (the) national interest.'

'Acha, toh tu mujhe national interest sikhayega (So, now you will teach me about national interest)?' Arun Nehru replied scathingly.

In the months that followed, Siddiqui wrote about 'what Nehru was up to'. Later, in May 1985, when the draconian law, Terrorists and Disruptive Activities (Prevention) Act (TADA), was brought in to combat terrorists in Punjab, Siddiqui was the first journalist to be arrested under it. It was a law which was misused more against political opponents and dissenters than against terrorists.

Such was the clout Nehru wielded in those days that editors used to be 'terrified' of him.

'Tell your friend,' Nehru had told Buta Singh, referring to G. S. Chawla, a journalist with the *Indian Express*, 'Main usko toh theek kar doonga.' (I will fix him.) Buta Singh was then the home minister and Nehru was minister of state under him in 1985–86. But Buta Singh used to refer to Nehru as sir.

By now Arun Nehru was also building his own team who would be loyal to him. The key members were Mrs Gandhi's aide M. L. Fotedar, Cabinet Secretary P. K. Kaul, Law Minister Shiv Shankar, Gopi Arora, a sharp bureaucrat in the PMO, all of them hardliners on Punjab and Kashmir—like Nehru. A number of Youth Congressmen who had been part of the Sanjay brigade, and had resisted Nehru to begin with began to gravitate towards him. Like Sanjay, he was tough and decisive, and could be abrasive to boot.

But Indira Gandhi was not prepared to listen to anything negative about her family, be it Rajiv or Nehru. If anyone complained to her about them, she would visibly show her annoyance.

■

Indira Gandhi gave Rajiv and Arun Nehru and their friends a free hand. In November 1982, Nehru—backed by Rajiv—dissuaded Indira from signing an agreement with the Akali Dal, which could have retrieved the situation in Punjab, prevented Operation Bluestar, and possibly her own assassination. This was to be a turning point in the Punjab story.

When Sanjay Gandhi was alive, he had zeroed in on Jarnail Singh Bhindranwale as the man the Congress should build up as a counter to the Akali Dal in Punjab. The Akalis had opposed the Emergency and Sanjay wanted to teach them a lesson. Zail Singh, then home minister—he would address Sanjay as Rehnuma (Merciful)—had identified Bhindranwale, a small-time charismatic preacher who could mesmerize audiences with his rendition of the Gurbani, the Sikh scriptures. It was an open secret in Punjab that the Congress had propped him up. Zail Singh had even paid the bill for a press conference that he had organized for Bhindranwale!

However, Bhindranwale soon became unmanageable—he got Hindus murdered, ran a parallel government in Punjab, and dispensed summary justice wherever his writ could be enforced. In time, he demanded the creation of a separate homeland for the Sikhs—Khalistan.

As the situation deteriorated, Indira Gandhi decided to reach out to the Akalis to counter Bhindranwale's challenge. They too had adopted a militant stance and launched a dharma yuddh for action on the 1973 Anandpur Sahib resolution for a 'radical devolution of power'.

Indira Gandhi deputed senior Congress leader Swaran Singh to talk to the Akalis. He managed to reach an agreement with them—and they agreed to suspend their agitation. Home Minister P. C. Sethi was to announce the terms of the agreement in parliament. But when he made the speech, it was very different from what had been agreed upon with the Akalis. At 11 p.m., on 3 November 1982, the night before the announcement was to be made, Indira had changed Sethi's speech.

At the last moment, Arun Nehru, Rajiv Gandhi and their friends had prevailed upon Indira Gandhi not to go ahead with the agreement. It would be seen as a 'surrender' to the Akalis—and could put off the Hindus in Haryana. Elections were due in the state soon—and it could create problems for the Congress.

Indira could see the advantage of a tough line against the Akalis. It was likely to get her the support of the Hindus, who were unhappy with the demands for a separate state of Khalistan. It could help the Congress not just in Haryana but also in the general elections a year down the line.

Zail Singh, who had by now become president—and was helping Arun Nehru—told Indira that it should be Rajiv, not Swaran Singh, who should get the credit for any breakthrough.

The Akalis felt betrayed. They boycotted the Asian Games which were to start two weeks later. Bhajan Lal, then chief minister of Haryana, supported by Arun Nehru and M. L. Fotedar, decided to frisk every Sikh going to Delhi for the games. Sikhs were taken out of their vehicles and subjected to a treatment they found humiliating. It led to widespread anger—and alienation—among the Sikhs. After that, the situation spun from bad to worse.

Bhindranwale and his supporters took refuge in the Golden Temple at the end of 1983. They began to fortify the shrine.

'I've told Mummy so many times,' an exasperated Rajiv told journalist Tavleen Singh, 'that we must do something. But she listens to her senior advisors. They tell her she shouldn't do anything that would upset the Sikhs.'

Rajiv, Arun Nehru, Arun Singh, and Vijay Dhar—the 'baba log' or 'computer boys' as they were called—had put into place a contingency plan for a military operation in Amritsar at the beginning of 1984 itself. It was an 'invasion blueprint'. The idea was to flush out Bhindranwale from the Golden Temple. But Indira 'delayed and resisted'. 'She was scared of attacking a house of God,' Arun Nehru told Indira's biographer, Katherine Frank. Instead, she conducted pujas. She kept hoping that some miracle would occur. Finally, the situation deteriorated to such an extent that Indira had to send the army into the Golden Temple in a military operation code named Operation Bluestar on 1 June 1984. It killed Bhindranwale, destroyed portions of the Golden Temple, and wounded the Sikh psyche. It was an action which was to lead to her assassination on 31 October 1984—and the mass murder of innocent Sikhs in its aftermath.

.

Despite the turbulence that the Punjab developments had unleashed in June 1984, weeks later, in July and August of 1984, the Congress's baba log went on to destabilize the duly elected Opposition governments of Abdullah in Srinagar and N. T. Rama Rao in Hyderabad. In Kashmir, they propped up a breakaway faction led by G. M. Shah, who was Farooq Abdullah's brother-in-law. In Andhra Pradesh, the Congress supported N. Bhaskara Rao, who broke away from NTR. In both instances, the technique was the same—encouraging defection and misusing the office of the governor to install a rival government supported by the Congress. Both operations were mounted by Rajiv, Arun Nehru, and their team.

To destabilize two Opposition governments in the aftermath of Operation Bluestar, with its fallout in a border state of India, seemed a senseless course of action. But Indira Gandhi was putting in place a constituency for the general elections that were due in January 1985—hoping to encash the anger of the Hindus all over the country. She also wanted to take control of the government machinery in as many states as possible when she went in for general elections. By the beginning of 1984, she had got a sense that she may not get a majority in the next election—and had to double her efforts in order to win somehow.

Indira Gandhi's assassination on 31 October 1984 was to change all that. The December 1984 election that followed turned out to be a shaken nation's homage to the slain leader. It was a 'sympathy vote'—to give her son Rajiv Gandhi a flying start as the prime minister of India.

IV

'In 1984, after Indira Gandhi's death, I was doing the planning for the Congress,' Arun Nehru claimed to me proudly. 'My strategy was to target 8 to 10 of the main Opposition leaders. So we put Madhavrao Scindia vs Vajpayee, Amitabh Bachchan vs H. N. Bahuguna, C. K. Jaffer Sharief against George Fernandes.'

He and Arun Singh had convinced Rajiv to strike while the iron was hot. They decided to go in for immediate elections while the rage and sorrow were still fresh in people's minds—and not wait for early 1985 when polls were due.

Rajiv Gandhi had won the country's sympathy for the poise and gravitas he had shown over those three days when Indira Gandhi's body had lain in Teen Murti House. With his dignified demeanour, he had half won the election in those hours when he stood by his mother's body—and then performed the last rites.

Rajiv campaigned relentlessly. All through November and December that year, he zig-zagged across the country, covering 19,000 kilometres in fifteen states in just twelve days, addressing ten meetings a day. He made more or less the same speech in rally after rally. Poignant and well-crafted, it carried a personal account of Indira Gandhi's tragic end woven into it. And how it should not be in vain. 'She was killed by people who hoped to break India into fragments.... The need of the hour is for all people to rise and protect India's unity and integrity'.

But, on 19 November 1984,which was his mother's birthday, he decided to up the ante. The script had been carefully crafted and designed to draw the agitated Hindus to his side. He virtually endorsed the anti-Sikh killings that had taken place after Indira Gandhi's death. 'When a big tree falls,' Rajiv said, 'the earth shakes'—suggesting that the anti-Sikh riots were a natural response to the assassination. It was a sentence he was to take a long time to live down.

Throughout the campaign, slogans had rent the air—'Rajiv Gandhi ka ailan, nahin banega Khalistan (Rajiv Gandhi has made it clear that there will not be a Khalistan).'

This was the theme of the first political ad campaign that was put out by Rediffusion, a Bombay-based advertising firm hired to put together a $100 million election campaign in 1984. It warned voters that the Punjab crisis, if unchecked, would break up India.

'Created...by Arun Nehru's friends in Rediffusion,' former journalist Raghunath A. S. was to write later, 'the campaign depicted Sikhs as the enemy.'

Nehru however, called it 'the cheapest election we fought'. Nobody got more than (₹) one lakh. The whole election did not cost more than ₹12–13 crores,' Nehru told me.

When Rajiv Gandhi hit the campaign trail, people noted a distinct change in the man who had lived a quiet life only four years earlier. 'Gone is the comfortable slouch,' wrote journalist Sunil Sethi, 'the diffident approach with people, or the first signs of a double chin. This is definitely a determined, belligerent, chin-up Rajiv Gandhi.' It was also a very different Rajiv from the one who had campaigned for his party in the January 1983 state elections in Karnataka and Andhra Pradesh—trying to explain abstract concepts like political freedom, or the value of hard work, to puzzled audiences. The Congress had lost both states.

All the Opposition heavyweights lost in the 1984 general election. The Congress won 84 out of 85 Lok Sabha seats in UP. The party came to power with an unprecedented majority of 404 Lok Sabha seats of the 514 seats elected. This tally went up to 414 when elections which had been delayed in Assam and Punjab were held in 1985. Not even Rajiv's grandfather, Jawaharlal Nehru, had managed to do better.

■

The man in the eye of the storm sat quietly at 1, Safdarjung Road, as the results poured in on 28 December 1984, showing a landslide for the Congress. He sat munching a toasted sandwich, dressed in slacks, Puma sneakers, and a smart green sweater with leather patches on the shoulders. He had continued to stay at 1, Safdarjung Road, as the PM House at 7, Race Course Road was still being readied. Rajiv Gandhi betrayed none of the excitement that raged outside. It was a Rajiv who was a far cry from the white-kurta-pyjama-clad figure haring around the country during those gruelling weeks of campaigning in November and December 1984.

Congratulatory phone calls were pouring in non-stop from all corners of the country. Rajiv even teased Haryana chief minister Bhajan Lal for not getting 11 seats out of the 10 the state sent to the Lok Sabha! When a visitor congratulated Rajiv for a victory which neither his mother nor his grandfather had managed to clock, Rajiv remarked modestly, 'What can I say?' In those hours, he was the boy next door—the politically correct Rajiv was to surface in the days that followed.

■

On 31 December 1984, Rajiv Gandhi was sworn in as the prime minister for the second time. He had been unanimously elected as the leader of the CPP. This time Arun Nehru did not have to lobby for his cousin; it was a given that he would become PM again.

The ceremony took place in the same Ashoka Hall in Rashtrapati Bhavan under its glittering chandeliers where he had sombrely taken the oath of office and secrecy two months earlier after his mother's assassination. A more buoyant Rajiv was now in evidence. The Congress was upbeat.

Rajiv's quiet, moustachioed friend Arun Singh sat in the front row with the Gandhi family. He had already been brought into the Rajya Sabha and appointed parliamentary secretary in November, a position revived after a gap of eighteen years, with powers equal to those of a deputy premier. The mega star Amitabh Bachchan, who had won as MP from Allahabad, sat amidst the guests, watching his close friend take oath.

Arun Nehru, who had been made a junior minister in the Ministry of

Power, though his powers were to go way beyond his designation—was happily back-slapping the new ministers. He almost 'toppled the dignified former Foreign Ministry official Natwar Singh to the ground'; Kunwar Natwar Singh was to be installed as a junior minister!

In the preceding hours, the two Aruns had sat with Rajiv, poring over the list of names to decide who would be in the cabinet—and who would be out of it.

Contrary to popular perception, Nehru, though a third cousin, was not really a 'friend' of Rajiv's.

'I don't remember seeing him at the PM House coming to meet Rajiv and Sonia, either when Indira Gandhi was PM or after Rajiv became prime minister,' recalled Vivek Bharat Ram, who Rajiv's friend. 'I saw Arun Singh coming to see him at home. Rajiv and Sonia had rooms on the right side of the PM House.'

Rajiv and Arun Singh went back many years. They were together in Doon School and later at Cambridge.

'Arun Singh was deferential to Rajiv as prime minister, but Arun Nehru was far from deferential,' recalled journalist B. N. Uniyal. Once a group of politicians was waiting outside the PM's office in parliament, Uniyal recalled, for Rajiv to come out. When he did, everyone stood up. Only Nehru kept sitting.

Arun Nehru made a point of addressing Rajiv, when he was PM, by his first name in front of colleagues and officials. Later, when V. P. Singh became prime minister in 1989, he would address him as Vishwanath. This would make the Janata Dal leaders, many of them stalwarts with long innings in politics, very uncomfortable. It was not just a reflection of the corporate culture he brought with him. They saw it as an attempt by Nehru to throw his weight around, demonstrate his proximity to the leader, to put others at a disadvantage.

Once, when Nehru had addressed UP chief minister Sripat Mishra as Sripat, Mishra politely put him in his place. 'Arunji, kuch toh umar ka lihaz kariye (Arunji, have some respect for age).'

After Rajiv Gandhi became prime minister, Arun Singh was given the bungalow at 1, Race Course Road, next to the PM's. There was only a wicket gate separating the two houses. The two friends had easy access to each other. Their wives, Sonia and Nina Singh, also hit it off. (Later they were to fall out.)

On 31 December 1984, Rajiv Gandhi had decided to revamp his cabinet; it comprised a mix of experienced and new faces. Treading cautiously, Rajiv kept as many as seventeen portfolios. The biggest surprise was the ouster of Pranab Mukherjee, who Rajiv had retained as finance minister in his first cabinet. 'I kept waiting for the call [to come from the prime minister]', Mukherjee would say later.

To the surprise of many, the more junior V. P. Singh became finance minister instead. When Indira Gandhi was alive, she had wanted VP to be part of Rajiv's team as she felt his clean image would be an asset. VP had been an unwavering supporter of Mrs Gandhi and her family, even when they were at their lowest ebb. It was Arun Nehru who had determinedly kept Mukherjee out—he saw Mukherjee as a threat to Rajiv. The choice of S. B. Chavan for home minister also showed the imprimatur of Nehru. Giving the ministry to an easy-going and pliant minister meant the prime minister—or whoever acted on his behalf, like Nehru—would have a direct say in the affairs of Punjab and Kashmir. Soon it would become clear—that Nehru was going to be the power behind the throne. Within weeks, he began to be seen as the de facto prime minister.

Though the minister of state for Power, in those early days, he was the man who had the most power in Rajiv's coterie. And he had the prime minister's ear.

■

Rajiv Gandhi's new cabinet made news. Particularly the induction of V. P. Singh as finance minister. But so did the exclusion of R. K. Dhawan, for years Indira Gandhi's powerful private secretary—and her man Friday—who was unceremoniously shown the door. If there was someone most recognized in the Congress circles, after the Gandhi family, it was Dhawan. With his ouster, a more confident Rajiv came to the fore, one who could be his own man.

On 1 January 1985, R. K. Dhawan drove to 1, Safdarjung Road, as he would normally do every morning. A bachelor, his day used to begin early and ended after Indira Gandhi had finished for the day. Seen as her shadow, he wielded enormous power, controlling access to her durbar, and carrying out sensitive political assignments on the PM's behalf. He was responsible for the rapid rise of certain industrialists. With a clipped black moustache, slickly combed black hair, shining black shoes, constantly puffing away at his cigarette, he had started off as a stenotypist, brought to the PM's household by his cousin Yashpal Kapoor, a chubby looking Punjabi. Indira chose to keep Kapoor, Dhawan, and later M. L. Fotedar as her personal/political aides, preferring them to people from the civil services, like P. N. Haksar or P. N. Dhar whom she had chosen in her first stint as prime minister.

When the gates of the PM's residence did not open for his car, Dhawan shouted at the guards, using choice epithets in Punjabi. But they had their instructions; they told him to leave his car outside and walk to the reception. A furious Dhawan parked his car outside the Gymkhana Club on the opposite side and walked in. When he demanded to speak to the prime minister, the staff at the reception, who had done his bidding for years, told him curtly that he should go back home and call the PM on the phone.

Dhawan was out. He was not even allowed to take any of his papers or belongings or money that were in his office. They were later packed and sent to him. Other staff members like Nathu Ram, who was Indira Gandhi's attendant and knew all about the comings and goings in the PM House, was also sent packing. Indira had trusted him with even the keys to her bedroom.

'It was Sonia Gandhi who decided that they wielded too much power (in the PM House) and should go,' disclosed journalist Pankaj Vohra, who had covered the politics of the period and knew both Dhawan and Fotedar well. Dhawan's exit also suited Fotedar and Nehru. It enabled them to get control of the PM House.

It is not publicly known that R. K. Dhawan, who had remained loyal to Indira Gandhi all through, had considered turning an approver in 1977. This was after she went out of power, and the Shah Commission was probing charges against her, Sanjay, and Dhawan.

One morning, Congress heavyweight Sitaram Kesri phoned Janata Party MP Krishan Kant. Kant had by then quit the Congress, having opposed the Emergency.

'Dhawan wants to meet you,' Kesri told Kant. 'I am sending him to you.' Dhawan walked across to Kant's house at 2, Telegraph Lane, from his brother's house nearby, where he was then living. Dhawan wanted Kant to convey to the Janata leadership that he wanted to turn approver.

'Don't even consider such a step,' Kant advised him, 'you owe a great deal to her.'

'Don't act in a hurry,' he said, 'this government is not going to last very long.'

Dhawan did not raise the matter again.

Dhawan believed there had never been a private secretary like him. Once when Pankaj Vohra had gone to see him at his 141, Golf Links house, and regaled him with the latest political gupshup (gossip)—about the growing power of Ahmed Patel in the Congress, this was sometime in 2008—Dhawan shouted an abuse in Punjabi, downed his whisky in one gulp, and said with a flourish: 'There can never be anyone as powerful as R. K. Dhawan.'

But after 1984, the all-powerful R. K. Dhawan was out. Fotedar gained influence in the PM House from 1984–87, after which Rajiv shunted Fotedar out to the Steel and Mines Ministry to get him out of the way. In their place, Rajiv brought in Vincent George as his private secretary.

When Rajiv Gandhi took over as prime minister in 1985, the cynicism and drift which had marked the last years of Indira Gandhi's rule seemed to have become a thing of the past. As the country's youngest ever prime minister, just forty years old, Rajiv Gandhi promised political stability and hope. When he began to signal a break from the past, even though he had been part of that past, people believed him. A tired nation was ready to move on.

In those first few months in office, Rajiv Gandhi could do no wrong. One of his first acts as prime minister was to enact an anti-defection law in January 1985 to put an end to large-scale defections. The shift of MPs from one party to another—what came to be known as the 'Aya Ram, Gaya Ram' phenomenon—for personal or political gain had become the bane of Indian politics.

Over the course of 1985, Rajiv Gandhi would sign two accords— in Punjab and Assam—and another one in Mizoram followed in 1986. All three were border states and had been wracked by insurgency and violence. Punjab had been in the grip of militancy since the late 1970s, which turned into a movement for a separate nation of Khalistan. Assam had been rocked by an anti-foreigner stir led by students and youth to deport foreigners who had come in illegally from Bangladesh. Mizoram continued to be roiled by an insurgency that had lasted sixteen years. Rajiv Gandhi's accord on Mizoram, when the insurgent Mizo National Front (MNF) gave up its demand for independence, turned out to be one of his most enduring legacies; it was to pave the way for peace and prosperity in the state.

Rajiv Gandhi went on to set up six technology missions under Sam Pitroda. These were on drinking water, immunization, literacy, oilseeds, and dairy production. It was the sixth one, on telecommunications, which had the most far-reaching impact. Public call office booths mushroomed everywhere, even in the far-flung areas of the country, connecting India's villages to the world. In 1986, Rajiv's government set up the Mahanagar Telephone Nigam Limited (MTNL) which expanded the reach of the telephone. Next, railway reservations were computerized. All this laid the ground for mobile telephony that changed the lives of ordinary Indians in ways that they could not have imagined. Those working in towns could now talk on a daily basis to their loved ones back in the villages instead of visiting them once in two years.

In 1988, Rajiv Gandhi lowered the voting age from twenty-one to eighteen, through a Constitution Amendment Bill—giving young people the chance to shape politics. He initiated the devolution of democracy by giving greater autonomy to the panchayati raj system and to local governments. These bills could not be passed during Rajiv Gandhi's term. They were enacted during P. V. Narasimha Rao's premiership as the Constitution (Seventy-third Amendment) Act, 1992 and Constitution (Seventy-fourth Amendment) Act, 1992—and provided reservation of one-third of positions in local governments for women.

Over the years, this helped create a pool of women who had acquired experience of governance in local governments—and were ready for a larger role. This was also to be another of Rajiv Gandhi's lasting legacies—and that story is far from over.

While Rajiv Gandhi took the first steps towards opening up the economy, it was the overspending during his term that led to a balance of payment crisis which P. V. Narasimha Rao had to deal with within hours of taking over as prime minister in 1991. Rajiv also gave the go-ahead to get India ready for nuclear testing; this was finally executed by Atal Bihari Vajpayee in 1998. Above all, Rajiv envisioned taking India into the twenty-first century as a modern, scientifically-oriented, tech-savvy, and forward-looking nation.

Two issues were to blight Rajiv Gandhi's premiership. The first was his handling of the Shah Bano judgment in 1985. The second was the Bofors gun deal in mid-1987, in which Rajiv, and others linked to him, were accused of taking kickbacks on the sale of the Swedish Bofors howitzer to the Indian Army. As the 'Mr Clean' of Indian politics, Rajiv had vowed to clean up the arms trade and banned commissions in arms deals when he came to power. Although no evidence was found directly implicating Rajiv in any wrongdoing, his family's connections to some of the middlemen accused of taking kickbacks—like Italian businessman Ottavio Quattrochi—damaged his reputation. V. P. Singh attacked him relentlessly on Bofors during the 1989 general election, which Rajiv lost.

But it was the Shah Bano missteps that cast a longer shadow on the country. The consequences of his actions would long outlive Rajiv's term as prime minister.

V

As was the case every year, 15 August in 1985 was a hot and muggy day in Delhi. But Rajiv Gandhi walked up the ramparts of the Red Fort with a spring in his step to unfurl the national tricolour on Independence Day. He had watched his mother do the honours for years. For him, it was the first time. As the young prime minister spoke, he struck a note of optimism which resonated with the country.

In the evening, Rajiv had another 'first' to his credit—and that was to sign the Assam Accord with leaders of the All Assam Students' Union and the All Assam Gana Sangram Parishad. For five years, they had been leading the movement for deportation of 'illegal' immigrants from Bangladesh who had come to Assam and settled there over the years. The agreement sought to resolve the identity issues thrown up by the movement in the Northeastern state. A month earlier, in July, he had signed an accord with Sikh leader Harchand Singh Longowal to resolve the vexed problem in Punjab.

The young PM used to revel in the cloak and dagger drama, and nocturnal meetings he would often call that were part of his decision-making process.

A day before the accord was signed, Rajiv Gandhi rang up Arun Nehru at 2 a.m. 'Come and have a cup of coffee with me. We are signing the Assam accord,' he told his cousin excitedly.

Nehru went across to see him.

'Rajesh Pilot has got the accord done.' Rajiv looked very pleased with himself.

'The Home Minister knew nothing about it,' he said gleefully. 'He learnt about it later.' Later, in the 1990s, this is what P. V. Narasimha Rao also did—he used Rajesh Pilot in Kashmir and in Ayodhya, cutting out Chavan, who was again home minister and otherwise quite close to Rao.

On 15 August 1985, upbeat Assamese leaders gathered at the PM House along with eminent citizens; they had been specially invited to witness the historic event. After the customary tea laid out for his guests, a buoyant Rajiv Gandhi did what would have been commonplace for any prime minister—to give an instruction to a junior minister. But that directive was to unleash forces which would overwhelm his government four years later.

After the function ended, instead of leaving, S. B. Chavan and senior officials from the Home Ministry walked back into the PMH. Arif Mohammed Khan, Chavan's deputy, was part of the group. They waited for Rajiv to come back after seeing off his guests.

As soon as everyone was seated, Rajiv asked Khan, 'What is your opinion on Shah Bano (judgment)?' Though the Shah Bano debate had been raging in the country for over three months, and Khan was a Muslim minister in Rajiv's cabinet, he had said nothing on the subject. This was unlike many other Muslim ministers who had made no secret of their opposition to the judgment.

Khan wondered why the PM had suddenly asked him for his opinion. Had he heard about his views from Chavan?

Only days earlier, the home minister had called a meeting in his office in North Block. He wanted to discuss what the government's response should be to the criticism of the judgment by powerful sections of the Muslim community.

The issue had come to a head with G. M. Banatwalla, an MP from the All India Muslim League (AIML), moving a private member's bill in the Lok Sabha in early May. The AIML was an ally of the ruling Congress in Kerala. It was a right-wing party founded in 1948 to promote the interests of Muslims. Banatwalla was also one of the leading lights of the All India Muslim Personal Law Board (AIMPLB), a non-governmental body of Muslims created in 1973 to ensure that Muslim Personal Law continued to be followed by the community. In 1937, the British had enacted a law

called the Muslim Personal Law (Shariat) Application Act, 1937, to provide
for the application of personal laws to Muslims. Anchored in religion,
it dealt with matters such as marriage, divorce, succession, inheritance,
and the custody of children. Before the Shariat Act came into existence,
Muslims in India followed local and religious customs in the way they
organized their personal lives.

Banatwalla's bill, however, was not about Muslim Personal Law. It
proposed an amendment to the country's Code of Criminal Procedure, to
exclude Muslims from the purview of Section 125—which provided for relief
to be given to the destitute, including divorced Hindu or Muslim women,
or a parent or anybody unable to look after themselves. It was under this
section that the Supreme Court had ruled that maintenance be paid to Shah
Bano after she was divorced by her husband. Banatwalla chose to highlight
his opposition to the judgment using the route of a private member's bill.

It was not uncommon for members of parliament to bring a private
member's bill to exert pressure on the government to move an official
bill on the subject. Usually taken up for discussion on Friday afternoons,
these bills were selected by lots. As luck would have it, Banatwalla's bill
got selected and was listed for discussion. The discussion on it continued
for many Friday afternoons. All who spoke on the issue happened to be
Muslims, except for one Janata Party MP.

In the 1980s, even private members' bills were given importance by the
government. This was why the home minister had called a meeting of his
officials to consider their response to Banatwalla's bill. The officials were
wrangling about the stage at which the home minister should intervene
in the debate. Suddenly, Chavan cut them short; he asked Khan for his
opinion. Khan, who had been silent until then, decided to be forthright.

'What Banatwalla is saying is all wrong,' he said, 'and his stand is not
in accordance with what the Quran says.'

Khan now had everyone's attention. For a start, he said, CrPC Section
125 was rooted in the theory of social justice. 'It has nothing to do with
personal law, as is being made out by the Muslim Personal Law Board.'
Nor did the law kick in automatically after divorce. It had to be invoked
by a woman if she faced economic hardship. In 1978, when the CrPC was
revised, the responsibility for a divorced woman in distress was passed
on to the former husband, if the woman could not look after herself. (In
the case of parents it was passed on to the sons.) However, even if the
AIMPLB's argument were to be accepted, that maintenance should be paid
only for the three month period of iddat, there was nothing to prevent
the husband 'from doing charity to a destitute stranger' who had after
all been his wife.

Khan cited verses from the Quran which laid down that 'even on the
occasion of divorce, which announces the annulment of the relationship,

do not refrain from showing goodness, consideration, and concession'. It was 'blasphemy for anyone to object to money being given to a destitute'.

The officials present at the meeting were impressed.

'We did not know this,' they said.

A smile lit up Chavan's face. 'Baat toh sahi hai (What you are saying makes sense),' he said.

So, when Rajiv Gandhi asked Khan for his views on 15 August 1985, Khan repeated what he had earlier told Chavan.

'Then why don't you speak (in parliament)?' the PM asked him.

'I haven't said anything so far,' Khan replied, 'because I did not know how you planned to deal with this.'

'No, no, we cannot agree to what these people are saying,' Rajiv told him, referring to the opposition mounted by the Muslim clergy and sections of the community.

Later, said Khan, Rajiv Gandhi wrote similarly strong words on the file relating to the issue. 'File pe toh Rajivji ne aur bhi sakht likha hai (what Rajiv wrote in the file was even stronger), that no compromise can be made with these fundamentalist elements.' Rajiv Gandhi's first instinct was to oppose the bill. He was a 'modern' leader with liberal traditions who wanted to position India for the twenty-first century.

'Arif will intervene first in the discussion,' the prime minister directed Chavan, 'and you should speak after him.'

■

On 23 August 1985, Arif Mohammed Khan intervened in the Lok Sabha in the debate on the Banatwalla private member's bill. His words were greeted with a thumping of desks, as his supporters endorsed his words. Passionately defending the Shah Bano judgment, Khan projected a 'progressive' point of view. 'We should have better practices these days,' he said. '...only if the downtrodden are uplifted can the Islamic tenets be said to have been followed and justice done.' When he was done, fellow MPs said he had made a brilliant speech and rushed to congratulate him.

When Khan reached home that evening, to his surprise, there was a letter waiting for him. It was from the prime minister. Within an hour of his speech, it had been delivered to his official residence at 3, Sunehri Bagh Road. 'Rajiv praised me generously for what I had said in the Lok Sabha.' So did the next day's newspapers.

■

Arif Mohammed Khan had been exercised about the issue of triple talaq from an early age. His curiosity about this form of divorce in Islam stemmed from an incident that took place when he was ten years old. Khan was in the eighth standard at the time. The incident occurred in his mother's village, Bassi, in UP's Bulandshahr district. 'Something happened in my family—extended family—for there was rishtedari (kinships) in the dozen or so villages around—which had shocked me.'

In the village in those days, when the padlocks that were used to secure the front door were unlocked, the unfastened locks would be left hanging from the door latches.

A villager had uttered the word taala (lock), but others around him insisted that he had pronounced the word talaq. 'Woh aadmi yeh kehta tha ki maine toh taala kaha tha, aur doosre log yeh kehte the ki nahi tune to talaaq kaha tha (The man said, I have uttered the word taala but others were sure he had said talaq).'

The man kept reiterating, 'I had the lock in my hand and I had only uttered the word, taala.' But people who were present there insisted he had said talaq thrice. He remonstrated, 'Maine teen baar kaha hai ya chatees baar kaha hai, maine taala kaha tha (Whether I said it three times or thirty-six times, the word I uttered was lock).'

Over the man's protestations, he and his wife were forced to separate. Those who maintained they had heard the word talaq enlisted the support of the local mullahs. 'I found this ridiculous,' Khan said.

Later, the man tried to get together with the wife he had been forced to divorce. The curious part of the story, Khan said, was that a patch-up was not possible. 'Society poora danda leke khadi ho gayi ki nahi bhai, toone talaq kaha hai (Society stood there with a stick insisting that he had said talaq).'

The upshot of it all was that the woman had to marry someone else as religious custom dictated before she was able to reunite with her first husband.

'People felt very bad. But nobody dared say anything in front of the mullahs. I never forgot this incident,' Arif said. It spurred him to read the Quran closely, to learn what it said about marriage, divorce, and Muslim Personal Law. While at Aligarh Muslim University, he studied the issue in some depth, read commentaries and interpretations of the holy book, and discussed its tenets with experts. So when the Shah Bano judgment came, Khan had done a fair amount of thinking on the subject.

Following Arif Mohammed Khan's intervention in parliament on 23 August 1985, the pressure on Rajiv Gandhi began to mount. This now came from powerful sections of the Muslim clergy who saw the judgment as interference in the personal law of the community. Rajiv tried to engage with them. He held many meetings with Maulana Abul Hasan Ali Nadwi, the chairman of the AIMPLB, and other representatives of the organization. Interestingly enough, the AIMPLB was set up with the blessings of Indira Gandhi. She had seen it as a way to win over the political allegiance of Muslim voters. Ali Mian, as Maulana Nadwi was popularly called, handed

Rajiv a memorandum. It argued that the judgment was an interference in Muslim Personal Law and the freedom of religion guaranteed them in the Constitution (Articles 25, 26, and 29). Ali Mian was 'backed by the entire Islamic world'.

The AIMPLB insisted that the divorced woman could not be in touch with her former husband on an ongoing basis, after the divorce had taken place. 'So, she could not be taking money from him every month.'

The clergy and political leaders aside, ordinary Muslims, too, came out 'very strongly' against the judgment. Muslims protested on the streets in their lakhs, holding demonstrations in Delhi, Mumbai, Kolkata, Patna, Kanpur, Hyderabad, and other cities. This also exerted its own pressure on the AIMPLB.

The first big meeting against the judgment was held in Siwan in Bihar. Though a local initiative, it attracted three lakh people—it was this meeting which signalled to the AIMPLB that Muslims were now ready to agitate against the judgment. For a majority of Indian Muslims, 'Shah Bano' was becoming even more important than the dispute over the Babri Masjid in Ayodhya. For many in the community regarded their identity as inextricably linked to their personal laws.

These protests in 1985 were the first real signs of large-scale assertiveness by Muslims after Independence. There had been demonstrations by the community earlier, of course. Like Muslims elsewhere in the world, they had protested when the holy Al-Aqsa Mosque in Jerusalem was attacked in 1969. In 1977, after the Aligarh riots, the community staged silent protests, demanding their fundamental rights be respected. On a few other occasions, too, when there were riots or violence against the community, there were localized protests. But there had never been anything to compare with the outrage that erupted after the judgment. As Shahid Siddiqui explained, until 1985, 'We used to mostly express our power through the exercise of the vote.'

Several Muslim leaders in the Congress criticized Arif Mohammed Khan for his stand. Given the reaction of the community, Muslim MPs and ministers in the Congress were worried. They did not want to antagonize members of the AIMPLB. Or go against Muslim opinion. C. K. Jaffer Sharief, a senior Muslim minister in Rajiv Gandhi's cabinet, was agitated. So also was Najma Heptulla, a Congress MP and deputy chairperson of the Rajya Sabha. All through 1985, she played a decisive role in facilitating negotiations between the AIMPLB and the government. Ali Mian gave her full credit for the role she had played.

At a protest meeting held at India Gate, Heptulla, Begum Abida Ahmed, wife of the former president Fakhruddin Ali Ahmed, and other prominent Muslim women attacked Khan for his views.

Undeterred, Khan hit back. 'Everyone has a right to their views,' he quipped. 'But one thing I do know. Najma Heptulla pays more money to her hairdresser than what the court has allocated to Shah Bano!'

The next day his comments were picked up by the media. The divide inside the Congress Party was deepening.

•

Soon after Khan's intervention in parliament, an agitated Ziaur Rahman Ansari met Rajiv Gandhi. 'If Arif [Mohammad] Khan, who is a minister, can speak in a debate on a private member's bill, why can't I speak?' Ansari was a senior Muslim minister in Rajiv's cabinet. A highly-regarded intellectual in the Muslim community, his knowledge of Arabic was phenomenal. He threatened to quit if he was not allowed to speak. He had arrived for the meeting with the prime minister armed with his resignation letter. 'Rajiv took the resignation letter, tore it, and threw it in the dustbin,' recalled Aziz Qureshi (later to become governor of Uttarakhand), who had accompanied Ansari to the meeting.

'Who is stopping you from speaking?' Rajiv tried to mollify the flustered Ansari.

Ansari spoke in parliament for three hours, first on 22 November and then again on 3 December 1985. He spoke as passionately as Arif Mohammed Khan had done. He lambasted the Shah Bano judgment as 'prejudiced'. The judges, he charged, were not competent to interpret the Quran and the Hadith.

Coming as it did after Khan's defence of the judgment, Ansari's speech sent a contrary signal—that Rajiv had now changed his mind. The Muslim community had managed to prevail upon Rajiv Gandhi, and the prime minister had fielded Ansari to counter Khan. 'It is clear beyond doubt,' the *Times of India* wrote in an editorial, 'that Mr Gandhi gave Mr Ansari the go-ahead signal. In plain terms Mr Ansari too was not acting on his own initiative.' Even though he had got Khan to make a strong defence of the Shah Bano judgment, Rajiv Gandhi realized that he had to placate an agitated Muslim opinion.

•

Pulled in two directions, till mid-November 1985, Rajiv Gandhi was still uncertain about what he should do.

On 16 November 1985, Khan was in his constituency, Bahraich. He had gone on a visit to a place called Sisiya, 150 kilometres away from the district headquarters. It was there that the local district magistrate, who had desperately been looking for him, caught up with him. 'There was a phone call from the PM House,' he told Khan. 'The message was that you have to accompany the PM to Oman tonight. A helicopter has already left Lucknow and will pick you up in Bahraich and take you back to Lucknow. So you had better cancel everything and leave immediately.'

Khan rushed to Bahraich; he reached Delhi by nightfall on 16 November 1985. He reached the airport by 2 a.m., all set to leave with the prime minister.

'Soon after I boarded the flight, an officer told me, "Sir, Khurshid Alam Khan was to be the accompanying minister, his name had come." This was not surprising for he was minister of state, External Affairs. "But the prime minister cut out his name and added your name," the official said. Then, warming up, he volunteered more information, "He (the PM) mentioned he was doing it because rumours were afloat that he was going to disown the stand taken by Arif Mohammad Khan. It is essential I take Arif with me at this point to scotch those rumours",' the official quoted Rajiv Gandhi as having said.

The prime minister and his team arrived in Oman on 17 November 1985 on a two-day visit to the capital of Muscat. Since he was the minister accompanying the PM, Khan's suite was next to that of Rajiv Gandhi in the hotel where they were staying. In the morning, Khan walked into the prime minister's room. Rajiv was having breakfast. 'Rajiv repeated what the official had told me the previous night as the reason why he had asked me to accompany him.'

Then he asked Khan, 'Why are you not campaigning about the stand you have taken?'

'I am not campaigning,' Khan replied, 'because I am not sure what is going to be the final outcome....'

He knew that the government was talking to members of the AIMPLB. He told Rajiv Gandhi as much. 'Then, I told Rajiv that I would have no problem if a middle ground can be found.'

'This is precisely the note I had struck at the end of my speech in parliament,' Khan reminded Rajiv, 'that there should be no agitation on this issue. It is a legal and constitutional issue. And public emotions should not be aroused on it.... It is not as if some way cannot be found out of this impasse.'

'Nahi, koi sawaal hi nahin inke saath samjhauta karne ka (No, there is no question of a compromise with these people),' Rajiv told Khan.

Then he added, 'I will instruct (Vincent) George to talk to the AICC people and make the necessary arrangements. You get into a full-scale campaign against these people (AIMPLB).'

'But I decided to wait,' Khan revealed. 'Because I was getting information of a different kind—that the negotiations with the Personal Law Board people were progressing well.' And he knew he was not being included in those negotiations for a definite reason—the AIMPLB had obviously set a condition that he be kept out of the talks. 'If I am not included in these negotiations, it means the government has agreed to their condition to keep Arif out,' Khan was to say later.

Khan did not seek the help of the AICC office bearers, as suggested by the prime minister. Nor did he get in touch with Vincent George, Rajiv Gandhi's private secretary. Nor for that matter did he contact Rajiv Gandhi. But the episode showed that till mid-November 1985, Rajiv was still uncertain. Even as he dithered, the situation, complex as it was, rapidly grew more vexed.

∎

M. J. Akbar was an educated and articulate Muslim, and a leading journalist who had established a rapport with the prime minister. He spoke in an idiom that Rajiv understood. Akbar was against the Shah Bano judgment, like the majority of the Muslim community. He went on television with Arif Mohammed Khan who opposed him. The debate became the talk of the town.

Wajahat Habibullah, who worked in Rajiv's PMO, described the role Akbar played in influencing Rajiv Gandhi. At the time, Habibullah was director in the PMO, a position he had also held during Indira Gandhi's tenure. He had been at Doon School with Rajiv and they had been friends ever since. Months into Rajiv's premiership, he was elevated to the joint secretary level. Habibullah was also in charge of the National Integration Council (NIC) and programmes for the welfare of the minorities. 'I was looking after minority matters. But there was no term like minority affairs at the time,' Habibullah said.

The flurry of petitions to the government by Muslim organizations like the Jamiat-e-Islami and the AIMPLB to reject the Supreme Court decision had all landed on Habibullah's desk. They compelled him to go deeper into 'the whole question of personal law and its application in India'. Personal laws, he concluded, had value in fostering social relations within a community. But Habibullah felt that these laws should be 'reviewed' in view of the practice in some other countries. And this should be done 'by the community itself'.

He was clear, however, that the government should not intervene in any way in the Shah Bano matter. Though many Muslim organizations had argued that the Supreme Court had no right to rule on a matter concerning Muslim Personal Law, Habibullah felt it had every right to rule because it was the 'supreme' legal authority in the country. If the community had problems with the decision, it could move the Supreme Court for a review. The maximum the government should do, he felt, was 'not to intervene in the matter'. There would be no end to it, if the government started to get involved in personal laws. It had to be left to the courts.

Habibullah put down his recommendations in a note to the prime minister. 'I sent out a single note...it must still be there,' Habibullah said.

Normally the PM would return it with his comments. But this file did not come back to him.

Then, one day, Rajiv Gandhi called Habibullah. Rajiv's style of functioning was different from that of his mother. When Indira Gandhi wanted to see Habibullah, she would send a formal message, couched in old-world courtesy, through her personal aide R. K. Dhawan—'Madam aapko yaad kar rahi hain (Madam is remembering you).' Rajiv was more informal in his dealings with his officers. That winter day towards the end of 1985, Rajiv called Habibullah on the secure RAX line.

'Will you come over?' he asked without preamble. Habibullah walked across to the PMO in South Block. When he entered the room, he saw M. J. Akbar sitting there. There was a nip in the air that day, he was to recall later, and Delhi had started to become cool.

'Come in, come in, Wajahat,' Rajiv greeted him breezily. And then he added, 'You are one of us.'

What is this? Habibullah thought to himself. Of course I am one of 'us'. He must have looked mystified but chose to remain silent. He was soon to discover what Rajiv meant.

Rajiv came straight to the point. Referring to the Muslim ire over the Shah Bano judgment, the prime minister said, 'Akbar feels that if we keep quiet and don't say anything on this case, the Muslim community will feel that...I am ignoring them. They might feel that they are not one of my own.'

At this point, M. J. Akbar took over—and spoke, 'at some length', about why the judgment should be undone. Rajiv had got huge support from the Muslims in the 1984 elections, he argued. Akbar talked about meetings where members of the Muslim community would say, 'Rajiv toh hamare hain (Rajiv is one of us).' This represented a shift from 1977, when the community had deserted Indira Gandhi because of the enforced sterilization of Muslim men. But if Rajiv went ahead and accepted the Supreme Court's verdict, Akbar warned, they would conclude that Rajiv did not 'really think of them as part of his family'.

It was M. J. Akbar's 'educated advice', Habibullah felt, which brought about a turnaround in the PM's stand.

'I must admit,' Wajahat Habibullah conceded years later that 'I and (or for that matter) Akbar'—had both made an "error" of judgment in 1985. We took this flurry of petitions by the clerics as...the voice of the Muslim community. That distinction, "now so clear (to me)" was "not clear then". And both Akbar and I being of a somewhat Westernized bent, like Rajiv himself, were not aware, nor sensitive to the difference between general opinion and the opinion voiced by the clerics.'

The tendency to rely on religious middlemen to make political decisions was not new in India. It had existed since British times. Ever since the uprising of 1857, Islamic clerics had taken it upon themselves to represent the community before the British government. This continued later with the Congress Party; over time they became the voice of the Muslim community.

That day, it became clear to Habibullah that Akbar's words had Rajiv's approval. He realized why the prime minister had called him to his office. Rajiv wanted to bring him around to a viewpoint different from the one he had taken in the note he had sent the PM.

The meeting ended. Rajiv gave Habibullah no instructions. Later, Habibullah learnt that the file was sent to the Ministry of Law and Justice. From then on the file moved between the Law Ministry and the PMO. But it never came back to Habibullah's desk. The matter was out of his hands.

■

The debate over the Shah Bano judgment divided the Congress Party right down the middle. It was not just the Muslim leaders like Ziaur Rahman Ansari, C. K. Jaffer Sharief, Najma Heptulla, and Salman Khurshid who wanted to undo the judgment. Senior party leaders like P. V. Narasimha Rao, Arjun Singh, N. D. Tiwari, and S. B. Chavan, were also in favour of amending the law. Ranged against them were Congressmen like Arun Nehru, Arif Mohammed Khan, D. P. Tripathi, and Sitaram Kesri.

In those early months of his premiership, Rajiv Gandhi would often turn to senior leaders for political advice. Though he was worried about the Muslims taking to the streets, the prime minister's mind was influenced not just by those like M. J. Akbar, but also these senior leaders—Rao, Arjun Singh, Tiwari, and Chavan. These men had headed governments in large states—Andhra Pradesh, Madhya Pradesh, Uttar Pradesh, and Maharashtra—which had sizeable Muslim populations, and he consulted them on how to handle the snowballing Muslim reaction.

Rao told Rajiv that 'prolonging this affair' would only be counter-productive. Arjun Singh felt that they should not alienate the leadership of the Muslims. Tiwari typified the Congress mindset—that the party's vote bank comprised Brahmins, Dalits, and Muslims, and the Muslims should not be antagonized. Surprisingly, Chavan too was of the same opinion, although he used to be snidely called a 'Sanghi' for what some of his partymen felt were his pro-RSS views.

But, surprisingly, it was Chavan who had advised Arif Mohammed Khan 'to be careful', as seen earlier. 'Though Rajiv had asked me at PMH to speak in parliament, in Chavan's presence, he (Chavan) had later advised me not to speak.'

'He met me separately, "Arif, mat bolo. Iss maamle mein mat pado (Arif, don't speak, don't get entangled in this affair)."'

It was not just Chavan who counselled Khan to tread with caution, '(M. L.) Fotedar had also said the same thing to me.'

'But,' Khan told Fotedar, 'the PM has asked me to speak.'

'Aap PM se baat kar leejiye. Mat boliye is maamle mein.' (You talk to the PM, but don't speak on this issue.) They did not want to make the going tough for Khan; he was seen as a young and promising leader in the Congress.

'I knew that Rajivji would not have changed his mind,' Khan told me, 'and given in to the pressure of the Personal Law Board people but for these senior leaders.'

Rajiv Gandhi was also mindful of international Islamic opinion, though this was not the primary consideration for him.

Events started to move at a cracking pace in December 1985. By now, Rajiv Gandhi had got intelligence reports that the overwhelming sentiment in the Muslim community was against the Shah Bano judgment. The results of the assembly elections in Assam and by-polls in seven Lok Sabha and nine assembly seats—they were held on 16 December 1985—made Rajiv Gandhi sit up. In Assam, the Congress lost badly to the political newbie Asom Gana Parishad (ASP) formed only sixty-seven days earlier, after the Assam Accord. Normally, the incumbent government had the advantage in the by-polls. But the Congress surprisingly lost in three Lok Sabha and five assembly by-polls only a year after its unprecedented victory in 1984. Even its heavyweight leader Siddhartha Shankar Ray lost to CPI (M)'s Somnath Chatterjee in Bolpur in West Bengal.

The message of the by-polls was unambiguous. Muslims were unhappy with Rajiv Gandhi's handling of the Shah Bano judgment and were moving away from the Congress. 'Though I kept my campaign very secular,' Syed Shahabuddin of the Janata Party was to say, 'not even mentioning the word Shah Bano once, there is no denying the unease in the Muslim mind about the centre's ambivalence regarding the Shah Bano case.' He won from the Muslim-dominated constituency of Kishanganj.

A. F. Golam Osmani, the president of the United Minorities Front which ate into the Congress's Muslim vote in Assam, blamed the prime minister for the Congress's defeat: 'This young, nice prime minister, who wants to be good to everyone, is destroying his party in its 100th year.'

Rajiv Gandhi, his colleagues began to say, could be persuaded by the views of the last person he had spoken to. This was one reason why he had been swinging from one point of view to the other for much of 1985.

In December 1985, Rajiv's views were undergoing a change once again. He was given a detailed briefing by a professor of law in Delhi University, Tahir Mahmood, on Islamic concepts of marriage, divorce, maintenance. He convinced Rajiv about the rightness of going in for a bill to undo the judgment.

What also bothered Rajiv was what Sonia had said to him around this time—the quote with which I started this chapter. He wanted to ensure that a poor, aggrieved, divorced Muslim woman would get a fair sum of money as maintenance to keep body and soul together.

■

Soon after the by-poll results, seventeen AIMPLB members met the prime minister; they were accompanied by Tahir Mahmood and Congress leader Salman Khurshid. Rajiv told them that he wanted to make sure that the Muslim Women's Bill gave the Muslim woman a reasonable and fair sum of money—which even the Supreme Court judgment (under Section 125 of the CrPC) had failed to do, despite ordering the husband to pay maintenance.

'Are you looking for safeguards for the woman, or do you want the husband to be punished?' asked a surprised member of the AIMPLB. Once they realized that Rajiv was really interested in more money to be paid to the divorced Muslim woman, they agreed to it. Rajiv said he wanted to bring the bill immediately as an ordinance, with the centenary celebrations of the Congress in Mumbai only four days away.

Within three hours, the AIMPLB had sent him their draft of the Muslim Women's Bill. It was handed over to Law Minister Ashoke Sen to work on. But the decision got postponed by a month. An article had appeared in the *Pakistan Times* which had criticized the Indian Muslims for insisting that the Shah Bano judgment was against the shariat. Rajiv urged Najma Heptulla to check this out—and this took a few weeks to do.

Finally, Rajiv decided to go in for a law to nullify the Shah Bano judgment. He instructed Ashoke Sen to frame a law and take the help of Ziaur Rahman and other Muslim leaders, including members of the AIMPLB, to draft it.

The pressure of the Muslim community, the opinion of senior leaders in the Congress, the advice of people like journalist-turned-politician M. J. Akbar, and the results of the December 1985 by-elections clinched the decision for Rajiv Gandhi.

■

Around this time in late 1985, counter pressures began to mount on Rajiv. Arun Nehru, who was opposed to the Muslim Women's Bill, warned Rajiv that his 'capitulation' to 'Muslim fundamentalists' was not going down well with a large number of MPs within the Congress.

'You didn't become Prime Minister just like that,' Nehru remonstrated with his cousin. 'Don't forget, you became PM when more than 5,000 Sikhs were killed.' Nehru was reminding Rajiv that it was the anti-Sikh violence after Indira Gandhi's assassination that had consolidated Hindu opinion behind Rajiv in the 1984 elections. If Rajiv persisted in placating the Muslim community, Nehru warned, it could cost him his 'support base among the Hindus' which 'was becoming shaky'.

This was not all. 'If you want to come back to power you will have to do three things,' Nehru told his cousin unambiguously. 'Build a temple in Ayodhya, enact the Uniform Civil Code, and abrogate Article 370. Uski abhi se tayyari kar ke chalo (You had better start getting ready for it from now onwards).' He felt that if the Congress took these steps, it would be able to retain the support of the Hindus.

'We will take the wind out of the BJP's sails totally,' Nehru told Rajiv.

The three issues had come to be identified with the BJP as its 'core issues', though the party adopted the construction of the Ram temple in Ayodhya as part of its political agenda only in 1989 at its meeting in Palampur.

Arun Nehru reminded his cousin not to undo the gains they had made, by bringing in the Muslim Women's Bill.

'What does Rajiv think he is doing?' he had remarked irritably at one meeting, in the presence of officials, about Rajiv's proposed move.

Arun Nehru was in touch with the VHP which had also stepped up pressure on Rajiv Gandhi towards the end of 1985. It organized a high-powered group of religious leaders to lobby around 250 Hindu MPs of all parties, including the Congress. How could Rajiv forget the 'Hindu vote bank' which had got him 414 seats in the elections, they asked. Some discussed, in undertones, whether the Muslim Women's Bill could be defeated on the floor of parliament if there were an upsurge of opinion against it across parties.

It was around this time that Rajiv first began to wonder whether Arun Nehru was trying to corner him on the bill. He began to suspect—there were many in the party who told him this—that the move to mobilize the MPs against the Muslim Women's Bill may not just be against the proposed legislation. It could be against his leadership, and could snowball into a move to replace him as prime minister.

VI

When the final draft of the Muslim Women (Protection of Rights on Divorce) Bill, 1986, was ready, M. L. Fotedar phoned Arif Mohammed Khan. He asked Khan to come over to the PM House. 'The draft of the bill is ready, please go and see the law minister now,' he told Khan. The prime minister had given instructions that Ashoke Sen should show Khan the draft. Sen was a lawyer of renown and had also been law minister under Jawaharlal Nehru. 'Sen received me in his study and handed over the draft to me,' Khan recalled. 'I read it. Then I re-read Section 3...three or four times.'

The section called for a 'reasonable and fair provision to be made and paid *within* the period of iddat'. A lawyer by training, Khan was quick to understand the implications of the phraseology used.

Khan asked Sen, 'Have they (the AIMPLB and others involved) agreed to this?'

'Yes,' Sen replied.

'This is not what they have been demanding,' Khan looked at Sen enquiringly. 'They had wanted to confine the husband's liability *for* the period of iddat only.' However, the wording of Section 3 of the bill stipulated that the amount (to be given the divorced woman) was to be fixed and paid *within* the iddat period, and not just for the iddat period. There was a fine but clear difference between the two.

Khan said: 'This means the court can now decide on the fair amount to meet the future requirements of the divorced wife.' 'Yes,' Sen replied, 'but they have agreed to it.'

'Congratulations,' Khan told him. 'For this is an improvement [on their demand].'

When Khan got up to leave, Sen turned to him and said, 'Arif, I am pleading with you to keep quiet. None of them has understood this provision.' When he went out to see Arif off, Sen folded his hands, 'Arif, please don't share this with anyone. No one.'

'He did not say please don't share it with the Muslim leaders,' Arif mused later. In other words, he did not want Arif to mention this even to the prime minister, though he did not say it in so many words.

The AIMPLB had been involved in the drafting of the bill. Among its advisors, as already noted, were the Congress minister Salman Khurshid, Tahir Mahmood, an expert in Muslim law, and Justice M. A. Ahmadi, who later became the twenty-sixth chief justice of India. The government had also consulted MPs, lawyers, judges, clerics, and scholars while drafting the bill.

Some were to pick up the 'catch' in the bill—but only when it was too late. When he found out, Syed Shahabuddin, who was an important voice of the Muslims, wanted to move an amendment to the bill. But by then, the government let it be known that if anyone pressed for an amendment, the whole exercise would be off.

The Muslim Women's Bill was deliberately drafted by Law Minister Ashoke Sen in such a way that it would undo the Shah Bano judgment, satisfy an irate Muslim community, but not fall foul of the courts in the future. The wording of the relevant section seemingly left Muslim Personal Law untouched, but it allowed for fairer compensation to be paid to the divorced woman for her entire lifetime and not just for the iddat period, as insisted upon by the conservative Muslims. The bill also made the divorced woman's relatives entitled to inherit her property, and the Waqf Board, if she did not have such relatives responsible for her care.

The AIMPLB had no problem with enhancing the financial settlement for the divorced woman. What they were adamant about was that the payment should be a one-time affair, only *for* the iddat period (three menstrual cycles) and not beyond it.

Congress leader Mani Shankar Aiyar was to say years later that the 'cleverly worded section' devised by 'Rajiv Gandhi and his legal advisors' had 'resolved the dilemma' before the government.

Was Rajiv aware of this bit of legal dexterity?

'Ashoke Sen did not inform Rajiv Gandhi about it (the catch in the bill). I am 100 per cent sure of this,' Khan told me. But why would Sen want to withhold the information from the prime minister, unless there was a larger plan afoot against him? The question hangs there unanswered even thirty-seven years later.

■

On 15 January 1986, Rajiv Gandhi announced that he would enact a law to undo the Shah Bano judgment. He was speaking at a public meeting at Delhi's Siri Fort Auditorium, which had been organized by Ziaur Ansari.

In his address he promised to introduce the Muslim Women's Bill on the first day of the Budget Session of parliament which was to start on 5 February 1986. The Muslim Women's Bill created a stir from the moment it was announced. Within hours, the government found itself on the defensive, and had to scurry for cover. It had to look for ways to deflect attention from the bill and find 'a balancing act'.

The bill could not be tabled, as promised, on the first day of the Budget Session of parliament. The Muslim Women (Protection of Rights on Divorce) Bill was finally introduced only on 25 February 1986 by the law minister in the Lok Sabha. Rajiv Gandhi made a spirited defence of it. He acknowledged that the Shah Bano judgment had caused uncertainties in the minds of 'certain communities'. He defended their right to their own personal laws; it strengthened secularism, rather than weakened it. He also argued that women would get more under the bill than under Section 125 of the CrPC (under which Shah Bano was awarded her maintenance by the Supreme Court). The CrPC gave women only a pittance. 'Muslims (generally) do not accept parliament's right to amend their laws,' Rajiv Gandhi told the assembled MPs. 'Now they are themselves asking us to legislate on this (aspect).' That was a good development for the future.

Three days after the bill was introduced, Justice V. R. Krishna Iyer, a former judge of the Supreme Court, warned—his words were to turn out to be prophetic—that it would awaken 'the sleeping Hindu giant' and generate competitive communalism in the country.

The bill was eventually passed three months later in May 1986 by both houses of parliament as the Muslim Women (Protection of Rights on Divorce) Act, 1986. Women activists in different parts of India wore black bands in protest; it was a toned-down victory for the Muslims, and the debate in parliament reflected a new reality—a communal divide all over North India they had not expected.

■

Arif Mohammed Khan had made up his mind that he would resign the day the bill was introduced in parliament. Having passionately defended the court judgment on the floor of the house he knew it would become untenable for him to continue in government if it rolled back the judgment.

The moment the bill was introduced, Khan walked back to the Lok Sabha. He sat down on a bench, and wrote out his resignation letter. He then walked across to the prime minister's office in Parliament House—and left the letter there. He did not go home that day. Instead, he went to a friend's house in Defence Colony where he spent the night. He was apprehensive that those opposed to him might fetch up at his doorstep and create an ugly situation. The next morning he went back to his office. He had an appointment to see the Egyptian ambassador. He told his secretary to cancel all his appointments. He collected his things, and made his way to parliament. As soon as he entered the parliament building, he found Arun Singh pacing about restlessly.

'I have been looking for you,' Singh said. He took Khan to the anteroom next to the PM's office.

'You have done an honourable thing,' he said. 'No one can find fault with you.' But he urged him to take back his resignation. 'It will create problems for Rajiv.'

'I'll take it back. But I will be as good as dead politically.... Having defended the judgment for fifty-five minutes, I will now be defending the exact opposite for fifty-five minutes.' It would not work, he told Singh.

Arun Nehru also sought him out and tried to persuade him to take back his resignation. 'For one and a half hours,' Khan recalled, 'he put a lot of pressure on me.' Though both had been moving in step against the bill, Nehru knew quitting the government would weaken Khan's position.

'I was in parliament and I saw Arif in the House visibly upset,' Arun Nehru told me. 'I forced him to tell me what had happened.'

Nehru then marched off to see Rajiv.

'What are you doing?' he asked the PM. 'Arif was made deputy minister at your behest. He was your confidant. Today he has resigned.'

Rajiv gave him 'a long explanation', and ended by saying, 'you talk Arif out of it.'

Khan refused to take back his resignation.

Nehru went back to Rajiv again. 'Why are you making an enemy of this chap?'

Rajiv asked him to speak to Khan yet again.

Again, Khan said he could not take back his resignation. '(But) Arif (then) gave two or three small requirements which were inconsequential like adjustment of some people in the (UP) Pradesh Congress Committee.'

'I took Arif to Rajiv,' Nehru continued, 'and said he is not going to come back to the ministry but told him about what Arif wanted.'

'OK,' Rajiv said, 'I will deal with it.' It was a very cordial meeting.

Two hours later, Rajiv called Nehru. 'Don't do anything,' he said. 'Hold on for a while'.

Nehru protested: 'Rajiv, you had said this before Arif. It is a breach of trust.' The PM had obviously come under pressure from the anti-Arif lobby in the Congress to desist from doing what Khan wanted.

'Rajiv's behaviour was inexcusable,' Nehru told me. It made matters worse when, a few days later, Nehru, as minister of state for Internal Security, received a report from the IB. 'Arif is going to be physically attacked' it warned.

'I got security sanctioned for an escort in the front and behind him,' Nehru said. 'Sure enough, he was attacked. Rajiv did not say anything. You can't ditch people like this.'

When Khan walked into the Central Hall of Parliament after submitting his resignation, there was thunderous applause from the MPs who were sitting there. 'Mujhe jahaan tak yaad hai,' Khan recalled, 'ki jab main resign karne ke baad Central Hall mein aaya hoon, toh paanch minute tak poora central hall khada ho gaya thaa (From what I can remember, when I went to the Central Hall in Parliament after resigning, for five minutes everybody there stood up and applauded).'

The applause was significant because it came essentially from Congress MPs. 'Rajivji ghabraye toh usi se thae (Rajiv had become worried because of this applause by Congress MPs).'

Another Congress leader who tried to reason with Khan that day was Narasimha Rao. Recounting what Rao had told him, Khan said, 'I am telling you the exact words...he said.'

Rao told him. 'Arif, tum bahut ziddi aadmi ho (you are a very stubborn man). Why don't you get it into your head that we are in the game of politics? We want votes. Hum apne vote ko kyon khrab karaen (Why should we spoil our votes)? You tell me one thing, are we social reformers? That is not our role.

'If the Muslims don't want social reform, and they want to continue to labour under this obscurantism and backwardness,' he said, 'let them.'

'(His next) sentence stunned me even more. He said, "Agar yeh (the Muslims) gadde mein pade rehna chahte hain toh pade rehne do (If they want to remain in a gutter, let them remain there)."'

Then Rao fired his final shot, 'Even Shah Bano has now said that she will give up the maintenance allowed her (by the court). So what is your problem, Arif?'

∎

While the politicians, clergy, and vocal sections of the Muslim community were wrangling over the controversy, the woman at the centre of it all, Shah Bano, had come under immense pressure. Her community wanted her to fall in line with traditional Islamic law. Finally, Shah Bano gave in.

'Prominent Muslim leader Syed Shahabuddin visited our house,' Shah Bano's son, Jameel, said later. He was trying to explain why his mother had changed her mind. 'So did the ulema from Indore and other cities, who told us that the (Supreme Court) verdict was against the shariat. We didn't know much about it (shariat provisions for maintenance, etc.) then...our mother was illiterate.' Clergymen from India and abroad 'offered money and even a job abroad (for refusing maintenance).... Journalists...started landing up.... The pressure became such that...(we even felt) it would've been better if we (had) lost (the case in the Supreme Court),' said Jameel.

Massive protests held across the country only increased the strain on the family. 'Even in Indore there was a lakh strong rally which passed in front of our house...If every rallyist threw a pebble each, our kuchha house would have crumbled.'

It was then that Shah Bano received a message from Rajiv Gandhi. He wanted to meet her. Shah Bano and Jameel travelled to Delhi in early December 1985, where they met the prime minister.

The PM told them the situation was 'very critical'.

'We have to find a way (out),' Rajiv said.

'I told him I'd since read up on shariat directives about marriage and maintenance,' Jameel said, '...there was no provision for maintenance, except for money to be paid during iddat and mehr (money to be paid at the time of divorce).'

'Rajiv asked us to announce that we were refusing the maintenance (awarded by the Supreme Court),' Jameel recalled.

After returning to Indore, Shah Bano held a press conference. She announced she was not taking the maintenance ordered by the court because it was against the shariat. She did not mention what the prime minister had said to them. Shah Bano and her family also decided to withdraw a case for the recovery of 'mehr', 'which was 3,000 kaldars (silver coins)'.

Jameel said: 'I thought my mother will live for another two, five, ten years. But if we agree (to accept the Shah Bano judgment), we'll be forever branded as the people who got the government, or the courts, to interfere in the Shariat. There's no point in living with such a taint on you.'

The most poignant part of the Shah Bano story was what happened to Shah Bano herself, the indigent woman at the centre of the drama which was to change Indian politics. When she died in 1992 of a brain haemorrhage, she was not even being paid the ₹179.20 per month which the Supreme Court had ordered her husband to pay.

Fifteen years later, on 28 September 2001, a five-judge bench of the Supreme Court clarified that Section 3(1)(a) of the Muslim Women (Protection of Rights on Divorce) Act, 1986 was not linked to the iddat period but 'extends to the whole life of the divorced wife unless she gets married for a second time'. The apex court interpreted the section to mean that a 'fair and reasonable' amount had to be paid her not 'for' the iddat period but 'within' the iddat period. It was to take care of her for the rest of her life.

Ashoke Sen, the law minister who had drafted the law in 1985, had succeeded. But many Muslims felt cheated. The promise to them, that the law would undo the judgment which they saw as interference in the Muslim Personal Law, had not been kept. But soon after the law was introduced, and they had caught the 'catch' in the law in mid-1986, Ali Mian told his supporters not to make an issue of it. They had, after all, been consulted during the drafting of the bill. It would only show them up in a poor light. Later, the court held that the Muslim Women's Act was 'not unconstitutional'. Nor did it offend Articles 14, 15, and 21 of the Constitution.

The Shah Bano verdict divided India as few legal battles have done. And the woman at the heart of it got no succour. The case became less about legality or about the rights of women, and more about political one-upmanship, along Hindu–Muslim lines.

VII

'Taala khulwa do,' Arun Nehru advised the prime minister (Get the locks opened). This was in the third week of January 1986. A worried Rajiv had called his cousin over to get his advice. On 18 January 1986, R&AW and IB chiefs had both reported to Rajiv Gandhi that unhappiness was growing amongst the Hindus over the government's decision to undo the Shah Bano judgment.

Nehru suggested that the locks—there were two locks at gates 'O' and 'P'—be opened at the enclosure in the Babri Masjid. As noted, a Ram idol had been clandestinely placed in the sanctum sanctorum by militant Hindus in December 1949. The mosque, which became a disputed structure, had been locked up, and neither Muslims nor Hindus were allowed entry. Hindus were allowed to offer prayers from outside the locked grille. The Shri Ram Mukti Yajna Samiti, a front for the Vishwa Hindu Parishad, had organized a Rath Yatra from Sitamarhi (where Sita is said to have appeared) to Ayodhya on 25 September 1985, calling for the liberation of the Ram Janmabhoomi.

If Rajiv got the locks opened and a temple built there, 'Hindus khush ho jayengae (The Hindus will be happy),' Nehru told Rajiv. Many Hindus, he told his cousin, were feeling aggrieved with Rajiv's 'appeasement' of Muslims.

Arun Nehru did not pull his punches. He told the prime minister that he was losing ground. It was not just conservative and fundamentalist Hindus who were upset with him, even liberal opinion was now turning against him. The editor of the *Times of India*, Girilal Jain, had penned a blistering piece against Rajiv Gandhi, which would sway the middle class. They had, until now, regarded Rajiv as their new messiah. Another eminent editor, Arun Shourie, had written two equally critical pieces in the same paper—flaying the prime minister for his turnaround and for betraying Arif Mohammed Khan; he also criticized Rajiv for ignoring the advice of his own departments—the Law and Home ministries—not to overturn the Shah Bano judgment.

Rajiv Gandhi asked Arun Shourie over. They met in the PM's office in Parliament House. Narasimha Rao and H. R. Bhardwaj were also present. 'I found Rajiv completely innocent of Muslim Personal Law, of case law in India and even the bill (he was planning to pass),' Shourie recalled. 'I told the prime minister the bill would stoke a reaction. Already people were beginning to feel that the state was bending before extremists. This had happened in Punjab (and it had claimed the life of his Mother, Prime Minister Indira Gandhi.)'

'How could paying ₹179.20 a month to a seventy-three-year-old destitute woman endanger Islam?' Shourie asked the PM. Women's groups were also on the warpath.

'Taala khul sakta hai kya (Can the locks be opened)?' Rajiv asked Arun Nehru, according to Arif Mohammed Khan who told me this story.

'Examine it, can this be done?' Rajiv told his cousin.

'I will find out what can be done,' Nehru said.

Nehru then (according to what he told Khan), spoke to Vir Bahadur Singh, the Congress chief minister of UP, where the disputed Babri Masjid was located.

Unknown to Rajiv, Vir Bahadur Singh had already been on the job. A month earlier, on 19 December 1985, the UP chief minister had visited Ayodhya to attend the Ramayan mela celebrations in the temple town. While there, Singh asked officials to show him the entire file on the Ayodhya dispute. Going through it, and briefed by officials, he discovered that the locks had been put there by an 'administrative'—and 'not a judicial'— order in 1949. He 'reportedly found no specific court order regarding its closure'. During the visit, he met with members of the VHP to gauge their thinking on the issue.

Since Vir Bahadur Singh was a protégé of Arun Nehru, it is not inconceivable that Nehru had put him on the job even before he called on Rajiv and suggested the opening of the locks. Singh felt indebted to

Nehru for having installed him as CM in UP in September 1985, after Rajiv took over as PM. On 18 September 1985, UP chief minister N. D. Tiwari had suddenly written to Rajiv Gandhi expressing his desire to step down as CM. There was only one name mentioned by all the MLAs as his successor—Vir Bahadur Singh. The squat and rustic Vir Bahadur Singh, who knew UP like the back of his hand, took over as the new chief minister of the state on 24 September 1985. The next morning Tiwari took a flight to Delhi to be sworn in as the minister of Industry in Rajiv's cabinet. During the 1985 elections to the UP assembly, of the 269 Congress MLAs who won, a majority (around 150) were Arun Nehru–Vir Bahadur Singh followers. When Indira Gandhi was alive, she had shot down Nehru's idea of making Singh the chief minister. But in September 1985, Nehru had his way—and firmed up his grip in UP.

Nehru, according to Arif Mohammed Khan, reported back to Rajiv on the opening of the locks.

'Tell Vir Bahadur, khulwaye (Tell Vir Bahadur Singh to get it opened),' the prime minister directed Nehru.

Nehru called the chief minister from the prime minister's office.

'DM se kaho ki taala khole (Tell the DM to get the locks opened),' Nehru told Singh in the presence of Rajiv. 'In how many days can the locks be opened?'

Then, suddenly he handed the phone to Rajiv. 'Lo PM se baat karo (Here talk to the PM),' Nehru said.

Nehru was to tell Arif Khan later, 'I did not want it said later that Arun Nehru had given instructions to Vir Bahadur Singh (of his own accord).'

'It was Rajiv who gave the instructions to Vir Bahadur,' Nehru told Khan.

'I don't know whether what Arun Nehru told me was correct or incorrect,' Khan told me years later, 'but this is what he told me.'

At the time, the situation was such that if Nehru gave directions, they were seen to be coming directly from the prime minister. 'All I can say is that Arun Nehru was managing the whole affair (from Delhi),' Vir Bahadur Singh told friends, when he became a union minister in Rajiv Gandhi's cabinet in 1988.

With clear instructions coming from Delhi, the UP CM moved with despatch. He first called on Mahant Avaidyanath, the head of the influential Gorakhpur peeth in eastern UP; Avaidyanath had been appointed as the head of the Ram Janmabhoomi Yagna Samiti on 18 July 1985. They enjoyed a cordial relationship. Like Avaidyanath, Vir Bahadur Singh also belonged to Gorakhpur. It was through him—and through the local officials—that Singh sent a message to the VHP, suggesting that the VHP approach the court for opening the locks. This time they would get the response they were looking for. 'The authorities (the allusion was to the district magistrate and superintendent of police) informally asked the VHP to move an application,' K. R. Malkani, was to write later, 'for the unlocking of the premises, with assurances of (a) positive response,' Malkani was the editor of *Motherland*, a paper sympathetic to the RSS–VHP.

But the VHP decided not to take the bait. 'The VHP...was interested in unlocking but not in going to court,' Malkani revealed. Having agitated for years to have the locks opened, they wanted to take the credit for it, and not let others run away with the issue.

Arun Nehru, who had wanted to consolidate Hindu sentiment behind the Congress, had established his own direct line of communications with the VHP—one of his links to the VHP was B. P. Singhal, VHP leader Ashok Singhal's younger brother. In 1986, B. P. Singhal was additional secretary in the Ministry of Home Affairs, working directly under Arun Nehru when he was minister of state, Home, in charge of Internal Security.

Ashok Singhal had told me during the course of an interview in April 1986 that the decision to open the locks had been taken 'right at the top'. 'Arun Nehru masterminded this coup,' Singhal had said. We had met at the VHP office, then in South Extension in New Delhi.

From what Ashok Singhal told me that day, Arun Nehru had conceived the idea, sold it to Rajiv Gandhi and then executed it. The VHP had been given the 'assurance', in advance, that the 'locks' at the Ram Janmabhoomi would be opened.

'Rajiv Gandhi had indicated in no uncertain terms that the gates of the Ram Janmabhoomi must open to devotees before Shivratri on 8 March 1986,' Singhal said.

VII

The political baptism of Rajiv Gandhi—and of Arun Nehru—had taken place under Indira Gandhi in her most Hinduized phase. Like her, Nehru too was clear that the Congress needed to consolidate the Hindus behind it. He used to pride himself on being a 'hawk'. The easy-going Rajiv, on the other hand, went with the flow—and with what his mother wanted.

Indira Gandhi, as we saw in the last chapter, had turned increasingly religious after her defeat in 1977.

What happened at Meenakshipuram worried her. On 18 April 1981, 800 Hindus belonging to the Dalit Palla caste had been converted to Islam in the temple town of Meenakshipuram in Tamil Nadu. There was an outcry against it by the RSS. When she came back to power in 1980, she had become even more conscious of the changing mood of the Hindus—and the need to reach out to them.

It was the RSS which had sent her word that Karan Singh was the best Hindu face the Congress should project. His Hindu credentials were impeccable, he headed the Vaishno Devi Trust. But she had been furious with him for deposing against her at the Shah Commission probing Emergency excesses. He had left the Congress and won as an independent in the 1980 elections. Though there had hardly been any contact between Indira Gandhi and Karan Singh between 1975–80, she decided to patch up with him after 1980.

In 1981, Karan Singh launched the Virat Hindu Samaj; he did this in collaboration with the Vishwa Hindu Parishad. Ashok Singhal was the VHP's general secretary; the RSS backed the effort. And it had Indira Gandhi's tacit approval.

Karan Singh organized virat Hindu sammelans (mega Hindu conventions) all over the country to create Hindu unity. Though he denied Indira Gandhi's hand behind it, he conceded that 'being the canny politician that she was, she used these sammelans' to her advantage. She was happy enough to let the impression gain ground that the 1981 initiative had her blessings.

Rajiv Gandhi and Arun Nehru had also seen Indira Gandhi tacitly support the Ekatmata Yatra launched by the VHP in 1983. With the backing of eighty-five main Hindu sects, the VHP undertook yatras to touch 3 lakh villages to 'unite Hindu society'. The ninety-two religious caravans moved through different parts of the country. The trucks carried an 8-foot vessel with water from the river Ganga and a picture of the goddess Bharat Mata astride a lion. With that, Mother India entered the pantheon of 33,000 gods and goddesses of the Hindu religion.

People flocked to see the Ekatmata Yatra. They would buy the 50 cc bottles of Ganga Jal (holy Ganga water) as the speakers warned of 'Hinduism in danger', and the 'pampering of Muslims as a vote bank'. It was a curtain-raiser for L. K. Advani's Ram Rath Yatra seven years later in 1990, from Somnath to Ayodhya.

Indira Gandhi had almost attended a meeting of the yatra. But she decided against it at the last moment. 'The Ekatmata Yatra in 1983 by the VHP was funded by Indira Gandhi,' revealed Anil Bali.

A quick learner, Arun Nehru had noticed how Indira Gandhi used the yatra to her advantage, without coming upfront. She got senior party leaders to condemn it. But she chose not to say anything herself. She knew how to play the game both ways. She had also been quietly encouraging new Hindu organizations that had suddenly mushroomed—Hindu Manch, Hindu Suraksha Samiti, North India's Hindu Shiv Sena (different from the Shiv Sena in Maharashtra).

More significantly, she enabled the VHP to hold its first dharam sansad (religious convention of Hindu preachers) on 7–8 April 1984 at the government's prestigious conference centre, the Vigyan Bhavan in Delhi. The meeting, which could not have been held without clearance from the top, demanded the return of three temples to Hindus—the Ram

Janmabhoomi in Ayodhya, the Kashi Vishwanath Temple in Varanasi, and the Shri Krishna Janmasthan in Mathura.

During the course of an interview in April 1986, VHP leader Ashok Singhal had told me that Indira Gandhi had contemplated using 'Ayodhya as an electoral issue' at an 'appropriate moment'.

Clearly, she had become more mindful of the sensibilities of the Hindus than about the sensitivities of the Muslims or the Sikhs. CPI (M) leader Harkishan Singh Surjeet had remarked sarcastically that the interests of the Hindus of Haryana now weighed more with Indira Gandhi than the settlement of the Punjab problem.Thrice an agreement had been reached on the dispute between Punjab and Haryana over Chandigarh. Each time she 'backed out', he said.

Indira Gandhi was fast acquiring the image of a pro-Hindu leader. And that is exactly what she wanted.

■

From the time he became an MP, Rajiv Gandhi knew that his mother was reaching out to the RSS. During the Emergency years, the RSS had sought her out, but she had been cool towards them. In the 1977 elections, she had asked for their help, as we saw in the last chapter. But by then, they were committed to supporting the Janata Party.

But Indira Gandhi had refused to meet any of the RSS leaders personally—as had Sanjay Gandhi.

But in 1982, almost halfway into her term, she asked Rajiv to meet RSS leader Bhaurao Deoras and open a dialogue with him. The meetings, fixed by Kapil Mohan, were not public knowledge. Even Arun Nehru did not know about them. Bhaurao, brother of RSS chief Balasaheb Deoras, looked after the political wing of the organization, and was tasked with befriending Rajiv.

Rajiv met Bhaurao thrice between 1982–84, when Indira Gandhi was still PM, and once in early 1991, when he was out of power. The first meeting was held in September 1982 at the 46, Pusa Road residence of Kapil Mohan. Mohan's friendship with Bhaurao went back many years. The second meeting also took place at Pusa Road, the third one was held at Anil Bali's residence in Friends Colony. The fourth meeting was held at 10, Janpath.

Anil Bali used to escort Rajiv Gandhi to these meetings. Subhash Arya, a BJP leader who was very close to Bhaurao, would accompany him. The first meeting was by way of an icebreaker. Bhaurao and Rajiv hit it off well and talked about all manner of subjects, including the Asian Games which Rajiv was organizing at the time, the rise of the communists, the limitation of the policy of reservations for the Scheduled Castes and Scheduled Tribes. Both were affable personalities; they were to enjoy a 'cordial relations right through', Anil Bali said. 'Bhaurao used to feel that Hinduism would be safe with Rajiv.'

'I am an eyewitness to Rajiv Gandhi doing a charan sparsh (touch the feet) to Bhaurao,' Banwarilal Purohit disclosed years later. Purohit was a Congress MP in 1984 and 1989, then joined the BJP and later became the governor of Tamil Nadu, and of Punjab.

K. N. Govindacharya, who was mentored by Bhaurao, recalled the day when he had returned after meeting Rajiv for the first time. 'I happened to be at Jhandewalan (where the RSS headquarters in Delhi was located) when Bhaurao came back... He said it was like his meeting with JP when he was underground (about which he had been very happy),' Govindacharya told me.

Bhaurao was a diabetic. 'We would make a point of getting fresh jamun juice for him (whenever he came to Pusa Road),' said Pushpa Mohan. Or Anil Bali would take the jamun juice to Jhandewalan 'whenever I went to meet him there'—Bali would be asked my Kapil Mohan to pass his message to RSS leaders.

Bali kept Indira Gandhi posted about every development that had to do with Jhandewalan. They had decided that he would report to her every Saturday morning. He would arrive at her residence at 7.45 a.m. and be out of the house by 8.15, before her other aide R. K. Dhawan arrived 'so that Dhawan didn't get to know anything'.

The nodal person who was facilitating these meetings, according to Anil Bali, was Indira Gandhi's political secretary, M. L. Fotedar. 'If there was one person who was a Hinduizing influence on Rajiv Gandhi between 1985–87 (after Indira Gandhi's death and when Rajiv was PM), it was Fotedarji.'

'Indiraji once told me,' Fotedar had revealed during the course of a conversation, "Tell Rajiv not to talk of this (his talks with the RSS) at the dining table". She knew that Sonia was dead against the RSS.'

Rajiv had gifted a Contessa car to Bhaurao after he became PM. He wanted to make it easier for him to move around, disclosed Pankaj Vohra. 'I even remember the colour of the car—it was chocolate in colour,' Vohra recalled.

After he became prime minister, Rajiv did not meet Bhaurao. But they remained in touch. Halfway into his term, the RSS had made a request to Rajiv to facilitate the telecasting of the Ramayana serial by Ramanand Sagar on Doordarshan—it had run into hurdles. Congress leader H. K. L. Bhagat, later to become minister for Information and Broadcasting, was alarmed when Rajiv mentioned the RSS request to him; he warned Rajiv that it would open a Pandora's box—and generate a climate in favour of the BJP–VHP–RSS-led Ram Janmabhoomi movement.

When Bhaurao heard that there was resistance from within the Congress to the idea, he wrote to Rajiv. 'Chiranjeevi Rajiv, Ramayana agar Bharat men nahin dekhi jayegi to kya New York maen dikhayi jayegi (May you live long dear Rajiv, if Ramayana will not be shown in India, where will it be shown—in New York)?'

Rajiv did not pay heed to Bhagat's apprehensions. The telecast of the Ramayana serial started on 25 January 1987. It went on till 31 July 1988—watched by 650 million people. Once, Home Minister Buta Singh got a cabinet meeting postponed because the Ramayana was going to be telecast at that time!

On Sunday mornings, the streets in Indian cities would be deserted, with families glued to their TV sets to watch the Ramayana, with many paying obeisance to their TV sets. As H. K. L. Bhagat had predicted, the TV serial created a religious fervour amongst the Hindus of an unprecedented kind.

In early 1989, a concerned Bhaurao was to advise a beleaguered Rajiv to advance the general elections due at the end of the year. Rajiv was then fighting with his back to the wall, facing corruption allegations in the deal to purchase the Bofors guns from Sweden.

'Bhaurao sent the message through me to Rajiv in January 1989,' Anil Bali revealed. The Opposition parties had not yet regrouped. Striking early would help Rajiv get the better of an Opposition on the offensive. Bhaurao's advice to Rajiv came, and this was curious, when the BJP had decided to support his rival V. P. Singh. But Rajiv did not pay heed to it. The IB had assured him that the party would win 300 seats.

In November that year, Banwarilal Purohit was to reveal years later there was a 'secret pact' between the RSS and Rajiv Gandhi, on the 'shilanyas' to lay the foundation stone of the Ram temple announced by the VHP. 'As the Congress pointsman at that time, I facilitated a meeting between then RSS chief Balasaheb Deoras and Rajiv's special emissary, Bhanu Prakash Singh. It was a secret one-to-one that lasted an hour....' Purohit was to state. 'Soon after that, Deoras had a meeting with the then Union Home minister Buta Singh in New Delhi where the deal was endorsed,' claimed Purohit.

But Buta Singh ridiculed Purohit's claim. It was, however, widely known at the time that Buta Singh had come to an understanding with the VHP. 'I remember Singh used to often come to Jhandewalan in those days,' recalled Subhash Arya.

Rajiv did not stop the shilanyas. There was an outcry from the Muslim community. It cost the Congress the Muslim votes in the 1989 elections—and helped V. P. Singh come to power.

Months later, Rajiv Gandhi was to tell Syed Shahabuddin that Buta Singh and N. D. Tiwari had 'misled' him in 1989.

'I will tell you what RG told me in 1991 March, two months before he died,' Shahabuddin told me.

'Shahabuddin saab, you are right,' he had said. And he had pulled out the file on Babri Masjid to show him. 'Two men have deceived me—N. D.

Tiwari and Buta Singh (who had negotiated the understanding with the VHP and the RSS). They both told me that the shilanyas site was outside the disputed area.' But, in reality, the site had been placed under the status quo order by the court, not to be touched.

'He (Rajiv) admitted (that day) that the shilanyas was done in violation of the court order,' Shahabuddin said, 'just as the introduction of the idol (in the Babri Masjid) in 1949 had been against the law.'

It was, however, the fourth meeting Rajiv had with Bhaurao that showed the cordial relationship they had developed over the years. The meeting, held at Rajiv's initiative, took place at 10, Janpath, in 1991, weeks before Rajiv died. The Chandra Shekhar government was in power at that time, propped up by the Congress. Sharad Pawar had told Rajiv that Chandra Shekhar was on the verge of a breakthrough in the Ayodhya talks which had been going on between representatives of the Hindus and Muslims. If Chandra Shekhar succeeded, Rajiv's associates warned him, he would overnight become a national hero. This could lead to a realignment of forces and affect the internal politics of the Congress, given the long-standing relationships Chandra Shekhar had with leaders inside the Congress.

Rajiv requested Bhaurao to reject the formula evolved by Chandra Shekhar. Bhaurao listened carefully to Rajiv, who had just returned from a trip. He was tired and hungry. While they were waiting for tea, Rajiv started to cut apples in the fruit bowl that lay on the table.

'He was cutting the fruit clumsily,' Anil Bali recalled. 'But he persisted. He served them each a piece of the apple he had cut.'

Bhaurao said little at the meeting. When he came out of 10, Janpath, he remarked to Bali, 'Bahut shaleen ladka hai (He is a very courteous boy).'

Bali drove Bhaurao back to Jhandewalan. As he bade him goodbye at the RSS headquarters, Bhaurao turned to Bali and said quietly, 'Rajiv ko bol dena ki theek hai (Tell Rajiv, we will go along with what he has asked). He will hear of our decision tomorrow on All India Radio.'

An elated Bali rushed back to 10, Janpath. He gave Rajiv Bhaurao's message. Rajiv took Bali outside the house. 'You don't know what is bugged and what is not,' he said. They walked in the driveway of 10, Janpath.

'We talked in whispers...I told him what Bhaurao had said. Three times he put his hand on my back,' Bali recalled. 'It indicated his... appreciation.'

The solution which had almost been worked out by Chandra Shekhar suddenly came unstuck. It is open to conjecture whether the Bhaurao–Rajiv parleys were really responsible for the RSS decision to call off the talks. For decisions such as these would hardly be contingent on one request, even though it was made by a former PM. Though Chandra Shekhar was talking to representatives of both the communities, including the VHP, the RSS had been wary of him. Like Rajiv, they may have apprehended that Chandra Shekhar would hog all the credit for building the temple, which they felt was their due. The RSS—and Rajiv—knew that Chandra Shekhar himself was capable of playing the Hindu card to his advantage. (Also see Chapter 4 on P. V. Narasimha Rao.)

Rajiv Gandhi withdrew support to the Chandra Shekhar government soon thereafter. Just as RSS chief Balasaheb Deoras had supported Indira Gandhi in the 1980 general elections, because they saw her as a 'Hindu' leader who could represent the interests of the community, they were also cultivating Rajiv Gandhi. The Deoras brothers, Balasaheb and Bhaurao, found Rajiv 'innocent', who could be 'moulded'. He neither carried ideological baggage nor did he have any ideological moorings. He represented political stability which the RSS found alluring.

•

Indira Gandhi went out of her way to keep Rajiv's meetings with Bhaurao under wraps. She did not even let Arun Nehru get wind of it. Though Indira depended on Nehru, she did not trust him fully—and was sharp enough to sense his ambitions.

When Rajiv first met Bhaurao in September 1982, Indira Gandhi was on an official visit to Moscow. On her return, Anil Bali was at the airport to receive her. She saw him and waved out to him.

'Did it go well?' she asked, the moment she saw him; she was referring to the Rajiv–Bhaurao meeting.

'Yes,' said Bali.

'The meeting lasted four and a half hours,' a pleased Bali told her.

'Do not speak to anyone about this,' she instructed Bali, her voice lowering a shade.

'Nobody,' she said, looking at him sternly.

'Tell Kapil Mohan also not to say anything,' she then added. 'He is a loudmouth.'

'Does that include Arun Nehru?' Bali asked.

'What do you mean does it include Arun Nehru?' she reacted sharply. He had asked the question on the spur of the moment. Nehru now appeared to be calling the shots in the Congress—with Indira Gandhi's blessings.

'He would be the last person to talk to,' she told a surprised Bali. 'Not a word to Arun Nehru,' she said with finality.

•

The RSS, and more specifically Bhaurao, influenced Rajiv's decision to open the locks at Ram Janmabhoomi on 1 February 1986. This was confirmed to me by BJP leaders Govindacharya and Subhash Arya, both very close to Bhaurao, and also by Anil Bali who had access to the Gandhi family.

'Bhaurao felt the lock-opening would create a national consensus on social and cultural issues in the country,' Govindacharya told me. 'Ram

Janmabhoomi ka taala kholo,' Bhaurao had sent Rajiv word, 'Hinduon ke neta bano (Open the locks and become a leader of Hindus).'

After the locks were opened, according to Bali, Bhaurao wrote to Rajiv, 'You have taken a historical step. Hindu Hridaya samrat bano aur rajya karo (Become a king of Hindu hearts and rule).'

In the 1984 elections, Nanaji Deshmukh, associated for years with the RSS, had openly exhorted people to vote for Rajiv: 'Naa jaat par naa paat par, mohar lagegi haath par (Vote not on the basis of caste, but for the symbol of the hand).'

On his part, Rajiv Gandhi never once openly acknowledged that he was in touch with the RSS.

VIII

It was a cold day in Faizabad on 1 February 1986. The soporific atmosphere that usually hung over the district courts in the small town near Ayodhya in UP was missing that day. Instead, the court was agog with expectation. The case was coming up for the opening up of the locks at the Babri Masjid where the idol of child Ram was worshipped from across padlocked grilles. There was 'hulchul' in the courtroom. Curious onlookers walked in from adjoining courtrooms to see what would happen.

The room—as most district courtrooms in the country—was run down. The paint was peeling off, marks of water seepage from the previous year's monsoon scarred the walls. But two stenographers sat expectantly facing the judge's desk, waiting for Judge Krishna Mohan Pandey to arrive. They sat there, poised behind their Remington typewriters, to type out the judge's order. Surprisingly, the judge had admitted the petition.

The judge had reserved his order the previous day—31 January 1986—and was to deliver it on 1 February.

To one side stood the expectant district officials. On the other side sat Umesh Chandra Pandey; he was the petitioner and a Congressman. Since the VHP had refused to approach the court, the Congress Party had got a local junior advocate, Umesh Chandra Pandey, to move the application. It was common knowledge that he was the son of a former Congress president of Faizabad.

Curious members of the VHP were also in the court to see what the judge would say. By now word had reached the VHP cadre that the top leadership of the Congress had decided to facilitate the opening of the locks.

It was on 21 January 1986 that petitioner Pandey had moved the court of Hari Shankar Dubey for the opening of the locks at the Babri Masjid. Dubey's was the munsif sadar (lowest court) in Faizabad. Pandey appealed that worshippers be allowed to pray directly to the Ram idol. On 28 January, the munsif declined to give a ruling. Since the case related to the title suit before the High Court he would have to examine the files which were with the higher court before he could give his view.

Knowing that a petition was moved almost every year, and the plea was always rejected, the munsif must have thought it was better to play safe. The case was a hot potato and had been pending for more than three decades.

Without a ruling by the munsif's court, Umesh Chandra Pandey immediately filed an appeal in the Faizabad District Court on 31 January. The district judge—and this too was surprising—decided to hear the matter on the same day.

Suspecting the central government's hand behind the moves to get the locks opened, Mohammed Hashim asked to be impleaded in the case. He was one of the plaintiffs in the title suit for the disputed structure, which was awaiting a hearing. Like Hashim, there were many others who believed that the judge had been given instructions by Delhi to open the locks.

It was rumoured that a senior judge of the Supreme Court had spoken to Judge Krishna Mohan Pandey to give a verdict in favour of opening the locks.

Surprisingly, Judge Pandey rejected Hashim's application outright. But he immediately admitted the plea of petitioner Pandey, who had nothing to do with the earlier case. Umesh Pandey pleaded that the locks be opened immediately. The structure, he argued, had been locked by the court in 1949 by an administrative, and not a judicial, order.

Every year, when there would be a plea to open the locks, the district officials would file a counter affidavit to oppose the plea. They would argue that the locks were necessary to maintain peace in the area. The court would then reject the plea.

That day the officials were present themselves in court, District Magistrate Indu Kumar Pandey (not related to the petitioner or to the presiding judge) was there as was senior superintendent of police, Karamveer Singh.

'The DM and SSP came to the court personally,' Judge Krishna Mohan Pandey was to recount later. They argued that locking the temple was not part of the main Ayodhya title suit. It had been put there, at the instance of the district administration then, as action under Section 144 of the CrPC.

'I asked them (DM and SSP) in open court,' Judge Pandey said, 'have you consulted the state government?'

'This is not the court's concern,' the officials responded. 'We are the government on the spot, and we will manage the law and order (situation).'

'If there is a law and order problem,' the judge asked the officials again, 'will you be able to handle it?'

'We told the district judge we will be able to handle the situation,' DM Indu Kumar Pandey confirmed to me.

But Judge Krishna Mohan Pandey decided to reserve his judgment (on

31 January 1986). 'I thought if the government does not know, and this was a sensitive issue, then at least they will be alerted.'

'When I reached my chamber,' the judge said, 'my peshekar (clerk) exclaimed, sahib, there is a Doordarshan team outside. In those days there were no private TV channels, only the public telecaster, Doordarshan.'

'I thought to myself,' Judge Pandey said, 'who will send a Doordarshan team here?' There was no Doordarshan office in Faizabad. The team would have come from Lucknow, a three-hour drive away.

On 1 February, the district judge walked into the courtroom all set to deliver his verdict. 'Before I headed to the courtroom,' Judge Pandey recalled, 'my peshekar told me, "Today there are 8-9 Doordarshan people outside and there are two camera teams...Then I felt reassured that the government wanted this (the opening of the locks) to happen".'

On entering the courtroom, Judge Pandey knew what he had to do. He ordered that the locks on the disputed structure be opened forthwith. In a 1,000-word judgment, Judge Pandey relied on the assurances given by the district officials to allow direct 'darshan' of 'Ram Lalla'. They had told him that namaz had not been offered in the mosque for thirty-six years, and the locks had been put there for the safety of the idol.

'Heavens are not going to fall by opening the locks at gates "O" and "P",' the judge declared in the packed courtroom.

The verdict was announced at 4.40 p.m. After that, the DM and the SSP made a point of personally escorting the district judge to his residence.

The local administration in Faizabad had posted a large number of policemen at the court site to maintain law and order. But there was no trouble.

The rusty locks were broken open at 5.19 p.m. A Doordarshan team at the spot captured for posterity the surging crowds who entered the structure after the opening of the locks.

As the district judge read out his order, Arun Nehru sat ensconced with the UP CM Vir Bahadur in the CM's office in Lucknow, closely tracking the developments in Faizabad. 'I was told this by a Congress leader from UP who sat in the anteroom,' Wajahat Habibullah told me.

Twenty-four years later, on 30 September 2010, the Allahabad High Court was to hold the district judge Krishna Mohan Pandey's order illegal. In a severe indictment of Judge Pandey, a three-judge bench said his order was responsible for the demolition of the Babri Masjid on 6 December 1992. The appeal before his court had been untenable because the munsif court had not given a ruling; it had only fixed the next date for hearing. Since the files of the case were with the High Court, it averred, neither the munsif nor the district judge had the right to take a view in the matter. But by then too much water had gone down the Ganga; it was too late to undo the decision to open the locks at the disputed structure.

The VHP took the credit for the lock opening. They had created the jan jagran (mass awareness) for it by leading Rath Yatras throughout the country.

■

Five days after the opening of the locks, on 6 February 1986, Arif Mohammed Khan decided to meet Rajiv Gandhi. 'Shah Bano will now take a back seat,' he warned the prime minister. 'Instead, Ayodhya will become the rallying cry of the VHP.'

'I have no such fears,' Rajiv told Khan confidently. The prime minister was certain of riding out the storm, if any.

The PM then confided in Khan, looking pleased with himself, 'I had alerted the concerned parties on the other side (Muslim organizations) about what I was planning to do (opening the locks).' He had taken the AIMPLB into confidence, he said. He had personally spoken to Ali Mian about the proposed lock-opening before it happened.

A few days before Khan met Rajiv, Ali Mian had made a statement making light of the opening of the locks. It was carried on 3 February 1986 in the *Kaumi Awaz*, the Urdu paper of the *National Herald*, which reflected the view of the Congress Party. Downplaying the lock-opening, he said, 'Aur bhi bahut si masjidon par gairon ka kabza hai (There are also many other mosques which are under the control of others).' With his statement he was underplaying the importance of what had happened.

But the Muslim community reacted sharply. 'Everything was pre-planned,' remarked advocate Abdul Mannan angrily. '...the state police and the Provincial Armed Constabulary (PAC) had been deployed much before the district judge had even pronounced his judgment.'

Ordinary Muslims became increasingly agitated. On 5 February 1986, many leaders of the community and lawyers for the Sunni Waqf Board met in Lucknow. Twenty-three Muslim MLAs were also present. They decided to form the Babri Masjid Movement Coordination Committee. This would become the apex committee to fight the battle on behalf of the Muslim community to protect the Babri Masjid. Syed Shahabuddin dubbed the temple opening as a 'unilateral seizure' of the Babri Masjid—which 'eroded' their 'faith in secularism'. He was a Janata Party MP and chief of another influential organization to safeguard Muslim interests—the All India Muslim Majlis-e-Mushawarat.

Soon after the opening of the locks, I travelled through several parts of UP and found the state to be extremely tense. The communal divide had seeped right down to the villages. In February and March, in the aftermath of the lock-opening, communal clashes had taken place in Moradabad, Meerut, Bijnore, Pilibhit, and Shahjehanpur. Units of the PAC were posted in villages in Moradabad district. Both communities saw the decision to open the locks as 'political'—as a 'ladoo' given the Hindus to offset the sop given to the Muslims in the form of the Muslim Women's Bill to set aside the Shah Bano judgment. And yet neither community was pleased.

Shafiqur Rahman Barq, convenor of the Babri Masjid Action Committee in UP, threatened, 'If the Babri Masjid is not restored to the Muslims, they will begin to hate the Congress (I). Congressmen will not be allowed to enter Muslim areas even to beg for votes. I am saying this with full responsibility.'

■

'Rajiv may have had discussions with (Arun) Nehru and others on the opening of the locks, but he did not give the go-ahead for it,' claimed Wajahat Habibullah. 'He was presented with a fait accompli.'

It was Rajiv, Habibullah said, who had told him this. In September 1986, when Rajiv was on tour in Gujarat, Habibullah had accompanied him. He was sitting in the front of the PM's plane. There was no one else seated there at the time. Rajiv came out of his cubicle, saw Habibullah, came over to sit beside him—and started chatting. The conversation veered around to the events of the preceding months. Though he was still in the PMO, Habibullah had not been involved in the decision to open the locks. 'Possibly you calculated there would be no (adverse) reaction to it,' Habibullah said, broaching the subject with Rajiv.

'Look,' Rajiv cut him short, 'interfering with places of worship of any religion is wrong and should never be done.'

Habibullah was taken aback.

'But,' he couldn't resist saying, 'you were the PM. It was under your government that these locks were opened.'

'Yes, but I don't know yet who ordered it,' Rajiv said. 'I did not know anything about it till after the locks were opened.'

Habibullah looked at him with disbelief.

'I am trying to find out who is responsible,' the PM told him. 'I suspect Arun,' he went on. 'Arun Nehru and Fotedar. But I still don't know for sure... And when I find out I am afraid I will have to take action.'

'Yes, Rajiv Gandhi also told me that he had not given the order to open the locks,' Shahid Siddiqui was to concur later.

M. K. Narayanan, who was director of the IB at the time, was also to say years later, 'I don't think Rajiv Gandhi was aware of the opening of the locks, though I am not 100 per cent sure. (But then) no PM is omnipotent.'

And yet, it seemed inconceivable that the prime minister of India could have been kept in the dark about such a major development pertaining to a hot button issue, with multiple intelligence agencies briefing him on a daily basis. There are several statements by various individuals that I have quoted in this chapter that indicate that Rajiv was in the loop. And even if in the unlikely event of being unaware of what had been decided, it seems incredible that he was not able to find out who was behind the opening of the locks even eight months after it happened (which was when the conversation with Habibullah took place). He had all the powers of the Indian state at his command.

By claiming that he did not know about the lock-opening before it happened, he also showed himself up as a novice. Could Rajiv Gandhi be offering an alibi for what he later considered an error of judgment? Was he preparing the ground to sack his cousin, which is what he did a few weeks after his conversation with Habibullah—yet another fascinating twist to the Shah Bano story?

'It is not possible that Rajiv Gandhi did not know about the opening of the locks,' said a senior Congress leader who had been close to both Arun Nehru and to Rajiv. 'It is, however, possible that he was not given the whole picture, and told the implications of the decision.'

IX

'The differences between Rajiv and Arun Nehru started over Bofors,' remarked a friend of Rajiv Gandhi not in politics.

Differences between the two cousins had started to surface in the first few months of Rajiv coming to power.

Arun Nehru had been dealing with the Swedish government for the purchase of the 155 mm howitzer guns from the Bofors company in Sweden. Then suddenly Rajiv pulled him out of the talks. 'In July 1985, Rajiv Gandhi told me not to bother further about the Swedes and that he would (himself) deal with Mr Palme (Olof Palme, then prime minister of Sweden),' Nehru testified to the CBI when the matter was being investigated years later.

Rajiv Gandhi took charge of dealing with the Swedes himself and finalized the deal in March 1986.

In September 1985, Rajiv moved Arun Nehru from the Power Ministry to the Ministry of Home, as minister of state for Internal Security. Nehru had got into a wrangle with the Swedish government over the setting up of a power plant in India.

Despite their growing differences, Rajiv moved cautiously in those early months as prime minister. Rajiv, for all his naiveté knew that he could not shunt his cousin out to an inconsequential ministry, without inviting his animus. Arun Nehru had become too powerful.

Rajiv Gandhi told Arun Nehru he was specially creating the internal security department for him. 'I never wanted it,' Nehru recalled to me. 'I was forced into it.'

Arun Nehru's differences with Rajiv started immediately after he took over. 'We started scrapping from day one,' Nehru said.

Rajiv, he said, held a 'derogatory view' of the Delhi Police.... 'I said to him that they will report to me. I have to defend them. It is my team now.'

Nehru claimed with pride that all the intelligence agencies reported to him when he took over as minister of Internal Security. 'When I became the minister of Internal Security...the chiefs of R&AW, IB, CBI used to meet me and send reports to me.'

'Rajiv Gandhi did not have time to meet them, so they met me,' he told the CBI.

'It was inconceivable for the intelligence chiefs not to report to the prime minister,' M. K. Narayanan said.

It was customary for the director, IB, and chief of R&AW to walk into the prime minister's office every morning and brief him/or her. That had been the convention since the days of Jawaharlal Nehru. The DIB would brief the home minister separately; he was not supposed to brief the minister of state, Home—unless there were express instructions from the prime minister to do so. The intelligence agencies at the time 'still stuck to form, even if the substance of their role had been diluted'.

'No bureaucrat could breach the brief of the prime minister,' said senior journalist B. N. Uniyal revealed.

However, Arun Nehru, according to Narayanan, would go out of his way to keep himself abreast of the goings-on in the government. 'Sometimes he would invite me for lunch, and chat. He would order lunch from the nearby Taj Hotel.'

'But,' said Narayanan, 'he was overstepping his boundaries, and that was the main problem.'

When the intelligence chiefs briefed the prime minister, no other minister was supposed to be present. 'But sometimes Arun Nehru would drop in to see Rajiv in the morning and would continue to sit there when the intelligence chiefs came in,' Uniyal revealed.

The intelligence chiefs also give 'political intelligence' to the PM; every prime minister stashed this information away in some dossier in his office to be pulled out and used at the appropriate moment. Every PMO has had dossiers on opponents. 'It was a way to bring opponents, inside and outside the party, "in line",' said Uniyal.

But very soon, 'Rajiv Gandhi was upset over this (state of affairs),' Arun Nehru was to say later.

'Rajiv directed the (intelligence) directors not to send reports to me. So, they used to give verbal reports to me.'

'Basically all this was on the surface,' Nehru explained. 'Rajiv had a constant fear, fuelled by others, and they would tell him this, that I may turn out to be better than him. My working style was so aggressive.'

Rajiv's suspicions grew.

'People were saying he (Arun) is very arrogant,' Arun Nehru said. 'The problem was that Rajiv did not meet anyone. He used to take one week to give time...they would come to me.... Once Rajiv and I had an argument.

He used to sit in my study and joke, "In your study I am surrounded by books". I said, "Rajiv, when I sit in your study I am surrounded by screwdrivers." He used to ask me what good is your sense of history. Any information I want I can ask ten experts to give me. They will give me a report on anything.'

'With hindsight I realize that I came into politics from a three-thousand-people company. I was used to managing people. Rajiv had never managed people all his life. When Indira Gandhi was PM the responsibility was hers. When I look back, his (Rajiv's) biggest error was to think whatever Mummy had done, he could do better. He reversed everything she had done.'

The differences between the two cousins had also surfaced on the Punjab Accord. When Rajiv began negotiating with Sant Harchand Singh Longowal in July 1985, Nehru, who used to pride himself on being a hardliner since Indira Gandhi's days, was against it. 'I opposed him,' Nehru revealed. He felt Rajiv was giving up his trump card the (anti-Sikh consolidation of Hindus), which had brought him to power. Rajiv Gandhi signed the Punjab Accord with Longowal on 24 July 1985.

The approach of the two cousins also diverged over the Assam and Mizoram accords. As PM, Rajiv believed that with the massive mandate he had been given, he should resolve problems that had become intractable. Arun Nehru thought Rajiv Gandhi was naive to believe he could do what his mother had not been able to achieve. '(The trouble is) you want confrontation, I want conciliation,' Rajiv told Nehru.

■

Arun Nehru held Sonia Gandhi responsible for his break-up with Rajiv. 'Sonia was behind him (Rajiv)...People forget that earlier Sonia Gandhi was the bahu, only packing Indira Gandhi's clothes for tours. That was her maximum involvement. Then she became the maharani and Prime Minister Rajiv Gandhi's wife....

'Even before he became PM Sonia used to brief Rajiv, saying he (Arun Nehru) is clever, he is a Nehru, and is more popular with the party.... My relationship was with Indira Gandhi. I could not care less for the domestic lobby or the kitchen cabinet.'

Sonia suspected that Arun Nehru was keeping surveillance on Rajiv and the family. Nehru would get their personal letters opened. Nehru did not deny it. 'Sonia Gandhi had told Rajiv that I was holding them under surveillance.'

'Arre bhai,' he said airily, with a flourish of his hand, 'the security of the PM House was (now) my business.'

From the beginning, Sonia was upset with Arun Nehru's arrogant ways, particularly the way he would speak to Rajiv. He was insolent, could be dismissive of him and even snap at Rajiv in public.

'Mitra bhi agar Raja ho jaye toh aap usko "hey rajan" bulate hain (Even if a friend becomes the ruler, you address him with respect due to him),' remarked B. N. Uniyal who covered the political events of the period closely.

'Arun Nehru never liked the family's proximity to Quattrochi, and the holidays they went on together,' Dinesh Trivedi revealed. 'He would warn Rajiv, "You are the prime minister and she is your wife...(and you have to be careful)."' Ottavio Quattrochi—an Italian businessman based in India who came to be charged in 1999 of receiving kickbacks in the Bofors case—was known for his proximity to Sonia and to the prime minister. The Quattrochis were frequent visitors to the PM House.

■

The visit of Pope John Paul II to India in February 1986 brought the differences between Rajiv–Sonia and Arun Nehru to a head. 'Arun Nehru did not want Sonia to go to the airport to receive the Pope (when he arrived in India),' two of Nehru's close associates, who rose to hold high positions, told me. 'He said you will have to kneel before the Pope as his the custom and kiss his ring,' one of these associates said. 'This would not be acceptable to people (here) that the prime minister's wife did that.' Though the papal ring is a powerful symbol of the pontiff's authority and kissing it is a sign of obedience and respect, Nehru wanted to protect the Hindu image of his cousin.

'Sonia did not go to the airport to receive the Pope.' Only President Zail Singh and Prime Minister Rajiv Gandhi received the Pope at the airport when he arrived in India on 1 February 1986. Sonia met the Pope at Rashtrapati Bhavan in the evening.

'Sonia might not have forgotten about it,' Nehru's associate said, 'but things became different during UPA-II, and the family seemed to have made up.'

■

'Shah Bano was not just about Shah Bano; it was also about the shahi gaddi (royal throne) in Delhi,' quipped Shahid Siddiqui.

'Arun Nehru felt that he was the "real" blue-blooded Nehru,' said a Congressman known to be close to Nehru and to Rajiv. 'He thought he could become prime minister. And, he was playing his game in a calibrated, calculated fashion.'

In the early days, 'Rajiv Arun Nehru se bahut ghabrate thae (Rajiv used to be wary of Arun),' revealed journalist G. S. Chawla, a keen observer of the political scene at the time.

As Rajiv Gandhi became comfortable with exercising the levers of power, he started to resent his cousin's overbearing ways. The differences between the two started to surface in mid-1985 itself, but very few were aware of it. While Rajiv was willing to allow Arun Nehru to become a 'power centre', he was not prepared to let him become the 'alternative power centre'. For Nehru had begun to be seen as the de facto prime minister.

Rajiv Gandhi became worried about the potential Arun Nehru had to engineer a revolt in the party, if the dissatisfaction of Hindu MPs against him continued to grow—another reason why he would have opted for the lock-opening. Nehru was, after all, an 'insider', and a 'Nehru' at that. Since Indira Gandhi's days, he had come to acquire a grip over the party organization.

Nehru was candid when he admitted, many years later, that 'they (Congress leadership) were afraid that I was positioning myself (to replace Rajiv). And (then) VP was positioning himself (for prime ministership).' Then he asked, quite belligerently, 'What is wrong with positioning? If someone is good, why not? Who does not position himself?' He conceded that 'it was a power game' in the 1980s. And he also admitted, again quite frankly, that 'I was 50 per cent of Rajiv's problems.'

∎

Rajiv had a showdown with Arun Nehru in early May 1986. He had put up with his abrasive ways for eighteen months. They had an angry exchange.

An upset Nehru took off with his family for Kashmir. They stayed there at a state government tourist resort in the picturesque surroundings of Dachigam. He would go for long walks—as he had been told to lose weight. At 3 a.m. on 31 May 1986, he suffered a heart attack.

Earlier in the day, he had met Governor Jagmohan. Jagmohan immediately drove across to Dachigam and took Arun Nehru to the Sher-e-Kashmir Institute of Medical Sciences, 16 kilometres away. The governor ensured that cardiologists and medical experts were at hand when Nehru arrived at the hospital at 6 a.m. Jagmohan's proximity to Nehru was well known. It was Jagmohan who had sacked the government of Farooq Abdullah in July 1984, and installed G. M. Shah in his place, at the instance of Arun Nehru. In 1990, when V. P. Singh came to power, Arun Nehru would send him as governor.

While he was in hospital, Nehru received a stream of visitors. P. Chidambaram arrived from Delhi. He was minister of state for Personnel, Public Grievances and Pensions and was obviously sent by Rajiv Gandhi; he was later to replace Nehru as MoS, Internal Security. President Giani Zail Singh also came. 'He came through the bathroom door, not from the front entrance,' recalled journalist G. S. Chawla, known for his proximity to Zail Singh. The PMO ensured that Dr S. P. Manchanda, a neurosurgeon in Bombay, and Professor Khaliullah, an eminent cardiologist in Delhi would be available to Nehru in Srinagar. The doctors ordered complete rest for him for at least two months. In Delhi, the grapevine was now abuzz that it was the end of the road for Nehru. Many expected the prime minister to come to Srinagar. But Rajiv did not visit his ailing cousin. This was the first visible sign of the rift between the two. Out of action for several months, Nehru's influence began to wane. Rajiv Gandhi was now contemplating dropping his cousin from the ministry. He had said as much to Natwar Singh in July 1986, and to Wajahat Habibullah two months later.

■

The date for the cabinet reshuffle was fixed for 22 October 1986. Hours before the reshuffle, Rajiv Gandhi asked Arun Nehru to come and see him. He told his cousin that he was going to make changes in his cabinet.

'He offered to send me as high commissioner to UK,' Arun Nehru told me.

'It will help you get the necessary treatment,' Rajiv told Arun. 'You can always return in six months' time.'

'I am not stupid,' Nehru retorted. 'You want me out.'

'I will drop you,' Rajiv threatened.

'You (can) do it.'

'We had a very bad meeting,' Nehru recalled. 'That day I told him, now I am going to fight you.'

The meeting ended with Rajiv Gandhi asking Arun Nehru to resign. Other ministers who were dropped wrote in their resignation letters that they would be ready to work under Rajiv in whatever capacity he wanted. Nehru refused to make such a commitment. He just wrote in his resignation letter, 'I thank you for the opportunity you have given me to work with you.'

Rajiv Gandhi scrawled in his big, bold handwriting on the letter, written with the thick-nibbed Montblanc pen he used—'Accepted'.

Then he left for the ceremony at Rashtrapati Bhavan. As Rajiv rushed out, he hastily motioned to his political aide M. L. Fotedar to come with him in the car.

'Kya hua (What happened)?' Fotedar asked him on the way.

Rajiv told him.

'What do you think will happen now?' Rajiv asked Fotedar. 'We should wait for the repercussions,' said Fotedar, who knew Nehru well. The car turned into Rashtrapati Bhavan.

The prime minister's face wore a worried look.

After the swearing-in, a restive Rajiv again asked Fotedar to accompany him back to Race Course Road.

'Rajivji was tense,' Fotedar said afterwards.

As the car reached Race Course Road, they saw Sonia Gandhi and Gandhi family loyalist Captain Satish Sharma waiting in the portico. Sonia had a wide smile on her face.

'I understood then why Arun Nehru had been dropped,' Fotedar said later.

Within hours of Arun Nehru being removed on 22 October 1986, V. P. Singh went to see Nehru. They spent a couple of hours together. 'From then on, VP realized that things were up for him also,' Nehru told me.

Publicly, Arun Nehru appeared completely unconcerned. He met people, talked to the media, as if nothing had happened. He gave the impression that he would be taken back in the government soon. But he was biding his time. He struck only when he was ready—and that was a year later in 1987. (See Chapter 3.) Swedish Radio did a programme 'Dagens Eko' which was based on the testimony of a former employee of Bofors—that Bofors had paid bribes to Indian politicians.

'It was Arun Nehru who leaked the Bofors story to the Swedish Radio,' H. R. Bhardwaj told me. 'We knew it.'

Bofors was to blight Rajiv Gandhi's remaining years in power. It scuppered his chances of re-election in 1989—and brought V. P. Singh to power.

X

Three days before he died on 21 May 1991, Rajiv Gandhi had hosted an iftar party at 10, Janpath. He had been out of power for a year and half—and was confident that he was coming back to power.

After most of the guests had left, he sat down with a small group of people. They had specially been asked to stay back by Congress leader Salman Khurshid. They were mostly professors from Aligarh Muslim University and from Jamia Millia Islamia Central University. Khurshid wanted Muslim intellectuals to give Rajiv their feedback about his prospects in the general elections that were due mid-1991.

Rajiv went around the room to get everyone's views. Most were upbeat—Rajiv had a great chance in UP, they said. Then it came to Qurban Ali, a journalist.

'What they are telling you is all wrong,' Qurban said. He had Rajiv's attention.

'You did a great favour to the Muslims by bringing in the (Muslim Women's) Bill to undo the Shah Bano judgment,' he said.

'But you compensated for it by opening the locks of the temple.... And it led to the worst kind of carnage all over—Barabanki, Malliana, Hashimpura, Bhagalpur,' he said. These were places synonymous with terrible killings of Muslims.

At this point, Rajiv interrupted him, 'But, you know who got the unlocking (at the Babri Masjid) done.'

'Yes, and since you won't take the name of the person, I will name him,' Qurban Ali said. 'It was Arun Nehru.'

'Yes,' Rajiv said.

'But you were the prime minister.'

Rajiv was quiet.

Ali couldn't help adding, 'At the time of the shilanyas also, there was a formal agreement between the Congress and the VHP (to lay the foundation stone of the Ram temple at Ayodhya in the middle of the poll campaign in 1989).'

Again Rajiv was quiet. He did not deny the uncomfortable observations. By this time, Khurshid was beginning to look distinctly unhappy. The meeting ended abruptly.

Many Congressmen used to say that Rajiv would have been very different in his second term. 'Rajiv was no longer as naive as people thought,' the wily H. R. Bhardwaj had said about Rajiv when he was out of power. Out of power, he had gained a greater understanding of Indian society, of people, and the political system. But destiny was not to give him a second chance.

∎

Rajiv Gandhi's decisions to contain the fallout of the Shah Bano judgment were influenced by several undercurrents. The first was the Muslim protests. New to the top job, he was unnerved by the large number of Muslims who came out on the streets to oppose what they saw as interference with their personal laws. Apart from pressures within the country, he was also aware that he would have to face international pressure. This propelled him to go in for the Muslim Women's Bill to placate an irate community.

Also, he had not expected a backlash amongst the Hindus. Once again, Rajiv wilted under pressure, this time from the Hindu groups, ranging from hardliners like the Vishwa Hindu Parishad to liberal Hindus.

While modern and secular in his outlook, hoping to ready India for the twenty-first century, Rajiv Gandhi did not fully understand the hold of caste or community on vast sections of Indian society. He could not comprehend why the Hindus should be exercised about the Muslim Women's Bill, which had nothing to do with them. Nor why the opening of the locks at the Babri Masjid should create such turmoil amongst the Muslims. His Westernized thinking led him to make the biggest miscalculations of his career. As a result, he displeased both Muslims and Hindus—and lost the support of both in the elections that followed in 1989, his majority slumping from 414 to 197 seats.

The Congress never recovered after that. Nor did it get a majority on its own in parliament. That a prime minister with such an unprecedented majority could be buffeted around the way he was damaged Rajiv Gandhi's standing. The country had wanted a strong leader after Indira Gandhi's assassination—and given him a mandate, which has not yet been bettered.

Besides dealing a blow to the party's electoral chances, Rajiv Gandhi's actions over the Muslim Women's Bill had other consequences. That the 'courts did not matter, political agitations did. So did electoral vote banks'. It also gave a greater fillip to the Hindu right-wing agenda, especially in North India—than any other single decision till then had done. Moving around Uttar Pradesh in April 1986 (to write a three-part piece on the 'communal divide' in the state for *The Statesman*), I was shocked to find how deep the Hindu–Muslim divide had become, creating fertile ground for the politics of Hindutva to take off—pursued by the BJP.

It was also at this time that 'Muslim appeasement'—to undo the Shah Bano judgment under pressure from fundamentalists in the Muslim community—entered the political lexicon and national discourse.

The VHP and Hindu hardliners tasted blood with the opening of the locks at the Babri Masjid. It was to embolden them to demolish the Babri mosque on 6 December 1992, even as forces of the mighty Indian state looked on helplessly, unable to prevent the demolition—and nobody was punished for it.

Three decades later, Narendra Modi would reap the harvest of what was sown during Rajiv Gandhi's term.

CHAPTER 3

THE CRAFTY PRIME MINISTER
WHO REMADE INDIAN POLITICS

V. P. Singh's Mandal Gambit

I

The reporter dashed out of the Central Hall of Parliament shouting, 'It is Devi Lal for PM.' He was rushing to file his copy. He worked for the wire service United News of India (UNI), and was headed to the press room on the first floor. Everyone within earshot was flabbergasted. They had expected Vishwanath Pratap Singh to be the new prime minister. It was under his leadership that the National Front, a coalition built by V. P. Singh, had won the most seats in the recent general election. Almost instantly, the news wires were humming: 'Devi Lal is the new prime minister of India.' Devi Lal, the maverick Jat leader, was the chief minister of the state of Haryana. A couple of people standing next to me groaned in disappointment. It was 4.10 p.m. on 1 December 1989.

I was taken aback by this turn of events. I had just come to parliament after meeting Om Prakash Chautala, Devi Lal's eldest son. He had been leading the campaign to make his father prime minister. A journalist colleague, Harish Gupta, whom I had bumped into, was with me. We had found Chautala eating lunch. He did not look up from his thali to greet us. He looked morose, was monosyllabic in his responses, virtually admitting that the game was up for his father—and that V. P. Singh would be prime minister.

All day, there had been frenetic political activity in the country's capital. At 28, Lodi Estate, V. P. Singh's residence, hundreds of people had hung around expectantly, some spilling into the house, others standing outside on the lawns, a few even pressed up against the walls of the kitchen. They waited for news on who would be the next prime minister. They knew senior leaders were huddled in groups in various parts of the city, holding parleys.

Devi Lal had projected V. P. Singh for prime minister all through the election campaign in 1989. But, after the polls, he decided to make a bid for the top job himself. An agitated S. N. Singh, VP's personal secretary who had been with him since his early days in Allahabad, remarked, almost in tears, 'Even Rajiv Gandhi did not humiliate Raja sahib (V. P. Singh) like this. Some of the Janata Dal leaders have ganged up against him....' he added, his voice trailing off. They were determined to deny VP what many across the country felt was his due—India's prime ministership.

Elsewhere in the capital, Haryana Bhavan was also buzzing with activity. The day had started very early for Devi Lal. He had been camping in the national capital for some days. Devi Lal had viewed himself as the kingmaker in the loosely knit group of political parties that had fought the election on a common platform—until he began to glimpse the possibility of becoming prime minister himself. Politicians, journalists, academics, and political activists who had worked for the defeat of Rajiv Gandhi, walked in and out of Haryana Bhavan that morning, hoping to confer with Devi Lal.

There was another hive of activity at 14, Akbar Road, the residence of Arun Nehru, at one time the most powerful minister in Rajiv Gandhi's government until Rajiv sacked him and he made common cause with V. P. Singh. He had stayed by VP's side after their exit from the Congress in 1987 and helped craft the Janata Dal in 1988. He had just been elected to the Lok Sabha from Bilhaur in UP, and had emerged as VP's right-hand man in those days. 'I told VP two...days before the election (of the leader), leave this to me and you stay out of it,' Nehru told me.

The fourth hub of action that day was Orissa Bhavan. Here, too, hectic negotiations were taking place under the watchful eye of another powerful politician, Biju Patnaik, the chief minister of Orissa.

Rushing from one place to another, I was a couple of minutes late arriving at parliament. The meeting of the Janata Dal Parliamentary Party (JDPP)had just started. It would pick the party's leader who would then become the country's next prime minister.

President R. Venkataraman had been waiting for the Janata Dal and its allies to choose their leader, who he could then invite to form the new government.

The doors of the domed Central Hall were now shut. Scores of journalists were standing outside waiting impatiently to know who would be the next prime minister of India.

In the general election just concluded, the country's grand old party, the Indian National Congress, had been trounced. It had lost 217 seats of the record majority of 414 seats it had won in the 1984 general election. Yet, it had still managed to win 197 seats, the largest number of any of the parties contesting the polls. Rajiv Gandhi, the leader of the party—and the outgoing prime minister—had submitted his resignation to President Venkataraman on 29 November. He had decided not to stake his claim to form the new government despite leading the single largest party in the Lok Sabha. This had ended the president's dilemma. He had been poring over legal precedents on whether to call the single largest party to form the government, despite it losing its majority. Or to invite the second largest party which had vanquished the incumbent. Rajiv was clear that he did not have the stomach to run a coalition government. No one in the Congress disagreed with Rajiv's decision. Not so with the winning side, the Janata Dal. It seemed to have the numbers, but there were squabbles over who would be leader.

The Janata Dal that V. P. Singh had put together in 1988 had been victorious in 143 Lok Sabha constituencies. It could form the government with its allies—the ruling coalition would need at least 263 seats for a simple majority in the Lok Sabha. Prior to the elections, VP had put together the National Front, a coalition with the Janata Dal at the centre, supported by regional outfits—the TDP of Andhra Pradesh, DMK of Tamil Nadu, AGP of Assam and a breakaway faction of the Congress, the Indian Congress (Socialist). To VP's delight, the Janata Dal had managed a strike rate of 60 per cent in the polls. It had done particularly well in UP and Bihar where he had led the campaign. The party had won 54 of 85 seats in UP and got 32 out of 54 seats in Bihar. However, his southern allies had let him down. The TDP had got only 2 seats, and the DMK drew a blank. The Congress (S) got 1 seat. And the AGP got none.

As in 1977, when the northern states had deserted the Congress, in 1989, too, it was the South which had stayed with the Congress. The BJP and the Left parties decided to support the ruling coalition from the 'outside'—and not join the government. Both these groups had gained from the 'VP wave' in the country. The BJP's tally had gone up from 2 Lok Sabha seats in 1984 to 85 in 1989; the Left parties had together mopped up 52 seats between them, mainly from West Bengal. With the support of the BJP and the Left parties, the National Front tally in the Lok Sabha added up to 283, a comfortable majority in a house of 525 MPs. (Later, more parties lent their support to the new government.)

As the president waited for word from the Janata Dal, the party made no move to stake its claim to form the government. The problem lay not with the arithmetic, but with the chemistry between the leaders. From 28 November to 1 December 1989, the struggle had intensified on who would be prime minister. V. P. Singh was the natural choice; it had been in his name that the elections had been won. But Devi Lal was eyeing the top slot. So was the old war horse Chandra Shekhar, who was determined to prevent VP from becoming prime minister. 'Vishwanath if you contest, I will also contest,' he told VP bluntly. He was not prepared to accept the leadership of a man he considered far junior to him. To him VP had been a courtier of the Gandhi family, when he had taken on the rich and powerful as the admired 'Young Turk' in the Congress and later battled Indira Gandhi herself during the 1975–77 Emergency. However, when it became clear that he would not have enough support within the party, he decided to back Devi Lal. Devi Lal had funded most of the candidates; he was confident he would have their backing.

As the delay over government formation grew, criticism mounted against the Janata Dal leadership for its inability to choose a leader. Finally, a meeting of the JDPP was called on 1 December.

Inside the Central Hall, the tense meeting had started at 4 p.m. On the dais sat the veteran socialist Madhu Dandavate. Appointed the returning officer, he had to ensure a smooth and fair election. Seated beside him were the three possible contenders—V. P. Singh, Chandra Shekhar, and Devi Lal.

Dandavate called the meeting to order—and invited nominations for the leader of the JDPP. V. P. Singh sprang up, 'I propose Devi Lal's name,' he said. It was immediately seconded by a smiling Chandra Shekhar. There was a shocked silence in the room. Since there was no other nomination, Dandavate declared Devi Lal elected. And the UNI reporter rushed out with his scoop before the rival agencies could beat him to it.

It was then that the tall and rustic Devi Lal rose slowly to his full height. He was casually attired in a white kurta and dhoti and a brown cardigan. 'The election has been fought against corruption,' he said slowly, '...and the battle has been led by V. P. Singh.' He continued: 'Aur phir Haryana maen jahan mujhe log tau keh kar pukarte hain, main wahan tau hi ban kar rehna chahta hoon (In Haryana people know me as uncle and it is as uncle I want to remain in Haryana),' he said with a flourish. 'I propose V. P. Singh's name as leader of the parliamentary party.'

Then he declared triumphantly, 'VP ho gaya (VP is the winner).' The assembled parliamentarians broke into thunderous applause. There was so much commotion and excitement that for a few seconds no one seconded Devi Lal's proposal. Then, Ajit Singh, the chief of the Rashtriya Lok Dal, and son of former prime minister, Charan Singh, stood up. 'I second the proposal,' he shouted over the din.

Madhu Dandavate asked if there were any other nominations. There was silence. He declared that V. P. Singh had been elected leader of the JDPP.

'Kill, kill, kill earlier story,' the wires buzzed again.

N. T. Rama Rao of the TDP, clad in his saffron robes, now took the stage. He went through the motions of electing V. P. Singh as the leader of the National Front Parliamentary Party—a formality, as only three MPs had won seats from parties other than the Janata Dal.

V. P. Singh was now set to lead the new government. There was excited chatter in the Central Hall which was witnessing yet another political milestone. It had seen Jawaharlal Nehru make his epochal 'tryst with destiny' speech at midnight on 14–15 August 1947, announcing India's independence. The same Central Hall had seen the adoption of the tricolour, the national anthem, and the republic's Constitution under its impressive domed hall.

Chandra Shekhar now sat in a corner near the main entrance of Central Hall. His nostrils flared, his face was red with anger. He had been duped—and humiliated—publicly. The understanding, he said bitterly, as I talked to him, was that Devi Lal would be prime minister. That is what he had been told by both Biju Patnaik and Devi Lal at Orissa Bhavan only two hours earlier. 'Iska anjam acha nahin hoga (This does not portend well for the future),' he warned.

'Biju had called me to Orissa Bhavan and told me that VP would propose Devi Lal's name and I would second him,' Chandra Shekhar said. He then flounced out of parliament, and headed to his 'ashram' at Bhondsi in Gurgaon. Biju Patnaik rushed after him to placate him.

'Biju came to see me and offered me the deputy PMship,' Chandra Shekhar revealed. '(Later) Devi Lal called me and offered me any portfolio. I refused.' When Chandra Shekhar became prime minister eleven months later, after the V. P. Singh government had been toppled, Patnaik said to him. 'Arrey Ballia, if I had known you would run a government like this, I would not have done what I did. He was referring to double-crossing me,' Chandra Shekhar added.

The charade, or the 'formula' as it was called, to install V. P. Singh as prime minister, had been worked out in Orissa Bhavan only a few hours before the JDPP meeting. It had been decided that VP would first propose Devi Lal's name and he in turn would crown VP. That is how VP became the seventh prime minister of India.

That evening, at 7 p.m., V. P. Singh called on President R. Venkataraman. He was accompanied by Madhu Dandavate and a couple of others. They handed him the official document stating that VP had been elected as the leader of the National Front Parliamentary Party. There were also the supporting letters from the BJP and the Left.

The president invited V. P. Singh to form the new government. He said he would swear him in the next day. The change of guard, he said, should take place without further delay. The other ministers could be sworn in later. Venkataraman gave VP thirty days to prove his majority on the floor of the house. The swearing-in ceremony was fixed for 12 noon on 2 December 1989.

∎

Every prime minister, from Jawaharlal Nehru onwards, had reached the pinnacle in highly unusual circumstances. But how V. P. Singh finally reached the top was somewhat like a fairy tale—and gave an insight into the working of the Delhi durbar. Just as it had dramatically decided successions in the Mughal and imperial courts in the past, it continued to do so in the democratic India of 1989.

As we have seen, the jockeying to become prime minister had reached fever pitch on the morning of 1 December 1989. Devi Lal had started to work the phones at dawn. The Haryana chief minister was an early riser. As he went for his morning walk in the compound of Haryana Bhavan at 5.30 a.m., his mind was working furiously—weighing up the pros and cons of the emerging situation.

All through the election campaign Devi Lal had projected V. P. Singh for PM. But within hours of the election results being declared on 28 November 1989, he had changed his mind. Chandra Shekhar had encouraged him to make a bid for prime ministership. He was moving through Om Prakash Chautala. Devi Lal began to tell visitors, 'What is the Janata Dal without me? ...I made the Janata Dal. I am the one who has spent the money on the elections.'

He then sent a message to the BJP leaders, seeking their support. The party was already backing his government in Haryana. He deputed 'godman' Chandraswami, and his aide Kailash Nath Aggarwal, known to most as Mamaji, both known for their political fixing abilities, to meet BJP leader Atal Bihari Vajpayee. Mamaji urged Vajpayee to make Devi Lal prime minister—and to join the government. Devi Lal would be ready to support the BJP's demand for a Hindu Rashtra. But Vajpayee and L. K. Advani were cool to the idea. They supported V. P. Singh for prime minister, for he had the people's mandate.

As Devi Lal ambled around the lawns at Haryana Bhavan, his mind went over the bitter argument he had had the previous evening with the Janata Dal leader Som Pal. Pal, who was related to him and called him Mamaji (uncle), had quit the Congress along with VP—and made a strong pitch to make him PM. 'Mamaji, all through the campaign, you had said again and again that V. P. Singh will be prime minister,' Pal had reminded Devi Lal. 'Now, stick to what you had promised.'

'Chandra Shekhar plans to contest (for the leadership of the JDPP),' Devi Lal had countered.

'The numbers are stacked heavily against Chandra Shekhar,' Som Pal shot back. 'We have done our arithmetic.' He then reeled off the names of MPs who could be expected to go with Chandra Shekhar and with Devi Lal—they were in a minority.

'But Chandra Shekhar is not agreeing,' Devi Lal had persisted. 'And your man (VP) does not want (a) contest.'

V. P. Singh wanted to be elected unanimously. A contest would divide the party at the outset, he said. He did not want the government to start on a discordant note. VP would have won hands down. But he was apprehensive about other factors at work. Industrialists had sent their representatives to Delhi within hours of the results, armed with big money. They were putting up the newly elected MPs in five-star hotels to influence them. These were powerful businessmen against whom VP had carried out raids for tax evasion and financial misdoings when he was finance minister in Rajiv Gandhi's government. He suspected that they were now conspiring with Chandra Shekhar and Devi Lal to deny him the party leadership. Though many of the Janata Dal MPs wanted him to be PM, their loyalties might get divided, if it came to a vote. For Devi Lal had funded the campaign of many.

As he mulled over the events of the last hours, it was becoming clear to Devi Lal that the majority now favoured VP.

As a plan began to take shape in his head, he asked to speak to some of the leaders loyal to him. If he wasn't going to get the top job, he had to strike a hard bargain. First, he called up Som Pal, and asked him to come over immediately. A Jat, not known to mince his words, Pal came straight to the point. 'Mamaji, running the central government is not like running the Haryana ministry.... In Haryana, it took you a couple of years to lose steam,' he told Devi Lal bluntly. 'In Delhi, it will not even take you two months.'

Then he held out a sop to Devi Lal, 'If you support VP as PM...you can become the deputy prime minister. We can talk about it.'

But the wily Devi Lal already knew that. He had heard that V. P. Singh was ready to make him deputy prime minister. Som Pal was not the only person who had told him this. At one stage, VP had toyed with the idea of having two deputy prime ministers—Devi Lal from the North and N. T. Rama Rao, chief minister of Andhra Pradesh, from the South. '(However) I was advised by P. Upendra of TDP that I would be inviting trouble,' VP said to me.

Devi Lal's eyes were now set not just on the deputy prime ministership. He also wanted to be home minister. Suddenly, as if he had just made up his mind, he turned to Som Pal and said, 'Send Arun Nehru to me.' So far he had refused to talk to Nehru, who was acting on behalf of VP. Som Pal rushed out of Haryana Bhavan to find Nehru.

■

'Did we fight Rajiv Gandhi to create a mess like this?' lamented editor Kuldip Nayar, who sat with Devi Lal later that morning. With him was J. D. Sethi, a well-known academic, who had accompanied Nayar. They wanted VP to become prime minister—as did many professionals and much of middle-class India. They had come to see Devi Lal to persuade him to back VP for PM.

Nayar used to claim proudly that he had played a role in the making of three of India's prime ministers—Lal Bahadur Shastri, V. P. Singh, and I. K. Gujral. Nayar became press secretary to Shastri, was India's high commissioner in London in 1990 during VP's premiership, and Gujral sent him to the Rajya Sabha in 1997.

Chautala, who had been told by Chandra Shekhar not to let his father out of sight, was grumbling to his father, 'Babuji, berhagarak karne wale hain Kuldip Nayar aur Sethi (Kuldip Nayar and Sethi are going to spoil things).' At 8 a.m., the newspaper editor Ashwini Kumar Chopra marched into the room. Devi Lal had called him an hour earlier and asked him to come over. On seeing him, Chautala became even more derisive, 'Lo teesra bewakoof aa gaya (Look, a third fool has come).'

'What do you suggest (I do)?' Devi Lal asked Chopra, ignoring the jibes of his son.

'What do you mean by asking that? Get on with forming a government,' Chopra replied. 'You make VP prime minister and you become home minister.'

'Home minister ban jayoon (Shall I become home minister)?' Devi Lal exclaimed, as if the idea had occurred to him for the first time.

'Usme kya hoga mere paas (What will I get under it)?'

Chopra started to reel off the perks that he thought Devi Lal might find attractive. 'Intelligence Bureau, Border Security Force, and a plane of the BSF, which only the home minister can use.... Then there is the ITBP [Indo-Tibetan Border Police]. It too has a helicopter.' He would be able to make police appointments and get information from the IB. 'Raja ki jaan tote maen hoti hai (A ruler's heartbeat lies in his parrot). Keep the tota with you,' he advised.

'You cannot become PM,' Ashwini Kumar Chopra told Devi Lal firmly.

'That's what we have been telling him,' Nayar said.

Nayar, Sethi, and Chopra walked out of Haryana Bhavan together—and decided to make their way to Arun Nehru's house. Nehru had emerged as the chief negotiator on VP's behalf, and was known to be a tough bargainer. He had let it be known to the Janata Dal leaders that VP must be chosen 'unanimously'. Or, he warned, 'we will go through with a contest'. It had been a war of nerves between him and Devi Lal. Nehru had been waiting for Devi Lal to blink first.

'I used to give it back to Devi Lal,' Nehru said later. 'You run a little state like Haryana, and you think you know everything.... Finally, he would climb down.'

'Biju (Patnaik) had once told me that if you don't give into his bullying and shout back at him, he will go under the table,' Nehru had remarked.

'We don't care about Devi Lal,' Nehru told Nayar, Sethi, and Chopra in his usual belligerent fashion when they met him at his residence. But he knew that the clock was ticking away. He agreed to talk to Devi Lal, provided there was no badtameezi (misbehaviour). 'You get Devi Lal to call me.' The excited trio rushed back to Haryana Bhavan.

■

Meanwhile, Som Pal had driven to VP's residence, instead of going directly to Arun Nehru. He thought he should first apprise him of the latest developments. Together they decided to head to Nehru's house. They were joined there by the journalist Santosh Bharatiya, editor of *Chauthi Duniya*, who was also close to VP. Very quickly, Som Pal apprised Nehru about his conversation with Devi Lal that morning—that Devi Lal was now willing to be persuaded. A pleased Nehru took off to Haryana Bhavan. At noon, Nehru called VP and asked him to reach Orissa Bhavan immediately. He too would be reaching there soon.

At Orissa Bhavan, as VP, Som Pal, and Santosh Bharatiya got into the lift, Biju Patnaik walked in. When Bharatiya greeted him, 'Dada, how are you?' an irritable Patnaik snapped back, 'Are you a doctor or what?' His grumpiness showed them that, till then, no agreement had been sewn up. Patnaik and Nehru had been working together in those hours to find a solution.

Upstairs, Biju Patnaik took VP and Nehru into Room 301 that had been allocated for his use. It was here that the Orissa chief minister held all his 'exclusive meetings' with senior leaders. Lesser lights sat in adjoining Room 302, which was allocated to Srikant Jena, who later became a minister in the United Front Government in 1996–97. But in those hours, he was constantly at Patnaik's elbow. Unknown to most, Patnaik and Nehru had been moving in step.

Patnaik had been sceptical about the possibility of a unanimous election in favour of VP. 'It cannot be done,' he had told Nehru bluntly. 'Chandra Shekhar will contest.' Patnaik had been working on Devi Lal to persuade him to accept VP as prime minister. 'Only Biju could have...persuaded Devi Lal (to agree to give up the PMship),' Chandra Shekhar was to say later, 'Arun Nehru could not have convinced Devi Lal.'

Biju Patnaik now called Devi Lal over to Orissa Bhavan. The atmosphere crackled with tension. No decision was yet in sight.

Sharad Yadav took Arun Nehru aside and beseeched him, 'Somehow find a way out. Devi Lal wants to be deputy prime minister and home minister.'

'Never,' Arun Nehru replied.

'What then?' asked an anxious Sharad Yadav, a senior Janata Dal leader who was in the Devi Lal group.

'We will make him deputy PM and give him agriculture,' Nehru replied unperturbed. 'After all, he is the leader of the farmers.'

'De doh (Give it to him),' VP told Nehru at one point. 'Arun, don't push things so hard that the party breaks.'

But Nehru wanted to hold firm till the end. 'Devi Lal was aggressive and unreasonable,' recalled Nehru. 'All of us had come out of the Congress culture. We were not used to his methods. I told VP, "Why succumb to this fellow? It won't stop at this".'

'Main samjhata hoon (I'll try and convince him),' Yadav offered.

The final solution was hammered out in Orissa Bhavan just over an hour before the JDPP meeting was to take place. VP told me the 'formula' was the brainchild of Devi Lal. 'I think it was Devi Lal's own idea that his name be proposed first.'

'Hamari izzat, hamari pagari bacha lijiye (Please save my honour),' he told VP, whom he had taken into Room 301.

'Hum aapke liye kuch bhi kar sakte hain (I can do anything for you),' VP assured him.

Devi Lal then said, 'Hamara naam propose ho jaye, phir hum withdraw karlenge (Once my name is proposed, I will then withdraw from the race).'

'Aap withdraw kyon kar lenge, aap hi ban jaeeye (Why should you withdraw, you can become PM?),' VP told him in his inimitable, polite manner.

'Dande maregi public (People will beat us),' Devi Lal replied.

But before talking to VP, Devi Lal had spoken to Biju Patnaik and Nehru in Room 301, and expressed his dilemma. 'Us (Chandra Shekhar) se vaada kiya hai ki main banoonga, chahe ek minute ke liye hi kyon naheen ho (I had promised Chandra Shekhar that I will become PM, even if it is for one minute).' Then he added, 'Usee (VP) ko banayenge. Soch raha tha kaise karaenge (However, we will make VP PM, I have been trying to figure out how to do it).' Devi Lal had later told Kuldip Nayar what had transpired at Orissa Bhavan.

The 'formula' was actually the brainchild of Arun Nehru. 'The formula,' Arun Nehru told me, 'was (evolved) to salvage Devi Lal's pride.... I had the power of attorney of all (the others).... It happened in the course of a conversation at Orissa Bhavan. It was not (previously) thought out.'

'It was Arun Nehru's idea,' confirmed S. P. Shukla, who was secretary of the commerce ministry when Nehru was the minister in 1990. 'He shared this with me unsolicited when...we went on a tour to Mexico. He was quite free with me. For Nehru it was all a question of how to manage people.'

Arun Nehru finally convinced Biju Patnaik that it was the only way out of the impasse. But, before agreeing, Patnaik decided to make a last-ditch effort to persuade Chandra Shekhar to accept VP as PM. He asked Chandra Shekhar over to Orissa Bhavan. Srikant Jena escorted him upto Patnaik's room. Chandra Shekhar remained unyielding. He left Orissa Bhavan in ten minutes. This was just before 3 p.m. Patnaik had told Chandra Shekhar only one part of the deal—that Devi Lal's name would be proposed by V. P. Singh, and he, Chandra Shekhar, would second it. A pleased Chandra Shekhar agreed readily.

Patnaik decided the 'formula' had now become inevitable.

'We told Devi Lal that he should tell Chandra Shekhar what the samjhauta (deal) was,' Arun Nehru said later.

'I will inform him,' Devi Lal assured him.

'But he did not do it. Later he told me,' Nehru said, '(that) if he had told Chandra Shekhar, he would not have agreed.'

The moment Chandra Shekhar left Orissa Bhavan, Patnaik rushed Jena to Parliament House. 'Go immediately to Central Hall, tell Madhu Dandavate...that first VP will propose Devi Lal's name and then Devi Lal will formally withdraw and propose V. P. Singh's name.'

'You also tell some MPs about this quietly,' Patnaik told Jena, 'so that they don't get a shock.'

'What...if Devi Lal accepts VP's proposal and rushes to Rashtrapati Bhavan to stake his claim to be PM?' Jena thought to himself anxiously. That was a risk they had to take.

'VP ko banana hai (VP has to be made PM), this is the consensus' Patnaik told Jena.

At 12 noon, on 2 December 1989, President R. Venkataraman administered the oath of office and secrecy to V. P. Singh as prime minister. He also swore in Devi Lal. Devi Lal was supposed to take the oath as a 'minister' and then be designated deputy prime minister afterwards. This was the precedent followed when Sardar Patel became deputy prime minister in 1947, and then again when Morarji Desai took over as deputy PM in 1967 under Indira Gandhi. And also when Charan Singh and Jagjivan Ram were sworn in as deputy prime ministers under Morarji Desai in 1978. But while taking oath, Devi Lal did not repeat the word mantri (minister) after the president. Instead, he kept saying oop pradhan mantri (deputy prime minister) while describing himself. President Venkataraman corrected him gently. But Devi Lal continued as if he had not heard. The president then gave up.

After the swearing-in ceremony, an excited Devi Lal, got into the official car designated for him and ordered, 'Chamra kholo', referring to the leather that encased the flag on the bonnet of the official car, which had a red light; his voice boomed with authority.

Then he asked Ashwini Kumar Chopra who had accompanied him to Rashtrapati Bhavan, 'Where is my office?'

For all his guile, there was a rustic simplicity about the Haryana strongman.

'South Block,' his aide Deepak informed him.

'Let's go to office.'

Chopra then corrected them, 'South Block is the PM's office. You have not yet been given a portfolio, you have become deputy PM without portfolio.' Uncertain about what to do next, they decided to go to Raj Ghat instead—and pay homage to Mahatma Gandhi. Then they returned to Haryana Bhavan in what was an anti-climactic end to a historic morning. Devi Lal got Agriculture, not Home. It was part of the deal that had been struck at Orissa Bhavan. For all his feigned ignorance, Devi Lal was privy to it.

But the day was not yet over. That evening Kuldip Nayar called on Devi Lal to chat with the new number two in government. When Nayar arrived at Haryana Bhavan, Devi Lal's family was dissecting what oop pradhan mantri entailed in terms of power and other benefits.

Suddenly Devi Lal interrupted them, 'Woh oop bhi uttar jayega (That deputy will also disappear soon).' Within hours of crowning V. P. Singh, Devi Lal was already coveting the throne. He would tell whoever called on him in the days that followed that he had crowned VP—and that he was beholden to him. 'It is because of me that he is prime minister today.'

'You should not talk about political morality,' he told VP three months later when the shenanigans of Devi Lal's son, O. P. Chautala, were to convulse the Janata Dal. 'You became the prime minister because I told a lie.' In the months that followed, it was the kingmaker, Devi Lal, who was to destabilize the VP government.

The genesis of V. P. Singh's problems, which played out over the next eleven months, lay in how he came to be elected on 1 December 1989. Chandra Shekhar never forgot it, nor forgave him for it. He fuelled the unhappiness against VP, and worked through Devi Lal. So did Rajiv Gandhi, whom VP had dethroned, who was waiting to strike as soon as an opportunity presented itself. The machinations of these senior politicians, the instability inherent in the Janata Dal regime, which they fomented, and the ambition of the BJP to expand its footprint led V. P. Singh to opt for Mandal. But it hastened the fall of his regime.

II

At 5.30 p.m., on 8 December 1989, the phone rang shrilly in the office of *Kashmir Times*, a newspaper in Srinagar. The Hizbul Mujahideen had kidnapped Rubaiya Sayeed, the daughter of the newly-appointed home minister of India, Mufti Mohammed Sayeed, the voice at the other end of the line told the staffer who picked up the phone. The informant said he belonged to the Jammu and Kashmir Liberation Front (JKLF) seeking 'azadi' for Jammu and Kashmir. Rubaiya would be held hostage till the government released five militants who were in its custody. They were JKLF 'area commander' Sheikh Abdul Hameed, Ghulam Nabi Bhat, the younger brother of the hanged terrorist, Maqbool Bhat, and three others.

The news stunned the government. It decided to release the militants to secure the release of the home minister's daughter. But giving into pressure did nothing for its image.

VP's woes had begun within a week of his taking over. Even before he could settle down as PM, there was Kashmir erupting and the chastened Indian peacekeeping forces were returning from an unsatisfactory operation in Sri Lanka. The situation with Pakistan was tense. 'I did not go to the press or to the cabinet (about it),' VP told me, 'but I did spend time in the operation theatre with the (armed forces) chiefs about what I should do.'

But it was not Kashmir, Sri Lanka, or Pakistan that was to threaten his ministry. His government was bedevilled by the rivalries that characterized the Janata Dal he had put together. The unrest began in Uttar Pradesh, which was VP's 'karmabhoomi', integrally linked to his politics. It was the VP wave which had led to the Janata Dal victory in the state elections in UP in November 1989. The party had been invited to form the government in Lucknow. Mulayam Singh Yadav staked his claim to be chief minister but the senior Janata Dal politician Ajit Singh wanted to contest against him.

'Aap UP ke pachrhe maen mat parho (Don't get entangled in the UP mess),' VP counselled Ajit Singh.

'If Mulayam Singh is not allowed to become CM,' he reasoned, 'the party's break-up will start from tomorrow itself.' And Mulayam Singh Yadav 'could go with the Congress'. VP assured Ajit Singh that his supporters would be appointed as ministers in the UP government. 'I see a bright future for you here at the centre,' VP held out a sop to Ajit Singh. But Ajit Singh contested against Mulayam Singh—and lost. Both Mulayam Singh Yadav and Ajit Singh blamed V. P. Singh for the contest. 'Mulayam Singh believes to this day that VP Singh was behind Ajit,' Som Pal said.' Ajit Singh used to say that it was VP who had initially encouraged him to take on Mulayam Singh Yadav and later got him (Ajit) defeated—when it became clear that Yadav could create problems for VP. The contest deepened the divide inside an already fractious Janata Dal right at the outset.

■

Essentially, three Ms—Meham, Mandal, and Mandir—defined the eleven-month-rule of the V. P. Singh government. 'Mayhem in Meham', the media headlines screamed after the by-election in Meham in Haryana on 27 February 1990. When Devi Lal moved from Haryana to Delhi as the deputy prime minister, he had installed his oldest son, Om Prakash Chautala, as chief minister of the state. He did not consult VP before making the move. Chautala now had to be elected to the state assembly within six months. He decided to contest from Meham in February 1990, a constituency Devi Lal had won in 1987.

With the election, all hell broke loose. It led to incidents which were 'a cross between a horror movie and burlesque theatre'. Chief Minister Chautala allegedly used open intimidation and booth capturing to get the better of his rival, Anand Singh Dangi. Dangi was a rebel Janata Dal leader. In the post-poll violence that rocked Meham, eight people were killed, and this included an independent candidate, Amir Singh. Chautala allegedly led groups of hoodlums through the villages of Meham even as the infamous 'green brigade' of his father, Devi Lal, stuffed ballot boxes and captured booths.Those who stood in Chautala's way, including journalists covering the elections, were badly beaten up. Chautala denied the allegations against him.

On 8 March 1990, the Election Commission countermanded the election. 'The entire election process was vitiated,' the ECI ruled, in a strong indictment of Chautala. There was a public outcry—and demands for Chautala's resignation. Every day, at the daily press briefing held at the Janata Dal headquarters at 7, Jantar Mantar Road, the media grilled Janata Dal spokesperson, Jaipal Reddy. The question remained unchanged— when will Chautala resign? This went on week after week. But Chautala refused to resign.

Finally, on 16 March 1990, VP called a meeting of the Political Affairs Committee of the Janata Dal—to defuse a tense situation which was spinning out of control. Several Janata Dal leaders—Ajit Singh, George Fernandes, Madhu Dandavate, and Nathuram Mirdha—demanded that Chautala step down immediately. Devi Lal was furious. He said he would not put up with these 'riff raff talking about principles', knowing that offence was the best form of defence. 'Who asked Ajit Singh to go to Meham?' he thundered, as soon as the meeting started. Ajit Singh, by now a bitter rival of Devi Lal, had visited Meham and reported back on the widespread violence there. 'I know my being deputy PM is a thorn in the side of many,' he went on aggressively. 'I am resigning right away.' With these words he walked out of the meeting in a huff. The Janata Dal leaders looked at each other nonplussed. They thought that Devi Lal was throwing yet another tantrum. But an hour later he sent in his letter of resignation as deputy prime minister.

Senior Janata Dal leaders rushed to his residence at 29, Willingdon Crescent, to placate him. In the hours that followed, he realized that the response to his resignation had been lukewarm. Devi Lal allowed himself to be 'persuaded' to take back his resignation. But the damage had been done—his shenanigans had further dented the party's image.

Though Devi Lal was less offensive in the cabinet meetings than he was in party fora—he would be mostly silent in the cabinet—there too he had once ticked off Cabinet Secretary Vinod Pande unceremoniously, 'Ae Pande tujhe kya pata hai iske bare maen (Oh Pande, what do you think you know about this)?' He did not spare V. P. Singh either. On one occasion, before the government was formed, he had shouted at an agitated VP, who walked out of the meeting, 'Jaata hai to jaa (Get out, if you want to).' It was Sharad Yadav who had rushed out to bring VP back.

'When Devi Lal first gave in his resignation,' VP was to recall later, 'my first inclination was to accept it.' He then added, rather ruefully, 'Your first instincts are often right. I was trained under Indira Gandhi. It was afterwards that I got the (other) training—panchayat karo (come to some kind of a compromise)—instead of taking a firm stand.'

Given the beating his government's image had taken after Meham, VP considered going in for a mid-term poll. 'In April (after Meham), I wanted to go in for parliamentary elections along with the elections to the assemblies of Bihar and Bengal,' VP said. 'I wanted to go (to the people) on the ground that I did not have a majority. (I) was very clear that (this time) I would gain in the South also.' VP consulted Arun Nehru. Nehru advised him against it. 'He told me the moment it comes up in the cabinet and before I (V. P. Singh) go to Rashtrapati Bhavan, the BJP will immediately withdraw support.' In that case, the president might not order an election. For elections had taken place only a few months earlier. 'He is likely to give the Congress a chance to form the government,' Nehru said. 'It will become counter-productive.' So VP continued to put up with Devi Lal's shenanigans.

■

'Devi Lal was a divine gift to us,' Rajiv Gandhi's aide M. L. Fotedar told me. 'We (had) decided the day VP took oath that he must step down by November 1990.... Even RV (President R. Venkataraman) was privately against VP at the time.'

Meham was the best news that Rajiv Gandhi could have hoped for. It gave him the opportunity to fast forward his decision to topple the National Front government.

Around February–March 1990, unhappiness had started to surface in the Congress Party against Rajiv Gandhi's leadership. Many disaffected Congressmen were now looking at the Janata Dal—and their former colleague, who was now prime minister—with interest. A worried Rajiv called N. K. Sharma—a tantric widely known as Panditji—whom Rajiv would consult from time to time and use for troubleshooting assignments. Sharma had enamoured himself to Rajiv—and was later to worm his way into the P. V. Narasimha Rao durbar. 'Dethrone the VP government,' Sharma advised Rajiv. VP's growing appeal to Congressmen would end, he argued, if he began to look unstable. 'We have to make the government look unattractive.'

In March 1990, Rajiv Gandhi established a direct link with Devi Lal. They were part of a group which went to Jammu and Kashmir on 8 March 1990 to study the situation in the troubled valley. Rajiv's courtiers had by now figured out that Devi Lal was the weakest link in the Janata Dal government. 'Devi Lal had already told me that the PM was not listening to him on issues concerning the farmers,' recalled N. K. Sharma, who knew Devi Lal well.

On 20 May 1990, Rajiv Gandhi sent an SOS to Sharma. It was around midnight. By the time Sharma reached 10, Janpath, it was 1.30 a.m. Rajiv loved these nocturnal hush-hush strategy planning sessions. He had got word that night that the JDPP was to meet the next morning. And that there was a plan afoot to corner and 'humiliate' Devi Lal.

Rajiv Gandhi had heard that the erstwhile Jan Morcha leaders—Arun Nehru, Arif Mohammed Khan, and others who had quit the Congress with VP—would create a 'hungama' at the meeting and demand Chautala's resignation. He had been tipped off by some officers who had remained in touch with Rajiv, and would give him feedback from time to time. Rajiv felt that Devi Lal could turn the tables on his opponents, 'if he takes Chautala's resignation with him to the meeting'.

'We have to talk to Chaudhary sahib (Devi Lal) right now, and pursue the strategy we had devised (to win him over to our side),' Rajiv Gandhi told Sharma.

'At this time of the night?' Sharma was incredulous.

'Tomorrow I will have three people who will be able to talk to him,' Rajiv said. 'You are the only one who can do it now.'

By then it was 2 a.m. Sharma drove to Devi Lal's residence at 29, Willingdon Crescent. Devi Lal was very angry at being woken up. Finally, he agreed to go along with what was being suggested. Sharma went back to 10, Janpath. Rajiv was waiting for him. Sharma told him what had happened.

Devi Lal had asked Sharma to come back to him in the morning. When Sharma arrived at his house at 5.30 a.m., he asked, 'Panditji, will you repeat what you told me last night?' When Sharma did so, Devi Lal asked his staff to call Om (Om Prakash Chautala), and asked him to rush to Delhi immediately. Chautala, however, refused to resign—and Rajiv Gandhi's plan could not be put into motion. But the episode brought Devi Lal closer to Rajiv.

By now, the BJP also joined the ranks of those who were demanding Chautala's resignation. Finally, with pressure mounting on all sides, Chautala quit on 22 May 1990.

All through this period, the distance between Devi Lal and V. P. Singh had grown. By June 1990, they were barely on talking terms. In a sulk, Devi Lal took off to the Jindal Naturecure Institute (JNI), a leading naturopathy hospital outside Bangalore, for treatment. Rajiv Gandhi now had another plan up his sleeve. He spoke to Devi Lal on the phone. When he put down the receiver, he said to Sharma, who was present, 'I don't understand what he says. You go there and talk to him and call me back.' Rajiv asked Sharma to persuade Devi Lal to sign a letter attacking Arun Nehru and Arif Mohammed Khan; it would widen the dissension within the Janata Dal.

'I took with me the draft of a letter. It was against Arun Nehru and Arif, calling for action against them.... This letter was drafted by T. N. Seshan (who had been cabinet secretary to Rajiv Gandhi when he was PM),' N. K. Sharma revealed.

On his arrival at the Jindal Centre, Sharma showed the letter to Devi Lal. 'Devi Lal copied it verbatim on the letterhead of the deputy PM, and signed it. He then addressed the letter to the PM.' The letter was being urgently awaited in Delhi—so that it could be released to the press. But Sharma missed the Bangalore–Delhi flight. Instead, he had to take a flight to Mumbai. 'I was told that somebody would meet me at the Mumbai airport with my boarding card for the connecting flight to Delhi.... As soon as I came down the aircraft stairs, there was a person waiting there with my boarding card.... The person was a very important industrialist.... He personally wanted to see the letter I had brought from Devi Lal.' The industrialist's presence on the tarmac showed that the anti-VP campaign now had the support of powerful entities in the corporate world who were working for his ouster. Sharma landed in Delhi late at night and drove straight to 10, Janpath.

Devi Lal's letter was not released to the press immediately, for some patch-up moves between Devi Lal and VP got underway. With Devi Lal on the warpath, Som Pal decided to go to Bangalore to see if he could tone down the tau. He was accompanied by Ranjit Singh, Devi Lal's younger son, who was at odds with his older brother, Om Prakash Chautala—and was supporting VP. The duo arrived at the Jindal Centre on 26 June 1990. They woke up Devi Lal from his siesta at 4.30 p.m. Ranjit told his father, 'Babuji aapke dushman aapki halat Charan Singh se bhi badtar kar daenge (Your enemies will reduce you to a state worse than that of Charan Singh).'

'VP is neglecting me,' Devi Lal let off a litany of complaints. 'He does not consult me on the appointments of UPSC members, ambassadors, governors.'

'These are very small issues,' Som Pal tried to pacify him. 'They can be sorted out between you and the PM.'

'The likes of Arun Nehru are bent upon sidelining me and VP has fallen in their trap,' he grumbled. They assured him that the PM would address his grievances. Devi Lal was due back in Delhi on 7 July. It was decided that he would meet VP soon after he came back.

On their return to Delhi, Som Pal and Ranjit Singh briefed the PM about Devi Lal's grievances. VP said he would address them. When Devi Lal came back to Delhi, VP immediately invited him to dinner at the PM House on 8 July. Som Pal dropped Devi Lal off at Race Course Road.

The phone rang early the next morning at Som Pal's house. It was Devi Lal. He was elated with what had transpired at the dinner with VP. 'Some people have deliberately created these misunderstandings between us,' he told Som Pal. 'Come and have breakfast with me at 9 and I will tell you about it,' he said enthusiastically.

VP also called Som Pal at 8 a.m. He was curious to find out what

Devi Lal had thought of the dinner. 'Devi Lal phoned this morning and said he was very happy with the dinner,' Som Pal told a pleased VP. Then, unable to overcome his curiosity, Som Pal asked VP, "Did Devi Lal raise the issue of making Chautala chief minister again?"'

'Yes,' VP replied.

Som Pal had warned VP that while Devi Lal was complaining about neglect, 'his ultimate aim is to put Chautala back in the saddle as CM'. Knowing 'Mamaji' as well as he did, Som Pal saw Devi Lal's blistering attack on Arun Nehru and Arif Mohammed Khan as a bargaining chip with V. P. Singh.

'What have you done?' asked an agitated Som Pal who was now really worried. 'This will create complications.' But VP was confident of riding out the crisis.

An hour later Som Pal's misgivings intensified at the breakfast with Devi Lal. The deputy prime minister was suspiciously full of praise for his boss: 'V. P. Singh is a fantastic person. Bahut zordar admi hai (He is a fantastic man). He was so nice. When I raised the Chautala issue,' he said, "Chaudhury sahib Haryana to aapka hai. Janata Dal banane se pehle apne jeeta thaa. Aap aur Haryana ke MLAs jaisa chahen vaisa karen (Chaudhary sahib, Haryana is yours. You had won the state even before the Janata Dal was formed. You and the MLAs of Haryana do what you feel best)".'

Som Pal now knew the situation was headed for a showdown. He pleaded with Devi Lal to wait for a month before making any move to reinstall Chautala. 'Let the dust settle down first,' he said. 'But he started shouting at me.'

'If the government goes,' Som Pal said, also raising his voice, 'the blame will be yours, Mamaji.'

By giving in to Devi Lal's demand to get his son reinstated as Haryana chief minister, VP had hoped to buy peace and time.

Devi Lal did not waste any time reinstalling Chautala as chief minister. On 11 July 1990, he called Som Pal to his office at Krishi Bhavan at 4 p.m. 'When I arrived, he handed me a two-page statement by Banarasi Das Gupta (the man who had replaced Chautala as CM). It said he was resigning as CM of Haryana,' Devi Lal wanted Som Pal to take it to V. P. Singh.

'The prime minister and the deputy PM want me to shift to the centre,' Gupta claimed in the statement. Devi Lal summoned the state legislators to Haryana Bhavan in Delhi. On 12 July 1990, Om Prakash Chautala was re-elected chief minister of Haryana.

■

That day, a worried Arif Mohammed Khan made an overseas call. He told Arun Nehru who was in London that Chautala had been reinstated as

CM. His reinstallation had invited widespread criticism; there was outrage in the Janata Dal and the National Front. Arun Nehru flew back to Delhi the next day—on 13 July. He rushed to the PM House. Chautala's return as CM was disastrous, a livid Nehru told VP—and he must go without delay. From the PM House, Nehru drove to 14, Akbar Road, to meet his colleagues. Arun, Arif, and Satyapal Malik decided to resign from the government; the letter was typed out on an ancient Remington typewriter by a steno hastily requisitioned.

'We had gathered at Arun Nehru's house in the evening,' recalled Satyapal Malik. 'I had gone there around 8.30 p.m. and Arun told me we had to resign.... Ajit Singh was also there. He was also to resign with us.' But later Ajit Singh changed his mind.

Within hours, their letter was leaked to the press. VP called Arun Nehru at 10 p.m.—they were having toast and cheese and coffee when the call came. The PM asked them to come over.

'We went to VP's house around 11 p.m., and told him about our desire to resign from the government,' Satyapal Malik said.

'Agar aap yeh kar rahen hain, toh main bhi yahi karoonga (If you are resigning, I too will put in my papers),' VP replied.

But VP sent in his resignation not to the president of India, but to the Janata Dal president, S. R. Bommai. The government was now teetering on the brink. As Bommai rushed from leader to leader to get their advice on how to tackle this new crisis, six ministers of state and deputy ministers quit within a few hours. Suddenly, neither VP nor Nehru were the issue any more. It was Devi Lal who found himself centre stage again in the next act of the drama as it unfolded. As VP had expected, pressure started to build up from all sides—the regional satraps and the BJP and Left leaders were vociferous in their demand—for VP to take back his resignation, and for Chautala to quit as CM.

Devi Lal struck back. He released the letter he had written earlier—it was dated 15 July 1990, to the PM making serious charges of corruption against Arun Nehru and Arif Khan—which N. K. Sharma had brought to Delhi, and which was in all probability held back because of the patch-up efforts which were underway. The letter created an uproar. Devi Lal added to the tumult by making daily statements about the 'Congress culture' which had vitiated the atmosphere within the Janata Dal. Mediators swung into action again. But this time, their efforts were to no avail.

■

The politically astute V. P. Singh had played his resignation card to turn the tables on his Jan Morcha colleagues, to delink himself from Devi Lal, and to regain his pre-eminent position within the coalition.

He knew he was caught in a pincer movement.

For, by July 1990, Arun Nehru was disillusioned with the government—and vocal about his dissatisfaction: 'It has now become very difficult to remain in this government or to run it.'

While in London, Nehru had revealed what was on his mind to Kuldip Nayar, the Indian high commissioner in the UK: 'VP is a self consuming target. We decided to utilize him. We knew he would destroy Rajiv Gandhi first and in the process he will destroy himself.'

'Kuldip Nayar told me this afterwards,' the senior Janata Dal politician Surendra Mohan said to me. 'In other words, the way would be cleared for Nehru for the top job.'

The move by the Jan Morcha group to go back to the Congress was corroborated by others. 'Arun Nehru had got in touch with Rajiv sometime in May–June 1990,' confirmed Fotedar. 'He (Arun Nehru) was constantly giving Rajiv information (about what was going on in the Janata Dal).' VP was aware that his former colleagues had opened up channels of communication with Rajiv Gandhi—and confirmed this later.

'I had asked VP why the Janata Dal had collapsed so quickly,' the former Congress politician Dinesh Trivedi told me. He was close to Arun Nehru, having quit the Congress and joined the Janata Dal. 'Ask your friends (he was referring to the Jan Morcha leaders),' VP replied cryptically. He then added, 'Arun Nehru and all of them wanted to go back to the Congress.'

'This was in the pre-Mandal (days),' Trivedi told me. Arun Nehru and his group had moved through M. L. Fotedar and Captain Satish Sharma. 'When Rajiv realized that the government could collapse, he hurried (up) the process.'

H. R. Bhardwaj also revealed that Rajiv Gandhi had asked him to rush back from London in June 1990, saying the 'VP government is going'. 'I had the feeling that Rajiv Gandhi was behind the resignations of Arun Nehru and Arif Khan from the VP government in July 1990,' to precipitate a crisis within the Janata Dal, Bhardwaj told me.

'VP used to be wary of Arun Nehru (and what he might do),' K. N. Govindacharya remarked. 'He was not so worried about what Rajiv Gandhi would do.'

■

Besides the wars that were on in the Janata Dal, VP had to confront another storm that was gathering force—the BJP was now getting ready to desert him, if needed. A hush-hush meeting of senior members of the BJP took place in Delhi on 1 July 1990.

'It was a secret meeting where they decided they would hold a Rath Yatra in the country,' Prem Shankar Jha told me. Jha was media advisor to the prime minister at the time. 'The PMO had got this information—that they (BJP) may bring down the government at the end of the Rath Yatra on 30 October 1990, when the kar seva was to be done in Ayodhya.' The party wanted to go back to one of its core issues to expand its footprint in the country—the building of a Ram temple in Ayodhya.

In June 1990, at its meeting in Haridwar, the VHP had already upped the ante and called for kar seva to be held in Ayodhya from 30 October to 2 November to start the construction of a Ram temple. When the VP government took over in December 1989, the VHP had given it six months' time to resolve the issue. Its deadline was up in June 1990.

'When I took over, I had thought that the BJP will take two years before it pulled the plug,' VP told me. Now everything was getting fast forwarded.

VP now knew he had to contend simultaneously with three forces which wanted to corner him—the ambitious Devi Lal backed by Chandra Shekhar; Rajiv Gandhi determined to bring him down by considering even a rapprochement with Arun Nehru and his colleagues; and an offensive mounted by the BJP on an issue which was likely to be emotive.

■

On 1 August 1990, V. P. Singh sacked Devi Lal from his ministry. 'I was in favour of asking him to resign,' VP was to say many years later. 'But Biju Patnaik and Arun Nehru...told me...you have to be tough. Sack him. They knew a sack would make the break irretrievable.' An agitated UP chief minister Mulayam Singh Yadav confronted VP. 'You could have managed it differently,' he said, his voice laced with censure. 'If Devi Lal had been in your cabinet,' VP asked Yadav, 'saying the things he had been saying, what would you have done?' Yadav replied reluctantly, 'I would have dropped him.'

The night before Devi Lal was dropped from the government, Som Pal was with V. P. Singh at his residence. They talked late into the night. 'You should resign tomorrow and then call for a mid-term election,' Som Pal told VP, 'there is no need to go in for Mandal.' Som Pal knew VP was contemplating implementing the report. Surendra Mohan had also advised VP to go in for a mid-term election. 'You have been a leader of consensus, and that image will remain. And you will live to fight another day.'

Som Pal warned VP: 'If you go in for Mandal, it will be others, not you, who will benefit from it.' Recounting that conversation to me, Som Pal said, 'VP was under the impression that Mandal would divide every party, including the Congress, right down the middle along Other Backward Classes (OBCs) and non OBC lines and it would help him politically.'

History was to prove Som Pal right. But, in July 1990, VP did not want his government to go. Nor did he want an early election.

■

Paradoxically, V. P. Singh had not always been for Mandal. 'I had (once) asked him about his views on reservations,' Dinesh Trivedi recalled. Even as late as 1987–88, VP was of a different view. "Even if you have 100 per cent reservation, it won't make a dent," VP had replied. "How many people will get jobs? Where are the jobs?" In those days, he did not talk about reservations. He would talk about increasing jobs in the market.'

The Janata Dal's 1989 election manifesto included Mandal as one of its promises. The OBC MPs of the party, especially those from UP and Bihar, who were a significant proportion of Janata Dal MPs, were for Mandal. It was just a matter of when it would be implemented.

With the war in the ruling Janata Dal now out in the open, VP knew that if he had to save his government, he had to push back with something big. With Devi Lal's exit, the stage was now set for Mandal— the implementation of the recommendations of the Mandal Commission Report, which advocated 27 per cent reservations for the socially and educationally backward classes in central government jobs.

'Mandal was the realization of the Janata Dal politically,' VP was to say of his decision years later.

III

The secure RAX phone in Sharad Yadav's bedroom rang late at night. The minister for Textiles and Food Processing looked at his wristwatch. It was well after 10 p.m.—and the date 1 August 1990. He would remember the time and the date long afterwards. Yadav picked up the receiver. It was the prime minister on the other end. V. P. Singh came to the point quickly, 'Sharad bhai, ab toh Devi Lalji ke saath kaam karna mushkil ho gaya hai (Brother Sharad, it has now become very difficult to work with Devi Lal).' Alarmed, and sensing trouble, Yadav shot back immediately, 'Nikalna mat (Don't throw him out). I will go and see him tomorrow and see what I can do. After that, I will come and talk to you.'

VP replied sagely, 'Hum tho, Sharad bhai, nikaal chuke hain (Brother Sharad, I have already sacked him).' The normally unflappable Sharad Yadav was taken aback. Yadav used to pride himself on managing contradictions others could not handle. 'Yeh aapne kya kiya (What have you done)?' While VP was explaining why it had become untenable for Devi Lal to continue, Yadav's mind began to work furiously. He was quick to realize that his own position in the Janata Dal could be weakened without Devi Lal around. The battle within the party had escalated between Arun Nehru, Arif Mohammad Khan, Satyapal Malik, and others who had come with V. P. Singh from the Congress and Devi Lal and others who represented the Lohia stream of socialists and pro-farmer MPs in the Janata Dal. Yadav belonged to the second group.

The conflict was not just between differing ideologies and personalities jostling for position. It was also between two different styles of functioning. The erstwhile Congressmen were used to working under a single leader and falling in line once fiats were issued to resolve a conflict. The socialists were more anarchic in the way they operated. Each one considered himself the leader. Their ego clashes had brought down the first non-Congress government at the centre in 1979, halfway through its term. Earlier, their individualistic agendas had played havoc with the non-Congress governments which had come to power in 1967 in the north Indian states.

That night, on the phone, VP made an offer to Sharad Yadav. It was couched in courteous words, 'Jo Devi Lalji ki sthiti thee woh ab aapki rahegi (You will enjoy the same standing now as Devi Lal had).'

Sharad Yadav was sharp enough to realize that the PM had sensed his fears. Since the government was formed, VP had not given Yadav his due. Even though Yadav saw himself as one of the senior leaders in the Janata Dal, VP had kept him out of the powerful Political Affairs Committee. Nor had he been given a weighty ministry; instead, he was relegated to the less important food processing and textiles departments. But a sullen Sharad Yadav had kept his counsel—waiting for the right moment to arrive when he could strike back.

That night, he did not ask the PM to elaborate on what he implied by 'Devi Lalji ki sthiti (standing)'. He would find out soon enough though, in the weeks that followed—VP was to strengthen Yadav's position in the government and make him a part of the Political Affairs Committee.

Clearly, the PM was out to drum up support for himself. He wanted Sharad Yadav's backing. Suddenly, VP ended the conversation. 'It's quite late, Sharad bhai, I will call you in the morning.'

As he was talking to the PM, a plan was taking shape in Sharad Yadav's mind. This was an opportunity he could not let go of. He put the phone down, deep in thought. His hand reached out for the bell by his side, and he asked for a fresh paan to be brought for him. Reclining against the long, rounded cushions on the settee in his sitting room, he began to put the plan into place. It revolved around the Mandal Commission Report; the Janata Dal manifesto had promised that it would be implemented. From time to time, there would be demands at party meetings for its implementation. As the minutes ticked away that night, Sharad Yadav decided that if the PM enforced the Mandal Commission Report, he would stay by his side. He would then be able to emerge as a leader of the OBCs, championing their rights. If not, he would remain with Devi Lal. Having made that decision, he started calling up prominent OBC leaders, many of them his protégés—Nitish Kumar, Mulayam Singh Yadav, Lalu Yadav—and told them what he had decided.

The next morning, the RAX phone rang early. It was the PM again.

'Can you come over for breakfast at seven?' Sharad Yadav agreed readily. By now, he knew what he had to do. The moment he sat down with the PM for breakfast at Race Course Road, Sharad Yadav lost no time setting about convincing VP why he should go in for 'Mandal' immediately. Their meeting lasted 'for two hours'.

'The previous night I had not mentioned the word Mandal, thinking that the PM may not like the idea,' Yadav recounted later. Soon after the National Front government came to power, the prime minister had appointed Devi Lal as chairman of the committee to look into the implementation of the Mandal Commission Report. 'This had been signal enough for me that the PM was in no hurry to bring in Mandal,' Sharad Yadav revealed. 'For I knew Devi Lal was not for it, because Jats were not included in the list. And I used to have fights with Devi Lal on (the implementation of) Mandal.'

Devi Lal's views on Mandal were no secret. Soon after the National Front government came to power, he had made a statement, in mid-December 1989, that reservations should be on the basis of 'economic' and 'educational' criteria, and not use a social (in other words, caste) yardstick.

He had made these remarks in the context of extending reservations to the Scheduled Castes (SCs) and Scheduled Tribes (STs) which were coming up for renewal. This aroused the ire of the SCs and STs. It had also angered the Mandalites in the party. They accused Devi Lal of taking a position at variance with the Constitution. For Article 15(4) provided for reservations only on the basis of 'social and educational'—and not economic—backwardness. Angered by Devi Lal's comments, Ram Pujan Patel, a prominent Kurmi leader from UP, who later joined VP's cabinet, shot off a letter to the prime minister. He accused Devi Lal of being 'against the Constitution, the Mandal Commission, and the Janata Dal manifesto'. 'Devi Lal can hardly be expected to do anything for the backward classes,' he wrote angrily, 'when he is openly talking about...economic criteria for Dalits.' Nevertheless, the prime minister—who wanted to keep all options open—continued to retain Devi Lal as the chair of the committee.

But, now that Devi Lal had been fired from the cabinet, Sharad Yadav decided to step up the pressure on VP to implement the Mandal Commission Report immediately.

At 9.30 a.m., VP rose from the breakfast table. As the PM was leaving, Yadav delivered his parting shot. 'You should announce the decision to implement the Mandal Commission Report before 9 August.' That was the day Devi Lal planned to hold a massive rally at the Boat Club. Yadav feared—and the PM knew this—that Devi Lal could demand the implementation of the Mandal Report at the public meeting to create problems for VP. It could make him a pied piper for the OBC MPs in the Janata Dal, and enamour him to the backward classes all over North

India. This would divide the Janata Dal right down the middle—and sound the death knell of the VP government.

VP heard Yadav out. But he did not say much. For he had already set in motion steps to implement the Mandal Report. He had called a meeting of the National Front Parliamentary Party that very day; it was to be held in the Central Hall of Parliament. The ostensible reason for it was to discuss Devi Lal's sacking. But he knew Mandal would come up for discussion, as it did in most party meetings. He had already alerted a couple of MPs. They were to ensure that the issue was raised. Once it came up, it would acquire its own momentum.

Like Indira Gandhi, VP also believed in laying out his chessboard. He would then wait for his opponent to make the first move—before making his counter-move and then a sustained attack to checkmate the adversary. Now, he was carefully setting the stage for Mandal.

■

As the forces began to mass against him by July 1990, VP knew he would have to push back quickly. Given the contradictions that beset his coalition, he would have to be ready if an early election was sprung on him. He had been the darling of the middle classes because of his crusade against corruption and his promise of a clean government. But they were becoming disenchanted with the open wrangling in the Janata Dal. He had learnt, years ago, from Indira Gandhi, that it was important to get the support of the poorer sections, not the middle class, in order to win elections. 'For long term survival,' VP would say, 'it is the poor who give stability, whichever the party.' He now needed to acquire a mass base, not just a following amongst the middle classes and the intelligentsia, if he had to take on both the Congress and the BJP in the next round.

As expected—and scripted—the MPs raised the demand for Mandal at the 2 August 1990 meeting of the National Front Parliamentary Party. VP had come prepared. He told them that he had already put fourteen joint secretaries of central ministries on the job. They would identify discrepancies in the backward class lists classified by Mandal and those with the states. At the time, twelve out of twenty-five states already had quotas for the OBCs. VP went into great detail to explain why he had undertaken the exercise. For example, he explained, in UP, a Mallah was a backward caste, but in Delhi a Mallah was a scheduled caste. A Bania (trader) was a backward in Bihar but not so in the rest of North India. A Kurmi was considered a 'backward' in UP, Madhya Pradesh, and Bihar. So also in Maharashtra, where Kurmis were known as Kunbis. But this was not the case in Gujarat. It was social and educational factors, and not caste alone, which determined backwardness, he said. 'The idea,' he told the assembled group, 'is to remove these discrepancies.'

But the MPs were in no mood for data or explanations. 'We should not hold up the announcement. The discrepancies can be dealt with later,' many said. Around two dozen MPs spoke at the meeting. Most demanded that the Mandal Report be implemented right away. Echoing the views of Sharad Yadav, some warned that if Mandal was not enforced immediately, Devi Lal would hijack the issue at his 9 August rally and put the government on the mat. The MPs were worried that a showdown with Devi Lal would bring on an early election.

They were also quick to point out that the Mandal Report could be implemented through a simple gazette notification. 'No legislation is required to do this,' explained Rajya Sabha member Satya Prakash Malaviya.

Then, Hukum Narayan Yadav, an OBC MP who belonged to the Chandra Shekhar camp, got up. Taking a personal swipe at the prime minister, he taunted VP, 'As long as a savarna (upper caste) is a prime minister, the Mandal Report will never be implemented.'

A stung VP reacted sharply, 'OK, let us decide right now the date when we should bring it.'

'We should announce it on the first day of the parliament session,' suggested some. Parliament was to start on 7 August 1990. VP agreed instantly.

VP had already pulled out the Mandal Report, forgotten for ten years in a dusty almirah of the Government of India—and made up his mind to adopt it. All he wanted was an endorsement from the MPs. He got the formal go-ahead from them on 2 August 1990.

IV

It was ten years earlier that Bindeshwari Prasad Mandal had asked to meet Giani Zail Singh urgently. Then the home minister, Zail Singh was not really surprised. He guessed that Mandal wanted to present his report on reservations for the OBCs. For Zail Singh, it was yet another report which would gather dust. But he told his secretary to make sure that the 'official' dealing with the 'backward issue' was present at the meeting. B. G. Deshmukh was the officer who had overseen everything to do with the Mandal Commission from the time it was set up on 1 January 1979.

When B. P. Mandal arrived in North Block, which housed the Home Ministry, there were very few people around. As it was the last day of 1980, much of North Block was deserted, and the usual bustle of government offices was absent.

Mandal was accompanied by a couple of his colleagues, including the commission's member secretary, S. S. Gill. It was an icy cold winter day in Delhi. The delegation was ushered into the home minister's spacious office. Zail Singh got up and shook hands with each one of them. He motioned to B. P. Mandal to sit in the chair across from him. Mandal did not waste any time with the usual pleasantries. Without any preamble, he handed over the report to Zail Singh. The home minister did not look at it, nor did he ask any questions about the report. Soon, the smartly clad waiters in North Block brought in tea and biscuits for the guests. Tea was served in white bone china cups laid out on a starched white tray cloth, a ceremonial remnant from British days. The tea over, and sensing that the appointment with the minister was coming to an end, Mandal got up and shook hands with Zail Singh again. The others in the group did likewise. All of them trooped out of the home minister's office in what had been an anti-climactic end to almost two years of work.

As they descended the wide red sandstone steps of North Block, B. P. Mandal turned to Gill, and said in a voice laced with scepticism, 'Saab, aap ne report par bahut mehnat ki hai. Par aaj hum iskaa visarjan kar aaye hain (You have worked very hard on the report but today we have performed its final immersion ceremony).' When he had handed over the report to the home minister, B. P. Mandal was sure no action would be taken on its recommendations. He turned out to be right; for ten years there was no move to implement it. Little did Mandal know that one day he would become a household name—and the subject of animated discussion all over India. And his report, one of the most controversial documents in independent India, would haunt Indian politics for decades afterwards.

■

B. P. Mandal had got into top gear to finish the report as soon as Indira Gandhi came back to power in January 1980. 'The government has changed,' he warned his colleagues. 'This government won't have the same commitment to the idea (of reservations for the OBCs).' Till then, he had taken his own time over it. When Morarji Desai had commissioned Mandal to prepare the report, he had been in no hurry to complete it. He remained laid back when Chaudhary Charan Singh took over from Morarji Desai as PM for five months. It was only in 1980 that he quickly finished the report—and lost no time in submitting it to the government.

The report was essentially written by member secretary S. S. Gill. 'Every word of the report was written by me,' Gill said. 'B. P. Mandal was a nice man...(but) he was basically interested in getting his MoS status (as chairman of the Second Backward Classes Commission).' B. P. Mandal had been given the ranking of a minister of state in the central government.

To Gill, an urban Punjabi who had little idea of the caste system in India, it had been 'an education' to learn about the social structure in the country's heartland. 'That was when my interest in sociology started and I took it very seriously.' The Mandal Report is probably the only government report which became a bestseller—after VP announced its adoption. There was such a flurry of interest in it, Gill said, that a reprint had to be ordered of an otherwise dull document. Yet, according to its unacknowledged co-author, 'those who implemented it had not read the report'. 'But,' Gill said, 'if you don't understand caste you can't really understand...its ramifications.'

The Mandal Report relied on caste as a yardstick for determining backwardness, though it was not the only criterion it used. It also used lack of education and economic deprivation as benchmarks. But, in the final analysis, it relied more on 'social backwardness' (in other words discrimination on the basis of caste) to identify the backward classes.

Gill would write a chapter at a time and send the draft to members of the commission for their comments. The members were mainly interested in ensuring that the maximum possible reservation was given to the OBCs. The SCs/STs already had 22.5 per cent reservations in jobs and in legislatures, provided for by the Constitution—this was in proportion to their population because of the level of their deprivation.

Gill told members of the commission that they could not expect 'more than 27 per cent reservation' for the OBCs. He came to that figure by halving the percentage of the total OBC population in the country, which was estimated to be 52 per cent based on the 1931 census. 'That meant 26 per cent.' But members of the commission kept demanding the 'maximum possible reservation'. 'The figure,' Gill said, 'was finally fixed at 27 per cent. The idea was to give it a rational basis.'

Gill was also constrained by a 1963 Supreme Court judgment—and referred to it in the report. The apex court had ruled in the *M. R. Balaji vs State of Mysore* case that reservations had to be 'capped at 50 per cent'. Since the Scheduled Castes were given 15 per cent reservations and the Scheduled Tribes allocated 7 per cent, the OBC quota, to be safe, had to be fixed at 27 per cent.

•

A quick look now at the story of reservations in India—to understand why V. P. Singh became the messiah of an idea that had been around since Independence—and led to the Mandal Commission Report (which over time was shortened to 'Mandal' which became part of the country's political lexicon).

After India gained independence, the Constitution banned untouchability and discrimination on the basis of caste, sex, religion, race, or place of birth (Article 15). It also provided for group rights by way of affirmative action (Article 15(4)), stipulating that special provisions (reservations) could be made for 'socially and educationally backward classes' (SEBCs) of citizens. Or for the Scheduled Castes (SCs) and Scheduled Tribes (STs). (The officially designated SCs and STs are Dalits and indigenous tribals, and are among the most disadvantaged groups in India.) In addition, the Constituent Assembly added Article 340 to specifically provide for a commission to be set up to improve the conditions of backward classes.

Just to provide context, even at the risk of oversimplifying a complex subject, the caste system that inheres among Hindus has been defined as the hierarchical order that came into being over centuries and structured Hindu society into four groupings or varnas—the Brahmins who were priests, intellectuals, and officials; the Kshatriyas, warriors and rulers; the Vaishyas who were traders; and the Shudras who comprised the large bulk of lower castes who were workers and service providers. A fifth group of people were excluded from the caste system; they were deemed 'untouchables', shunned for centuries, and compelled to do menial work by the so-called higher castes. After Independence, untouchability was banned and those belonging to this group would come to be known as Dalits.

In modern times, social reform, education, urbanization, increasing affluence, migration, and inter-caste marriages, especially in urban India, dented the inflexible hold of the caste system. But, at another level, with the onset of democracy, as political parties used caste as a tool to mobilize distinct groups to support them, its hold became even more unyielding. In earlier years, lower castes would hide their caste by adopting surnames which were used by upper-caste families. Now it is not uncommon for people to flaunt their lower-caste identity—or even pretend to belong to the lower castes—to get the economic and political benefits that accrue from a policy of reservations for these marginal communities. This trend was to gain momentum after the acceptance of Mandal. While Mandal divided society, it also became an equalizer.

•

After Independence, the ruling Congress relied on the support of the upper castes, who had been dominant in the freedom movement. Though small in number, they were able to come to power because the other groups were fragmented. In fact, in the early years of the Indian republic, most state governments were led by Brahmin chief ministers.

This began to change in the mid-1960s, with the rise of the peasant and middle castes. The abolition of the zamindari system in 1951, land reforms over a period of two decades (1950–72), and the Green Revolution in the 1960s to increase food production had improved the financial conditions of some of the dominant backward classes like the Yadavs, Kurmis, and Koeris. As they became prosperous, they wanted a greater share in the power structure. In the 1967 state elections, the Congress lost in nine states in North India and the governments which took charge were headed by non-Brahmin chief ministers—a sign of the devolution of power that was taking place. These governments were underpinned by the OBCs and intermediate castes (such as the Jats) which supported non-Congress parties like the Bharatiya Lok Dal led by kisan leader Charan Singh.

While caste was all along a factor in voter choices, it was not talked about so openly in the years after Independence. India's first prime minister, Jawaharlal Nehru, himself a Kashmiri Brahmin, was opposed to using religion and caste in politics. 'I don't think Nehru really understood caste,' S. S. Gill said.

With one person one vote becoming a reality, the lower castes began to realize the importance of their numbers—and demand a bigger say in the decision-making processes.

In the early 1950s, backward class leaders approached Prime Minister Nehru for reservations in government jobs. He set up the First Backward Class Commission on 29 January 1953 to look into the conditions of the Socially and Economically Backward Classes (SEBCs). It was headed by Dattatraya Balakrishna Kalelkar, a freedom fighter and social reformer, popularly known as Kaka Saheb Kalelkar. He submitted his report to the government at the beginning of 1955. He listed 2,399 castes as backward, entitled for help, and recommended that anything between 25–40 per cent of jobs be reserved for them in central government services.

When the Kalelkar Report came out, Punjala Shiv Shankar and two other OBC leaders from Andhra Pradesh went to meet Nehru. Nehru was popularly called Panditji—the title connoted his caste—even though he was dismissive of caste. They met him at Teen Murti House to press for the implementation of the report. 'We got the impression that he wanted to implement it (the Kalelkar Report), but he did not say so directly,' recalled Shiv Shankar, a staunch advocate of reservations for over four decades. Nehru heard them out. At the end, he told them, 'Aap home minister se mil leejiye (You go and meet the home minister).'

Govind Ballabh Pant was the home minister. 'We went to see Pantji in his office. There were three of us—I, Bujjan Narsimloo, who was a Congress corporator from Hyderabad, and Gouthu Latchanna, MLA, who had been a minister in Andhra Pradesh in 1953.... (But) we came away with the feeling that Pantji had reservations and wanted the report to be shelved.... But, again, (like Nehru), he did not say so directly.'

Pant felt that the implementation of the Kalelkar Report would divide Indian society. As it turned out, the report was neither tabled in parliament nor discussed. Interestingly, even though the report's author, Kalelkar, was sympathetic towards the downtrodden, he had opposed caste as a criterion to determine backwardness. Since there was no unanimity on the report, the government found it easier to ignore it. In 1961, however, it decided it would leave it to state governments to decide who would qualify for reservation. But it ruled out reservations for OBCs in the central government.

The state governments set up their own commissions. In the years that followed, fifteen such commissions were set up. The southern states—Tamil Nadu, Andhra Pradesh, Kerala, Karnataka—led the way. The states fixed their own quotas. While Karnataka went in for 50 per cent reservations, Punjab opted for 5 per cent.

When the Janata Party was formed in 1977, it promised to implement the Kalelkar Commission Report in its manifesto. But once the party came to power, as often happens, it took no action. However, the situation hotted up when the Janata Party chief minister of Bihar, Karpoori Thakur, a socialist, decided in March 1978 to go in for reservations for the OBCs. He decided to implement the recommendations of the Mungeri Lal Commission in Bihar to reserve 26 per cent government jobs for the OBCs. It was in 1959 that socialist icon Ram Manohar Lohia had first flagged the idea of reserving 60 per cent of government jobs for OBCs at the third national conference of the Socialist Party. In 1978, Karpoori Thakur coined the slogan, 'Sasopa ne bandhi gaanth, pichde paanve sau maen saath (The SSP has made a resolve that the backwards will get representation of 60 out of 100)'—which was to reverberate in the Hindi heartland for years afterwards.

Karpoori Thakur had hoped that his reservation move would help him consolidate his hold on the fractious Janata Party government. Instead, his problems multiplied. The decision triggered off widespread violence in the state. The upper castes retaliated in protest. The national leadership set up a committee to go into the matter, committees being a tried and tested way to defuse tensions. Finally, a compromise was evolved. Karpoori Thakur agreed to modify his policy. He decided to give 3 per cent reservations to women of all castes and another 3 per cent to the poor of all castes. This effectively reduced the quantum of OBC reservations to 20 per cent. He also decided to keep the creamy layer amongst the OBCs—those whose income was more than ₹1,000 every month—out of the ambit of the decision. This had the pro-reservationists up in arms and divided the Janata Party right down the middle. The erstwhile Congress (O) and Jan Sangh faction in the Janata Party, which had a following amongst the upper castes, opposed Thakur's move. The BLD led by Charan Singh and socialists, who derived their support from the OBCs, supported the decision. Interestingly enough, Jayaprakash Narayan wanted reservations to be based only on economic and not on social criteria.

Reservations became such a combustible issue that Prime Minister Morarji Desai decided to set up a new commission to look into the matter. The Second Backward Class Commission, as it was called, was set up on 1 January 1979, and notified on 1 February 1979. Desai appointed a former chief minister of Bihar, Bindeshwari Prasad Mandal, to head it; soon enough, it came to be known as the Mandal Commission. Desai wanted to retain the support of the OBC MPs, who were becoming increasingly restive, buy time for his beleaguered government, and keep his challenger, Charan Singh, in check. As we saw in Chapter 1, an assertive Charan Singh had mounted a formidable challenge to Desai's leadership in the second half of 1978.

■

Once the Mandal Report was submitted to Indira Gandhi's government on 31 December 1980, the Opposition demanded that it be tabled in parliament. The Janata Party was in the Opposition now. Charan Singh led the attack on the government. Facing him was Law Minister Shiv Shankar, an OBC (Kapu) himself who, like Charan Singh, had been an avowed advocate of reservations for the OBCs. 'I once went to Charan Singh for some work when he was home minister,' Shiv Shankar told me. 'He immediately told his officials, "Kaam kar doh, hai toh backward (Do what he wants done, after all, he is a backward)!"' (When B. P. Mandal was finalizing his report, it was Shiv Shankar who had quietly advised the commission not to adopt economic criteria as a basis for reservations.)

As the Opposition voices became louder for the report's implementation, Indira Gandhi decided to call a meeting of the Political Affairs Committee to take a view on it. Present at the meeting were P. V. Narasimha Rao, Kamalapati Tripathi, R. Venkataraman, Pranab Mukherjee, and Zail Singh. Except Zail Singh (to whom the report had been submitted by B. P. Mandal), all the others opposed the report's implementation. They criticized it for relying on caste as a basis for identifying backwardness.

Indira Gandhi seemed undecided. Though she had come back to power because of a Hindu, upper-caste consolidation in her favour—it had also been a backlash against the 'backward' caste politics of the Janata Party—she also knew she could not annoy the backward classes.

She called Shiv Shankar to her office. 'Shiv Shankarji, kya karaen (What shall we do)?' she asked him. Shiv Shankar was silent for a few moments. He was aware of her dilemma. He decided to be candid. 'You can't turn this down easily,' he said. 'This is a matter involving 52 per cent of the population. You will have to place it before the house. But even before tabling it, you will have to be clear on what the ATR (Action Taken Report) should say.' Indira Gandhi was thoughtful. Then, choosing her words carefully, like the skilled politician she was, she said, 'Aisa ATR likhiye ki saamp bhi mar jaye aur laathi bhi naa toote (Please draft the ATR in such a way that it kills the snake but does not break the stick with which it is killed).' Shiv Shankar prepared the draft of the ATR. He took it across to her. Indira glanced through it. She looked pleased, but did not say anything. The draft stated that while the government accepted, 'in principle' the recommendations of the Mandal Commission Report, it was appointing a 'ministerial committee to go into all its implications'. It also decided to constitute an officials' committee to examine its findings.

Indira Gandhi then looked at Shiv Shankar, 'Who will head the committee of ministers?' Without waiting for his answer, she asked him if he would be willing to chair it. He agreed. But she encountered resistance from within the Political Affairs Committee. It came 'from four of the Brahmin members,' Shiv Shankar recalled. 'They were P. V. Narasimha Rao, Pranab Mukherjee, R. Venkataraman, and Kamalapati Tripathi.' She decided to put off the decision. Nothing happened for a few months. Then, one day, she appointed Rao chairman of the committee, taking the line of least resistance.

Rao was a master of indecision. If he was opposed to something, he prevaricated and put off the decision. The committee, of which Shiv Shankar was also a member, would faithfully meet twice a year. But nothing came of these meetings.

'Shiv Shankarji, what's going on in the committee?' Indira would politely ask him from time to time. He would not have much to report. 'When I would force an issue in the committee,' Shiv Shankar recalled, 'Narasimha Rao would turn to the officials present, and instruct them, "Acha, iski implications study kariye (Please study the implications of what has been suggested)".' The officials would spend the next one year 'studying' the implications. And so it went on.

For all practical purposes, Indira Gandhi had put OBC reservations on the back-burner. The committee outlived her—and was in existence until 1989, five years after she was killed. But it took no decision on the report. Indira had viewed the Mandal recommendations as one of the arrows in her quiver she might use at a later date. She knew, more than most, the significance of the emerging 'backward' politics in the country—in her case, it had prevented the Congress from being wiped out in the southern states in 1977. Moreover, when she was on the comeback trail during 1977–80, she had been careful not to alienate the OBCs in the South. It had paid her handsome dividends.

The backward classes movement had started in the South even before Independence—and she was familiar with this history. The South had gone in for reservations long before the northern states did so—in Mysore, for instance, the maharaja had gone in for reservations as far back as 1921. Devaraj Urs, the chief minister of Karnataka in 1977, a backward class leader belonging to the Asaru community, had successfully crafted an OBC–SC–ST axis, which had catapulted the Congress to power in Karnataka in the 1977 elections, notching up 26 out of 28 Lok Sabha seats, even as the party was wiped out all over North India. It was Urs who had suggested to Indira Gandhi that she contest from the lush green, coffee-plantation-dotted constituency of Chikmagalur in the 1978 by-election. She won the by-poll handsomely. There was no stopping her after that—and she bounced back to power in 1980.

■

Rajiv Gandhi, who succeeded Indira Gandhi, was not in favour of reservations. Coming as he did from an urban, Westernized, well-to-do background, he was opposed to Mandal. To him, it underscored the feudal and caste divisions in Indian society. Rajiv felt that 'other steps' should be taken to improve the lot of the backward classes. 'The Mandal Commission Report is a can of worms,' he told his aides dismissively, 'and I am not going to open it.' He had also shot down the proposal to go for reservations for OBCs in panchayati raj institutions, even though he was told that it would benefit the party electorally.

Though the Congress had gained from reservations for OBCs in the southern states, Rajiv still spoke critically of them. A month after V. P. Singh's decision on Mandal, Rajiv denounced the decision in no uncertain terms. He was speaking in parliament on 6 September 1990 as the leader of the Opposition. He spoke for two and half hours—in the longest ever speech delivered in the Lok Sabha. 'Ministers are provoking caste wars,' Rajiv Gandhi declaimed passionately.

V

The massive wooden door creaked loudly as the prime minister walked into the room for the cabinet meeting. His colleagues, who were waiting for him restlessly, looked up expectantly. The cabinet meeting had been called to discuss Mandal, but many of them did not know this. It was 6 August 1990, a hot and muggy day in Delhi, long to be remembered—and cited—afterwards.

V. P. Singh was dressed in an immaculately starched white kurta–pyjama. His attire normally indicated the role he saw for himself at that particular moment. When he donned his sherwani and winter cap, the head of government, the chief administrator, was on display. It would also signal a 'secular' VP, party leaders would joke. When he dressed in a white kurta–pyjama, the politician in him came to the fore.

The ministers had trickled in for the meeting earlier in the afternoon. Alighting from their cars outside South Block, which housed the PMO, they walked in and took the lift up to the room on the first floor where cabinet meetings were normally held. The officials had already taken their seats by the time the ministers began to arrive. B. G. Deshmukh, the principal secretary to the prime minister, sat next to Vinod Pande, the cabinet secretary. Pande, a bachelor from Allahabad, was also a novelist and had shared VP's father and older brother's interest in astrology. He had predicted that VP would become prime minister one day. This was when VP was finance minister and Pande, the revenue secretary under him (from 1985–87). VP trusted him and had brought him in to head the civil service. When he was inducted as 'Cab Sec', many were apprehensive about what Pande, though an upright officer, might do, given his reputation as a maverick. But they knew that he was VP's man and his word could not be disregarded.

B. G. Deshmukh had been principal secretary to Rajiv Gandhi when he was prime minister. Normally, when there was a change of government in Delhi, there was also a change of the top officials. Each PM wanted to have his own team, though the bureaucracy in India is supposed to be apolitical. Deshmukh had offered to resign soon after VP was sworn in. But the new prime minister asked him to continue. By retaining him, VP, who knew the ropes of administration well enough, having been a minister in the commerce, finance, and defence departments in the Congress governments of Indira Gandhi and Rajiv Gandhi, wanted to send a message to the bureaucracy that he was not going to be vindictive.

VP's cabinet meetings were usually informal. Ministers and officials felt free to speak up. As he himself once put it, in an uncharacteristic moment of candour, 'I never had problems in my cabinet. It was the party which proved to be my undoing.'

On this day, the prime minister came straight to the point. He took his seat and began without wasting time on niceties, 'We will first discuss the implementation of the Mandal Commission Report.' There was consternation on Deshmukh's face. This was new to him. This had not been part of the agenda. And bureaucrats do not like being taken by surprise. The PMO was clearly not in the loop, and had had no warning of this. Though VP's PMO was not as powerful as Rajiv Gandhi's or Indira Gandhi's, the PMO was not usually ignored and decisions were normally routed through it.

Deshmukh looked at Vinod Pande enquiringly. Pande looked visibly unhappy. He looked down but the expression on his face showed that he had an inkling of what was going on. Deshmukh decided he would voice his objection. He turned to the PM and said flatly that he 'had no notice' that this was the subject the PM wanted discussed. He needed 'time to collect the material and prepare a note', he said. The PM showed signs of impatience with his principal secretary. A note by the PMO, which Deshmukh wanted to prepare, was clearly a bureaucratic ploy to buy time. Deshmukh was taken aback when the normally courteous V. P. Singh brushed aside his request, rather brusquely.

VP turned to Ram Vilas Paswan instead. He asked his minister for Social Welfare to go ahead and make his presentation. A socialist in his early years, Paswan was an avowed supporter of Mandal. VP had decided not to work through his most senior bureaucrat. He did not want to risk last minute bureaucratic delays. Instead, he had given the go-ahead to Paswan to get the paperwork ready for the cabinet meeting. The work was done essentially by the Ministry of Social Welfare, and its secretary, P. S. Krishna.

'I had called Ram Vilas Paswan and told him that irrespective of the (party) committee (that had been set up to take a view on Mandal), you process it departmentally and bring it before the cabinet,' VP said to me. Paswan had walked into the room with a bundle of papers. As he warmed up, Paswan made a case for the implementation of the Mandal Commission Report. It was a promise made in the Janata Dal's manifesto. The time, he said, had come to redeem the pledge. He spoke for around ten minutes. When he had finished, VP turned to Sharad Yadav, and asked him to say a few words. Yadav also spoke in favour of the proposal. After Yadav had finished speaking, VP looked around the room and asked if any of his other colleagues wanted to express a view. Ajit Singh, minister for Industries, was for going ahead, provided Jats were included in the Mandal list. Mufti Mohammed Sayeed, India's first Muslim home minister—from Jammu and Kashmir—pleaded for more time. The decision could lead to a serious law and order problem in some parts of the country. He wanted time to alert the paramilitary forces in case they were needed.

Two people had expressed themselves clearly against the proposal. They were Arun Nehru, minister for Commerce, and Chimanbhai Mehta, minister of state for Education with independent charge, who was from Gujarat. 'Is sae duvidha hogi (This will create a dilemma),' Chimanbhai Mehta cautioned the prime minister. He reminded VP of the wide-scale riots, arson, and killings that had taken place in Gujarat in 1985. The unrest had been sparked off by anti-reservationists protesting the hiking of the OBC quota from 10 per cent to 28 per cent in technical and medical colleges. It had brought down the government of Madhavsinh Solanki in 1985. In his measured manner, Mehta pleaded, 'Sir, don't do it. We did it in Gujarat. It will create many problems.'

Arun Nehru was not present at the cabinet meeting but had attended the Cabinet Committee on Political Affairs a day earlier. 'Vishwanath, politics is not arithmetic,' he had told the prime minister. 'We should think very seriously before doing it.' Nehru's absence at the cabinet meeting showed that while he was opposed to the move, he did not want to be seen to be openly confronting the PM.

Then the cabinet secretary, Vinod Pande, spoke up. He made a case for reservations to be given to the economically weaker sections. That, he said, should take place on the same lines as was done by Karpoori Thakur in Bihar in 1978. Pande also reminded the meeting about the large-scale violence reservations had led to in the state. Pande was known to have the ear of the prime minister. But, on this occasion, VP wasn't listening to him. In desperation, an unhappy Pande looked to Finance Minister Madhu Dandavate for help. Pande and Deepak Nayyar, who was chief economic advisor to the VP government, had discussed the matter with Dandavate a day earlier. They had asked him to persuade the prime minister to desist from making the move. They thought they had convinced him. But Dandavate, a socialist, was a long-standing supporter of Mandal. Although he had not said anything to Pande and Nayyar, 'I supported the (VP) move 100 per cent,' he told me later.

A few days earlier, Vinod Pande, Finance Secretary Bimal Jalan (who would go on to become the governor of the Reserve Bank of India for two terms) and Deepak Nayyar had pored over the Mandal Commission Report and its annexures. 'I had a one-on-one discussion with VP on it,' Nayyar said, 'to dissuade him.'

'Deepak, you leave politics to me,' the normally polite VP said shortly to Nayyar, 'and I will leave economics to you.'

At the cabinet meeting, VP turned to Paswan again, after Pande had spoken, to indicate that he should continue. Sensing the undercurrents in the room, Paswan said he was going to implement the Mandal Report recommendations only 'partially'. 'I have not gone the whole hog,' he said in a conciliatory tone. Trying to soften the blow, he conceded that accepting the entire list of OBCs could cause problems. He would include only those castes, he said, which were common in the central list and the state lists. The final list was therefore going to be much 'smaller' than envisaged earlier. He was not going to provide for reservations in promotions. He then went on to list the sectors where reservations would not apply—education, atomic energy, space, defence departments, hospitals, the army, and the judiciary. And Mandal, he assured his colleagues, was to apply only to central government jobs and to public sector units.

VP heard his colleagues out. But he hardly said anything himself. He did not attempt to answer any of the specific questions the ministers raised. 'No one really resisted it in the cabinet. Maybe there was some sort of comment of caution,' VP said years later. 'But no one opposed it frontally. No one said, "This is wrong". Any "no" would have registered in my mind. Devi Lal never said anything...because by then he had been removed from the cabinet.'

It was clear to everyone present that V. P. Singh was determined to push through the decision that very day. All he wanted was the formal approval of the cabinet. The meeting did not last very long, Jaipal Reddy recalled. There were a couple of other items on the agenda. But they were disposed of in a few minutes. No one remembered afterwards what they were. When it was finally all over, V. P. Singh declared, 'This, then, is the consensus.' He looked around at his colleagues, and said, 'The cabinet approves the decision to implement the Mandal Commission's recommendation for job reservations for the backward classes.'

VP then turned to B. G. Deshmukh. 'Can you prepare a note for me so that I can announce the decision in parliament tomorrow?' he asked his glum-looking principal secretary.

Then the prime minister told Deshmukh, 'Please speak to Shiv Shankarji about it before drafting the statement.' As noted, Shiv Shankar was a votary of Mandal, but he had not been able to get the Mandal Report accepted by the Congress governments.

Deshmukh was surprised by VP's words to him. He just nodded unhappily. He turned to his secretary and passed on the instructions. But the prime minister's request intrigued the principal secretary. It was hardly a secret in Delhi's political and bureaucratic circles that there had been no love lost between V. P. Singh and Shiv Shankar. In 1986, it was Shiv Shankar who had lobbied for VP's dismissal as finance minister. In 1987, he had pushed for his expulsion from the Congress Party. Shiv Shankar had hoped to get the finance portfolio in 1984, when Rajiv Gandhi had made VP the finance minister. But, by the end of 1986, Shiv Shankar's fortunes had begun to dip. He had ceased to be in the inner coterie of Rajiv. Unlike VP, who quit the Congress in 1987, Shiv Shankar stayed on in the party. But he became disenchanted with Rajiv. He had kept in touch with VP after he quit the Congress.

Unknown to most, the man who had influenced V. P. Singh to go for Mandal was Shiv Shankar. 'Shiv Shankar advised VP to go in for Mandal... and become another Ambedkar,' H. R. Bhardwaj told me. When Deshmukh went across to meet Shiv Shankar, with a draft of the GO (government order), Shiv Shankar 'rejected it outright'. 'It was such a mundane type of writing that it couldn't fit the description of social justice,' Shiv Shankar recalled contemptuously. 'I redrafted the GO myself, sharpening the formulation of social justice. I must say every word of mine was retained in the GO.'

After the cabinet meeting, VP called Ram Vilas Paswan and Social Welfare Secretary P. S. Krishnan to his residence. Krishnan was one of the two senior bureaucrats convinced of the need to implement Mandal, the other one being Commerce Secretary S. P. Shukla. He had been assigned the task of putting into place the nuts and bolts of the move. VP went over with him the points he would make in parliament the next day.

Having got the decision out of the way, VP now turned to tackling the parties which gave his government external support—the BJP and the Left groups—a task he had deliberately left till the last moment. He knew they were not going to welcome the decision. But he also knew that they would not pull the plug on him. Neither party, VP had calculated, wanted elections. They did not want to risk the Congress coming back to power.

'It's the one time I did not consult them,' VP admitted, 'I merely informed them.'

He spoke first to BJP leader L. K. Advani, and then to Harkishan Singh Surjeet, general secretary of the CPI (M). Advani tried to talk VP out if it. They could discuss it at length 'at the weekly Tuesday meeting which was only two days away', Advani suggested. After he became PM, VP would meet with the senior BJP leaders every Tuesday to apprise them of what was happening in government and take their suggestions on board. He would do the same with the Left leaders. 'No, I cannot wait,' the normally accommodative VP told Advani. 'I have to announce it tomorrow.'

Later, VP despatched Som Pal to meet Advani to explain the situation to him in detail. 'If the Janata Dal is bent upon playing the Mandal card,' Advani told Som Pal frankly, 'the BJP will be forced to play the Mandir card'—shorthand for the building of the Ram temple in Ayodhya.

V. P. Singh announced the decision in both houses of parliament on 7 August 1990—two days before Devi Lal's rally at Delhi's Boat Club. The cabinet decision was sent to the Department of Personnel and Training. It issued an office memorandum on 13 August which listed 1,200 OBCs common to the Mandal Commission and the state government's lists as potential beneficiaries of the policy. There was now no going back on the decision.

Mandal, unquestionably the most far-reaching decision of V. P. Singh's career, was to change the course of Indian politics. It occurred during the third phase of his political career. I will now look at the first two phases—the feudal and loyalist phase as a Congressman during Indira Gandhi's rule and the rebel phase when he fell out with Rajiv Gandhi. They give a glimpse into VP's personality, mental make-up, and ways in which he dealt with challenges, all of which had a bearing on his decision to finally go in for Mandal.

VI

In December 1981, a lunch party was in progress at a two-storeyed bungalow at 82, Shah Jahan Road. The houses with sloping roofs that lined one side of the tree-lined avenue in Lutyens' Delhi resembled Swiss chalets and housed senior members of parliament. There was laughter and banter at the lunch—and the political chit-chat that characterizes such occasions in the country's capital. The words spoken were couched in politeness and courtesy, a hallmark of feudal families. Sant Bux Singh was the host. An MP from Uttar Pradesh from the ruling Congress Party, he had invited two of his brothers, Chandra Shekhar Prasad Singh and Vishwanath Pratap Singh, and a friend, Devendra Nath Dwivedi, to the exclusive event. At the time C.

S. P. Singh was a judge in the Allahabad High Court in Uttar Pradesh and V. P. Singh was the chief minister of Uttar Pradesh.

That winter afternoon, even as the brothers joked and laughed as if they did not have a care in the world, there was something forced about the bonhomie that prevailed. Suddenly, pointing to his two brothers, C. S. P. Singh turned to Dwivedi and asked jokingly, 'Devendra, which one of them is the chaiin (the crafty one)?' Before Dwivedi could reply, VP protested. 'Dada bhai, surely you don't consider me chaiin?' He laughed to hide the embarrassment he felt. 'I am a simple person,' he said. And added, 'Why don't you rephrase your question? Why don't you ask who is the bigger chaiin of the two of us?'

C. S. P. Singh laughed. 'No, no, we know who the bigger chaiin is and that is Raja Bahadur.' (Raja Bahadur was an honorific frequently used for VP, as the owner of the estate of Manda, an erstwhile princely state.)

C. S. P. Singh was not trying to put down VP. He was very fond of his younger brother. He was going out of his way to show courtesy to his half-brother, Sant Bux, as often happens in traditional families. It was an attempt to balance his obvious affection for VP—and, by so doing, make Sant Bux feel good. Even though he was half teasing his brother, C. S. P. Singh was acknowledging a reality that day—V. P. Singh had shown more political savvy and craftiness than his older brother, Sant Bux Singh, who had entered politics first. It had created tensions between the two.

The three Singh brothers were Rajputs and belonged to the Dahiya clan in Uttar Pradesh. They were the sons of Bhagwati Prasad Singh, the raja of the Dahiya estate, who had married three ranis. The eldest rani died without giving birth to a child. Sant Bux Singh was among five children born to the second rani. C. S. P. Singh and V. P. Singh were among the three children of the third rani sahiba. The children grew up referring to them as Bari Ma (Big Mother) and Choti Ma (Small Mother).

V. P. Singh was born on 25 June 1931. The young Vishwanath was taken away from his biological family at the age of five and given in adoption to the childless raja of Manda, Ram Gopal Singh. Manda was a neighbouring estate, larger than Dahiya, and comprised 500 villages. Its raja had become an alcoholic after the death of his wife—and wanted to adopt a child. That is when the manipulation and the manoeuvring started in Dahiya. The elder rani wanted C. S. P. Singh to be adopted. That would have left the way open for her son, Sant Bux Singh, to become the raja of Dahiya. However, it was VP's horoscope that 'matched' the requirements of the Raja of Manda.

Bhagwati Prasad Singh agreed to give away five-year-old VP, hoping to consolidate the two neighbouring estates in the future. VP had all the material comforts in his adoptive home, and a retinue of servants in tow.

But he had very little other company. Loneliness marked his early years. He was allowed no contact with his natal family—this was one of the conditions laid down by his adoptive father. His was a troubled, even traumatic childhood. Initially, his adoptive father asked his estate manager, a Scotsman called Captain Cook, and his wife, to take care of him. Mrs Cook was a great disciplinarian but was not particularly interested in VP. When his adoptive father took seriously ill with tuberculosis, VP was sent to school in Dehradun. After a couple of years there, at Col. Brown Cambridge School, and just as he was settling down, he was brought back home. This time, his adoptive father, although still very ill, kept him in Allahabad. VP lived in an enormous two-storeyed mansion called Aish Mahal which was part of the Manda estate. He attended the Boys' High School and College in the city. It was in Allahabad that he picked up the threads of the relationship with his brothers again.

One day, an older boy walked up to him in school. He bent down and whispered in his ear, 'I am your brother.' Looking around to see if anyone could hear him, he said, 'Do not say a word to anyone or they will not let us meet.' C. S. P. Singh then bought his younger sibling an ice cream. VP recalled years later that he could still remember its flavour. 'It was magnolia.' In the weeks that followed, VP grew very close to C. S. P. Singh. As he hated studies, C. S. P. Singh would often do his homework on the quiet, and bring it back the next day.

Sant Bux Singh treated his younger half-brother differently. Initially, he was more curious about the Manda estate, which everyone knew VP would inherit. He and his other brother Har Bux Singh would sometimes surreptitiously accompany him in the 'buggy' of the Manda estate to see the sprawling Aish Mahal where he lived.

A year after VP's move to Allahabad, his adoptive father died. The responsibility of looking after VP and the estate was transferred by the government to Amar Singh Mathur, a civil servant. Mathur and his family moved in with VP in Aish Mahal. The young VP grew to love them and Mrs Mathur gave him the affection he had longed for. But when VP was ten years old, his biological father brought him back to Dahiya again, over the child's protests that he did not want to leave the Mathur family. His father feared for his life—and the property left to him by his adoptive father. People had challenged his adoption in court and laid claim to Ram Gopal Singh's property after his death. VP was enrolled in the same school as his brothers but very soon his father sent him off yet again, this time to Varanasi to study at the famous Udai Pratap College where many Rajput children went.

Talking about his unsettled existence in his most formative years, VP said, 'I was insecure, very insecure.' His lonely childhood was also to make him a loner in politics.

■

It was when VP was in college that he started to look up to Sant Bux Singh. Under the influence of his older sibling, who was 'erudite and articulate', he began to advocate the abolition of the zamindari system. He spoke at debates about it. His empathy for the poor was visible in those early years, and he also came under the influence of socialists and communists in his college days. VP donated 200 bighas of his own lands to the Vinoba Bhave-led Bhoodan movement.

VP got his earliest lessons in how to win elections when he worked for his brother's election campaign in Fatehpur in the 1967 Lok Sabha polls. He camped for a month in the UP town 135 kilometres from Allahabad. It is here that he picked up the tricks of the trade which were to stand him in good stead in later years. He saw how his brother's poll team analysed voters' lists, categorized names according to the polling booths, decided on which areas to visit and those to leave out. Sant Bux Singh sent a postcard with a message and his photo to many in the constituency; he then followed it up with personal visits to them. To save money, the team borrowed vehicles from friends. Family members would drive the vehicles to prevent their misuse.

VP and his three brothers would resort to subterfuge during the campaigning. They would go to the villages at night, each one pretending to be the candidate. They would talk to the villagers in groups, and since the places where they spoke were dark and poorly lit, the villagers couldn't make out the face of the candidate who was doing the talking. Before long, his opponents began to wonder how one single candidate, Sant Bux Singh, could cover so much ground personally! Though it was a Rajput-dominated constituency, and Sant Bux Singh was a Rajput, victory was not a given. Nationally, the Congress, led by Indira Gandhi, just managed to get through in the 1967 election. But Sant Bux Singh won handsomely. Later, he would tell people how hard VP had worked to get him elected.

VP realized the importance of optics in politics early on. In December 1965, when Lal Bahadur Shastri came to Manda, VP put a tilak on Shastri's forehead. He slashed his thumb with a blade and then smeared his blood on the visiting leader's forehead in the traditional method that Rajputs used to welcome a returning hero. Shastri had just won the 1965 war with Pakistan in September. He was so moved by the gesture that he declared VP would be his fifth son. Two decades later, Shastri's wife, Lalita, refused to campaign for her son, Sunil, in the 1988 by-election in Allahabad because he was pitted against VP, who had by then quit the Congress. She said she did not want to be forced to choose between two sons.

Soon after college, VP began to toy with the idea of going into politics.

It seemed the natural thing to do; as the Raja of Manda he was expected to solve people's problems. Later VP admitted that a desire for recognition and to leave a mark in public affairs also had something to do with his entry into politics. In 1969, encouraged by Sant Bux Singh, VP decided to contest from the Soraon assembly constituency, one of the five assembly segments in Phulpur in Uttar Pradesh. It was in Soraon that VP displayed his chaiin characteristics to the full, compelling Indira Gandhi to allocate the seat to him and not to the incumbent. He managed to get a Dalit candidate to withdraw in his favour. The upper-caste votes were not even 5 per cent in Soraon. It was basically a constituency dominated by SCs, OBCs, and Muslim voters; and established Congress leaders had revolted against VP's candidature.

'Forget the leaders, go to the people,' one of his team members told him. VP started going door to door. He would visit Dalit homes at night, and sit around the fire with their families. Till then the Congress leaders had come only to the borders of their hamlets. Dalits were a very visible part of his campaign. 'My jeep used to be loaded mostly with Dalits,' he said to me. It was during his campaign in Soraon that he began to understand the aspirations, and angst, of the OBCs and the Dalits. 'My own election gave me an insight of the fire burning below,' VP was to say years later. VP won from Soraon.

As the brothers reminisced at the December 1981 lunch in Delhi, Devendra Dwivedi regaled them with stories. The most popular one was about how VP had secured the Congress ticket for his first parliamentary election in 1971. It was from the prestigious Phulpur Lok Sabha seat, a constituency from which Jawaharlal Nehru had once won. Congress heavyweight H. N. Bahuguna had asked Dwivedi to convince VP to stand from Phulpur. He wanted a consolidation of the Brahmin and Thakur votes to take place. (Bahuguna was a Brahmin and VP was a Thakur.) Bahuguna calculated it would help him in his own constituency, Allahabad, which was adjacent to Phulpur. Dwivedi took VP to meet Bahuguna, who as general secretary of the AICC was responsible for ticket distribution.

They travelled in VP's Fiat car to Bahuguna's house. There was a large crowd of people outside waiting to see Bahuguna. 'As I entered...Bahuguna told me, "Inko andar lekar jao (Please take him inside)".'

'We went into a room inside.' Bahuguna finally came into the room where they were seated. 'Inko taiyyar karna hai (We have to ready him to contest),' he told Dwivedi, without preamble.

At this point VP spoke up, 'Bahugunaji, humko rehne deejiye (Bahugunaji, please leave me out of it).' Bahuguna looked at him, nonplussed. There were 1,000 people outside, all seeking nomination, and here was this man, refusing a party ticket.

'Bahugunaji, humare paas paisa nahin hai,' VP said. 'Humare bahut mukadme chal rahen hain (I have little money. I have many legal cases going on against me).'

'You don't worry about money,' Bahuguna assured him. 'We are going to be giving ₹1 lakh to each candidate.'

Bahuguna prevailed upon a reluctant VP to contest from Phulpur. Powerful in UP at the time, Bahuguna presented VP's candidature to Indira Gandhi as a fait accompli. Though she did not like the fact that the decision had been made without her clearance, she went along with the plan.

Indira Gandhi had liked V. P. Singh from the beginning. He was devoted to her and looked upon her as his political mentor. When the excesses of the 1975–77 Emergency began to be probed, and dozens of Congress leaders turned against her, VP stuck by her. When Indira was arrested in December 1978, he was one of those who went to jail in protest.

VP's elevation as the chief minister of UP was one of those quirky lucky breaks that came his way, thanks to his loyalist persona. When Indira refused to agree to Sanjay becoming the chief minister of Uttar Pradesh in June 1980, as we saw Chapter 1, Sanjay chose VP to head the country's largest state. Initially, VP was reluctant to take over as chief minister. But he allowed himself to be persuaded by Sanjay and took charge on 9 June 1980—just two weeks before Sanjay died in an aircrash. Being a reluctant politician as opposed to one who was seen to be grasping power was a strategy he would use to great effect during his political career.

In his early days as the CM of UP, he did not display a preference for any ideology. Nor did he have strong views on any political subject. He was pragmatic, discreet, and known for a quiet efficiency—and, of course, loyalty to the Nehru family. But he also proved to be a good administrator, though he often used unorthodox methods to get things done.

Once, when there was a shortage of electricity in the state and the chairman of the electricity board kept insisting that people were getting eight hours of power supply, VP called him to the CM's office one morning. He told the surprised official, 'We are going from Lucknow right up to Bullandshahr.... I told him to sit in the helicopter (which was ready for take-off).' VP had already carried out 'raids' and found that apart from the shortage of electricity in many parts of the state, power was being diverted to a few industrial houses.

As they flew around the state, VP would ask the pilot to randomly land in places. The villagers would gather around the helicopter, and VP would ask them about the electricity available to them. They confirmed they did not get bijli for more than three hours. In Bullandshahr, at a public meeting, VP introduced the chairman to the gathering, 'You have heard what the people have to say,' VP told him in front of the crowd. 'If you can correct the situation, come (back) to Lucknow, if not, go home.'

VP left him there, and flew back to Lucknow. The electricity situation improved in UP.

What the Singh brothers did not talk about that December day was something that had rankled with Sant Bux Singh for years—and dated back to 1974. That year, VP had outmanoeuvred his older brother and was inducted by Indira Gandhi into her cabinet. She appointed him deputy minister of commerce on 10 October 1974 under D. P. Chattopadhyaya. At the time, VP was only a backbencher in parliament, and rarely spoke in the house. Sant Bux Singh, on the other hand, was educated at Oxford, an eloquent speaker, an able parliamentarian, and a foreign policy specialist. It was his name which had been doing the rounds in Congress circles as a possible inductee into the ministry. But VP emerged as the dark horse. In 1974, Indira Gandhi was not looking for an independent-minded minister like Sant Bux. She was looking for 'loyalty' which VP was known for, even though he was a 'novice' compared to his brother. The relationship between the two brothers changed irrevocably after that. VP rose in the Congress Party hierarchy faster than Sant Bux Singh.

■

Three months after the lunch at Sant Bux Singh's home, tragedy struck the Singh family. On 20 March 1982, C. S. P. Singh and his fifteen-year-old son, Ajit, were gunned down by dacoits in the middle of the night, close to Allahabad, in what appeared to be retaliation for his brother's campaign to rid UP of dacoits. They had gone for a 'weekend shoot'.

It was C. S. P. Singh who had brought brotherly affection and warmth to VP's lonely life as a boy. For hours, VP sat inconsolably beside the body. His brother had paid the price for his office, he kept repeating over and over again.

When VP had taken charge as chief minister, the state was overrun by dacoits. Murderous gangs terrorized people in the towns and villages. The gang headed by Phoolan Devi, a woman dacoit who was an OBC, and was later elected to parliament, had killed over twenty Thakurs in Behmai, leading to retaliation by the Rajputs. On 23 November 1981, VP vowed to rid UP of the dacoit menace. If he did not succeed, he would quit as CM, he said. In the forty-one days that followed, 299 'dacoits' were eliminated in 'encounters'. VP had given the police carte blanche to deal with the most notorious ones. But soon they came under fire themselves. There was an outcry against the government's 'encounters'. Civil rights groups and the media, probing the encounter deaths, charged VP's government of inflating the figure, and nabbing small-time criminals and innocent people.

It is during these months that VP's first brush took place with Mulayam Singh Yadav, then leader of the opposing Lok Dal in UP. Yadav was agitated about the issue because a large number of those killed were OBCs and Dalits.

On 28 June 1982—three months after C. S. P. Singh had been gunned down—ten Yadavs and six Dalits were shot dead in another gruesome episode. VP decided to resign. He called a press conference and announced his resignation. It was after making the announcement that he sent his letter of resignation to the governor, C. P. N. Singh. He did not want to be pressured to take it back. He took this step without consulting the party high command, even though he knew he might invite Indira Gandhi's wrath.

While he had kept to his word of quitting if he could not deal with the dacoit menace, he was sharp enough to know that with the situation deteriorating, it was only a matter of time before he was replaced. An innate sense of political timing, which he learnt from Indira Gandhi, and an ability to take a risk, not knowing what the consequences of his action would be, were also to stand him in good stead, especially in the later years. It was in those days that he also learnt the value of 'resignation' as a tool to further his political goals. He had already learnt the value of 'reluctance' to grasp power as a political weapon.

His resignation as the chief minister of UP defused some of the anger that had been building up against him. As he went around the state, he found the move had enhanced his stature. By taking on the high command, he was now being seen as a leader in his own right.

His resignation annoyed Indira Gandhi, but as on earlier occasions, she soon forgave him and brought him back to the centre as commerce minister on 29 January 1983, and made him a Rajya Sabha member.

Two months before she died, in the run-up to the general elections which were due in early 1985, she appointed him president of the Uttar Pradesh Congress Committee. VP's star was once again rising. But in the next phase of his political career, VP the Congress loyalist, would give way to VP the Congress rebel.

VII

The political history of independent India might have been different had Rajiv Gandhi and V. P. Singh not fallen out in 1987. VP might not have become prime minister and the story of affirmative action for the OBCs might have taken a different trajectory. Their relationship was marked by periods of great camaraderie as well as deep mistrust and bitterness.

When Rajiv Gandhi contested the Lok Sabha election in mid-1981 from Amethi in UP, VP went there to campaign for him. He was chief minister of the state at the time. 'I have seen them lie down on the same charpoy on a tour of Amethi,' recalled H. R. Bhardwaj, the Congress politician. 'I remember this distinctly. We were electioneering in Amethi, and Rajiv was drawing huge crowds. We were at this guest house near the canal, where we had stopped for refreshments. There was time only for half an hour's rest. Rajiv and VP had a dip in the canal. But there was only one charpoy to rest on. Both of them lay down on it in their kachcha-banians after bathing.'

In the 1970s, and till the mid-1980s, VP's loyalty to the Gandhi–Nehru family, first to Sanjay, then to Indira, and finally to Rajiv Gandhi was unquestioned. Before she was assassinated, Indira had expressed the hope that VP would be part of Rajiv's core team. She saw his clean image and loyalty to the Nehru–Gandhi family as an asset.

VP first became unhappy with Rajiv Gandhi in December 1984 over his decision to pit Amitabh Bachchan against the UP strongman, Hemvati Nandan Bahuguna, from the Allahabad parliamentary constituency. The Machiavellian Bahuguna had quit the Congress in February 1977 along with Jagjivan Ram, and joined the Janata Party, which he left to rejoin Indira Gandhi in 1979, after the collapse of the Janata experiment, only to break away again in 1980 to float his own party. He was defeated by the Congress in the famous Garhwal by-polls in 1981, amidst allegations of massive rigging by the Congress, all under the leadership of VP.

VP's unhappiness over Rajiv's decision was only the beginning of a fluctuating relationship between the two. 'One day at midnight—this was just before the 1984 elections—Rajivji called me to 1, Akbar Road,' H. R. Bhardwaj recounted. As he entered the house, he saw VP sitting there. At the time, VP was the chief of the UP Congress, and had a major say in who would get the party tickets in the state. Ignoring VP, Rajiv took Bhardwaj inside. Amitabh Bachchan was sitting there. 'Do you know him?' Rajiv asked Bhardwaj. 'He is an actor,' Bhardwaj replied. 'But I knew his father.'

Harivansh Rai Bachchan, Amitabh's father, was an eminent Hindi poet. The Nehru–Gandhi family had been longstanding friends of the Bachchans. Sarojini Naidu had first introduced Harivansh Rai and his wife, Teji, to Jawaharlal Nehru at Anand Bhavan in the early 1940s. He had called them 'the poet and the poem'. Teji Bachchan went on to strike up a friendship with Indira Gandhi which lasted over the decades. Sonia Gandhi stayed at their home when she came from Italy to marry Rajiv in 1968. Later, when Rajiv was at Cambridge, he would hang out with Amitabh when he came home for the holidays. At this time, the Bachchans were living at 13, Willingdon Crescent, in Delhi as Harivansh Rai had been nominated to the Rajya Sabha in 1966, soon after Indira became prime minister. The Gandhis lived in 1, Safdarjung Road, and the two houses were near enough for them to meet frequently. The Bachchan and Gandhi boys would swim together in the pool in Rashtrapati Bhavan.

∎

Rajiv Gandhi told Bhardwaj to take Amitabh Bachchan to Lucknow. 'But you have to do it quietly. No one should know. Bahuguna ke khilaaf larhana hain inhe. Par Bahuguna ko pata nahin lagana chahiye.' (We have to pit him against Bahuguna but Bahuguna should not get a whiff of this.)

Amitabh Bachchan had agreed to contest the election 'to stand by Rajiv' after Indira Gandhi's assassination, even though, as he told Rajiv, 'I don't know the "p" of politics.'

Having given his instructions to Bhardwaj, Rajiv Gandhi then walked with him to the visitors' room where V. P. Singh sat waiting for them. He had taken over as the UP Congress chief on 1 September 1984, after being commerce minister for nineteen months. Worried about the Congress's prospects in Uttar Pradesh, Indira Gandhi had sent him to UP to revive the party there. Rajiv wanted to firm up Bachchan's candidature from Allahabad immediately. But the Congress ticket had already been given to K. P. Tiwari, who was a follower of V. P. Singh.

There is nothing more unpalatable for a politician than to lose his hold over his constituency. In 1980, Indira Gandhi had given VP the Congress ticket from Allahabad. She had preferred him to H. N. Bahuguna. After that, VP had regarded Allahabad as his turf. Manda, of which he was the raja, was only 70 kilometres from Allahabad. VP had known that Bahuguna would be a formidable foe in Allahabad this time round. But he had faith in Tiwari; he had won from Allahabad when VP had vacated the constituency after becoming the chief minister in June 1980.

As president of the Congress in UP, VP's word was decisive in every constituency. But he did not get his way in his own constituency—Allahabad—where it mattered the most.

That night, VP did not say much.

'There's no problem,' he told Rajiv Gandhi politely. 'We'll change him (Tiwari).' But the decision troubled him. To compensate Tiwari, it was decided 'that night itself' to induct him in the UP ministry. K. P. Tiwari took oath the next day. Later, he was made a member of the legislative council (MLC), rewarded for having made way for Amitabh Bachchan.

The next morning, Arun Nehru, who was overseeing the 1984 poll strategy, escorted Amitabh and Jaya Bachchan to Lucknow. Bhardwaj accompanied them. They drove straight from the airport to the CM's residence in Lucknow.

'It was decided that the Bachchans would then go onto Allahabad incognito.' The idea was to catch H. N. Bahuguna unawares. That is why Amitabh Bachchan filed his nomination papers only at the last moment—at 3.30 p.m. Nominations closed at 4 p.m. It left Bahuguna no time to shift to another constituency. He was trapped.

When Amitabh Bachchan arrived in Allahabad to campaign, euphoric women threw their chunnis at him. 'There were 1,785 chunnis thrown,'

D. P. Tripathi told me. 'I know because I got them counted.' Bachchan's film-star glamour drew large crowds to his meetings. He was also known for his proximity to Rajiv Gandhi. It made the established politicians of Uttar Pradesh envious—and insecure. VP was not alone in feeling threatened by Bachchan. He avoided addressing rallies with him; he agreed to be present only when Rajiv came to Allahabad to campaign for Bachchan on 18 December 1984. Amitabh Bachchan went on to defeat Bahuguna, polling 68 per cent of the votes cast.

Thereafter, VP felt that he had been 'exiled from Allahabad'. (The word he used was 'bedakhal'.) Slowly he found himself left with little say in the affairs of Allahabad. He could not even 'decide who would be in the telephone advisory committee or any other government body'. 'You are creating problems for me in the future,' he complained to Arun Nehru. 'Forget it,' Nehru dismissed VP's qualms with a customary wave of his hand. 'We have to defeat these (Opposition) people first.'

Arun Nehru's strategy—to field figures like Amitabh Bachchan against H. N. Bahuguna and Madhavrao Scindia against Atal Bihari Vajpayee in Gwalior—worked. The bigwigs in the Opposition were vanquished in the 1984 election. (In the event, Bachchan's tenure in politics was short-lived; after an enthusiastic start, he began to neglect his constituency and his constituents soon grew disenchanted with him. A few years later, in mid-1987, he resigned as MP, after allegations were levelled against his brother Ajitabh. And the Raja of Manda was to regain his importance in Allahabad.)

In December 1984, Rajiv Gandhi gave V. P. Singh the biggest job of his political career, which was to become the springboard for even bigger things. Rajiv appointed VP as the finance minister in his new cabinet replacing the veteran Pranab Mukherjee. Rajiv didn't trust Mukherjee given his prime ministerial ambitions, which I have detailed in the previous chapter. The new PM also wanted a face which would be a break from the past. He told journalist M. J. Akbar: 'The finance minister has to be very tough.... I don't think he (Mukherjee) was tough enough.' VP turned out to be tougher than what Rajiv had bargained for.

V. P. Singh's first budget as finance minister in 1985 was welcomed by industry and business. It came as a big relief to them after Indira Gandhi's socialist policies. They started to look at VP with interest. The new finance minister had lowered income tax and wealth tax rates, abolished estate duty, raised the income tax exemption limit, and mooted a host of other market-friendly measures. Some corporate leaders hailed it as the 'best ever in independent India'. However, their initial enthusiasm for him began to peter out, when the new finance minister began to conduct raids against economic offenders and top industrialists allegedly involved in sharp business practices.

When VP began to go after big businessmen, he told his trusted men in the Department of Revenue Intelligence and the ED that nobody was sacrosanct. He had inducted Vinod Pande as revenue secretary and appointed Bhure Lal to head the ED.

VP had got to know Lal when he had issued orders for his arrest, as the collector in Allahabad. Indira Gandhi had been jailed in 1978 and VP along with many others had courted arrest to show their solidarity with her. Both Pande and Lal were upright—and loyal to VP. He knew he could trust them. The bulldoggish Bhure Lal went after big business without fear. 'Prime minister Rajiv Gandhi had said he wanted an honest government and the Raja (VP) took that seriously,' Lal said. 'If you are serious about catching the economic offenders, information starts to flow in on its own. Even family members gave us information (against the errant businessmen).'

VP would repeatedly urge Pande to 'catch the bigger fish'. Pande used to hang a picture of a fish in his office. After every such conversation, he would come back to his office and draw a bigger fish around the one he had drawn earlier.

First, VP carried out raids industry wise—starting with real estate developers. Then it was the jewellery and diamond businessmen. Next, big names among Bollywood producers like N. N. Sippy and Subhash Ghai were targeted. And so it went. High-profile businessmen found their names for all the wrong reasons on the front pages of newspapers as the finance minister's campaign against shady business dealings and tax evasion intensified.

This went on for all of 1985. When asked about it, VP replied enigmatically, 'I have only turned the ignition.'

On 6 December 1985, in the early hours of the morning, Bhure Lal and his team raided the home of the eighty-two-year-old industry doyen, S. L. Kirloskar. They took him to the police station. His interrogation went on for eighteen hours. The arrest sent shock waves throughout the financial world. Another prominent business titan, Lalit Thapar, chairman of Thapar Industries, was arrested at 1 a.m., for alleged foreign exchange violations by his companies. Better connected in Delhi, his arrest rocked parliament. This time around, even the PMO sought an explanation from the finance ministry. But as it turned out, Thapar apologized and accepted most of the charges levelled against him. In return, the ED agreed to drop the criminal charges against him. Other prominent industrial houses which were hauled up included Bajaj Auto, Voltas, and Bata. Allegations levelled against many of those in the dock included money laundering, violation of foreign exchange rules, under-invoicing and over-invoicing, acquiring benami shares, insider trading, and defrauding the public by artificially pushing up the prices.

VP was now targeting bigger and bigger fish. And then he went after one of the biggest of them all—Reliance Industries started by Dhirubhai Ambani in 1967. To raise funds, Reliance had been issuing both convertible and non-convertible debentures for retail investors (at different interest rates). Later, it got special permission from the finance ministry to convert even non-convertible debentures into shares. On 10 June 1986, VP banned 'all conversion of non-convertible debentures into shares'. Reliance, which had just issued two fresh series of such debentures ('E' and 'F' series), which the market had expected to be converted like the earlier ones, saw its share price slump as a result. VP also ordered a probe into the role the banks had played to help Reliance.

Some of his cabinet colleagues were furious with him. N. D. Tiwari had once remarked in disgust, 'Aisa shaneechar bitha diya hai sir par (What kind of a demon have they imposed on us?)' VP, he charged, was impeding the industrialization of the country.

Initially, Rajiv Gandhi gave V. P. Singh a free hand to move against Reliance, even though during his mother's premiership Dhirubhai Ambani had been viewed with favour. A story which used to do the rounds in the late 1980s—and became part of the country's political folklore—was a meeting that Dhirubhai Ambani had allegedly had with Rajiv. Ambani told the PM that he 'was holding a huge amount of funds on behalf of Rajiv's late mother and wanted to know what to do with the money'.

Eventually, V. P. Singh did not raid Dhirubhai Ambani. He had already faced a lot of flak for the detention of the eighty-two-year-old Kirloskar—and had begun to lose the prime minister's backing. Consequently, he told Bhure Lal not to arrest Ambani.

The turning point came when Lal hired a foreign detective agency, Fairfax, to probe Reliance's foreign dealings. Amitabh Bachchan complained to Rajiv Gandhi that agents on behalf of Fairfax had gone to interrogate his brother Ajitabh in Switzerland where he had acquired a house. VP said these were fake agents to malign him in Rajiv's eyes. The prime minister's friends told him that VP was using the Fairfax agency to keep tabs on Rajiv himself.

The appointment of Fairfax led to an uproar in parliament. Attacking V. P. Singh, Congressmen questioned how the finance ministry could hire a foreign detective agency. Who, they asked, was paying the agency? They called VP a traitor and a CIA agent.

Later, in 1989, the Congress Party was to charge V. P. Singh with having an illegal account abroad in the name of his son Ajeya Pratap Singh in Saint Kitts. The document turned out to be a forgery. The government's dirty tricks department was very active in those weeks.

'Fairfax' and 'Saint Kitt's' were to become symbols of the fallout between Rajiv Gandhi and V. P. Singh.

It was around this time that Rajiv's attitude towards VP underwent a change. Till September 1986, VP had Rajiv's backing for the raids. However, even though the prime minister was no longer as enthusiastic as he had once been about going after big business, having told his finance minister to be 'tough', Rajiv was finding it difficult to tell him to call it off. At one point, Rajiv told VP, 'Jitna soft kar sakte ho karo (Soften the blow as much as you can).'

VP replied, 'Yeh jail maen nahin hain, kya itna kam soft hai (That these people are not in jail, isn't that soft enough)?'

On 17 September 1986, Rajiv Gandhi addressed a FICCI meeting in Calcutta. Agitated industrialists confronted the PM—they complained they were being humiliated by his finance minister. FICCI president Rama Prasad Goenka who sat on the dais with the prime minister said a 'raid raj' had been unleashed in the country. Rajiv did not rebut Goenka. Instead, speaking to reporters afterwards, he said the arrest of L. M. Thapar had not been 'as per my guidelines'. His indirect censure of the finance ministry was reported widely in the media.

V. P. Singh was not in the country at the time. He was in Uruguay participating in a global trade meeting at the head of a high-level Indian delegation. The newspapers had praised his role at the General Agreement on Tariffs and Trade (GATT) talks in Punta del Este—for having won a victory for the Global South, 'without inflicting a defeat on the North'. But when VP got word of what had transpired in Calcutta, he rushed back to India. He went immediately to see Rajiv Gandhi—and offered to resign. Rajiv calmed him down. He did not have anything in mind, he said, when he had made that remark.

Business groups however kept up the pressure on Rajiv. They told the prime minister his finance minister was spinning out of control.

VIII

'It was in 1985 that V. P. Singh began to see the possibility of becoming prime minister,' remarked Som Pal.

'I think the possibility had occurred to him even when he was chief minister of UP,' Devendra Dwivedi told me. With the raids, and his crusade against corruption, many suspected that VP had started to position himself for the top job towards the end of 1985.

In September 1985, *Imprint* magazine decided to do an article on V. P. Singh. Amrita Shah was deputed by editor R. V. Pandit to do a piece on him. The magazine carried a striking photograph of him on the cover, in which he looked a bit like Mahatma Gandhi. 'The composure, composition, and expression were just right,' according to Som Pal. VP took great pains to ensure that Amrita Shah had access to all the information she wanted. He asked Som Pal to accompany her to Western UP, where he was well-regarded, to enable her to meet people in the villages. Her profile covered both his time as chief minister of UP and as finance minister—and described him as a leader who could be trusted by the people of India. The article had a ripple effect. Many other pieces began to appear on him in the media.

'This was VP's first exercise in PR. What came later was not an accident.'

■

As the number of raids went up in the rest of 1985 and 1986, so did VP's popularity. People now saw him as a man of integrity who was taking on the corrupt and the powerful—a leader capable of taking bold decisions. It was the prime minister who was losing ground and seen to be shielding the dishonest. V. P. Singh was now replacing Rajiv Gandhi as the Mr Clean of Indian politics. In August 1986, *India Today* did a survey. It revealed that V. P. Singh was now only a shade behind Rajiv Gandhi in the popularity charts. During his two years as finance minister, VP had conducted 6,000 raids, searched 100,000 premises, and interrogated half a million people. During this period, the nature of the finance ministry had also undergone a change—from being a purely policymaking body it had evolved into an institution that sought to punish the economic offenders.

■

'It was Quattrochi who was one of the reasons for my differences with Rajiv,' VP revealed. He was referring to Ottavio Quattrochi, the Italian businessman based in Delhi who was later to be implicated in the Bofors scandal. As a friend of the Gandhis, Quattrochi was prone to throwing his weight around in government circles. 'He had been asking me for an appointment,' VP said. 'I wasn't giving it. I had thought if there is a tender, I can call people.... Then Rajiv asked me to meet him. I said OK. He gave me a memorandum. I got it processed...Banta nahin thaa (But I could not make out a case to favour him). .... I didn't do anything.

'Rajiv sent for me (again) and said, "You (now) have this (project) examined from these angles." He dictated five to six points.... Those points were all those which had been used by Quattrochi in his representation.

'I got it reprocessed. There was (again) no change of recommendation from the (finance) department.... I sent the file to the prime minister. It was given to someone else, was approved, and sent back.' Quattrochi secured the contract for the project, bypassing the finance ministry.

'Either you trust me that I can handle them (the projects),' an unhappy VP complained to the PM, 'or there is no point in my staying on.'

At this stage, some of VP's well-wishers alerted him that the PM's attitude towards him was changing. In September 1986 itself, Som Pal had warned VP that he could be moved out of the finance ministry.

'I had gone to meet him,' Som Pal recalled. 'I told him of a conversation I had picked up in Bombay, that he would be out in a week's time.'

But VP was unfazed. 'No,' he assured Pal, 'there is nothing to worry....
I enjoy the total confidence of Rajiv Gandhi, he knows all about it (what
I am doing).'

In early December 1986, Som Pal warned VP yet again. 'I had heard
in the political circles that he would be moved out in a week,' Pal said,
'This time there were signs of worry on his face.'

'I am a disciplined soldier of the party,' VP replied defensively. 'Whatever
they give me, I will do.'

On 21 January 1987, V. P. Singh was moved out of finance.

'I need a responsible person to head the defence ministry,' Rajiv Gandhi
explained to V. P. Singh. Though he had defence under him, he said he
wanted 'a full-time minister' and could not leave defence 'to juniors'. He
was alluding to Arun Singh, his friend of long-standing, who was minister
of state, Defence. At this time, Rajiv was also unhappy with the role
played by the chief of army staff, General K. Sundarji, and Arun Singh in
scaling up Operation Brasstacks, a large-scale military exercise launched
in Rajasthan on 18 November 1986, which had led to a stand-off with
Pakistan on the border, and almost brought both countries to war.

By transferring V. P. Singh, Rajiv Gandhi thought he would be solving
two problems at once—moving VP out of finance where he had alienated
too many influential businessmen—some of whom were his friends—and
putting him in charge of defence where he could monitor the actions of Arun
Singh and General Sundarji. Although the PM tried to put a positive spin
on the transfer, his exit from the finance ministry stung the Raja of Manda.

■

It was a bright, sunny winter day in Delhi on 24 January 1987, but
V. P. Singh sat all alone inside his residence. The crowd that would mill
around in the garden, or sit on the veranda waiting to have a word with
him, was missing. Congressmen were quick to sense he had fallen out of
favour. He had been removed as finance minister three days earlier.

When Som Pal went to see him that morning VP said wryly, 'Aiye
Sompalji, what you were saying, one part of it has come true.'

Som Pal told him, 'Khapaenge aap yehan bhi nahin (You won't fit
into defence either).' Both Pal and VP knew that the defence establishment
was also riddled with corruption, right from the recruitment of soldiers
to the elevation of generals, from purchases to expenditure. Both knew
that VP was not going to stop his 'crusade' against corruption. But that
day, VP was cautious, 'Dekhaenge. Abhi to hum machine ko study kar
rahen hain (We will see. At the moment I am studying this machine).
Without studying, agar keel paech haath ko lag gaya to garhbarh ho
jayegi (Without a study of its nuts and bolts, if I touch the wrong place
by mistake, everything will go wrong....). Whatever I do will be after a

study and I will do it in my own way. Chahe kuch bhi ho, hum to apne tareeke se kaam karenge (No matter what anyone says, I am going to do what I have to do).'

V. P. Singh's opportunity to strike came soon enough. It came over the navy's purchase of HDW submarines from Germany. VP ordered an enquiry into the deal. He had received a telegram from the Indian ambassador in Germany that the price of the HDW submarines could not be reduced. This, the ambassador said—and he quoted a German official—could not be done because a heavy commission of 7 per cent was being paid to an Indian agent. VP questioned the defence secretary, S. K. Bhatnagar, about it. Bhatnagar told him that a big business family was behind the deal. VP put all the information on file, and ordered a departmental enquiry. He also issued a press release about what he had done. Again, there was an uproar in parliament. VP was present in the house when agitated MPs demanded more information. He confirmed to them that his ministry had issued a press note.

Within minutes, the prime minister summoned VP to his office—this was on 9 April 1987. Rajiv Gandhi was livid. 'He was red in the face,' VP recalled. 'How do you know that the telegram that you received is correct?' Rajiv asked.

'How do you know it is incorrect?' VP responded. 'It came through a coded procedure, the decoding was done in the PMO and the defence ministry. It came through a secret channel, there is no reason to suspect it.' VP went on, 'It is not garbled. But even if it is not correct, an enquiry will reveal it (the truth), and the ambassador will deny it. If it is incorrect, it is also a serious matter, and needs to be looked into.'

'What will be the result of the enquiry?' Rajiv asked VP irritably.

'It is your policy not to have middlemen,' VP replied coolly.

In October 1985, an enthusiastic Rajiv Gandhi wanting to cleanse the system after his historic victory, had announced a ban on defence agents in the negotiation of defence deals. Till then global defence companies would work through Indian agents who would then get big commissions, and would influence who got the contracts. Rajiv ordered that from then on the government would directly negotiate the arms deals.

The parting of ways between Rajiv Gandhi and V. P. Singh came on 11 April 1987. Dusk had fallen over Delhi. All day VP had left messages at the PM House, asking for an appointment with Rajiv. But he had heard nothing back. It was unusual for a senior minister to request an urgent meeting with the prime minister and get no word back. The silence carried its own message. VP then sat down and wrote out a letter resigning as defence minister. The evening wore on but there was still no word from Race Course Road.

Finally, VP asked his son, Abhay, to drive him to the PM House. Abhay, a physician, took him there in his Maruti 800 Omni. Highly conscious about his image, VP did not want to go in his official car to submit his resignation, even though Rajiv lived only a three-minute drive away at 7, Race Course Road. He was not at home. VP left his resignation letter with M. L. Fotedar and walked back to the car. VP and his son drove back home in silence. Later that evening he heard that the prime minister had accepted his resignation.

■

Seventy kilometres from Delhi, a heated family discussion was in progress in the small town of Baraut, in western UP. It was the day after VP quit as defence minister—and the papers were full of his resignation. 'We decided to meet as a family when we heard that V. P. Singh had resigned,' recalled Som Pal. 'We were discussing what I should do. My mother said to me, "You must stay with V. P. Singh".' The family council decided that Som Pal should drive to Delhi the same day and meet VP. The next morning, when he arrived at 1, Rajaji Marg, there were around 100 people at the house. But the atmosphere was one of mourning. 'What has Rajiv done (by accepting VP's resignation)?' many lamented, 'You were doing such good work,' others told VP, 'and the Congress was getting the credit for it'. VP did not look unduly worried. He tried to quieten his agitated supporters. 'Don't worry. Everything will be all right. I have a good equation with Rajiv. We will only work under his leadership.' Clearly, VP was hopeful that his differences with Rajiv would be sorted out.

Som Pal, who had brought a garland for VP to compliment him for his decision to resign, felt disappointed. 'If you wanted to work under Rajiv's leadership, why did you resign?' he asked VP. 'I wanted to congratulate you for throwing away this yoke.' Then he added, 'I am with you.'

VP did not say anything. 'But I thought I saw approval in his eyes,' Pal said. As he was making his way out, one of VP's attendants, Gulab Tiwari, ran up to him. 'Sahib wants to see you,' he said. Pal went back into the house. VP put a hand on his shoulder, and said, 'In a day or two, I want to talk to you about the political situation. I am going to Lucknow tomorrow, you come and see me on the 17th.'

'Who is going with you to Lucknow?' Som Pal asked.

'Come if you can,' VP replied.

As it turned out, they flew to Lucknow that very evening by the 6.30 p.m. flight. As they drove to the airport, Pal tried to convince VP to strike out on his own, 'You will not be able to adjust inside the Congress now. The sooner you come out of the Congress, the better...it has become immaterial whether you come out or they throw you out.' The Congress politician V. N. Dixit, who was also accompanying VP, was aghast. 'Som Palji, what advice are you giving Raja sahib?' he exclaimed. 'He should not leave the Congress.'

'Som Palji, you are asking me to leave the organization in which I have spent twenty years. How can I leave it so quickly?' As VP spoke, his eyes became moist. Dixit touched Pal's arm, motioning him to stop. Till then, VP had given no indication to his supporters that quitting the Congress was even remotely on his mind. But then the Raja of Manda was not given to letting his left hand know what his right hand was doing.

At Delhi airport, they saw four ministers from the Congress government in UP; none of them even looked towards V. P. Singh. Even Sanjay Singh, the state transport minister who was married to VP's niece, Garima, only did a formal namaste from a distance. In less than a week, Congressmen, quick to sense the direction of the wind, were giving VP short shrift.

In the aircraft, V. P. Singh, V. N. Dixit, and Sanjay Singh sat in the first row. Som Pal was seated in the third row. After take-off, VP got up from his seat, walked back to where Pal sat, and occupied the empty seat next to him. 'What is to be done now?' he asked Som Pal. Had VP not been toying with the idea of quitting the Congress, he would not have sought out Som Pal that day. Soon, Pal was in full flow. 'The modality of how you quit (the Congress) is unimportant.... You will have to decide whether you want to remove the Congress in 1990 or in 1995. But if you want to do it in 1990, you will have to bring all the non-Congress parties together on one platform.'

V. P. Singh did not need to be told that he would have to act quickly. Or the goodwill for him would soon peter out. There was no knowing the events that might overtake them by 1995. Som Pal then talked about the possibility of the BJP and Left parties supporting VP. At this point VP looked at Pal with interest. It was possible, Pal pressed on, for both parties to support him. Though their ideologies diverged, their areas of influence were different. 'And, both parties realize they cannot come to power at the centre on their own.'

Though he did not react to what Som Pal was saying, in the not-too-distant future, VP was to do just that—bring the entire Opposition together on a common platform.

■

On 14 April 1987, three days after V. P. Singh resigned as defence minister the Bofors scandal broke—it would become VP's passport to the premiership. As mentioned in the previous chapter, Congress leader H. R. Bhardwaj told me that they suspected that Arun Nehru had leaked the Bofors story to Swedish radio.

The Swedish broadcaster announced that the Swedish armaments company had paid commissions to middlemen who included Indian politicians, officials, and arms dealers for the purchase of the 155-mm howitzer guns by the Indian Army, despite the fact that PM Rajiv Gandhi had outlawed the practice of commissions. In the days and months that followed, 'Bofors' became the ammunition VP needed to take Rajiv head on. Everywhere he went, he spoke about Bofors and the foreign accounts of Rajiv. Though he could not substantiate any of the charges, VP's reputation grew as a crusader against corruption in high places.

'Is maen kitna Bofors hai (How much Bofors is there in this)?' People would ask derisively whenever there was the hint of a bribe. And though no evidence was ever found linking Rajiv Gandhi or members of his immediate family to the kickbacks in the Bofors deal, they damaged Rajiv's image irreparably. No matter how vigorously Rajiv protested his innocence, the stain did not wash out. The next months after VP's resignation were to be tumultuous.

■

On 25 June 1987, Arif Mohammed Khan, who had by then quit the government, threw a party at his residence. It was V. P. Singh's birthday, and the party was in his honour. Several dissatisfied Congress MPs were present. There was the once powerful Arun Nehru, who had been sacked by Rajiv Gandhi as minister of state for Internal Security in October 1986 and V. C. Shukla, who had served as Information and Broadcasting minister during the Emergency under Indira Gandhi. Shukla was in touch with President Zail Singh who, it was rumoured, might sack the prime minister on corruption charges and swear in someone else in his place. Dissatisfaction with the prime minister was growing both within the party and in the country. After his resignation from the government, many unhappy Congress leaders had begun to watch with interest VP's next moves.

Many mediapersons had also been invited to the party. Several of us arrived at Khan's residence at 3, Sunehri Bagh Road, expecting to find a good story with so many dissident Congressmen present.

The signal that went out after the evening was that V. P. Singh had joined hands with Arun Nehru against Rajiv Gandhi. The next day's papers said as much. The event had been crafted to get a sense of 'kaun kitne paani maen hai (To test the waters)'.

'I was told, you must come to the tea party. We have to push the Raja to take a position,' Satyapal Malik recalled. Malik, a Congress MP at the time, would join hands with VP, Arun Nehru, and Arif Mohammed Khan.

Arif Mohammed Khan and Arun Nehru had been working in tandem, and wanted VP to make a final break with the prime minister. Although he had quit the government, VP was still in two minds about the next moves he should make. Rajiv Gandhi had continued to reach out to him through emissaries like his young minister Rajesh Pilot. Before that Rajiv also met VP personally twice to affect a patch-up.

'The first time he called me, I went, thinking that perhaps he wanted to smoothen things out,' VP recalled. 'I told Rajiv, now we are not talking as PM and his minister. We are talking as Rajiv and Vishwanath. I asked him, what is this, every day Kalpnath Rai and K. K. Tewary make statements that I am a CIA agent.'

Rajiv said, 'Nahin nahin, gussa hai party maen (No, no, there is anger in the party). It is an expression of it.'

'I have run this machine with your mother,' VP was blunt. 'I know where every nut and bolt and wire is joined. K. K. Tewary and Kalpnath are loudspeakers. The microphones are installed in this very office.'

'No, no,' Rajiv said. 'I'll tell them kum karo (to reduce it).'

'What do you mean "kum karo"?' said VP indignantly. 'If I feel you are playing games with me...we cannot have a genuine dialogue (this way).... You can call me an incompetent minister or a lousy party man,' VP continued, 'but if you challenge my love for the country, then, Rajiv, I will dig in and fight. Itihas maen is issue par logon ne sar kata diye. Is par hum khatam ho jayenge (History has shown that people have given their lives for the country, if their patriotism is challenged. I too will do the same. It is immaterial to me what then follows).'

'The next day,' VP went on, 'I saw the papers had written—that it was I who had sought an appointment to see Rajiv (to patch-up). These were small games being played by the PMO.'

After a few days, Rajiv called VP over to his house again. 'It must have been around 11 p.m.' VP recalled. This time the PM went on the attack, 'When Indira Gandhi lost (the elections in 1977), you left her side.'

VP replied: 'Jo aap keh rahe hain, dharti phat jaani chahiye (What you are saying is so untrue that the earth should open up).'

'We used to go and see Indiraji at her Willingdon Crescent house.' A stung VP then said to Rajiv, 'Sanjay was around, but...you were not there and now you are telling me that I was not there with her.'

Rajiv was silent.

'If this is what you (really) think,' VP said, 'you can take it that Vishwanath is dead.' He stood up to go.

'No, no, Vishwanath,' he said, 'sit down.'

Rajiv told VP that without the Congress, he would not survive even for three months.

'Rajivji, if I can stand firm for three months toh main kharha reh jaunga. Meri toh problem hi pehle teen maheenae ki hai (Rajivji, if I can stand firm for three months, I will be able to stand on my own. My problem is of the first three months).' VP knew that if he stayed the course for the first weeks, he would generate enough momentum to take off—and that is exactly what happened.

It was a rainy day on 15 July 1987 when a group of dissident Congressmen drove to Haridwar to address a political meeting. They wanted 'to test the waters' and see what kind of public response they would get. VP accompanied them. A large number of people were patiently waiting under their umbrellas for them. Arif Mohammed Khan mounted a blistering attack on Rajiv Gandhi. VP too went on the offensive against the government, dubbing the fight as 'aar paar ki larhai (fight to the finish)'. That night Arif Mohammed Khan, Arun Nehru, and V. C. Shukla, all former ministers in the Rajiv Gandhi government, were expelled from the Congress. But VP's name was not on the list of those who had been shown the door. He issued a tough statement against the Congress high command—for taking action without even hearing what the leaders had to say in their defence.

Rajiv had moved strategically by not expelling VP along with the others. The idea was to delink him from them. Rajiv hoped that with the others out of the way, VP's position inside the Congress would get weakened. If he supported the expelled leaders, disciplinary action could be taken against him for anti-party activity. Rajiv did not want to be seen to be taking action against VP for his anti-corruption crusade, which would make him a hero. VP saw through Rajiv's game.

He phoned Arun Nehru that night. 'I am sticking with you,' he said. 'This is to tell you that I have burnt all my boats.' VP announced his resignation from the Congress the next day. He first made the announcement to the press in Haridwar. It was only after that, that he sent his letter of resignation on to Rajiv. He did not accept it—not immediately.

Rajiv's final bulawa (invitation) to VP came on 19 July 1987. It was the day the *Indian Express* carried an exposé against Ajitabh Bachchan, Amitabh Bachchan's brother. It charged Ajitabh with buying a ₹45 lakh flat in Montreux, Switzerland, in April 1986, when he was still living in Delhi. The story raised questions about the legality of the acquisition.

VP immediately wrote to the prime minister urging Rajiv to 'unturn this stone' to find out what lay under it. VP demanded that either the *Indian Express* should be prosecuted, if its charge was proved wrong, or legal action should be taken against Ajitabh. VP was keeping up the pressure on the prime minister.

This time the prime minister sent media proprietor Narendra Mohan as his emissary to VP. Mohan was the chairman of the widely read Hindi paper *Dainik Jagran*. Mohan urged VP to meet Rajiv again.

'Let us set an agenda and then let a discussion be held on it,' VP said, 'or...I have (already) written letters to Rajiv (and said what I had to).'

'Ab chaliye bhi (Now, come with me),' Narendra Mohan cajoled him, 'yeh larhai theek nahin hai (this fight is not good for anyone). He wants you to return to the government. You can take any ministry you want, including finance....'

VP said, 'When Indiraji took away my ministry, and made me PCC chief, she did it in a way that I felt honoured. Today, I am finding this humiliating. That is the difference between Indira Gandhi and Rajiv Gandhi....' Then he added with an air of finality, 'There is no question of meeting him.'

Having taken on Rajiv Gandhi on corruption, and having 'burnt his boats', he knew he would be finished politically if he were to return to the Congress for the sake of a ministry.

That afternoon, on 19 July 1987, V. P. Singh was expelled from the Congress Party. 'I was at (Ramakrishna) Hegde's house when the news came. Hegde turned to me and said, "Congratulations, you are a free man now. You have been expelled from the Congress".'

IX

'Chalaen (Shall we go)?'

With that one word to a group of mediapersons who had gathered outside his house at 1, Teen Murti Marg, Vishwanath Pratap Singh embarked on a journey that was to snowball into a movement against corruption and make him the country's seventh prime minister—all in twenty-eight months.

At 5.50 a.m., on 26 July 1987, attired in his customary white kurta–pyjama, he emerged from his residence to greet supporters who were going to accompany him. He was off to his first public rally in the western UP town of Muzaffarnagar, located in the sugar bowl of India, a week after his expulsion from the Congress Party. It would be a test of how the Indian heartland viewed his expulsion. Outside was a long line of cars that would follow him to Muzaffarnagar. The convoy of around fifty vehicles was stopped several times on the 120-kilometre stretch from Delhi to Muzaffarnagar. Groups of people standing by the roadside would raise full-throated slogans, 'V. P. Singh sangharsh karo, hum tumhare saath hain (V. P. Singh fight on, we are with you)'. 'Gali gali maen shor hai, Rajiv Gandhi chor hai (Every alley is resounding with the sound Rajiv Gandhi is a thief)'.

The vast Inter-college ground in Muzaffarnagar was packed. The crowd had been waiting for him for four hours. Moving around, I realized this was not a staged event—as political gatherings usually tend to be, full of paid supporters orchestrated by the party in question. Many people had made their way to the venue on their own, atop hundreds of tractors which were parked around the ground. Or they had come on foot, or in buses they themselves had hired. Those gathered were people who had come to assess for themselves a man they saw as an alternative to the government in power. The atmosphere crackled with expectancy. Slogans rent the air here too, 'Raja nahin, faqir hai, desh ki taqdeer hai (He is not a raja but a mendicant, he is the country's destiny).'

VP addressed the crowd along with his colleagues who had been expelled or suspended from the Congress—Arun Nehru, Arif Mohammed Khan, Satyapal Malik, and Ram Dhan, who was a senior Dalit leader.

V. P. Singh, no great orator, spoke about local issues first. Then he ripped into Rajiv Gandhi and the Bachchans. 'My only fault,' he said, 'was sharing this information about corruption with the people.' And the crowd shouted, 'V. P. Singh aur bhanda phorho, aur bhanda phorho (V. P. Singh expose them even more, expose them even more).' By the end, enthusiastic youngsters had got on to the stage, wanting to see the leaders at close quarters and touch them. They threw flower petals at them. The stage almost gave way and the politicians had to fight their way out of the crowd with great difficulty. Muzaffarnagar showed the changing mood in heartland India. People were becoming disillusioned with Rajiv and saw him as a protector of the corrupt. They were beginning to view VP as their saviour. The slogan 'Takht badal do, taj badal do, beimaano ka raaj badal do (Change the throne, change the crown, change the rule of the corrupt)' captured the prevalent mood.

■

The success of the Muzaffarnagar meeting led to intense discussions within the VP group. They would meet at his house every evening to strategize. They drew up a list of 200 Congress MPs and MLAs who were disenchanted with Rajiv Gandhi—and could join them. They decided they would launch a new non-political organization—the Jan Morcha—and not a political party. It would enable dissatisfied Congressmen and Congresswomen to associate with them without attracting disciplinary action, which joining a political party would have done.

Publicly the group talked about changing a corrupt system. Privately, they knew that more Congressmen would join their ranks only if the Congress did not get a majority in the next elections. VP's idea at the time was to create an alternate Congress to the Congress led by Rajiv Gandhi, and not an anti-Congress political front. The Jan Morcha was launched on 2 October 1987—and was headed by the Dalit leader Ram Dhan.

■

'Raja sahib wants you to go and see Devi Lal now,' Santosh Bhartiya told Som Pal. Pal and Bhartiya had emerged as the key lieutenants of V. P. Singh. That day both knew what Pal had to do.

VP had been closely tracking the elections in Haryana. The results were declared on 16 June 1987. Devi Lal had scored a huge victory. His party, the Lok Dal, at one time headed by Charan Singh, had won 60 seats on its own, and its ally, the BJP, had got 16 (out of a total of 90). Rajiv

Gandhi's Congress got a drubbing, winning only 5 seats. The message was clear. For all his massive majority in the Lok Sabha, Rajiv had begun to lose ground halfway into his term.

Som Pal met Devi Lal in Chandigarh. He urged 'Mamaji' to play 'a role in national politics', and to 'back VP as a prime ministerial candidate of the Opposition'. Devi Lal ridiculed the idea. 'Haryana has shown the way to the country,' he told Pal. 'By the next election, a non-Congress Opposition will form the government at the centre.... Sarkar tho humari hee banegi (You see, we will form the government next time),' he said confidently. 'Anybody coming out of the Congress cannot become the leader,' he said contemptuously. 'But,' he offered by way of a concession, 'V. P. Singh is welcome to join my party.' Then, he added, as an afterthought, 'I hear he is a good and an able man. Usae hum "wazir-fazir" bana daenge (We can make him a minister when we form a government at the centre).'

But a few days later, Devi Lal rang up Som Pal. 'I am coming to Delhi on 27 July and want to see you.' A mystified Pal went to meet him in Haryana Bhavan. As he entered the CM's room, Devi Lal said abruptly, 'I want to meet V. P. Singh.' Intrigued by the change of heart that seemed to have taken place in Devi Lal, Pal asked him, 'Mamaji, what has made you change your mind in such a short time?' Devi Lal replied, 'I sent a dozen CID men to do a quick survey in Delhi and the neighbouring districts of western UP. They came back with the report that VP has already become a great favourite of the people.' Devi Lal offered to meet VP the next morning, over breakfast. 'We can meet either at Haryana Bhavan or at VP's Teen Murti Marg residence, whichever is more convenient for him.'

VP, in his polite fashion, said that since Devi Lal was senior, and also the chief minister, he would go to see him at Haryana Bhavan. Som Pal drove VP there. 'When they finished,' recalled Pal, 'I was called inside. I was told that a meeting should be arranged somewhere in UP or in Rajasthan which would be addressed by the two leaders (to kick off their joint campaign).'

VP and Devi Lal decided to hold their first joint meeting on 9 August 1987, the anniversary of the Quit India movement. They selected Sangariya in Ganganagar district in Rajasthan as the venue. It was a small town, with a population of only 30,000 people. But it was near the border, and only 3 kilometres from Devi Lal's own village, Chautala. They had chosen the venue strategically. The idea was to enable people from Haryana villages to come in large numbers and to ensure an impressive turnout.

The meeting was a great success. Devi Lal was now convinced that joining hands with VP would be politically beneficial. He reached out to other Opposition leaders to join them.

Although there were some hiccups, such as Devi Lal's initial opposition to having fellow Jat and rival Ajit Singh (who headed Lok Dal (Ajit)), another rump party of the erstwhile Lok Dal his father Charan Singh had led, different groups began finally to coalesce around V. P. Singh.

■

'It was when I started to get such a strong and wide response, (that) I felt that...a real alternative to the Congress could be possible...(and) would be a contribution to the country's democracy,' V. P. Singh told me.

He figured there were three options before him. One, to select eminent people from all over the country and form a new party. Two, to bring together existing political collectivities and forge a new party. And three, to continue as a front, and create a movement for social change. 'Personally, I would have opted for continuing as a front, and creating a movement of people.' Ram Dhan warned him against forming a party. Sarvodaya leader Acharya Ramamurti felt that this 'urja' (energy) VP had unleashed 'should not be...consumed by politicians' but used for bringing change. However, this was really not the view of most of the political leaders who wanted to join VP—Orissa's Biju Patnaik, Karnataka's R. K. Hegde, Haryana's Devi Lal. Also, most of his colleagues in the Jan Morcha were for contesting elections, and not just being a part of a movement for social change. The eventual consensus amongst all those who were considering throwing in their lot with him was in favour of launching a political party.

The question now arose, whether to do this by 'selecting good people from around the country and from within existing parties' or by bringing together existing political entities. Cherry picking 'good people' from various parties to form a new entity would have further fragmented the Opposition. 'Every party in the Opposition would have been split,' VP said. 'In Karnataka...the government would have fallen.' Even the BJP might have split.

'At that time Atal Bihari Vajpayee, Jaswant Singh, and Bhairon Singh Shekhawat were ready to join a new party,' VP claimed. (Vajpayee would later deny this.) On the other hand, BJP leader Jaswant Singh warned VP not to bring together existing parties.

In the end, VP concluded that the only way to take on the Congress was to unite the existing Opposition parties. No group was strong enough on its own to mount a challenge to Rajiv Gandhi with his 414 Lok Sabha seats. A brand-new party would not be able to defeat an established organization like the Congress. VP knew that he would have to bring the entire phalanx of anti-Congress forces together on a common platform. He hoped the Jan Morcha would 'act as (the) cement between the big boulders' in the Opposition. But the more realistic H. N. Bahuguna told him, and his warning turned out to be prophetic, 'Vishwanath, cement can join one boulder with another, but (it) cannot join a boulder with a piece of wood.'

V. P. Singh also knew he would have to contend with the mega egos of the various Opposition leaders, all used to having their way. A Congressman all his life, VP now had to navigate the minefield called Opposition politics—a very different ecosystem from the one he was used to. 'Managing contradictions is an art,' VP used to say optimistically, 'which consists of identifying the common...interest and not the differences.... I could identify the common interest—which was to defeat the Congress.... My aim was that there should be no voice of the Opposition left out of this formation. I could marshal all these forces to a common point of defeating the Congress, and this worked.'

■

The Allahabad by-election in June 1988 gave a fillip to the Opposition unity that VP now sought. There had been talk of Amitabh Bachchan standing again as the Congress candidate. The moment VP heard that Bachchan might stand, he decided he would contest—to take him on as a candidate of the united Opposition. For VP, it would have been a vindication of honour. At the last minute, Bachchan decided not to stand. The Congress fielded Sunil Shastri, son of Lal Bahadur Shastri, whose family VP had great regard for. The idea was to make it difficult for VP to fight Shastri. VP campaigned extensively, riding pillion on a two-wheeler scooter, his head wrapped in a towel in the searing June heat. It was a style contra-distinct from that of the Congress. He emphasized austerity, but he also spoke of national issues. The Congress focussed on wooing different castes. Devi Lal sent his 'green brigade' of volunteers to campaign for VP—they wore green headbands to distinguish themselves from other campaigners. VP defeated the might of the Congress—and won handsomely. And he managed to prove that he could win even without the Congress's electoral machinery. Cartoonist R. K. Laxman was to capture the essence of Allahabad: the cartoon he drew showed the wreckage of a huge tank lying by the wayside while V. P. Singh rode away on a motor cycle; in the turret was Sunil Shastri telling PM Rajiv Gandhi on a walkie talkie, 'Rajiv, he rammed his bicycle into mine and drove away.'

Allahabad had a demonstrable effect on the Opposition parties. They saw what was possible if they joined hands to take on the Congress.

■

On 27 July 1988, V. P. Singh announced the formation of the seven-party National Front comprising the Janata Party, Lok Dal (B), Congress (S), TDP, DMK, and AGP. The Jan Morcha which was only a non-party platform also joined the alliance. Officially, the National Front was launched two months later with great fanfare on the Marina Beach in Madras (Chennai). 'The National Front is a chariot of God Aditya (sun),' thundered Andhra

Pradesh Chief Minister N. T. Rama Rao. 'This chariot of ours will dispel the gloom and shadows that thickened through the passage of the last few decades of national history.' Rama Rao became the chairman of the front and V. P. Singh its convenor. The event boosted VP's profile; suddenly the southern part of the country also started to view him as the prime ministerial candidate of the Opposition.

On 11 October 1988, which was the birthday of Jayaprakash Narayan, VP announced the formation of a new party, the Janata Dal; it would be the centrepiece of the united Opposition. After prolonged and tortuous negotiations, he had succeeded in getting the centrist parties in the Opposition—the Janata Party (which now included the Lok Dal (A), Lok Dal (B), Congress (S), which was a small breakaway group of the Congress, and his own Jan Morcha—to dissolve their respective identities and merge with the new party. The Janata Dal was launched at a convention in Bangalore hosted by Karnataka chief minister Ramakrishna Hegde. The merger did not come about without glitches. There was an open spat between Chandra Shekhar and Hegde, both from the Janata Party, and an equally ugly war of words between H. N. Bahuguna, who headed the Lok Dal (B) named after him, and Devi Lal. 'Not a hero but a zero', Devi Lal lashed out at Bahuguna for boycotting the Bangalore meet.

Unlike Bahuguna, the wily Chandra Shekhar came to the launch of the Janata Dal—he thought it would be better to be in than out, if there was the likelihood of the new grouping coming to power. Chandra Shekhar and Bahuguna were both opposed to VP's leadership. Hegde and Devi Lal stood by VP.

■

Having created the instrument to take on the Congress, VP flung himself into the battle to dethrone Rajiv Gandhi. By now, the momentum on the Bofors case against Rajiv was beginning to peter out. This was despite the additional information published by *The Hindu*, and *The Statesman*, and *Indian Express*, from time to time about front companies of Indian agents who were paid for the deal. Under pressure from the Opposition, Rajiv had set up a Joint Parliamentary Committee (JPC) on 6 August 1987 to identify the recipients of the ₹64 crores of commissions paid by Bofors to clinch the deal. The JPC in April 1988 exonerated the government of any wrongdoing. But the government's woes were not over yet. On 18 July 1989, the report by the CAG, the official government auditor, was tabled in parliament. It indicted the government on Bofors.

The CAG report was for Rajiv Gandhi what the Allahabad judgment had been for his mother, Indira Gandhi, in 1975 which had disqualified her from parliament. Opposition MPs demanded a debate in parliament. Lok Sabha Speaker Balram Jakhar refused. For three days, the MPs stalled parliament, demanding that Rajiv quit and order fresh elections. 'The CAG report has ended the 1984 mandate for Rajiv,' V. P. Singh thundered.

On 24 July 1989, on a cloudy Monday in Delhi, seventy-three MPs belonging to twelve parties walked into parliament and submitted their resignations from the Lok Sabha. It was a move that caught the Congress by surprise. If Rajiv Gandhi did not resign on Bofors, it was better that they did so, the MPs said. The resignations were a turning point in the battle to dislodge the Congress. VP had convinced the Opposition stalwarts about the impact en masse resignations would have. The MPs agreed to go along with his plan, even though it meant a loss of salary, allowances, travel expenditure by rail and air—there were still three months to go before elections were due. Even more important, they would have to forego the lifelong monthly pension which they would have got if they were to complete their full term.

With this move, V. P. Singh had managed to unsettle the Congress. More significantly, the resignations brought the BJP and the Left parties, for all their disquiet about each other, to stand behind VP. Vajpayee declared, 'From Left to Right we have now all come together to defeat a common enemy.' N. T. Rama Rao had worked the phones to the Left leaders Jyoti Basu and E. M. S. Namboodiripad and BJP stalwarts Atal Bihari Vajpayee and L. K. Advani to bring them on board. The BJP had only two Lok Sabha MPs but the Left had fifty-two MPs. At a dinner hosted by N. T. Rama Rao for the Opposition leaders, Madhu Dandavate had quipped, 'Now we need Comrade Vajpayee and Pandit Namboodiripad to work together to oust Rajiv!'

Suddenly, Bofors had come back centre stage as a poll issue. When elections were announced on 17 October 1989, the slogan rent the air all over North India, 'Gali gali maen shor hai, Rajiv Gandhi chor hai'. Rajiv Gandhi's credibility had taken a knock. The Congress went into the elections on the defensive. Its party managers knew it was not a happy position to be in.

V. P. Singh remained unrelenting in his attack on Rajiv Gandhi. Once, while travelling with VP to Uttar Pradesh in 1989, I had asked him whether he was concerned that Devi Lal and Chandra Shekhar might not allow him to become PM. 'I don't care who becomes prime minister,' he said with a vehemence which took me aback. 'But this man (Rajiv) must go.' I had wondered that day whether he had suffered any unknown slights at the hands of Rajiv which lent his fight an additional edge.

V. P. Singh turned out to be a brilliant tactician—accessible, and accommodating towards the allies, often letting them take the credit. And yet he did not allow the initiative to go out of his hands. Continuing to build the momentum against Rajiv Gandhi, he criss-crossed UP and Bihar, deputing his colleagues to look after the other states. As his car would race through the countryside by night to get from one election meeting to the next, it would pass small groups of poor villagers standing by the roadside holding up kerosene lamps in order to get a glimpse of the 'raja turned faqir'. Every time he spotted one of these groups, he would stop the vehicle, and exchange a few words with the villagers before moving on.

■

V. P. Singh's poll strategy was simple: strike at Rajiv Gandhi and demolish the Congress. As he had done in Muzaffarnagar in July 1987, so also during the election campaign in October 1989, he spoke of local concerns alongside national issues. And, at every rally, he would ask, 'Bofors ka dalaal kaun hai (Who is the middleman/broker for Bofors)?' The audience would shout back lustily, 'Rajiv Gandhi.' VP's message had percolated down to the villages.

Rajiv Gandhi, on the other hand, hired an agency to mount a high-voltage Congress campaign. It described the Opposition as 'scorpions and fighting roosters'. This did not connect with ordinary people. He also made other mistakes. He had kicked off his election campaign from Ayodhya on 3 November 1989, by declaring that he would bring a Ram rajya in the country. He was now fighting on the BJP's turf, using its terminology. Then he allowed the VHP to lay the foundation stone for the Ram temple in Ayodhya on 9 November 1989. 'It was that day ...for the first time... that I felt we had a chance (of winning),' V. P. Singh told me.

A section of the Muslims now threw their weight behind VP, despite his alliance with the BJP. His partnership with the Left parties also netted the coalition a major haul of seats.

The Janata Dal won the second largest number of seats in the elections. When Rajiv Gandhi declined to form the government, as the leader of the largest party in parliament with 197 seats, but still short of a majority, V. P. Singh was sworn in as the seventh prime minister of India on 2 December 1989. He headed what was probably the most contradiction-ridden government in India's history, even as it represented the widest possible shades of opinion from the Left to the Right. Shaky from the first day, few thought it would last its full term. It was at the height of its deepest crisis that VP played the Mandal gambit. It unleashed a reaction he had least expected.

X

The aftermath of the Mandal decision was as dramatic as the decision itself. The Mandal story is incomplete without a look at its fallout—which set the country's political agenda for three decades and more. Mandal unleashed forces which VP had not anticipated. Even though he used to pride himself for his ability to 'manage contradictions'—these were to finally devour his government.

On 19 September 1990, Rajeev Goswami, a twenty-year-old student of Delhi's Deshbandhu College immolated himself near his campus in protest against Mandal. As the flames began to envelop his torso and head, the boy screamed in agony. He tried to beat out the fire with his green kurta-clad arms; his stupefied friends stood around, watching helplessly.

Agitated by the Mandal decision, nine days earlier, a group of students had sat on a dharna outside their college. But they had not received the media attention they had expected. It was then that they decided to go in for something more dramatic—self-immolation. Two of Rajeev's friends were to set themselves alight along with him. But they backed out at the last moment. Spectators watched Rajeev shrieking in pain and thrashing around. But no one stepped forward to help. It was the police who finally put out the fire.

Rajeev Goswami's screams became the defining moment of the anti-Mandal agitation. Before the flames were finally doused, he had received 50 per cent burns all over his body. It was said at the time that he had planned to douse only his ankles and legs with kerosene and set them alight. His friends were then to rescue him. Whether he himself decided at the last moment to pour kerosene all over his body or others did it for him has continued to remain a mystery. Rajeev had told his mother the night before, 'Hum sirf tamasha karne jaa rahe hain.' (We are only going to indulge in some dramatics.) Somewhere, the plan to stage a drama went horribly wrong. The critically injured Rajeev was rushed to Safdarjung Hospital. Two days later, the intersection near Safdarjung Hospital was renamed by students as Qurbani Chowk (Sacrifice Circle).

The second immolation took place in Delhi a few days later. A young man drove to the AIIMS intersection on his motorbike, calmly parked it on one side of the road, took out a bottle of kerosene from his bag, poured it over himself, and set himself ablaze. A crowd of students who were there, waiting to get word about Rajeev inside the burns unit, rushed over to the burning man to try and save him. 'As I got to the spot where he was...I saw an image I will never forget,' wrote Parag Vohra, a student who witnessed the incident. 'A pair of melted Nikes was all there was left of an individual.' The man died. People did not even remember his name afterwards. Rajeev Goswami survived, only to die fourteen years later on 24 February 2004 at the age of thirty-three of jaundice-induced complications. His body had been irreparably damaged by his attempt to immolate himself.

■

'I had expected opposition to Mandal,' V. P. Singh told me years later, 'and was prepared for it. But I had not expected immolation by students.'

The prime minister expected the middle class and upper castes not to support Mandal. It went against their interests. 'You cannot argue out an interest,' VP shrugged philosophically. 'You can only compromise with an interest...I had even thought it (Opposition) may take place in the villages of UP and Bihar.... But,' he said again and again, 'not...immolations.'

In the beginning, the anti-Mandal protests were limited to candlelight vigils and silent marches in Delhi University. There were a few incidents of students smashing the glass panes of Delhi Transport Corporation (DTC) buses. The politically affiliated students' unions, the Congress-aligned National Students Union of India (NSUI) and the pro-BJP Akhil Bharatiya Vidyarthi Parishad (ABVP) were initially cool to the protests. They jumped in only when they got the go-ahead from the political parties they were aligned with.

But Rajeev's immolation galvanized young people all over India. The situation grew violent as the number of immolations increased. The government had to call out the army in Chandigarh; in other places, the police opened fire. Sixty-three youngsters died by immolating themselves. Ultimately, the figure went up to 200.

Officially, the BJP and the Congress did not take an anti-Mandal position. They were only unhappy that they had not been consulted—and condemned the manner in which it had been implemented.

A day after the cabinet decision, that is on 8 August 1990, when the Rajya Sabha debated Mandal, BJP leader Pramod Mahajan had suggested only economic criteria to be built into the decision.

However, after Rajeev Goswami's immolation attempt—it happened a week before Advani's Rath Yatra was to start in September—the BJP panicked. For students all over North India went on the rampage against Mandal—in city after city. When Advani and Madan Lal Khurana went to commiserate with Rajeev's parents at the Safdarjung Hospital, they were hooted at by the protesting students. Khurana was roughed up. Advani and Khurana were told to publicly denounce the Mandal Commission Report. Or they should not come to sympathize with the students. Since Advani could not disown Mandal—it was part of the BJP's manifesto—he only condemned the police excesses against the students.

As the student protests spread, Advani could see support for the BJP ebbing away. Students gathered outside the BJP's Delhi office to protest. Advani knew that unless the party acted, the middle classes and the upper castes, who were most agitated by Mandal, and who were the backbone of the BJP, would desert them.

There was another reason for the BJP's worry. BJP leaders suspected that V. P. Singh had played the Mandal card because he was getting ready to go in for an early election.

When VP had asked Vajpayee what had suddenly set the BJP against the government, as VP said to me, the BJP stalwart had replied with candour, 'Your speech on August 15 (1990).... It was for the first time that a holiday had been announced on Prophet Muhammad's birthday.'

VP remonstrated that the BJP had not objected when 'Rajiv was increasing holidays all the time with one stroke of his pen'.

Vajpayee: '(But) we felt this is like a manifesto...and you could go in for elections.' He added, 'Before (you did) that we had to act.'

VP: 'Mandal toh aapke manifesto maen bhi thaa, usi se prerna lee hai (Mandal was in your manifesto I have taken inspiration from it).'

'Prerna laete rehte (You could have continued to take inspiration from it),' Vajpayee was quick with his riposte, 'par prakriya kyon kar dee (Why did you have to implement it).'

■

'I was very clear,' V. P. Singh told me, 'that my government would last not more than two years.' This had become clear to him the day he took over as prime minister. He was also clear that it would be the BJP 'which will bring down the government'.

'I was clear because BJP was the aspirant for the same chair....' But the contradictions inside the coalition he led—and Devi Lal in particular—were to hasten the downfall.

K. N. Govindacharya was also clear that the BJP's real adversary in the future would be V. P. Singh. 'Our fight is ultimately going to be against V. P. Singh,' Govindacharya prophesized. 'This is ideologically inevitable.' The BJP's high profile general secretary said this to me on the day—and I found this astonishing—that VP was sworn in as prime minister with the support of the BJP. I had gone to the BJP office on Ashoka Road in Delhi on 2 December 1989 and was chatting with Govindacharya about the day's events. As we stood there outside the media room, he recalled what VP had told him in early 1989, before the National Front came to power. 'Govindji, first this government (of Rajiv Gandhi) has to go. Only then can either you or I move forward.'

That day VP had talked at length about the importance of vote banks. 'You can create an organization as much as you like. But if you ignore vote banks, you will not be able to win.' VP then told Govindacharya about the vote bank he hoped to create to defeat Rajiv Gandhi's Congress. 'I can break half the forward castes (who are with the Congress). Some of your supporters (also upper castes) may also come with us. (But) we have to ensure that we do not antagonize the backward classes. They are by inclination with the Opposition. The Dalits will not come with us in a hurry because they feel obliged to the Congress, right from (Mahatma) Gandhi's time.... (However) without the Muslims breaking away from the Congress, the Congress will not lose.

'...If I am seen with you blindly then all will be over. Then we will continue to sit in the Opposition.... We will try to get the Muslim vote, you try to consolidate the Hindu vote through the Ram Janmabhoomi (movement). You can abuse me, I won't feel bad about it. But I can't share a platform with you, please don't feel bad about that...please explain this to your people.'

Govindacharya's conversation with V. P. Singh took place soon after a public meeting held in the western UP town of Mathura. When VP had arrived there, he found BJP flags flying on the dais along with the Janata Dal flags. He threw a tantrum. 'I will not go on the stage till the BJP flags are removed.'

V. P. Singh phoned Govindacharya from Mathura. 'Please, talk to your people and get the BJP flags down,' he said. The flags were brought down in full view of the public. Only then did VP address the rally. With this action, he sent a clear signal to the Muslims that he was distancing himself from the BJP. 'I could do it (bring down the flags),' Govindacharya said, 'because I had the support of the organization then.'

'Once Rajiv goes,' VP told Govindacharya that day, 'we can fight each other. We will see later who gets the better of whom.'

■

'The decision to hold the (Somnath to Ayodhya) Rath Yatra was made (as early as) on 29 June 1990,' Govindacharya told me. Informal consultations had gone on inside the BJP all through June 1990. As mentioned earlier, it was at a secret meeting in Delhi on 1 July 1990 that the decision was firmed up. This was five weeks before VP decided to go ahead with Mandal in August. The preparations for the yatra had got underway in July 1990 itself.

'The idea for the Rath Yatra was mine,' the normally self-effacing Govindacharya revealed. He had discussed it with Bhaurao Deoras, who was in charge of the political wing of the RSS. 'Bhaurao used to encourage new ideas,' Govindacharya said.

Bhaurao gave his backing to Govindacharya to go ahead with the plan. Even though Govindacharya did not say so, given the way the RSS functioned, his proposal would have been discussed at various levels of the Sangh's decision-making hierarchy, and green-lighted only after that.

By then the BJP had already adopted mandir (the proposal to build a Ram temple in Ayodhya) as part of its agenda. This was done in mid-1989 at its national executive meet in Palampur in Himachal Pradesh. Till then, only individual BJP members, like Vijaya Raje Scindia and Vinay Katiyar, had supported the VHP's temple plan.

Initially, several senior BJP leaders were reluctant to include mandir in the Palampur Resolution. They had received only a lukewarm response to the idea. 'I remember Sushma Swaraj speaking in Himachal Pradesh,'

Govindacharya recalled. 'When she referred to the Ram Janmabhoomi movement, the crowd was silent. When she started speaking about the farmers' needs, her words were greeted with a huge applause.' But the RSS and the VHP stepped up pressure on the BJP to commit itself to the construction of the temple.

It was Bhaurao Deoras who managed to convince Advani. Then Vajpayee also decided to go along with the plan. But, after the National Front came to power, the moderate streak in Vajpayee would reassert itself. Whenever Mandir came up in the internal meetings of the BJP, Vajpayee would argue, 'What's the hurry? It can wait for a while.... If we push hard with these "hard" secular people, the alliance can break.' He did not want to do anything which would bring the Congress back to power. The BJP leaders could not forget that their alliance with VP had yielded the party 85 seats, up from the paltry 2 it had got on its own in 1984. They were willing to put Mandir on the back-burner for electoral gains.

But the post-Meham shenanigans in the Janata Dal had convinced many in the BJP–RSS–VHP family that the countdown had begun for the VP government. The VHP, as seen, had already announced another kar seva in Ayodhya on 30 October 1990 to start the construction of the temple.

It was at this stage—in June 1990—that Govindacharya spoke to Advani about undertaking a Rath Yatra.

'Though I was young, Advaniji used to listen to me and give weight to what I had to say,' Govindacharya said. 'That was because of the Sangh (RSS). In a way, he considered me as Bhaurao's representative (in the BJP).' Govindacharya reminded Advani of the phenomenal success of the VHP's Ekatmata Yatra in 1983. As we saw in Chapter 1, this yatra was responsible for generating an outpouring of Hindu religious fervour. 'The BJP's role today could be to create a similar...atmosphere in the country,' Govindacharya told Advani persuasively.

'Baat toh sahi hai (It sounds good),' Advani replied. 'Do one thing,' he told Govindacharya. 'You talk to the others also—to Atalji, Sikander Bakhtji, Rajmataji....'

Govindacharya proposed four yatras from different parts of the country which would converge in Ayodhya in time for the 30 October kar seva. 'The idea was for Advani to set out from Kanyakumari or Kalady,' Govindacharya recalled. 'Sikander Bakht would start his yatra from Mumbai, Vajpayee from Jammu and the Rajmata (Vijaya Raje Scindia) from Kamakhya (Assam). And they would meet in Ayodhya on 30 October (1990) to participate in kar seva there....

'(However), when I talked to the other three, they declined.... Rajmataji said she could not do it for reasons of health. Sikander Bakht said no one would listen to him, but "I will join it once in a while". Atalji was outright dismissive, "I don't believe in this nautanki (theatrics)...."'

Govindacharya reported back to Advani. It was decided then that only Advani would lead the yatra. 'We will do one thing,' Advani offered. 'If I start from Kalady, it will become too religious an agenda.... I have been thinking maybe I should start from Somnath. The issue should remain political. For, after all, we are in this work for the BJP (as a political party).'

BJP leader Pramod Mahajan, with his go-getting ways, was roped in. He was tasked with taking care of the logistics, and to get the rath (chariot) constructed. 'You leave all that to me,' Mahajan said reassuringly. He was known for mounting big events, given his contacts with Mumbai's corporate world—and leveraged them for the Rath Yatra. Arun Jaitley was to look after the press and publicity at the Delhi end. And Govindacharya was tasked with the daily planning of the yatra.

'The Rath Yatra was decided much before (the Mandal decision),' Govindacharya told me emphatically. 'It was also decided in July (1990) itself that we would announce it publicly only on 15 or 16 September. Till then it was to be kept under wraps.... The yatra was to start on 25 September.'

As planned, the yatra was announced on 16 September 1990. But because V. P. Singh had adopted Mandal by then, the BJP billed the Rath Yatra a response to his decision.

■

Mandal was a reaction to Mandir—not the other way around—as is widely believed. Even the Rath Yatra was not a response to Mandal. The decision to hold it, as just seen, was made over a month earlier, on 29 June 1990—forty days before Mandal was announced by V. P. Singh on 7 August 1990.

The BJP had piggy-backed on the VP wave, its tally jumping from 2 seats to 85 in 1989. Painstaking ground work—which had been done in UP to bring about 'one-on-one' contests, pitting one candidate from the Opposition against the Congress candidate to prevent a split in the Opposition vote—had helped. This was done in most of the Lok Sabha constituencies in the state in an impressive show of opposition unity. But after Meham, the BJP felt the government may not last long. It decided to go back to Mandir to mobilize people along religious lines—and get ready for early elections.

VP played the Mandal card to checkmate Devi Lal, as we have seen. But, more important, he was trying to put in place an alternate support base around the issue of 'social justice'—made up of the OBCs, Muslims, and a section of the upper castes, including his own—knowing the plans the BJP had up its sleeve. But things didn't quite work out the way VP had planned.

Mandal lent the Rath Yatra, which had anyway been planned, an urgency. The BJP could not risk its voter base fragmenting along caste lines. It feared it would lose its supporters, angry about Mandal, if it continued to support the V. P. Singh government.

The youth who immolated themselves in August and September 1990 and led the agitation against Mandal sensed shrinking opportunities; it created a sense of victimhood in them. All at once, the upper castes became 'a solid rock'. Mandal united a disparate group of people—Gandhians, Marxists, religious fundamentalists, and secularists—as nothing else could have done. Many turned to the BJP for protection and support.

The strong opposition from the upper castes created a counter political consciousness amongst the OBCs about their identity—which otherwise might not have happened so quickly.

■

One day, during this period, an unsigned letter arrived at Bhure Lal's residence. It was from Rashtrapati Bhavan and it was meant for V. P. Singh's eyes. From President R. Venkataraman, it suggested the prime minister refer Mandal to the Supreme Court for its view, under Article 143 of the Constitution. It might defuse a situation which was becoming increasingly flammable.

Bhure Lal took the letter to V. P. Singh. VP was inclined to accept the suggestion. But the Mandalites in the party prevailed on him not to do so.

VP knew he could not go back on his Mandal decision—even if he had wanted to. Any backtracking would have brought the OBCs out on the streets, leading to more clashes and violence. Now, he could only go forward. VP held firm.

'There was a lot of politics behind Mandal,' VP was to say years later. 'The first reaction (opposition by students to Mandal) was genuine. Later, it was fuelled by politicians for their own ends.'

VP, however, made a last-ditch effort to save his government. He promulgated an ordinance on 19 October 1990 even as the Rath Yatra was moving inexorably towards its end. The idea was for the government to acquire the undisputed land (27 hectares) around the disputed structure, and allow the VHP to start kar seva there. The disputed Babri structure would remain with the government till the Supreme Court decided the tricky question—whether a temple existed there in the past. The VHP and BJP agreed to the plan. 'If you win in court,' VP told the BJP leaders optimistically, 'you can extend the temple. If you don't, you have a temple next door.'

'(Then) I will (also) accompany you to offer kar seva,' he told the BJP leaders cheerfully. At this point Bhairon Singh Shekhawat quipped, tongue-in-cheek, 'If you will do kar seva, what will there be left for us to do!'

It was chief minister of UP, Mulayam Singh Yadav who shot down the proposal. 'Not even a sparrow will enter Ayodhya,' he said, a remark which was to be quoted for years afterwards. He refused to allow kar sevaks to enter Ayodhya. Within two days, VP had to withdraw the ordinance. 'The same day I rang up Lalu (Yadav) at 9 p.m. and told him to arrest Advani. We went in for a red alert. But I needed one day's breather for further consolidating the administrative machinery.... I told Lalu to arrest (Advani) after 2 a.m. so that there was nothing in the press the next morning, and (BJP) supporters did not go out of hand.' VP had learnt this trick from Indira Gandhi. She would announce a controversial decision late at night so that the press missed its deadline. A day-late headline had less of an impact.

Advani was arrested by Lalu Yadav at 4 a.m. on 23 October 1990 in Bihar's Samastipur district. The BJP withdrew support to VP's government. The BJP's letter of withdrawal was already with Vajpayee. He went to the president and handed it over. Later Vajpayee told VP, 'Aapne Mandal kiya, toh humne Kamandal kar diya (You went in for Mandal so we went in for Kamandal).' Kamandal is a reliquary that Hindu ascetics carry.

■

'Rajiv helped to make the Rath Yatra a success,' disclosed H. R. Bhardwaj enigmatically, 'so that VP would be forced to arrest Advani and the BJP would withdraw support to his government.' Though Bhardwaj did not state it explicitly, the Congress had given its help to mobilize the crowds for the Rath Yatra without coming upfront. Then Bhardwaj added as an afterthought, 'Rajiv was not as naive as people believed.'

Once it became clear that the VP government was on its last legs, Arun Nehru sent a message to Rajiv Gandhi. Many in the Janata Dal, he said, would be willing to support him if he made a bid for the prime ministership. It would be a homecoming for those who had left the party in 1987. For a few days it had seemed that Rajiv Gandhi might take over as prime minister again. 'I know this. Even the neighbouring countries... had been alerted....' said Dinesh Trivedi.

'We were all set to join the Congress. Even the day and time of (our) joining had been fixed,' said Trivedi. 'I think it was (just) before the confidence motion in the first week of November (1990). The decision to join (the Congress) was made at 9 a.m. It was to be announced at 6 p.m. the same day.... There was euphoria, that things were finally falling into place. And that Rajiv would take over as PM. And the same old team would be back. Arun Nehru was to be rehabilitated. He had matured. He would often say, "We are trained as Congressis, used to following the middle path".'

Congress stalwart H. K. L. Bhagat was supporting Arun Nehru's return to the party. On the face of it, so were M. L. Fotedar and Satish Sharma. 'But (in reality) Fotedar, Satish Sharma, and R. K. Dhawan sabotaged it,' Trivedi disclosed. Even though initially Fotedar and Satish Sharma had helped Arun Nehru re-establish contact with Rajiv Gandhi, 'they really apprehended Nehru's return to the Congress.' The coterie around Rajiv feared that the two cousins, Rajiv and Arun, would together begin to dominate the Congress again—and they might be relegated to the margins.

The erstwhile Jan Morcha group also suspected that Sonia Gandhi had a hand in stopping the re-entry of Arun Nehru into the Congress.

■

It was President R. Venkataraman who torpedoed the proposal to make Rajiv Gandhi prime minister when the VP government fell. He told M. L. Fotedar that he would be ready to swear in a Congress government immediately. But it would be on condition that Rajiv Gandhi agreed to swear in Pranab Mukherjee as prime minister.

Rajiv Gandhi was scheduled to see Venkataraman later that day. Fotedar had gone to sound out the president in the morning.

'RV (Venkataraman) was personally against Rajiv,' H. R. Bhardwaj had told me. He thought it was because Indira Gandhi had shown a preference for P. V. Narasimha Rao, whom she had retained in her ministry, while shunting Venkataraman out of the government to the ceremonial position of vice president in August 1984.

A shocked Fotedar reported back to Rajiv Gandhi what President Venkataraman had said to him. 'Rajiv was thoughtful for a long time,' Fotedar recalled. 'But he did not say anything.' It was then that he decided, finally, to support Chandra Shekhar as prime minister.

■

When the VP government was teetering, one of his associates had rung up a top Mumbai industrialist. 'We keep hearing you are unhappy with the government.... Surely, that cannot be the case,' he said rather unctuously. The industrialist cut him short. 'Do you think I am a chutiya (an asshole)?', he said brutally. 'This man (V. P. Singh) has tried to finish us. Do you think we will sit back and not destroy him?'

Right through his premiership, V. P. Singh had to contend with Rajiv Gandhi out to trip him, an irate Chandra Shekhar fuelling trouble, a maverick Devi Lal becoming more and more demanding, and in the final round, an assertive BJP withdrawing support to his government. Then there was the industrialists' lobby which wanted to get even with him for the raids he had conducted against many of them when he was finance minister. A combination of all these forces, and more, ensured that his government lasted only eleven months.

■

On 7 November 1990, Vishwanath Pratap Singh lost the confidence motion in parliament. His eleven-month-old government passed into history. His bete noire Chandra Shekhar became prime minister—heading a group of sixty breakaway Janata Dal MPs, supported from the 'outside' by the Congress led by Rajiv Gandhi. Chandra Shekhar's government lasted only for seven months, three of which were as the head of a caretaker government. But that's another prime ministerial story.

XI

'Jab tak samaj maen vishamta hai, tab tak samajik nyay ki avashyakata hai (As long as there are disparities in society, there will be a need for social justice).' 'These words were spoken not by V. P. Singh,' VP said in 1999, expressing immense satisfaction. 'They were spoken by Atal Bihari Vajpayee (about the need for reservations for OBCs).' Vajpayee's words showed how Mandal had altered the country's political agenda, compelling successive governments to accept the reality of job reservations for OBCs as 'irreversible'. No prime minister could undo the process.

If anything, PMs after VP extended the ambit of job reservations for the OBCs. Atal Bihari Vajpayee's government gave reservations to Jats, including them in the OBC category in Rajasthan, where they were more backward than the Jats in Haryana or UP.

Prime Minister Manmohan Singh went a step further in 2006 and took the decision to reserve 27 per cent of the seats for OBCs in centres of higher education, including elite institutions.

▪

In the days after the Mandal decision, many challenged the government's decision in court. On 1 October 1990, the Supreme Court put the decision 'in abeyance'. The court's stay came as a relief for the beleaguered VP government, which was under attack from all sides.

The Supreme Court clubbed all the petitions together in what came to be known as the *Indira Sawhney vs Union of India* case. Two years later, in 1992, the highest court in the land upheld the validity of the government's decision to reserve 27 per cent jobs in the central government for the OBCs. It also found caste an acceptable determinant of backwardness. The verdict also held that the number of reserved seats could not exceed 50 per cent of the total seats on offer. However, the court asked the government to exclude the well-off sections from the list of beneficiaries—which it did by way of another memorandum it put out on 8 September 1993.

By now Narasimha Rao was in power. It fell to him to enforce the Mandal Commission Report—the same Narasimha Rao who, as we saw earlier in the chapter, had chaired the Indira Gandhi-appointed ministerial committee on the Mandal Commission Report—and sat on it for nine long years without anything coming out of the exercise.

The Rao government fixed ₹1 lakh of yearly income as a key criterion for eligibility. Later this was to increase to ₹8 lakhs. Thereafter, Mandal became the official policy of the Indian government. Those who tried to undo reservations had to beat a hasty retreat. The RSS had attempted to question reservations during the 2015 Bihar elections. But very quickly it had to backtrack. The fear of losing reservations made the OBC groups club together; this was one reason why the BJP lost that election and the Lalu Yadav–Nitish Kumar combine won.

In October 2017, the G. Rohini Commission was set up to categorize the OBCs into subgroups—and to collect data about their populations—to ensure a more equitable distribution of the benefits of reservations to a larger number. According to data available till 2018, only ten communities had hogged 97 per cent of the reserved jobs meant for the OBCs. And as many as 983 OBC communities, out of 2,600, had got no representation at all in jobs. The commission, which was to help the government streamline its policy of reservations, was supposed to submit its report in three months' time—by January 2018. Instead, till September 2022, it had got as many as ten extensions.

No regime after V. P. Singh tried to undo the policy of reservations for the OBCs. They had only tried to bring more communities within its ambit.

■

'Mandal changed the grammar of politics,' VP said about his decision. With Mandal, caste became more of a political category than just a hierarchical social formation with only rituals, occupation, and prejudice defining it. As we have seen, the politicization of caste had begun even before independence, when the British accepted it as a category in the 1931 census. These groups began to demand patronage on the basis of their numbers. But VP's decision gave the process an impetus—as never before.

Mandal also gave a fillip to regional parties, and identity politics—and thereby to coalition governance. Caste-based regional parties grew in North India like the RJD, Samajwadi Party, and Janata Dal (U) in UP and Bihar. Smaller caste-based groupings mushroomed—for instance, the party representing the Rajbhar community, the Kurmi-dominated Apna Dal, another party of Nishads, all three in UP alone—and these in turn were wooed by mainstream parties. Their numbers had begun to matter.

Their growing clout enabled the OBCs in the Hindi heartland—as also the Scheduled Castes—to make tactical alliances with upper castes at election time from a position of strength. When Dalit leader Mayawati aligned with the Brahmins in 2007, winning an absolute majority on her own in UP to become chief minister, she had come a long way from the war cry given by her mentor Kanshi Ram, 'Tilak, Tarazu, aur Talwar, Inko maro joote chaar'. (The slogan referred to the Dalits kicking the upper castes, with the tilak representing the Brahmins, tarazu or scales the Banias, and the talwar or sword representing the Rajputs).

Though atrocities against the Dalits and the most backward castes still continue, gone are the days when higher caste toughs could en masse stamp the ballot papers on behalf of Dalits or the Most Backward Classes (MBCs), hijacking an election.

The more dominant amongst the OBCs, like the Yadavs and Kurmis— or the 'creamy layer' among the OBCs—gained more. But with time, power started to devolve to the non-Yadav/Kurmi OBCs, or MBCs— the Mahadalits, the more deprived amongst Dalits—and the 'Pasmanda Muslims', the more backward among the Muslims.

Mandal also heightened caste consciousness in the country. The upper castes would lament that it had divided society. But for Mandal's beneficiaries, caste became a badge of honour to wear—diluting the odium that had surrounded their status. Discriminated against for centuries, affirmative action was a means to their empowerment—an opportunity to catch up.

In practice, of course, there was a fine line between casteism and social justice. When a socialist worker had once remarked to Sharad Yadav that their battle had originally been about 'social justice', Yadav shot back, 'Make up your mind, do you want social justice or do you want a Yadav raj?' His response showed how quickly a new set of Brahmins could emerge.

■

The new OBC constituency VP had courted did not embrace him as their leader. They turned more to their own caste leaders. But his decision threw up a new OBC leadership which ruled India in the two decades that followed. Mulayam Singh Yadav, Lalu Prasad Yadav, Nitish Kumar, Akhilesh Yadav, Uma Bharati, Kalyan Singh, Shivraj Chouhan, Ashok Gehlot, and others went on to rule their states—UP, Bihar, Madhya Pradesh, and Rajasthan.

In 2014, when the 'chaiwallah', Narendra Modi took over the reins of the country, he became the first MBC—he belongs to the Ghanchi or the oil-presser's caste—to become prime minister of India.

VP would repeatedly say that Mandal meant 'satta maen shirkat' (participation in power). It had to be 'shirkat, not sahuliyat' (wielding of power, not doling out of patronage). He viewed Mandal not just as 44,000 jobs reserved for the OBCs in central government services. It was about OBCs exercising the levers of political power—which would give them upward mobility and economic gain.

The Mandal story is far from over as power continues to devolve to the smaller groups amongst the OBCs—and amongst the SCs—who want their place under the sun, as they realize the strength of their vote in a democracy. Knowingly or unknowingly, V. P. Singh tapped into the aspirational revolution that was taking place amongst the OBCs—and enabled it to grow into a political force.

XII

Lantern-lit boats
Littered on the sea
Which one will take me?

Towards the end of his life in 2003, strapped to a hospital bed in Apollo Hospital in New Delhi, V. P. Singh read out to me a couple of poems he had written. 'One morning I woke up very early, and looked out of the window,' V. P. Singh mused, 'I saw lantern-lit boats sail towards me.' He was at the time staying at the Raj Bhavan in Mumbai by the seaside. 'These were small boats out at the sea with lights on them.... In our religion and mythology, they say you undertake your last journey by boat.'

VP's kidneys had got damaged in 1994 after a dharna at Mumbai's Flora Fountain. He was now tied to the dialysis machine every second day. Then he got myeloma, a form of blood cancer, which damaged 50 per cent of his bone marrow. The doctors advised chemotherapy—but he managed to avoid it.

He was in a reflective mood that day. Suddenly, he said, 'All my life I scribbled.'

'Now,' he added, 'I need an eraser.'

'You come to a stage when you ask—what is the meaning of all this?'

After going out of power in 1990, he had gone back to painting and writing poetry, which he had started to do in his earlier years—first in Hindi, then in English, between interludes of dialysis. The Mandal messiah was looking back at his life's journey. Some of the images he saw now inhabited his poems.

'I used to play with paper boats in my childhood.... When you are finishing your journey, you are reminded of your... paper boats.'

Suddenly I found afloat
My childhood paper boat
It signalled
'Come it's time to go.'

■

Vishwanath Pratap Singh was arguably the most controversial prime minister India has had.

Undoubtedly, he was chaiin or politically crafty—and he could be tough. But there was also an emotional side to him, which his poetry reflected—

and it defined this complex personality. VP was a contradiction in many ways—feudal and yet not feudal, a loyalist and rebel at the same time, a man of character and a political hypocrite. Many who knew him well said that it was impossible to know the 'real' VP or where his loyalties lay. While he was a loyalist par excellence in the early phase of his political career, he would often say in later years that there was 'no such thing as loyalty in politics', it was all about the convergence of interests.

What V. P. Singh did, no one else who had left the Congress over the years had managed to do. Neither Chandra Shekhar, nor Sharad Pawar, nor Ramkrishna Hegde, nor Mamata Banerjee, nor Jagan Mohan Reddy. They too had, like VP, severed relations with the Congress leadership in the 1970s, 1980s, and 1990s in the last century, and also in the twenty-first century. Hegde, Pawar, Banerjee, Reddy went on to replace the Congress in their states and became chief ministers, ironically sometimes in alliance with the Congress they had quit. Chandra Shekhar had become prime minister at the head of a rump supported by the larger, domineering Congress. But none had managed to create a national alternative to the Congress—like VP did, though it lasted just under a year.

He brought together almost all the anti-Congress forces, of the Right, Left, Centre, and the regional parties on one platform in the first truly national coalition. It was a three-tiered arrangement, in what was a rare show of Opposition unity. He gave the regional parties a stake in national governance at the centre. 'Even when the DMK did not have a single MP, I brought it into the cabinet,' he would say. 'The idea was that once they start to participate in the management of the country, there would be no fissiparous tendencies.' He saw this as one of his major achievements.

Mandal speeded up the downfall of the Congress Party which fell between the two stools of caste and community, popularly referred to as the 'Mandal versus Kamandal' face-off.

Breaking the 'hegemony' of the Congress Party, VP inflicted such a body blow on the Congress that the grand old party of India—which had ruled the country for four decades, until VP took over (barring the interregnum when the Janata Party ruled (1977–79)—never recovered after that. Nor did it get a majority on its own. P. V. Narasimha Rao came to power in 1991 at the head of a minority government and Manmohan Singh headed a coalition for ten years from 2004–14.

VP's emergence as Rajiv Gandhi's successor marked the end of the rule of the Nehru–Gandhi family. No member of India's first family, has since then, till the time of writing, led a government.

V. P. Singh's name continues to arouse passions—reviled by some, revered by others. Some see him as a cunning politician who in a desperate attempt to retain power let a genie out of the bottle which could not be put back. Others call him the messiah of social justice, and that is the way he liked to see himself.

'Some run governments,' he told me, speaking about the processes he had unleashed. 'I ran history. It will define governments and coalitions in the time to come.'

CHAPTER 4

THE PRIME MINISTER
WHO REFUSED TO DECIDE

P. V. Narasimha Rao and the
Demolition of the Babri Masjid

I

'I heard you were doing puja after twelve o'clock on 6 December,' Nikhil Chakravartty, a left-leaning journalist said to Prime Minister P. V. Narasimha Rao. He had come to see the PM at 7, Race Course Road, a couple of days after 6 December 1992, when the Babri Masjid was razed to the ground. It wasn't really a statement, more a question, part-serious and part-tongue-in-cheek. But Chakravartty was curious to know what the prime minister had been doing when the mosque was being demolished on that fateful day.

At noon on 6 December, a frenzied mob had rushed into the precincts of the Babri Masjid, climbed up the three domes of the sixteenth-century mosque in the temple town of Ayodhya in Uttar Pradesh, and set about systematically destroying the building with ropes, shovels, and pickaxes. By 4.55 p.m., the structure, which Hindus and Muslims had wrangled over for forty-three years and more, had been flattened. Neither the police stationed around the mosque, nor the paramilitary forces, which had been sent there a month earlier by the central government to deal with precisely such an eventuality, prevented the mobs from pulling down the structure. The prime minister, the chief minister of the country's largest state of Uttar Pradesh, and the many agencies of the government that could have saved the mosque, watched helplessly.

A stung Rao shot back at Chakravartty, 'Dada, you think I don't know politics. I was born in rajniti (politics) and I have only been doing politics till today. Jo hua voh theek hua.... (What happened, happened for good.) Maine is liye hone diya...ki Bharatiya Janata Party ki mandir ki rajniti hamesha ke liye khatam ho jaye (I allowed it to happen because I wanted the BJP's temple politics to finish forever).'

Chakravartty could speak to the prime minister freely because besides being a journalist, he had for years been a friend of Rao. He was accompanied by three other journalists—Prabhash Joshi of *Jansatta*, R. K. Mishra of *Blitz*, and Ram Bahadur Rai who had worked closely with Joshi at *Jansatta*.

'They used to meet Rao frequently,' Rai recalled. 'That day I happened to accompany them.'

In the five months before the fall of the Babri Masjid, Chakravartty, Joshi, and Mishra had been assisting the prime minister to find a way out of the impasse at Ayodhya. Hindu organizations insisted that a temple be built at the spot where the mosque stood—which they claimed was Lord Ram's birthplace—and the Muslim groups were determined to save the structure they viewed as a mosque. The trio had held many behind-the-scenes parleys with both sides of the dispute.

All through the day on 6 December, Delhi was gripped by rumours that the prime minister had been sleeping while the mosque and its domes were brought down. Others said he had been doing puja. After the first dome collapsed, President Shankar Dayal Sharma shot off a sharply worded letter to the prime minister to stop the mob from bringing down the mosque.

The prime minister called a meeting of the union cabinet that day to take a decision—but it took place only at 6 p.m. By then the Babri Masjid had been reduced to rubble. For the central government to intervene, and take over direct control of the state government, it had to impose President's Rule in Uttar Pradesh. But the president could do this only on the aid and advice of the council of ministers. The prime minister called its meeting only after everything was over.

■

Within minutes of Chakravartty and his colleagues leaving, Rao expressed similar sentiments to another visitor, Rashmi Kant, a young film-maker from a well-known political family in Delhi. As the four journalists were trooping out, he was coming in to see the prime minister. As he watched them leave, he could not help wondering what they had come to see him about.

Usually he would come with Home Minister S. B. Chavan and Yunus Saleem, who had been the governor of Bihar. It was Saleem who had first asked for his help to bring around Kashmiri militants—so that they could be rehabilitated. They would usually be asked by Rao to come at night when he was done for the day. They would find the PM in a white banian, a lungi, and white slippers, sitting beside a heap of files lying on the sofa on his right side. The upholstery of the dull beige sofa had clearly been chosen by the government's Public Works Department (PWD). The film-maker was fascinated by how a subconscious tic would manifest itself—and Rao's hand would rub his stomach in a circular movement as he listened intently to his visitors.

In December 1992, Rashmi Kant had come to see Rao alone. He was surprised that he had been given an appointment so soon after the demolition.

'I started off by asking him about Ayodhya,' Kant told me.

'Yeh tho hona hee thaa (This had to happen, it was inevitable),' Rao said, much to the surprise of his young visitor. In other words, he had been expecting what had happened on 6 December.

The prime minister's face was 'emotionless'.

'You look pressured,' he tried to be sympathetic.

'What do you expect me to be?' Rao shot back irritably.

'Yeh log jo abhi gaye hain (These people who have just gone),' he went on. He was referring to Nikhil Chakravartty and the journalists who had just seen him.

'Yeh bhi keh rahen hai ki daer ho rahi hai, jaldi karo. They were also advising, it's getting late, you must make haste and act),' the PM went on. As he said this, Rao waved the document he was holding in his hand. What the prime minister was referring to was a suggestion many had voiced, apart from the journalists who had just left, that he ban major Hindu right-wing organizations such as the RSS, VHP, and Bajrang Dal—which he was to go on to do on 10 December 1992.

In the days after the demolition, Rao had come in for a barrage of criticism, from within his party and from the Opposition, the media, and the public, for allowing the Babri Masjid to be razed to the ground. There was now growing pressure on him to re-establish the secular credentials of his government.

'Kya karoon, saari umar clerk hee tho raha hoon (What can I do, all my life I have been a clerk),' Rao said, his words tinged with an unexpected bitterness. He was making a sarcastic reference to being portrayed as a ditherer and not as a bold leader but used as the party's draftsman, writing its many resolutions and manifestos, agonizing over which sentence would remain and which comma and full stop had to be deleted. Rao was a man of detail, and weighed the pros and cons of a decision to a fault—and this included the way he handled the Ayodhya tangle, leading to its destruction.

'I don't know whether he was happy or unhappy (that day), but I got a sense that it (demolition) had come as no surprise to him,' recalled Rashmi Kant.

■

Years after the demolition, senior BJP and RSS leaders were to claim that they had warned Narasimha Rao that the Babri Masjid would be brought down on 6 December 1992. They had alerted Rao, they said, so that he could make the necessary arrangements to manage the aftermath of the demolition.

'Kushabhau Thakre (President of the BJP) told me this,' Som Pal, the Janata Dal leader turned BJP MP, revealed. 'He said unse baat ho gayee thee ki 6 December ko aisa karenge (We had told Rao we will do this on 6 December).'

'You work out how you manage the situation,' Thakre said 'they' had told Rao.

'RSS chief K. Sudarshan also confirmed this to me,' Som Pal said. 'Sudarshan told me, "Humari understanding ho gayi thee (We had come to an understanding with PV)".'

Thakre and Sudarshan came out with this information when Som Pal related to them an encounter he had had with Rao. This was exactly a year after the demolition of the mosque. On 5 December 1993, Rao had asked to see Som Pal. Having ridden out the Babri storm, he was consulting leaders from different political groups on how to rejuvenate the Congress Party.

'I don't know what got into me, and maybe I was being mischievous, when I said to PV,' Som Pal reminisced. 'Maybe history will judge you differently in the future.... The Babri was a festering sore and I suppose some surgery had to be done.'

PV smiled. Som Pal went on, 'It was a smile of recognition and there was a glitter in his eyes. The way he smiled, I got the sense that he seemed pleased with what I had said. And that he approved of what had happened.'

■

The demolition of the Babri Masjid was not just about the destruction, by a frenzied mob, of a disused structure at which Muslims had stopped praying—and which many Hindus looked upon as the birthplace of Lord Ram.

PV was later to attribute it to the breakdown of trust between the central government and state government, essential for the functioning of a federal polity. Till the demolition, according to Rao, opposing political parties used to be elected to office at the centre and states. Despite their diverse views, they were expected to act 'in harmony' for 'the national good'. But after the demolition, this became more difficult, Rao himself was to say in *Ayodhya*, a book he authored which was published after his death in 2004. What had taken a beating on 6 December 1992 was 'good faith in a federal structure'.

Besides affecting the relationship between the centre and states, the temple movement had pitchforked the country's politics 'right into the religious ambit'. Secularism in independent India had been seen as 'sarvadharma sambhav' or respect for all religions—as opposed to an absence of religion in matters of state, as was the case in some Western democracies. But the temple movement changed all that; it forced even the secular parties to follow the BJP's path, 'if only to counter' the challenge posed by it. It gave respectability to the communal card for short-term electoral gains.

Even decades after Rao's death on 23 December 2004, the question that refuses to go away is this: could Pamulaparti Venkata Narasimha Rao have done more to protect the Babri Masjid? How culpable will history hold him for what happened in Ayodhya on 6 December 1992, an event which was to shape the country's politics—and its social relations—in the decades that followed, and continues to blight its path?

While there were many who were responsible for the 6 December tragedy, the ultimate responsibility for saving the mosque lay with the prime minister. This is the story of how—and why—Narasimha Rao failed to protect the Babri Masjid in what was the ultimate 'non-decision' by the ninth prime minister of India.

II

P. V. Narasimha Rao had not expected to become prime minister of India. Denied a ticket by Rajiv Gandhi in May 1991 to contest the Lok Sabha elections he had decided to retire from politics. Speculation was rife in the weeks ahead of the 1991 elections that Rajiv suspected him of aiming for the top job—and that was a reason why he was sidelined.

Rao let it be known that he had been asked to head the Sri Siddheswari Peetham, a matha in Tamil Nadu with which he had been associated over the years. He would give up all worldly associations when he accepted the position.

Nevertheless, since it was election time, and he was the chairman of the Congress coordination committee for elections, he was electioneering for the party. But his heart was not in campaigning. He had already started packing his bags for his return to Hyderabad, his home town. He had put half of his books and papers in crates and sent them back home. But although he had publicly declared that he was joining a matha, he was a die-hard politician—and still looking for an opportunity which could enable him to continue in an active political role. He had quietly said to N. Janardhana Reddy, chief minister of Andhra Pradesh, with whom he enjoyed a rapport: 'Khayal rakhna. Keep in mind a Rajya Sabha seat for me, should the opportunity arise.'

■

On 20 May 1991, Narasimha Rao was in Ramtek, a constituency in Maharashtra he had earlier represented. It was one of the 204 Lok Sabha constituencies in which the first phase of voting was taking place.

That day, Rajiv Gandhi, who was on the campaign trail in UP, had sent a message to Pranab Mukherjee and M. L. Fotedar. He asked them to meet him at Palam airport. He was going to halt in Delhi only for a few hours and wanted a word with them.

When he landed at Palam, Rajiv looked tired and dishevelled. The

Congress leaders suggested he head home and freshen up before taking off again on a tour that was proving to be hectic. At home, he spoke to Mukherjee and Fotedar separately. Having finished with Mukherjee, he turned to Fotedar. 'Kitnee seataen (How many seats)?' Before Fotedar could reply, Rajiv said, sounding confident, 'We will form the government.' Then, for a couple of minutes, he dwelt on who should be part of the new government he would form. He was certain he was coming back to power. Then he turned to go. As he was leaving, he looked back and said, 'Achcha Fotedarji, ta-ta.'

'He had never used that word earlier,' Fotedar said afterwards. It would be the last time they would ever meet.

That night Rajiv Gandhi flew to Orissa, addressed a meeting there, and headed to Tamil Nadu the next afternoon. It was one of those curious coincidences that Indira Gandhi had also been in Orissa a day before she was gunned down. Jawaharlal Nehru, too, had been in Orissa just days before he died.

The next night, on 21 May 1991, at 10 p.m., Rajiv was blown to bits at a poll rally in Sriperumbudur. A LTTE suicide bomber had detonated a bomb strapped to her chest as she bent to touch his feet. Seconds before he was assassinated, Jayanthi Natarajan had been standing next to Rajiv. She had been translating for him, from Tamil into English. Rajiv turned to her and said something. But his words were indistinct. Then she clearly heard him say, 'I am telling you to go.' She thought he wanted her to find out about the two journalists from foreign newspapers who had travelled to Sriperumbudur with him. As Natarajan started to walk away, there was a muffled explosion. She fell down with a thud. When a dazed Natarajan got up, she saw a grisly scene spread out before her—amidst the carnage, the white Lotto shoes that Rajiv had been wearing caught her eye.

'Several guys bundled him up, and (G. K.) Moopanar and I and some others took him to the general hospital which was more than an hour away, opposite the railway station.... It must have been around 11 p.m. when we reached there.... I had to sign and identify the body.... The doctor was so angry. "You have no shame bringing this to me? He was such a handsome man and you bring me this bundle and call him Rajiv Gandhi...."'

At the hospital, Rajiv Gandhi was declared dead. Later, at around 3 a.m., the body was taken to the mortuary for the post-mortem. Outside the building, crowds had begun to gather.

The Tamil Nadu governor, Bhishma Narain Singh, arrived around 4 a.m. He asked, 'Who died?'

'Rajivji,' Natarajan replied.

'I know that,' he said.

'Who were the important people who died?' the governor asked again.

'Everyone is important,' Natarajan said irritably, referring to the sixteen people who had died, including Rajiv Gandhi and his assassin. The governor ignored her comment.

Soon thereafter, Natarajan and Moopanar accompanied the coffin to Chennai's Meenambakkam airport. At 6 a.m. the plane carrying Sonia Gandhi and Priyanka landed. (Rahul was not in Delhi that day.) 'Priyanka fell on the coffin and cried,' recalled Natarajan. 'Sonia was very restrained. She was wearing dark glasses. She did not speak with anyone.'

The aircraft took the body back to Delhi.

■

Narasimha Rao landed in Delhi on 22 May 1991 in the morning, and made his way to Rajiv Gandhi's residence at 10, Janpath. His private secretary Ramu Damodaran had called him the moment the news came of Rajiv's assassination. Shocked Congressmen and Congresswomen had started to gather at 10, Janpath, as soon as word spread about the death of their leader. Many of the senior Congressmen—like Pranab Mukherjee, and Rajiv's aides R. K. Dhawan and M. L. Fotedar—had spent the night on the lawns of 10, Janpath, waiting for the body to arrive. Arrangements were underway for the funeral.

'Who will lead the Congress Party now?' was the question that was being discussed in undertones by those gathered. Standing next to Rao, Pranab Mukherjee said to him, 'Aap ban jao (You take over).'

'Abhi to arthi nahin uthi hai (The body has not yet been cremated),' Rao replied, his face set in his familiar pout. 'People will say, you are playing politics. Jis ko sab mil kar karenge woh banega (Whoever everyone wants will become the party leader).'

'But your name is being considered seriously,' Mukherjee persisted.

Privately, Rao hoped so. But in public, he remained non-committal. He did not really trust Mukherjee. He was not sure whether Mukherjee was making this suggestion to throw him out of the race by appearing eager prematurely. Or he was only repeating what others were saying.

Later that day, Rajiv Gandhi's body was taken to Teen Murti Bhavan, residence of the first prime minister of India and Rajiv's grandfather, Jawaharlal Nehru. The body of the slain former prime minister lay in state for people to pay their last respects. As people thronged the building to pay homage, some recalled that this was where the bodies of Jawaharlal Nehru and Indira Gandhi had also lain in state. Many Congressmen did not know what had hit them. Mani Shankar Aiyar sat alone in a corner on a parapet, his head in his hands, quietly grieving for his friend and boss.

That afternoon, Bhuvnesh Chaturvedi, a Congress leader from Rajasthan, went to call on Rao at 9, Motilal Nehru Marg.

'You should become the candidate (for Congress president),' Chaturvedi told Rao.

'It should be unanimous,' Rao replied.

'This was enough indication (to me) that he was willing,' Chaturvedi said later.

■

'George, Arjun Singh, and I had decided we should make Sonia Gandhi president of the Congress,' Fotedar claimed. Vincent George was Rajiv Gandhi's personal assistant and Arjun Singh a senior leader in the Congress.

Rajiv Gandhi's wife Sonia was not a member of the Congress Party. But it would have been easy enough to get her enrolled as a member—and then elected as Congress president.

The Congress Working Committee, the apex decision-making body of the party, was due to meet that evening at 5 p.m., to decide who should take over as the Congress president after Rajiv. It was to be a meeting of the 'extended' Working Committee. Besides the CWC members, Congress chief ministers and special invitees were also to be present at it.

'Arjun Singh, G. K. Moopanar, Sitaram Kesri, and I went to see PV just before the CWC (meeting),' Fotedar recounted. 'Rao sahib, we have decided to get Sonia Gandhi to take over the presidentship of the Congress,' Fotedar told him.

'Arjun Singhji, what's your opinion?' Rao asked him.

'Sir, I will propose her name,' Arjun Singh replied. Rao was quiet. Then without saying more, he decided to accompany them to the CWC meeting.

Kesri asked Rao to preside over the meeting. The CWC met in the big room in the AICC headquarters which was used for media briefings. In the middle of the meeting, suddenly N. Janardhana Reddy walked up to Fotedar and whispered something in his ear. Fotedar stepped out of the meeting with Reddy. 'Fotedarji, the atmosphere is favourable for Sonia Gandhi,' Reddy reported. 'But you will have to talk to Sharad Pawar and Karunakaran.'

'What about the rest?' Fotedar asked him.

'The rest are OK.'

Fotedar called Pawar out of the meeting.

'I have a request to make,' he told Pawar. 'If you don't support it, please don't oppose it either. We want to carry the resolution unanimously.... We want to have Sonia Gandhi as president.' Pawar agreed to support the resolution. For Pawar, too, the situation had undergone a dramatic change with the assassination. Rajiv Gandhi had tried to replace the Maratha strongman as chief minister of Maharashtra in 1990, suspecting him of hobnobbing with former prime minister Chandra Shekhar. But Pawar upstaged Rajiv—and the legislature party voted overwhelmingly for him. Fotedar was one of those who had urged Rajiv not to precipitate matters till the elections were over. Pawar knew this.

Arjun Singh proposed Sonia Gandhi's name for presidentship of the Congress. Kesri seconded it. The entire house supported it. The only 'discordant' note was struck by Karunakaran: 'Let us ask Soniaji if she is ready.' Karunakaran was close to Rao, and was seen to be batting for him. 'Is this the time to ask her?' Fotedar brushed aside his suggestion. 'Let's pass the resolution first.' The resolution was passed unanimously. It requested Sonia to take up the leadership of the Indian National Congress. Rao showed no resistance to the idea. Nor did he project himself as an alternative candidate.

'After the CWC meeting, I saw some of the leaders embrace each other in one of the rooms at AICC headquarters,' Bhuvnesh Chaturvedi recalled. 'They thought they would be able to control Sonia just as the Syndicate (of senior Congress leaders) had thought they could control Indira and had voted against Morarji (Desai) in 1966.'

At 6.30 p.m., a delegation of senior Congressmen went across to meet Sonia Gandhi at 10, Janpath, which was adjacent to the AICC headquarters at 24, Akbar Road, where the CWC meeting had taken place. They requested Sonia Gandhi to take charge of the party. Sonia listened to them politely. But she turned down their request.

At 8 p.m., Fotedar went back to 10, Janpath. He requested George to send in a note to Sonia Gandhi. Whatever her final decision, he wrote on the chit, she should wait for a day before making it public. She agreed.

The next morning's papers carried headlines that the Congress had requested Sonia Gandhi to take charge of India's grand old party. Fotedar had asked Sonia to defer making her decision public by a day because he felt that the CWC's decision should first receive wide publicity. Her 'no' should come later. If both were reported in the media simultaneously, the 'import of her decision' would be lost. If she declined, the decision could be projected as a 'sacrifice' on her part. 'She will be required in the future,' Fotedar said. 'She will be a leader in reserve.'

Fotedar was not alone in viewing Sonia Gandhi as a leader in the future. Long before she actively entered politics in 1997, or became a member of the Congress Party, she had begun to be seen as a power centre within the party. It was what Rao had to contend with during his premiership.

∎

'(Since) you are not interested in becoming prime minister,' Natwar Singh said to Sonia Gandhi, a few days after Rajiv's death, 'you must decide who should be the next prime minister.' By now the world leaders who had come for Rajiv Gandhi's funeral had departed. The time had come for hard decisions.

'Why don't you consult P. N. Haksar?' he suggested. Haksar had once been a trusted advisor to Sonia's mother-in-law, Indira Gandhi, and was still held in esteem by the family.

'I will let you know,' the cautious Sonia was non-committal. She called him back a day later and asked him to invite Haksar to 10, Janpath. Haksar made a suggestion. 'You (should) send Aruna Asif Ali and Natwar to Shankar Dayal Sharma,' he told Sonia, 'and tell him that Soniaji has requested him to become Congress president and prime minister (if the Congress won and came back to power).' Sharma was then the vice president of India. Haksar had zeroed in on his name because he was an experienced administrator, belonged to the Hindi heartland—and was a Brahmin. The Brahmins had been a core constituency of the Congress in North India but had begun to desert it for an ascendant BJP. Haksar felt he would be able to handle the uncertainties created by Rajiv Gandhi's assassination.

Aruna Asaf Ali and Natwar Singh went across to 6, Maulana Azad Road. Sharma listened to their proposition gravely. Then he delivered his bombshell. 'It is very gracious of Soniaji to make the offer,' he said. 'Mera swasthya saath nahin dega, haath jorh ke shama kar deejiye (My health will not permit it, so with folded hands I ask you to excuse me).'

The surprised messengers rushed back to report to Sonia—and to Haksar. 'Send now for P. V. Narasimha Rao,' advised an unperturbed Haksar. Three other names had also been talked about in Congress circles for the party presidentship—Arjun Singh, Sharad Pawar, and N. D. Tiwari. For many, Rao was the obvious choice. He was experienced, non-abrasive, and low-key. Old and frail, he was seen as someone who wouldn't be around for too long. He had just had heart surgery. Since he did not have a mass following, he was not seen as a threat to the more ambitious politicians in the party.

It was Sonia Gandhi's nod for Rao which came as a clincher, though she made no public statement about it. There were those like R. D. Pradhan, former home secretary and a one-time advisor to Sonia Gandhi, who tried to distance her from the decision—and denied that Sonia had a hand in the selection of Rao.

On 29 May 1991, P. V. Narasimha Rao was elected as the president of the Indian National Congress.

■

As soon as he was elected president of the Congress, Rao started to campaign for the party in UP. He wanted to test the waters in the Hindi heartland. Salman Khurshid took him to his constituency in Farrukhabad. As soon as he arrived at the first meeting, and much to his annoyance, Rao was greeted with slogans. They were not about him, but were raised in favour of the UP Congress chief N. D Tiwari. 'Desh ka neta kaisa ho, Narayan Dutt Tiwari jaisa ho (What should the country's leader be like? He should be like Narayan Dutt Tiwari).'

'PV felt very bad,' recalled Bhuvnesh Chaturvedi. 'The slogans erupted when Narayan Dutt Tiwari was introducing PV to UP.' To Rao, the reception at Farrukhabad was confirmation that he would either have to line up UP behind him, or manage to rule without being dependent on the state.

∎

'Maa bete ka balidan, yaad karega Hindustan (The sacrifice of mother and son will always be remembered by India)'. The slogan about Indira Gandhi and Rajiv Gandhi's martyrdom rent the air throughout the Congress campaign for the last two phases of the 1991 general election. Voting during these phases took place on 12 and 15 June 1991 mainly in the southern states, though some seats also remained to be contested in the North.

The sympathy vote for Rajiv—though it was nothing like what had been seen after Indira Gandhi's assasination in 1984—enhanced the Congress tally. In Rao's own state of Andhra Pradesh, there was a marked improvement in the performance of the Congress. It won 20 out of 27 seats in the second phase compared to 5 out 15 seats in the first phase.

With the Congress doing poorly in the North, political power was shifting southwards. The four southern states—Andhra Pradesh, Karnataka, Kerala, and Tamil Nadu—elected 88 MPs to the Lok Sabha. The northern states of UP, Bihar, and Madhya Pradesh, on the other hand, sent only 33 seats. It was a sharp decline from the 171 the Congress had won from these states in the 1984 general elections.

When the final results were in, the Congress had won the most seats—232—though it was short of an absolute majority in parliament. Now, very quickly—and quietly—Rao put his confidantes to work to rustle up support for his candidature as prime minister. He utilized the services of 'godman' Chandraswami, tantrik N. K. Sharma, and Captain Satish Sharma who was a friend of Rajiv Gandhi and had access to Sonia Gandhi.

Most of the powerful Congress leaders from the South, G. K. Moopanar, K. Karunakaran, N. Janardhan Reddy—all 'except for Shiv Shankar'—mobilized support for him. So did the experienced Congress politician from West Bengal, Siddhartha Shankar Ray, who also enlisted MPs to back Rao for PM.

After the elections, Arjun Singh's name had surfaced briefly as one of the contenders for the top job. But it petered out very quickly; the Congress had not done so well in his home state of Madhya Pradesh.

It was Sharad Pawar, the Maharashtra strongman, who emerged as the serious challenger to Rao. Under his leadership, the Congress had won 37 out of 48 Lok Sabha seats in Maharashtra. He had also funded many Congress candidates across the country, particularly those in the fray in the second phase of elections, giving them two to four lakh rupees apiece.

In 1989, Rao himself had depended on Sharad Pawar to win his Lok Sabha seat from Ramtek. Pawar was confident that besides those who had won from Maharashtra, many of the southern MPs he had helped would back him.

To begin with, many favoured Pawar. Their number started to swell. Operation Pawar was being carried out from N. K. P. Salve's house on Aurangzeb Road. Salve and Najma Heptulla and Suresh Kalmadi were mobilizing support for their leader.

Pawar insisted on an election by secret ballot. At a dinner for his newly elected MPs, they passed a resolution for a 'conscience vote' to select the leader.

But the risk-averse Rao did not want a contest. Playing the southern card, he pitched himself as the Telugu bidda (Telugu son of the soil), who, if chosen, would be the first prime minister from the South. He also stepped up pressure on Pawar to withdraw. Subramanian Swamy, who was batting for Rao at the time, announced a press conference, and let it be known that he would expose Pawar's involvement in a land scam.

Suspense mounted on 19 June 1991. Hectic parleys got underway to find a compromise solution. Finally, Pawar realized the numbers might not favour him. He would claim later that he had lost out to Rao because 'Sonia Gandhi would not have brooked an independent-minded PM.'

Pawar sent word to Rao that he would be willing to settle for the deputy prime ministership. But he wanted Rao to invite him for talks.

'Panditji,' Rao told N. K. Sharma, 'I won't phone him.' In the war of nerves that was on, it would be seen as a sign of weakness. Sharma, whom Rao was using as an intermediary, decided to phone a senior Congress leader he knew. 'Please go to Salve's house and bring Sharad Pawar to PV's residence at 9, Moti Lal Nehru Marg,' he said, and put the phone down before any questions could be asked. In twenty minutes, the Congress leader arrived at Rao's residence with Pawar. All he had told Pawar was that 'an invitation had come for him from 9, Moti Lal Nehru Marg'. He did not reveal that the phone call was from Sharma.

Rao and Pawar talked for forty-five minutes. 'You come here (to Delhi) as minister, and take any portfolio you want. Someone of your choice will become the chief minister in Maharashtra,' Rao made the offer to Pawar. Then, he pitched the appeal at an emotional level: 'I am an old man...you are much younger, you have your whole life ahead of you, your chance will come.' On 20 June 1991, Pawar withdrew from the race. On the same day, Rao was unanimously elected leader of the CPP. As the leader of the single largest party in parliament, he was now all set to be invited by the president to form the government—and become the next prime minister of India.

The first move Rao made as the leader of the CPP was to call on Sonia Gandhi. At 10, Janpath, when Rao was inside with Sonia, 'a group of us were sitting (outside) in George's room,' N. K. Sharma recalled. 'There were tears in George's eyes'. Kesri also became emotional. 'I asked them why they were they crying... "If Rajiv had been alive," George said, "he would have been elected leader of the CPP today".'

On 21 June 1991, P. V. Narasimha Rao was sworn in as the ninth prime minister of India. He made Pawar defence minister in his cabinet. It was a portfolio the Maratha leader had sought. His mentor, Y. B. Chavan, had also been defence minister. But Rao did not give Pawar the deputy prime ministership he coveted. He did not make the mistake V. P. Singh had committed when he became PM, anointing Devi Lal as deputy PM as part of a compromise package. He had invited trouble for himself by creating a rival power centre in the government.

Throughout the battle to become prime minister, Rao displayed a deft political touch. Afterwards, his partymen could only guess at what had worked in his favour in getting the better of Pawar—the offer of a position to him, or the stick he had wielded through others like Subramanian Swamy, or the nod Sonia Gandhi had given for Rao, or in all probability, a combination of all these factors. All through, Rao neither appeared too eager to become prime minister, nor did he, at any point, rule himself out of the race.

Within one month, from the day Rajiv Gandhi's body was brought to 10, Janpath, Rao had done the impossible. A man who had been denied a Lok Sabha ticket, who was reconciled to becoming a hermit at a religious matha in South India, P. V. Narasimha Rao was now set to head the world's largest democracy.

III

An IB officer had once alerted Narasimha Rao to people who could pose a problem for him in the future. An unfazed Rao replied sagely, 'I am a Brahmin. I know how to deal with these people (adversaries).' He considered his Brahminical antecedents a good enough credential to get the better of his opponents.

Born on 28 June 1921, Rao was a Telugu Brahmin and a Niyogi Brahmin at that—a subcaste known for its sharp intellect, scholarship, and administrative skills. The Telugu Brahmins were divided into two major groups—the Vaidiki Brahmins who learnt the scriptures and chose the priesthood as their profession and the Niyogi Brahmins, who became administrators, landlords, military men, scholars, and rulers. Many of them, like Rao, had become successful politicians. Prominent among them were B. Pattabhi Sitaramayya, freedom fighter and president of the Indian National Congress (1947–48), S. Radhakrishnan, who went on to be the president of India from 1962–67, T. Prakasam, the first chief minister of Andhra Pradesh, and Burgula Ramakrishna Rao, the first chief minister of Hyderabad state, with whom Narasimha Rao had worked closely.

Rao's Niyogi genes led him to quit farming—his father had 200 acres of dry land in Vangara in Warangal district in present-day Telangana—and pursue higher studies in Nagpur, Pune, and Hyderabad.

Besides his Niyogi Brahmin antecedents, the village Vangara where his family lived and farmed was also to influence his political persona. Vangara lay at the junction of multiple linguistic influences—and made him who he was. Rao had described Vangara in the then princely state of Hyderabad, as 'geographically a bridge between the North and the South'.

The residents of this small inhabitation spoke Telugu, Hindi, Marathi, Kannada, and even a smattering of Odia. Rao became proficient in ten languages, including his mother tongue, Telugu. In addition to Telugu, he learnt to speak Hindi and English in school. He could recite scriptures in Sanskrit he had learnt from his unlettered father; he become fluent in Urdu which was spoken in nizam's rule, and proficient in Persian which was the language of the court. Having spent many years in Nagpur for study, he spoke Marathi fluently—and decided to learn Tamil when he had gone to Chennai in 1968 for a writing break. During his lean political years, he attended classes in Jawaharlal Nehru University in Delhi to learn Spanish. Once asked if he had read Gabriel García Márquez's *Love in the Time of Cholera,* he replied nonchalantly that he had read it in the original Spanish!

His father gave the four-year-old Narasimha in adoption to a Brahmin family in the neighbourhood in Vangara. They had no children and did not want the nizam to take over the lands of an heirless couple. Like V. P. Singh, who too was given in adoption by his father to another raja to consolidate the landholdings of both families, so too was Rao taken away from his natal family. Like VP, he too had a lonely childhood—and became a loner. He was married off at the age of ten, and his wife Satyamma was to look after their lands in the village and their eight children till the end of her life. Rao on the other hand went on to join the Congress Party and pursue a political career amidst the bright lights.

Barring Jawaharlal Nehru, Rao was the most erudite prime minister India has had. But more than Nehru, he understood the complexities of Indian society and the hold caste and religion exercised on the Indian psyche. By the time he became prime minister, he had also had two decades of administrative experience. He had been chief minister of Andhra Pradesh. At the national level, he came to hold weighty portfolios like Foreign Affairs, Home, Defence, and Human Resource Development under Indira Gandhi and Rajiv Gandhi.

■

In this younger days, Rao had been a gunrunner. For a year, he was based in a camp in Chanda in Maharashtra and would ferry arms to groups working for the ouster of the nizam of Hyderabad. A major factor that shaped Rao's political thinking was his participation in the anti-nizam movement, against the Muslim ruler of the princely state of Hyderabad. In 1938, the Congress in Hyderabad had launched a satyagraha against the nizam and the seventeen-year-old Rao sang the banned national song 'Vande Mataram' with other Hindu students in his college in Warangal. The principal expelled 300 students, including Rao. The nationalist chancellor of Nagpur University, heard about the expulsions and offered admission to many of these students, including Rao. Rao went to Nagpur to complete his college education; later he was to return to the city to do his law degree.

•

Narasimha Rao's guru—and mentor—was the saffron-robe-clad Swami Ramanand Tirtha, part sadhu and part politician, part socialist and part spiritualist. He could justify Gandhian non-violence as well as violence to achieve his objectives—and was president of the Hyderabad state Congress. Rao worked under him when Tirtha led the anti-nizam movement between August 1947 and September 1948. Tirtha also went on to influence S. B. Chavan and Veerendra Patil, later to become the chief ministers of Maharashtra and Karnataka.

Unlike other princely states, which had merged into India after Independence, the nizam opposed the integration of Hyderabad with India. In September 1948, Home Minister Sardar Vallabhbhai Patel sent the police into Hyderabad and annexed the state. When Hyderabad finally merged into the Indian union, it ended more than two centuries of rule by the nizams. But it was marked by violence, and around 40,000 Muslims were killed.

After the liberation of Hyderabad, many of those who had led the anti-nizam struggle, like Rao and Tirtha, decided to enter politics. Rao became the president of the Karimnagar district of Congress. He contested the Lok Sabha elections from Huzurabad in Hyderabad in 1952—but lost. Subsequently, he became an MLA from Munthani in 1957, and represented the constituency for twenty years. From 1962 onwards, for nine years, he was a minister in the state government, holding important portfolios like education and health.

The anti-nizam movement had brought together three diverse religio-political streams—the Indian National Congress which sought the integration of India as a modern secular nation; the Hindu Mahasabha and Arya Samaj movements, which were opposed to the nizam as an Islamic ruler and emphasized Hindu thought and philosophy; and the communists who fought against the nizam, in favour of the peasants in Telangana—for land to be given to the tiller. All three streams were to influence Rao's thinking.

•

It was his stint as chief minister of Andhra Pradesh which was to affect Rao profoundly as a politician. He was chosen by Prime Minister Indira Gandhi to head the government of Andhra Pradesh in 1971 because he came from the backward region of Telangana (in the united Andhra Pradesh), and he was a Brahmin. Till then the powerful landed community, the Reddys, had dominated the politics of Andhra Pradesh. Besides Tirtha, Rao had also been influenced by Nehru's leftist thinking; he believed that the state had to be the main arbiter for development. The socialist Rao was to legislate far-reaching land reforms as chief minister—and he strictly enforced the land ceiling.

Indira Gandhi, who was in a leftist mode at the time, backed his land reforms. But he invited the wrath of the landed interests and they struck back when given an opportunity in 1972. Instead of backing off, he took them head-on—and decided to pack his ministry with more OBCs and Dalits. But protests grew over the land reforms. Under pressure, Indira Gandhi decided to sack him. She imposed President's Rule in Andhra Pradesh—and did not reinstate Rao as chief minister.

The Andhra experience taught Rao many lessons. One was not to bite off more than he could chew. He also learnt the value of 'ambivalence', as a way to deal with difficult situations. When Ramanand Tirtha was pitted against Burgula Ramakrishna Rao for an important position in the Indian National Congress, both had sought Rao's support. They headed two factions within the party. This created a huge dilemma for Rao. For he was close to both of them. He had worked under Ramakrishna Rao after studying law from Nagpur. Tirtha was his spiritual and political mentor. Somehow, Rao managed to avoid taking sides and did it without alienating either. In the process, he learnt what it meant to walk the 'middle path'.

Rao also learnt in those days the importance of staying on the right side of the high command—in a party like the Indian National Congress.

IV

The Chanakya of Indian politics—that is how Narasimha Rao was popularly known—was the first South Indian to become prime minister. Till then, barring Morarji Desai, who was from Gujarat, India's prime ministers had all been from Uttar Pradesh in the North.

Though a master of statecraft and realpolitik, Rao was not a mass leader. He was, arguably, India's most uncharismatic prime minister—as charismatic as a 'dead fish', in the words of a Congressman, Jairam Ramesh. His colleagues saw him as cold, clinical, and calculating.

He would usually only provide information to his colleagues—and officials—on a need-to-know basis. And he used their services as required— and was one of those PMs who did not have a coterie. Hardly anyone was given the full picture—this enabled him to control the situation like a master puppeteer.

It was his inability to connect with the masses which did him in when he was up for re-election in 1996. And yet, despite attacks from senior Congress leaders within his party, no mass following to speak of, the challenges of governance at the head of a minority government, inheriting an economy in the doldrums, faced with militancy in the border states of Kashmir and Punjab, and an aggressive Hindu nationalism on the rise, Narasimha Rao completed his term in office. He was the first Congressman who did not belong to the party's first family, the Nehru–Gandhis, to do so.

It was during Rao's tenure (1991–96) that the political centre of gravity moved to the south of the country. Coincidentally, or by design, this happened at the same time that the Congress lost in Uttar Pradesh, never to recover the state again. Rao was often blamed for deliberately allowing UP to slip out of Congress hands. The loss of UP, the Nehru–Gandhi family's home state, naturally weakened their political base.

■

Narasimha Rao did not think much of the Nehru–Gandhi family or their capabilities. He had a complex relationship with Indira Gandhi, Rajiv Gandhi, and with Sonia Gandhi.

Though he owed his rise to Indira Gandhi, and was seen as an Indira loyalist, Rao was deeply hurt when she replaced him in 1973 as chief minister of Andhra Pradesh. Though he sulked for a time, he did not abandon her—and was rewarded for his loyalty. In 1980, Indira Gandhi made him foreign minister and then home minister, the position he held when she was assassinated in 1984. At one time, she had even contemplated sending him to the Rashtrapati Bhavan in 1982, though she finally opted for Zail Singh as president.

Privately he disapproved of her decision to impose the Emergency—and would write under a pseudonym, for the magazine *Mainstream*, edited by his friend Nikhil Chakravartty. He criticized the imprisonment of Opposition leaders and the imposition of press censorship. But having been appointed a general secretary of the party by Indira, after he had moved to Delhi in 1976 from Andhra Pradesh, he did not oppose her openly.

His opinion of Indira Gandhi was scathing in a novel he wrote. Initially entitled *The Other Half,* and later published as *The Insider*, its author had its central character (a politician who was an alter ego of Rao) say of Indira: 'Indira Gandhi will never, repeat never, get over her...very complex...feeling of inferiority...and an admission of inadequacy inside, coupled above all with a consuming passion to attain immortal fame eclipsing her great father.'

He was even more critical of Rajiv Gandhi's capabilities—and would express his angst in private to Nikhilda. Though a senior minister in his cabinet, Rajiv would often keep Rao waiting. On one occasion, Rao waited in the visitor's room for two hours after Rajiv had summoned him to 7, Race Course Road for urgent consultations. Inside, Rajiv sat chit-chatting with his friends Romi Chopra and Rajeev Sethi.

'Why do you put up with all this?' Chakravartty asked an agitated Rao. 'Why don't you take a stand?'

'Kya stand loon (What stand can I take)?' PV replied. 'He will say, "Jao phir chutti karo (Go, pack your bags)".'

In 1991, that is precisely what Rajiv Gandhi did—he sent Rao packing. Although Rajiv justified his decision by saying that he wanted to bring in a younger team, he had taken strong exception to an article that appeared in *Mainstream*, which Rao was suspected of having written. It was published shortly after V. P. Singh had trounced Rajiv Gandhi in the 1989 general elections. Entitled 'The Great Suicide', and penned under a pseudonym, 'Congressman', it was a blistering attack on Rajiv. It called him a 'praise addict' who had frittered away the massive mandate given him in 1984 because of his immaturity and arrogance.

Rao's relationship with Sonia Gandhi was equally complex. Initially, he obliged her—and accepted her suggestions for who should be in the cabinet after he took over as prime minister. 'Kaisi lagi cabinet (How did you like the cabinet)?' he had asked Bhuvnesh Chaturvedi after the oath-taking ceremony on 21 June 1991.

'Why are you asking for my opinion?' Chaturvedi had replied in his blunt fashion. 'This is not your cabinet, and you know this.' Apparently, the prime minister had sent President R. Venkataraman three different lists of those to be included in the cabinet—each iteration revising the previous one and the president had made a derisive comment about it to Chaturvedi.

'What can I do?' Rao said, expressing helplessness. '(Vincent) George says this is Sonia Gandhi's choice and adds more names.'

During the first year of his premiership, he did his best to keep Sonia Gandhi in good humour. Even though he was prime minister, and she an ordinary citizen, he would regularly call on her. He would go across to her residence at 10, Janpath, rather than have her come to the PM House at 7, Race Course Road—and keep her briefed about what the government was doing. He also made sure that whatever she needed for the smooth functioning of 10, Janpath, was taken care of.

It was a year after he took over as PM that he began to suspect that she might have political ambitions. That was to be the turning point in their relationship.

'Do you think I should enter active politics?' Sonia had asked Rao in 1992, and he told me this during the course of an informal chat. 'What would you advise me if I was your daughter?'

'Since you are asking me to advise you as if you were my daughter,'

Rao replied, 'I would say, "no".'

'But if your children are interested,' he continued, 'I will groom them. I will take them with me on some of my tours.'

It was from then on that Rao became wary of what Sonia might do. Later that year, their relationship grew more strained after the demolition of the Babri Masjid. It had made Sonia very unhappy—and she suspected he had deliberately allowed the structure to be brought down.

From 1993 onwards, Rao had come under criticism for kowtowing to her. His visits to 10, Janpath became less frequent and petered out. The distance between them grew. His rivals within the party influenced Sonia against him, and in 1995, she openly criticized him for the first time—and she did so in the Gandhi family pocket borough of Amethi—for not doing enough to pursue the probe into Rajiv Gandhi's assassination. This was a clear signal to Rao that she was now planning to come into active politics.

Rao reacted to her charge in his own inimitable fashion—illustrating his style of functioning. He thrived on confusion, which sometimes he himself created to send multiple signals simultaneously.

Around this time, suddenly the Home Ministry moved a note in the cabinet that the Jain Commission probing Rajiv Gandhi's assasination should be disbanded. Rao shot down the proposal firmly. It was however curious that Home Minister S. B. Chavan, a confidante of Rao, should take such a far-reaching step without the PM's clearance. But Rao obviously wanted to show Sonia Gandhi that he, as the PM, was as exercised as she was about finding Rajiv Gandhi's assassins.

Then to further emphasize his resolve to bring the guilty to book, Rao put a minister in charge of monitoring the progress of the probe to speed up the investigation.

The minister asked for a particular official to be appointed to assist the commission. The request was put up to Rao for clearance. But the file did not come back from the PM's residence. Normally, a file that was sent to him in the evening, would be returned the next morning, the PM having duly signed it, 'except those files he did not want to clear'.

The minister, no pushover, came back to see the PM. Why was so much time being taken to appoint the bureaucrat, he asked. Rao called in his aides. He scolded them in front of the minister. 'What has happened to the file? Why has it not been sent to me?' They reminded him it had already been referred to him for clearance.

'You should put important ones in a brown cover,' he said querulously, 'so I know which the important ones are. Please start doing this.'

They sent him the file in a brown cover. It was still not returned with his signature. Most people would have given up at this stage. You don't keep meeting the prime minister again and again about an official's appointment. But not so this minister, he sought a meeting with the prime minister yet again.

Rao called in his staff yet again. This time he admonished them in even stronger terms.

'Can't you people even handle a simple matter?'

They insisted the file had been sent to him in a brown cover. 'This shows you are sending me too many brown files,' Rao said irritably. He then assured the minister that he would look into the matter promptly. Nothing happened. This time around, even the go-getting minister knew better than to show up in the prime minister's office a third time.

Narasimha Rao knew how to tire out people when he did not want to take a decision.

■

'No decision is also a decision', Rao would often say, giving a philosophical twist to what some felt was only dithering on decisions. 'PV thanda karke khate hain (PV believes in first cooling the food and then eating it),' Bhuvnesh Chaturvedi would say loyally about his boss.

Pout—a nickname the media gave Rao, because of the frown that would perennially sit on his face—weighed the pros and cons of a decision to such an extent that often he did not get around to making it. But those who knew him better used to say that Rao used prevarication only as a political tool. 'It was only when he did not want to take a decision that he would postpone it,' said one of his secretaries who had observed him closely. 'But he knew exactly what he wanted.'

He could be decisive when he wanted to be. It took him only a few hours to take the far-reaching decision to go in for economic reforms in June–July 1991. India had barely three weeks of foreign exchange to pay for imports and was on the verge of defaulting on its financial obligations. Rao moved swiftly to get through the crisis by securing a bailout from the International Monetary Fund (by pledging the government's gold reserves). Along with his finance minister, Manmohan Singh, he went on to institute massive economic reforms. The economy recovered over the next months, and Rao was hailed as the father of the economic reforms.

While Rao dithered in the run-up to the Babri Masjid demolition, he acted firmly, as we shall soon see, after the tragedy played out.

'Silence', 'ambivalence', 'evasiveness', and 'histrionics'—these were weapons he used effectively to get what he wanted done. And he thrived in the midst of confusion—using dissimulation and smokescreens to keep his opponents guessing.

■

During his first year in office, instances of the way Rao managed his minority government were legion. He relied heavily on the support of Opposition leaders and kept them in good humour. Many of the Opposition leaders who visited him at the PM House remained 'anonymous'; they were shown in the register merely as a 'reserved' appointment, so there was no record of them having met him. He had given instructions to the PMO that if they asked for any 'work to be done', be it the grant of contracts or the transfer of officers, it should be done with despatch. Throughout his tenure as PM, he went out of his way to win over the leaders of other parties— Lalu Yadav, Mulayam Singh Yadav, Jyoti Basu, H. D. Deve Gowda. Since he had to run a coalition government to begin with, he knew he had to keep politicians of other parties happy: 'Na jaane kis bhesh main Narayan mil jaye (We have no idea in what garb God could appear).'

Sometimes his strategy paid off. N. T. Rama Rao who headed the Telugu Desam—a regional outfit opposed to the Congress in Rao's home state Andhra Pradesh—decided not to field a candidate against Rao in a by-election in November 1991 to enter parliament. Rao won from Nandyal with a record 5.8 lakh votes. 90 per cent of those who cast their vote opted for him.

Rao knew he could not rule like Indira Gandhi or Rajiv Gandhi. They had commanded a brute majority, which he did not have. He had to rule by consensus. And by persuading opposing parties not to impede the functioning of his government.

■

'PV bahut zaalim hain (PV is very ruthless),' Bhuvnesh Chaturvedi once quipped about his boss. Conciliatory towards Opposition leaders, he could be tough with his party colleagues, particularly those who were potential rivals.

He kept Pranab Mukherjee, who was the most senior member of the Congress, out of his cabinet in 1991. Mukherjee was hoping to get the finance portfolio. He had backed Rao's candidature for PM. 'Pranab had asked me to put in a word to PV to give him finance,' Bhuvnesh Chaturvedi told me. Rao told Chaturvedi, 'It will be problematic'—and cited Mukherjee's alleged proximity to a large industrial conglomerate for not acceding to the request.

When the list of ministers came out, an expectant Mukherjee was 'surprised' to find his name missing. He boycotted the oath-taking ceremony. Rao called him that night—and offered him the less important post of deputy chairman of the Planning Commission. Mukherjee said he would 'think it over'. Rao replied, 'You can think for as long as you want, but I expect you to join on Monday. The notification is going to be issued.' Mukherjee wrote in his memoirs, 'I had no option but to comply with the orders.' A few days later Rao told him, 'Pranab, I can't tell you why

I did not take you into the cabinet. Perhaps a day will come when I can speak to you about it.' That day never came. And Mukherjee remained deputy chairman of the Planning Commission.

Then there was Arjun Singh: he was to remain a thorn in Rao's side all through his premiership. He and Fotedar had supported Rao's candidacy as PM—on the condition that Rao would step down as president of the Congress within three months. 'Why three months,' Rao assured Arjun Singh and Fotedar, 'I will leave the post in forty-five days.' Those forty-five days never came. 'As soon as there is a consensus on some name, I will step down,' Rao would tell them every time they brought up the subject. Rao calculated that a consensus on who could replace him as party president was near impossible—Arjun Singh would not accept Sharad Pawar and vice versa. And he was not going to create a challenger who could destabilize him. He had initially made Arjun Singh the leader of the party in the Lok Sabha, to keep him in good humour—and give his government a smooth start. Rao could not be leader in the house because he was not an MP. He had to get elected to parliament within the statutorily provided six months. In those months, Arjun Singh would make all the conciliatory noises. 'Unki meherbaani hai ki mujhe leader banaya, rakhenge tho bhi theek, nahin tho bhi theek hai (It's his goodness that he has made me a leader. If he continues with me, it is fine. But otherwise also it is fine).' But when Rao became an MP and replaced Arjun Singh as the leader of the Congress Party in the Lok Sabha, Singh resented it. He emerged as Rao's arch-opponent in the months that followed. When he and Sharad Pawar won convincingly in the election to the Congress Working Committee at Tirupati in April 1992, Rao moved swiftly to clip their wings. He got some of the newly elected nominees to resign on the ground that women and Dalits had not found representation on the body—and the CWC needed to be reconfigured. As a result, all the new CWC members, including Singh and Pawar, had to resign. This enabled Rao to reconstitute the party's apex decision-making body—and strengthen his grip over the party.

Eventually, in 1995, Arjun Singh would go on to split the Congress to form the Congress (Tiwari) along with Narayan Dutt Tiwari, M. L. Fotedar, Sheila Dikshit, and others. Though Arjun Singh had tried to pit Sonia Gandhi against the prime minister, she did not openly cast her lot with the Congress (Tiwari) when it broke away from the parent party. Throughout his tenure as prime minister, Rao had the measure of his opponents within the party.

■

Rao had a complex relationship with the BJP. He handled the saffron party very differently from the way his predecessors had dealt with it.

As we've seen, Rao had shown an interest in Hindu thought and philosophy from an early age, not just because of his Brahmin antecedents but also because of the anti-nizam movement he had participated in.

Rao first met RSS leaders Balasaheb Deoras and his brother, Bhaurao Deoras, in Nagpur—and they befriended the young Rao. This was before Balasaheb became the RSS chief. In those days, Rao lived in 'a one-room quarter in Sona Gali' and studied at the Law College in Nagpur.

Rao was in a new city, away from familiar surroundings. 'The Sangh has this speciality of befriending people, meeting them over a cup of tea, even when they may not be immediately useful,' revealed Govindacharya, who was himself mentored by Bhaurao. 'Rao and Bhaurao continued to meet each other and got to know each other well.' Rao kept in touch with the Deoras brothers over the years. But he enjoyed a special rapport with Bhaurao, who, as noted, looked after the 'political wing' of the Sangh, and had become powerful when Balasaheb was ailing in the 1980s and early 1990s.

The Sangh (RSS) had also got to know R. K. Khandekar during this period. 'I had been a swayamsevak since I was six and used to attend the RSS shakhas,' Khandekar told me. 'At that time, every second house in Nagpur had a swayamsevak in it. The children at the shakhas were taught about Hindu unity.'

'Rao sahib knew this (about my being a swayamsevak) when he took me on.' Khandekar had come to Delhi to work with Y. B. Chavan; he was then employed by the veteran Congressman Vasant Sathe—before joining Rao's team. He was to become a trusted aide of Rao when he became PM. 'By the end, he trusted me so much that anything I said got done'. Khandekar also took care of the money that came to Race Course Road for Rao's political activity. Khandekar travelled with Rao, juggled his appointments, undertook sensitive political assignments for him, taking confidential messages to leaders from the PM.

He even kept an eye on his clothes. Once, Rao was to call on Queen Elizabeth II, when on a visit to England. He had got ready, and was about to leave when his private secretary, Ramu Damodaran, noticed his socks. Their colour stood out in complete contrast to the shirt he was wearing. 'Look at the socks he is wearing,' Damodaran exclaimed in exasperation. Damodaran, who had been part of the Indian Foreign Service before joining Rao, knew the importance of dress in international diplomacy. He told Khandekar to tell the PM to change his socks, 'but please do it discreetly and tell him in Marathi.' Khandekar uttered a few words in Rao's ear in Marathi, and then rushed to his own room to get a new pair of socks for him. He used to carry an extra set of clothes for Rao, 'even a pair of goggles'.

Sometimes called Narasimha Rao's 'R. K. Dhawan', Khandekar was the go-between Rao used when the PM had to send messages to BJP–RSS leaders. Or to receive those visitors whose name did not go in the PM's formal 'manifest'.

Coincidentally, or otherwise, Rao's travails on Ayodhya were to start soon after Bhaurao's death in May 1992—six months before the demolition of the Babri Masjid. It was soon after that, that the VHP upped the ante again on temple construction. Rao no longer had a trusted point of contact within the RSS. Bhaurao had kept in touch with Rao even after he became prime minister. Rao had once remarked to Bhaurao—this was sometime in early 1992—'Give me a warning if you ever decide to bring down the Babri mosque.'

The BJP claimed they did—if one were to believe Kushabhau Thakre and K. Sudarshan, whose comments appear earlier in this chapter.

■

'PV would have actually finished the BJP if he had continued in power a little longer,' Bhuvnesh Chaturvedi once remarked to me. His strategy was to weaken the BJP—but not by confronting it head-on.

The BJP advocated the construction of a Ram temple and a Uniform Civil Code in the country. It was committed to undoing the special status given to Jammu and Kashmir at the time of its accession to India—and espoused Hindutva to bring about national unity. Rao knew he could not meet the BJP's challenge by coming across either as anti-Hindu or anti-Ram—or by countering its nationalistic rhetoric. He wanted to position the Congress as a pro-Hindu party (without being anti-minority), and take away from the BJP its Hindu plank.

Apart from Bhaurao in the RSS, Rao enjoyed a rare rapport with Atal Bihari Vajpayee. Both came to each other's rescue at various points in their career. While releasing a book of Vajpayee's poems, on 13 October 1995, Rao had hailed him as his 'guru'. Vajpayee immediately shot back, calling Rao a 'gurughantal'. (This epithet could either mean a very cunning person or a great teacher.)

By design, and by inclination, Rao had all along cultivated the 'moderate' elements in the BJP—Vajpayee, Jaswant Singh, and Bhairon Singh Shekhawat were his friends. By constantly strengthening their position, he hoped to weaken the hardliners like L. K. Advani, and sharpen the divide in the BJP. To begin with, even the more hawkish Advani had seen Rao not just as the 'most scholarly prime minister' after Nehru, but also as one who understood 'the trials and tribulations of Hindus', having fought against the fanatical nizam's rule in Hyderabad.

As part of his strategy to woo the BJP, after becoming PM, Rao gave the deputy speaker's post in the Lok Sabha to the party's stalwart, S. Mallikarjunaiah. This pleased the BJP but made the Left parties, whose help he also needed, resentful. So when he enacted the far-reaching legislation—Places of Worship (Special Provisions) Act, 1991, which froze the status of religious places as they existed on 15 August 1947, apart from that of the disputed Ram Janmabhoomi–Babri Masjid structure under legal scrutiny—he made it appear that it was done to please the communist parties. He knew they were worried about the BJP's temple politics.

The way he handled the BJP's Ekta Yatra in December 1991, from Kanyakumari to Srinagar, was another example of the deft Rao touch. Murli Manohar Joshi, then BJP president, had announced the yatra, to draw attention to Congress's 'inability to handle the problem of terrorism and secessionism' in Kashmir. This was fourteen months after L. K. Advani had undertaken his Somnath to Ayodhya Rath Yatra. With the Ekta Yatra, Joshi hoped 'to divert attention from the temple issue', which had come to be associated with Advani.

Travelling in a DCM Toyota van, through fourteen states of India, the 15,000-kilometre journey was to culminate in a flag-hoisting ceremony in Srinagar on Republic Day in 1992. Joshi would have calculated that Rao would be forced to arrest him before the yatra entered Srinagar. That would make him a hero—and a symbol of national unity.

Knowing the nationalistic sensitivities around the Kashmir issue, Rao did not publicly criticize Joshi's initiative. He manoeuvred the situation in such a way so as to 'create doubts about its motives'.

The banned militant organizations Jammu and Kashmir Liberation Front (JKLF) and Hizbul Mujahideen, had threatened that they would not allow the BJP to hoist the national flag in Srinagar. As it turned out, on 23 January 1992, three days before Joshi was to reach Srinagar, six BJP supporters were gunned down in the state when militants opened fire on the buses carrying party members to Srinagar. The BJP decided to reduce the number of people who would travel to Srinagar for the flag hoisting.

It was at this stage that Rao intervened. He offered to fly Joshi from Jammu to Srinagar in a military plane. Joshi now had little option but to accept. He unfurled the national flag at Lal Chowk on 26 January 1992—as planned. But it was hoisted against the backdrop of gunfire and grenades exploding in the city under a curfew, with hardly anyone seen on the streets. (Jammu and Kashmir was at the time under President's Rule, and under the charge of Rao's central government.) An event which was meant to be witnessed by thousands had only sixty-seven BJP members and security personnel as spectators. It was not a leader thundering from Srinagar for national unity but one who had to be protected himself by armed security personnel. What had been billed as a historic event turned out to be an anti-climax. Murli Manohar Joshi did not get a second term as BJP president.

'Had Rajiv been alive, he would have stopped the Ekta Yatra,' Rao remarked to some of his colleagues. 'And the message would have gone (out) that the BJP wanted to unfurl the tricolour in Srinagar but the central government had stopped it.'

Rao's strategy all along had been to make the BJP look like 'another Congress'—and not 'a party with a difference'. Towards the end of his term, the 'Great September Revolt' took place in Gujarat in March 1995, and forty-seven BJP MLAs headed by Shankarsinh Vaghela revolted. The rebel MLAs were holed up in a hotel in Khajuraho, threatening to bring down the newly formed government of CM Keshubhai Patel.

Though Vajpayee worked out a compromise, and a Vaghela loyalist, Suresh Mehta, replaced Keshubhai, the strife in the party made an anguished Vajpayee weep in front of colleagues. Pulling up the collar of his kurta, Advani too lamented, 'We could always hold it high. We cannot do it any longer.' Suddenly, the BJP had lost its sheen—and begun to resemble the 'faction ridden, power hungry' Congress (I).

The 'master puppeteer' behind the scenes was none other than P. V. Narasimha Rao. Shankarsinh Vaghela was in touch with Gujarat Congress chief Prabodh Raval, who was 'our man', disclosed Bhuvnesh Chaturvedi. 'We told Raval that we had sent another PCC President to Gujarat,' Chaturvedi revealed.

'Who?' Raval had asked.

'Naresh Chandra,' Chaturvedi said.

Naresh Chandra, governor of Gujarat, was never in touch with the PM directly, he moved through a senior secretary to the government of India.

Operation Khajuraho was to set a new trend in Indian politics, of parties flying their legislators to five star hotels, to keep them safe from the Opposition's predatory ways.

After this incident, the phrase 'Congressisation of the BJP' gained currency.

'This was no accident,' remarked Chaturvedi. 'It was done in a planned manner by P. V. Narasimha Rao.' He wanted to project the Congress, 'good or bad', as the only party of governance which alone knew how to rule.

V

It was in mid-1992, a year after Rao had taken over as PM, that the VHP upped the ante again on Mandir.

Till then, the BJP had liked the way Rao had handled the difficult situation he had inherited. The RSS mouthpiece *Panchjanya* wrote in Rao's favour. RSS chief Balasaheb Deoras had good things to say about him.

During Rao's first year in office, the BJP–VHP combine had lain low, satisfied with the 120 seats the BJP had won in the 1991 elections. But by mid-1992, they were a worried lot. For Rao was rapidly consolidating his position. He had successfully grappled with the grim economic crisis the country faced when he took over. He had been quick to position India for a unipolar world after the dissolution of the Soviet Union in December 1991. He reached out to the strategically-located and mineral-rich Central Asian republics, after they became independent following the Soviet Union's collapse. (Rao was to visit four out of the five republics between 1993 and 1995—Kazakhstan, Uzbekistan, Turkmenistan, and the Kyrgyz Republic.) He put in place a Look East Policy in 1991 for greater cooperation with the Southeast Asian nations. Soon thereafter, on 29 January 1992, Rao took the far-reaching step of recognizing Israel—and informed PLA leader Yasser Arafat, who was in India at the time, before announcing it.

On 7 August 1991, India's surface-to-surface missile, Prithvi, was launched. On 3 November that year, Trishul, the short-range surface-to-air missile, was tested—infusing the country with a sense of pride. More significantly, Rao had managed to scale down the caste versus religion confrontation that had polarized Indian politics—after V. P. Singh's controversial decision to implement the Mandal Commission Report, and L. K. Advani's Rath Yatra for the construction of a Ram temple in Ayodhya. He defused the tensions that had built up in Punjab and in Jammu and Kashmir, with demands for secession gaining ground in both states—and managed to hold elections in Punjab in February 1992, with the Congress forming the government there.

A worried BJP decided it had to get the political initiative back—and it encouraged the sants to revisit the temple issue. The sadhus and sants met in Ujjain in May 1992 and announced they would resume their kar seva on 9 July.

Now it was a worried Rao who despatched his political secretary Jitendra Prasada to meet them—and dissuade them from going ahead with their plan. Prasada fixed a meeting for them with the prime minister. Rao received them at the PM House. Those who came were well-known names like Mahant Avaidyanath of Gorakhpur, Swami Vamdev, Swami Chinmayanand, and Pejewar Swami from the Udipi math in Karnataka. The sants told the PM they had come to personally apprise him of their proposed kar seva on 9 July 1992, for they did not want him to be surprised.

Rao heard out the sants—but did not say much. Silence was a weapon Rao had honed. Once, when asked how he had managed to repulse so many attacks that had come his way, Rao remarked, 'Moonh jo band rakha hai (Because I have kept my mouth shut).' When he remained quiet, some would interpret his silence to mean a yes. Others read it as a no. Nobody could be sure about what he wanted.

Just as the religious heads were about to leave, Rao broke his silence. He had his punch lines ready. 'I too want the construction of the mandir,' he told them. 'And I want this matter to be resolved quickly....'

They looked surprised. Unfortunately, the issue had become politicized, Rao said. The need was to keep politics out of it. The sants urged the prime minister to pick up the threads from where Chandra Shekhar had left off, when there had almost been a breakthrough. Documents had been exchanged between both sides to support their respective claims. The VHP had shown that the masjid had not been in use since 1936. The All India Babri Masjid Action Committee (AIBMAC) had built a case that the story of Ramayana was mythological and not historical. Rao assured them he would pick up from where Chandra Shekhar had left off—and restart the dialogue between the VHP and AIBMAC.

Rao let the sants go away with the impression that he had agreed to reopen negotiations on their suggestion. All that the PM was looking for at that stage was to ensure their kar seva remained tokenistic.

∎

The telephone rang shrilly, drowning out the hum of the old air conditioner. Devendra Dwivedi, additional solicitor general of India, was poring over some case papers in his study at home. It was late in the evening in end June 1992, a few days after Rao had met the sants. Dwivedi picked up the receiver absent-mindedly.

'Kaho, Devendra, kaise ho (Tell me, Devendra, how are you)?' said the prime minister amiably. 'Bahut din se dikhe nahin. Kya ho raha hai (I haven't seen you for many days. What is happening)?' The PM sounded as if he had all the time in the world to chat with Dwivedi, who was a constitutional expert, and belonged to the old school of 'cerebral' Congress politicians like Rao himself. A politician from Varanasi in Uttar Pradesh, he had been a Rajya Sabha MP a little over a decade earlier—and had emerged as a close advisor to Rao.

Dwivedi knew that PV rang him only when he needed something. That day he had a hunch as to what might have triggered the call. The prime minister had held a cabinet meeting that day—and came under fire. With the VHP announcing its kar seva from 9 July 1992, Rao's rivals in the Congress had begun to unsheath their knives. Rao's ministerial colleague, Arjun Singh, had told the PM bluntly that he was not doing enough to resolve the Ayodhya problem. During the year Rao had been in power, Arjun Singh had taken to writing him letters finding fault with one or another aspect of policy, which he would leak to the press. He had made 3,000 photocopies of one of his vitriolic missives and sent them to party leaders seeking their comment. He was trying to arrogate to himself the role of the party chief, much to Rao's annoyance.

Within an hour of the cabinet meeting, one of the ministers present there had called Dwivedi and given him the low-down. And so, when the PM phoned, Dwivedi told him he had better watch out. For the honeymoon period was coming to an end. The VHP's kar seva, Rao knew, would trigger problems for him inside his own party.

'Toh kya karna hai (So what is to be done)?' Rao asked Devendra Dwivedi.

'I think you should talk to the BJP,' Dwivedi replied.

'Maain tumhe kal bulata hoon (I will call you tomorrow),' Rao said, sounding pleased with Dwivedi's suggestion. 'I have a tight day tomorrow but...you keep yourself free.' The next day, Dwivedi waited all day. But no call came. Eventually Rao called him at 8 p.m.

'I have been thinking about...what you suggested. I want you to do something,' Rao said. 'You are the best person to talk to the BJP, you have a good relationship with them,' the prime minister said. Dwivedi was a critic of the BJP but enjoyed a comfortable relationship with the party's senior leaders.

'OK,' Dwivedi agreed.

'You talk to the BJP leaders right away,' Rao told him.

'What? Now?' Dwivedi expressed surprise.

'Yes, now,' the PM replied.

Narasimha Rao had an uneasy relationship with L. K. Advani at the time. And Advani, though not the party chief, was the most powerful figure in the BJP.

Dwivedi put the receiver down and dialled Advani's number. He was not at home. Dwivedi asked to speak to Advani's wife. After a wait of five minutes, Kamla Advani came on the line. Dwivedi introduced himself. He told her he wanted to 'speak to Advaniji urgently'. She asked him to leave his number, and said she would inform her husband. In ten minutes Advani called back. He was at the residence of Murli Manohar Joshi. Joshi, then BJP president, had invited all the BJP MPs to dinner that evening. But 'it will get over in 15-20 minutes', Advani told Dwivedi. He would head home, he said, and asked Dwivedi to come over at 10 p.m.

'I remember I reached there at 10.07.' Advani was already there, waiting for him. 'We talked till 12.30 a.m.' Advani suggested that Dwivedi should also talk to Murli Manohar Joshi. Joshi was sensitive about not being given his due as party president. Dwivedi went to meet Joshi the next morning. He also spoke to Atal Bihari Vajpayee.

The next day Dwivedi phoned Rao, and told him what had transpired at his meetings with the BJP leaders. Narasimha Rao sounded pleased. Now that Dwivedi had prepared the ground, the PM invited both Advani and Joshi to RCR. He also spoke to Vajpayee. All three agreed to give Rao time to find a solution. 'The PM spoke to both Vajpayee and me to prevail upon the leaders of the temple movement to give him some time,' Advani confirmed. They agreed that the kar seva announced by the VHP in Ayodhya should only be tokenistic—which is what Rao wanted. And it should be followed by negotiations.

As planned, the kar seva started on 9 July, though the court had stayed it. All through the kar seva, Rao remained the monarch of all the confusion that prevailed, skilfully navigating the contradictions. Officially, the central government's position was articulated by the Home Ministry—that the 9 July kar seva was a violation of the court's orders. At the same time, Home Minister S. B. Chavan worshipped at the makeshift temple inside the disputed structure when he went to Ayodhya to assess the situation on the ground!

Publicly, the VHP declared that neither the government nor the courts could stop it from constructing the temple. For the land belonged to Ram Lalla. Despite the court's restraining orders, the kar sevaks went on to build a chabutra (platform) at a place christened the Singhdwar (gate to the temple) not far from the spot where the shilanyas (laying of the temple's foundation) had taken place on 9 November 1989, during Rajiv Gandhi's premiership.

Rao remained unfazed by the court's stay—and allowed the kar seva to continue unchecked. He did not want to antagonize the VHP—and he wanted to buy time. He had already brought around Advani, Joshi, and Vajpayee. He now reached out to VHP leader Ashok Singhal, seeking four months' time to find a way out. Finally, the VHP agreed. It stopped the kar seva on 26 July and decided to give Rao three months to find a solution. (Though a hardened politician, Rao now became cautiously optimistic that a way out may be possible. He hoped both sides would at least agree to abide by the court verdict.)

As soon as the kar seva ended, Dwivedi went to see Rao. 'He is a cold man, but he got up and caught me by both my shoulders. "Devendra, I want to really thank you". The PM then asked, "What is the next step?" Rao himself provided the answer to that question. "You should continue to talk to the BJP".'

'I must have the authority to do so,' Dwivedi countered. They discussed various possibilities. One way of going about it, Dwivedi suggested, was for him to head the proposed Ayodhya Cell.

'Done,' Rao replied.

Then they discussed the constitution of the Ayodhya Cell and who could be part of it. 'It could comprise me, (Home Minister) Chavan, and Naresh Chandra,' Dwivedi suggested, warming up to the idea.

The PM agreed. 'I am going to Ballia the day after. I will do it when I come back'.

In the days that followed, Dwivedi did not hear back from Rao. He would learn later that the idea (of Dwivedi heading the Ayodhya Cell) had been shot down by the PMO. How could the additional solicitor general of India, the officials argued, head a cell of which the Home Minister was only a member? The Brahmin lobby within the Congress—including Jitendra Prasad, Rao's political secretary—also had no wish to see Dwivedi, a fellow Brahmin, becoming powerful. 'After this, PV started to avoid me,' Dwivedi recalled.

On 2 August 1992, Rao appointed Naresh Chandra as the head of the Ayodhya Cell in the PMO.

VI

'I inherited the Ayodhya dispute,' Rao would often lament. 'It is not a problem of my making.' But he was familiar with all the ins and outs of the longstanding tangle. Rajiv Gandhi had made him head of a committee of ministers in 1987 to advise on Ayodhya. He had seen the twists and turns in the drama—including the fiasco that had occurred in 1986 when Rajiv had the masjid unlocked, and the blunder he made in 1989 when he allowed the VHP to do 'shilanyas', and lay the foundation stone for the temple at Ayodhya.

Rao decided to set up the Ayodhya Cell to monitor the functioning of the Home Ministry and keep direct control over the temple issue. The cell comprised representatives from the Home Ministry, Law Ministry, and the PMO and was principally meant to facilitate coordination between them. It had joint secretaries from these three departments—Vinod Dhal from Home, S. C. Jain from Law, and Nishikant Sinha from the PMO.

Naresh Chandra was designated senior advisor to the prime minister. 'I was officially neither a secretary to the Government of India, nor a secretary to the Ayodhya Cell, nor a secretary to the prime minister,' Chandra said to me, his face crumpling with laughter as he recalled Rao's ingenuity. He was given a rank equivalent to that of cabinet secretary, the most senior officer in the Government of India, so that his word could not be ignored. 'In the way he designed the post, and this was typical of the way Rao functioned, I headed the cell but could not be "held to account",' Chandra said. That is why the Liberhan Commission, set up by Rao on 16 December 1992 to fix responsibility for the demolition 'could not call me for questioning'.

If there was an official considered close to Rao, and privy to his thinking, it was Naresh Chandra. Chandra had held all the important positions in the Government of India—cabinet secretary, home secretary, defence secretary. Tall, portly, and good-humoured, his affable exterior masked a steeliness. He could be really tough when it came to taking decisions that he considered to be in the 'larger national interest'. Successive prime ministers had utilized his services in out-of-the-ordinary situations. He was known to be politically sharp and discreet.

Rao told Chandra to collect all the papers about the dispute and authenticate the records relating to negotiations conducted by previous governments. Chandra was not only trusted by Rao, he was a living encyclopaedia on Ayodhya, having been home secretary when V. P. Singh was prime minister and L. K. Advani took out his Rath Yatra—and when a serious effort was made by two governors, Krishan Kant and Yunus Saleem, to break the Ayodhya impasse. Chandra was cabinet secretary when Chandra Shekhar was PM and a whisker away from a breakthrough.

Oddly enough, Rao asked neither Krishan Kant nor Chandra Shekhar—he enjoyed cordial relations with both—about why their efforts had not yielded results. 'Not one of my successors had talked to me even for five minutes about what I had done on Ayodhya,' an aggrieved Chandra Shekhar once said to me.

Given the rapport he enjoyed with Rao, Krishan Kant thought Rao might seek his help on Ayodhya. More so as Rao and Kant—he was governor in Andhra Pradesh when Rao was PM—shared the same guru in Sivanand Murthy, a former IPS officer who had taken to spiritualism at the age of twenty-five. Murthy had prophesied that Rao would become prime minister—and predicted that Kant would become vice president a year before it happened.

'Guruji what will happen to the Babri Masjid?' Rao had once asked Sivanand Murthy. Even as prime minister, he would openly address Murthy as 'guruji', visit him a couple of times a year at his ashram at Vishakhapatnam and spend hours with him talking about Hindu thought and philosophy.

Hearing Rao's question about the fate of the Babri Masjid, Murthy closed his eyes for a few minutes. Then he replied, 'I don't see it there.'

This deeply affected Rao—it also underlined the superstitious side of his personality. 'From then on, I think somewhere inside him, he reconciled to the fact that Babri Masjid would go,' disclosed a senior government official who spent several years in Andhra Pradesh, and knew Sivanand Murthy well.

■

When Rao formed the Ayodhya Cell in August 1992, he went 'over and over again' with Naresh Chandra the major milestones in the long history of the conflict.

The basic facts about the Babri Masjid, and the controversy surrounding it, are well known. I will limit myself to a quick recap. The mosque was constructed by the Mughal general, Mir Baqi, in 1528 on the orders of Emperor Babur. On this rested the Muslim claim to the structure. For Hindus, Ayodhya was holy because they believed it to be the birthplace of Lord Ram. Many of them believed the mosque was built where a temple had earlier stood. This led to a long-standing dispute over the structure between the Hindus and the Muslims. There were a few clashes between the two communities in the nineteenth century. By 1885, the outer part of the structure had been converted into Hindu places of worship. It included a 'Ram Chabutra' where an idol of Lord Ram was placed; the inner part of the structure remained a mosque where the Muslims offered prayers. In 1934, Hindu rioters demolished a portion of the mosque; it was rebuilt by the British. After 1934, Hindu protestors averred that Muslims no longer worshipped at the mosque—a claim that was immediately contested by the Muslims.

It was in December 1949 that the mosque was declared a 'disputed structure' by the Faizabad court. This was after an idol of Ram Lalla was smuggled into the sanctum sanctorum of the structure. This was a turning point in the Ayodhya story. I have dwelt on it in some detail because it was the Gangotri from where all else flowed in the decades that followed. Rao had studied this episode meticulously, particularly the similarities between the situation in 1949 and the one he faced in 1992.

The politics behind it interested him even more—the tussle between the traditionalist Hindu opinion in the Congress represented by Govind Ballabh Pant and Sardar Vallabhbhai Patel on the one side and the secularist push that Nehru wanted to give the party on the other side.

The action in 1949 took place in the dead of night on 22 December. It was just before midnight, and pitch dark around the mosque. Not surprisingly, the area was deserted and the outline of the three domes could be barely seen. The soft murmur of the Sarayu River could be heard in the stillness of the night, as a group of people stealthily made their way to the building. They had already brought around the guard on duty, who offered them no resistance. They had to enter the mosque before midnight when the change of guard took place. The intruders scaled the wall and went inside. The outer compound had several structures including a couple of small temples. The inner compound housed the mosque. Once inside, they took the idol of Ram Lalla they had carried with them—and placed it under the central dome of the mosque. And they waited for dawn to break. When they saw the first glimmer of light, they lit a lamp before the idol and started chanting prayers to the chimes of bells, cymbals, and conches they had brought with them.

Very quickly, word spread that Ram Lalla had miraculously manifested himself within the mosque—'Bhaya prakat kripala Deen Dayala (God has manifested himself).' The devotees began to gather there to offer prayers.

The 'miracle' story had been in the making for a couple of months. The All India Ramayana Mahasabha, formed by the Hindu Mahasabha, which was the precursor of the Bharatiya Jan Sangh and the Bharatiya Janata Party, had placed an idol of Ram Lalla on a platform outside the masjid. It organized prayers for the idol to move inside the mosque, in what it believed would be a miracle. But for three weeks no miracle had taken place—until the night of 22 December 1949.

It is not so known that Nanaji Deshmukh, a senior RSS leader, and till 1977 considered amongst the top three of the Bharatiya Jan Sangh, along with Vajpayee and Advani, was part of the group which smuggled the idol of Ram Lalla into the Babri Masjid on 22 December 1949. For many years, the RSS had been chary about admitting its involvement in the 1949 episode.

'One day I had gone to meet Nanaji Deshmukh at the Deen Dayal Shodh Sansthan where he used to sit as its adhyaksh (president),' Ram Bahadur Rai, a senior journalist, told me. That day, 'he started to talk about events in Ayodhya as they had panned out.'

Nanaji was in an expansive mood. He revealed that he had been in the group which went to the mosque to install the idol that night. Besides himself, the group, according to Nanaji, included 'Abhiram Das, Bhaiji Hanuman Prasad Poddar, Mahant Ramchandra Paramhans, and Shakuntala Nair'.

'I was a part of the plan,' Nanaji told Rai. 'And it was all Hanuman Prasad Poddar's planning.' Countering the lore that had been passed down for forty years, that a miracle had occurred that day, Nanaji Deshmukh told Rai, 'Sach yeh hai ki murtiyo ko Sarayu mein vidhivar snaan karaya gaya. Unki puja archana hui, aur raat ko Abhiram Das murtiyon ko sar par rakh kar le gaye ...Shakuntala Nair ne unse apne sir par lekar rakha (The truth is that the idol was taken to the Sarayu River, bathed in it, and readied with the chanting of prayers, and then at night Abhiram Das placed it on his head and took it...then Shakuntala Nair (wife of the district magistrate K. K. K. Nair) had transferred the idol to her head....)'

'(Unhone) Vistar se varnan kiya,' Ram Bahadur Rai said. 'Yeh log aaye, murtiyan stapith ki. Raat me gayae (He told me in great detail, how they had gone there, and installed the idol). And it was found at 5 a.m.'

■

Word reached Prime Minister Jawaharlal Nehru in Delhi. He ordered that the idols be removed forthwith and the mosque restored to its old status. In Lucknow, the chief minister of UP, Govind Ballabh Pant, came under pressure from Nehru to act quickly. But this did not happen.

At the local court, K. K. K. Nair, who was the district magistrate of Faizabad and the top bureaucrat in the district, was sympathetic to the Hindu Mahasabha. He manoeuvred the situation in such a way that Nehru's instructions were disregarded.

Nair told his superiors in Lucknow that the issue was an emotional one, involving the sensibilities of thousands of people. It had to be handled with care. Or it could have huge law and order ramifications.

On 23 December 1949, a police FIR was filed to investigate the matter, which named Abhiram Das and around sixty others culpable of illegal entry into the mosque. With the installation of the Hindu idol, the mosque had become a 'disputed structure'. The city magistrate Guru Datt Singh, working under Nair, 'attached' the structure, and appointed a receiver.

The Faizabad court ordered on 16 January 1950 that Hindus could worship the Ram Lalla from behind the locked gates and it could not be removed by anyone. With the Hindus allowed to offer prayers, the Muslims stopped offering namaz. For all practical purposes, the structure ceased to be a mosque.

The midnight entry planned by the Hindu Mahasabha came after a resolution it had passed four months earlier. On 14 August 1949, it had vowed to free all the temples where Muslims had constructed mosques— including the Ram Janmabhoomi in Ayodhya, the Vishwanath Temple in Kashi, and the Krishna Janmasthan in Mathura.

•

The Hindu Mahasabha had been emboldened because of the charged communal atmosphere that prevailed after the country's partition in 1947. The outcome of a by-election in Ayodhya in 1948 had also given the Mahasabha new heart. The Praja Socialist Party, which had been part of the Congress since its inception in 1934, had quit it in 1948. Its leader, Acharya Narendra Dev, had resigned, necessitating a by-election. Even though he had left the Congress, Nehru wanted him to win, given his Left-wing, progressive views, with which the PM agreed. The Congress had first selected a candidate who would put up only a notional fight against Narendra Dev. But UP (United Provinces at the time) CM Govind Ballabh Pant, sympathetic to Hindu sentiments, chose Baba Raghav Das to contest against Narendra Dev. Das, a proclaimed Gandhian and a sadhu from eastern UP, led a 'communally vitriolic attack against Dev'—and especially appealed to orthodox Hindus. He even distributed tulsi leaves during his campaign to win people over—and was backed all through by G. B. Pant. For Pant, it was an opportunity to keep control of the Congress in UP—and to marginalize Narendra Dev who was his rival in UP and enjoyed Nehru's confidence.

For the Hindu Mahasabha and its leaders like Mahant Digvijay Nath, who was head of the Gorakhpeeth in Gorakhpur, the tug-of-war inside the Congress was an opportunity to push forward with their agenda. They had been lying low, after their suspected involvement in Mahatma Gandhi's assassination in January 1948. They decided to place the Ram Lalla in the Babri Masjid to arouse Hindu sentiment in their favour—and do it surreptitiously so that they did not come directly into the government's firing line.

Raghav Das defeated Acharya Narendra Dev—and became a giant killer. Mahant Digvijay Nath exulted afterwards that 'the Congress leaders had to appeal to the Hindu feeling of voters'.

Home Minister Sardar Patel, a strong presence in Nehru's government, backed Govind Ballabh Pant. Pant regarded Sardar Patel as his leader. Even though an anguished Nehru had written Pant repeatedly and even offered to visit Ayodhya himself, his writ finally did not run. The conservative Hindu opinion in the Congress had prevailed.

What happened in December 1949 reflected the Hindu versus secular conundrum inside the Congress which was to surface from time to time in the years that followed. Nehru chose not to push beyond a point to get his way in 1949. He was able to get a firm grip over the party only after Sardar Patel's death in December 1950.

■

There were several similarities between 1948–49 and 1991–92, which held Rao's interest—and he discussed these with Naresh Chandra. On both occasions, it was a tussle within the Congress which influenced the central government's line on the temple issue. In 1949, there was the Pant–Patel duo sympathetic to the Hindu cause pitted against the 'secular' Nehru. In 1992, there was a standoff between Rao and Arjun Singh, with Singh using secularism as a weapon to get the better of Rao, accusing him of pursuing a soft Hindutva line. It is a matter of interest that the 'secularists' lost out on both occasions, despite the influence Nehru wielded after Independence. Rao, on the other hand, was heading a shaky minority government in 1992.

As in 1949, so also in 1992, the government, both central and state, just watched helplessly as rioters went into the mosque and broke the law. On both occasions, Congress governments were in power and displayed a marked reluctance to act decisively. In both cases, the mob got the better of the authorities. And, in both instances, responsibility for the lawlessness could not be pinned on anyone—or the guilty punished. The authority of the Indian state lay in tatters both times. Both 1949 and 1992 were pre-planned. Subterfuge was used in 1949 as also in 1992—in 1949, a Ram idol was stealthily smuggled into the Babri Masjid; in 1992, despite assurances that the mosque would not be harmed, Kalyan Singh allowed the demolition to take place.

VII

Never had a dispute polarized the country as much as Ayodhya did. The court cases over Ayodhya constituted the biggest and most protracted legal battle in independent India's history—all over just 1,500 square yards of land. It fashioned India's politics for three decades, and the story may not yet be over. Even though a Ram temple will rise where the masjid once stood, after the Supreme Court judgment in 2019, there are renewed demands to 'liberate' the sites in Mathura and Varanasi, where temples stand next to mosques. Before I deal in detail with the events of December 1992, and the run-up to it, it would be useful to recap how the courts dealt with the issue. And equally important, to look at why the mediation efforts to resolve the crisis failed. They formed the backdrop against which Narasimha Rao had to make his decisions.

The first legal suit over the Babri Masjid was filed by Mahant Raghubir Das in 1885. He appealed to the court to allow him to construct a Ram temple on the Ram Chabutra in the outer precincts of the mosque. The court turned down his plea on the grounds that it would lead to a law-and-order problem to have a temple so close to the mosque. After the Ram Lalla idol was surreptitiously placed inside the mosque on the night of 22 December 1949, locks were put on the structure by the order of a magistrate under Section 145 CrPC. Shortly thereafter, in January 1950, the court ordered that the idol could not be removed and that puja could be allowed from outside the gates. The Allahabad High Court confirmed this order in 1955. In 1959, the Nirmohi Akhara filed a 'title suit' for the ownership of the disputed land. So did the Sunni Waqf Board in 1961, seeking the removal of the idol. Until then the Muslim community had not taken too much interest in what was happening.

On 1 February 1986, the district judge in Faizabad passed the order for the opening of the locks at the Ram Janmabhoomi–Babri Masjid (as we saw in Chapter 2). Hindus could now worship at the disputed structure. This provoked a reaction from the Muslims; they formed an All India Babri Masjid Action Committee of eminent Muslims in 1987 to safeguard the mosque—and held protest rallies throughout North India. It created a counter-reaction amongst the Hindus, deepening the communal divide. In 1989, the five original title suits, which had been filed till then contesting the ownership of the site, were consolidated and transferred to the Allahabad High Court so that they could be taken up together.

Apart from the ongoing litigation to decide the ownership of the disputed land in Ayodhya, the courts came into the picture again after Kalyan Singh took over as CM of UP in June 1991—and vowed to construct a Ram temple in Ayodhya. He acquired '2.77 acres' of disputed land around the mosque and began demolishing structures that stood on it, in preparation to build the temple. While the Allahabad High Court allowed the Kalyan Singh government to acquire the land around the mosque and demolish buildings on it, it prohibited the construction of permanent structures on it.

By now Rao was the prime minister.

The VHP and various sants announced that kar seva would take place on the site on 9 July 1992. A case was filed in the Supreme Court on 23 July 1992 challenging their actions. The apex court upheld the ruling of the Allahabad High Court—that no construction activity of any kind should take place on the land that had been acquired by Kalyan Singh. The Allahabad High Court would have to decide the validity of the acquisition of 2.77 acres of land acquired by the UP government. (While the figure of 2.77 acres is often mentioned while referring to the disputed site, the actual acreage was only 1,500 square yards or 0.309 acres—as documented by the Supreme Court.)

The Supreme Court judgment in 1992 was where matters stood legally—when Rao had to deal with the snowballing crisis. (After the mosque was demolished, the battle continued in the courts until 2019, when the Supreme Court finally decided to give its go-ahead for a temple where the Babri Masjid had once stood.)

■

The first serious attempt to peacefully unravel the Ayodhya tangle was undertaken by two governors jointly—Krishan Kant (of Andhra Pradesh) and Yunus Saleem (of Bihar), one a Hindu the other a Muslim. This was during V. P. Singh's term as PM in 1989–90, though Kant and Saleem took the initiative even before VP came to power. They informed VP about what they were doing—and he endorsed their efforts. Saleem told me that he had gone to meet Krishan Kant after the terrible communal violence which broke out in Lucknow, Meerut, Malliyana, and Hashimpura—following the opening of the locks at the Ram Janmabhoomi–Babri Masjid structure in February 1986.

'I went to (meet) Krishan Kant at his house at Telegraph Lane,' recounted Saleem. They were friends and belonged to the same party, the Janata Dal. 'The situation is deteriorating, can you do something?' an anguished Saleem asked Kant. A few days later Kant called Saleem. 'I have contacted the Shankaracharya of Kanchi (Kanchi Kamakoti Peetham, in Kanchipuram, Tamil Nadu), Jayendra Saraswati. He is ready to talk. But he has kept a precondition—that two people will not be involved (in the effort), (Syed) Shahabuddin and Imam Bukhari. I have suggested your name and that of Ali Mian (for the talks).' As we have seen, Ali Mian a renowned Islamic scholar, headed the AIMPLB. He was initially reluctant. But eventually he agreed to get involved—and included his disciple, Abdul Karim Parikh, in the effort. The wily Parikh was a businessman, pragmatic, and from Nagpur with links with the RSS leadership there. 'You fix a meeting with the Shankaracharya and we will go to him together,' Ali Mian told Kant and Saleem.

By this time, Krishan Kant and Yunus Saleem had been appointed governors of Andhra Pradesh and Bihar respectively. As governors, their movements were restricted. They could not travel without the permission of the president. 'If we were to go to Madras to meet the Shankaracharya of Kanchi, the president would have wondered what we were doing.' Kant decided to take the president, R. Venkataraman, into confidence. 'I told him everything,' Kant said. 'If you succeed in this,' the president told him, 'and can bring about a compromise, it will be the greatest event of this century, even greater than the freedom of India.'

Krishan Kant saw the Shankaracharya of Kanchi 'at least a dozen times' in the weeks that followed. On 19 March 1990, Kant, Saleem, their ADCs, and Ali Mian, Abdul Karim Parikh, and Ali Mian's personal attendant, Abdul Razak, travelled to Chennai. There, they met the two shankaracharyas, Jayendra Saraswati and Vijayendra Saraswati. On the second occasion, their sons Junaid and Rashmi also accompanied them.

Ali Mian made a reference to these efforts in his seven-volume memoir, *Karvaan-e-Zindagi*, of which Yunus Saleem translated an excerpt as follows: 'When Mohammed Yunus Saleem and Krishan Kant met me and informed me that the shankaracharyas, the senior and the junior, are prepared to help and try and reach some kind of a formula which may save the situation so that the mosque may be saved and the temple may be constructed at a distance.... I agreed to participate in the discussion.'

Ali Mian laid down three conditions—that the talks would not be considered formal; he would not sign off on any solution on his own; and he would come to see the shankaracharya with his associate Abdul Karim Parikh.

Besides the two shankaracharyas, the group also met the senior head of the Kanchi math, the parmacharya. 'I remember he was lying curled up on a cemented platform,' recalled Kant. 'He did not say anything but just nodded his approval,' Saleem said. 'I remember him nodding.'

The shankaracharya and Ali Mian decided to broaden the discussion and involve more religious heads of both communities. They called the 'Muslim divines' and the 'Hindu sants' to the negotiating table. On the advice of Ali Mian, forty Muslim scholars from all over India came to Bihar Bhavan. Similarly, the Hindu sants were gathered in Andhra Bhavan. The two governors were upbeat that they were making progress.

A joint meeting between the two sides was held in the conference room of Andhra Bhavan in Delhi. They resolved that the issue should be decided peacefully; that the masjid would not be disturbed nor would attempts to build a temple be stopped; that a kar seva, which was going to take place on 30 October and 2 November 1990 would be held peacefully as planned; that a trust would be formed with one nominee of Ali Mian and one of the shankaracharyas, and a representative of the Government of India. And that the shankaracharya and Ali Mian would jointly announce the solution. But suddenly things began to go awry.

On the verge of a breakthrough, the talks were sabotaged. There was a leak from the Home Ministry. The shankaracharya informed Krishan Kant that Ashok Singhal of the VHP had come to see him. Singhal had told him that Subodh Kant Sahay—then minister of state (Home) who was coordinating efforts on Ayodhya, and was close to Chandra Shekhar— had urged him to get the shankaracharya to disengage from the effort.

The VP Singh government was on its way out, Sahay said, and Chandra Shekhar would form the next government. All efforts to mediate should be postponed until then. The VHP stepped up pressure on the shankaracharya to distance himself from the effort—which he did.

Krishan Kant and Yunus Saleem had envisaged the creation of a cultural centre in Ayodhya, while building a temple and retaining the existing mosque—to demonstrate India's syncretic culture. Ali Mian had promised to bring around the All India Babri Masjid Action Committee. 'You leave the VHP to me,' the shankaracharya would tell Krishan Kant repeatedly.

Kant had also made a point of keeping Atal Bihari Vajpayee in the loop, and Jaswant Singh was also present at one of these meetings. He knew the BJP would have to approve any solution that was worked out.

In the end, a sincere and well-meaning effort did not work out because of political one-upmanship—and a desire for credit—that some of those at the top wanted.

■

'Where are you?' Chandra Shekhar asked VHP leader Ashok Singhal. It was 10 November 1990—the day Chandra Shekhar had taken over as prime minister. Singhal replied they were in a meeting 'at Vijaya Raje Scindia's house'.

'Come and meet me at the PM House,' Chandra Shekhar told him.

With those words, Chandra Shekhar initiated the second serious effort to resolve the Ayodhya tangle. Unlike Kant and Saleem, who had moved through religious figures on both sides, Chandra Shekhar decided to negotiate directly with the VHP. Chandra Shekhar wanted to waste no time; he was aware that his government may not last long. For his sixty-three member Janata Dal (S) was being supported by Rajiv Gandhi's Congress Party from the 'outside', and that was not a stable arrangement.

When Singhal and the VHP leaders turned up at the PM House, Chandra Shekhar came straight to the point, 'How do we resolve the Ayodhya problem?' They repeated their demand that the temple must be built where the Babri Masjid stood. If it was not done, 'khoon ki nadiya beh jayengee (rivers of blood will flow)', one of them said polemically.

'I won't let one brick fall,' Chandra Shekhar retorted.

'Is there any way (forward)?' Singhal asked the PM towards the end of the meeting,

'Baatcheet karo (Start a dialogue),' Chandra Shekhar suggested.

'How?' they asked. 'The Babri Masjid Action Committee won't be ready.'

'You talk about yourself,' Chandra Shekhar told them. 'Are you ready?'

The VHP agreed to start a dialogue with representatives of the Muslims. Chandra Shekhar then talked to the Babri Masjid Action Committee, urging them to defuse an explosive situation, which could singe the six lakh villages in India where Hindus and Muslims lived side by side.

Ten days later, talks started between the two sides. Chandra Shekhar appointed a committee comprising Bhairon Singh Shekhawat, Sharad Pawar, and, later, Mulayam Singh Yadav to find 'a way out'. He could not have zeroed in on more pragmatic politicians in India, to grapple with an issue which had become intractable.

On 1 and 4 December 1990, meetings were held between the VHP and Muslim leaders. They decided to ascertain whether a temple had existed at the spot where the Babri Masjid stood. Both sides agreed to furnish the evidence they collected to the Home Ministry, and then meet again in January.

Bhairon Singh was dealing with the BJP and VHP. Pawar handled the 'Nagpur end' (RSS), and worked through RSS leader Moropant Pingle, whom he knew well, and who was the Sangh Parivar's point person on Ayodhya. 'Tantric-godman' Chandraswami also helped to 'get the sadhus together.' He 'reached out to 200 sadhus,' including Nritya Gopal Das, who headed the largest temple in Ayodhya, and Ram Chandra Paramhans, who headed the Ram Janmabhoomi Nyas, a body which was tasked to undertake the construction of the temple.

Once asked why he had used the services of 'godman' Chandraswami, who had attained a certain notoriety, Chandra Shekhar replied cryptically 'Kaun mahatma hai aur kaun duratma hai, kaam zaroori hai (Who can say who is a good soul and who is a bad spirit, what is important is to get the work done).' Later, Chandraswami was to undertake a similar exercise for Narasimha Rao.

Chandra Shekhar told Om Prakash Chautala to keep the sadhus 'happy' and provide them vehicles, mushtandas (security guards), and whatever else they wanted.

Given his rapport with the Muslim religious leadership, Mulayam Singh Yadav talked to those heading the Darul Uloom Nadwatul Ulama, an Islamic institution in Lucknow that attracted Muslim scholars from all over the world. He also met Ali Mian. 'There was a readiness on both sides to find a solution,' Chandra Shekhar told me.

Several meetings took place between the AIBMAC and the Ram Janmabhoomi Nyas. It was decided that the site would be excavated. And if it were found that the mosque had been constructed after breaking a temple there, the Muslims would give up their claim. But, 'if there was no structure', Chandra Shekhar told the VHP, 'then we could build a grand temple on the banks of Bhagirathi and Sarayu.' This was the basis of the formula Chandra Shekhar was working on.

Soon after he had met the VHP leaders, Chandra Shekhar called Syed Shahabuddin for consultations. Shahabuddin was very close to the prime minister, and led the Babri Masjid Movement Coordination Committee (BMMCC) which had been formed on 5 February 1986 after the opening of the locks at the Ram Janmabhoomi–Babri Masjid structure by Rajiv Gandhi.

'Bhai, woh (VHP) log aaye thae, unke paas saboot tha ki wahan mandir thaa (Brother, the VHP people had come, they say they have proof that there was a temple here),' Chandra Shekhar took Shahabuddin into confidence. Shahabuddin was astonished that Chandra Shekhar seemed inclined to believe the VHP's version.

'You are the PM of India, not the chief justice,' Shahabuddin shot back. 'You give your judgment after listening to both sides. You tell the VHP, if they have proof, they should give it before the court. I give you my word of honour that I will accept the court verdict. But I will not accept you as a judge and arbitrator.'

To speak to Chandra Shekhar in this vein was not easy for Shahabuddin. For it was Chandra Shekhar who had helped build his political career. There was a time when Shahabuddin used to sit in a rickety chair at the Janata Party's office at 7, Jantar Mantar Road, and reply to the Urdu letters that would come there. Later, in 1979, Chandra Shekhar made him a Rajya Sabha MP, and there was no looking back for him after that.

Shahabuddin said to me later, 'I spoke like this to a man whose secularism I would have vouched for. But (I did so because) I suspected Chandra Shekhar's motives.... I'm saying this for the first time to anyone. He wanted to build his political future on this action. He wanted to take credit for persuading the Muslims to come around so he could say "Maine Muslims ko tayyar kiya (I got the Muslims ready)".'

Chandra Shekhar also approached other senior AIBMAC leaders, like Sultan Salahuddin Owaisi (who was with the All India Majlis-e-Ittehadul Muslimeen and an MP, and the father of Asaduddin Owaisi) and senior advocate Zafaryab Gilani. The VHP experts came to a meeting with the Muslim leaders. The Muslims got their experts, including four historians of Aligarh University, who supported their view. The Muslims argued that the mosque had to be protected to uphold the rule of law. For the VHP, it was 'a matter of faith'.

Chandra Shekhar was hopeful that the VHP would 'agree to leave (aside) their claim on Kashi and Mathura—if an agreement took place on Ayodhya'. This was one of the main concerns of the Muslim community at the time. The VHP had been demanding not just a temple in Ayodhya and at Kashi and Mathura, but also getting back 3,000 temples where they claimed mosques had been built.

'Vishnu Hari Dalmia...told me that Chandra Shekhar had pleaded with him to give up Varanasi and Mathura and they had said a categorical no,' averred Romesh Bhandari, who was then governor of UP. However, both sides agreed to abide by the court verdict, and that was a step forward.

Chandra Shekhar talked to C. Ranganath Misra who was the chief justice of India. He asked Justice Misra to determine whether a Ram temple at Ayodhya was actually destroyed to build a mosque there. 'I told him, you give your verdict in one month.'

According to Chandra Shekhar, the chief justice agreed to fast track his verdict: 'Misra said he would do it (give the verdict) in three months.'

"But,' Misra added, 'it will have to be mandatory, not recommendatory.'

Chandra Shekar agreed. 'OK. It will be mandatory.' The prime minister assured the chief justice—as well as the VHP and the AIBMAC—that the government would implement the order of the Supreme Court.

The government's interlocutors had reached out to powerful figures in the Arab world to bring around the Muslim side. They contacted the Saudis. 'The crown prince was involved, his help was taken, and through him the religious heads were spoken to.... We moved through religious and diplomatic leaders.'

The Saudis also contacted prominent religious heads in Mecca. They said that 'Jhagrhe ki jageh naek Musalmaan nahin jaata (A devout Muslim does not pray at a disputed site).' The religious heads of the Kaaba 'were (even) in a mood to give it in writing—asking the Muslims not to go into it (mosque) since it was under dispute.' 'We were briefed by the top Muslim leaders (in India) that this could be a way out, and the fight would end,' said one of the interlocutors.

The situation was moving towards a settlement. The three-member committee met the prime minister again to get his final nod. 'Go ahead,' Chandra Shekhar told them. The VHP had even decided to call the AIBMAC leaders for dinner to celebrate the breakthrough.

It was at this time that Sharad Pawar reported to Rajiv Gandhi 'in detail'—that the agreement was almost through. He did it 'in good faith', he said later.

'You are spending so much time here (in Delhi),' was all Rajiv Gandhi said to Pawar, after hearing him out. 'Who is going to look after the state?'

A few days later, a revolt erupted against Pawar in Maharashtra. It was fuelled by central leaders Vilasrao Deshmukh, Sushil Kumar Shinde, S. B. Chavan, and V. N. Gadgil. They demanded Pawar's resignation as chief minister. But Pawar managed to keep his flock together—and the rebels were finally left with the backing of only 11 out of the 210 MLAs.

But whispers grew in Delhi's power circles that Chandra Shekhar 'was gaining ground'. Rajiv Gandhi's coterie suddenly sat up. His advisors warned him that if Chandra Shekhar managed to effect a breakthrough on the Ayodhya issue, he would become a popular leader nationally. He might also find support inside the Congress, and in time, either capture the party or split the Congress. He had after all been a Congressman once, and had old connections with party leaders and Congress chief ministers. The coterie feared that Sharad Pawar may join hands with Chandra Shekhar.

Towards the end of his premiership, Narasimha Rao had reached out to Chandra Shekhar with a view to inducting him into the Congress to offset the growing influence of Sonia Gandhi in the party. But he got cold feet at the last moment.

In February 1991 Rajiv Gandhi decided to withdraw support to the Chandra Shekhar government. Rajiv's relationship with Chandra Shekhar was anyway at a low ebb by this time. The reason given was that 'two Haryana sub-inspectors' were found snooping around the Gandhi residence at 10, Janpath, a bungalow Rajiv Gandhi had shifted to after he ceased being prime minister.

Prime Minister Chandra Shekhar resigned on 5 March 1991, and with him went another chance of the Ayodhya dispute being resolved peacefully.

Later, when I asked him about it, Chandra Shekhar shrugged philosophically, 'I can't say if it (resolution of the problem) would have happened.... I think thora khoon kharaba hota, par implement ho jata (There might have been a little bloodshed, but it would have got implemented).' But I feel I was successful in throwing some cold water on a troubled situation.'

■

The episode Rao studied most carefully, according to Naresh Chandra, was how Mulayam Singh Yadav had successfully managed to prevent the kar sevaks armed with pickaxes from swarming the mosque on 30 October and 2 November in 1990. 'This...he...discussed in great detail with me,' Chandra revealed.

Chandra had told him how thousands of kar sevaks had gathered in Ayodhya on the VHP's call by 30 October 1990. Their number would have been much larger but for the precautionary measures that the government headed by Mulayam Singh Yadav had put in place. He had arrested more than 1.5 lakh kar sevaks in UP. At this time, the central government led by V. P. Singh was teetering on the brink. As seen in the last chapter, the BJP had just withdrawn support to it, after Lalu Yadav arrested L. K. Advani in Samastipur in Bihar, cutting short his Rath Yatra on 23 October 1990.

In UP, Mulayam Singh Yadav faced a tense situation. Raj Bhargava was the chief secretary and Naresh Chandra the home secretary at the centre, both were overseeing the arrangements that had been put in place to protect the mosque. The Home Ministry had given clear instructions to the state government that nobody would be allowed to enter the structure. But on 30 October, the personnel of the UP PAC guarding the structure allowed a security breach to take place. They lifted the barrier which was meant to keep the kar sevaks out. There were reports also of a sadhu having driven a PAC van through the barrier. Around forty excited youth entered the structure, according to Chandra, and started to break down the walls with pickaxes. It was filmed by the IB and the film was sent to the Home Ministry in Delhi, where officials scrutinized it in detail to figure out what the VHP intended to do.

The police opened fire to deal with the crowds, though there were no casualties. And the situation was brought under control. But the ease with which the kar sevaks had entered the Babri Masjid had encouraged them.

The Home Ministry decided to send the central forces—Border Security Force (BSF) and Central Reserve Police Force (CRPF)—to the spot. 'I was monitoring the situation hour by hour,' recalled Naresh Chandra.

The Government of India's instructions were clear. The central forces would not open fire. If absolutely necessary, the firing would be done by the UP Police.

'I gave strict instructions to the senior police officers that the UP PAC must act (if necessary), or very strong action will be taken against them.'

'We told them, "If you allow the kar sevaks to enter (the structure), the BSF–CRPF fellows will deal with you...they might attack you from behind". We had tried this in Punjab when we had put everybody under the Punjab Police.'

On 2 November 1990, the kar sevaks assembled at the Babri Masjid in even larger numbers. They surged forward to enter the structure as they had done two days earlier. The police had to open fire to control them. 'The official figure of the dead was twelve but really eighteen were killed.' Later, Mulayam Singh Yadav disclosed that twenty-eight people had died in the firing that day. Atal Bihari Vajpayee put the figure of the dead at fifty-six.

In 1990, Mulayam Singh Yadav had given a free hand to the bureaucracy to deal with the brewing crisis.

'I had 90,000 people confined in cantonments,' recalled Naresh Chandra. 'Dozens of culverts bringing these people by bus routes were blown (up) in UP. Trains were cancelled at will.'

Chandra had delegated the power of the home secretary to Raj Bhargava, who was in the hot seat, so that he could take decisions on the spot. 'The chairman Railway Board was told that if the chief secretary says that cancel this train, you cancel (it). Keep it in Bihar, MP—it can't enter UP. So all this had to be done to reduce the count there (in Ayodhya). Once the crowd collects (and becomes unruly), you will have to shoot.'

Raj Bhargava kept Mulayam Singh Yadav informed at every stage. Even though he had a tense relationship with Prime Minister V. P. Singh, Mulayam Singh cooperated with the centre and did not interfere with the security arrangements the Home Ministry had put into place. The plan suited Mulayam Singh down to the hilt. He had declared that not a parinda (bird) would be able to enter the structure on that day. His tough handling of the situation on 2 November to protect the mosque made him the darling of the minorities—and earned him the title 'Mullah Mulayam'. Such was the faith of the Muslims in him that they used to say after the demolition on 6 December 1992, 'Had Netaji (Mulayam Singh) been in charge (of UP), he would not have allowed this to happen.'

While he had scrutinized Mulayam Singh's strategy to protect the mosque, Rao was not convinced it would work in 1992. There was an essential difference between 1990 and 1992, he told Chandra. In 1990, UP CM Mulayam Singh Yadav saw himself as the protector of the Babri Masjid. In 1992, UP CM Kalyan Singh viewed himself as the builder of the Ram mandir.

'This time you will not be able to stop the kar sevaks coming into Ayodhya on the border as had happened in 1990,' Rao told Chandra. 'Besides UP, the BJP (is) also in power in the neighbouring states of Madhya Pradesh and Rajasthan.' And to deploy such a massive force 'to seal the borders between states is impossible'.

Moreover, unlike Mulayam Singh, who was not shy of opening fire to stop the kar sevaks from damaging the mosque, Rao was averse to firing on them. But then, Mulayam Singh was wooing the Muslims, Rao was cultivating a Hindu constituency. As it was to turn out, a pro-temple Kalyan Singh also gave orders against firing on the kar sevaks on 6 December 1992. Much later, in 2007, Rahul Gandhi claimed that the Babri Masjid would not have fallen if a member of the Nehru–Gandhi family had been at the helm. Chandra Shekhar had once remarked to me, 'Agar main hota, toh 2,000 log bhi mar jaate na, I would have protected the (Babri Masjid) structure (If I had been there, I would have protected the structure, even if 2,000 people died).' His cabinet secretary Naresh Chandra agreed that he was capable of taking a strong decision. But P. V. Narasimha Rao was no Chandra Shekhar.

VIII

'No journalist can be a friend, though a friend can be a journalist,' Narasimha Rao had once remarked to a colleague. Though he distrusted journalists in general, he had enlisted a team of senior editors he was comfortable with, as we saw at the beginning of the chapter—Nikhil Chakravartty, Prabhash Joshi, and R. K. Mishra—to help with the Ayodhya negotiations.

He had appointed all three members of the National Integration Council, a body of eminent political and civil society leaders set up in 1961 to resolve problems dividing the country.

Five months before the crisis spiralled out of control, on 27 July 1992,

Prime Minister Rao told parliament he wanted to 'defuse the situation', 'avoid a confrontation', 'bring about a reconciliation', and move towards an 'amicable settlement through negotiations'. He recalled the Congress Party's commitment, in its 1991 manifesto, to finding a negotiated settlement to the dispute, respecting the sentiments of both the Hindus and the Muslims.

As he spoke in parliament, Rao sounded upbeat; the VHP had ended the kar seva and given him three months' time to find a solution.

The normally sceptical Rao had become cautiously optimistic—that a way out of the imbroglio may be possible. If not, he hoped, as Chandra Shekhar before him had done, that both sides would at least agree to abide by the court verdict.

Frenetic activity ensued. From August to October 1992, Rao pressed into service several interlocutors to open channels of communication with both sides of the dispute. At the formal level, he appointed one of his junior ministers, P. R. Kumaramangalam, to talk to the leaders of the various political parties; by doing so, control would remain with him.

Like Chandra Shekhar, he also used the controversial godman Chandraswami to mobilize the sadhus and sants. Also helping with religious players was the tantric, Pandit N. K. Sharma. Again, like Chandra Shekhar, Rao brought in political interlocutors Sharad Pawar, Bhairon Singh Shekhawat, and also roped in Digvijay Singh and Kamal Nath. Besides the senior government officials, Naresh Chandra brought Kishore Kunal, an IPS officer, who was the DIG, CISF, and close to the VHP, to work with him.

The negotiations between the VHP and the AIBMAC restarted on 3 October 1992, picking up from where they had left off in February 1991, when Chandra Shekhar was prime minister. The second meeting between the groups took place on 16 October 1992; they exchanged documents and their responses to each other's papers and arguments.

Rao was criticized for deploying too many players. Sometimes they worked at cross purposes, trying to upstage each other. It only compounded the confusion that prevailed. It was curious that Rao chose not to opt for a structured dialogue. Nor did he formally authorize an individual or a group to talk with both sides. Senior Congress leader Pranab Mukherjee was to say later that Rao 'should have entrusted the task of tough negotiations to a more senior and seasoned politician familiar with politics in UP—like N. D. Tiwari.' Home Minister S. B. Chavan, Mukherjee felt, could not grasp the emotive aspects of the problem, and Kumaramangalam was too 'young' and 'inexperienced'.

While his interlocutors were holding meetings with the parties to the dispute, Rao himself was in direct touch with many of the sadhus and Muslim clergy. He used to talk to the sants in Sanskrit. He would sometimes sit on the floor of his office with them and recite the Upanishads and they would be charmed. And he would talk to Muslim leaders in Farsi. They too would be impressed. He was familiar with both Muslim and Hindu cultures. And this way, he remained the master puppeteer with all the strings firmly in his control.

'It was this mobilization (by the PM) that created a panic in the VHP'. Given the rapport he was beginning to build with the sadhus, the VHP began to suspect that Rao himself wanted to build a Ram temple in Ayodhya—and would marginalize them. Though Rao was to disclose his plans to build the temple to his trusted aide P. V. R. K. Prasad only after the demolition took place, he may have started to toy with the idea. After all, the Congress Party had in its 1991 manifesto, committed itself to building a temple in Ayodhya.

'PV's talks with Hindu sants and Muslim fakirs was to finish the BJP's hold on them,' Chaturvedi admitted. 'Once trust was created (between the communities) and the temple was built, the Hindus would have considered PV as their leader.'

It would have given him enormous clout with the voters, especially in UP, where he had no political influence.

'PV had once talked to K. K. Birla about (the latter donating) ₹2 crores for building the temple,' Bhuvnesh Chaturvedi revealed. 'He had also talked to Ali Mian (about it).' Some feared that Rao wanted to create 'some kind of a confederation of Hindu churches' which could emerge as an alternative influence to the VHP. If such a grouping had come about and delivered on the construction of a temple in Ayodhya (without destroying the mosque), it might have acquired a position of power even on issues other than the mandir.

Just as Rao seemed to be making headway, the VHP suddenly had a rethink. This was towards the end of October 1992. The Dharam Sansad decided on 30-31 October 1992, at its meeting in Delhi to resume kar seva in Ayodhya on 6 December 1992. Its announcement turned out to be another turning point in the Ayodhya story.

■

'The day the kar seva was announced, Rao sahib got a sense that "dal maen kuch kaala hai (something is very wrong somewhere)",' R. K. Khandekar, who had trained as a RSS worker in his youth, recalled. 'Till then meetings with the Hindu sants and Muslim clergy...were going on smoothly. He had been optimistic that a way out could be found....

'To announce the kar seva in the middle of the negotiations showed they (the VHP and other members of the Sangh Parivar) did not want a settlement,' Khandekar said. 'It was then that Rao sahib began to feel it may not be possible to save the Babri Masjid.'

Rao now changed his strategy. In the weeks that followed, he did everything possible to buy time, hoped for the best—and prepared for the worst. After all, an attempt to demolish the mosque had been made two years earlier in October–November 1990 when Mulayam Singh Yadav was the chief minister of UP.

Rao may well have calculated that if the mosque was brought down, it would remove an intractable problem which had fuelled the BJP's rise; and its disappearance might take the wind out of the BJP's sails—and could push the increasingly insecure Muslims back into the Congress' arms. That was not the way things turned out.

■

No sooner had the VHP made its startling announcement than Rao's detractors in the party began to get ready for battle. On 6 November 1992, Arjun Singh met M. L. Fotedar.

'Arjun Singh had come to see me at 6, Kushak Road. He was with me for two hours,' Fotedar recalled. 'I told him my information was that the Babri Masjid would be demolished. And that the PM would not act fast. I also told him that I would like him (Arjun Singh) to take the initiative and resign, if such a thing happened.'

'I am not telling you to jump alone,' Fotedar told Arjun Singh that day, 'I can also do it, but it will be more effective if you take the lead because you have a state with you.... I will do it (resign) myself. You can even take my resignation now and you can send it on afterwards.'

Though neither Arjun Singh nor Fotedar was to resign on D-Day, they began to step up pressure on Rao to impose President's Rule in Uttar Pradesh. They moved through the Cabinet Committee on Political Affairs which began to meet frequently from 20 November onwards.

■

'The time for talks is over,' police officer Kishore Kunal told Naresh Chandra soon after the VHP made its announcement.

'Ab toh yudh hone wala hai (Now it is going to be a full-fledged war),' he said. He decided to return to his job at the CISF.

A few days later, Naresh Chandra called up Kunal—and asked him to return to Delhi immediately. Kunal took the next flight to Delhi. He went straight from the airport to meet Chandra. 'This time it is not me who has called you,' Chandra told him, 'Sharad Pawarji has been looking for you.' Chandra spoke to Pawar on the phone. Pawar asked Kunal to come over at 4 p.m. that day. At their meeting, according to Kunal, Pawar said: 'Kunalji, ab toh ghoshna inhone kar di hai. Aap sadhu samaaj ko thoda sa phod dijiye, todh dijiye (Now these people have made the announcement about holding the kar seva. You break the ranks of the sadhus and create confusion amongst them)....' Pawar then elaborated, 'Jo VHP ke saath log jude hue hain, unko kuch udhar se tod karke idhar mila dijiye (You bring over some of the people who are with the VHP to this side).'

'Toh maine kaha, sir, yeh mera swabhaav nahi hai (I said this is not in my temperament),' Kunal told Pawar. 'Yeh kaam maine zindagi bhar nahi kiya hai (I have never done this all my life).'

Kunal then told Pawar the situation could still be retrieved, even though a solution looked difficult.

'How?' Pawar asked.

Kunal discussed the 'possibilities' with the Maratha leader. Pawar liked what he heard.

Immediately, Pawar dialled the PM on the RAX line. Rao asked him to come over immediately with Kunal. At 7, Race Course Road, Pawar first went in alone to see Rao. Then Kunal was called in to join them. The moment he entered the room, Rao started off by saying, 'I am not going to sack the UP government. Kalyan Singh's is a duly elected government.' Since Kunal was known to be close to the VHP, Rao obviously wanted this message to be relayed to them. 'What do you have to suggest?' Rao then asked Kunal. 'There is a solution,' Kunal said, coming straight to the point. 'You make Ayodhya, Faizabad, and Nandigram into a union territory.' (Kishore Kunal's idea was to convert Ayodhya and the surrounding areas into a territorial unit that could be directly ruled by the central government.)

He had the prime minister's attention. 'If Mulayam Singh or the Left (parties) question your decision,' Kunal went on, 'you can tell them that since we were not sure that Kalyan Singh would...protect the mosque, we took direct charge of the area in this way.... And if the BJP and the VHP question your action, you can tell them you are giving Ayodhya a Vatican type status by converting it into a union territory. That should please them.'

This proposal, he suggested, could be part of an overall plan, which would freeze all Ayodhya-related litigation for ten years, and enable temple construction, without altering the structure. It could be done immediately by an ordinance, Kunal said. Lal Narayan Sinha, who had been a top legal functionary in Indira Gandhi's government, had been working on it, he told the PM.

'It is a good suggestion,' Rao said. He 'seemed enthused' about the idea.

'Where is the ordinance?' Rao then asked him.

'Sir, I am a police officer and I don't know how to make an ordinance.'

'When will I get it?' Rao asked.

'You will get it by tomorrow morning.'

After the meeting, Kunal phoned Lal Narayan Sinha and asked him to prepare the ordinance. He got a pilot friend to fly it from Patna to Delhi—and took it across to Sharad Pawar. 'I gave both the ordinance and the formula to him.... I told him, sir, please get this circulated, it will be accepted... I had told Ahmed Bukhari (of Delhi's politically influential mosque, Jama Masjid) about it and he too liked the formula.'

However, nothing came of Kunal's plan. Senior officials in the government—and the group of journalists working on another formula—did not think it was 'feasible'. The three editors, R. K. Mishra, Prabhash Joshi, and Nikhil Chakravartty had also worked out a three-point formula. They had shown it to Rajju Bhaiya (Professor Rajendra Singh, who was the sarkaryavah or general secretary of the RSS) on 1 December at Keshav Kunj, Jhandewalan, the RSS's headquarters in Delhi. Their plan recommended kar seva on the 2.77-acre-plot around the disputed area; an expeditious judgment by the Allahabad High Court to decide the legality of the takeover of 2.77 acres by the UP government; and an assurance by the Sangh Parivar that they would protect the structure. However, nothing came of either plan.

Many formulae were doing the rounds in those days to avert the impending crisis. Ved Pratap Vaidik, the editor of *Bhasha* and a friend of Rao's had phoned the PM on 20 November 1992, and suggested he acquire rubber bullets to be used in Ayodhya, if necessary. He and defence analyst K. Subrahmanyam had been discussing ways in which the kar sevaks could be controlled on 6 December without injuring them. 'The PM started to laugh. Arre bhai, the VHP has promised that the kar seva will be done peacefully. The RSS has given me the promise. Why are you getting so worried?' Rao said.

■

During November and the first five days of December 1992, Rao tried to get the RSS–VHP–BJP to defer the kar seva which would give him more time; he devised ploys to divide and weaken his opponents, as we have just seen. And he built alibis for himself which could insulate him from blame were the unthinkable to happen.

He hoped the courts, the National Integration Council, and the UP governor would act as shields to protect him from any adverse fallout should the situation deteriorate.

Rao called a meeting of the NIC on 23 November 1992. It authorized the PM to take whatever step was necessary to protect the structure, although it was only half an authorization because the meeting was boycotted by the BJP leaders. But a day after the NIC meet, 'the PM finally gave clearance for moving central forces into UP'. The home secretary deployed 20,000 central forces in Ayodhya, the 'single largest mobilization...for such an operation since independence'. By 26 November, they had taken up position in Ayodhya, ready for their orders. Not unexpectedly, the UP chief minister protested vehemently.

■

The Allahabad High Court and the Supreme Court were seized of the matter. Rao hoped that if they delivered clear rulings, it would absolve him of any responsibility. The Supreme Court was holding hearings almost daily. There were several Public Interest Litigations before the apex court. Many of them were contempt proceedings against the Kalyan Singh government—for violating the High Court's order prohibiting any construction activity in July 1992.

The Supreme Court sought a categorical assurance from the UP government that it would protect the structure. It had been dissatisfied with Kalyan Singh's initial response; it threatened to appoint the central government as 'receiver' of the whole property if Kalyan Singh's assurance was unsatisfactory. Finally, Kalyan Singh gave the court categorical assurances on 27 and 28 November 1992 to protect the structure, and not carry out any construction during the kar seva on 6 December.

The apex court chose to believe the chief minister of UP.

•

After Rao initiated the negotiations with both sides in August 1992, the RSS and BJP leaders had urged him again and again to get the Allahabad High Court's judgment expedited. L. K. Advani told Kamal Nath, one of Rao's interlocutors, 'Whatever the judgment, it will help.' Rajendra Singh also asked Rao for a quick judgement by the High Court. Essentially, the court had to rule on the validity of the UP government's acquisition in 1991, of 2.77 acres of disputed land. If the Allahabad High Court held the acquisition to be legal, the construction of the temple could start there. If it was found to be illegal, the land would revert to the original owners—2.09 acres would go to the Ram Janmabhoomi Nyas which had bought it and the rest to the Sunni Waqf Board. The kar seva could then begin on the land owned by the Nyas. Kalyan Singh had helped the Nyas acquire a large swathe of 42 acres of land around the structure in March 1992.

Initially, Kamal Nath turned down Advani's suggestion. It was not possible, he said, to ask the court to expedite its verdict. But he came back to the BJP leader in the second week of October—and put forward another proposal. The government would hand over the 2.77 acres of land to the Ram Janmabhoomi Nyas, with the understanding that the land would not be touched till a judicial verdict was given. And the Nyas in turn would agree to abide by the court's view. As noted, the Ram Janmabhoomi Nyas was a trust formed by members of the VHP to oversee the construction of a temple in Ayodhya.

'Would this be acceptable to the BJP?' Nath asked Advani. 'I did not hesitate even for a minute to state that the proposal would be acceptable,' Advani replied.

A couple of days later, Rao invited the now retired BJP–RSS leader Nanaji

Deshmukh to meet him. During the conversation, Deshmukh referred to Kamal Nath's proposal. To Deshmukh's surprise, Rao denied any knowledge of it. 'There is no such proposal,' he said flatly. It was common knowledge that Kamal Nath would report the proceedings of his meetings with Advani to the prime minister. Later, when Advani met the PM, Rao dismissively referred to his ministers as 'har-fan-maula' (jack-of-all-trades).

Kamal Nath told me years later that Rao had gone back on what he had earlier agreed on. 'What Advani said was correct,' asserted Kamal Nath. Though Rao had initially considered the proposal, by the end of October 1992, he had changed his mind.

'The prime minister's refusal to get the court to expedite its verdict was one of the reasons for the breakdown of the talks,' Kishore Kunal was to say later. It remained one of those inexplicable mysteries of the Babri Masjid affair.

Rao was to later tell the Liberhan Commission he set up to probe the demolition, 'How could the central government make any such request even if it wanted to, when it was not a party to the proceedings before the Allahabad High Court?' Had Rao disclosed this to the representatives of the temple movement, an astonished Advani retorted, 'We would have followed a different course.'

The Allahabad High Court's stand was equally curious. It had reserved its judgment on 4 November 1992.

On that day, Ashok Singhal was travelling from Allahabad to Delhi. So was the chief justice of the Allahabad High Court. Singhal and the judge that, given the importance of the case, the court should give its verdict early. The chief justice told him he 'was sure it would come before the end of November'. This had earlier been 'privately hinted (to Singhal) by the PM'.

The BJP concluded that the 'PM's advisors—in the PMO, Ayodhya Cell or Intelligence Bureau—had advised him that a showdown was (now) inevitable and it was better to have it now rather than later, close to elections.'

The judgment came on 11 December 1992—after the mosque had been reduced to rubble.

■

Pressure had been mounting on P. V. Narasimha Rao since July 1992 to impose President's Rule in UP. The central government could then directly rule the state—and protect the masjid. Rao's detractors in the Congress had been demanding it. So had the Opposition MPs.

Home Secretary Madhav Godbole would raise the issue with the PM repeatedly. '(The PM) would hear me out,' Godbole told me ruefully, 'but he would mostly keep quiet.... At the end he would say, "Let me give it a thought". And that would be the end of the matter. It was like a wife says to her husband, "Let's see"—what she actually means is "no".' Godbole claimed his plan had the backing of his boss, Home Minister Chavan.

He had first prepared a contingency plan in July 1992, when the VHP had held its kar seva. It was revived again in November 1992. In fact, Godbole had proposed that action be swiftly taken first under Article 355 and be done 'at midnight' on 22 November 1992. Article 355 empowered the central government to protect states against external aggression and internal disturbance. It would give the security forces enough 'lead time' to take over the complex immediately—at midnight. This would then be followed up with the notification of President's Rule under Article 356 the next day, which would have taken a little longer. Godbole had chosen the dates carefully—it would enable the government to announce its action on the opening day of the winter session of parliament on 24 November 1992. He knew that the Opposition would corner the prime minister on Ayodhya.

But Rao did not think much of the plan. Sharad Pawar, who was defence minister, also met with the same response from Rao when he advocated central rule.

Given the mounting pressure on him to impose central rule in UP, Rao chose the UP governor as the third alibi he built for himself. He said he couldn't go in for central rule unless the UP governor recommended it. Godbole didn't agree. 'I mentioned to the PM that...the governor's report could be dispensed with...since the government of UP was not being carried on according to the Constitution,' Godbole said to me. He cited a precedent when prime minister Chandra Shekhar had imposed President's Rule in Tamil Nadu on 30 January, 1991—he had not relied on Governor S. S. Barnala's report.

Chandra Shekhar had told me he had imposed President's Rule after receiving intelligence reports about the ruling DMK's unwillingness to deal firmly with the LTTE's terrorist activities. When he had asked the governor for a report, Barnala had sent him an unofficial note expressing his inability to give it. Chandra Shekhar had asked Naresh Chandra to keep the letter in his safe custody. 'I still have that letter somewhere in my almirah,' Chandra confirmed to me.

But Rao insisted that he could act only if the governor made a case for central rule citing a constitutional breakdown in the state. Rao did not want to be held responsible afterwards.

The prime minister called the UP governor to Delhi on 26 November. Governor B. Satya Narayan Reddy had been appointed governor by V. P. Singh, when he was PM. Reddy was from Andhra Pradesh, Rao's home state. He was an old socialist who had joined the TDP. But it was said of him that he would do 'nothing without the go-ahead of PV'.

Governor Reddy met the prime minister and the home minister in Delhi. 'During his discussion with the home minister, he had agreed to send his report that evening for taking action under Article 356 of the Constitution,' Godbole recalled. But then, the governor suddenly did a turnaround. He told the home minister that it would 'not be advisable for me to take any action under Article 356'. For the government of UP had filed an affidavit in the ongoing hearings in the Supreme Court on 27 and 28 November 1992—and assured the court that it would protect the disputed structure. On 1 December 1992, Governor Reddy sent a secret note to the prime minister. He made a strong case—but it was not for President's Rule. It was against it. He went to the extent of stating that President's Rule would endanger the disputed structure.

Many suspected governor Reddy of arguing against President's Rule at the instance of Rao—to help the PM ward off pressure for central rule.

'Satya Narayan Reddy would not have put down an alphabet, a comma, a full stop without asking Rao,' said an insider who knew Reddy well. When the demolition was underway on 6 December 1992, Governor Reddy had been frantically trying to get in touch with Rao on the phone in the afternoon. He did not want to accept Kalyan Singh's resignation without getting the PM's nod.

Even President Shankar Dayal Sharma was full of disquiet about the role the governor had played, according to Fotedar. The president had told him this when Fotedar met him on 6 December 1992.

The governor's letter to the PM let Rao off the hook—and gave him a perfect alibi when he came under attack for his failure to take pre-emptive action to save the Babri mosque Masjid. It was cited by Rao for long afterwards as the reason why his hands were tied.

It is not that prime ministers had been above asking a governor to act against a chief minister. Only a couple of months earlier, Rao had himself asked for Andhra Governor Krishan Kant's help to replace the then Andhra Pradesh chief minister Janardhan Reddy, once his acolyte, with Vijay Bhaskar Reddy. Kant told him that the situation did not warrant President's Rule. And that Rao must act politically (and not through the governor)—if he wanted a change of guard in the state. Rao did act politically and replaced Janardhan Reddy in October 1992.

■

It was the day before the UP governor wrote to the prime minister that Rao actually came closest to considering President's Rule in the state. On 30 November 1992, he had called a meeting of the CCPA. All the members of the committee were present—besides Rao, there was Home Minister S. B. Chavan, Defence Minister Sharad Pawar, and Finance Minister Manmohan Singh. In a last ditch effort to avert a showdown with the BJP, the CCPA was meeting to decide whether to refer the Ayodhya cases to the Supreme Court under Article 138(2) of the Constitution to determine whether a temple existed under the mosque. Under Section 138(2), the Supreme Court's view would be binding on all the parties. But it required the state government to buy in to the plan.

Rao summoned Kalyan Singh to Delhi. While the CCPA was in session, a restive Kalyan Singh sat in the visitor's room at 5, Race Course Road. In a war of nerves (that politicians are so adept at), the prime minister first kept the UP chief minister waiting for a while. Then he sent Sharad Pawar to talk to him. A few minutes later, he joined them. But very soon, Rao and Pawar returned to the meeting. 'Kalyan Singh has refused to accept action under Article 138(2),' an unhappy Rao told his waiting colleagues. The UP chief minister was only prepared to accept a non-binding advisory reference under Article 143.

'President's Rule has now become inevitable,' Rao said shortly, much to the surprise of his colleagues, the pout on his face deepening. 'Let Godbole prepare...a cabinet note', he said with finality. The CCPA agreed.

Godbole rushed back to North Block. He prepared the note at top speed. He made forty-five copies of it. They were to be given to the ministers the next day at the cabinet meeting which was to take a formal decision on President's Rule in UP.

But the next day was another day. The meeting of the cabinet never took place. Rao backed off—and relied on 'procedure' to do so. Normally, the Home Ministry sent a note to the cabinet secretary on a matter it wanted the cabinet to clear. The cabinet secretary then had to obtain the formal approval of the prime minister—before it was put up before the cabinet. The prime minister's nod never came.

■

Rao did not want to impose President's Rule in UP for a variety of reasons. He would repeatedly say that President's Rule could not be imposed in apprehension of a breakdown of the 'Constitutional machinery'; the breakdown had to take place before central rule could be imposed.

Legalities apart, Rao would have shied away from it because he saw it as political hara-kiri. His law secretary P. C. Rao convinced him that it might invite strictures from the Supreme Court. Legal strictures would have given his colleagues in the Congress like N. D. Tiwari, Pranab Mukherjee, and Arjun Singh the opportunity they had been waiting for—to mount an attack on him. Others would have also condemned him for the arbitrary use of power. The BJP might have brought a no-confidence motion against him, which he feared might get carried.

Rao never forgot that he was a 'compromise' choice of his party. He was not a leader elected in his own right. In December 1992, he still headed a minority government. If he imposed President's Rule it wouldn't just stop there—he might have to use force to protect the mosque, if the responsibility to safeguard the mosque was passed on to the central government.

'When PV was visualizing what will happen...in Ayodhya, it was not in the air,' Naresh Chandra said. 'He knew that even after President's Rule he may have "to shoot a lot of people". People think that everything will be hunky dory if there is President's Rule...(If that were the case) then Kashmir would have been set right, Punjab would have been set right. According to conservative estimates, at least 50 to 100 people would have been killed in Ayodhya, if President's Rule was imposed. And this was the report and the oral submission given by the Governor of UP, no less.'

It was a risk Rao was not prepared to take. It is another matter that the failure to protect the mosque led to around 1,000 people being killed in communal riots that engulfed the country after the demolition.

Rao could have created conditions to justify the imposition of central rule—a route many leaders are not averse to taking. 'Suppose P. V. Narasimha Rao had given free reign to munshis (managers) like me,' Naresh Chandra told me, 'ki yaar dekho isko kisi tarah se President's Rule karana hai (see, my friend, we have to somehow impose President's Rule) then, you can create a situation administratively to justify it.'

Chandra was alluding to using the government's Dirty Tricks Department (DTD). The DTD was a generic term used for illegal and below-the-belt steps taken at the instance of the government—to down its opponents. The Prime Minister's Office, under different prime ministers, had often been accused of dirty tricks. Former West Bengal governor Gopalkrishna Gandhi once called the CBI the 'Department of Dirty Tricks' for the notorious hatchet jobs it undertook for the government.

Chandra then raised the unspoken question: 'How far are you willing to go for that strategic advantage to the country? Do you allow a few bad things to be done, by the state, for the larger interest of the state? I think in India we have not answered this question frankly. Because it's a slippery slope.'

According to Chandra, top bureaucrats in Rao's government were hesitant even to raise such a question with him. They were not sure how it would be received.

'(While) these unorthodox options...might have yielded results', they were not seriously considered. If Rao thought about these options, 'he didn't share it with anybody, not even with me.'

■

On 2 December 1992—three days after his infructuous meeting with Kalyan Singh—Rao phoned Mani Shankar Aiyar. It was 5 a.m. on a dark, cold morning in Delhi. In a tear-choked voice, he expressed his helplessness about the rising tensions in Ayodhya—and sought Aiyar's advice. At dawn, a concerned Aiyar rushed across to see the PM. He suggested that Rao send an all-party team of MPs to Ayodhya—it might help defuse the situation. Rao agreed with Aiyar. But he did nothing. It is possible that he had reached out to Aiyar to send a message to an agitated Sonia Gandhi, and worried secularists, that he was exercised about the issue—and doing all he could. Aiyar, with his proximity to the Gandhi family and his unabashed secular credentials, was the best means to convey that message.

The situation ratcheted up in intensity on 3 December, with BJP leaders L. K. Advani and Murli Manohar Joshi starting their yatras from Varanasi and Mathura to mobilize people for the kar seva on 6 December.

On the morning of 5 December 1992, a last ditch effort was made by Naresh Chandra and B. P. Singhal, a bureaucrat who had joined the BJP—and who, as we have seen, was VHP leader Ashok Singhal's brother. They decided that the UP government would petition the Allahabad High Court that very afternoon requesting it to deliver at least the operative part of the judgment immediately—and its plea would be supported by the central government. The UP government made its plea. But the counsel for the centre did not show up in court.

A day earlier, on 4 December, Rao had sent rival-cum-ministerial-colleague Arjun Singh, who was his sternest critic on Ayodhya, to UP to ensure that adequate arrangements had been made in the state to protect the mosque. The idea was to prevent Singh from attacking the PM afterwards—if things went wrong. Singh came back and informed the PM that the situation was 'under control'.

But in his memoir Arjun Singh wrote that he had gone to Lucknow of his own accord and had a breakfast meeting with Kalyan Singh. He did not go to Ayodhya as planned, he said, because Kalyan Singh told him it would agitate the kar sevaks gathered there.

Upon his return to Delhi, Arjun Singh rang Home Secretary Godbole. 'So, is everything safe now, home secretary saab?' he asked Godbole. 'Can I go for my function?' He said he was due to attend an event on 6 December outside Delhi. Godbole, a straightforward civil servant, 'didn't realize what...was going on.' Naresh Chandra told me that Singh was planning to leave the capital so that if things whirled out of control on 6 December, he could say he had been assured by the top officials that everything was under control. Not being on the spot would also leave him with more options in an evolving situation. The straight-shooting Godbole gave Arjun Singh the low-down on the companies, vehicles, armed battalions that he had sent to Faizabad.

Arjun Singh then rang Naresh Chandra. 'Toh bhai Naresh Chandraji, you now have everything under control. There is this function, I've made a promise to go, toh main chalaa jaata hoon.' Chandra, realizing what Arjun Singh was about, replied, 'Sir, hum log kya control karenge, humaare control mein hi nahi hai (Officers in Delhi have no powers, nor can they guarantee anything).'

Singh said, 'But Godbole was saying this....'

Chandra: 'He has sent the forces there...(the) Home Ministry has more control than retired officers sitting as advisors in the PMO. And you know, sir, advisors are not supposed to take any action. Only talk.'

Singh started to say, 'No, no, do you then think....'

Chandra cut him short, 'Dekhiye, sir, my knowledge is not as good and up to date as yours, because you were in Lucknow. And you have had talks with the (UP) CM. So I was hoping you will give us some kind of guidance.'

Arjun Singh became defensive, 'The UP CM was saying that everything is under control....' And then he rang off abruptly.

■

'On December 4, I asked Naresh Chandra,' Kishore Kunal was to recount later, 'sir, 250 companies have gone to Ayodhya, one and a half lakh kar sevaks reached there yesterday, what will happen the day after tomorrow?'

'I just asked Narasimha Raoji this very question,' Chandra replied. He had just returned from the PMO.

'The PM told me, "Maain Supreme Court ke dwaar par Hanumanji ki tarah baitha hua hoon (I am seated at the door of the Supreme Court for instructions like Hanuman did at the door of Lord Ram)".'

'Jaisa Supreme Court ka direction hoga, waisa hi karna hai (I will do what the court directs),' Rao had told Chandra.

All that the Supreme Court did was to appoint a district judge of Meerut as its representative in Ayodhya to be its eyes and ears. It asked him to inform the court of what was going on in the temple town every half hour. He was also given a wireless set to communicate with the apex court!

'The state has abdicated its authority,' an agitated Kunal remarked. He felt 'really apprehensive' about what lay ahead.

At midday on 6 December, Kunal received a call from Lieutenant General S. K. Sinha, who had been governor of Bihar. 'Babri Masjid has fallen'.

'How can that be?' Kunal was shocked. 'There is such a large force stationed there.'

'(The) BBC is saying it,' Sinha replied.

He immediately called up Ram Chandra Paramhans who headed the Ram Janmabhoomi Nyas Kunal had known him for years. Paramhans was unambiguous about their plan when he told Kishore Kunal, 'Hum log usko gira karke, leepa-pothi karke, sab baraabar kar denge zameen ko (We are going to bring it down, flatten the ground, and rearrange things).' That is exactly what happened.

IX

6 December 1992—the day the Babri Masjid fell—was a Sunday. It would be remembered afterwards as 'Black Sunday'. The events of that day changed the trajectory of Indian politics, and the last word of that story has still not been written.

Although it was the weekend, by 9.30 a.m. Ved Pratap Vaidik was in his office in the Press Trust of India building on Parliament Street in central Delhi.

Vaidik was also a friend of Narasimha Rao. 'Narasimha Rao is my closest friend,' he would claim. Although there were those who thought he was simply dropping names, not uncommon in journalistic circles, senior officials in the PM's establishment vouched for his proximity to Rao. That morning, before he left for the office, Vaidik called Rao. 'How are you?' he asked the PM.

'Haath par haath dhare baithe hain,' Rao replied non-commitally. 'Dekhein aapke mitra log kya karte hain (I am sitting here twiddling my thumbs. Let's see what your friends get up to).' There was an underlying sarcasm in the PM's words. He was referring to Vaidik's 'friends' in the RSS and the BJP—many of whom were also his friends. Vaidik was close to several prominent figures in the RSS, particularly its senior leader, Rajendra Singh. Vaidik had met many senior functionaries of the RSS with his father, an eminent member of the Arya Samaj movement in Indore, who had been courted by the RSS—and later Vaidik got to know them as a journalist.

For all their banter, Rao and Vaidik were worried men that morning, anxious about what the coming hours would bring. Vaidik had sent an ace reporter, Yogesh Mathur, to Ayodhya and told him that *Bhasha* had to be the first to break the news of what happened in Ayodhya that day. He later claimed that his organization was the first media organ to put out the story. 'PTI picked it up from us.' There were no mobile phones in those days. Vaidik knew that public telephone lines could be unreliable. He could not take a chance when a breaking story as big as Ayodhya was about to hit the headlines. He called an old friend, Shitila Singh, who ran an organization called Jan Morcha in Faizabad. 'I want a telephone facility,' he told Singh. 'My phone is yours,' Singh had replied obligingly.

∎

The day had begun for Rao at 7 a.m.—much before Vaidik's call. He had first phoned BJP leader Vinay Katiyar, a leading light of the temple movement. He wanted the latest update on the situation in Ayodhya. Rao had started to cultivate Katiyar a few months earlier. Since his relationship with L. K. Advani had become strained because the BJP leader had criticized Rao's role in the Harshad Mehta stock scam in April 1992, he needed alternative sources in the BJP to get information. 'Don't worry,' Katiyar reassured Rao. 'The kar seva will only be symbolic, as we had decided.'

It was only after calling Katiyar that the PM spoke to the IB chief, V. G. Vaidya. 'Preparations are going on for the kar seva,' Vaidya informed the PM. The prime minister then went through his usual morning drill—a workout on the treadmill, breakfast, and a physical examination by his physician, Dr Srinath Reddy, who was also from Andhra Pradesh. They conversed in English interspersed with Telugu about the huge numbers of kar sevaks gathered in Ayodhya, which was front page news in the *Times of India* that day.

Then came another call. Rao decided to take it. It was from the tantric N. K. Sharma, who was helping him deal with his critics in the party. Sharma, as seen earlier, had also acted as a 'political go-between' in Rajiv Gandhi's durbar. 'Arjun Singh is angry,' Sharma warned him. 'Your loyalists have been attacking him.' Arjun Singh, as noted, had been leading the attack on Rao for not doing enough on Ayodhya. Singh was peeved that Rao's supporters had mounted a counter-attack against him.

The phone calls over, Rao planted himself in front of his computer—he could spend hours working on it, it was his favourite pastime. It was also a stress-buster. Though an old school politician, Rao was among a handful of his tribe comfortable with the new technology. He had started using a computer in 1985, long before many of his colleagues even knew what one looked like. He had asked his younger son, Prabhakar, to get one for him—after a derisive comment by Rajiv Gandhi, then prime minister, that the 'old guard in my party will not understand' his desire to import computers.

Being a Sunday, the PM had no official engagements. Apart from his doctor, he had no other visitor that morning. R. K. Khandekar, the officer on special duty (OSD) to the prime minister, recalled how 'grim' Rao looked. 'He had only one thing on his mind that day and that was (the) Babri Masjid.'

At around 10.30 a.m., a restive prime minister called up his cabinet secretary, S. Rajgopal. 'What's happening?'

'I am leaving for office, sir, and will let you know,' Rajgopal responded. On Sundays, Rajgopal would usually visit his elderly mother. 'I was about to leave and go and see her but then decided to go to office instead.' He was as worried as his boss about what would happen that day. He had taken over as cabinet secretary only four months earlier. Rao had not really involved him on Ayodhya—except for whatever came up in meetings of the Cabinet Committee on Political Affairs.

The day-to-day responsibility for the Ayodhya issue vested in with the Ministry of Home Affairs—and with the Ayodhya Cell in the PMO, headed by Naresh Chandra. The Ayodhya Cell was expected 'to guide the home secretary', as the prime minister did not think the Home Ministry could deal with the situation as he wanted. Rao knew that the home secretary, Madhav Godbole 'was an upright officer, and the best you could get', but found him 'opinionated and obstinate'.

Vaidik's phone rang a couple of hours after he had spoken to Rao. It was Yogesh Mathur on the line. The reporter's excited voice crackled on the line. 'Pehla dome gir gaya hai (The first dome has fallen),' he told his boss. Vaidik was stunned. He put the receiver down, and dialled the PM's number. Without any preliminaries, he told the PM what he had heard. Rao had already got word. 'Yes, Vaidya phoned me on the RAX. He told me,' said Rao.

■

It was a cloudy morning in Ayodhya on 6 December. Lakhs of kar sevaks had started to gather near the Babri Masjid.

The kar sevaks had washed the Ram Chabutra that morning. Around 500 sadhus sat on it to offer a symbolic puja. Senior BJP leaders, L. K. Advani and Murli Manohar Joshi arrived around 10.30 a.m. They were accompanied by Vinay Katiyar, the founder-president of Bajrang Dal, the youth wing of the VHP, and Ashok Singhal, president of the VHP. Both were instrumental in bringing the temple issue centre stage. Seeing them, the crowd became excited. Katiyar and Singhal moved towards the dais where they were to address the gathering.

Just before noon, about 150 people suddenly broke through the security cordon. They started pelting stones at the policemen standing there. In a few minutes, around a thousand men had climbed over the barricades that had been erected around the mosque and stormed the building. The police forces guarding the structure put up feeble resistance—but were swept away. By 12.20 p.m., around eighty members of the mob had managed to climb atop the domes, and hoisted saffron flags there. 'Then began a frenzied demolition with shovels, iron rods and pickaxes.' Within minutes, the crowd within the barricades had swelled to 25,000. 'As the kar sevaks chipped away at the structure, some of the BJP–VHP–RSS leaders present there pleaded with them to stop,' Narasimha Rao would write in his book about the incident. But no one heeded their pleas. The Babri Masjid was demolished in just over four hours. By 4.55 p.m., it was all over.

There was disbelief all around. Many had thought that as long as the top leaders of the BJP, Atal Bihari Vajpayee and L. K. Advani, were around, they would somehow find a way of preventing the mosque from being harmed. That belief turned out to be nothing but naiveté.

■

Praveen Jain, a photographer, had arrived in Ayodhya two days earlier to cover the kar seva. He was working with *The Pioneer* and had been assigned this task by his editor, Vinod Mehta. On 4 December 1992, Jain had bumped into B. L. Sharma aka Prem, a BJP MP, at a press conference. The briefing was held by the VHP for mediapersons present in Ayodhya. Ashok Singhal was present at the press briefing. The journalists were given ID cards to cover the event on 6 December 1992.

Jain had known Prem for years. 'I had known him since the days he used to come to the *Indian Express* in Delhi with press releases. Since then, he was a friend. Later, he became an MP...I had asked him what would happen on 6 December,' Jain said.

By way of a reply, Prem offered to accompany Jain to the site. 'He gave me a (ID) card of the VHP...and a yellow kar sevak scarf. This enabled me to enter (the area) as a VHP photographer... "If anyone asks (anything), (you) say you are from the VHP."'

On 5 December, Jain made his way to the site. No other mediaperson was there. 'I took the pictures without any problem. There were some naqab posh (masked) people there with their faces covered. They were training people on how to demolish the mosque. They had rods and hammers,' Jain said. 'Everything was pre-planned. I am saying this because the same method was used the next day to break the mosque. They even had ropes. There was a small tila, a raised piece of land, there. People...were climbing this hill, using the ropes...(they) were totally professional people, in terms of knowing how they will break it,' Jain recalled. That evening, he sent these photos to his editor in Delhi. But the office decided 'to wait' and 'be sure'. 'At the time, no one really believed that the Babri Masjid could be destroyed the next day.'

■

On the night of 5 December, there was a secret meeting held in Ayodhya. Senior RSS and VHP leaders were present there; they went over the plan for the next day. It was decided that while the sants and sadhus would do the kar seva on the chabutra as planned, there would be an attack on the structure from the south and the east side. The VHP's secret plan was being fine-tuned till the early hours of the morning. The kar sevaks were given orders to 'seal' Ayodhya. That is why numerous obstructions like iron rods and barricades were found on the Faizabad–Ayodhya Road. The task of demolishing the structure had been assigned to five groups. One of these groups was told to keep the media quiet, by force, if necessary. On the day of the demolition, Jain and other mediapersons were on the rooftop of a three-storey building not far from the mosque so as to get a good view of the whole area. They saw the frenzied kar sevaks enter the Babri Masjid and start to destroy it with pickaxes. Soon after the destruction began, a group of people came into the building where the journalists had positioned themselves. They started to beat them up, identifying them by the ID cards hanging around their necks. They attacked photographers, broke their cameras, and targeted foreign journalists in particular. Many ran for their lives, others were badly injured.

'I first ran towards the platform from where the BJP leaders had addressed the crowds,' Jain recalled. 'I beseeched Advani, who knew mediapersons from Delhi personally, to help.' But 'they looked the other way'. Then Jain 'ran all the way' to his hotel, Shan-e-Awadh. On the way, 'I watched with horror Muslim homes being set on fire.' Riots had broken out by then. Years later, Praveen Jain would relive the trauma of that Black Sunday when he had to give evidence in one of the Babri Masjid demolition cases—and deposed before the Lucknow bench of the Allahabad High Court.

■

On the morning of the tragedy, Delhi was basking in bright winter sunshine. Senior BJP leaders had congregated around 10 a.m. at the party office at 11, Ashoka Road. They sat together on the lawn outside the sprawling bungalow. In those days, Delhi did not have the polluting cover of smog it would acquire in later years. 'The sun was as sweetly warm as the nip in the air was refreshing,' K. R. Malkani remembered afterwards. He was vice president of the BJP and the editor of the RSS mouthpiece, *Organiser*.

Like many around the country, they awaited news from Ayodhya. Senior BJP vice president Sundar Singh Bhandari had just returned from Ayodhya. He was holding forth on what he had seen—two lakh enthusiastic people gathered in the temple town to offer kar seva. Another lakh were expected to join them that morning. The Kendriya Marg Darshak Mandal, the highest decision-making body of the VHP, had declared that the kar seva would be 'tokenistic'. The kar sevaks would only carry earth to a previously excavated hole just south of the Ram Janmasthan (the spot where Lord Ram was believed to have been born) and fill it up. Then, they would fetch water from the nearby river, Sarayu, and wash the platform they had built in July during an earlier kar seva.

Malkani was already working on the draft of a press note he was to release to the media in the evening. Suddenly, Malkani saw BJP Rajya Sabha MP Ashwini Kumar come hurrying out of the office. He whispered in Malkani's ear, 'We won't need the press note now.'

Malkani rushed inside. He was told Sunderlal Patwa had called from Ayodhya—that the mosque was being destroyed. Patwa was chief minister of Madhya Pradesh and had gone to Ayodhya for the kar seva.

Later that evening, Malkani was to describe the day's events as 'unfortunate'. They had wanted the disputed structure to go, 'but...we wanted it gone through a due process of law'. The party took 'moral responsibility' for what had happened.

X

It was a few minutes before noon when the phone rang at 5, Race Course Road. The prime minister was at his desk—and picked up the receiver on the secure RAX line. It was IB chief, V. G. Vaidya. Frenzied kar sevaks had broken into the Babri Masjid and clambered atop the domes and had set about breaking it. The UP police had not been able to stop them. Vaidya conveyed this information to Rao in Marathi. He was a Maharashtrian, and since Rao was proficient in Marathi, they used to converse mainly in that language.

Rao was sitting with a friend who had just arrived when the phone rang. 5, RCR, with its wood panelling and paintings, was the most beautifully decorated of all the four houses—3, 5, 7, 9 Race Course Road—allocated for the prime minister of India. While Rajiv Gandhi had used number 5 as a guest house for his special guests, Rao used it for holding secret political meetings of which no record was kept.

'For about ten minutes, the prime minister sat in his chair motionless, as if in a state of shock', recalled the friend who was with him. He did not utter a word. 'I had never seen him look so dazed. He knew his political future was now at stake.'

In those moments, Rao would have gone over the contours of the strategy he would have to put into place to contain the damage that had been done. There was the possibility of a communal flare-up in Ayodhya. The law and order situation could spin out of control. Large groups of rioters—and kar sevaks present in Ayodhya—were running around, celebrating the ongoing destruction of the mosque. With the kar sevaks uncontrolled, there was every likelihood of the Babri Masjid being totally destroyed. Rao must have considered whether he could—or should—stop the demolition, even at that late stage. Then there was the problem of when to sack the UP government, which he would have to do. And the question of how soon to call a meeting of his cabinet. He knew there would be demands for his resignation.

After the first 'ten minutes or so', the prime minister started to work the phones and was at it 'for the next two hours'. But he did not take the calls of his political colleagues, who were frantically trying to reach him. He spoke only to Home Minister S. B. Chavan. Others like Arjun Singh, P. R. Kumaramangalam, M. L. Fotedar, even Madhu Limaye said later what Rao's aides had told them—that they had instructions that the

PM 'was not to be disturbed'. The inability to reach Rao at the peak of the crisis led to the rumour that the prime minister was either sleeping or doing puja while the Babri Masjid was being razed to the ground.

Politicians from every major party were calling one another frantically. They wanted to find out exactly what was going on. Everyone was at sea. Even those who were expected to have some news, given their proximity to the prime minister, were clueless.

'Apne buddhe premi se baat hui kya (Have you managed to talk to our old lover boy—a sarcastic reference to Rao)?' Jitendra Prasad, the PM's political secretary, asked Vaidik, on the phone.

'Kya chal raha hai (What's going on)?' an anxious Atal Bihari Vajpayee asked Vaidik. But Vaidik had little to tell them—except for his morning call to Rao.

Finally, the PM decided to take the call of his strident critic, Fotedar. 'I spoke to Narasimha Rao at 1.40 p.m,' Fotedar said. Since his early days with Indira Gandhi as her political aide, Fotedar had the habit of noting down the precise time of his meetings and conversations with political leaders.

'I told Rao to do two things. To come on television and radio and console a grieving nation. And to order 100 to 200 helicopters to take a round of the area and if necessary to start teargassing from the air so that the crowds dispersed.... If we can save at least one pillar of the structure, we can tell the nation that the government had tried to save it.... Otherwise,' Fotedar warned a silent Rao, 'the Congress will be finished.'

Rao took neither suggestion. But by 1.40 p.m., when he decided to take Fotedar's phone call, he had made up his mind on what he had to do. For, half an hour later, he called Fotedar back and asked, 'Should we hold a cabinet meeting?' Fotedar replied, 'You should take action first and then hold the cabinet meeting.' Without realizing it at the time, Fotedar was making a case for delaying the cabinet meeting—which is what Rao wanted.

•

Just as the prime minister was personally tracking the Ayodhya developments that morning, so were his top officials. The conscientious home secretary, Madhav Godbole, and his wife, Sujata, were due to go to a wedding reception. So Godbole had planned to go to the office around noon. But, like his other colleagues, he too felt uneasy and headed instead towards North Block. He arrived there at 9 a.m.

'I was assuming everything would be peaceful, but I did not want to take a chance,' Godbole said. 'We were monitoring the situation from my office in North Block.' On reaching the office, Godbole called IB chief Vaidya for the latest feedback. Then he spoke to R. K. Wadhera, the director general (DG) of the Indo-Tibetan Border Police (ITBP), a paramilitary force that was established in 1962. Wadhera was stationed in Faizabad, just 7 kilometres from Ayodhya, with his battalions in readiness. As noted earlier, the central government had dispatched around '20,000' men from the Central Paramilitary Forces (CPMF) to Ayodhya. They were stationed at nearby Faizabad, ready to assist the state government in the event of a crisis.

They included men from the CRPF, CISF, ITBP, Rapid Action Force (RAF), and even some from the elite National Security Guard (NSG). They were equipped with an array of 'soft' weapons like 'stun grenades', 'rubber pellets,' and 'rubber bullets'.

'Please do not wait for my go-ahead,' Godbole instructed Wadhera—if a request for help came from the state government. In normal circumstances, Wadhera would need to be authorized to act by Godbole. 'Don't waste any time,' he said repeatedly to Wadhera. Till 11 a.m. 'everything seemed to be okay'.

Just before noon, there was the shrill ring of the phone in Godbole's office. It was the IB chief again. 'A group of kar sevaks have entered the masjid and got on top of the dome,' Vaidya told Godbole.

The IB chief said he had already informed the prime minister. 'I don't know if I was the first person to tell the PM,' Vaidya would say later. 'Of course, it is the duty of the DIB to inform the PM immediately, which I did... But an octopus does not have do paet, it also has dus pair (does not just have two stomachs it also has ten feet).' He used the colloquial expression to indicate that Rao had many independent channels of information. 'The PM had so many political sources, and he would have known immediately if there was an attack on the Babri Masjid.'

Vaidya had also informed the home minister, S. B. Chavan, who in turn spoke to the PM. Godbole, too, got on the phone and informed the home minister immediately. Then he called the cabinet secretary, Rajgopal, and Naresh Chandra.

'Oh my God,' exclaimed Rajgopal. 'This can't be happening. Yeh tho nahin ho sakta (This is not possible),' Chandra was incredulous. Godbole himself was shocked. 'I hadn't thought that they would go to the extent of going to the top of the mosque.'

In the tense weeks before the demolition, the top officials of the prime minister's team had been divided on taking pre-emptive steps to save the structure. For weeks, Godbole had argued that Kalyan Singh, the BJP chief minister of UP, should be sacked and central rule imposed in the state. However, both Chandra and Rajgopal had opposed the idea of using Article 356 to impose President's Rule in UP. Chandra knew L. K. Advani and Murli Manohar Joshi well—and believed their assurances that the mosque would not be touched. He also believed that the RSS and the VHP would not destroy the structure because it had been used as a temple since 1949 with an idol of Lord Ram worshipped there. Amar Nath Verma, the prime minister's principal secretary, was non-committal; he took his cue from his boss. Those opposed to central action argued that Kalyan Singh had after all given a solemn promise to the Supreme Court only ten days earlier that his administration would protect the mosque.

Then Godbole got on the phone to Lucknow. The chief secretary was not available. He finally got hold of the director general of police (DGP)—and told him to rush 'the central forces immediately' from Faizabad to Ayodhya. 'We will have to get the CM's permission,' countered the DGP, making the position clear. 'We can only call the central forces if he agrees.'

By around 1 p.m., the five top officers of the Indian government were in North Block, where a control room had been set up. Besides Godbole, S. Rajgopal, V. G. Vaidya, and Naresh Chandra, the law secretary, P. C. Rao, had also arrived. They were worried men—and knew the initiative had moved out of their hands. 'We felt our options had closed. Now it was left to the state government to decide whether to call the central forces or not.' However, even if the central forces were called out, they would be at the disposal of the state government.

∎

'Aap Shankar Raoji (S. B. Chavan) se baat kar lo (You talk to S. B. Chavan),' Rao told Vaidik when he had called the PM to tell him about the demolition. This was an unusual request. For the PM knew that the officials would by then have informed the home minister of the latest developments. Besides, Chavan had himself spoken to Rao.

It must have struck the politically savvy Rao that somebody would have to take responsibility for the demolition. As the minutes ticked by, this had begun to dawn on many in the corridors of power. Chavan's name had begun to be mentioned as a possible fall guy. In the hours that followed, Rao had also asked Ghulam Nabi Azad, then parliamentary affairs minister, to talk to Chavan. As Chavan sensed the mounting heat, the home minister made himself incommunicado. He took off for the ashram of the controversial godman and political fixer Chandraswami to seek his counsel.

'Chavan was really a dummy home minister,' Rao's aide, R. K. Khandekar, would say. Despite their proximity, Rao 'did not really rely' on S. B. Chavan. Rao had decided to induct his 'old and trusted friend' Chavan into the ministry because it would make it easier for the PM to be his own home minister. Rao had sidelined Chavan during the Ayodhya negotiations. He would only be present at formal meetings, not in the parleys Rao had with the Hindu sants and Muslim clergy.

As instructed by the PM, Vaidik called up the home minister. His wife picked up the phone. 'Abhi toh woh so rahein hain (He is sleeping at the moment),' she told a surprised Vaidik.

'Is everything all right?' he asked.

'He took a long walk this morning, and went off to sleep after breakfast,' she explained. Vaidik left a message with her. 'Please tell him bahut bada sankat paida ho gaya hai. Masjid ka dome gir gaya hai (Please tell him there is a big problem, a dome of the mosque has been brought down).' That Chavan was 'sleeping' was obviously a way to dodge those the home minister wanted to avoid. For he had been in touch with key officials and the prime minister.

Chavan also spoke to Kalyan Singh at 12.25 p.m., urging him to use the central forces stationed at Faizabad to remove the intruders from the disputed structure. He also called up Governor Reddy, seeking his intervention to save the structure.

■

All through the tense hours of the afternoon, Governor Reddy tried frantically to reach the prime minister. He wanted to know what to do in the situation that was evolving by the minute. With the PM not taking his calls, Reddy reached out to Vaidik instead. Vaidik knew him well. Both had gone to jail in 1965 for taking part in a Bharat bandh called by socialist leader Ram Manohar Lohia. Though Vaidik was based in Indore, and Reddy in Hyderabad, they had kept in touch over the years.

'Doctor saab, Kalyan Singh meri jaan kha raha hai (Kalyan Singh is after my life),' a distraught Reddy told Vaidik that afternoon. 'Governor House ke nahi (He is outside Governor's House, I have not responded. Shall I agree to see him? What shall I do)?'

'What can I say?' Vaidik replied. 'Rao saab se poochhiye (You ask Rao).'

'Rao saab ko chaar baar phone kar chuka hoon,' Reddy replied. 'Mera phone hi nahi le rahein. Aap unse baat keejiye. Main kya karoon (I have called Rao saab four times. He is not taking my calls. You talk to him. Ask him what I should be doing)?'

When Vaidik spoke to the prime minister in the afternoon, to relay the governor's message to him, Rao ignored the governor's query. Instead, he vented his spleen on the VHP–BJP. 'Unhone aashvaasan diya thaa.... Ab itna galat kaam kar diya (They had assured me...What they have done now is very wrong).'

Trying to be helpful, Vaidik suggested, 'You tell Jaffer Sharief (the then railway minister) to send ten to twenty trains and empty out Faizabad.' But Rao continued to speak about the betrayal. 'Mere saath bahut bada dhokha hua hai (They have betrayed me).'

'Rao saab, Raja ko kabhi nahin kehna chahiye ke mere saath dhokha hua hai,' Vaidik found himself telling the PM, as if from a 'guru to a chela'. (Mr Rao, it doesn't speak well of a ruler to admit that he has been cheated.) Vaidik said he was paraphrasing Kautilya to the prime minister. Narasimha Rao became silent.

■

At around 3 p.m., the prime minister met Home Secretary Godbole. After that Rao separately met Naresh Chandra.

Godbole told the PM that Kalyan Singh had finally asked the central forces to move towards Ayodhya. But he had given a clear order that they were not to open fire on the kar sevaks—even though crowds were obstructing the movement of the forces, preventing them from reaching the mosque. Halfway there, given their lack of progress, the magistrate accompanying them told them to return to Faizabad.

'I had asked Kalyan Singh to give me a written order for the district magistrate to shoot, if necessary,' the UP CM's principal home secretary at the time, Prabhat Kumar, was to say later. 'Instead, Kalyan Singh put it down in writing that the police will not open fire on the kar sevaks.'

Rao listened intently to Godbole, the frown deepening on his face. He did not say much. Godbole got the sense that the PM was listening, but that 'he knew all about' what he was being told.

While Godbole was with the PM, a call came from the governor. This time the PM took the call. Reddy told him that Kalyan Singh had resigned.

Rao put down the receiver and turned to Godbole, 'What is to be done now?'

'Kalyan Singh should not be allowed to go honourably,' the home secretary said. 'We should first impose President's Rule before accepting his resignation.' The PM picked up the phone and asked to be connected to the governor again. When Reddy came on the line, Rao told him not to accept Kalyan Singh's resignation. He should keep it pending and wait for word from Delhi. The cabinet would meet at 6 p.m. and take a view on the dismissal of the government.

The prime minister may have wanted to mollify the home secretary, having rejected his earlier advice to put the state under central rule. He knew that hard questions would now be asked about why he had not imposed President's Rule in Uttar Pradesh, when he still had the time to do so.

■

Cabinet Secretary Rajgopal's office got a call from the PMO 'in the afternoon' to call a meeting of the cabinet. The phone call was intended for Rajgopal's colleague 'who normally organized the cabinet meetings and had the phone numbers of the ministers', Rajgopal said. But the 'colleague was not at his residence. Being Sunday, he could not be traced.' The PMO instructed the cabinet secretariat to fix the cabinet meeting, but to do so only after 'ensuring' that some of the senior ministers, especially Arjun

Singh, who had travelled out of Delhi that day, were present. Fotedar got word about the cabinet meeting only around 5 p.m.

'We waited till 6 o'clock, because Arjun Singh was not in Delhi,' Naresh Chandra was to explain later. 'It took us time to get him back here.... Narasimha Rao did not want to start (the meeting) in his absence. As soon as he came, the (cabinet) meeting started. That (was) the reason for the delay....'

The delay in calling the cabinet meant that Rao had ruled out any immediate intervention to stop the ongoing demolition. By the time the cabinet met, six hours after the demolition had started, the structure had been pulled down.

■

Naresh Chandra arrived at 7, Race Course Road, 'around 4.30 pm', well before the cabinet meeting had started. Unlike the 'stoic' demeanour the PM had presented to Godbole, Chandra found the prime minister 'really agitated'. Rao was much more informal with Chandra than he was with his home secretary. PV did not waste any time on preliminaries.

'How did this happen?' he asked Chandra.

'We have to get all the facts from the IB,' Chandra started to say.

'But I got a mouthful from him. Uspe woh humaare upar hi bigad gaye.' (He began to get angry with me.)

Trying to calm the PM down, Chandra tried again, 'We'll hold the IB's feet to the fire and make them....'

Before Chandra could finish his sentence, Rao cut him short, with a sharpness that was uncharacteristic of him: 'IB!! Don't talk of IB.'

'He was very angry, I got a bit of a shock.'

Only minutes earlier, Rao had been placatory towards the home secretary, who had all along been warning of this eventuality. But with Chandra, he ripped into the IB and laid the blame at its door. Intelligence failure was the line he stuck to in the weeks and months that followed. And, he blamed Kalyan Singh for his failure to honour the assurances he had given. In those hours, he had identified the two fall guys he would go for.

'What was happening in Ayodhya was open knowledge...for the whole world to see,' Vaidya said later in defence of the Intelligence Bureau. As a senior bureaucrat this was as open as he could get to admitting that he had briefed the PM about the build-up that was taking place in Ayodhya. As seen earlier, it was a daily convention for the IB and R&AW chiefs to brief the PM with the sensitive information that could only be conveyed to the PM orally. Vaidya added, 'Everyone (and he was including the PM in this) knew the situation could spin out of control.'

When they came to meet the prime minister, Naresh Chandra and

Madhav Godbole had already prepared the papers that would be needed to impose President's Rule in UP. 'We were ready,' Chandra said. 'The moment the cabinet okayed President's Rule, we would rush the papers to the president for him to sign.'

Forty-five sets of papers had been prepared for the process of sacking Kalyan Singh, dissolving the UP assembly, and promulgating President's Rule in Uttar Pradesh.

■

'I was having tea and pakoras with a couple of senior ministers, when I got the news that kar sevaks had breached the Babri Masjid,' said the man at the centre of the storm, UP chief minister Kalyan Singh. They were sitting on the terrace of his official residence on Kalidas Marg in Lucknow, also soaking in the winter sun.

'I received a phone call from the Ayodhya police control room,' Kalyan Singh told me. 'They said one part of the dhancha (structure) was being demolished.' He continued: 'This was around 12-12.15 p.m. It was only at around 4.30 p.m. that I got to know that the entire structure had been brought down.'

'I immediately ordered the state police to stop them,' Kalyan Singh said. He gave orders that the police should do everything possible to evacuate the mosque. But he also gave clear instructions that 'the police must not fire at the crowds'. A police firing, and the stampede that would follow, would have killed many. Kalyan Singh estimated that there were 300,000 gathered in Ayodhya that day. 'By asking the police not to fire, I saved the lives of thousands of Ram bhakts, though I was not able to save the dhancha,' he said.

As the afternoon wore on, the effort to manage the situation turned into a battle of wits between the PM and the UP chief minister. Both knew that Kalyan Singh's exit was unavoidable. The question was how it would be done—and who would be able to score a political point. Like Narasimha Rao, Kalyan Singh, too, said he felt 'let down'. The chief minister was angry that he was caught off guard and the VHP had kept him in the dark. They should have warned him if they intended to demolish the structure, an aggrieved CM told his close associates. Though he was the CM, it was the VHP—and Vinay Katiyar—whose word held greater sway with the local administration in Faizabad and Ayodhya.

Kalyan Singh had taken over as UP chief minister in June 1991. It was around the same time that Rao had become prime minister. A protégé of L. K. Advani, Singh had begun to hype the temple issue as soon as he came to power—to become acceptable to the BJP's core constituency for which it was an article of faith. As a backward class leader—he belonged to the Lodh community. He was one of the few politicians'who benefitted from both the Mandal phenomenon and the Mandir movement in the 1990s.

On the evening of 5 December, the day before the demolition, Kalyan Singh had begun to feel uneasy. He had got word that an aggressive group amongst the kar sevaks wanted the kar seva to be more than symbolic. He asked L. K. Advani and Murli Manohar Joshi to leave for Ayodhya immediately. They were to arrive in the temple town on the morning of 6 December—but decided to get there on the night of 5 December.

On 6 December, like Rao, Kalyan Singh also started his day by phoning Vinay Katiyar. Advani and Joshi were at Katiyar's house in Ayodhya, having breakfast. VHP leader Ashok Singhal was also with them. The chief minister appealed to Advani: 'Please ensure that everything goes smoothly with the kar seva today.'

However, that is not the way things panned out. As soon as the intruders climbed on to the domes, Kalyan Singh knew it was the end of the road for him as chief minister. He knew that if he did not resign, he would be sacked. He had, after all, given an undertaking to the Supreme Court— and he had repeatedly assured Rao—that he would protect the mosque. It would be better to submit his resignation to the governor, he decided, before the centre could dismiss him.

Kalyan Singh asked to see the governor immediately. Before resigning as chief minister, 'I called up Atal Bihari Vajpayee at 5 p.m. and informed him about my intention to resign.' Kalyan Singh said. 'He gave me his consent.' 'I submitted my resignation to the governor around 5.15 p.m. But my government was overthrown by the centre at around 9 to 9.15 p.m. This was the first time in history that a government was overthrown which did not exist in the first place,' he remarked wryly.

■

In New Delhi, the prime minister prepared for the cabinet meeting. Rao was now in damage control mode. His major challenge would be to contain Arjun Singh. Minutes before 6 p.m., the ministers began to troop in to the PM House on 7, Race Course Road.

The atmosphere in the meeting room was 'despondent'. Ministers conversed in hushed undertones. M. L. Fotedar arrived fifteen minutes late. When he entered the room, his colleagues were all seated. So was the prime minister. 'What is this cabinet (meeting) for?' Fotedar asked, his tone clearly sarcastic.

Madhavrao Scindia, minister for Civil Aviation, and V. C. Shukla, minister for Parliamentary Affairs, looked up, surprised, 'Don't you know?'

'No,' replied Fotedar, with a straight face.

'The Babri Masjid has been demolished,' they said.

Fotedar: 'Is that so?'

'We have come here to dismiss the (UP) government and dissolve the assembly,' someone interjected.

Fotedar: 'Which assembly are you going to dissolve? He (Kalyan Singh) has (already) resigned.'

According to Fotedar, everyone looked surprised.

'The PM asked the cabinet secretary to find out. He came back in five minutes and said, "Yes, sir, Doordarshan is saying it".'

Fotedar had come to Race Course Road directly from Rashtrapati Bhavan. He had met the president, Shankar Dayal Sharma, at 5.30 p.m. When Fotedar was with the president (between 5.30 p.m. and 6 p.m.), Sharma had received a message that the chief minister of UP had resigned. Fotedar had found the president extremely agitated. 'Shankar Dayal Sharma was genuinely in tears,' Fotedar said.

Earlier in the day, when Shahid Siddiqui and a group of Muslim leaders went to meet the president at 3 p.m., 'he showed us a letter he had written to the prime minister. That letter is not yet released. It was a very strong letter (in which) he held the prime minister responsible for the demolition. It was written after the first dome fell and it urged the PM to take action quickly.' From the way Fotedar spoke, the president had obviously also told him about his missive to the PM. 'I told the president to go on the air (and address the nation),' Fotedar said. 'But the PM's office did not permit it. Only his (the president's) statement was telecast.'

At the cabinet meeting, Fotedar turned to Rao, 'Mr Prime Minister, this CM has resigned and thrown this illegitimate child (the government) in the Hazrat Mahal park. You have to accept this constitutional responsibility and own this illegitimate child.' He told the PM that he 'must accept moral responsibility for it'. Others remember Fotedar shouting at the PM. At one point, Fotedar 'started to cry'. An upset C. K. Jaffer Sharief warned that the country would have to pay a heavy price for what had happened. Most ministers didn't say anything. The atmosphere in the room was heavy.

■

An hour into the meeting, Rao stepped out to meet a delegation that had arrived to see him. It comprised agitated Muslim leaders who had been trying to get through to him all day. The group was led by Syed Shahabuddin, Shahid Siddiqui, Maulana Parikh (an associate of Ali Mian of Deoband), Sulaiman Sait, and many others. They had met in the home of Sulaiman Sait that afternoon after news of the demolition broke. During the day they had tried to contact Rao and Chavan but were told they 'were resting'. Finally, at 5 p.m., they received word from the Prime Minister's Office asking them to come to Race Course Road at 7 p.m.

'Bahut bura ho gaya, bahut bura ho gaya (It's terrible what's happened, it's terrible what's happened),' Rao lamented, as he entered the room.

'Rao sahib, gumbad gir gaya (Rao sahib, the domes have fallen),' they said to him, several of them speaking at the same time.

'Usse bhi zyada,' Rao said. 'Sab kuch gir gaya, sab kuch gir gaya. Leken mein banaoonga doobara. Sab kuch banaoonga (Not just the domes, everything has collapsed. But I will construct it again).'

At this point, Shahabuddin broke down. 'He was an emotional man,' Siddiqui said to me. For years, Shahabuddin had advocated the Muslim point of view on Ayodhya. 'Aap banwa deejeye (Please get it reconstructed),' he beseeched Rao.

At this point, Siddiqui suddenly lost his cool. 'Shahabuddin sahib, yeh aadmi!' he said angrily, 'hum inse kehte rahe din raat aur inhone bachaya nahi. Ye jab bacha nahi sakae, to yeh kya banwayaengae. Inki himmat nahi. Isko bachane ke liye humne saari power di thee inhe (This man, we kept beseeching him to save the mosque but he did not do so. If he could not save it, what reconstruction will he do now? He does not have the courage. We had authorized him with all the power at our disposal to do what was necessary (to save the mosque).' Siddiqui was referring to the meeting of the NIC on 23 November 1992 which had authorized the prime minister to do whatever was necessary to save the structure. Siddiqui was agitated all the more because he had met the prime minister the night before the demolition. And Rao had assured him once again that the masjid would not be harmed.

Suddenly, Siddiqui recalled what Rao had said to him before the 1991 elections. He had gone to see him at the instance of Rajiv Gandhi, armed with suggestions for the welfare of Muslims to be included in the Congress manifesto. Rao was in charge of the manifesto drafting committee and Siddiqui told him about his ideas.

'Haan. Musalman ka vote chahiye. Hindu ka toh vote hee nahi chahiye,' Rao had remarked sarcastically. 'Hindu ki toh koi aukaat hi nahi hai iss desh mein, aapki party mein (Yes, you need the votes of Muslim, you don't need the votes of Hindus, what importance do Hindus have in this country anyway, and in your party).'

Siddiqui was taken aback: 'Sir, aapki party hai. Meri toh koi aukaat nahi hai. Mujhe toh kaha thaa ki minority ke baare mein kuch deejiye, toh main yeh de raha hoon (Sir, this is your party, I have no position in it. I was told to give something on the minorities, so I am giving it).'

But Siddiqui quickly regained his composure that 6 December evening. 'Rao sahib, please do one thing,' he told the PM, speaking more calmly. '(Today) there is neither a masjid nor a mandir there. Please don't change that status quo. It should not be turned...into a temple. Then we can solve the problem forever. Divide the land. Let the mandir be constructed on one side and the masjid on the other.'

'No, no, I am going to rebuild the mosque,' Rao told the delegation. 'The cabinet meeting is going on, and I am going to take the decision.' The prime minister announced his decision to rebuild the mosque the very next day, 7 December, during a speech he made in parliament. 'The demolition of the mosque was a most barbarous act,' Rao declared 'the government will see to it that it is rebuilt.'

∎

After the delegation of Muslim leaders had left, the PM went back to the cabinet meeting. Nobody really asked Rao to resign. Fotedar was the sharpest in his criticism of Rao—that the government had failed to protect the mosque for all the forces the centre had stationed near Ayodhya. Fotedar had repeatedly pleaded with the prime minister in several cabinet meetings, as he put it—on 18 November, 22 November, and again on 4 December—to dismiss the BJP government in UP and suspend the assembly. If the mosque remained unharmed on 6 December, he argued, they could always 'restore the assembly' afterwards. Even in July 1992, when a kar seva had been held at the mosque, he had advised the prime minister not to permit it. Each time the PM would make the same promise—that he would 'save the mosque at any cost'.

At the cabinet meeting on 6 December, Arjun Singh did not demand Rao's resignation. He only took the Home Ministry to task for not being adequately prepared. Had Arjun Singh resigned that day, Rao's exit would have become unavoidable. Agitated Congressmen would have gravitated towards Arjun Singh, and stood behind him. Singh could well have replaced Rao as prime minister.

Despite his disappointment with the prime minister, Fotedar, too did not resign. Even one resignation at the cabinet meeting that evening would have exacerbated the crisis facing a beleaguered Rao. Arjun Singh was to explain later why he did not resign, 'I did not think it proper to enter into an open confrontation with him (PM) there and decided to adopt a conciliatory tone.'

∎

At around 9.30 that night, Arjun Singh drove to Fotedar's residence at 6, Kushak Road. Anil Bali joined them. Bali had grown close to Fotedar after Rajiv Gandhi's death. 'I kept beseeching them to resign,' Bali recalled. 'Both kept saying that if they resigned, "Desh toot jayega (The country will break)." I got a sense that Shankar Dayal Sharma had managed to persuade Fotedar when he had met him that evening (to dissuade) Arjun Singh from putting in his papers.' Given the politics of Madhya Pradesh, to which both Arjun Singh and Dr Sharma belonged, Bali felt 'the president did not want Arjun Singh to become prime minister'. The president would have argued that Arjun Singh was not likely to get the backing of other Congress leaders. And that it would be better for Singh and Fotedar to continue in government and oppose Rao from the inside, than be out in the cold. Though no one openly demanded his resignation, the knives were out for Rao within minutes of the conclusion of the cabinet meeting. Knowing Vaidik's proximity to Rao, Arjun Singh called him at 10.30 that night. 'Dekhiye, Narasimha Raoji ne (mosque) girwaya hai (I know Narasimha Rao has got the mosque destroyed). Aapne milke saazish ki hai (You people have conspired to do it),' he fulminated. He obviously wanted Vaidik to convey to Rao that he was not going to remain conciliatory. 'Hum Narasimha Raoji ko dekh lenge,' the normally restrained Arjun Singh said. 'Hum aapko bhi dekh lenge (I will deal with Narasimha Rao, and I know how to deal with you also).'

An angry Vaidik shot back, 'Aap Narasimha Raoji ko dekh lena. Aap mujhe dekhne ki baat mat karna. Agar main raajneeti karne laga hota, toh main aapko Delhi nahi aane deta (You deal with Narasimha Rao, but don't talk about dealing with me. If I had played politics, I would not have let you enter Delhi to do your politics),' he told Singh.

■

Just after 7 p.m. that evening, the union cabinet had recommended the removal of the chief minister of Uttar Pradesh, the dissolution of the state assembly, and the imposition of President's Rule in the state. Around 7.30 p.m., Home Minister Chavan rushed to Rashtrapati Bhavan, armed with the papers for the president to sign. The president signed the proclamation for central rule at 9.10 p.m. The prime minister addressed the nation at 9.30 p.m.

At the cabinet meeting, Arjun Singh had suggested that the PM address the nation that night. 'He immediately accepted this suggestion,' Singh stated. Rao asked Arjun Singh, Fotedar, and Madhavrao Scindia to prepare the draft of his speech.

After his speech that night, Rao set about dousing the many fires which had been lit. At 10 p.m., he drove to Rashtrapati Bhavan to apprise the president about the day's events—and to mollify him. Many difficult decisions lay ahead and Rao knew that a non-cooperative head of state could be problematic. After all, the president had the power to swear in anybody as prime minister and give him time to prove his majority.

After weeks of dithering in the run-up to the demolition, things suddenly began to move at breakneck speed. Lights burned late into the night in the offices in North Block and South Block. The prime minister's instructions to the officers were now clear—and unambiguous. With President's Rule in place in UP, advisors to the governor had to be appointed immediately. The central government had to get on with governance in Lucknow.

Godbole had already prepared a shortlist of advisors. It was part of the contingency plan he had prepared in November 1992. But the PM had his own ideas. He cut out all the names Godbole had identified. Even in the midst of the crisis, he gave instructions that from then on, the cabinet secretary, and not the home secretary, would appoint the advisors. After talking to the PM, Rajgopal chose Ashok Chandra and B. K. Goswami as advisors. Even the home minister was not consulted. The PM did not want to take any chances. Having advisors with ideas of their own could prove problematic. At 1.30 a.m., the cabinet secretary and the home secretary briefed the new advisors. Then they boarded a BSF plane for Lucknow. It was another matter that they had to return because of bad weather that night, and go the next day.

Suddenly, the PM displayed no signs of indecision or paralysis; he was moving with firmness and authority. By the end of the day, Rao had won the first round—he had survived the attack from within the cabinet and was still prime minister.

At 11 p.m., Vaidik rang up Rao to tell him about Arjun Singh's threatening message. 'Rao sahib has high fever,' an unperturbed Khandekar informed him. 'He is sleeping.'

XI

The story of the demolition is not complete without a look at how P. V. Narasimha Rao dealt with its aftermath—only to understand how the ninth prime minister of India contained the damage that had been done to his premiership.

After the demolition, a makeshift temple came up on the spot where the mosque had stood a few hours earlier. It was put in place on the nights of 6 and 7 December. Rao did nothing to stop it, though by now, the central government was in charge in the state.

Rajesh Pilot, the minister of Internal Security, and Rao's blue-eyed boy, made a bright suggestion to his boss. He told the prime minister that a dome could be salvaged from a dilapidated mosque in Gonda in eastern UP and brought to Ayodhya to be a symbolic stand-in for the destroyed mosque. 'Uska gumbad toota pada hai. Hum yahan deewar bana ke us gumbad ko rakh denge (Its dome is lying there broken. We can bring the dome here and build a wall around it).' It could mitigate some of the damage done by the demolition, Pilot felt.

Rao told Pilot to go ahead with his 'dome' plan.

'Rajesh Pilot and I knuckled down to it,' Shahid Siddiqui said. By now communal riots had erupted in many parts of the country. 'We needed an army helicopter to pick up the gumbad. And for this, we needed the permission of the home and defence secretaries. But Rao said "no" to them.'

'The order (not to do it) has come from the top,' a disappointed Pilot told Siddiqui. The plan, like so many others, died stillborn.

On 8 December 1992, L. K. Advani was arrested along with Murli Manohar Joshi, Ashok Singhal, Vishnu Hari Dalmia, Vinay Katiyar, and Uma Bharati. They were accused of a criminal conspiracy and incitement which led to the destruction of the mosque. Advani, who had first called 6 December 'the saddest day of my life', but later dubbed it as 'a day of Hindu awakening', was released by a court order on 10 January 1992.

On 10 December, the government banned the RSS, VHP, Bajrang Dal, Jamiat-e-Islami Hind, and Islamic Sevak Sangh. Six months later, on 4 June 1993, a tribunal headed by Justice P. K. Bahri, a Delhi High Court judge, was to strike down the ban on the RSS and the Bajrang Dal. But he stopped short of doing it for the VHP, because of its role in the Ayodhya demolition. The tribunal felt that the government had failed to prepare a comprehensive case against the three Hindutva organizations.

On 13 December 1992, Rao ordered the CBI to probe law and order infractions related to the demolition. On 15 December 1992, the central government dismissed the BJP governments in Madhya Pradesh, Rajasthan, and Himachal Pradesh, for their failure to control the communal riots. As with UP, the centre took direct control of these states. On 16 December, the prime minister constituted a commission of enquiry to fix culpability. It was headed by Justice Manmohan Singh Liberhan, a sitting judge of the High Court of Punjab and Haryana. After seventeen years of enquiry and forty-eight extensions, the commission found that the demolition was 'preplanned', carried out with 'painstaking preparation'—and was 'not intended to be tokenistic'. Such a plan could not have been kept a secret from the chief minister of UP or the head of the RSS, the commission ruled. Though it indicted sixty-eight leaders for the act of destruction, no one was punished.

Rao took these steps to counter the growing clamour inside the Congress for 'action'. He had come in for huge criticism also for the Hindu–Muslim riots the demolition had sparked off—which left 1,200 dead and 4,000 injured. Expectedly, the BJP brought a no-confidence motion against the Rao government in parliament on 16 December 1992—which he survived.

Three weeks after the demolition, the Rao government decided to take over 67 acres at the Ram Janmabhoomi–Babri Masjid site in the interest of public peace and harmony. It did this through an ordinance on 7 January 1993—the Acquisition of Certain Area at Ayodhya Act—which later became a law. The central government also referred the core question, of whether a temple predated the mosque on the disputed site, to the Supreme Court. This time Rao made a reference not under Article 138 of the Constitution, that he had asked Kalyan Singh to accept, which would be binding on the government. He did it under Article 143 of the Constitution, which was only a recommendation—which Kalyan Singh had been willing to agree to. As it turned out, in 1994, the Supreme Court 'respectfully refused' to go into the issue.

All of a sudden, the dithering PM was showing resolve—and pulling out all the stops to do the very things he had wavered on, to save himself and his government.

■

After the demolition, the plethora of legal suits filed in the Ayodhya case diverged into two streams—civil and criminal. Apart from the ongoing civil cases, criminal cases to fix liability for the demolition were filed against kar sevaks and BJP and VHP leaders. It was only in 2002 that the Allahabad High Court began its hearings. This was thirteen years after the civil suits to decide the ownership of the disputed land were clubbed together and transferred to the Allahabad High Court.

In July 2003, the Allahabad High Court ordered an excavation to be carried out at the disputed site. This was done by the Archaeological Survey of India (ASI). Its report stated that there was a structure beneath the disputed structure, which included temple walls and pillars. This was recorded in the court proceedings. But Muslim groups disputed the ASI's findings. On 30 September 2010, the Allahabad High Court finally delivered its judgment. It divided the disputed land into three parts, and gave it to Ram Lalla Virajman, Nirmohi Akhara, and the Sunni Waqf Board. All three went in appeal to the Supreme Court. The Supreme Court stayed the Allahabad High Court's judgment on 9 August 2011.

On 9 November 2019, the Supreme Court handed down its final ruling in the civil litigation in the Ayodhya matter. A five-judge Constitution bench unanimously settled the longstanding land dispute. It allowed Hindus to build a Ram temple at the site, while sanctioning 5 acres to the Muslims to build a mosque elsewhere in the temple town. The court directed that the 2.77-acre disputed site be handed over to a trust to be formed by the central government. The Narendra Modi government chose not to entrust the construction of the temple to the Ram Janmabhoomi Nyas which had led the movement for the Ram temple. Rather, it constituted a new trust—Shri Ram Janmbhoomi Teerth Kshetra—to raise the temple. On 5 August 2020, the foundation stone of the Ram Janmabhoomi temple was laid by Prime Minister Narendra Modi. The judgment may not have brought justice to the aggrieved parties, but it brought closure to an issue which had sharply divided India for over seventy years.

The two criminal cases to fix liability for the destruction of the Babri

Masjid saw many twists and turns. First, the trial court dropped the charges against the accused on technical grounds. The CBI challenged the trial court's verdict. Then, in 2017, the charges were restored against the BJP leaders who had been initially accused, and the two separate cases were merged. Finally, a special court in Lucknow acquitted all the thirty-two accused, including L. K. Advani, Murli Manohar Joshi, Kalyan Singh, Uma Bharati, and Vinay Katiyar for the charge of criminal conspiracy (on 30 September 2020), twenty-eight years after the Babri Masjid was brought down. In a ruling which came in for criticism, the court held in its 2,000-page judgment that the demolition was not preplanned but happened on the spur of the moment.

Soon after the mosque was pulled down, riots erupted in the country's financial hub in Mumbai. First Muslim protests over the demolition turned violent. Soon afterwards, the Hindus, mobilized by the Shiv Sena, hit back. The consummate player that he was, Rao used this opportunity to send a reluctant Defence Minister Sharad Pawar back to Maharashtra to take charge as chief minister.

'I was called (to) the PM's residence,' Pawar was to recall years later. 'I was not willing to go.' The meeting went on for six hours. Finally Pawar relented. But he always felt that his 'ghar wapasi' (homecoming) had cut short the national role which he may have otherwise been able to play.

Less than a week later, on 12 March, a series of twelve bomb blasts ripped through hotels, banks, and markets in different parts of Mumbai, killing 257 people on a single day, injuring 1,400.

On 20 March 1993, Rao phoned his defence secretary, N. N. Vohra, in the evening. 'I want you to take over as home secretary from 8 a.m. tomorrow,' he said. Vohra was taken aback, for the next day was a Sunday. 'You come to my residence tomorrow morning at 6.30 and we will talk.'

When Vohra arrived at the PM House next morning, Rao was exercising in the veranda on his stationary bike, wearing baggy shorts which came down to his knees. Vohra waited for the PM to finish, looking through the morning papers. Soon a cup of coffee arrived. When the PM had finished exercising, he told Vohra, 'I want you to look into how three and a half tonnes of explosive material came into a metro city of the country.'

'I had given myself ninety days to complete the report. But I finished it in eighty-five days,' Vohra said. He made a ten-page note which 'summed up the assessments made and suggested the way forward. Since some members of the committee were hesitant to speak out openly at the meetings chaired by Vohra, he met them individually and 'got their inputs in writing'. Vohra made three copies of the report—one was given to Home Minister S. B.

Chavan, another to Rajesh Pilot, the minister of state for Internal Security, and the third was kept in the home secretary's confidential record. All the 'supporting material,' Vohra said, 'were kept in the DIB's TS [top secret] vault'.

The ten-page report mentioned that Dawood Ibrahim and the Memon brothers were involved. Vohra suggested the setting up of a committee under him to take the enquiry further.

Then, one day, Vohra got a message from the home minister. Chavan asked him to 'withdraw the report'. Being a seasoned bureaucrat, he did nothing. A couple of weeks later, he got another message, this time it was to 'cut out a para'—this para had stated that the 'mafia had replaced established authority in several parts of the country'.

Vohra then met the PM over his findings. 'I informed him,' Vohra said, 'of the very large spectrum on political and other persons who were involved in varying networks.' His investigation had documented the links a large number of prominent political personalities—many of them top names—had forged with the mafia in real estate, tobacco, liquor, highways, and other sectors. He did not name anyone. But anyone intelligent could have made out who he was referring to, Vohra told me. The annexures ran to around 1,000 pages. Vohra had established a clear nexus between the criminals, police, and politicians. 'It has taken deep roots. It was so deep seated that it was not going to go away easily.'

In the months that followed, the government gave assurances 'thirteen times' on the floor of parliament, in 1993 and 1994, that the Vohra Report was under its 'serious consideration'. Despite these 'assurances', no action followed. Before he retired, on his last day in office on 31 May 1994, Vohra made a case for further action on the report. 'I left a handwritten note,' he said, '...that given the thirteen assurances to parliament, the report should be sent to the Committee on Assurances (of parliament).' (This committee, set up in the Rajya Sabha in 1972, scrutinized assurances given by ministers in parliament to see whether they had been implemented.)

Rao did nothing about the Vohra Report. Nor did his successors. Nor were the annexures ever made public. But their very existence was enough to silence those who might have created problems for Rao. That seemed to be enough for the PM.

■

'Aisi baat hai,' police officer Kishore Kunal told me, 'Narasimha Raoji jahaan Ram Lallaji virajman hai, waheen mandir banaana chahte thae (The fact is that Narasimha Rao himself wanted to build the temple where the idols were kept).'

Rao instructed his media advisor, P. V. R. K. Prasad, to create a trust which could build a temple where the mosque had once stood.

On the Sunday after the demolition (13 December 1992), Prasad had gone to see Rao. He had found the PM alone and in a reflective mood. 'We can fight the BJP, but how can we fight Lord Ram?' he asked Prasad pensively. 'When we say that the Congress is a secular party, it does not mean we are atheists,' he went on. 'How far are they (BJP) justified in hoodwinking people by monopolizing Lord Ram under the pretext of constructing a temple in Ayodhya?'

He then referred to the Congress's commitment in its 1991 manifesto to construct a temple in Ayodhya and said, 'Our aim should be to achieve both (temple and mosque), not through the courts nor through the politicians.'

He tasked a surprised Prasad to create 'a representative and apolitical committee comprising all Hindu heads of maths and peethams representing the whole cross section of Hindus.' He reeled off the names of people who should be members—the heads of Adwaita, Dwaita, and Vishistadwaita peethams, the shankaracharyas of Sringeri, Kanchi, Dwarka, Badri, and Puri. Then he added others like 'Tamil Nadu Jiyars', and 'Andhra Jiyyangars', heads of Vaishnav maths belonging to the Ramanuja tradition in the North and heads of Udipi and Uttaradi maths belonging to the Dwaita tradition. He continued rattling off names, and ended with the 'mahants of Ayodhya'. He had obviously given a great deal of thought to the project.

Prasad took him at his word. He began working, along with Kishore Kunal and Naresh Chandra. Rao also asked Digvijay Singh, then chief minister of Madhya Pradesh, to help. Digvijay Singh took Prasad in his plane to meet some of the religious heads. Rao met some of them himself. Many of the heads of leading Hindu sects, representing almost the entire body of Hindu religious opinion, agreed to be part of the trust. They were told to keep things under wraps. The trust was finally registered in 1995.

Rao asked Prasad to convene its meeting. And then, suddenly, he seemed to lose interest. 'Wait until the elections are over', he told a baffled Prasad. And that, according to Prasad 'was the end of the story'.

Had Rao been committed to building a temple at all costs, he would have started its construction in 1995 itself. But Rao was interested in the politics of the temple. Ayodhya was one area, he had told colleagues, 'where we cannot take on the BJP successfully'.

By the end of 1995, with the Babri Masjid gone, the temple had ceased to be the emotive plank that it had been when there was a dispute over the mosque. Rao was now looking at other issues which might garner him votes in the 1996 general elections which were around the corner. He considered going in for a nuclear test, but ruled it out when information about it leaked to the Americans. Finally, he opted for corruption as the issue to flog. He initiated action in the 'hawala' scam in which many of his own party colleagues were involved. But it did not cut ice with the voters. Even during the campaign it was clear which way the wind was blowing; people would walk out of his meetings when Rao would start to speak. The Congress failed to get a majority. The BJP, the party with the largest number of seats, fronted by Atal Bihari Vajpayee, was invited by the president to form the government.

XII

Thirty years after the demolition, questions continue to tantalize. Did Narasimha Rao know that the Babri Masjid would be demolished on 6 December 1992? Did he collude with Hindu fundamentalists in their effort to bring it down? Could he have done more to save the mosque?

As seen throughout the chapter, it is difficult to believe that Rao did not have an inkling that a group of people within the VHP–Bajrang Dal–RSS might bring down the structure. His intelligence agencies would have alerted him. It is also likely that his contacts among the BJP–RSS family—like Kushabhau Thakre and K. Sudarshan as mentioned earlier—had alerted him about their impending move. And, there were rehearsals going on in plain sight in Ayodhya on how to demolish the structure in the hours before it happened. The prime minister of India could not but be aware of this, given the multiple agencies which provided him feedback.

There is no conclusive evidence to prove that Rao colluded with the BJP and the RSS to bring down the structure. But he would have known that the mosque was in danger—and chose not to take the hard political decisions required to protect it. He may have reconciled himself to the inevitability of the mosque going, thinking it would remove, once and for all, what had become a festering sore for the Hindus, fuelling the BJP's politics. As mentioned, he had wanted to build a temple himself on the same spot where the Babri Masjid stood, which he hoped would enable him to become a saviour of Hindus—but lost interest in the project in 1995. For by the end of his term as prime minister, the temple had ceased to agitate Hindus.

Could Rao have done more to save the mosque? The choices he faced were no easy ones. But he could have persuaded the Allahabad High Court to give its verdict before 6 December 1992 in the national interest as was being demanded by the BJP–RSS–VHP combine. This might have defused an escalating situation, and given him breathing room. But, inexplicably, Rao chose not to do it. He may have calculated that the balance of advantage for him lay in letting the mosque go, if it came to that, than to give the BJP a fresh lease of life. A court verdict would have enabled the BJP either to start building the temple with renewed vigour or step up its agitation for the temple.

And, if there had to be a showdown with the BJP, which he now saw as inevitable, he wanted it to be over in 1992 and not take it closer to elections in 1996.

That may be why Rao chose not to call in the army a few days ahead of 6 December, before the kar sevaks gathered there. V. P. Singh had made this suggestion to him at the end of November 1992, when Rao had sought his advice. But all Rao did, by his own admission, was to 'alert' the army—not have it man the barricades! Nor did he exercise other options.

Though he cited legal reasons for not resorting to Article 356—that President's Rule could be imposed in UP following a breakdown of the Constitution, and not in apprehension of a breakdown—it is the political fallout of such a step that Rao worried about. He knew that sacking the Kalyan Singh government for demanding a Ram temple could inflame Hindu sentiment all over North India, particularly in UP, given the mood in the country's largest and politically influential state. It would only end up giving a fillip to the BJP, as nothing else would have done. It could, as he was to argue later, have invited strictures from the Supreme Court, giving his opponents inside his own party the chance they were waiting for to dethrone him. As he was to say in his book, *Ayodhya*, 'Along with the Babri Masjid, it was me whom they were trying to demolish.'

With the demolition, the temple issue went on the back-burner temporarily. In the months that followed the demolition, the BJP had difficulty generating a sense of victimhood amongst the Hindus; it lost the north Indian states of Madhya Pradesh and Himachal Pradesh in less than a year, and a non-BJP party led by Mulayam Singh Yadav formed the government in Uttar Pradesh in mid-1993, along with the Bahujan Samaj Party.

The temple ceased to be a vote-catching ploy for the BJP after December 1992, though the party continued to flag it. It would be included in its manifesto, mainly to keep its core constituency happy. The BJP brass sensed that they had milked the temple electorally as much as they could. In the 1996 general elections, the BJP's main poll plank was not the temple, but the corruption inside the Rao government. With its cry, 'Abki baari Atal Bihari', the party trumpeted the leadership of its charismatic leader, Atal Bihari Vajpayee. In 1998 and 1999, it put Ayodhya—and its other two core commitments of abrogating Article 370 and enacting a Uniform Civil Code—on the back-burner to forge alliances with other parties and form a national government. The BJP had added other issues to its temple agenda, as it sensed a changed mood in the country.

P. V. Narasimha Rao may have achieved a short-term gain by defusing the Ayodhya crisis during his premiership. Rao did not calculate the damage—or he chose to ignore it—the demolition would do to the Muslim psyche. The Congress lost Muslim support. But, even more significantly, it dented the confidence of the community in the ability of the Indian Constitution—and the Indian state—to safeguard their lives and their rights. It made them feel helpless, insecure, and 'second-class citizens' in their own country. Also, Rao did not factor in the long-term damage the demolition would inflict on India's plural social order, and its multicultural heritage.

The demolition strengthened the idea of an aggressive Hindu nationalism as nothing else in the history of independent India had done—ushering in the beginnings of a shadow Hindu raj. It was to lead to the rise and rise of the BJP.

■

Rao's political career went into a tailspin after his government was voted out of power in 1996. His own party shunned him. Very few senior leaders kept in touch with him, barring exceptions like Manmohan Singh. He was forced to resign as the leader of the CPP and as party president, having to make way for Sitaram Kesri. Cases were initiated against him for corruption. It saddened and troubled him—and till the end of his life, the demolition of the Babri Masjid continued to weigh on Narasimha Rao's mind.

In hospital, in November 2004, he refused one day to eat, indicating that he saw no point in living. For a day he sat on a chair placed next to his hospital bed in Delhi's AIIMS, adamant that he would not take any food or water. His desperate daughter Vani Devi sent word to the Congress leadership asking them to help. The Congress leader, Shivraj Patil, called her on 24 November 2004, and said Sonia Gandhi, Ahmed Patel, and he would visit Rao. They arrived at the hospital at 10.30 p.m. Cajoling the ailing leader to give up his obstinacy, Ahmed Patel picked up a glass of water and asked him to drink it. At this point, Rao not known to lose his cool, suddenly blurted agitatedly, 'You people accuse me of breaking the mosque. Now, you give me water.' Rao's biographer Vinay Sitapati was to write.

'Who has not done a mistake?' Rao went on, '(But) why should I be blamed for something I have not done?'

Sonia Gandhi sat there listening. But she did not say much. His visitors finally left at 2.30 a.m. The next morning, he was his normal self—and started to eat. He then asked his children, 'Did I speak more than I should have?'

Narasimha Rao died a month later—on 23 December 2004. When his body draped in the national flag was brought to the Congress headquarters, it was stopped at the gates which had been shut. The flower-bedecked cortege was not allowed entry into 24, Akbar Road—for his party colleagues to pay their last respects to a man who had served the Congress for half a century.

Just as the demolition troubled Rao till the end of his life, his role in it troubled the Congress leadership—and they did not forgive him till the end.

CHAPTER 5

THE PEACEABLE PRIME MINISTER
WHO ROARED

A. B. Vajpayee Authorizes the
Testing of Nuclear Devices

I

Atal Bihari Vajpayee knew he was late for the emergency meeting Prime Minister Morarji Desai had called as he hurried into South Block. The meeting was supposed to be a 'hush-hush' affair. Delhi, he thought, was already very hot, even though it was only the month of April in 1979. But it was much cooler inside the red sandstone building he stepped into, which housed the PMO.

Desai had summoned his top four ministers to meet with him urgently. The portly Babu Jagjivan Ram, the defence minister, had been the first to walk in. Dressed in his trademark khadi Gandhi cap, he was a familiar figure on Raisina Hill, having been a minister since the days of Jawaharlal Nehru. He was followed by Charan Singh, now the finance minister, but known more as a kisan leader. Only three months earlier, Desai had made Jagjivan Ram and Charan Singh deputy prime ministers. It was part of a truce he had effected in his dissension-riven government. The balding H. M. Patel, the home minister, came right behind—and Patel was followed by Vajpayee who was the external affairs minister of India.

An edgy Morarji Desai sat in his office, impatiently waiting for his colleagues to arrive. Looking sterner than he usually did, he wanted to be done with this meeting. Left to himself, he would not have called it.

The four ministers took their seats—and waited expectantly for the PM to tell them why he had called them at short notice. The PMO had given them no reason why the prime minister wanted to meet them so urgently. Normally, they would have been accompanied by their department secretaries. But, this time, they were told to come alone. The ministers were members of the Janata government's apex decision-making body—the Cabinet Committee on Political Affairs.

Morarji Desai lost no time in coming to the point. He had called them to discuss what the government should do about its nuclear programme. Vajpayee, Ram, and Patel were now really curious. They knew that Desai was opposed to India developing nuclear weapons. Till now he had been reluctant even to discuss the subject. Desai informed them they could not postpone a decision any longer. For Pakistan was on the verge of acquiring nuclear weapons.

What had prompted him to call this 'secret' meeting was a report, he said. It had been submitted by K. Subrahmanyam, chairman of the Joint Intelligence Committee of the government. Subrahmanyam had stated that Pakistan 'was only a screwdriver away from a bomb'.

'In 1979, I produced a report that Pakistan was going in for nuclear weapons,' the tall and unsmiling Subrahmanyam told me in his flat in Vasant Kunj in New Delhi.

As soon as he had finished the report, Subrahmanyam had handed it over to the cabinet secretary, Nirmal Mukherji. Glancing through it, a worried Mukherji warned Subrahmanyam, 'Morarji is going to be very displeased with this report.'

'It's my duty to produce this report,' replied Subrahmanyam, who was known to take his work very seriously, 'and yours to give it.'

India 'going nuclear' was an issue close to Subrahmanyam's heart. 'Normally at these meetings,' Subrahmanyam recalled, 'I would keep the minutes.' But that day, Mukherji told him 'to stay out'.

'Subbu, you...don't attend the meeting,' he instructed Subrahmanyam. 'Don't allow any of the other secretaries to come in either,' the cabinet secretary added.

'We did not even inform the secretaries—except the foreign secretary (Jagat Mehta).' Besides the ministers, there were only two officials present at the CCPA meeting that day. They were the specially invited Atomic Energy Commission chairman, Homi Sethna, and Nirmal Mukherji.

As the meeting got underway, the prime minister did not hide his displeasure with the report. He had been 'greatly surprised' by Subrahmanyam's findings, he said cuttingly. The report recommended that India needed to act immediately—and this would have meant going against the PM's anti-nuclear position and his policy of reaching out to Islamabad. But given the gravity of the report's findings, Desai could not put off the meeting. For it would have to take a view on whether India should develop nuclear weapons. The meeting went on for one and a half hours.

After it ended, the cabinet secretary came out hurriedly to brief Subrahmanyam. He had to prepare the minutes—and had been told to wait in the anteroom.

'How did it go?' Subrahmanyam asked him eagerly.

'The decision,' Mukherji replied blandly, 'was that we should proceed with our efforts.'

Realizing the import of what Mukherji was saying, Subrahmanyam asked, 'Is this unanimous?'

Mukherji laughed. 'No,' he said, 'it was a split verdict. It was 3:2.'

'Morarji must have been opposed to it,' Subrahmanyam was curious. 'Yes,' Mukherji replied.

'Guess who the second person was?' Mukherji asked Subrahmanyam. 'Was it Charan Singh?' he asked Mukherji.

Subrahmanyam knew that H. M. Patel and Jagjivan Ram had favoured moving ahead with India testing a bomb. 'I had already talked to H. M. Patel and Jagjivan Ram. And I knew they were for it.' And, he also knew that Vajpayee's parent party, the Bharatiya Jan Sangh (the precursor of the BJP) had since December 1962 openly advocated that India become a nuclear-weapon state (NWS). Vajpayee had himself spoken in parliament in favour of a bomb in 1964.

'No, it was Vajpayee,' Mukherji said, to Subrahmanyam's surprise. Subrahmanyam confirmed to me later that 'Morarji and Vajpayee were opposed to going ahead. H. M. Patel, Jagjivan Ram, and Charan Singh were for it.'

■

Subrahmanyam's report made the politicians and the scientists in India sit up. 'They (Pakistan) had got new centrifuge technology. It could be used to enrich uranium to make nuclear weapons,' Subrahmanyam said.

The scientists were particularly worried because 'in 1979 we (also) had new evidence about A. Q. Khan'. They had got word that nuclear scientist Abdul Qadeer Khan—known as the father of Pakistan's nuclear bomb—was using the centrifuge technology to develop the bomb in Pakistan. In his report, Subrahmanyam had stated quite unambiguously 'that Pakistan was now going nuclear using this new technology'.

Khan had left India for Pakistan in 1952 and had thereafter been working in Europe. It was in September 1974, four months after Indira Gandhi had tested India's 'peaceful nuclear device' on 18 May, that the Bhopal-born Khan wrote to Pakistan premier Z. A. Bhutto—and offered his expertise to Pakistan. He now began to work with the Pakistan Atomic Energy Commission. Bhutto gave him autonomous control over Pakistan's uranium enrichment programme that would be used to make the atomic bomb. Khan focussed on developing Pakistan's indigenous uranium enrichment capability in Kahuta. It was much later that Khan was to go rogue—and was accused of selling nuclear secrets to North Korea, Libya, Iran, and other countries.

The first person to realize what Pakistan was up to was actually nuclear scientist K. Santhanam—known to colleagues as Santy. He had started off as a strategic analyst with R&AW. Later, in 1986, he joined the Defence Research and Development Organisation (DRDO), the country's premier R&D organization to cater to the needs of the defence set-up.

'I exposed Pakistan's programme (back in 1976),' Santhanam disclosed.

'(But, at the time,) no one would believe it, including the bigwigs in Trombay like (Homi) Sethna.' Homi Sethna was the chairman of the Atomic Energy Commission (AEC) when Indira Gandhi was prime minister. It was after Subrahmanyam submitted his report that the scientific establishment began to take serious note of what Santhanam had been saying.

Pakistan laid the foundations of its nuclear programme after India divided the country in 1971 with the creation of Bangladesh, the erstwhile East Pakistan. It decided to 'go nuclear' in January 1972 because it felt it did not get all the help it wanted—even though it was getting assistance from China. China had shared with Pakistan its nuclear bomb designs from its Lop Nor tests on 16 October 1964. Over the years it was to provide 'significant assistance' to Pakistan's nuclear weapons programme. Pakistan's arsenal was essentially of Chinese design.

'(Z. A.) Bhutto (had) convened a meeting of nuclear scientists...the Pakistanis felt the Americans and even the Chinese had not helped them as they expected,' said strategic analyst C. Raja Mohan. Later China became 'extraordinarily' generous with Pakistan because Pakistani nuclear scientists had shared with it secrets about the high-speed centrifuge technology to enrich uranium to make it weapons grade.

■

A day after the CCPA meeting, Subrahmanyam confronted Vajpayee.

'How could you oppose it?' he asked Vajpayee. 'You have been for it all along.'

'No, no, now the most important thing is to stop Pakistan from making the bomb,' Vajpayee replied defensively. 'And we should not provoke them.'

While Morarji Desai's position was well known, Vajpayee's stand at the CCPA meeting had come as a shock to Subrahmanyam. For, until then, Vajpayee had been seen as a nuclear hawk. Subrahmanyam remembered Vajpayee thundering in parliament, days after China had detonated a 16-kiloton bomb in its first nuclear test, becoming the fifth nation to join the exclusive nuclear club: 'The only answer to an atom bomb is an atom bomb, nothing else,' he had thundered.

The Chinese test had caused consternation in India, coming as it did two years after the Indo–China war in 1962. Worried about the threat it could pose to India's security, an assertive Jan Sangh, the Opposition party to which Vajpayee belonged, introduced a motion in the Lok Sabha on 27 November 1964. It called for India to manufacture nuclear weapons. The Jan Sangh took Prime Minister Jawaharlal Nehru to task—and did so repeatedly in the months that followed—for ignoring the danger China posed to India, particularly after its entry into the nuclear club.

■

Vajpayee's changed stance had also surprised his ministerial colleagues. It was not just that he had echoed at the United Nations General Assembly (UNGA) assurances given by PM Morarji Desai. During his two-day visit to Washington on 13–14 June 1978, Desai had pledged that India would not 'manufacture or acquire nuclear weapons even if the rest of the world did so' and that it 'abjured nuclear explosions even for peaceful purposes'. Or that, like Morarji, Vajpayee too wanted to improve relations with Pakistan. To find a solution to the Kashmir problem was one of the dreams Vajpayee had harboured since his early days in the Jan Sangh when he had worked with its founder, Syama Prasad Mookerji. But, in 1979, as External Affairs minister, Vajpayee may have been conditioned by the need to stay on the right side of the prime minister. And to carve out a niche for himself, which was distinctly different from his party's position. It was to help him shape his persona as a leader who was a moderate, not a hardliner.

■

This was not the first time that Vajpayee changed his position on the nuclear issue. In the 1950s, he was a pacifist. In the 1960s, he became a hawk, in line with his party's position that India needed to acquire nuclear weapons. In the 1970s, he was back to becoming a dove.

In the 1950s, he had even written an anguished poem, 'Hiroshima ki Peeda' (The Agony of Hiroshima). The poem was about the devastation caused by the atom bombs that were dropped on Hiroshima and Nagasaki in Japan, on 6 and 9 August 1945. They had killed around 210,000 people. In the poem, he posed questions, feelingly, to the scientists who had invented the bomb. Did they, even for a moment, feel remorse about what they had done, Vajpayee asked emotionally. Were they able to sleep at night when they learnt about the devastation their invention had caused?

The questions he posed seemed to reflect his own inner turmoil about the dangers nuclear weapons posed to humanity.

Sometimes at night,
Suddenly, sleep deserts me,
My eyes open,
I begin to ponder—those scientists who invented nuclear weapons,
On hearing of the gruesome human destruction,
Of Hiroshima and Nagasaki,
How did they ever sleep at night?

■

There was a twist to the April 1979 CCPA meet—that did not come to light. Although Subrahmanyam had been told by the cabinet secretary that the CCPA had decided 3:2 to keep the strategic nuclear programme going, there had actually been a vote on whether to take the next steps to weaponize. In other words, whether India should develop nuclear bombs and delivery systems. This time, by a 3:2 vote, the CCPA decided against India developing nuclear weapons. This vote was not minuted.

After the meeting, Subrahmanyam told Krishan Kant, who had all along been his comrade-in-arms 'for the bomb', that Morarji Desai had exercised his 'casting vote'.

The PM exercises his casting vote only if there is a tie. In other words, his other ministerial colleagues were evenly divided 2:2. Given his known position, Morarji's vote would obviously be against India going on to acquire nuclear weapons. But he may have wanted to maintain an ambivalence about the government's position so as not to make India vulnerable in the eyes of its adversaries, particularly Pakistan.

When it came to the official record, the minutes simply said the country would continue with its strategic nuclear programme. This was consistent with the stand taken by every government since Independence—except for a brief interregnum when the Janata Party came to power in 1977 and 'discontinued the nuclear programme started by the Congress Government'.

Subrahmanyam told me he wrote out the minutes 'in my (own) hand' and sent them to Morarji Desai. The prime minister signed the minutes immediately. Morarji Desai at the time was also the minister for Atomic Energy.

'I took a Xerox copy of the minutes,' Subrahmanyam said, 'and flew down to Bombay and handed it over to Sethna.'

AEC chairman Homi Sethna called on Morarji Desai not long after the CCPA meeting. He asked the prime minister point blank, 'Do you want me to do it (to test)?'

'As long as I am prime minister, I will never permit an experiment,' Desai told Sethna. But Desai gave him permission to 'refine' the design of the explosive device. The scientists were trying to 'miniaturize everything' and reduce the weight and diameter of the device. However, it was clear that it would be far short of a bomb. What the prime minister authorized the scientists to do was to continue India's ongoing nuclear programme, expanding research, upgrading nuclear technology, and refining infrastructure and design—but stopping short of weaponization.

∎

As a proclaimed Gandhian, Morarji Desai's aversion to India producing nuclear weapons was no secret. Soon after he took over as PM in March 1977, the US ambassador to India, Robert R. Goheen, had called on him. He raised the issue of India's nuclear policy with the new PM—and said he was speaking to Desai 'on behalf of US President Jimmy Carter'. He asked the PM if he planned to greenlight a nuclear device. Even as the ambassador sought assurances from Desai, he also held out a veiled threat: any fuel the US supplied for the Tarapur nuclear power plant would have to be used only for generating power and not in a nuclear device. At this, Desai became really indignant. There was no question of India not standing by its agreed commitments, Desai replied. The PM, who was known for his self-righteousness, stated this 'vigorously' and 'emotionally'.

Despite the CCPA's decision in April 1979 to 'proceed' with the nuclear programme, not much happened during the remaining months of the Janata government. The Morarji government fell three months later.

However, in one of those rare ironies that are ever present in politics, Vajpayee, a peacenik in the 1950s, a hawk by 1964, a nuclear dove again in 1979, was to make history two decades later. In 1998, as prime minister, he ushered India into the nuclear weapons club. He would justify it by saying that nuclear weapons prevented war. And that if India had to live in peace with its neighbours, it was necessary to have a credible nuclear deterrent.

II

'I am the longest prime minister in waiting,' Vajpayee once quipped in 1988, to his friend, Janata Party leader Krishan Kant. The comment was made half in jest. But it expressed an underlying frustration. The job was a long time coming. Even after he became prime minister for the first time in 1996, he had to suffer two abbreviated terms before he eventually served out a term. This too was cut short by a few months because he decided to call for early elections in 2004.

It was India's first prime minister Jawaharlal Nehru who had initially spotted Vajpayee's talent in the 1950s. Vajpayee first came to Nehru's notice in 1958. He had spoken during a debate on foreign policy in the Lok Sabha. Nehru had been impressed with his oratory and grasp of foreign affairs. When Nehru replied to the discussion, he—the PM also held charge of Foreign Affairs—suddenly switched from English to Hindi halfway into his speech. He did it deliberately to enable Vajpayee, who was more comfortable with Hindi, to catch all the nuances in the PM's response to his speech.

In 1960, Nikita Krushchev, the premier of (the then) Soviet Union came to India. It was a high-profile visit. The government laid out a banquet for him. Vajpayee, already an MP, was invited to it. Standing next to the Soviet leader, Prime Minister Nehru was introducing the Indian guests to him. When it came to Vajpayee, Nehru said of Vajpayee, 'This is our future prime minister.' Nehru encouraged Vajpayee in those early years—he once instructed an Indian ambassador posted in the US to 'introduce' Vajpayee to people 'who mattered' as 'he (had) potential....'

Even though Vajpayee would criticize the prime minister, Nehru continued to support the young MP. When Vajpayee had gone to campaign against the Congress in Nehru's constituency during the 1962 general election—Nehru had pulled up the Congress workers who were gunning for Vajpayee, 'Aane do na. Woh...acha bolta hai. Bolne do na (Let him come, this youngster speaks well, let him speak).' Then he had added, 'Jisko vote dena hai toh doh, nahin dena toh mat doh (If voters want to vote for me, fine, if they want to vote for somebody else, that too is fine).' Vajpayee was later to repeat those very words while referring to Shivraj Patil—he was to become the Lok Sabha speaker and India's home minister—when he went to campaign against him in his constituency, Latur, in 1996. Hearing Vajpayee speak good words about her husband, Shivraj Patil's wife, Vijaya, had teased him afterwards, 'Was it you who invited him to speak at the rally or was it his party?' But then, like Nehru, Vajpayee also believed that while electoral battles had their place in a democracy, relations between political opponents did not always have to be adversarial.

∎

A quick look now at Vajpayee the person and the politician to better understand why and how he took the decision which made India a part of the nuclear league. His unconventional lifestyle was at odds with the puritanical features of his party—and yet he managed to hold his own. What has never ceased to interest political observers is how he came to be a moderate in a hardline Hindu party.

I also dwell on how prime ministers from Nehru onwards dealt with the nuclear question, and kept the programme going—which gives insights into why Vajpayee decided to exercise the nuclear option in 1998.

The Vajpayee family were originally from UP. They belonged to the temple-lined Bateshwar village in Agra district—famous for its legend that Lord Shiva, when not in the mountains, sat under the bat (banyan) tree here to meditate. Vajpayee's grandfather, Shyam Lal Vajpayee, was a Kanyakubj Brahmin and migrated to Morena in Gwalior district of Madhya Pradesh. Vajpayee's father, Krishna Bihari Vajpayee, then moved to Gwalior and became a schoolteacher there. Atal Bihari was born to him and his wife, Krishna Devi, on Christmas Day in 1924—and grew up in a two-storeyed house in one of the narrow by-lanes of Gwalior. Poetry came naturally and early to the boy. He picked it up from his father who had become renowned for his compositions. The young Atal Bihari would recite poems as he walked to school, clutching his father's finger, and Krishna Bihari would correct his language and pronunciation.

Though some in the literary world did not think much of his poetry, it got play in later years because of who he was. It was the poet in him who could communicate at the popular level the complex political messages that people could relate to.

He was recognized as a public speaker not only because of his poetic turn of phrase—but also for the legendary pauses in his speeches, which made him the orator he was. Many went to his rallies just for the pleasure of hearing him speak. He was also known to speak extempore. In 1934, when he was still in school in Ujjain, he learnt a lesson which was to influence his oratory and that was never to do rote learning.

Having learnt by heart a speech he was to deliver in school on the Indian Railways, he suddenly forgot his lines and became tongue-tied. From that day onwards, he would work very hard on his speeches, creating a mental corpus of information, stories, anecdotes, and metaphors—to use as and when he needed to make a point. It was a trove of information he could draw upon and he always preferred to speak extempore. Vajpayee was just not himself when he had to read his speeches or follow notes.

Politics, he would sometimes say wistfully, had interfered in his journey as a poet. One of his more famous poems was about his jousting with death—when he was in hospital in New York in 1988.

He sent the poem to the Hindi magazine *Dharamyug* for publication. 'These lines may not be upto the mark as poetry,' he wrote to the editor, 'kintu yeh meri zindagi ka dastavez hai (…but these words capture the story of my life).'

The poem was published. It was hailed as an example of Vajpayee's never-say-die spirit in the face of adversity.

Toote hue sapno ki, kaun sune siski,
Antar ki cheer vyatha, palkon par thithki,
Haar nahin manoonga, raar nahin thanoonga,
Kaal ke kapal par, likhta hoon mithata hoon,
Geet naya gaata hoon.

(Who will listen to the sobs of broken dreams, the pain inside makes its way to the lids but does not flow out, I will not accept defeat, I will start the struggle afresh, I will write and unwrite my own destiny, And I will sing a new song.)

Another of his well-known poems was about his battle against illness—cancer.

'Kal agar kaal aakar mere dwar par dastak de, toh main usi shaan se uske saath chal kharha hoonga (Tomorrow if death knocks on my door, I will go with it without demur),' Vajpayee wrote. '…Kintu yadi maut mere sath khel karegi…toh us sae main larhoonga. Akhri dam tak doh doh haath karoonga (But if it plays games with me, then I will fight it. And I will fight it till my dying breath).

With these words, Vajpayee was describing what he had felt when he learnt he had cancer in the winter of 1988. His cancer was one of those carefully guarded secrets about Vajpayee. Few knew about his ailment.

'I didn't know he had cancer,' a surprised Yashwant Sinha said to me in 2021; Sinha had been finance minister under him. After the treatment he underwent, the disease did not reappear.

'He got cancer in the late eighties,' revealed Shakti Sinha. 'The two, kidney and cancer, were interrelated...it was confirmed. I knew about it.' Shakti Sinha told me.

Vajpayee was treated for cancer in New York. When people commented about his morose mood, reflected in his poem, he shot back, 'Meri kavita jang ka elan hai, parajaya ki prastavana nahin (My poem is a call for battle, it is not a proposal for defeat).' I write poetry to find strength, he used to say.

It was when Rajiv Gandhi died in 1991 that Vajpayee revealed how Rajiv had saved his life. 'When Rajiv Gandhi was the prime minister, he somehow found out I had a kidney problem and needed treatment abroad,' Vajpayee said. 'One day he called me to his office and said he was going to include me in India's delegation to the UN and hoped I would use the opportunity to get the treatment I needed.

'I went to New York and that is one reason I am alive today.'

Rajiv Gandhi gave instructions that Vajpayee should return to India only after his treatment in New York was completed. Neither did Rajiv ever speak about why he included Vajpayee in the Indian delegation, nor did Vajpayee ever mention it—till after Rajiv's death.

Successive prime ministers after Rajiv Gandhi also included Vajpayee in the Indian delegation to the United Nations General Assembly every year. Apart from attending the UN session, his yearly visit to New York would enable him to get his annual check-ups done.

That no prime minister leaked information about Vajpayee's cancer was a sign of the regard his opponents had for him. His cancer story illustrated his across-the-board relationships with politicians of all hues.

■

Affable and 'zinda dil', Vajpayee had a zest for the good things of life. He would enthusiastically tuck into samosas and jalebis and kebabs and loved his drink at night. He had once instructed Brajesh Mishra to inform journalist Rajdeep Sardesai where he could get the best steak in New York! On his various trips there, he explored the different global cuisines offered by New York city. He was particularly fond of Mexican food, according to his friend Mukund Modi, a paediatrician who had a practice in East Brooklyn, and had known Vajpayee since the 1970s.

Vajpayee really liked getting away from India. It enabled him to 'merge in the crowd', meet with friends he had made abroad, visit the supermarkets, wear his safari suits, and eat the food he liked. New York was a city he particularly enjoyed—he liked the 'high-end politics' at the UN, and 'the comings and goings of leaders from around the world.'

If poetry, and an appreciation of the finer things in life, shaped Vajpayee's personality, so did Rajkumari Kaul. They had studied at the Victoria College in Gwalior in 1941 and had been drawn to each other. Vajpayee 'hoped one day to marry her', wrote his biographer Sagarika Ghose, but her family did not approve—and then they lost touch. They reconnected after sixteen years. Vajpayee was a first time MP and had gone to speak at Delhi's Ramjas College. B. N. Kaul, a professor in the college, had come to hear Vajpayee along with his young wife, Rajkumari. The meeting 'rekindled the flame' between Vajpayee and Rajkumari. Subsequently, Rajkumari and her family moved in with Vajpayee. Mrs Kaul became an established presence in the Vajpayee household when he became prime minister—and was 'Kaul aunty' to the world. Karan Singh, who had never met her at Vajpayee's house, only at parties at the home of a common friend, remembered her as a 'remarkable woman'.

Vajpayee's association with Rajkumari was one of those undefined relationships which made the Sangh leadership very unhappy—and snide remarks would be made in RSS and BJP circles about it. Much as the RSS disapproved of Vajpayee's 'romancing, whisky-drinking, meat-eating ways', they were 'helpless against his political stardom'.

But, unlike many politicians who had relationships which were speculated about, Vajpayee, till her death, owned his relationship with Mrs Kaul publicly. And no one could question him about it. Vajpayee adopted Mrs Kaul's children as his own. He was particularly devoted to her daughter Namita, popularly known as Gunnu—and to Namita's daughter Niharika. Gunnu came to be known as his 'foster daughter', and her husband Ranjan Bhattacharya as his 'foster son-in-law'.

'The heart of the relationship between Rajkumari and Vajpayee,' political scientist Vinay Sitapati was to write in his book *Jugalbandi*, 'was intellectual'. She came from a Kashmiri Pandit family and was connected to the powerful 'Kashmiri mafia' in Delhi, comprising P. N. Haksar, R. N. Kao, P. N. Dhar, D. P. Dhar, T. N. Kaul, the 'panj pyaras' of the Delhi durbar under Indira Gandhi. Well-read and fluent in English, Mrs Kaul brought to the provincial politician Vajpayee a different world view of India. Friends recalled 'Rajkumari arguing with Vajpayee on politics'. Rajkumari Kaul was to become one of those influences in Vajpayee's life which was to make him a 'moderate'.

■

Vajpayee's brush with the RSS came early and it was to shape the politician in him. He started to attend the RSS shakhas while at school and became a vistarak (full-time worker) in 1946. By then, the RSS had grown into a well-trained force of 100,000 swayamsevaks. Vajpayee was drawn to the idea of Hindu nationalism, and impressed by the austere living of RSS's full-time pracharaks. On their part, the RSS pracharaks were enthused by his oratory and singled him out for attention.

In the early 1940s, Vajpayee had been attracted to the ideas of socialism and had also dabbled with communism in 1944, and joined the All India Students Federation (AISF). But, as India gained independence in 1947, convulsed as it was by the bloody Partition and Hindu–Muslim violence—by then he had done his MA and enrolled for a law degree—the twenty-three-year old Atal Bihari Vajpayee decided to become a full-time pracharak of the RSS.

The RSS asked him to be the joint editor of its newly launched magazine *Rashtradharma*, and in 1948 to become the editor of its new weekly *Panchjanya* in Lucknow. It is here that he worked closely with the legendary RSS organizer—the UP secretary of the RSS—Deen Dayal Upadhyaya who supported his rise. Vajpayee had moved to Delhi in 1950. When Syama Prasad Mookerjee launched the Bharatiya Jan Sangh on 21 October 1951, with the help of the RSS, it was only natural for the politically-inclined Vajpayee to join him.

Having been banned after Mahatma Gandhi's murder, the RSS now sought to create a political platform—the Bharatiya Jan Sangh. There was no looking back for Vajpayee after that.

■

Vajpayee first met Lal Krishna Advani in Kota. This was in 1952. Advani was also a RSS pracharak, having migrated to Rajasthan from Sindh in Pakistan. A few years later, in 1957, Deen Dayal Upadhyaya asked the English proficient Advani to assist Vajpayee with his parliamentary work. Vajpayee had just become an MP. Thus began a partnership which was to last half a century. Advani would later speak about 'the chaat we would go and have at Delhi's Bengali Market', or 'watch a film together to drown the sorrows of an electoral defeat'.

When the Congress lost the 1977 elections, and the Janata Party formed the government—the Bharatiya Jan Sangh had merged its identity in the Janata Party—Vajpayee became India's foreign minister. The socialists in the party demanded that the erstwhile Jan Sangh members should sever their ties with the RSS, now that they were members of a new party. Surprisingly, Vajpayee favoured the idea. He felt they should be loyal only to the Janata Party to which they now belonged—and end what had come to be called their 'dual membership' (of the RSS and the Janata Party). He also urged the RSS to open its doors to the Muslims. In a signed article in the *Indian Express* he wrote that the RSS should 'not seek a political role', and work only as a 'Hindu religious cum social cultural organisation'—and make it clear that by 'Hindu Rashtra it means the Indian nation which included non-Hindus as members'. His views did not enamour him to the RSS leadership. This was a time when Vajpayee was trying to secularize his image, and Indira Gandhi was projecting a 'Hindu' persona.

After the issue of 'dual membership' devoured the Janata government, and the party lost to Indira Gandhi in 1980, Vajpayee and Advani decided to launch a new party—the Bharatiya Janata Party (BJP)—in April 1980. Significantly, they chose not to revive the by now defunct Bharatiya Jan Sangh but to start on a clean slate. Vajpayee chose 'Gandhian Socialism' as his mantra for the newbie BJP. It was an attempt to identify the new party not so much with the Right or the Left but with Gandhi. Vajpayee did not opt for the doctrine of 'Integral Humanism' developed by RSS ideologue Deen Dayal Upadhyaya which was the official line of the Jan Sangh in 1965—it also rejected capitalism and socialism, and called for an indigenous model based on 'the values of sanatan dharma'.

But the BJP under Vajpayee's leadership did not take off. It was defeated in the polls it contested in 1981. It lost out to the Congress in its stronghold of Jammu in the 1983 elections held in Jammu and Kashmir. It had to bite the dust in the civic polls in Delhi in January of the same year. 'Atal Bihari atak gaya, kamal ka phool latak gaya (Atal Bihari has got stuck and the lotus has wilted as a result)', victorious Congress leaders raised full-throated slogans. With the Indira-Gandhi-led-Congress getting the better of the Vajpayee-helmed BJP in the election to the Metropolitan Council, the *New York Times* considered the local election significant enough to write about it.

In the 1984 general elections, the BJP was reduced to a mere 2 Lok Sabha seats—after Indira Gandhi's assassination. It was a tally lower than the 4 Lok Sabha seats its earlier avatar the Jan Sangh had won in the 1957 general elections, Vajpayee being 1 of the 4.

The second half of the 1980s was a particularly 'low' phase for Vajpayee. Backed by the RSS, Advani replaced him as party president in 1986. For the first time since he rose to prominence, Vajpayee was forced to the sidelines.

Advani now took centrestage. Till the end of the 1980s, he had seen himself as Vajpayee's number two. 'Advani will never be prime minister as long as Atalji is there,' Govindacharya, who often reflected Advani's thinking, had told me in 1989. 'That is the relationship they have.'

The relationship was to undergo a subtle change after Advani led the Rath Yatra from Somnath to Ayodhya in September 1990. Advani's popularity soared. Villagers would come upto the rath and touch it reverently. Women would perform aarti of the rath.

'I never realized that religiosity was so deep rooted in the lives of Indian people,' Advani remarked, 'it...made me realize that if I was to communicate the message of nationalism through the religious idiom, I would be able to transmit it more effectively.'

Till then, it was Vajpayee who had aroused the masses with his oratory. Now, for the first time, Advani began to be viewed as a leader who was hailed by the masses—and not just an efficient backroom organizer. Able to connect with the people during the yatra, he started to feel that he could be prime minister—it was a dream that was to remain unfulfilled. It was Vajpayee who went on to lead the country as prime minister.

Spanning more than half a century, their relationship as equals—even as they emerged as rivals—made Vajpayee and Advani the most distinctive political jodi of Indian politics—after Jawaharlal Nehru and Sardar Patel. Their relationship was to nosedive when Vajpayee did not take Advani into confidence, till the last moment, on his decision to greenlight the nuclear test, as we will see later in the chapter. Even as their rivalry sharpened when Vajpayee became prime minister, they never allowed their relationship to come to breaking point. Together they were to take their party to power, first in 1996, then in 1998, and again in 1999.

■

The most fascinating aspect of Vajpayee's political persona was the way he consciously carved out a moderate niche for himself in the RSS-backed, right-wing Bharatiya Jana Sangh and then in its subsequent avatar, the BJP. It was an image no other leader in the BJP could acquire—and it made him stand out.

As early as the 1950s, Vajpayee managed to leverage, though ever so subtly, Nehru's growing interest in him as a young MP—to acquire an image different from that of his party. Although he was a critic of the Nehruvian policy of non-alignment in the late 1950s, he became more Nehruvian in his approach during 1977–79 when he was foreign minister—even more so than many Congressmen. He had even called himself a 'champion of non-alignment' in one of his speeches in parliament.

In the process, he came to be seen as more 'moderate'—sometimes even left-of-centre—than his party, which was right wing, pro-market, and pro-America. Rajkumari Kaul, as we have seen, was an important liberalizing influence in Vajpayee's life, nudging him towards inclusive ideas.

In the early 1980s, Vajpayee had sensed the need to widen the BJP's base, which he felt should go beyond its forward caste Bania–Brahmin moorings. Months after the BJP's formation in April 1980, Chaudhury Radhakrishan, the first president of BJP in Punjab and a respected Gandhian, was escorting Vajpayee to address meetings in Punjab. On the way, they saw graffiti on a wall in big, bold letters, exhorting people to join the BJP, 'Bhajpa ke sadasya baniye (Become a member of the BJP)'. Reading it aloud slowly, Vajpayee punned on the word 'Baniye', and quipped, 'Yahi to dikkat hai, baniye hi baniye hain. Aur koi nahi (This is the real problem, it only adds upto the trading community of Banias, nobody else).'

His cryptic words had described the character of the party—an outfit of the upper castes. Vajpayee knew they had to cast the net wider and reach out to other communities. A few years later, Govindacharya called for 'social engineering' to bring the OBCs into the party fold. Later, as prime minister, Narendra Modi was to take backward class mobilization to a higher level, reaching out to the numerically large segment of the MBCs, as also the Dalits, in order to mainstream the party.

But for all his accommodative and easy-going ways, Vajpayee could show a steely side, which came to the fore when he was crossed. He made sure that K. N. Govindacharya never came back to the mainstream BJP because he had called Vajpayee the party's 'mukhota' (mask). (Govindacharya denied this and said that his words were taken out of context.) Vajpayee ensured that Govindacharya's political career was finished, even after the dust had settled on the episode.

Two other factors helped Vajpayee come across as a liberal compared to his party colleagues—his long innings as a member of parliament and a desire to improve India's relations with Pakistan. Though groomed as a pracharak in the RSS, it was parliamentary politics with its clash of ideas, an emphasis on dialogue—and the give and take it entailed—which made him more tolerant towards those across the political aisle. Vajpayee, who joined politics in 1951, was cast essentially in the mould of a parliamentarian—he was an MP for over fifty years, elected to the Lok Sabha ten times from different constituencies, and to the Rajya Sabha twice. He had also lost elections to the Lok Sabha five times. He had first won the Lok Sabha elections from Balrampur in 1957, lost from there in 1962, but determinedly wrested back the seat in 1967. Later, he was to represent Gwalior, New Delhi, Gandhinagar, and Lucknow.

When he was the head of his party in parliament from 1957–77, other BJP MPs like Balraj Madhok and Sundar Singh Bhandari would complain that with Vajpayee hogging all the limelight, they were not given the chance to speak in parliament.

Vajpayee loved being in parliament, and it was there that he struck many across-the-board friendships which continued till the end; he was particularly close to P. V. Narasimha Rao, a relationship which was, as we shall see, to influence his decision to go in for a nuclear test in May 1998.

Vajpayee's desire from the beginning to mend India's relations with Pakistan, without which the problem in Jammu and Kashmir could not be unknotted, also reinforced his image as a leader who could rise above his party.

He had started his political innings, as we have seen, under Jan

Sangh founder Syama Prasada Mookerji, who had been a member of the
Nehru cabinet, but had quit over differences with Nehru. Vajpayee had
accompanied Mookerji to Kashmir, to sit on a hunger strike in protest
against the special status granted to Jammu and Kashmir. 'Doh vidhan,
doh pradhan, doh nishan nahin chalega (Two constitutions, two prime
ministers, two flags, it will not do)'—was Mookerji's battle cry against
the state's separate constitution, prime minister, and flag.

Mookerji was arrested by Sheikh Abdullah. When he died in jail in
Kashmir on 23 June 1953, it affected Vajpayee deeply.

When he became foreign minister under Morarji Desai, Vajpayee went to
Pakistan in February 1978 on a visit he called 'historic'—and it liberalized
visa facilities. He was the first minister to visit both China and Pakistan
after the two countries had fought wars with India in 1962 and 1965. As
PM, he was to make efforts to better relations with Pakistan—he undertook
a bus yatra to Lahore in February 1999, and despite Pakistan retaliating
with an attack against India in Kargil, he invited Pakistan president General
Pervez Musharraf for summit level talks in Agra in July 2001 to resolve the
outstanding issues between the two countries. Though his initiative did not
succeed, it made him come across as a leader who was open-minded—and
wanted to improve relations with India's neighbours.

∎

Although Vajpayee was to dexterously position himself as a moderate
figure in the hardline Hindu party, he was known for his flip-flops on
the positions he took all through his political career. And what was
astonishing, he managed to get away with it. According to Sagarika Ghose,
'Vajpayee was a clever careerist.' He had learnt what 'strategic survival'
was all about; he could smell which way the wind was blowing—and
changed his stance accordingly. But he never strayed too far from the
mainstream party position.

His constantly changing position on important issues, like Ayodhya,
for instance, may explain why his views and actions on nuclear weapons
were so protean.

Ever since the BJP's Palampur convention in 1989, accepting the
construction of a Ram temple in Ayodhya as part of its agenda, Vajpayee
spoke in two voices. In April 1991, he said a temple was necessary 'to
restore national honour'. But, in December 1992, he called the demolition
of the Babri Masjid the 'saddest day of my life'. In May 1996, he almost
justified the demolition, saying that if religion-related problems were not
addressed, it would lead to another Ayodhya. But in December 1997,
he backtracked, declaring that Ayodhya 'will not be a major issue (for
the BJP)'. In February 1998, Vajpayee included the 'construction of a
Ram temple in Ayodhya' in the BJP's manifesto. But, in June 1998, he

gave an assurance that the judiciary 'will be unfettered in discharging its duty in the Ayodhya matter'. On 6 December 2000, he shocked many by saying that the Ayodhya agenda was still incomplete, calling the Ram Janmabhoomi movement an 'expression of national sentiment'—still to be fulfilled. He told reporters that the temple could be built on the disputed site and the mosque at another place in Ayodhya. But, four days later, on 10 December 2000, he backed down yet again and got the NDA to put out a resolution that the status quo in Ayodhya would be maintained till there was a judgment by the Supreme Court. On 1 August 2003, he went into reverse gear yet again; he promised to remove all obstacles for temple construction, urging opponents to 'come to their senses'.

There was perhaps no other well-known leader in India who would say something and then go back on it as frequently as did Vajpayee—despite this, he did not lose popular support. He had skilfully created the impression that he had to resort to doublespeak only to ward off pressure from the hardliners within the 'RSS family'. And that, at heart, he was really a liberal. That remained the popular perception about him. It made his appeal wider than the support base of the BJP.

Many of these flip-flops were dictated by political expediency—to avoid being cornered. Vajpayee's views were fashioned by a complex mix of influences. His politics was shaped by Hindu thought and philosophy, cultural inclinations, a respect for India's diversity and democracy, exposure to friendships formed across party lines—and a clarity about the role of the Opposition in a democracy. There was also a humanism born out of being a poet.

Som Pal, a V. P. Singh acolyte who joined the BJP, recalled an occasion when he was contesting against Ajit Singh from Baghpat in West UP. He was addressing a poll rally on 16 September 1999. L. K. Advani had come to campaign for him. Taking a swipe at Sonia Gandhi, who had been appointed president of the Congress, Som Pal thundered, 'Yeh apni party ka prashasan bhi gori chamrhi ke bina nahin chala sakte (These people cannot run even their party without a white person at the helm).' After the meeting, Advani complimented him for his 'jumla' (sentence); it was smart enough to be used elsewhere in their campaign. Nine days later, on 25 September, Vajpayee addressed a meeting at Baraut in the same constituency and Som Pal repeated the jumla. Vajpayee praised Som Pal's speech, but he also chided him, 'Never speak about anyone in that fashion again....You have a long innings in politics ahead of you.'

Vajpayee had spoken similarly to party colleague Sushma Swaraj when she had threatened to tonsure her hair, live on roasted chana, and sleep on the floor in protest against the move to make Sonia Gandhi prime minister in May 2004. 'What she is saying is not right,' he remarked unhappily to Som Pal who had gone to meet him. 'Who are we to decide who should be the leader of another party?'

Vajpayee's spontaneous response to the violence against the Sikhs in Delhi after Indira Gandhi's assasination on 31 October 1984 pointed to a leader who believed that India belonged to all Indians. Standing in his veranda, clad in a lungi, he had rushed out to save the Sikh taxi drivers outside his house as he saw smoke billowing from what used to be their taxi stand.

'Maaro mujhe maaro (Kill me, kill me),' he shouted. His colleague Jaswant Singh had to physically drag him back into the house at 6, Raisina Road. He kept saying agitatedly, 'Yeh toh nahi chalega, yeh toh nahin chalega (This can't be allowed, this can't be allowed).'

III

'What do you think, it's a gentlemanly game you are getting into?' Daniel Patrick Moynihan asked the young men sitting in front of him. At the time the US ambassador in India, he was speaking to foreign service trainees at an event organized by the Institute of Foreign Trade in New Delhi. This was one year before India tested its first nuclear device in 1974.

'It's a bloody game you are getting into,' he warned them brutally.

It was not just those men who heard Moynihan that afternoon who were to discover what the 'bloody game' was all about in the years that followed. It was also Indira Gandhi, first, and Atal Bihari Vajpayee later who were to realize what it meant to face stringent sanctions from the global community when they went in for nuclear tests in 1974 and 1998 respectively. Even the other prime ministers who did not test, but who kept India's nuclear programme going, had got a whiff of what the bloody game was all about.

The prime minister of India is the only person who is empowered to start a nuclear war. Or to respond to a nuclear strike by another country. A 'nuclear briefcase' goes with the PM wherever s/he goes; s/he has sole custody of it. It is a specially outfitted briefcase, to enable the PM to give the final go-ahead for the firing of a nuclear missile. But the PM's authorization does not automatically trigger the launch. The entire process is subjected to a series of checks and balances—as is the case in Western democracies with nuclear weapons, like the US—before such weapons blast off from their silos. In India, many of the protocols governing the launch of nuclear warheads are classified and not open to public scrutiny.

'No one sees these papers, not even the staff knows about it,' Inder Kumar Gujral, India's twelfth prime minister, told me. 'I had kept them at my residence under lock and key and the key never left my possession.

I got a room built that was safe.'

There is an unspoken convention that an outgoing prime minister briefs the incoming one on the country's nuclear preparedness—and hands over the 'nuclear briefcase'.

It is well known that Narasimha Rao followed the convention and briefed Vajpayee in 1996—urging him to test immediately. But the convention was not always followed. V. P. Singh said he was not briefed by Rajiv Gandhi. Chandra Shekhar complained he was not briefed by V. P. Singh. Narasimha Rao sent Naresh Chandra and A. P. J. Abdul Kalam to brief H. D. Deve Gowda. Deve Gowda said he didn't brief Gujral who 'knew everything' in any case, having been foreign minister under him. Gujral did brief Vajpayee in 1998 but he had anyway been brought up to date in 1996 by Narasimha Rao. It is not known whether Vajpayee briefed Manmohan Singh on the government's nuclear preparedness. Or for that matter if Manmohan Singh brought Narendra Modi upto date.

We have seen how Jawaharlal Nehru and Morarji Desai were philosophically opposed to the idea. Vajpayee made flip-flops at various stages of his political career. But, despite their opposition, neither Nehru nor Desai, nor any of the other prime ministers shut down India's strategic nuclear programme. Even Desai, who was the least enthusiastic about weaponization, kept the R&D and small table-top experiments going. As Gujral was to point out, 'Despite political differences, no prime minister acted in a manner which was less than responsible.'

•

India's first prime minister, Jawaharlal Nehru, was against the bomb. He saw himself as an apostle of peace, non-alignment, and nuclear disarmament in the world. But even at his most idealistic, Nehru was not totally against India building its infrastructure to exercise the nuclear option—should it be required. But he wanted to move cautiously. 'It is not generally known,' said the historian Sarvepalli Gopal, who was Nehru's biographer (and son of President Sarvepalli Radhakrishnan), that Nehru was 'against outlawing atomic weapons'.

His policy was not to use the bomb but to have it 'because we can't completely abjure from it'. Homi Jehangir Bhabha, who came to be known as the 'father of India's nuclear programme', wanted to ban the bomb, taking Nehru's public speeches seriously. Bhabha was the founding director of the Atomic Energy Establishment (AEET) at Trombay—it would later be named after him as the Bhabha Atomic Research Centre (BARC). He even wanted Nehru to amend the Constitution, and insert in it a section to outlaw the bomb. 'No, no,' Nehru told him. 'Don't go that far. This is a political decision not to be taken by nuclear scientists,' Nehru wrote on the relevant file.

There were reports at the time, which remained unconfirmed, that Nehru was going to collaborate with President Gamal Nasser of Egypt and President Josif Tito of Yugoslavia, two other important members of the non-aligned movement, to acquire the expertise to make the bomb so that 'they could form a powerful third force'. Yugoslavia had been able to make heavy water and the idea was for Egypt to make the plutonium with the help of the Soviet Union and Norway.

So, even as Nehru made speeches about why India should not make nuclear weapons, he wanted to ensure that India was not at a disadvantage or its security compromised. He sanctioned plans for Bhabha to set up the infrastructure capable of making nuclear weapons.

•

Lal Bahadur Shastri, Nehru's successor, also wanted atomic energy to be used for peaceful purposes. His view began to undergo a change after India's war with China in 1962 and with Pakistan in 1965. It was then that he began to feel that India should be able to exercise the nuclear option if needed. With a nuclear deterrent, India could better secure its borders. Accordingly, a plutonium reprocessing plant was started in 1965 in Trombay. On 5 April 1965, he sanctioned the setting up of a nuclear design group, Study of Nuclear Explosions for Peaceful Purposes (SNEPP). It could acquire and develop the technology and infrastructure necessary to explode a nuclear device. The group was headed by nuclear physicist Raja Ramanna. The SNEPP was the first step in the journey to make the bomb.

Weeks before he died, Shastri told Homi Bhabha to speed up plans for a 'Peaceful Nuclear Explosion' (PNE), to be conducted for non-military purposes. But Shastri died soon thereafter—on 11 January 1966. It was left to Indira Gandhi, who succeeded him, to initiate a PNE eight years later.

•

On a hot and muggy day in September 1972, Indira Gandhi took the first decisive step towards making India a nuclear-weapon state. She was the chief guest at the annual convocation ceremony of IIT, Bombay, at its prestigious Powai campus. She had sent word to Raja Ramanna to meet her there. He was director of BARC. Homi Sethna, the chair of the Atomic Energy Commission, was present. Sethna was also the chairman of IIT, Bombay.

After the convocation, Sethna escorted the prime minister and Raja Ramanna to his office. It was the prime minister's idea to use his room for the meeting—she wanted to meet the nuclear scientists in a place that wouldn't attract attention. If she had summoned them to the Prime Minister's Office, it would have raised questions. That day, she gave both of them the 'go-ahead' to put together a nuclear device—and get ready to test it. Ramanna was asked to oversee the bomb project—the design of the device would be completed under his guidance.

But they were told to await word from her on when to make it operational. She knew it would take approximately eighteen months to pull everything together for the test. 'Ramanna had told me this himself (later) in 1978,' K. Subrahmanyam revealed.

In April 1974, Indira Gandhi called a meeting of her core team of bureaucrats and scientists who were helping her with the nuclear programme. They included her principal secretary, P. N. Dhar; trusted advisor, P. N. Haksar (who had quit as principal secretary in 1971 but had continued to advise her), AEC chairman Homi Sethna, BARC director Raja Ramanna, army chief General Gopal Gurunath Bewoor, and Basanti Dulal Nagchaudhuri, who was DRDO chief and senior advisor to the defence minister. She discussed with them the pros and cons of 'going nuclear'. Interestingly, Indira Gandhi kept her political colleagues out of the loop so as to prevent information from leaking out—Vajpayee was to do the same twenty-four years later, when he decided to test in May 1998. Indira Gandhi did not even take Defence Minister Jagjivan Ram into confidence. Nor did she inform External Affairs Minister Sardar Swaran Singh. They were told only forty-eight hours before the test took place. Vajpayee was also to inform his defence minister and external affairs minister only two days in advance.

P. N. Dhar, who was an economist, was against the test—he was apprehensive about the sanctions that would be imposed by the US. This, he warned Indira Gandhi, was inevitable after the friendship treaty India had signed in 1971 with the USSR. At the time, the two superpowers were still locked in the Cold War. However, the scientists were raring to test. Political strategist that he was, Haksar wanted the test to take place closer to elections due in 1976; he felt Indira Gandhi may be able to harvest it electorally.

At the core group meeting, Indira Gandhi just listened—and doodled on the pad before her. She did not rebut any member of her team. After they had all had their say, she just made a brief announcement—that she would be going ahead with the test.

On 18 May 1974, at 8.05 a.m., India conducted a 'peaceful implosion', a nuclear test carried out underground. The test was code-named Smiling Buddha; it was conducted on Buddha Purnima. The announcement about it was low-key and routine. All India Radio aired it in one of its news bulletins. When asked about it, the prime minister played down its importance. The government described the device as a 'peaceful nuclear explosive'.

But Indira Gandhi had chosen the timing of the test very carefully. In 1974, she hoped to take advantage of a provision in the international Non-Proliferation Treaty (NPT), which allowed nations to conduct nuclear tests for peaceful purposes.

This was why the test was described as a 'Peaceful Nuclear Explosion'. She had hoped it might dilute the world's condemnation of it—which was bound to come. But neither the Americans nor the Russians bought India's explanation that the explosion was meant for peaceful purposes. Nor did the Pakistanis.

Indira Gandhi had taken the decision to test the bomb in 1972 itself. Having won the war with Pakistan in 1971 and created the new nation of Bangladesh, she had been hailed as 'Durga'. But by 1973–74, the euphoria over Bangladesh began to dissipate. The economy was in trouble, burdened by the cost of war and the influx of refugees from the new nation. Then came a drought. Oil prices were also rising. By 1974, the domestic situation deteriorated rapidly. The movement led by Jayaprakash Narayan against corruption and Congress's misrule gathered momentum; a railwaymen's strike led by the firebrand socialist leader George Fernandes virtually brought the country to a standstill. Strategic considerations apart, Indira Gandhi had to do something bold to seize the political initiative again. She would have calculated that if she tested, she would be hailed again as a strong leader—though she knew that sanctions would follow.

Indira Gandhi went in for the explosion. Almost instantaneously sanctions were imposed by the industrialized world, led by the US.

The Nuclear Suppliers Group (NSG), which was formed soon after India's test, restricted exports of key technology and materials to it and other countries who had not signed the NPT. The sanctions came as a huge 'setback' to India's nuclear programme, particularly 'for building power reactors'. They were so stringent that in the mid-1980s, the US even refused to sell India a super computer for weather-tracking purposes! It was categorized as dual-use technology, which could be used for creating a weapon. India was treated like a rogue nation even though there was nothing illegal about what it had done. It had simply exercised its right as an independent nation by refusing to sign the NPT, which was essentially a private treaty between the signatory nations. Additionally, PNEs were permitted even under the NPT.

There were other consequences of the 1974 test. The Chinese stepped up their help to Pakistan. They did not want India's influence to grow in the region—and came out in support of Pakistan. After Zulfikar Ali Bhutto's death in 1979, the Pakistan army took over the nuclear weapons programme. Less than a decade later, it was rumoured that Pakistan had the bomb. The US chose to look the other way. It needed Pakistan's help with its misadventure in Afghanistan. Because of the Pakistan factor, even Morarji Desai, who was dead against nuclear weapons, had not dared to mothball the nuclear programme in 1979 (as we saw at the beginning of the chapter).

In 1980, a triumphant Indira Gandhi returned to power, and she decided to go in for another test. The scientists knew that the rudimentary PNE of 1974 had to be improved. She brought Raja Ramanna, who had been transferred out by Morarji Desai, back as director of BARC in January 1981. He immediately suggested that India test the two weapon designs that had been developed in the years that the Congress had been out of power. By mid-1982, the shafts in which the explosion would take place had been dug and readied in Pokhran in Rajasthan. But, at the last moment, Indira lost her nerve. According to R. Venkataraman, who was defence minister at the time, she changed her mind from one day to the next. American satellites had picked up suspicious signs of an imminent nuclear test. These photographs were shown by US under secretary of state for political affairs, Lawrence Eagleburger, to India's foreign secretary, M. K. Rasgotra. Rasgotra had gone to meet him in Washington DC in May 1982, just before Indira Gandhi's visit to the US.

Indira Gandhi cried off because she knew the American response to a test would be punitive—and she also knew she had to contend with a difficult economic situation in the country. She was no longer the confident leader she had been in 1974—having lost her younger son Sanjay in a plane crash. She could also not forget that two years after the 1974 test, Henry Kissinger, the powerful US secretary of state, had warned one of her aides, 'Don't do it again. This time we will destroy you.' Within hours of giving the go-ahead, she asked 'RV' to call up V. S. Arunachalam who had taken over as director general of DRDO, and Ramanna—and tell them to call it off.

'Why?' a disappointed Ramanna asked her.

'We don't want our skulls to be broken,' she told him.

■

Rajiv Gandhi was the first prime minister to specifically authorize the assembly of nuclear weapons in 1989.

K. Santhanam explained the difference between the weapons Rajiv Gandhi had in the mind and the device his mother, Indira Gandhi, had tested. 'The PNE in 1974 was only a device. A weapon on the other hand is optimized for vector delivery.... A device to become a nuclear bomb for delivery has to be weaponized. This involves a great deal of complicated engineering. It has to be qualified for flight and must withstand the changes in temperature, environment, and low pressure when you go high, for it is a near vacuum 40–50 kilometres up there.'

Rajiv Gandhi's instructions, according to Santhanam, were to 'keep working', but 'every milestone has to be cleared by me'. He warned that there would be serious problems if the information leaked. 'Rajiv was persuaded by evidence that Pakistan was doing naughty things when he gave the go-ahead in '89.'

Rajiv Gandhi had started off as an advocate of nuclear disarmament. In May 1984, India had teamed up with five other nations—Sweden, Argentina, Tanzania, Mexico, and Greece—to initiate a six-nation, five-continent global initiative on disarmament. Days after he took over as PM, Rajiv hosted the first summit in Delhi in January 1985. Till 1988, he kept pursuing disarmament as a goal.

But he kept his options open. Like his predecessors, he too did not close down the country's nuclear weapons programme. It would come up for discussion at a small group he had especially set up in 1985. The idea was to review all strategic issues facing the country, of which the nuclear issue was one. Called the Interdisciplinary Group, it comprised Rajiv Gandhi, Arun Singh, MoS Defence, who was also Rajiv's friend, two Congress chief ministers, K. Karunakaran of Kerala and Hiteshwar Saikia of Assam, the Atomic Energy chief, Raja Ramanna, and Chief Economic Advisor Bimal Jalan. The cabinet secretary, the chairman of the Chiefs of Staff Committee, the two Intelligence chiefs, and the head of the Joint Intelligence Committee were also members of the committee. K. Subrahmanyam was the only member from outside the government.

At one of the monthly meetings of the group, Subrahmanyam was holding forth on why India 'should go nuclear'. When he finished, Rajiv Gandhi turned to him and asked, 'You've not dealt with any of the reasons why we should not sign the NPT.'

'You'll have to give me another session for that,' Subrahmanyam replied. At the next session he went over why India should not sign the NPT. At another meeting, Rajiv Gandhi said to Ramanna, 'Why don't you produce an alternative NPT which would be non-discriminatory?' Yet, even though Rajiv was pursuing disarmament as a goal, he allowed the team to continue the research. According to Subrahmanyam, 'he did not scrimp on money'.

Sometime in August 1985, Ramanna and Subrahmanyam proposed to Rajiv Gandhi that India should offer Pakistan the guarantee of no first use. And that both sides would sign an agreement not to attack each other's nuclear facilities. Rajiv told them to talk to 'my chaps'—Cabinet Secretary P. K. Kaul and Gopi Arora. Both shot down the idea.

'We can't do it,' they said.

'Why not?' Subrahmanyam asked.

'We would be admitting that either we have the nuclear weapons or we are working to make them.... We can't recommend this to the PM.'

Rajiv Gandhi also asked them to consult Narasimha Rao who was defence minister at the time. Rao told Ramanna and Subrahmanyam, 'Out of the two proposals you put forward, the one on non-attack is OK, but I don't agree with the one on no-first-use.'

'Why?' they asked him.

'You know our young PM is going up and down the country talking about the Pakistani bomb,' Rao told them. 'If now you offer a no-first-use, the Pakistanis will say "India has become afraid and is doing it out of fear".'

At one of the meetings he had with the prime minister—this was in October 1985—Subrahmanyam told Rajiv Gandhi, 'You can't go on postponing a decision on this (going nuclear). If you go on delaying, the defence expenditure will go through the roof. You shouldn't believe what people are telling you, that the US is putting pressure on Pakistan. You have no choice but to go for a weapons' program.'

Rajiv decided to go around the room—and asked for everyone's opinion. Most people sat on the fence. Bimal Jalan said a definite 'no'. 'We can't afford it,' he was clear, 'the economy would be ruined.' It so happened that the army chief, General Arun Shridhar Vaidya, was not there that day. He was represented by the navy chief, R. H. Tahiliani. Tahiliani played it safe. 'We will study this and tell you at our next meeting.' That very night, Ramanna and Subrahmanyam went to see Tahiliani at the Navy House in New Delhi. Tahiliani told them, 'I'm going to have a committee to examine the cost of this.'

'Before Vaidya comes back, you should, as the officiating chairman, appoint the committee,' they suggested, 'because we want the committee to be headed by Sundarji.'

General K. Sundarji was then the vice chief of the Armed Forces. 'He's the only fellow who knows the subject,' they said. Tahiliani appointed a committee headed by General Sundarji. It comprised Admiral K. K. Nayar, from the Navy, Air Marshal Johnny Green from the Air Force and the nuclear scientists A. P. J. Abdul Kalam and Rajagopala Chidambaram. They produced a report within ten days. It projected that in seven years' time India could have a minimum nuclear deterrent of a hundred missiles and warheads at the cost of ₹7,000 crores. The concept of a 'nuclear deterrent' first surfaced in this report.

The twenty-page-report was shown to Arun Singh, Ramanna, V. S. Arunachalam, who was the scientific advisor to the defence minister, and to Subrahmanyam. General Sundarji had personally typed it. He said he gave the only copy he had to Rajiv Gandhi.

It was at this stage that the idea of weaponization got a fillip from an unexpected quarter. In the last week of October 1985, Rajiv Gandhi met US President Ronald Reagan in the US. The meeting took place at the Waldorf Astoria in New York. The UN General Assembly was in session. Rajiv and Reagan had struck up a rapport when the Indian prime minister had visited the US on a state visit in June that year. The US hoped that India, under its young prime minister, would adopt a more 'balanced posture in relation with the United States and the Soviet Union'.

When they met in October 1985, Reagan told Rajiv Gandhi, 'Pakistan has already made a bomb.' When Rajiv started talking about disarmament, the US president cut him short, 'Don't talk theory, think of your own protection.' The diplomat S. K. Singh told me this. He had been the Indian ambassador to Vienna (1979–82) and privy to the details of the country's strategic weapons programme. He had also been on the board of governors of the international nuclear regulatory authority, the IAEA, headquartered in Vienna, and had closely tracked international opinion on the development of nuclear weapons. Singh was also in the loop when it came to Pakistan. In 1985 he was recalled from Vienna and posted to Pakistan as high commissioner.

S. K. Singh told me it was at this time that Rajiv Gandhi had given instructions to move towards weaponization. 'I was privy to the instructions that Rajiv gave, that nothing would be put on paper and that we would move full scale on weapons acquisition.'

This far, a lot of the information about Pakistan's nuclear weapons programme was unconfirmed. But after Reagan's words to Rajiv—that Pakistan already had a bomb—a worried PM asked S. K. Singh to confirm whatever he could about Pakistan's enriched uranium facility at Kahuta, 22 kilometres away from Islamabad.

'Rajiv had given me instructions to set up an intelligence-sharing device on top of the roof of my personal home. Two of Pakistan's listening posts were connected to me directly. The result was that I got information directly from the posts in (the) North West Frontier and South East Frontier.' He added, 'We had to provide proof to Britain and America (of what Pakistan was up to).'

One of the things he was asked to do, to get the hard information that was needed, was to set up a roadside barber shop near Kahuta. The idea was to obtain the hair of workers at the facility. 'Hair is a sensitive area of (the) human anatomy, which captures and conveys microns and atoms.' Singh said to me, 'Through the hair that was cut of the chaprasis, etc., who worked at Kahuta, we could make out that enriched uranium (was) being used there.... It confirmed what Reagan had told Rajiv.'

It had become clear to India that by 1987 Pakistan 'had the bomb,' said C. Raja Mohan. 'The question for India then was, what do you do?' India's resolve to accelerate the nuclear weapons programme came in early 1987. Pakistan threatened to go nuclear on India during Operation Brasstacks, a large-scale Indian military war-gaming exercise that took place near the border with Pakistan. Spooked by Brasstacks, the junior minister in the Pakistani defence ministry, Zain Noorani (at the time the president of Pakistan, Zia ul Haq, was also the defence minister) summoned the Indian high commissioner, S. K. Singh, to his office. Singh was called at 10 p.m. He was made to wait for two hours before Noorani called him in. He told Singh that he was coming straight from President Zia.

The Pakistan president wanted to convey a message to the government of India: if Indian troops infringed Pakistan's sovereignty and territorial integrity, Pakistan was in a position to inflict 'unacceptable damage' on India. (That was the phraseology employed for the use of nuclear force, S. K. Singh told me.) Pakistan later claimed that it was its nuclear threat which prevented India from invading it.

Presented with 'incontrovertible evidence' that Pakistan had the bomb in February 1987, Rajiv Gandhi decided to speed up India's nuclear weapons programme. He was anyway disenchanted with his initiative on disarmament, which had turned out to be a damp squib at the UN in July 1988.

On Saturday 18 March 1989, Rajiv formally gave the go-ahead for making weapons in sufficient numbers and perfecting the delivery systems. He gave the orders to Naresh Chandra, his defence secretary. That morning he was attending an air show at the Tilpat range, watching an impressive flypast, along with his wife Sonia. Naresh Chandra was also at the event, sitting right behind him.

As the show ended, Rajiv asked to have a word with his defence secretary. 'Rajiv said to me,' Naresh Chandra revealed to me years later, 'Yeh aapko karna hai (You have to do this).' The prime minister authorized Chandra to oversee the nuclear and DRDO programmes, and the readying of the missiles—and become the prime minister's principal troubleshooter in everything to do with the nuclear question.

It was around 1988–89 that Rajiv started to think about putting a command and control system in place. T. N. Seshan, the cabinet secretary, was 'entrusted...with finding an outer location from where the whole government could function in the event of a nuclear strike,' S. K. Singh said. 'Of course, the government would not be elaborate but there would be a team to look after defence, finance, external affairs, home, and the prime ministerial business.... It had to be underground...connected with radio and TV and new technology and communications and where intelligence could be fed and where it would be able to ensure that the public morale was kept up.... Gopi Arora, Seshan, and I were tasked to put the command and control system in place.... We were considering three places for the alternative government but they were not finalized. They were not near Delhi and the architectural plans for the underground site were made.'

Rajiv Gandhi kept every move of his on the nuclear issue a closely guarded secret. Only a handful of people were directly involved. Even strategic guru K. Subrahmanyam, who was deeply embedded in the system, did not get a whiff of it.

'I was told formally and officially about India's bomb (only) in July 1990,' Subrahmanyam said.

By then V. P. Singh had taken over as prime minister.

■

In July 1990, seven months after he took over as PM, V. P. Singh constituted a high-powered committee to oversee all matters relating to the nuclear bomb 'now that we had got it'.

It comprised Arun Singh, General Sundarji, who had by now retired as chief of army staff, but whose expertise on nuclear weapons was known, and K. Subrahmanyam and K. Santhanam.

'It was a secret committee,' K. Subrahmanyam said. It met half a dozen times. During Rajiv Gandhi's time, they discussed 'things like, suppose the capital was attacked, and the political leadership was wiped out, who would then push the button, all that was worked out.'

Said Santhanam, secretary to the committee: 'The idea was to flesh out the nuclear doctrine, which could be translated into operational details.' Like the blue book, he said, which laid down the standard operating procedure on the prime minister's security, the committee began working on a red book which would lay down what would be done in case of a nuclear war. The group tried to visualize the different scenarios that could emerge if a nuclear strike decimated the country's leadership—and discussed the three chains of command—political, technical, and administrative—which would have to kick in, if such an eventuality were to arise.

When the administrative chain of command was being discussed, the meeting was also attended by the cabinet secretary, and the secretaries for defence, home and foreign affairs.

'Gentlemen, we are here to discuss who will survive us,' said defence secretary N. N. Vohra jocularly to lighten the mood. 'It was hilarious,' recalled Santhanam afterwards. For implicit in Vohra's statement was the belief 'that if the IAS (Indian Administrative Service) does not survive, nothing survives.'

V. P. Singh was quick to understand the need for the strategic weapons programme to go into an overdrive. He had been defence minister during Operation Brasstacks, when Pakistan had threatened India with a nuclear attack in 1987. He knew that both Pakistan and China, India's less than friendly neighbours, possessed nuclear arms. India couldn't afford to be caught napping.

However, given the frosty relations between him and his predecessor, Rajiv Gandhi who had not updated V. P. Singh, some of the concerned nuclear scientists decided to get president R. Venkataraman to bring the prime minister up to date. It was only after this that V. P. Singh knew exactly how advanced the country's nuclear programme was. Dr V. S. Arunachalam, defence scientific advisor, had told the prime minister: 'Within a week to ten days we can deliver (a bomb), if need be....'

V. P. Singh was to say later, 'We had achieved it to the nanosecond.... We had reports that Pakistan was very near assembling one...(and that) it had the capability to do so.... My concern was that we should not be lagging behind. It would make Pakistan bolder on Kashmir....'

'Generally I'd known as defence minister (in 1987),' V. P. Singh continued, 'that our capability and stocks were there. And our nuclear explosion capacity was there.... When I became PM, all this had to be expedited. As PM, an emphasis was laid on...having an operational bomb.'

But in the end V. P. Singh decided not to go for a test. The border with Pakistan was 'in a critical condition'; Pakistani troops had 'dug in on our border after the exercises they had done'. Benazir Bhutto, the Pakistani prime minister, had talked about a 1,000-year war with India. Moreover, V. P. Singh explained, 'The explosion would have annoyed the US and China, when we needed them both.' Then he added wistfully, 'Decisions are not taken in a vacuum.'

■

When Chandra Shekhar took over from V. P. Singh as prime minister, he called up S. K. Singh, whom he knew well—and asked him to come over. Singh had resigned soon after VP took over.

Chandra Shekhar asked 'SK' to explain to him the command and control structure.

'You are the prime minister. Has no one briefed you?' an astonished Singh asked the new prime minister.

'No, no one briefed me,' Chandra Shekhar sounded annoyed, alluding to this act of omission by his predecessor V. P. Singh. There was no love lost between the two.

'If Parliament, South, and North Block are wiped out, where will the government run from? And at what stage would the different organs of the government and their nodal personnel have to be conveyed there?' S. K. Singh asked the PM.

'I don't know,' Chandra Shekhar said.

Then Singh said, tongue-in-cheek, 'Then you and ı are in the same boat.' Chandra Shekhar laughed.

Though opposed to the bomb right from the beginning, Chandra Shekhar did not stop the programme; he signed the bills to release the money for the ongoing nuclear programme.

It was only when Chandra Shekhar's successor, P. V. Narasimha Rao, took charge that India came closest to testing nuclear weapons. But Rao backed off at the last moment. However, he was the one who influenced Atal Bihari Vajpayee to test in 1998. And he readied India for testing, bringing the situation to a T-3 stage (three days before the explosion).

Even as we now look at how and why Vajpayee exercised the nuclear option, the story is not complete without delving into Rao's part in it. I will deal more comprehensively with the critical role Rao played in Vajpayee's decision-making in the section below. But, before that, a quick review of how H. D. Deve Gowda and I. K. Gujral, who followed Narasimha Rao, and preceded Vajpayee as prime minister, dealt with the nuclear issue during their brief premierships in 1996–97.

■

It was during Deve Gowda's stewardship of the country that a shift of policy took place. In February 1996, three months before Deve Gowda took over, the Narasimha Rao government had suddenly declared that nuclear weapons were not necessary for India's security. This was soon after Rao had decided against testing. But under Deve Gowda, India declared for the first time that it considered nuclear weapons 'a security issue'—and that the nuclear option was not just for peaceful purposes. This was declared at a conference on disarmament in Geneva on 20 June 1996.

It was I. K. Gujral, foreign minister under Deve Gowda, who was behind the policy change. 'It was Gujral who did it,' K. Subrahmanyam revealed, 'and the shift in policy took place under him.'

The scientists recalled their first meeting with Deve Gowda—it was nothing to rave about. 'When we went to meet Deve Gowda after he took over as PM, that is Kalam, Chidambaram, and I, he kept falling off to sleep,' recounted Santhanam. 'His head would fall.' At this meeting, Gowda postponed the decision to test. Three weeks later, he had another meeting with the scientists. At this meeting, he told them categorically, 'No, no. Not now.' But Deve Gowda did contemplate going in for a test at the tail end of his premiership as a ploy to deal with his domestic woes—and deflect the political pressure he was facing from the Congress, which supported his government. Finally, he decided against it.

I. K. Gujral was an avowed peacenik. He focussed on improving relations with India's neighbours in what came to be known as the Gujral Doctrine. What is not known is that he too had seriously considered a nuclear test in the final months of his prime ministership—after the Congress had withdrawn support to his government in 1997. It was while he was still in power for five months as the caretaker prime minister that Gujral considered the possibility.

'It was at that time that Gujral suddenly seriously considered whether he should go in for a test,' recalled N. N. Vohra who was his principal secretary.

'First, you have to know what stage we are at,' Vohra advised his boss. At the time, the principal secretary to the PM also functioned as the security advisor, Vohra said. He arranged for Gujral to meet with the scientists.

A. P. J. Abdul Kalam, then secretary DRDO and chief scientific advisor to the defence minister, was in Hyderabad at that time. On 2 and 3 January 1998, Gujral had to inaugurate the National Science Congress in

Hyderabad—and stayed with the governor, Krishan Kant.

'In his programme, I showed a private lunch between 1 and 2 p.m. and a time for rest between 2 and 5 p.m.,' Vohra said. The local politicians were told that the PM's appointments would start only after 5 p.m.

'At 1.45 we took Gujral to the Integrated Missile Development Centre (of the DRDO). The only two people who knew (about this) were Dr Kalam and K. Santhanam.' The meeting went on for three hours.

In the middle of January, 'Gujral sahib decided to go in for a test,' Vohra said. 'I had told him he should not do it, for the process for the elections had started... (But) from everything he said, I knew he'd made up his mind. He would make observations like who needed to be in the picture, who gets to know, etc.' The scientists were also meeting him directly, especially physicist R. Chidambaram, who was chairman of the Atomic Energy Commission, and was 'keen to get a validation of the researches done by his boys'.

Worried about the timing of the tests, Vohra then suggested that the prime minister talk to the president. It was President K. R. Narayanan who finally dissuaded Gujral from going ahead. It was after his meeting with Narayanan, that 'he stopped making those references' to testing a nuclear device.

■

It is interesting to note that all the prime ministers bypassed the established chain of command while deciding on the nuclear question; they ignored the defence minister, and engaged directly with the scientists. Indira Gandhi had kept her defence minister, Jagjivan Ram out of the loop, P. V. Narasimha Rao chose Naresh Chandra to be a bridge between him and the scientists, A. B. Vajpayee confided in Brajesh Mishra. The scientists involved also did not adhere to the bureaucratic hierarchies.

As Naresh Chandra explained in later years: 'The only way we could do all this was not to be part of the system.'

'There is no record of any kind of people who were really doing this stuff,' Naresh Chandra said. 'There were no urgent milestones or annual reports or targets to be met or to show time-bound results. The idea was to be well prepared and keep advancing in bits and pieces.' He then added, 'The scientific community is highly reliable, with committed people...and that helped.'

Then Chandra laughed, 'Even my brother Gary (Girish Saksena) did not know what Naresh was up to.'

IV

Before moving on to how the wily Narasimha Rao and the flip-flopping Vajpayee dealt with the nuclear question, a quick look at the international nuclear regulatory order the prime ministers had to navigate—and the strictures India had to deal with after 1974.

The story began with the bombing of Hiroshima and Nagasaki by the US with nuclear weapons in August 1945—towards the end of World War II. The terrifying consequences of the nuclear holocaust that killed 210,000 people and caused unimaginable devastation and suffering made the US determined to prevent any other nation from developing nuclear weapons. For it could jeopardize the US's security, and its survival.

The US prodded the newly formed UN General Assembly to develop measures to deal with the nuclear threat. The UNGA adopted a resolution to this effect on 24 January 1946 in London. This led to the formation of the UN Atomic Energy Commission, which aimed to regulate the use of atomic energy for peaceful purposes—and the elimination of atomic weapons which could be used for mass destruction.

However, despite the efforts of the US and the UN, they were unable to prevent other nations from acquiring nuclear weapons. The USSR tested a nuclear weapon in 1949, the UK in 1950, France in 1958, and China in 1964. (Today, there are nine nuclear-weapon states. Besides those who tested before 1968, the other four are India, Pakistan, Israel, and North Korea.)

In 1968, the US efforts to check proliferation finally had some traction. The world's first nuclear-weapon states—the US, USSR, UK, France, China— crafted the NPT—to prevent the spread of nuclear weapons, promote the peaceful use of nuclear energy, and generally move towards nuclear disarmament. The five nations with nuclear weapons had decided amongst themselves that 1 January 1968 would be the cut-off date for any other country which wished to acquire nuclear weapons to do so. Those who possessed nuclear weapons before that date would be called the NWS and those who did not have such weapons would be non-nuclear-weapons state (NNWS). NNWS which signed the NPT would have to refrain from developing or acquiring nuclear weapons in the future. And they would have to put all their civil nuclear facilities under the safeguards of the International Atomic Energy Authority (IAEA), a UN body, founded in July 1957.

As it took years, if not decades, to develop a viable nuclear weapons programme through above-board means, besides the five nuclear-haves, the nuclear option would really be unavailable to every other nation in the world. The NPT divided the world into nuclear 'haves' (NWS) and 'have-nots' (NNWS) 'legally' (i.e., through voluntarily contracted treaty obligations.) It was opened up for signature to the world's nations in 1968 and came into force in 1970. '[A]n international instrument, brazenly discriminatory in design, aimed at disarming the unarmed,' senior diplomat Saurabh Kumar said, citing the words of India's NPT negotiator Vishnu Trivedi. (Kumar was India's Ambassador to the IAEA at the time of the NSG meeting drama in Vienna in 2008.) India found the NPT 'discriminatory', and refused to sign it. Along with India, Pakistan and Israel also refused to sign the NPT.

For India, signing the NPT would have meant a huge handicap vis-à-vis China in hard, strategic terms. As China had tested its nuclear weapon in 1964, it was designated as NWS. If India had signed the NPT, it would have had to do so as a NNWS. This would have meant giving up its option to go for nuclear weapons for all time to come, no matter what the future brought.

After Vajpayee's party, the Bharatiya Jan Sangh, made a strong case for India going nuclear after China tested in 1964, the government decided on a two-pronged approach. The first was to step up diplomatic efforts to convince the international community to move towards universal disarmament, which both Jawaharlal Nehru and Rajiv Gandhi tried, with next to no success. The second was to acquire nuclear weapons capability. With India's efforts to promote universal disarmament going nowhere, exploding a nuclear device was the only response available to the country, given its nuclear-armed and belligerent neighbour, China. The test in 1974 was, in some ways, a delayed response to China's going nuclear in 1964.

India went about preparing for its nuclear explosion, putting in place a policy that was careful not to contravene the provisions of the NPT—so that it could take the moral high ground globally and yet ready itself to exercise its nuclear option, which it did in 1974.

Its scientific and nuclear establishment mastered the nuclear fuel cycle, which included the reprocessing of spent fuel from its civil reactors, which yielded plutonium, the raw material used for making a nuclear weapon more efficient—and compact—than enriched uranium. This apparent dual use of plutonium left India open to criticism suggesting that it was developing nuclear capability covertly—which was discounted. India also developed the capability to build—and operate—nuclear power plants and for conducting nuclear explosions—which were allowed by the NPT (though India had not signed the treaty) provided they were for peaceful uses of nuclear energy.

•

We will now fast forward to the 1990s. A new treaty to regulate nuclear weapons threatened to come into existence. The NPT had been extended periodically, every time its term was about to expire. Finally, it was extended indefinitely in 1995.

Soon after, in 1996, the Comprehensive Test Ban Treaty (CTBT) was adopted by the United Nations General Assembly on 10 September—another part of the international regulatory structure to prevent more nations from acquiring nuclear weapons. The CTBT went a step further than the Partial Test Ban Treaty (PTBT) of 1963. It banned nuclear tests, both for peaceful and military purposes, in 'all' surroundings.

The looming deadline of the CTBT was the immediate trigger for India to consider testing in 1994–95. When India was considering going for a test during P. V. Narasimha Rao's premiership, or when Rao urged Vajpayee to do it during his thirteen days as prime minister in May 1996, or when Vajpayee finally tested in May 1998, the decision was governed by the fact that the CTBT was about to come into effect. India's worry was that if it signed the CTBT, it would foreclose its nuclear option forever. If it refused to sign it, it would become a pariah in the global community—although Arundhati Ghosh, India's envoy to the UN in Geneva, had stated categorically in 1996, 'India will not sign this unequal treaty, not now, nor later.' But then, India did not want to be cornered. It was not known at the time that the US senate would not ratify the CTBT in 1999. As a result, the treaty was put on the back-burner. The CTBT could not come into force unless it was ratified by forty-four specific nations, which had nuclear power and research reactors (and this had to be confirmed by the IAEA). Eight of these countries did not ratify it. Three of them—India, Pakistan, and North Korea—did not sign it in the first place. And five nations which signed it did not ratify it—these were Egypt, China, Iran, Israel, and the US. And that is where it remains, though it surfaces from time to time in international fora.

V

'It was in 1994 that PV raised the matter with me first (about testing),' revealed Naresh Chandra, who was a senior advisor in the PMO at the time. Chandra would go on to become Rao's pointsperson on the nuclear question. Rao knew how closely Chandra had been involved with the nuclear issue towards the end of Rajiv Gandhi's tenure.

Rao, Chandra said, had been 'toying with the idea' since 1993. They—Chandra and the scientists—would assemble in the PM's Office at RCR. Rao would hear everybody out. Then he would put off a decision by saying, 'Baat kareinge fursat se (We will talk about it at leisure).'

He had got detailed studies done about the consequences of nuclear testing—especially its economic and security fallout. He got a lot of verbiage put out under the aegis of the National Security Council.

Unlike Rajiv Gandhi, who was direct in his style, Rao was more elliptical in his approach. He would ask, 'Kya karna hai (What is to be done)?' Or, 'Kya preparedness hai (What is the preparedness)?' His officials had to read between the lines to figure out what was on his mind.

One day, Rao asked Chandra: 'Do you know that they (Pakistan) can strike back in eight hours?' He was referring to the time Pakistan would take to hit back, if there was a nuclear strike by India. He asked Chandra to assess how long 'we would take' (to respond), if Pakistan struck first.

'I went through the whole process,' Chandra recalled. Such as, who had the key at the Atomic Energy Commission, the time it would take to coordinate between the government organizations, which held the fissionable material, and the DRDO which held the device. Then there was the question of charging the warhead, mating it with the delivery system, loading it, and revving it up.

Chandra came back to Rao with the information that the reaction time 'was probably around thirty-six hours'.

Rao's query showed Chandra that the PM was now seriously considering the possibility of testing. The AEC and the DRDO, which reported directly to the PM, were given adequate funds to get ready. Rao had asked Chandra to deal with the funds.

'Twice I got...a bulk of money' for the nuclear programme, which could not be shown in the books. Rao had told him to go to his finance minister Manmohan Singh. Manmohan Singh, according to Chandra, released the money for the programme year after year though no record of it was kept.

It was in mid-1994 that Chandra suggested to Rao that the Air Force be brought on board—and the defence secretary be briefed.

Cautious to a fault, Rao gave the go-ahead for Chandra to meet Defence Secretary K. A. Nambiar—but not in India. He suggested they meet in Paris. Nambiar was anyway going to Paris to attend a meeting. A team from the Defence Ministry was also going to be in the French capital attending an air show. The Naresh–Nambiar meeting would hardly attract attention, Rao reckoned. Chandra, who also had to go to the US to attend meetings in Washington and New York, could fly from there to Paris.

'I took the Concorde from New York to Paris,' Chandra recalled.

Chandra and Nambiar decided to meet at the art gallery at the Louvre. When Nambiar arrived at the world's largest art museum, he found Chandra pacing up and down restlessly. 'I was in the Louvre, hanging around, ostensibly checking on what paintings to buy for the Government of India, which we could not buy,' Chandra remarked, his face creasing into laughter.

One could only imagine the two men, the serious, poker-faced, low profile, South Indian Nambiar, and the tall and portly Chandra standing in front of the portrait of the *Mona Lisa*, admiring her enigmatic smile, while Chandra briefed the defence secretary on the latest developments in India's nuclear programme. It was inconceivable that any surveillance agency would have picked up their lip movements!

Narasimha Rao, who was in the US in May 1994 to meet President Bill Clinton, insisted that Chandra fly back to New York and report to him immediately. The Americans said afterwards that Rao had promised

Clinton that he would not conduct a nuclear test. But the canny Rao was keeping his options open.

Rao became serious about testing only in mid-1995. It was the indefinite extension of the NPT which convinced him to go ahead.

The NPT was given infinite life on 11 May 1995.

India was also riled that the US had introduced the Hank Brown Amendment, which had allowed the US a one-time transfer of military hardware worth $368 million to Pakistan. This undid the Pressler Law, under which the US had cut off aid to Pakistan and held up arms worth $1.4 billion that had been paid for. India protested. But the message coming through from the US was clear—that time was running out for India.

Though the officials had been holding meetings, with or without the prime minister till then, Rao, according to Naresh Chandra, had 'just been procrastinating'.

The first serious meeting that Rao had held with Chandra and the scientists was in Hyderabad in end-1994. It was the day Rao's grand-daughter got married.

It was a secret meeting, held in a sealed room at the DRDO office just outside of Hyderabad. It took place after the wedding ceremonies were over. Rao had invited Chandra to the wedding. The scientists—A. P. J. Abdul Kalam and R. Chidambaram—had gone to Hyderabad ostensibly for 'work'.

At the meeting, they discussed the state of preparedness of the nuclear establishment, and how many days it would take to test after a decision was taken. The scientists wanted the timetable to be advanced.

'We briefed PV completely on...the pitch, the likely consequences,' Chandra recounted.

Rao listened intently. From time to time, he would say 'achcha'. Even if he agreed on a point, the cautious Rao would still say, 'OK, we have to take a decision on this.' Though it was a close-knit group, and the deliberations confidential, 'he would put things in a way that nobody could allege (afterwards) that he was actively encouraging the blast programme.'

'I travelled back to Hyderabad with him by helicopter,' Chandra said, 'and we talked more.'

When Chandra questioned him about the timing of the final order, Rao said, 'Haan vaapis chal kar baat karenge (We will talk when we return [to Delhi]).' But that day, Rao did give the team the clearance to 'get prepared'—though still short of a final order to test. Rao asked Chandra to prepare a paper on it. 'I wrote this paper,' Chandra said.

Yet, Chandra and the scientists saw the meeting as a step forward. For now they had to await only the penultimate nod.

In the second half of 1995, three of the scientists—Kalam, Chidambaram, and Santhanam—went to Ahmedabad. By then, Chandra had been anointed the governor of Gujarat (on 1 July, 1995). 'We met at the Plasma Centre near Ahmedabad and not in the Raj Bhavan, so as not to invite any suspicion.'

It was around this time that Rao passed a written order—and this 'was the nearest he came to giving up his caution'—to set up a group with Naresh Chandra as its chairman to take a view on the nuclear programme.

'I remember words like "strategic weapons" were included in the order,' Naresh Chandra recalled, 'the intent was clear'.

'There was only one copy of it and that was with Kalam. He showed it to me. I told him to put it in the safe. That order was for our safety.'

■

In December 1995, P. V. Narasimha Rao authorized A. P. J. Abdul Kalam to go ahead, and allowed the timeline to come down to T-3. This meant he could do the test in three days.

'By December 1995, he (Rao) had made up his mind to put oxygen into the option,' said K. Santhanam. 'The T-3 was in December, but the (final) timing was the prerogative of the government....'

'It was Kalam who phoned me in Ahmedabad to tell me that PV had given the T-3 order,' Naresh Chandra revealed. 'When you get to T-3, you might as well do it,' Chandra said. 'I had told Kalam, Santhanam, and Chidambaram that you cannot hide T-3. It cannot be kept a secret for very long after that.'

'That was the closest Rao came to testing.'

But, in mid-December 1995 the American satellites picked up activity at the nuclear testing site in Pokhran (Rajasthan). The 'very sharp' US ambassador to India Frank Wisner had just returned to Delhi after a visit back home to Washington DC—and he came armed with photographs of the preparation underway in Pokhran. Cabling work had been going on—under the garb of fencing. India held that what was going on was routine maintenance work.

'Wisner came to me first,' Chandra recalled. He showed Chandra the photographs which showed suspicious movement in Pokhran. 'Maine bhaga diya (I shooed him off),' he said airily.

But, according to sources close to the nuclear establishment, Chandra, who had been trained, from his SDM (sub-divisional magistrate) days in Rajasthan, to read documents and memorize them, was sharp enough to pick up the details on the photos that Wisner showed him.

The photographs carried on the edges the date and timing of the satellite when it had gone over Pokhran. The two sets of satellite photos indicated the time taken by the American satellite to return to Pokhran. This information was passed onto the scientists. The scientists did their calculations. It was based on the movement of the earth and movement of the satellite. They worked out the time that the satellite would require to come back for its next round. This, they figured out, would be the time they would have to complete the work on the ground.

'Naresh Chandra...had told my father (Jaswant Singh) stories about how he had got the better of the Americans,' recalled Manvendra Singh. But he never spoke about them publicly.

After seeing Chandra, Wisner went to see Pranab Mukherjee, who was the External Affairs minister at the time. 'Mukherjee did not know (anything).' Soon after, when presspersons questioned Mukherjee about it, he told them, 'We have no such plans (to test).'

Wisner then went to A. N. Verma, Rao's principal secretary. Verma went 'ballistic' when he learnt about it. According to Naresh Chandra, 'Verma was not in the loop.'

Having drawn a blank, Wisner lined up a call from Clinton to Rao to make the government's assurances 'pukka' that there would be no testing.

'I was summoned (to Delhi) at short notice from Ahmedabad,' reminisced Chandra. 'I came immediately and went straight to South Block.'

No one was at the PMO except Deepak Bhojwani, the prime minister's private secretary who was 'in the loop'.

'What's the brief?' Chandra asked Bhojwani.

'You are the brief,' he replied.

He asked Chandra to prepare what Rao would say. 'Give the PM a statement and the questions and answers that will come (from the US president).'

'We got a PA with a top security clearance and attempted a formulation on what Rao should say to Clinton.'

On the other side, Bill Clinton, a staunch believer in non-proliferation, also had his brief. He too read from the prepared text. That is the way the US system worked.

Clinton started off with 'Mr PM....' and started reading, 'we are thankful to your foreign minister's statement that there would be no testing.'

Rao told Clinton. 'I have also seen press reports to that effect. Leave it to me, I will make it very clear shortly.'

While Rao was agreeing with Mukherjee's statement about no test on the anvil, he was also saying that there was something to be clarified—and thereby keeping his options open.

Clinton then asked Rao point blank whether India was going to test.

Rao said, 'No, no. Things are being exaggerated. It was a routine maintenance of existing facilities. I will make a statement soon.' He also talked about acting 'responsibly', which was neither here nor there.

Clinton 'kept praising India's stand and (kept saying) that he understood India's security concerns over non-proliferation and CTBT'.

Rao was very happy with the conversation.

'Galti ho gayi, Gujarat bhej diya (I made a mistake, I sent you to

Gujarat),' he said to Chandra, 'Washington jana thaa. Jayenge na (I should have sent you to Washington. You will go, won't you)?'

'I used to often wonder,' Naresh Chandra remarked years later, 'whether I had been sent as governor to Gujarat as a cover', so as to deflect attention from the possibility of testing.

Rao sent Naresh Chandra as India's Ambassador to Washington DC in 1996. The announcement was made in January of that year. Chandra was preparing to leave for the US when Rao's second conversation took place with Clinton in March 1996.

Rao's first conversation with Clinton had shown that his nuclear options were open. The second call was a clear sign that he had given up on it.

'The second conversation was desultory,' Chandra said, 'it was not good....The PM was off balance.'

'Clinton talked about CTBT. He talked about the non-proliferation regime not working, the pressure the regime was under, the fallout of testing by China.....

'We had prepared a different brief. The conversation became progressively difficult.

'At the end of it PV was saying, "No, sir. I get it, sir".'

'You either say sir in anger,' Chandra said, 'or to somebody senior.'

Or you say it tongue-in-cheek.

■

Why did P. V. Narasimha Rao get cold feet? The question has exercised scientists, policymakers, and the strategic community for over a quarter century.

Rao, as we saw earlier in the book, was given to having arguments with himself. He would internally debate an issue and see both points of view to such an extent that no clear picture emerged. Then he would decide to further mull over the issue—yet again putting off the decision. Having said that, when Rao wanted something done, he could be very decisive.

Clearly, in December 1995, Rao concluded that the balance of advantage lay in deferring the tests. Once he had come to that decision, it was immaterial whether he was caught out by the Americans or he allowed himself to be caught.

Some believe that the Chanakya of Indian politics had made a calculated decision to get caught out. He was quite capable of setting the stage for the Americans to trip him up. He would then get an alibi for not testing and have a legitimate explanation for the scientists and the strategic community—that was all keyed up and raring to go.

Curiously, the tests were being planned in the month of December when the weather is very clear in the Rajasthan desert, increasing the chances of being found out. Rao, who never fully showed his cards even with his aides or close associates and imparted information on a need-to-know basis, had surprisingly included a large number of people in the decision to test. The normally super-cautious Rao had also ordered several studies to be done, increasing the chances of word leaking out—and it did. At the T-3 stage, it was anyway very difficult to keep things under wraps. When Vajpayee was to test in 1998, as we will see, it was really only Brajesh Mishra—and the scientists—who knew the date and time. Others came on board only hours before D-Day and H-Hour.

In 1995, Rao was vulnerable both on the international front as also within his own party. He knew the US would slap legally mandated sanctions against India. So would the European capitals. Economically, India was coming out of a crisis, but the situation was still 'delicate'.

Finance Secretary Montek Singh Ahluwalia was asked to prepare a financial paper on the economic implications. Ahluwalia warned that the economy had not yet recovered from the crisis and the impact could be substantial. He was 'pessimistic' about testing.

Though the economy had picked up, Rao worried about what would happen were the US to impose an oil embargo on India; it would put pressure on the oil-producing Gulf states to follow suit. This would send the price of food items, fertilizers, pharmaceuticals spiralling, just months before elections were due in April–May 1996. He would have also worried about how Pakistan would respond to a test by India. For, though the situation in Punjab had improved, Kashmir was still unsettled. And China remained a wild card. Rao may well have calculated that he would need a lead time of eighteen to twenty-four months before the polls to contain the fallout. In December 1995, he had only five months.

What's more, Rao was really not sure of how his own party would respond. Sonia Gandhi was turning against him; she had for the first time publicly criticized him for soft-pedalling Rajiv Gandhi's assassination probe. Congress rebels like Arjun Singh had already formed a separate party, Congress (Tiwari), which was on the attack. If the situation were to become difficult after sanctions, which it could, his party could always dump him and go for another prime-ministerial face. As it is, he was not a charismatic figure—nor a mass leader.

The BJP, he knew, would support testing. But it too would not want him to run away with the credit on an issue it considered its own. It would have criticized Rao's handling of the sanctions and the economic distress that would flow from it.

In the end, Rao was not very convinced by the argument that testing would make him the strong leader India craved. Or that it would be a panacea for his woes. Indira Gandhi had tested in 1974 when she too was beleaguered. Within weeks, the gains had petered out. The nuclear blast, he suspected, might give him some temporary advantage. But it was

THE PEACEABLE PRIME MINISTER WHO ROARED

unlikely to create a national euphoria and win him the election.

'(A. N.) Verma played on PV's fears,' Chandra said, 'he was a shrewd politician and kept talking about a debacle (Rao might face in the impending elections in 1996).'

Apparently, Verma told Rao that if he went ahead with the test, 'toh America peeche parh jayega (America will get after you)'. And that 'the Americans would then back the BJP'.

As the year 1995 was ending, the choice staring Rao was between a nuclear explosion and going the 'hawala' way, making the issue of corruption his main poll plank in mid-1996.

Verma pointed Rao in the direction of the hawala scam. The scam involved politicians, including senior Congress leaders, for the alleged payment of black money using four hawala brokers. In 1991, a Kashmiri militant's arrest had led to raids and the discovery of foreign currency and diaries which contained details of payments made to leading politicians who were identified by their initials. The court had been monitoring the hawala probe.

Verma argued that Rao's image would get refurbished—and he would be seen as a leader who was cleaning up Indian politics. Among his team, the CBI Chief Vijay Rama Rao pushed the 'hawala line'; he was a man in A. N. Verma's confidence, according to Naresh Chandra. His MoS, PMO Bhuvnesh Chaturvedi argued for a nuclear test instead. So did Naresh Chandra.

Rao made a miscalculation by opting to take the hawala route. With the kind of scams that had dogged his premiership—the Harshad Mehta stock scam, sugar scandal, fertilizer and environment scams—his platform was far from clean. A fight against corruption was hardly likely to cut ice with people.

'Hawala was the biggest folly of his life,' said Naresh Chandra, who knew him more than most.

■

'The best window of opportunity (for testing) was 1994–95,' Naresh Chandra concluded. 'Par mauke par kuchh nahin kiya (He lost a golden opportunity).'

In 1994 and early 1995, the US, China, and France had also conducted tests. '(For) it was becoming some kind of a norm (then),' said Santhanam. '...If everyone was letting off crackers, it would go to page seven and not (remain on) page one for very long. Besides, there was no treaty we would have violated if we had tested. We had not signed the NPT, we were opposed to the CTBT (which was on the anvil). And conducting of tests on the ground was permissible.'

Years later when Naresh Chandra was in Washington as India's ambassador, people in the American establishment would ask him, 'Why didn't you do it when France and China did it in 1994?' 'Oos time queue maen nikal jaate (We would have escaped relatively unscathed then).'

Rao was optimistic that he would come back to power—and be able to test. He was hoping to get enough seats in 1996 to cobble together a coalition government. He did not want an absolute majority in the house, which he felt would be a risky proposition for him. For then, he would not be able to withstand the pressure to install Sonia Gandhi as the party leader. In 1995, she was showing signs of getting ready for an active political role. Rao had a better chance of becoming prime minister again only if the Congress was in a minority—and could lead a coalition government.

Having been the foreign minister, he knew only too well India's compulsions to test. It could not indefinitely hold back on the CTBT and become an outcast in the global community. He knew the political importance of possessing a nuclear deterrent.

Interestingly enough, though Rao cried off in December 1995, he continued to give the impression that he was keeping his options open—even though to go in for a test soon after being found out by the Americans, and deferring the decision for that reason, would have been difficult. But he continued to signal the scientific community that he had not foreclosed the possibility—throughout the first four months of 1996. He asked them to keep everything in a state of readiness. He even told Kalam this two days before the election results to be prepared. Once he realized he had lost the election, he took back his order.

'PV missed his tryst with destiny,' Naresh Chandra was to say years later. Rao's loss was to become Atal Bihari Vajpayee's gain.

VI

'We will fight the next election under the leadership of...Atal Bihari Vajpayee,' thundered L. K. Advani. He uttered those words in the middle of a speech in Mumbai in November 1995—six months before the 1996 general elections. 'And he will be our candidate for prime minister.' There was a stunned silence in the audience. For it was Advani who was seen as the BJP's rising star, and expected to be the party's candidate for the prime ministership.

Advani had given no warning of the words he was about to deliver. He was speaking on the second day of the 'mahaadhiveshan' (big meeting) in Mumbai held from 11 to 13 November 1995. One hundred thousand delegates were attending the gathering.

It was after Vajpayee had finished speaking on 12 May 1995 that Advani rose as the BJP president to make the last speech of the day. 'For many years, not only our party workers but also the common people have been chanting the slogan, "Agli baari Atal Bihari".' Here Advani paused. 'I am confident,' he said, 'that the BJP will form the next government under

Atalji's prime ministership.' There was a momentary silence. And then the audience broke into thunderous applause.

A smiling Advani turned to go back to his chair. But before he could take his seat, Vajpayee got up and took the mike. 'The BJP will win the election,' he declared, 'and we will form the government, and Advaniji will be prime minister.'

'Ghoshna ho chuki hai (I have already made the announcement),' Advani interjected going back to the mike. 'Toh main bhi ghoshna karta hoon (Then I am also making the announcement),' Vajpayee said, 'ki pradhan mantri (that the prime minister....)'

Advani was back at the mike, and completed the sentence for him, 'Atalji hi banaenge (Atalji will be prime minister).'

More applause.

Vajpayee turned to Advani, 'What did you announce? Kum se kum mujh se toh baat karte (You should have at least talked to me).'

Advani retorted, 'Kya aap maante agar humne aap se poocha hota (Would you have agreed if I had asked you)?' The good-natured jousting hid something that was more sharp-edged. For Advani and Vajpayee had been locked in a veiled struggle for the leadership of the party.

That evening, an astonished Govindacharya rushed into Advani's hotel room. 'How could you make such an announcement?' he asked his mentor agitatedly.

'Maine kiya jo mujhe theek laga,' Advani replied matter-of-factly. (I did what I felt was right.)

'If I had consulted (others), it would not have happened,' L. K. Advani said to me when I asked him about his surprise announcement. This was uncharacteristic of a leader who was seen as a man of the organization—and a believer in taking decisions after extensive consultations with party colleagues.

The timing of Advani's announcement was curious. For it was his political star, and not Vajpayee's, which had been on the rise after the Rath Yatra he had led in 1990. It was Advani's leadership which had taken the party to an unforeseen tally of 120 Lok Sabha seats in the 1991 elections. It had altered the balance of power between him and 'Atalji'. Till then, Vajpayee was seen as the top leader of the BJP, and Advani a number two.

Many suspected that, in 1995, Advani had made a virtue of a necessity. He may have declared Vajpayee as the party's prime ministerial candidate, having got wind that P. V. Narasimha Rao was going to hasten the filing of chargesheets in the hawala case against politicians, including him—which might have thrown him out of the prime-ministerial race.

In January 1996, two months after his momentous announcement in Mumbai, Advani was chargesheeted in the case. He promptly resigned as an MP—and said he would not contest elections till he was acquitted.

He did not fight the 1996 polls and returned to parliament only in 1998 after his name was cleared—the Supreme Court did not find substance in the charges against Advani and other senior politicians who were charged.

Advani believed that Narasimha Rao had played a part in speeding up the chargesheet against him and others in order to help Vajpayee. It had opened the way for Vajpayee to become the BJP's prime ministerial candidate in the 1996 general election.

'PV helped Vajpayee by pursuing the hawala case,' Bhuvnesh Chaturvedi admitted to me.

'The case was being pursued under the supervision of the Supreme Court, but PV knew it would help (Vajpayee).' Chaturvedi continued: 'Advani asked me at a function, "Aapne mujhe kisi ke kehne par prosecute kiya thaa (Did you prosecute me at the instance of someone else)?" He was referring to Vajpayee, though he did not take his name.'

'Kisi ke kehne par nahin (No, we did not act at the instance of someone else),' Chaturvedi told Advani, 'woh toh Supreme Court ka adesh thaa (we were acting under the directions of the Supreme Court).' Advani was not convinced. He asked Rao the same question, when he met him at another function. 'PV denied it flatly.'

It is one of those conjectures of history that if the hawala probe had not been speeded up towards the end of 1995, would Advani have announced Vajpayee as the BJP's face for the 1996 election?

∎

In 1996, it was 'Abki baari Atal Bihari' and his charisma resonated with the voters. The twist in the fortunes of the BJP's top two leaders ensured that Vajpayee led the party's campaign in the 1996 election. Unlike other politicians who took part in more than a dozen rallies in a day the laid-back Vajpayee would address no more than four to five meetings. His day would begin in a leisurely way and campaigning would end soon after sundown. He loved to relax over a drink in the evening. He and Advani had agreed that Hindutva would be only one of the poll issues.

On 16 May 1996, the seventy-one-year-old Vajpayee was sworn in as the tenth prime minister of India. The BJP emerged as the single largest party in the Lok Sabha, notching up 161 Lok Sabha seats, 41 seats more than in 1991. Its three allies, the Shiv Sena, Haryana Vikas Party, and the Samata Party got 26 seats between them, taking the alliance's total tally up to 187. However, this was still well short of the 273 seats that were needed to have a majority in the Lok Sabha.

It was not clear who would support the party to form the government. Nor had Vajpayee staked his claim to form the government.

But in a move that took many by surprise, President Shankar Dayal Sharma invited him to form the new government, as the leader of the single largest party—but without ensuring how he would prove his majority in the house.

'Vajpayee was himself surprised that he had been called,' revealed Bhuvnesh Chaturvedi, who was a friend of Vajpayee and had talked to him. Some suspected that the invitation to Vajpayee to form the government was a khichdi cooked up by the president and the outgoing PM Rao together.

For some hours, an uncertain Vajpayee was not sure he should accept the president's invitation, Chaturvedi said. For he was far from sure that he would be able to get the support of other parties or of the independents.

He had reason to be cautious; the demolition of the Babri Masjid in 1992, had made many parties wary of the BJP—they treated it as a political untouchable. Vajpayee was given two weeks by the president to prove his majority. Immediately, he put senior party leaders, Bhairon Singh Shekhawat, Pramod Mahajan, and Jaswant Singh, to work. They reached out to the regional outfits.

■

Two days after Vajpayee took over as prime minister, Narasimha Rao phoned him. He wanted to call on the new PM. According to convention, the outgoing prime minister called on his successor. But Vajpayee insisted that he would visit Rao instead. It was in deference to a friendship which went back decades. Vajpayee went across to RCR. Rao had not yet moved out of the PM House. The meeting took place on 18 May 1996—and it was to have a far-reaching consequence. Rao briefed his successor on the country's nuclear preparedness, the urgent need to weaponize, the reasons he had been unable to test, and particularly the pitfalls Vajpayee must avoid. It was after this meeting that Vajpayee decided to 'go nuclear'.

Rao tried to persuade Vajpayee to go in for a nuclear test immediately—even before undertaking a majority test. He argued that if Vajpayee's government did not last, the next in line to form the government would be the United Front (UF) government; I. K. Gujral was expected to be foreign minister if the UF came to power and would be certain to oppose testing.

K. Subrahmanyam, who was told about the meeting by Rao himself, confirmed to me what Rao had told him about the meeting.

In 1999, Subrahmanyam was heading the Kargil Review committee, set up by the Vajpayee government (on 29 July 1999)—three days after the end of the Kargil War. Tasked to look into intelligence failures and 'make recommendations for the future', Subrahmanyam asked to see Narasimha Rao, along with the other committee members.

'You come and see me on your own first,' a chary Rao sent him word. Subrahmanyam went to see him alone. 'We want to talk to you about your Kashmir policy', Subrahmanyam told Rao. 'And about your nuclear policy.'

'I will talk to you on Kashmir,' Rao said, 'but I will not talk to you on the nuclear policy.'

'Why?'

Rao: 'No, I will not do that because the country was misled by people. And I had to set things right. Our people had been told that we were ahead of Pakistan on the nuclear programme....'

Subrahmanyam: 'Don't you owe it to the people to set the record straight?'

'No,' Rao said. 'I don't owe anything to anyone, except to one person. And that duty I have already discharged.'

'Who was that person?' Subrahmanyam was mystified.

Rao replied, 'Atalji, who took over from me. I told him everything.'

Later, Vajpayee was to give full credit to Narasimha Rao for getting everything ready to test. 'Rao told me the bomb was ready. I only exploded it,' an emotional Vajpayee said soon after Rao's death on 23 December 2004.

In conversations, Rao did not hide the fact that he had advised Vajpayee to test during his thirteen-day first term, even though he did not have a majority in parliament, 'I told Vajpayee to do it,' Rao told Naresh Chandra. 'Humne toh Atalji ko kaha thaa kar jaate, jo ayenge woh dekhenge (I had told Atalji to do it, whoever comes after you will handle the fallout),' Rao told Chandra.

In his meeting with Vajpayee on 18 May 1996, Rao appealed to the new prime minister at two levels. The first was 'emotional'. A test, he felt, would generate national pride. The second reason was related to security—if India did not test immediately, before the stringent provisions of the CTBT came into force, it would not be able to do so in the future. It is another matter that the CTBT did not go through. But Rao did not know this in 1996 when he was briefing Vajpayee.

Rao also warned Vajpayee not to make the mistake he had made in December 1995 when American satellites had caught the activity underway at Pokhran. K. Santhanam had explained how the Americans had caught wind of what was going on: 'The shafts had been sealed (from) 1983 onwards. Once the shafts began to be renovated, and water pumped out, the water was on the sand and the American satellite picked it up...it (the contaminated water) used to be red like sambar.'

Vajpayee listened intently to everything that Rao told him that day.

■

The Vajpayee–Rao relationship was unique in independent India's history. Though they belonged to opposing parties, and subscribed to different ideologies, they had a regard for each other, a trust they did not enjoy with their own party colleagues.

They went back a long way—and had come to each other's rescue at critical moments in their careers. As mentioned in Chapter 4, many also saw 'a Brahminical bond' between the two—both were Brahmins—and had respect for each other's intellect.

Rao and Vajpayee first got to know each other in 1977 when Vajpayee was External Affairs minister in the Janata Party regime. Rao then was a first time MP from Hanamkonda in Andhra Pradesh. When Rao became foreign minister in 1980, he would often consult Vajpayee. He had retained most of Vajpayee's staff.

Later, their common interest in Hindi literature—and in the Urdu language—drew them closer. Vajpayee's use of Urdu in his poems made them even more evocative. Rao, being from Hyderabad, appreciated Urdu. Vajpayee loved ghazals and one of his favourites, according to Karan Singh, and one he sometimes liked to sing was: 'Ranjishe hee sahi dil dukhane ke liye aa, Aa phir se mujhe chorhne ke liye aa.' Karan Singh had contested against Vajpayee from Lucknow but neither had attacked the other during the poll campaign.

In November 1995, Rao launched Vajpayee's book of poems, Meri Ikyavan Kavitayen. Many of us from the media attended the function at the FICCI auditorium in Delhi for the sheer magic only Vajpayee could weave with words. That evening was memorable for just two words uttered by two political maestros representing two mainline parties of India—the two words were 'guru' and 'gurughantal'.

While launching Vajpayee's book, Rao remarked, 'Atalji mere haal kaal ke guru rahe hain (Atalji has been my teacher in my bad times).'

In his reply, Vajpayee described the prime minister as a 'gurughantal' (guru of gurus). In fact, they would usually address each other as guruji. Not unexpectedly, their words made headlines the next morning.

In 1994, Vajpayee agreed to lead the Indian delegation to Geneva at the instance of PM Narasimha Rao. Pakistan had sponsored a resolution at the United Nations Human Rights Commission (UNHRC) censuring India's record on human rights in Jammu and Kashmir. It was an unusual move to let an Opposition leader head the official delegation to the UN and put the MoS, Foreign Affairs—Salman Khurshid—under him. But it signalled to India's neighbours that the government and Opposition in the country were moving in step on Kashmir. Thanks to the efforts of the delegation, the resolution was defeated.

Rao helped Vajpayee on numerous occasions. In October 1995, they were together in New York to attend a meeting of the United Nations General Assembly. 'Vajpayee was sitting between PV and me,' recalled Bhuvnesh Chaturvedi. 'He turned to me and whispered, "I want to talk to PV."' Chaturvedi told him, 'Come to the hotel in the evening.'

Vajpayee: 'Evening is no time to talk.'

'Then talk to him now'.

Vajpayee leaned across and said to Rao, 'Kalyan Singh humare bahut virodh maen hai, unko nahi banna chahiye (Kalyan Singh has been opposing me, he should not take over (as CM of UP).'

'Hmm, hmm', Rao first made non-committal sounds. Then he added, 'Dekhte hain, governor se baat karenge (Let's see, we will talk to the governor).'

When they returned to the hotel in the evening, Chaturvedi asked Rao, 'Karna hai unka kya (Do we help him with it)?'

'Haan keh do Voraji ko (Yes, tell Voraji to do what's necessary),' Rao replied.

Motilal Vora was the governor of Uttar Pradesh, and a quintessential 'loyalist'. Chaturvedi phoned Vora from New York, 'The PM is saying that Kalyan Singh should not become the CM.'

'But,' Vora said, 'he is sitting here in the outside room staking his claim to form the government.'

Chaturvedi was firm, 'He must not become CM.'

Vora: 'OK.'

In October 1995, Lucknow was convulsed by a political upheaval. On 17 October, the BJP had withdrawn support to the coalition government led by Mayawati of the Bahujan Samaj Party. She had been installed as chief minister on 3 June that year, with the BJP's support, after her alliance with Mulayam Singh Yadav of the Samajwadi Party came apart. Kalyan Singh, who was a protégé of L. K. Advani, had all along been opposed to supporting Mayawati. Finally, he had his way and the BJP withdrew support to her. It seemed that he might be able to cobble together a government. He claimed the support of a majority of Mayawati's fifty-nine MLAs. Vajpayee had got word of the goings-on in Lucknow. The installation of Kalyan Singh as the CM in Lucknow would mean power moving into the hands of Advani. This could create problems for Vajpayee, for he regarded UP his turf. It was vital that he be seen as the unchallenged leader from the state in the BJP—if he were to become prime minister. A majority of the country's prime ministers had roots in UP—Jawaharlal Nehru, Lal Bahadur Shastri, Indira Gandhi, Charan Singh, Rajiv Gandhi, V. P. Singh, Chandra Shekhar. Rao understood the importance of UP for Vajpayee—and decided to help his friend.

When Rao returned from New York on 26 October 1995, Motilal Vora was waiting for him in the technical area of Palam airport. It was unusual for a governor to receive the prime minister—and that too on his return from a foreign trip. The next night, on 27 October 1995, the UP assembly was dissolved and President's Rule imposed in the state. Vora did not invite Kalyan Singh to form the government.

Long after he ceased to be governor, I had asked Vora about the episode. He just smiled sagely.

■

While Rao helped Vajpayee by vigorously pursuing the hawala case, Vajpayee, too, came to Rao's rescue when he was in trouble. 'Vajpayee helped in getting Narasimha Rao acquitted (in the JMM case),' Bhuvnesh Chaturvedi told me.

In September 2000, the trial court had sentenced Rao—and Buta Singh—to three years' imprisonment in the Jharkhand Mukti Morcha case. On 29 September 2000, special judge Ajit Bharihoke had held the two guilty of bribing the JMM MPs to defeat the no-confidence motion against Rao's minority government (on 28 July, 1993).

Rao sought Vajpayee's help to close the case. Chaturvedi told me that he was the go-between.

'I went to see Atalji.' Chaturvedi recalled. 'He called Brajesh into the room. He told him, "Isko khatam keejiye".'

On 16 March 2002, the Delhi High Court was to acquit Rao and Buta Singh in the JMM bribery case, in which the two had been sentenced to three years imprisonment. Justice R. S. Sodhi of the Delhi High Court observed that the only witness, JMM MP Shailendra Mahto (he had turned approver), was a 'self confessed liar'—and set aside the 2000 trial court judgment against Rao and Buta Singh. Rao's lawyer R. K. Anand had argued that the entire prosecution case was based on just one witness who had contradicted himself a number of times. Four JMM MPs had allegedly been paid bribes.

'These are political decisions, the rest (the legal aspect) is mere detail that is worked out,' Chaturvedi added.

I. K. Gujral, by then a former PM himself, had also conveyed to Vajpayee that 'it isn't good to have prime ministers and former PMs proceeded against.' Krishan Kant, then vice president, had also spoken to Vajpayee to help Rao.

It was significant that the Vajpayee government decided not to appeal the High Court verdict. Instead, the CBI decided to drop the case. There were voices of protest by some BJP leaders, led by L. K. Advani. But Vajpayee held firm; he decided against going in for an appeal. 'Vajpayee tried not to damage PV—and vice versa.'

It was hardly surprising that Rao felt comfortable briefing Vajpayee on all aspects of the nuclear option.

■

Soon after his meeting with Rao on 18 May 1996, an excited Vajpayee rushed back home. 'Please get Kalam,' he instructed his newly appointed private secretary, Shakti Sinha. It took hours for Sinha to locate A. P. J. Abdul Kalam. He was the chief scientific advisor to the prime minister since 1992, and also secretary of the DRDO. More importantly, he had for several years been an advocate of India acquiring a nuclear deterrent. Finally, Sinha traced him in Kolkata. It was by then 9 at night. 'The PM wants to meet you,' Sinha informed him. He urged Kalam to take the morning flight to Delhi.

'Patakha chorhna hai (We have to let off the cracker),' Vajpayee told Kalam the moment he saw him the next morning. Kalam was accompanied by K. Santhanam. Kalam told the prime minister he needed some time. But Vajpayee gave him the go-ahead to get ready. 'We could have done it in those thirteen days when Vajpayee had made up his mind,' said Santhanam. 'But there was a higher level of advice to him—that he had not faced parliament. And what would be the authority of such a PM to...undertake an event which had wider national and international implications.'

Cabinet Secretary Surinder Singh was against the decision. Vajpayee should not take such a far-reaching step, he argued. It would not be fair to leave another government to pick up the pieces afterwards. The cabinet secretary would have worried about what the next prime minister would say to him if he was left holding the baby—that is if the Vajpayee government fell, which seemed likely.

For Vajpayee, it was not a simple decision to make. Had he gone in for a test, he might have possibly won the confidence vote in parliament. Some felt it might have generated the kind of euphoria which might have compelled some political parties to change their mind and support him. On the other hand, he had to think about his government's ability—and it was a fragile government—to handle a punitive American response which was bound to come. Knowing what had happened in 1974 when Indira Gandhi went in for a test, he was under no illusions about how the Americans would react.

Yet, he had been veering around to the view that the time had come to conduct a test; he was doubly convinced of it after his detailed meeting with Rao.

Vajpayee intensified his efforts to reach out to other parties to somehow cobble together a majority. He despatched George Fernandes to meet Bhuvnesh Chaturvedi for help. Fernandes urged Chaturvedi to 'please persuade' Chandra Shekhar to let the eight-member Samata Party, headed by Fernandes, join the Vajpayee government. Though Chandra Shekhar was not a member of the party—he had broken away from the Janata Dal in 1994—he exercised influence over some of its members who were his protégés. Chaturvedi agreed to speak to Chandra Shekhar. But he did not agree.

Vajpayee personally met Kanshi Ram, the chief of the Dalit dominated Bahujan Samaj Party, to seek his support. Since Kanshi Ram wanted to be prime minister himself, he was not going to support Vajpayee to become PM. He too refused.

Vajpayee then made his last desperate move. He asked George Fernandes to see Narasimha Rao—to seek the rival Congress's support to bail out his government. 'I myself made an appointment for George to see PV,' revealed Bhuvnesh Chaturvedi.

'It is not as if the Congress is in a position to form the government,' Fernandes argued with Rao, now no longer prime minister. But Rao refused.

Rao wanted Vajpayee to test. But he knew there was no way the Congress could support the BJP without committing hara-kiri. Even if he had wanted to bail out Vajpayee, he would not have been able to carry his party with him. Inside the Congress, the knives were out for him, after he had lost the 1996 election.

Vajpayee had hoped that if he could get even one other party to support the BJP and thereby break the 'untouchability' tag against it, other groups might decide to support him. This did not happen. And all options ran out for Vajpayee.

■

It was not just Surinder Singh who poured cold water on Vajpayee's plans to test. The ultimate clincher came from the Americans, who had begun suspecting that Vajpayee might go in for a test. The US's wariness of him was reflected in some of the emails sent to Washington by the US embassy in Delhi, which were declassified later in 2011.

Just before he left for Washington as Indian ambassador, Naresh Chandra had called on Vajpayee in Delhi in April 1996. Rao was still PM at the time. It was unusual for an ambassador-designate to call on an Opposition leader before going on a diplomatic assignment, IB chief V. G. Vaidya told me.

Chandra had met Vajpayee, it was said, at the instance of Narasimha Rao, who may have wanted to alert his successor. 'Rao had an inkling that the US would be lobbying to deny (the) premiership to Vajpayee in the event of a hung Lok Sabha (in 1996),' wrote Ashok Tandon, who was to become PM Vajpayee's media advisor.

When Vajpayee was sworn in as PM on 16 May 1996, the Americans were watching the situation hawk-like—and Vajpayee knew it. One day, during those thirteen days of his rule, Vajpayee called up Naresh Chandra in Washington.

'Wisner aa rahe hain (Wisner is coming to see me),' he said cryptically. 'Kya kehne aa rahe hai (What does he intend to say)?'

'We both knew it was an open line. We both knew what he was coming to say,' Chandra said later.

It was clear that Frank Wisner would try to ascertain whether the BJP government was planning to go ahead with testing. Somewhere the Americans had got wind of Vajpayee's inclinations.

'It will be a courtesy call,' Chandra told Vajpayee cautiously.

'Inki sun leejiye. Keh deejiye...that we attach importance to Indo–US relations (Hear him out, and say your piece),' Chandra told the PM. Vajpayee said his piece.

The Americans later revealed, through declassified documents, that Vajpayee had been all set to test. Wisner, who had met Vajpayee, was convinced from his 'body language' that he was committed to testing. In end December 1996, US Secretary of State Warren Christopher issued a warning to the Government of India—and it was delivered to Delhi through Naresh Chandra. By then H. D. Deve Gowda had taken over as PM. 'I remember one sentence from it,' Chandra recalled, 'that a test would have "devastating consequences" for India–US relations.'

Given the shaky footing he was on, Vajpayee decided not to go ahead with his plan to test. He conveyed this to the scientists.

Vajpayee's government lasted only thirteen days, the shortest span of any government in independent India. He resigned on 28 May 1996, but continued as caretaker prime minister for a few more days. H. D. Deve Gowda was sworn in as the next prime minister on 1 June 1996. Vajpayee had seriously considered the option to test in 1996 but didn't go ahead. But, during his fleeting tenure, he was convinced that if he got the chance again he would do it.

VII

'How are things going?' Vice President Krishan Kant asked a troubled Vajpayee. They were meeting a couple of weeks after Vajpayee took over for his second stint as prime minister on 19 March 1998. For Kant knew that Vajpayee had hit rough weather even before his ministry was constituted.

Vajpayee felt at ease with Kant and could speak freely about the problems he was facing with the BJP's allies—'Mamata, Samata, Jayalalithaa'—as the media came to christen his bringers of woe. The reference was to Mamata Banerjee's Trinamool Congress, George Fernandes's Samata Party, and J. Jayalalithaa's AIADMK, all three allies of the BJP, who were driving the prime minister to distraction.

Vajpayee had become prime minister again, just short of two years after he had demitted office in 1996. This time it was at the head of another BJP-led grouping called the National Democratic Alliance (NDA). The United Front government which had replaced him in 1996 had collapsed under the weight of its contradictions, having seen two prime ministers, H. D. Deve Gowda, and then I. K. Gujral, at the helm. In the mid-term polls which followed in 1998, the BJP won 182 seats, more than the 161 it had won in 1996, but still nowhere near the 273 it needed for a majority in the Lok Sabha. However, this time around, the BJP managed to get the support of fifteen parties after the election; it formed the National Democratic Alliance and put together a common programme which it called the National Agenda for Governance (NAG). Vajpayee sat at his dining table and dictated a draft of the NAG to his secretary Shakti Sinha. When Vajpayee met President K. R. Narayanan to stake his claim to form the government, he had the support of 267 MPs in the Lok Sabha. But the president then bowled a googly at Vajpayee—Narayanan asked him to provide letters of support from the parties backing the BJP. This included both the pre-poll and post-poll allies of the BJP. Sensing an opportunity, the supporting parties now began stepping up their demands in return for their support.

It started with tantrums by J. Jayalalithaa, the tough supremo of the AIADMK. Jayalalithaa was worried about the many corruption cases filed against her. She wanted economist Subramanian Swamy to be made finance minister. The normally accommodative Vajpayee put his foot down. There was no love lost between the two men. When Swamy was in the Jan Sangh years earlier, he had launched a vicious attack on Vajpayee. There was no way Vajpayee would accept Swamy as his finance minister.

By 12 March 1998, all the supporting parties had given Vajpayee their letters of support—except Jayalalithaa. She had thirty MPs from the AIADMK and its allies and their support was crucial for government formation. But she continued to hold out. The president gave Vajpayee two more days, until 14 March, to muster the requisite numbers.

An anxious Vajpayee rushed his senior party colleague, 'Major Sahib', as Jaswant Singh was called because of his army background, to bring around Jayalalithaa. After hours of hard bargaining, Jayalalithaa finally relented. She agreed to send her letter of support to Vajpayee on 14 March. But President K. R. Narayanan did not send his letter of invitation to Vajpayee immediately. He continued his consultations with other parties. It was only when Sonia Gandhi declined to stake her claim to form the government that the president invited Vajpayee to form the government.

But this was not the end of Vajpayee's troubles. The shenanigans continued, this time on who would be the new finance minister.

The prime-minister-designate had personally invited Jaswant Singh to be his finance minister. At 8 p.m. on 18 March 1998, he had sent the list of names of those to be sworn in as ministers to the president. Jaswant Singh's name was part of the list. The swearing-in was to take place the next morning at 9.30 a.m. 'I had myself typed the list,' recalled Shakti Sinha. Once the list was dispatched, Vajpayee and his family sat down to dinner.

Vajpayee had a high-powered guest that night—RSS joint general secretary, K. S. Sudarshan. Sudarshan had phoned earlier in the evening, asking to see Vajpayee. Vajpayee invited him to stay for dinner. Ranjan Bhattacharya, Vajpayee's foster son-in-law, who was in the hotel industry, made sure the meal did not have any tomatoes in it—Sudarshan was known to be allergic to them.

After dinner, Vajpayee took his guest to another room so they could talk in private. Unlike other RSS leaders, Sudarshan was known for his blunt manner. Without beating about the bush, he told Vajpayee not to induct Jaswant Singh and Pramod Mahajan in the cabinet. They had after all been defeated in the Lok Sabha elections. This posed a dilemma for Vajpayee—for they were two people he relied on and enjoyed a comfort level with.

Jaswant Singh was in favour of the liberalization of the economy, which had been initiated by Narasimha Rao. The RSS knew that Vajpayee also wanted to go down that path. It wanted the new government to pursue the path of swadeshi (self-reliance). They found Jaswant Singh's economic views problematic. After quitting the army, and before he joined the BJP, Jaswant Singh had been a member of the right-wing Swatantra Party, started by India's first governor general C. Rajagopalachari (Rajaji)—which believed in free enterprise and a market economy.

Keeping up the pressure, Sudarshan told Vajpayee he had come to see him with the blessings of the RSS chief Rajju Bhaiya. The RSS request made Vajpayee deeply unhappy. He, as the duly elected prime minister-designate of a billion Indians, was being asked to retract his word given to Jaswant Singh. He realized 'they' were clipping his wings even before he had taken off. But not wanting to start his premiership on a contentious note, he acceded to its request.

Shakti Sinha typed out another note around 2 a.m., which did not have Jaswant Singh's name in it. It was rushed to Rashtrapati Bhavan in the early hours of 19 March 1998.

The next morning, 19 March, was the day of the swearing-in. But it was quiet at Vajpayee's residence at 6, Raisina Road. Vajpayee sat down for breakfast at 7.30 a.m. He ate his papaya and toast unhurriedly. But he looked pensive—not upbeat, as he should have been. The swearing-in was scheduled for 9.30 a.m.

Driving to Rashtrapati Bhavan, a reflective Vajpayee asked Sinha, who was in the car with him, 'Finance ka kya hoga?'

He then added, 'What will happen if I retain the finance portfolio?'

'It should be fine,' Shakti Sinha replied. 'You can have a couple of good ministers of state in Finance.'

Vajpayee said nothing more for the rest of the journey. An eloquent speaker, he was not a very talkative man in person. At Rashtrapati Bhavan he greeted the long line of VIP guests, former prime ministers, and leaders of the Opposition who had gathered there for the ceremony. He was his usual smiling self. But by the time it came to the more formal part of the proceedings—when the new ministers took their oath of office and secrecy—he looked grave and troubled.

After the oath-taking was done, reporters crowded around the new prime minister. 'Why was Jaswant Singh's name omitted from the list of ministers?' they wanted to know.

'I will keep Finance myself,' Vajpayee replied casually. The TV cameras captured his words. The journalists then rushed to where Advani stood. They asked Advani the same question. Vajpayee should not retain Finance himself, Advani replied.

Within four hours, Vajpayee had to eat his words—once again. In what was a humiliating climbdown, he had to appoint Yashwant Sinha as finance minister, before the day was out. Yashwant Sinha had emerged as a last-minute compromise choice. He had been finance minister in the Chandra Shekhar ministry in early 1991 and had joined the BJP in 1994. 'Vajpayee was not keen on Yashwant Sinha,' revealed Shakti Sinha to me. At the time, Yashwant Sinha was seen to be close to the 'swadeshi' lobby in the RSS which pushed for economic self-reliance. However, later on, Sinha would change his stance and push the pro-liberalization economic agenda of the Vajpayee government. The prime minister had already signalled to the captains of industry that he did not view them with distrust.

After these initial hiccups, in the first fifty days of the new NDA government, nothing seemed to go right for Vajpayee. By caving into pressure from the RSS, and the BJP, the new prime minister had signalled that he could be pushed around. His allies were quick to pick this up.

Jayalalithaa, Subramanian Swamy, Ram Jethmalani, Ramakrishna Hegde, Buta Singh, Mamata Banerjee—all of them made their demands and put the new prime minister on the defensive. Though she lent her support to Vajpayee, Jayalalithaa was not an easy partner to work with. Her party AIADMK, now an ally in the NDA, had cornered fifteen ministerial berths including prized ones like Revenue, Banking, Law, and Surface Transport. She even told Vajpayee who to have in his cabinet!

From day one Vajpayee had been nervous about what Jayalalithaa might do. When she was scheduled to come and meet him first on 9 March 1998, he had gone out of his way to win her over. He even found out what should be served to her when she came calling on him. Did she like tea? 'No, please serve her coconut water,' her AIADMK pointsman in Delhi, R. K. Kumar, told the PM's aides.

Seeing her behaviour, other party chieftains also began to flex their muscles. When she attacked R. K. Hegde, now a minister in the Vajpayee government, for opposing her suggestion that Tamil be declared a national language, Hegde retaliated by calling Jayalalithaa and Subramanian Swamy 'insects'. Swamy called Ram Jethmalani, another minister in the government, 'Jhootmalani'.

In less than a month the situation was spinning out of control. Some in the BJP started to suggest that it would be better for Vajpayee 'to go back to the people' than submit to blackmail. By early April, people began to wonder how long the government would last.

Vajpayee was swamped by criticism from all sides—his own party, the RSS, the Congress, and the Left. Senior Left leaders like Harkishan Singh Surjeet and Jyoti Basu even dubbed his government 'anti-national'.

Criticism was not new to Vajpayee. Nor were feelings of despondency— this time at the way his long-awaited prime ministerial tenure was going. He had also felt dejected in 1984 when the BJP under his stewardship had got only 2 Lok Sabha seats. His career had hit low phases in the 1980s when he was sidelined and Advani promoted by the party and the RSS. But the despair he felt then was nothing like the dejection which hit him in 1998 as his government lurched from crisis to crisis.

'What has become of Atal Bihari Vajpayee's beatific smile?' Mani Shankar Aiyar of the Congress asked sarcastically. In just a month, gone was the 'bouncy, bubbly' Vajpayee. He had been replaced by an unrecognizable figure—'wan, fatigued, dispirited'.

'At one point things became so bad that he had made himself incommunicado,' Shakti Sinha was to recount later. In conflict situations, Vajpayee tended to go into a shell. He could be combative at the political level, but shunned conflict in interpersonal relations. Within weeks, the immense goodwill he had commanded began to erode. People began to ask: Does Vajpayee have what it takes to rule the country?

It seemed incredible that this should be happening to a leader with fifty years of political experience, who had no major charge levelled against him, whom the Opposition respected enough to call the 'right man in the wrong party', who was acceptable to the minorities despite being in the BJP, whose poetic heart, conciliatory image, and hypnotic oratorical skills had endeared him to millions.

Commentators urged him to do something 'bold'. Bring a Lok Pal Bill in parliament as he had promised. Or initiate legislation to reserve one third of the seats in parliament and legislative assemblies for women. It had to be something weighty and radical. As the clamour for big and decisive action ratcheted up, Vajpayee knew what he had to do. He had almost done it in 1996 during his thirteen-day government. He had given the go-ahead to the scientists to go for a nuclear test—only to pull back at the last moment. Besides his domestic woes, Pakistan had also provided India the immediate provocation for a nuclear test by testing its missile Ghauri on 6 April 1998.

In principle he had already made up his mind to test. It was only a matter of when. He chose the timing of his move very carefully. And one of the reasons for his timing was his 'shaky' position within the NDA—and within his own party. 'He wanted to acquire strength,' said Bhuvnesh Chaturvedi, who knew Vajpayee well. 'Secondly, the scientific establishment was ready.' As the head of Parliament's Standing Committee on External Affairs between 1996–98, Vajpayee had closely followed the global negotiations on the CTBT and become even more convinced about India's need to test soon.

And so, while the timing of the tests in May 1998 had everything to do with India's security imperatives, it was also designed to still the voices raised against Atal Bihari Vajpayee by his allies, his own party, and its ideological mentor, the RSS.

Vajpayee decided to go for the 'Big Bang' on 11 May 1998.

∎

Brajesh Mishra, Vajpayee's consigliere and national security advisor, agreed that 'Atalji also had his political considerations for opting for the test at that particular juncture.'

By the time Vajpayee started his second term, Mishra had emerged as his most trusted confidante and troubleshooter. They had first met when Vajpayee became foreign minister in 1977 and Mishra was an IFS officer. Mishra had hit the headlines in 1970 because of an incident that took place when he was posted as India's Charge d'Affaires in Beijing. At the May Day function, Mao Zedong shook Mishra's hand and sent a message to the Indian PM saying, 'We cannot go on quarrelling like this. We must become friends again.'

In the 1970s, the Vajpayee–Mishra relationship was 'official' but 'cordial'—the kind that usually exists between a bureaucrat and a minister. However, Mishra who joined the BJP in 1991, became close to Vajpayee during the seven years that followed, when he was handling the Foreign Affairs Cell of the BJP till 1998—and would often have a drink with Vajpayee in the evenings. 'We had many discussions. That brought us closer together,' Mishra said.

Vajpayee had known Mishra's father, Dwarka Prasad Mishra, the legendary practitioner of realpolitik and the Congress chief minister of Madhya Pradesh in the mid-1960s. Indira Gandhi would often seek the senior Mishra's advice after she became prime minister.

In early March 1998, Vajpayee asked Mishra over. The election results were not yet out but the poll surveys were predicting his victory. 'I want you to become my principal secretary,' Vajpayee said to Mishra.

'Look,' Mishra told him, 'I retired from the bureaucracy in 1987. Eleven years later you are asking me to again become a bureaucrat.'

Vajpayee: 'I want someone I can trust.'

Mishra accepted Vajpayee's offer: 'You cannot say no to a PM,' he laughed. The first order Vajpayee signed after taking over as prime minister was to appoint Mishra as his principal secretary. He was also made the national security advisor. But he came to be much more than that. Very quickly, he began to decode what his boss wanted done or not done. Vajpayee was not a nuts and bolts man, was laid back; he took instinctive, big-picture decisions and left the details to others.

'His instincts were marvellous,' Mishra said. 'Handling the details was my business. I always had the habit of briefing him (the PM) in detail every morning and every evening. Even (about) the smallest of things. So, he was never surprised with what the PMO or the NSA were doing,' Mishra said.

Vajpayee gave Mishra free access to him. He could walk into his room any time and get urgent decisions approved between official engagements. He took the load off Vajpayee as far as the nitty-gritty of governance went. 'He appreciated what I was doing because it was a combination of the national interest and his (own) interest.' Whenever a visitor raised any issue with Vajpayee, or wanted something done, the PM would tell them, 'Aap Brajesh se baat kar lo (Please talk to Brajesh).' When Vajpayee did not agree with Mishra's viewpoint, he would resort to ambiguity, 'We will talk about this later.' However, more often than not he would leave things to Mishra. Very soon, members of the party, ministers, and even government functionaries began to refer to Brajesh Mishra as the 'de facto prime minister'. In reality, he became the unofficial number two in government, although formally L. K. Advani was regarded as Vajpayee's deputy. No other principal secretary had been given such a free hand to take decisions—not even P. N. Haksar under Indira Gandhi. Even though he was essentially a bureaucrat, his remit was wide. Vajpayee also relied on him to take care of political matters—like forging cordial relations with Sonia Gandhi. Vajpayee did not needle Sonia Gandhi when he was in power nor she him, when the Congress-led UPA took charge. Sonia Gandhi once remarked to me, 'I like Vajpayee. I don't trust Advani.'

Mishra himself described his relationship with the PM as 'symbiotic'. 'It was no longer a case of PM and principal secretary. It was entirely a matter of trust. He was sure that I would do anything for him.'

'I had once told Atalji that it is my one-point agenda,' Mishra once remarked, 'that not even a whiff of a scandal should come out of the Prime Minister's Office or the PM House.' But his role went far beyond the management of 'potential' scandals, as we shall see.

VIII

On 6 April 1998, at 7.25 a.m., Pakistan test-fired a surface-to-surface missile from Malute in Jhelum cantonment. The Hatf–V Ghauri–I missile had a range of upto 1,500 kilometres, was able to carry 700 kilograms of warhead, and was designed at Pakistan's main nuclear weapons laboratory created by A. Q. Khan.

The missile that was tested traversed 1,100 kilometres that day—this range would enable the Ghauri missile to strike cities deep into the Indian territory such as Delhi, Mumbai, Kolkata, and Chennai.

The launch that Monday morning took India by surprise. In Delhi, Brajesh Mishra heard about the news from the ticker—and then from the intelligence agencies. He strode purposefully across to the PM's room to brief Vajpayee. India had to respond, he said, without beating about the bush. Or it could demoralize the country. The launch of Ghauri had given Vajpayee a reason to move ahead with the tests. Vajpayee agreed immediately. He asked Mishra to call an urgent meeting of the scientists.

The NDA government saw the missile's name as an additional provocation by Pakistan, as it was named after Muhammad Ghori. Ghori was a Muslim ruler belonging to Persia's Ghurid empire who had been victorious in battle over Prithviraj Chauhan, a Hindu ruler in the twelfth century. Ghori had defeated Chauhan at the Second Battle of Tarain in 1192.

Only two weeks earlier, Pakistan prime minister Nawaz Sharif had written to Vajpayee, promising to go the 'extra mile' towards creating 'good neighbourly relations', away from the 'old mindset of confrontation'. But on 6 April, Sharif who announced the successful launch of Ghauri, said, 'The public utterances of the BJP that India would go nuclear are a source of great concern for us.'

India Today quoted a Pakistan official as saying the 'main purpose of testing Ghauri was to send a signal to Delhi' that Pakistan could match any plans that India had of going nuclear. Some saw Ghauri as Pakistan's rejoinder to India starting production of the Prithvi missile, with a range of 250 kilometres, and storing it close to the Pakistani border in 1997.

Defence Minister George Fernandes responded sharply to the launch of Ghauri. He warned Pakistan that India was more than capable of taking care of itself. '...our understanding is that China is the mother of Ghauri,' he said. 'Everybody knows,' Fernandes added, 'that China has been supplying missile technology to Pakistan. It is up to the United States to take it up with Pakistan.' Pakistan claimed Ghauri was indigenously produced. But the Pakistani media had reported that the missile was developed with Chinese technology. India had growing evidence of China helping Pakistan with its nuclear and missile programme; it had supplied over fifty M-11 missiles to Pakistan between 1992 and 1994, and ring magnets to enrich uranium at Kahuta. India had specifically raised the issue of Chinese involvement because it was upset by the US's lukewarm reaction to the launch of Ghauri. New Delhi had watched with concern the growing defence ties between the US and China since Chinese President Jiang Zemin's visit to Washington in 1997. India soon realized that Washington was trying to 'whitewash' the Chinese connection with Ghauri, because of US President Bill Clinton's impending trip in June that year to Beijing.

Prime Minister Vajpayee was however more measured in his response to Ghauri than his defence minister. 'No nuclear race will be started due to the firing of Ghauri,' he said.

However, behind the scenes, the Pakistani missile launch galvanized the Indian government into action. Hours after the Ghauri launch, a concerned Brajesh Mishra called in security strategist K. Subrahmanyam for consultations.

'What can we do, Subbu?' Mishra asked Subrahmanyam.

'Our response should also be a missile test,' Subrahmanyam replied. 'But that depends on what's being done by your scientists.' He was alluding to the slowdown of the strategic nuclear programme during the two years of United Front rule from 1996–98. 'It never occurred to me,' Subrahmanyam was to say later, 'that they would go for the test.'

It was two days after the launch of Ghauri that Vajpayee gave the scientists the thumbs up. 'We decided on April 8 (1998) to go in for a test,' Brajesh Mishra told me, 'and gave the go-ahead to the scientists (that day).'

■

Unknown to most, Vajpayee had already initiated the process of exercising the nuclear option before Ghauri took flight. Within hours of taking over, the prime minister had called A. P. J. Abdul Kalam and R. Chidambaram to his office at Race Course Road. He had a 'cozy' relationship with Kalam; Kalam 'made it a point' to keep in touch with politicians. Vajpayee told the scientists to prepare the test site at Pokhran in the Thar Desert and to get ready to test. Brajesh Mishra was the only other person present at the meeting.

The scientists were half expecting the summons. The BJP had agreed to put its core commitments—building a Ram temple in Ayodhya, abrogating Article 370 of the Constitution, and enacting a Uniform Civil Code—on the back-burner, to be able to forge alliances with other parties, which had reservations about its Hindu nationalist agenda. But it had managed to persuade its partners to agree to the exercise of the nuclear option. This was part of NDA's National Agenda for Governance, released by Vajpayee. He had committed his government to revisit India's nuclear policy.

Though the PM did not give the formal go-ahead to the scientists at this meeting, 'we were activated by the end of March 1998,' Santhanam revealed. 'The actual day (of the test)...is chosen by the PM.... It is like building your house but deciding on the day of griha pravesh (housewarming) later. We were somewhere around T-3, that is three days' notice, by the end of April 1998.'

∎

A lot of field work had already been done at Pokhran—like the laying of the cables from the control room to the mouth of the shaft 2 kilometres away and then inside it. 'We didn't have (to start doing this from scratch),' Santhanam said, 'since the cables were buried under the sand and were intact (from previous preparations to test). We had to, of course, check out all the instruments.... The cables were in a very reasonable condition.'

Santhanam described in detail how the engineers and scientists had laid several hundred kilometres of cables in 1995, when Narasimha Rao had come close to testing. 'We had laid the cables by candlelight at night in 1995. So you can call it candlelit lay for cables instead of a candlelit dinner,' Santhanam laughed.

The satellites could not pick up candlelight unless the candles were seen in a procession in sequence. The shafts were very deep, more than 100 metres. 'The diameter was 2 metres and three of us could go down the shaft in a bucket,' Santhanam reminisced. When they reached the bottom, the bucket door opened and they could walk out into the shaft which was L-shaped. 'It was so dark inside and there was the sound of water falling. We were...with helmet and torch,' Santhanam recounted. 'It was bloody humid below. If you work(ed) a little bit you sweat(ed) like a pig. There were three close circuit cameras installed there and the images were conveyed to the control room 2 kilometres away.'

Sometimes, to the frustration of the scientists, the desert rats would nibble away at the cables. The scientists also found snakes there, 'though the pits were too wet for their comfort'.

One of the lessons the scientists had learnt during Rao's time was how to get around the prying eyes of the satellites in orbit. The satellites picked up any change in the desert. 'You take a picture on day one and then on day ten, and put the pictures on top of one another and cancel out what's common.' The end result was that what was new in the pictures could be seen. The computers did it by a method of 'digital image processing'. 'When you are at the T-3 stage,' Santhanam explained, 'the filling operation (of the shafts) has to be over in one night otherwise the change would be detected.

'For filling up we moved sand and made it appear as if there were sand dunes in the desert.' But natural sand dunes shaped by the wind had a way of leaning in one direction.

'Our sand dunes were in the opposite direction in 1998,' Santhanam said wryly. 'But by the time the Americans found out, the event was over.'

∎

Throughout the second half of March and the first week of April, while the scientists and engineers were making preparations in Pokhran, the prime minister held extensive discussions with Brajesh Mishra. He had told his principal secretary how they had almost done 'it' during his thirteen-day government in 1996, and why he had to cry off. Unlike in 1979, now Vajpayee was convinced that a credible nuclear deterrent was essential to prevent wars with the country's hostile neighbours. And, of course, there was the pressing need to do something big immediately to give his government credibility.

However, Vajpayee was worried about the fallout of the tests at all levels—global, geopolitical, economic, and political. Mishra assured the PM that the economy, which was by now doing well as compared to the Narasimha Rao years, could absorb the shock of sanctions. The country had $35 billion of foreign exchange reserves, which would help cushion any temporary strictures on trade, unless the US went to the extent of getting an 'oil embargo imposed', which could hit transport, energy, fertilizers, and make the situation untenable. But Mishra felt this was 'very unlikely'.

'I tended to take a long-term view of things,' Mishra said. Vajpayee was more worried about the immediate political fallout.

'We should do it (test) immediately,' Mishra told his boss. If it were delayed, he told the PM, the Americans would start to mount pressure on them to desist from taking such a step. 'We have to give a signal to the Americans that they have to take us seriously,' he told the PM. Vajpayee agreed with him.

For most people in the know of things, it was Brajesh Mishra who catalysed the decision which fundamentally changed India's foreign policy. He was not only committed to a nuclear deterrent, but was 'the real decision-maker' as far as nuclear tests went, according to K. Subrahmanyam. 'It was Brajesh Mishra who was the key enabler (of the tests),' disclosed the scientist R. Chidambaram, years later. 'The credit must be given to him. He complemented Vajpayee.'

'Brajesh played a key role in May 1998,' concurred Naresh Chandra.

In 1998, Brajesh Mishra was a key enabler of Vajpayee's decision to test. Ironically, it was another bureaucrat, his foreign secretary Jagat Singh Mehta, who had influenced his decision to oppose nuclear testing in 1979. Mehta wanted a shift from the country's complete dependence on the Soviet Union during Indira Gandhi's time to a new relationship with the US—and consequently with China and Pakistan. This was in tune with the thinking of Morarji Desai but also of Vajpayee himself at the time. Mehta felt that the future of the subcontinent lay in India making peace with its neighbours. He found Vajpayee 'very receptive' to the idea. Mehta was totally against the nuclear bomb. He felt that if India tested it would only encourage an arms race on the subcontinent. It was a mistake for Indira Gandhi to have gone in for the nuclear test in 1974, he felt, and for India not to have signed the Non-Proliferation Treaty.

Interestingly, both Jagat Mehta and Brajesh Mishra belonged to the foreign service, both had served in China in their early postings, both wanted to forge a new relationship with the US—although their views on testing were diametrically opposed. In 1998, Mishra understood that India's security situation had undergone a change. It was a case of 'now' or 'never'. The NPT had been extended indefinitely in 1995. The CTBT which sought to ban all nuclear tests had been adopted by the United Nations in September 1996—and awaited ratification. India had resisted signing both; it did not want to foreclose its nuclear option. But the window of opportunity that India had was small. It would eventually have to sign the CTBT if it was ratified and the rest of the world signed it. The plan was for India to test so it could weaponize—and then sign the CTBT.

(As already noted, the CTBT was never ratified but in March 1998 neither Vajpayee nor Mishra would know that.)

■

A week after Vajpayee had taken the decision to test, the US ambassador to the UN, Bill Richardson, arrived in New Delhi at the head of a delegation. He came as an emissary of US president Bill Clinton. Clinton was keen to get a sense of what the new Vajpayee government was planning to do on the nuclear front. Richard Frank Celeste, the US ambassador in Delhi, took Richardson to meet the PM. They also met Brajesh Mishra and other NDA leaders.

When Richardson called on George Fernandes, he asked the defence minister in his blunt fashion, 'George, there aren't going to be any surprises on testing, are there?'

'Absolutely not,' Fernandes replied, poker-faced. Although Fernandes did not know exactly what was being planned, he had a sense that Vajpayee would test sooner than later.

Vajpayee was trying to soften up the Americans in the run-up to the tests so as to contain the reaction he knew would come afterwards. Quietly, he opened another channel of communication with them. He sent word to the US ambassador, asking him to meet with Jaswant Singh "offline"—that is, in private. Jaswant Singh went to Roosevelt House, the home of the US ambassador in Chanakyapuri in Delhi. He told Celeste he had brought a message from the PM. He, Jaswant, would act as 'a discreet—and if necessary, secret—channel to Washington'. The US leadership could send any message which was of a sensitive nature through him to the prime minister. There would be a quick response, he promised. It would also prevent any 'leaks' from taking place, he added.

Despite the suspicions of the Americans, and the Pakistanis, and the curiosity of his political colleagues, the PM managed to keep the tests under wraps. Vajpayee and Mishra managed to staunch the flow of information by being highly frugal about sharing it. And those they had no option but to inform, because of the positions they held, were told only at the last minute.

■

'Brajesh Mishra called me on 8 May,' recalled General V. P. Malik, who was army chief in 1998. 'The prime minister wants to meet you,' Mishra said. That morning Mishra had suggested to the PM that the time had come 'to call the three chiefs and brief them now'. The other two chiefs also received similar calls. They were told to come to 5, Race Course Road, the next morning, on 9 May.

The PM delinked his briefing to the defence minister from the one he gave to the service chiefs. The service chiefs believed that their boss, George Fernandes, was told about the tests only on the day itself.

'When we (all three chiefs) arrived, Brajesh Mishra and Abdul Kalam were already sitting there,' recalled General Malik. 'It was around 9.30 or 10 in the morning,' he said. Without wasting any time, the PM gave them the news about the imminent tests. 'What do you expect by way of a reaction?' he asked the chiefs. 'What should we do to be ready for it?'

General Malik had come prepared with a one-page document which contained a plan for what 'our response should be....'

'When Brajesh Mishra had called, I had anticipated that something of this nature would be discussed.' General Malik suspected there was going to be a test very soon. The pits where the tests would take place—where work had been going on—were under the supervision of the army. 'By that time, I had begun to get information from the ground,' General Malik said. 'Whatever was going on in the Pokhran area, the army units (there) were informing us at the higher level. So I knew preparations were going on.... Normally in a matter like this someone on the ground in the army is taken into confidence...and in this instance it was the local formation commander. The director general of military operations (DGMO) was Lieutenant General Inder Verma and he was getting information from the ground and feeding me. Kalam would ring up and say such and such a thing should happen.'

Besides asking the chiefs about preparedness, the prime minister 'didn't say much'. Kalam did most of the talking. He explained to the chiefs what was being planned. 'Brajesh also talked.... One got the impression that it would happen in the next two to three days.... The exact day or time was not indicated to us even that day.'

'Before we left the Prime Minister's residence, Dr Kalam told me that twenty-four hours before the tests, there would be a requirement to move the villagers of Khetolai village (pop.: 1,200), located 5 kilometres from the test site, to an alternative location.' This move, General Malik said, had to be made by night, 'for which the local engineer regiment had been briefed.'

After returning home, General Malik instructed the operational staff to ensure that there was adequate transport at Pokhran for any task at short notice. 'The requirement to move residents of Khetolai villagers came sooner than expected, on 10 May.'

That day, General Malik said, 'We did not talk with the PM about the possibility of tests by Pakistan. In my note, or in the discussion that day, we did not anticipate that Pakistan will go in for tests although we had intel reports from earlier on Pakistan's capability in this field. It was only after our explosion that we began to think that Pakistan may also conduct tests.'

When he briefed the service chiefs, Vajpayee was not exercised about the long-term implications of the step he was about to take. He only wanted their views on what they should do immediately.

■

Having talked to the defence chiefs, Vajpayee then called his senior political colleagues.

'The PM told me that he had told his political colleagues two days before the test, i.e., on the 9th of May,' Brajesh Mishra told me. Those who were 'informed' included Home Minister L. K. Advani, Jaswant Singh, who was deputy chairman of the Planning Commission and emerged as the prime minister's point person on the tests, Defence Minister George Fernandes, and Finance Minister Yashwant Sinha.

'I am not sure whether the PM told them the exact date of the tests,' Mishra said evasively. He was hinting that even on 9 May, they were not told the exact date or time of the tests.

'On 9 May, in the afternoon, there was a meeting,' confirmed Shakti Sinha. 'It was attended by the PM, Advani, George Fernandes, and Jaswant Singh.' Except Jaswant Singh, the other two were members of the Cabinet Committee on Security. Vajpayee chose not to brief the Cabinet Committee on Security as a group—so he could have Jaswant Singh as his master of ceremonies.

Vajpayee knew Fernandes had been against the bomb, and Advani was for it. He might have calculated that Fernandes would be more circumspect about his views in front of Advani. But Fernandes had smelt the direction of the wind. Six days earlier, he had issued a statement, 'Earlier nuclear weapons were not ruled out, now they are ruled in.' The Chinese had reacted sharply and called it 'absolutely ridiculous'.

Yashwant Sinha was informed separately—and he remembered that day well. Summoned by the prime minister, he got to Vajpayee's house only to be told: 'Unke bedroom me ja kar miliye (Go into his bedroom to meet him).'

'You can imagine my feelings,' Yashwant Sinha said. 'Bedroom mae jaa ke milne ka kya matlab? Naukri janewali hai zaroor? Ki kuch baat ho gayi hai... (Going into the bedroom, what did it mean? That means I am about to lose my job. Something must have happened) It was with these thoughts that I went into his bedroom...' It turned out later that the bedroom was the most secure room in the house. Vajpayee was seated there waiting for him. After the initial pleasantries, he said, 'Humlog yeh karne ja rahe hain, around the 10th or the 11th.' (We are going to do this on the 10th or the 11th—alluding to a nuclear test.) 'I am telling you this because we have to now think in terms of a backlash on the economic front.... You have to be absolutely ready with a plan on how you are going to tackle the fallout.'

Sinha was stunned. The PM swore him to secrecy. 'I was so shocked and unnerved by this news,' he said, 'that I did not even ask him, "Who have you taken into confidence, who can I talk to, if I need to talk". I asked him nothing.' Sinha went on, 'I was aware of the gravity of the information which he had shared with me. I was (also) aware that Narasimha Rao had been stopped from testing by American pressure because the news had leaked out.... So, there was no question of sharing the information with anyone. I couldn't talk to anyone in the ministry. I couldn't quite call senior officials and tell them, "This is going to happen, what should we be doing?" So, I kept it within myself.... I kept thinking about the economic consequences, and what we could possibly do.'

■

There were indications that Vajpayee also took the RSS chief, Rajju Bhaiya, into confidence. As we have seen, he had run into trouble with the RSS over his plan to appoint Jaswant Singh as finance minister. He now wanted to keep them on his right side. So he gave them the minimum information that was necessary. That week, on 11 May 1998, that is the day of the tests, *Organiser*, the mouthpiece of the RSS, carried a banner headline on its cover, 'Nuclear India'. Nowhere did the issue say that the tests had taken place. It hit the stands hours before the test. The strap on the front page screamed, 'The testing time has come', making a case for India to acquire a nuclear deterrent. However, and this was the noteworthy part of the story, the edition was printed and ready for distribution on 11 May, which meant the RSS brass knew in advance that the tests were to happen very soon.

Another giveaway that the RSS brass had an idea of what was in the offing, was Rajju Bhaiya's visit to the BARC in Bombay only a few days before the test. The *Organiser* carried a report of the visit—the piece described 'Professor Rajendra Singh, the Sarsanghchalak of the RSS' as a 'nuclear physicist' who said that India must acquire a nuclear deterrent. 'We cannot afford to forego our nuclear option,' the RSS chief said while at BARC, 'when everyone around is arming...to the teeth.'

IX

On 11 May 1998, Yashwant Sinha got a call on his RAX phone. Jaswant Singh was on the line. 'Bhaiya, aap zara paanch number aa jaiye (Brother, please come to Number 5, Race Course Road),' Jaswant told Sinha. Bungalow number 5 was part of the PM House.

'Kyun (Why)? Ghatna ghat gayi hai kya (Has the event taken place)?' Sinha asked him. Jaswant Singh did not say anything. Besides Sinha, he had also called up George Fernandes. Vajpayee had personally called Advani and asked him to come over.

'When I went there,' Yashwant Sinha recounted, 'I found that apart from Jaswant Singh and Brajesh Mishra.... Advani and George Fernandes had (also) been called. So, the entire Cabinet Committee on Security was there.'

They were initially to meet in the morning. But the meeting was postponed because the tests had been delayed—the winds at Pokhran were blowing in the wrong direction, and would have carried the radioactive fallout towards villages. It was Buddha Purnima, as was the case in 1974 when Indira Gandhi conducted the first nuclear test and codenamed it 'Smiling Buddha'.

Vajpayee had moved into 3, Race Course Road, that very morning; the griha pravesh (housewarming) was supposed to bring good tidings. A tense prime minister waited for word from the desert, 900 kilometres away.

■

In Pokhran, the day had started early for the scientists. They had been told in the first week of May that 11 May would be D-Day. K. Santhanam, the mission director, recalled, 'We were to do it before 8 in the morning but the Trombay chaps (scientists attached to the Bhabha Atomic Research Centre) found that the wind was not favourable.... The scientific team waited on edge, until they were finally given the go-ahead. It came with a booming voice telling them, "Now favourable, saar".' Santhanam described what happened next. Before the explosion could take place, a key would need to inserted into the 'electro-relay-operated switches'. 'It's like your car key going into the switch,' Santhanam explained. As mission director, Santhanam handed over the key to the 'range safety officer', who then went around to see if the range was clear for the test. 'I handed the key to Vasudeva, who was the range safety officer...he gave it to one of the DRDO people who turned the key....' Santhanam then added, 'These were virtually the keys of the nuclear kingdom.' At that time they were so focused on what they were doing, that there was no question of feeling any excitement.

When the explosion took place, the whole ground rose and 'then it fell to create a crater'. From where the scientists sat behind glass and radiation shields, it felt like 'what can be called a bump tickle'.

But it was when 'we saw the crater that...the elation occurred'. The scientists dialled the PM's number on a secure line.

■

At 5, Race Course Road, the PM sat on a sofa awaiting word from Pokhran; Advani, Fernandes, Sinha, and Jaswant Singh sat around the dining table. The banter had slowly died down. Nobody spoke. Nobody moved. Then came the call that everyone had been waiting for. A tense Brajesh Mishra reached out for the phone after the first ring. 'First, Kalam spoke (to Delhi) in English, then Chidambaram spoke,' Santhanam recounted.

'Sir, we have done it,' Kalam told Mishra.

'God bless you,' the NSA told him and put the phone down.

In the minutes that followed, there were a lot of tears in that room. They were tears of relief, of a sense of pride, and of 'finally having done it'. Vajpayee's face, grim till then, suddenly broke into a wide smile.

The PM informed the president and the vice president—that India had exploded three nuclear devices at 3.45 p.m. on 11 May 1998. President K. R. Narayanan had been in Latin America and had returned to Delhi only the previous day. Soon after Narayanan's return to the capital, Vajpayee had driven to Rashtrapati Bhavan to brief the president about what they intended to do the next day. 'They timed it (the tests) in such a way that (the president) who was away in Latin America would be back in Delhi,' Subrahmanyam revealed later, 'so that he could avoid uncomfortable questions (while abroad).'

The prime minister then asked Jaswant Singh to call up K. Subrahmanyam and tell him that the tests had taken place. He was the first person outside the government to be informed. But by the time Jaswant Singh called, Subrahmanyam had already heard. 'The first person who told me about it was Krishan Kant,' revealed Subrahmanyam.

A week earlier, Vajpayee had personally gone to brief Kant before the VP left for Cairo on an official visit—without telling him the date and time of the explosions.

'Aap jo chahte rahen hain, woh hum karne jaa rahe hain (We are going to do what you have been wanting for a long time),' Vajpayee told Kant in his roundabout way.

Krishan Kant, who had openly championed the cause of 'India going nuclear' understood what the PM meant. He did not ask any questions. Vajpayee did not elaborate.

'Have you heard about it?' Kant asked Subrahmanyam.

'About what?'

Kant said, 'About the nuclear explosion.'

'No, I haven't.'

Kant: 'Just now the PM spoke to me... I have not told anybody this so far. You're the first person (I am telling.)'

'Jo humari baat hui thee kuch din pehle...woh humne kar diya hai (We have done what we had talked about a few days earlier),' the PM had told Kant.

Then Kant asked Subrahmanyam, 'What shall I say about it?'

'Don't open your mouth,' Subrahmanyam advised the vice president, 'till the government gives you the official version. You will have to get a brief from the PM (about what to say.)'

'I put the phone down and five minutes later the phone rang again,' Subrahmanyam continued. 'It was Jaswant Singh.'

He said, 'I must tell you that we have carried out a nuclear test. We felt you should be the first person to hear about it outside the government. The nuclear test included the thermo-nuclear test (aka the hydrogen bomb).'

After the initial flurry of calls, the group gathered at 5, Race Course Road, had to decide the next steps to take. 'We were supposed to... discuss...how to manage the consequences and how to announce (it) to the world,' Yashwant Sinha recalled. They decided that Vajpayee should address the media on his own. He would make the announcement from a podium on the sprawling lawns of 7, Race Course Road. It was Pramod Mahajan, the PM's political secretary—he had arrived at RCR by then— who thought of placing the national flag behind Vajpayee. This, too, was a last moment decision. It was decided that the announcement by Vajpayee would be a brief one. Brajesh Mishra and Jaswant Singh dictated it to Shakti Sinha who then took it to the prime minister. Vajpayee changed only one word in it. Very deliberately, he removed the word 'brief' to describe the statement he was to read. The statement was 'brief', but the wordsmith that he was, he did not want the word 'brief' to lessen its import. It was also decided that PM would take no questions. His office worked the phones furiously. Representatives of the media were asked to come over to RCR immediately.

Soon thereafter, Vajpayee emerged from his residence, walking slowly. He headed straight for the podium which stood forlornly on the manicured lawns of 7, Race Course Road, before the Indian tricolour which formed the backdrop. Pramod Mahajan and Shakti Sinha stood behind him.

The PM started to read out his statement. His tone was sombre. There was no triumphalism accompanying his words. He barely looked up as he read. This was uncharacteristic of Vajpayee who was used to making his points with a flourish. And this was a once-in-a-lifetime announcement he was making. After he had finished speaking, Vajpayee turned around and went back into the house. The press conference was over before you knew it. The PM fielded no questions. His six-sentence statement to the newspersons on 11 May 1998 was bare and matter-of-fact.

> Today, at 15.45 hours, India conducted three underground nuclear tests in the Pokhran range. The tests conducted today were with a fission device, a low-yield device, and a thermonuclear device (hydrogen bomb). The measured yields are in line with expected values.
>
> Measurements have confirmed that there was no release of radioactivity into the atmosphere. These were contained explosions, like in the experiment conducted in May 1974. I warmly congratulate the scientists and engineers who have carried out these successful tests.

As the PM had mentioned in his statement, apart from the hydrogen bomb, India tested an atom bomb and a low-yield fission weapon with a 'sub-kiloton yield' (below the equivalent of 1,000 tonnes of TNT.) A group of Western scientists were later to question India's claim of a 5- kiloton yield for the nuclear tests as overestimated.

Two days later, on 13 May, India was to conduct a second set of tests of 2 sub-kiloton tests. The five tests were codenamed Operation Shakti.

'India is now a nuclear-weapon state,' Prime Minister Vajpayee declared soon after the tests.

Like Indira Gandhi had done in 1974, Vajpayee also chose to play down the event. There was however a significant difference between 1974 and 1998. Indira had described the 1974 explosion as an 'implosion' meant for 'peaceful' purposes. Vajpayee chose not to describe the test in 1998 as peaceful. Neither his 11 May statement nor the longer official text released later that day had called the explosions 'peaceful nuclear tests'—even if India's intentions were peaceful. In other words, India would go in for weaponization. Vajpayee also ruled out signing either the CTBT or the NPT because they were discriminatory. But like Indira Gandhi, Vajpayee was also all too aware that the next, and more difficult, challenge lay ahead—of managing the fallout.

∎

As the politicians made their moves in Delhi, in Pokhran, the scientists anxiously measured radiation levels. They measured the impact of the explosions on the surrounding villages. Three groups got into three jeeps and drove in different directions. They also wanted to see if there had been any cracks in the houses in the habitations around.

The villagers were sharp enough to know that something major had just taken place; and this was a chance to make a bit of money. So some said,

'This cow and this camel are not able to walk.' The cop with the group would then pay them a sum of money. 'We gave them the cash and they were happy,' Santhanam said. Others would say: 'Crack abhi hua hai (Our houses have just developed cracks).' They too received instant compensation.

But it was not just the immediate effects of the explosions that needed to be monitored. Environmentalists were a worried lot—about the impact the tests would have on the health of the people in the area. Six months later, in November 1998, when journalist Kalpana Sharma visited Khetolai village, 5 kilometres from the test site, unhappy villagers told her they wanted a health monitoring centre to be set up there. For a study done after the 1974 implosion had shown an increase in the cases of cancer in western Rajasthan. What the villagers didn't know, Sharma wrote, quoting reliable sources in Jodhpur, was that they had cause to be worried—the government was planning 'a secret study' on the impact of the tests, because it was 'worried that the recent spurt of rain might have led to some contamination of the underground aquifers around the nuclear test site'.

Fifteen years after the May 1998 blasts, villagers around the site in Pokhran continued to complain of frequent cancer deaths. But authorities dismissed their complaints as having 'no scientific basis'.

■

After the phone calls he received, Subrahmanyam rang up the *Times of India*—and gave them the news. He was on the editorial board of the paper, and had been writing regularly for it. He had just reached home from the *Times* office—but told them he was rushing back to write a piece. H. K. Dua was the executive editor of the paper. He told Subrahmanyam, 'If they do not give you space on the edit page, I will give you space on the front page'. Subrahmanyam's piece appeared as 'news analysis' on the front page of the *Times of India* on 12 May 1998. The headline said it all: 'India now joins the club of five N-Weapon States'. His piece was read with great interest in the country and also by the international community. For, as the acknowledged leader of the pro-bomb lobby in India's strategic community, Subrahmanyam's views were closely tracked by strategic analysts and by the non-proliferation lobbies in Western capitals.

Subrahmanyam made three important points in his piece. India had announced that it would be joining the CTBT, and thereby foreclosing all further options to conduct tests. (This was an offer by India in those early hours after testing to tone down the sanctions it knew the US and the Western world would slap against it.) Secondly, he asserted, India was a 'reluctant nuclear-weapon state'. It was compelled to join the nuclear club because all its plans to move towards disarmament had been ignored by the nuclear-haves. They had got their nuclear weapons legitimized by the international

community, and done it through the 'unconditional' and 'indefinite' extension
of the Non-Proliferation Treaty (in 1995). India had been left with little
choice, given Pakistan's recent test of its missile Ghauri and the ongoing
'nuclear and missile technology cooperation between Pakistan and China'.
Thirdly, he called for India to 'immediately' declare a 'no first use policy'.
And he urged the government to invite China, Russia, and Pakistan to
join in 'a joint no first use declaration'. Vajpayee declared a moratorium
on further testing after the tests. But 'it took him four months to declare
that India would not use it first'.

■

When Vajpayee walked back into the PM House after making his
announcement to the presspersons at Race Course Road, his colleagues
were waiting impatiently for him. They would now have to discuss the next
steps they needed to take.

'It was...decided that Vajpayee should write a letter to (US President)
Clinton,' Yashwant Sinha revealed, 'and tell him that it was not Pakistan
but China we had in mind for going for nuclear tests.'

Vajpayee wrote to Clinton the next day. Alluding to China as the
reason for India's tests, he wrote, 'We have an overt nuclear-weapon state
on our borders, a state which committed armed aggression against India
in 1962. Although our relations with that country have improved in the
last decade or so, an atmosphere of distrust persists mainly due to the
unresolved border question.'

China, Vajpayee wrote, had helped Pakistan to become a 'covert nuclear-
weapon state', and 'this bitter neighbour' had committed 'three aggressions
in the last 50 years'. Pakistan, the PM asserted, had inflicted 'unremitting
terrorism and militancy' in different parts of India.

Expressing the hope that the tests would not damage India's relations
with the US, he said, 'We value our friendship and cooperation with your
country. We hope you will show understanding of our concern for India's
security.'

Vajpayee's letter to Clinton was published in the *New York Times*—
obviously leaked soon after it reached the White House. The leak came
as a huge embarrassment for the Vajpayee government. For the PM had
held China publicly responsible for its decision to test.

The US derided India for its rationale to test. It was only in later years
that the Americans, including Henry Kissinger, came to accept that India
had a case for a deterrent against China. Clinton treated the tests as a
personal affront. He erupted in a 'volcanic fit' when he heard about them,
according to foreign policy advisor and long-time friend, Strobe Talbott.
Stopping the proliferation of nuclear weapons had been a proclaimed
priority of the Clinton administration. The US president had taken 'a

personal initiative' to roll back the nuclear programmes of both India and Pakistan. In a strongly worded message, the US president called for India to 'cap, roll back and eliminate' its nuclear programme. The UN Security Council passed a similar resolution.

On 13 May, when India conducted two more tests, Clinton announced sanctions against India. He was in Germany at the time. The US froze all its aid to India, including its defence commitments—barring humanitarian assistance. The US government made it known that it was also opposed to international financial institutions like the World Bank lending to India. Japan also froze all aid which was more than $1 billion dollars, Germany announced a moratorium on its aid, which, at $300 million, was more than that of the US. France, however, said that sanctions made no sense. The UK and Russia also took a similar position, though the Russian premier Boris Yeltsin expressed his disappointment with India. China's reaction, initially subdued, sharpened after Vajpayee named China as the raison d'etre for the tests.

To begin with, Vajpayee was very depressed with the global community's response to the tests—even though he was expecting it. He immediately called a meeting of key secretaries to the government of India—to get their ideas on how to handle the fallout. Montek Singh Ahluwalia, who was present at the meeting said that if India continued with liberalization and economic engagement with the US, the international community would come around.

Vajpayee sent Brajesh Mishra to the world capitals to contain the damage. The immediate task before the government was to end its diplomatic isolation, and rebuild its relations particularly with the US. In Washington, India's ambassador to the US, Naresh Chandra, engaged in deft diplomacy; he disseminated India's viewpoint to the American think tanks and members of the US Congress—and countered the demand that India now sign the CTBT.

■

A day after the tests, Vajpayee invited Sonia Gandhi over. He told her the tests were a continuation of the polices followed by her mother-in-law, Indira Gandhi, and husband, Rajiv Gandhi. He later told his colleagues what she had said to him that day—that the '1988 decision' by Rajiv Gandhi (to make an adequate number of weapons) had been kept totally under wraps. But she had known that Rajiv had given his go-ahead for weaponization.

To begin with, the Opposition parties were flummoxed—uncertain about how they should react. Initially the Congress Party did not know whether to welcome the tests as a continuum of what had been started by Indira Gandhi and taken forward by Rajiv or to criticize the Vajpayee government. It ended up criticizing the timing of the tests.

Besides Sonia Gandhi, the PM decided to brief most of the Opposition leaders individually. In the months that followed, when Vajpayee came under increasing pressure to sign the CTBT, he decided to talk to CPI (M) leaders to help him ward off pressure. He invited H. K. S. Surjeet and Jyoti Basu, who had criticized the tests, for tea.

'What are people saying about the nuclear tests?' he asked Surjeet conversationally. Surjeet replied, 'People are opposed to it.'

Vajpayee: 'But there are no voices being raised.'

Surjeet was quick to realize that Vajpayee was asking them to start an agitation that India should not sign the CTBT.

Like other prime ministers before him, Vajpayee also used the Opposition leaders to ward off external pressures on the government. He had learnt this from Indira Gandhi. During the Bangladesh war, she had taunted him. 'Toh, aap log nahi chahete ke Bangladesh azaad ho (So, you people do not want Bangladesh to be liberated).'

'Nahi, hum poori tarah se aap ke saath hai (No, we are fully with you),' Vajpayee had responded defensively.

'I can't see any signs of it,' Indira Gandhi had quipped. 'You are not mounting any agitations.'

She later sent her aide R. K. Dhawan to Vajpayee asking him to create an atmosphere that the whole country was one on the issue.

In a similar vein, Vajpayee told the Left leaders, 'Kuch public opinion banaye (Create public opinion against signing the CTBT).'

X

On 28 May 1998, Pakistan carried out five nuclear tests in the beautiful granite hills of the Ras Koh range in East Balochistan. Before the dust had settled at the Chagai test site, it went in for a sixth blast on 30 May. Pakistan could now claim it had set off one more explosion than the five conducted by India. Announcing the tests, Pakistan's prime minister Nawaz Sharif declared: 'If India had not exploded the bomb, Pakistan would not have done so. Once New Delhi did so, we had no choice because of public pressure.' The tests heightened the tensions between the two neighbours. As with India, the world slapped sanctions on Pakistan. As the weeks went by, international pressure mounted on the two new nuclear states, India and Pakistan, to de-escalate tensions, show restraint, and reopen dialogue. Four months later an opportunity to do so presented itself—and both Vajpayee and Nawaz Sharif grasped it.

In September 1998, Vajpayee and Sharif were having lunch together in New York city, along with their official delegations. Both prime ministers had arrived in the city to attend meetings of the United Nations General Assembly. Jaswant Singh, Brajesh Mishra, Shakti Sinha, and some others were part of the Indian delegation. Among the Pakistanis was Sartaz Aziz, foreign minister of Pakistan. In stark contrast to the tension and threats of war of a few months earlier, there was banter and bonhomie between the Indians and the Pakistanis that afternoon. The two sides discussed how to improve relations between their countries.

The lunch had been set up a month earlier, when Vajpayee and Sharif had met on 29 July 1998 on the sidelines of the SAARC summit in Colombo. 'We had a one-on-one meeting with Nawaz Sharif in Colombo,' confirmed Brajesh Mishra. Both leaders had agreed to meet again in New York during the UNGA deliberations. At one point during the lunch, while the two sides were discussing the opening of land routes, Jaswant Singh suddenly suggested, 'Why shouldn't there be a bus from Delhi to Lahore?' Both prime ministers immediately 'jumped' at the idea of a 'bus' journey.

'The decision was that Atalji should first travel by bus to Lahore.... Vajpayee immediately saw the value of this.... It wasn't simply symbolic.... The idea was to improve relations with Pakistan and the bus became the means to do it, as a linkage and a symbol,' Jaswant Singh said. 'Nawaz Sharif was also agreeable because it related to Punjab from where he hailed.... It was to catch the imagination of people.'

Vajpayee's historic Lahore Yatra in February 1999, an event that was a consequence of the nuclear tests, served two purposes. It was calculated to put Pakistan at ease—and reach out for a new relationship with it. The yatra was also meant to signal the global community that India and Pakistan were mature enough to take care of their nuclear concerns and settle their issues 'bilaterally'.

In Lahore, Vajpayee declared at Minaret-e-Pakistan, the symbol of Pakistan's nationhood, that a strong Pakistan was in India's interest. His words were significant coming as they did from a prime minister belonging to the BJP, a party which had continued to harp on the idea of an akhand bharat in which Pakistan and Bangladesh would become part of a reunified India. The Indian prime minister took to Lahore the special Vajpayee touch. He said in one of his speeches: 'Yeh loha aur ispaat ki bus nahi hai. Yeh hamare dono mulko ke awam ke jasbaaton ke baat hai (This is not a bus made of iron and metals, it represents the sentiments of the people of our two nations).'

Unfortunately, the goodwill generated by the Lahore bus trip did not last long. Pakistan started a war in May 1999 on the icy heights of Kargil in the Himalayas. Although accounts vary on who on the Pakistani side was responsible for initiating hostilities (Nawaz Sharif said he was unaware of the action, though this has been disputed), the Kargil War was seen to have been initiated by General Pervez Musharraf, the Pakistani general who would topple Nawaz Sharif in a military coup in 1999.

Kargil was followed by the hijacking of an Indian Airlines plane to

Kandahar in December 1999 and the terrorist attack on the Indian Parliament on 13 December 2001. In response, India mobilized its armed forces for nine months under Operation Parakram on the border with Pakistan. Though Vajpayee invited Pakistan president Musharraf for talks in Agra in July 2001, to break new ground, the summit did not make any headway.

Vajpayee himself was pulled down in April 1999 by Jayalalithaa. Her party, the AIADMK, was a key constituent of the Vajpayee-led NDA but she joined hands with Congress leader Sonia Gandhi and brought down the Vajpayee ministry by one vote during a vote of confidence. Vajpayee would continue as caretaker PM until October when mid-term elections returned him to power later in 1999—and he remained in office till 2004.

Paradoxically, the nuclear tests were to change the relationship between India and the US—as Brajesh Mishra had predicted in April 1998. He had told Vajpayee that testing would compel the Americans to take India more seriously—this is exactly what happened. Within a couple of years, there was a marked improvement in India's relationship with the US.

Even as the US imposed sanctions after the tests, the Americans showed a willingness to talk to India seriously about security issues. For the Americans, the Indian tests had come as 'a very serious intelligence failure', particularly since 'one of the CIA's jobs is not to be fooled'. But there were Indians who suspected that the American failure was 'contrived'—to allow India to 'get on with it' and then sign the CTBT.

For Vajpayee, softening up the US was on top of his agenda. He deputed Jaswant Singh—by then he had been appointed foreign minister—to open a dialogue with the US. The talks between Jaswant Singh and US deputy secretary of State Strobe Talbott were to become one of the show pieces of India–US track two diplomacy. From July 1998 onwards, India and the US held eighteen rounds of talks to find a way out of the impasse. The two men, who had been friends, developed a greater rapport with each other. The talks petered out with India's refusal to sign the CTBT. But India and the US were to move towards a strategic partnership in the months and years that followed.

■

In the year 2000, Delhi rolled out the red carpet for US President Bill Clinton—as had not been done for a foreign dignitary in a long time. By now Clinton, who had been livid about India's nuclear tests, was speaking a different language. A US president was visiting India after a gap of twenty-two years, and the visit was a reflection of how Vajpayee—and Brajesh Mishra—had managed the fallout of the 1998 tests. Clinton had decided to come despite Vajpayee making it clear that there was no question of rolling back India's nuclear programme.

On 23 March 2000, day three of Clinton's high-profile visit, Clinton addressed MPs from both the houses in the Central Hall of Parliament. Accredited parliamentary correspondents were permitted to cover the event. Clinton knew how to strike the right chords that would touch his audience. He referred to Mahatma Gandhi, he lauded India's 'leadership in the region', he quoted Nobel Prize-winning economist Amartya Sen, cited the achievements of Silicon Valley, and spoke glowingly about India's panchayati raj institutions, and its devolutionary democracy. Clinton's words showed how well he had been tutored. He had been told the 'best way to drive (home) any message to India: wrap it in two layers, one that panders to its ego and the other(to)...its self-interest.'

After Clinton finished his speech and came down the aisle, we journalists watched the unprecedented spectacle of elected members of parliament suddenly start to behave like Bollywood film fans. MPs fell over each other to shake the US president's hand as he walked past. It might not be an exaggeration to say that at least 300 MPs would have shaken hands with Clinton that day. 'Many MPs would not have washed their hands for a couple of days to retain the Clinton touch,' quipped a young MP irreverently afterwards.

The anti-Americanism which had undergirded India's foreign policy during the years of the Cold War had begun to dissolve after 1998. In 2000, when Clinton came, the Indian lawmakers were a visible sign of the change that was taking place in the country.

Clinton's visit provided a new framework for the Indo–US partnership; it was an acknowledgement that India was now being seen in a different light—a rising power which could no longer be ignored. 'India's gamble' on nuclear testing had paid off, as Brahma Chellaney, columnist on strategic affairs, was to point out.

The visit turned out to be a defining moment in Indo–US relations. It was a precursor for the major shift in policy that was to take place during George W. Bush's presidency of the United States (2001–09). Towards the end of his term, when Vajpayee went to Washington DC in January 2004, a rethink was already taking place at the American end. India and the US announced the Next Steps in Strategic Partnership (NSSP), for cooperation in space, high-end technology, and civil nuclear energy—though at the time it was limited to 'regulatory and safety issues'. In 2005, Manmohan Singh would initiate a process that led to the two countries signing the Indo–US Civil Nuclear Deal—which took the relationship to an altogether new level. It resulted in billions of dollars in trade, and a growing defence partnership, among other things—and was, according to C. Raja Mohan, the 'single biggest consequence' of the 1998 tests. 'It is only by (our) going nuclear, (that) the Americans were willing to go along with us.' This would not have happened, if India had 'not come out of the purdah' and declared it had the weapons.

XI

After the PM's press conference on the tests on 11 May 1998, I had headed
to North Block from Race Course Road. I had hoped to catch Advani
to get his reaction to the tests. He agreed to see me—and we chatted
'informally'. I thought he would be surrounded by ecstatic partymen
celebrating the occasion. But he was sitting all alone in that large room
once used by India's iron man Vallabhbhai Patel, whom he wanted to
emulate, and whose photo adorned the wall behind him.

Advani looked pensive, not elated. As he talked, he became emotional.
I found it curious that he should talk less about the nuclear tests—though
he recalled the party's long-standing commitment to make a bomb—and
more about his struggles over the years to make the party a mainstream
force. He recalled with feeling the early years when he and Vajpayee had
launched the BJP. He spoke of the attempt on his life three months earlier,
going over the attack on him in Coimbatore on 14 February 1998 which
had almost killed him. Advani is an emotional man and as he went over
the events of that day, tears welled up in his eyes.

That evening I got the feeling that Advani was hurt—that Vajpayee had
taken a step as monumental as exercising the nuclear option, but when it
happened, he had not been part of crafting a decision, to which Advani
and the party had been committed for half a century. He was merely
informed, not consulted—and kept out of the loop till the last moment.
Vajpayee had chosen to 'rely on an official', as Advani saw Brajesh Mishra,
and not him, a political comrade of four decades' standing.

After 1984, when the party was down to 2 Lok Sabha seats under
Vajpayee's stewardship, it was Advani who had led the party. But in 1998,
for the first time since the BJP was formed, he had not been part of the
inner group which took a decision as big as the nuclear tests. For Advani
saw himself as the builder of BJP as much as Vajpayee. He must have
sensed that though he was the home minister of India, he was now no
longer going to be number two.

11 May 1998 was to throw up a more assertive Advani—though the
differences between him and Vajpayee were to come out openly only a
couple of years later. While the 1998 tests took India to the global high table
of nuclear weapon states, they generated tensions within the government
and the ruling BJP—which Vajpayee was less able to manage, and which
were to create problems for the prime minister in 2001–02. Above all,
they redefined the Vajpayee–Advani relationship—casting a long shadow
over the years of comradeship-cum-rivalry which had coexisted between
the two men. Till then, whenever differences had arisen, they would meet,
talk, and pull back from the brink.

I came away from North Block on 11 May 1998 with an indefinable
sense that Advani felt—though he did not say it explicitly—that his

contribution to the 'big moment' had not been acknowledged by Vajpayee.

∎

When Vajpayee became prime minister, it was clear that for all practical purposes, it would be Brajesh Mishra who would occupy the number two position. He was not just principal secretary to the PM, and national security advisor taking care of all security issues, he had become a friend and companion to Vajpayee. He would share a drink with him on most evenings.

Like Vajpayee's foster family—his companion of years, Rajkumari Kaul, foster daughter Namita, and foster son-in-law Ranjan Bhattacharya, and their daughter Niharika—Brajesh Mishra started to take care of Vajpayee. 'When the family were away, Brajesh or I would babysit him in the evening,' Ashok Saikia had once told me. Saikia was joint secretary in the PMO and a friend of Rajkumari Kaul's family.

For Vajpayee, being PM meant having a free hand to make decisions. He did not relish either Advani or the RSS brass breathing down his neck. In Mishra, Vajpayee had found both his sword and his shield.

This intensified the tussle between Mishra and Advani in the months that followed. Advani had wanted Vijai Kapoor, not Brajesh Mishra, to be made the prime minister's principal secretary. Party colleagues had told Advani that he, as the number two, must have a say in the decisions at the top. But Vajpayee ruled out Kapoor. That, according to Brajesh Mishra, was the beginning of the problem between them. Mishra admitted frankly that there were 'problems' between them. 'Advani suddenly found...my...strong influence on Vajpayee and he didn't like that.' Ministers and secretaries went to see Brajesh Mishra, sensing that power had been delegated to him by the prime minister. Mishra would tell them that he would 'talk to Atalji and (then) see'.

Said Brajesh Mishra, 'Advani didn't like it. Nor did Jaswant Singh.'

'The two of them got together and tried to get Atalji to divest me of one of the two jobs,' Mishra said. 'Either NSA or the principal secretary. The RSS also intervened.'

But Atalji held firm. 'If he goes I go', he was clear.

At one stage, Vajpayee asked Mishra to meet Advani to sort out their differences. He held 'two long meetings' with Advani. Advani, according to Mishra, started off by saying, 'I am not an ordinary home minister.'

'I know you are the senior leader of the party. If you have any problem,' Mishra told Advani, 'why don't you meet him (Vajpayee) and have lunch with him once a week and talk over things. You have known each other for forty to fifty years.'

Advani: 'If we have lunch neither he will talk nor I will talk.'

'You are the only person in the BJP who can pick up the phone day or night and call him,' Mishra replied. 'Do that, instead of thinking that

I am doing something contrary to what you think should be done.'

Mishra reported the conversation back to Vajpayee. Nothing came of the mediatory efforts. Having been acquitted in the hawala case in 1997, Advani would have felt he had as much right to the top job as did Vajpayee.

■

In April 1999, almost a year after the nuclear tests, Vajpayee's government fell. He lost a no-confidence motion by just 1 vote in April 1999. He was re-elected to power in October 1999, with his popularity at an all-time high. It was not so much the Kargil War which won him votes. It was more, I found as I travelled in the country in the run-up to elections, the sympathy people had for him. Many felt he had been wronged, brought down by Sonia Gandhi, Jayalalithaa, and Subramaniam Swamy who had joined hands to get him defeated.

By 2001, the euphoria was petering out. Advani, backed by the RSS brass, kept up the pressure on the prime minister. Things came to a head in 2002. The levels of distrust between the two leaders kept growing. There was a buzz in the corridors of power that Vajpayee might move to Rashtrapati Bhavan when the presidential elections took place in July 2002—and Advani would take over from him. An RSS leader even met Vajpayee and put this proposal to him—which he turned down. The year 2002 saw a visible weakening of Vajpayee. His prime-ministerial authority took a beating as an ascendant—and assertive—Advani came to the fore.

In the way Advani carried himself in those days, his words, his demeanour, body language, everything about him exuded a sense of confidence that he would soon be taking over as prime minister.

Three episodes that year symbolized the altered equations between the two men. After the Godhra killings in Gujarat in February end and early March 2002, Vajpayee urged the chief minister, Narendra Modi, to observe 'raj dharma', in other words to resign. But Advani, the younger group of BJP leaders and the RSS leadership backed Modi. Vajpayee had to climb down from his position at the Goa meet of the party's national executive in April 2002. A week later he was giving explanations for Modi's actions.

In early June 2002, *Time* magazine carried a piece by Alex Perry on Vajpayee. It wrote about a 'drunken' PM heading the Indian government. Whatever be the truth about who was Perry's informant, according to Shakti Sinha, the Vajpayee camp saw it as a 'hatchet job' carried out on behalf of Advani. Though the Home Ministry, in a show of disapproval, made Perry run around to get his visa extended, this made things worse for Vajpayee. It made him look vindictive.

Around the same time, moves were underway for who would be made president of India, when K. R. Narayanan's term came to an end in July 2002. Vajpayee wanted Krishan Kant to become the next president of

India. Both the BJP and the Congress had agreed to back Kant. His name was finalized after discussions between the two parties which were led by Brajesh Mishra and Natwar Singh. Vajpayee personally went to meet Kant. The prime minister informed the vice president officially that the NDA and the Congress would both support him for president—as they sat talking on the back veranda of 6, Maulana Azad Road. But Vajpayee was upstaged by Advani and a group of BJP leaders and A. P. J. Abdul Kalam, became president. It galled Vajpayee that he as the prime minister of India could not even have a say in who would be the president of the republic.

Ten years later, Brajesh Mishra said on Krishan Kant's tenth death anniversary, 'Humne toh kar diya thaa... Yeh to Advani ne garbar kar dee thee (We had got everything cleared, it was Advani who upset the plan).'

It was in mid-2002 that Vajpayee decided to sue for peace. He picked up the phone and dialled Advani. 'Tell Kamlaji, I am coming for lunch and will eat Sindhi kadhi,' he said. Their meeting lasted four hours. They went over the gilae-shikwae—and a truce was finally worked out. Vajpayee appointed Advani as deputy prime minister on 29 June 2002—this was something the RSS had been demanding for some time. According to Brajesh Mishra, Vajpayee had deferred to the RSS—Rajju Bhaiya was the RSS chief at the time—and made Advani DPM. After that Vajpayee kept giving in to Advani and the RSS; the last straw came with the announcement of an early general election in 2004.

After the assembly elections in the winter of 2003, when the BJP did well in north Indian states, Advani led a group of BJP leaders to see Vajpayee. Those who accompanied him included M. Venkaiah Naidu, Pramod Mahajan, and Ananth Kumar. Except Murli Manohar Joshi, most of the other prominent leaders were there in the group. They asked him to advance the dates of the next general election, which were to take place in October 2004. It was assumed that Advani would take over as PM after the elections. Vajpayee agreed.

'Why did you agree to this?' an upset Mishra confronted Vajpayee. 'It was the only time when I said this to Atalji.'

'The entire party came to me, what do I do?' a disheartened Vajpayee told Mishra.

But Advani's plan backfired. The BJP lost in 2004. The Congress formed a government at the head of a coalition. 'If Advani had waited till October (for elections as scheduled),' Brajesh Mishra said later, 'perhaps things would have been different.'

It was the end of the road for Vajpayee. He announced Advani as his successor in 2005 at a meeting in Mumbai's Shivaji Park. It was at the same grounds where Advani had projected Vajpayee as the BJP's prime ministerial candidate ten years earlier.

Advani did not make it to the top position he had long coveted. His bid for the prime ministership in 2009 failed. Though in power for five years, the Congress increased its tally from 145 to 206 seats. Vajpayee walked into the sunset. Advani too moved into the shadows that were rapidly lengthening.

Vajpayee had successfully managed the fallout of the nuclear explosion at the international level. But Pokhran II compounded an already complex situation within his government and inside the BJP—which was more difficult to handle.

XII

Was Atal Bihari Vajpayee an overrated prime minister? Some might say 'yes'—if he is judged by the achievements of his prime-ministerial tenure.

Vajpayee's premiership will, of course, be remembered for the nuclear tests he undertook, taking India into the big league of 'nuclear-have' states. And yet, ironically, he himself did not view them as the biggest achievement of his tenure. In fact, he felt the credit for testing should be given to Narasimha Rao. 'Rao told me the bomb was ready,' he said. 'I only exploded it.'

Vajpayee also followed liberal economic policies, but again he was only following the path shown by Rao when he opened up the Indian economy in 1991. Much of Vajpayee's premiership was a story of managing the conflicts inherent in the difficult twenty-party coalition he headed.

He was clearly not a hands-on administrator—interested more in making the macro decisions. He left the nuts and bolts of decision-making to Brajesh Mishra. Interestingly, Vajpayee wanted to be remembered more for his attempts to settle the Kashmir problem, the thawing of Indo-Pak relations, and his efforts to usher in permanent peace in the subcontinent.

He undertook the pathbreaking Lahore Yatra in 1999 to create goodwill between the two countries. But, as already mentioned, the Pakistan Army responded with the Kargil War. Its military leadership did not endorse the civilian government's decision to improve relations with India. Despite Kargil, Vajpayee made another effort to effect a breakthrough between the two countries—and held the Agra Summit in 2001. It did not succeed. As Murasoli Maran, a minister in the Vajpayee cabinet, was to reveal later in private, it was Advani who shot down the final statement that had been hammered out.

Vajpayee made efforts to resolve the Kashmir tangle—an issue which was close to his heart. In April 2003, he announced a three-word solution to the Kashmir problem—that it was through a spirit of 'Kashmiriyat, Insaniyat, Jamooriyat (Kashmiri identity, democracy, and humanity)' that a solution could be found. These were words uttered in Urdu by the leader of a party known for its Hindu and Hindi credentials. It was an idea that only Vajpayee could formulate, creating an ambience, which he often did, without spelling out the specifics.

The Vajpayee doctrine on Kashmir, as it was sometimes called, made the Kashmiris sit up and take note. But a solution to Kashmir or the Indo-Pak impasse eluded him—as it would the prime ministers who followed him. However, he saw his unremitting efforts to solve one of the most vexed problems facing the country as the contribution for which he most wanted to be remembered.

Vajpayee was a skilled chess master, who thought out his moves in advance to get the better of his opponents. though he did not always succeed. Essentially a non-confrontationist, he did not like conflict situations, and often backed down when pressure mounted. On Ayodhya, after opposing the kar seva which led to the demolition of the Babri Masjid, he defended it in his inimitable, roundabout way. In Agra, under pressure from Advani, he did not push for a breakthrough with Pakistan president General Pervez Musharraf. Or in Goa, where he had asked Gujarat CM Narendra Modi to follow 'raj dharma' after the Godhra riots and resign, he backed down under pressure from his party colleagues. He did not push to get the president of his choice installed in Rashtrapati Bhavan in 2002. The one instance where he refused to yield ground was when the RSS mounted pressure on him for the removal of Brajesh Mishra—where he threatened to quit as PM.

At heart, Vajpayee believed in give and take. Though he was groomed in the RSS and became a pracharak, it was the cut and thrust of parliamentary politics, and the many relationships he forged across parties in parliament over a period of almost fifty years, which made him what he was—a moderate in a right-wing party.

While his politics was located within the Hindu framework, he did not come across as being against the minorities, or the Muslims, in particular. And the image of a moderate stuck to him, for all the political somersaults he made for survival, and he made many. But people forgave him because they felt he made his flip-flops under pressure from the hardliners in his party. After working in the RSS-driven Jan Sangh, and its later avatar, the BJP, Vajpayee wanted to fashion a pro-Hindu, right-wing party which was 'inclusive' and mindful of India's plural ethos—and freed of backseat driving by the 'Sangh' leadership. He chafed against the pressure the RSS exerted on him from time to time, but lacked the courage—or the stamina—to break free and fashion a new instrumentality.

How then will Vajpayee be judged as a politician and a prime minister?

Vajpayee will be remembered not so much for what he did—like the nuclear tests he went in for. Or for other decisions he took or failed to take. He will be remembered more for what he was—a man who believed in walking the middle path. He believed a country as diverse as India could only be governed by a consensus. That will remain his enduring legacy.

CHAPTER 6

THE UNDERRATED PRIME MINISTER WHO TRIUMPHED

Manmohan Singh and the Indo–US Civil Nuclear Deal

I

On 18 July 2005, an elaborate banquet was underway at the White House in Washington DC. It was a dinner that would be remembered long after the dessert plates and cognac snifters were cleared away. Those present were aware that the event was being held to herald the beginning of a new and strategic partnership between India and the US.

An embossed invitation to the dinner had gone out to a select guest list from US president George W. Bush and First Lady Laura Bush. The evening was to be 'in honour of the Prime Minister of the Republic of India and Mrs Gursharan Kaur'. The tables in the State Dining Room that evening were covered in saffron-coloured silk and adorned with floral statues of trumpeting elephants made of pink roses. '[It] signaled it was no ordinary evening at the White House' read a report in the *Washington Post* the next day. The paper described the evening as 'A Bush dinner as rare as a pink elephant'. The dinner was meant to be 'a nod to India'. For George W. Bush was not given to throwing banquets. He preferred to retire to bed by 9 p.m.

Earlier in the day, Prime Minister Manmohan Singh and President Bush had issued a joint statement which laid out a framework for a strategic partnership between the two countries. The agreement was on joint India–US efforts on terrorism, security, trade, finance, investment, environment, and energy. The significant part of the agreement, however, was about 'nuclear energy'—which was to lead to the Indo–US Civil Nuclear Deal.

Ten days earlier, the soft-spoken Singh and the hearty Texan Bush had sat side by side at a meeting in Scotland. It was held at the exclusive Gleneagles Hotel in Auchterarder. They were both participating in the 31st G8 summit hosted by British Prime Minister Tony Blair. On this occasion, in early July 2005, five of the world's growing economic powers—China, India, Brazil, Mexico, and South Africa (who called themselves the G5)—had joined the world's top eight industrialized nations. They were France, Germany, Italy, Japan, the UK, the US, Canada, Russia, and comprised the G8. Climate change, carbon emissions, clean energy, and aid to Africa dominated the discussions.

The Glendevon Room at the grand and massive hotel, set amidst the rolling hills of Scotland, had been converted into a high security meeting area. In their first meeting, Bush turned to Singh and said: 'If the oil prices go up to $100, it hurts India...But it also hurts the United States.' Then, he added: 'So, we must work together to help India to get its nuclear security by increased emphasis on the availability of nuclear power.'

When the two leaders had met on the sidelines of the United Nations General Assembly a year earlier, Bush in his direct style had asked Manmohan Singh, 'What can I do for you?' Singh told Bush that the biggest problem India faced was 'of energy, and prices are going up'.

Manmohan Singh had first talked about cooperation with the US on civil nuclear energy when he was in New York soon after he took over as prime minister in September 2004.

That day in Scotland, without saying so explicitly, Bush and Singh put the Indo–US Civil Nuclear Deal at the centre of the new relationship they wanted to forge between their nations. The US under secretary of state for political affairs, R. Nicholas Burns and the Indian foreign secretary, Shyam Saran, sat in another room at the massive estate. Burns told Saran that day that the US objective was to 'confirm India's status as a full-fledged nuclear-weapon state with all the rights but also the obligations'. However, soon thereafter he was to go back on his statement, and called up to say that as a party to the NPT, the US could not explicitly recognize India as a nuclear-weapon state.

At Gleneagles, George W. Bush and Manmohan Singh struck up a rapport—which was to lead to a 'chemistry' between the two that was later talked about widely. For all their closeness, however, both knew only too well that national interest, not personal factors, determined relations between nations. Nevertheless, personal chemistry did smoothen the ride when the path became rocky in the months that followed.

'Dr Singh,' Bush was to tell the Indian prime minister, 'you are a good man. I look forward to doing business with you.' Manmohan Singh, fourteen years older than Bush, reciprocated Bush's sentiments, 'He (Bush) is very nice to me,' Singh was to remark to journalist Raj Chengappa, 'and of all the US presidents, he seemed the friendliest to India'.

Sitting in the large and beautiful Scottish estate that day which the media had described as the 'eighth wonder of the world' when the hotel opened in 1924, Bush remarked to Singh, 'A solid relationship is based on values as well as (common) interest.' Those words were to stay with Manmohan Singh for long afterwards.

∎

The dinner Bush hosted in honour of Singh ten days later was a black-tie affair. Prithviraj Chavan, the minister of state in the Prime Minister's

Office, who was a guest at the occasion, recalled: 'There was a special embossed programme, the guest list was published in the social pages of newspapers, a jazz group specially selected to provide the music...(the) Indians invited were carefully chosen—footballers, doctors, businessmen....' Bush had initially described the event as a 'family dinner'. But it became a black-tie affair, the first big social event in the White House in two years, and the fifth formal dinner given by Bush for any head of government. This did not go unnoticed in the higher echelons of the US administration. Nor was its importance lost on the 134 guests who were there.

Bush had turned out in a tuxedo; Singh wore a black bandhgala and his signature pale blue turban. Laura Bush was attired in bright colours associated with India—a yellow chiffon gown with orange flowery design. Mrs Gursharan Kaur chose to wear a sophisticated and understated black silk sari with a red border. US Vice President Dick Cheney, Defence Secretary Donald Rumsfeld, Supreme Court Judge Clarence Thomas, World Bank President Paul Wolfowitz, and US senators mingled with the Indian guests, and those from the Indian business diaspora. Besides the prime minister and his wife, the Indian delegation comprised External Affairs Minister Natwar Singh, Indian Ambassador to the US Ronen Sen, Deputy Chairman of the Planning Commission Montek Singh Ahluwalia, Minister of State in the PMO Prithviraj Chavan, National Security Advisor M. K. Narayanan, the PM's Principal Secretary T. K. Nair, and Foreign Secretary Shyam Saran.

US Secretary of State Condoleezza Rice mingled with the guests, a wide smile lighting up her face. She had reason to be pleased. The framework agreement had almost fallen through twenty-four hours earlier. Rice had just managed to retrieve the situation, with a timely intervention in the early hours of that morning.

President Bush and the First Lady escorted their guests into the State Dining Room. The US president raised a toast to his Indian guest. 'India and the US are separated by half a globe,' he said. 'Yet today our two nations are closer than ever before.' The Indian prime minister was equally effusive. He thanked the president for his generosity. 'Mark Twain once said the only foreign land he ever...longed to see was India,' Singh said. 'We have grown up learning the story of the unfinished voyage of Christopher Columbus: setting sail to reach India, he discovered America. I now invite the people of America to complete the voyage of that great explorer.'

Applause followed. Then, a four-course meal. There was asparagus soup, halibut, basmati rice with pistachios and raisins to give the Indian touch, and a salad of Bibb lettuce and citrus vinaigrette. This was followed by dessert—chocolate lotus blossoms with mango, and chocolate-cardamom, and cashew ice cream. And the choicest of wines complemented the food.

After dinner, the guests moved to the East Room where they were joined by 126 others for an evening of entertainment by the legendary Preservation Hall Jazz Band, considered a 'genuine American Art treasure'. George Bush had rolled out the red carpet for Manmohan Singh.

The atmosphere was upbeat. Many noticed the camaraderie between Singh and Bush. Both sides were on a high, having overcome the last glitches to finalize the joint statement—which would redefine their relationship as never before. But neither leader realized that night that it would take another thirty-nine months of painstaking, determined effort, on both sides, to bring the deal they had been working on to fruition.

II

'I am thinking in very bold terms,' an upbeat US Secretary of State Condoleezza Rice told Indian officials in New Delhi in March 2005. She had come to India on a flying visit and was speaking animatedly about her vision for Indo–US relations which could lead to a new partnership between the two countries.

The energetic and focussed Rice who was to become the prime mover in the Indo–US Civil Nuclear Deal, had immediately grasped the possibility of a 'strategic convergence' between the two countries. She had first expressed an interest in enhancing US ties with India during the 2000 presidential campaign in the US. In a widely quoted article in *Foreign Affairs*, Rice, who was to become one of the most powerful officials in the incoming Bush administration (as national security advisor in his first term and secretary of state in the second term), wrote that India was not a great power yet. But it had the potential to become one—and it should figure prominently in the US's calculations in a post-Cold War world—just as it did in China's concerns.

As the Republicans took over from the Democrats in the US in 2000, Rice was looking at how the US should redefine its national interest after the collapse of the Soviet Union in 1991.

'Great Powers,' she asserted, 'do not just mind their own business.' She viewed a rising China as a 'strategic competitor', not a 'strategic partner', as seen by Bush's predecessor Bill Clinton. While welcoming America's growing economic relationship with China, Rice could see the 'potential threat' it could pose to the stability of the Asia-Pacific region, even though its military power at the time was no match to that of the US. Her words were prophetic.

Rice made a strong case for the US to move away from viewing India through a narrow prism and instead to 'pay closer attention to India's role in the regional balance'. 'There is a strong tendency,' she lamented, 'conceptually to connect India with Pakistan and to think only of Kashmir or the nuclear competition between the two states.'

With Rice calling for a 'deep dialogue' with India, the Bush administration reached out to New Delhi in a new way in the months that followed.

India too was looking at an emerging global reality after the collapse of the Soviet Union in 1990 and the opening up of its economy in 1991. Russia had weakened, China was on the rise. While the US was not giving up the economic interest it had in China, it had started to look at India as a 'balancing factor'. India too was apprehensive, Foreign Secretary Shyam Saran was to reveal, that a US on the decline might cede to China a dominant role in Asia, which could go against Indian interests. These changing perceptions about each other led to the creation of the NSSP initiative on 12 January 2004—when Prime Minister Atal Bihari Vajpayee went to Washington. It envisaged cooperation between the two countries in the areas of civil nuclear energy, space, and high-end technology—but in an incremental manner.

■

'Someday the US will need to let India get out of the nuclear netherworld.' Brajesh Mishra, national security advisor to Vajpayee, had once said to Rice, when she was still the US's national security advisor during Bush's first term as President (2000–04). Those words were to stay with her. For, over the years, the nuclear issue had been a major irritant between the two countries.

The US sanctions against India after its 1974 'peaceful nuclear explosion' had made it a nuclear pariah globally. America had gone back on its agreement to supply fuel to the Tarapur reactors it had helped set up in India—and also refused to let India reprocess the spent fuel. The US had also helped to set up a global regime to prevent India from acquiring high-end technology or do trade in nuclear fuel even for its civilian reactors—unless it signed the Non-Proliferation Treaty and gave up its nuclear weapons. The tension between the two countries grew after India's nuclear tests in 1998. Hit by sanctions imposed by the US and other countries, India was penalized by the Nuclear Suppliers Group, a group of forty-five of the world's industrialized nations, which had come into existence after the 1974 nuclear test by India. They included nations with nuclear weapons. The cartel imposed a ban on the sale of nuclear fuel and sophisticated technology to India. As a result, India's civil nuclear set-up had struggled to meet the shortage of fuel, to run its existing nuclear reactors. It lacked spare parts and technology to upgrade its nuclear plants. The sanctions had also adversely affected the country's space programme and its defence establishment.

Soon after the NSSP in early 2004, Brajesh Mishra had sent word to his US counterpart, Colin Powell (in Bush's second term), that India was willing to put some of its nuclear reactors under safeguards—if the ban on the fuel supply imposed on it after 1974 and 1998 could be lifted. There was no response from the American side at the time.

It was only when Manmohan Singh succeeded Vajpayee in mid-2004 that the US began to look at India's core concerns—and consider the possibility of recognizing it as a de facto nuclear-weapon state. The US, which was revisiting its foreign policy at the time, calculated that strengthening its relationship with an India on the rise—even if it was an India with nuclear weapons—was in its interest. It could become a counterweight to an ascendant China in the Asia-Pacific region. The US, however, did not openly talk about containing China during 2005–08, when the Indo–US Civil Nuclear Deal was being negotiated. Nor did India. But China saw it as a ploy by the US to induct India into an anti-China formation to counter China's influence in the region.

•

Condoleezza Rice decided to pursue the nuclear deal with India as soon as she became secretary of state in January 2005. When she visited India in March 2005, and met Prime Minister Manmohan Singh and External Affairs Minister Natwar Singh, who hosted her, Rice told the Indian leaders that Bush now wanted to go beyond the NSSP forged during Vajpayee's time. She made a case for quickly concluding the NSSP—and suggested it be done by the time the Indian prime minister came to the US in July 2005. It was her first trip to South Asia and she was on her way to Pakistan. Few Indian officials had expected such an 'expansive presentation' from a new US secretary of state.

She also took Indian officials into confidence that Bush was going to sell F-16 fighter aircraft to Pakistan and that India, too, could buy 'advanced weapons'. Ten days later, the White House announced the sale of F-16s to Pakistan. Rice had persuaded Bush to delay the announcement until she returned from her trip to South Asia. It was what Rice said in private conversations that piqued India's interest.

During the journey home to Washington DC, Rice wrote out a memo for President Bush. In six pages, she summed up the outlines of her South Asian strategy. The memo proposed that the US administration should end its incremental approach towards India. It should 'simply go for broke' and cut a civil nuclear deal. She was clear about the 'broader strategic goal' to pursue—position India 'to become one of the United States's two or three closest partners'.

Over the next weeks, the hard-headed Rice convinced Bush, who was given to holding forth on freedom and democracy, that the US should deal with India as a great power in the making. It had to move beyond its attitude of 'restraining India' from going nuclear just because it had not signed the NPT. She saw a powerful India becoming a counterweight to China, although, in her memo, Rice did not state this explicitly. She also had a timetable in mind, particularly for the civil nuclear deal. While in

Delhi, she had told the Indian officials that both countries should aim to issue a joint statement at the forthcoming July 2005 summit between George W. Bush and Manmohan Singh (with which we began this chapter). And when Bush visited India in March 2006, the two leaders could finalize a schedule for the implementation of the deal.

Enthused by her words, officials on both sides knuckled down to work.

■

On 17 July 2005, the Indian prime minister flew into Washington DC aboard Air India One. He was accompanied by a high-level delegation. The prime minister was hoping to finalize an agreement with the US on cooperation between the two countries on civil nuclear energy.

Before arriving in Washington DC, Manmohan Singh had already made two strategic decisions. He had included Anil Kakodkar, the chairman of the Atomic Energy Commission (AEC), in the official delegation. He had a sense that the opposition to the proposed agreement was likely to come from the AEC back home. He also knew that if the agreement had the approval of the country's premier scientific body (the AEC), it would dilute some of the criticism that was bound to come, especially from the Left parties at home.

By now, the Left parties, which propped up his government, were a worried lot. They witnessed India was moving into the US orbit. They had ripped into the ten-year Defence Framework Agreement, to expand ties between India and the US in security-related areas—signed three weeks earlier by Defence Minister Pranab Mukherjee and US Defence Secretary Donald Rumsfeld. The Left leaders feared that India was giving away too much of its autonomy, and could become a client state of the US.

Manmohan Singh also apprehended that Sonia Gandhi might have reservations. He knew she wanted to keep the Left parties in good humour; their support was critical for the survival of the UPA government. This was of crucial concern for Singh as he owed his prime ministership to Sonia, and she controlled many of the levers of decision-making at the top.

His second strategic move was to send External Affairs Minister Natwar Singh to Washington DC a day earlier to clear the draft agreement that officials had been working on.

Besides being the foreign minister, Natwar Singh was trusted by Sonia Gandhi. She had relied on his advice on foreign policy long before the UPA came to power. Manmohan Singh was now relying on Natwar Singh to convince her of the need to forge a new relationship with the US.

■

Soon after arriving in the US capital, Manmohan Singh called a meeting of the Indian delegation. The group gathered at Blair House, the US president's guest house, where the Indian PM was staying. He wanted to discuss the draft agreement which had already been prepared. Present at the meeting was Foreign Secretary Shyam Saran who had been in the US capital holding preparatory discussions. Saran and Burns had worked on the draft agreement. This had then been vetted by Natwar Singh and Condoleezza Rice on 16 July. Everything was ready for the Indian prime minister.

Singh asked the draft to be circulated to everyone present. He then went around the room, seeking the comments of each one. Most felt the deal should be closed. Many in the Indian delegation were upbeat. A never-before partnership between India and the US was now in the offing. It was a historic opportunity which should not be missed.

However, there were some who feared that India might be getting too close to the US. Their main reservation, according to Shyam Saran, was about 'the constraints the framework agreement would impose on India's strategic (nuclear) programme'. These constraints consisted of 'safeguards' India would have to agree to put on its nuclear facilities. It would have to indicate which establishments it would open up for inspections by the UN's International Atomic Energy Agency (IAEA).

According to Anil Kakodkar, there were twenty-two power generating reactors in the country at the time.

At one stage, the US wanted all Indian nuclear reactors to be brought under the IAEA's supervision. This was unacceptable to India. The discussions then had moved on to which reactors would be classified as civil, and open for inspections, and which would be defined as military and out of bounds to outsiders.

At the meeting, National Security Advisor M. K. Narayanan, though 'positive' overall, had responded with 'caution'. Anil Kakodkar had serious reservations. 'We will benefit from nuclear commerce,' Kakodkar told the group. But he was concerned about the 'impact it will have on India's nuclear programme'. He—and the Department of Atomic Energy (DAE)—had been wary of the US's understanding of which of India's twenty-two nuclear reactors would be defined as civil and which of them would be classified as strategic installations. But Kakodkar was clear that this was a decision only India should make. Eventually, India was to classify its power generating reactors into two categories, agreeing to put fourteen under safeguards and keep eight for strategic (military) purposes.

Kakodkar was also worried about the impact the deal would have on India's plans to develop a 'three-stage nuclear fuel cycle' for its nuclear programme. What this was designed to do was to move the programme 'from the uranium-based reactors to fast reactors to thorium reactors'.

'That cannot be developed with foreign inspectors breathing down your neck,' Kakodkar told the delegation. 'They (inspectors) will look at it with great suspicion, that we are up to some mischief.'

India has large thorium reserves. But uranium was in short supply—a reason why its reactors were not running at full capacity. The three-stage programme aimed to develop the technology to overcome its uranium shortage and utilize its ample thorium resources to produce enough nuclear fuel. As Kakodkar put it, 'The strategy of exploiting thorium to the fullest is embedded in the three-stage programme to give long-term energy security to India.'

The Americans were proposing to put reactors using the three-stage nuclear fuel cycle in the civilian category. This, Kakodkar was clear, was totally 'unacceptable'. For, the three-stage nuclear fuel cycle required sensitive technology. It could not be kept under the 'civilian' category, it had to be put under the 'military'. 'Or,' Kakodkar did not mince his words at the Blair House meeting chaired by the prime minister, 'India would be "sacrificing" its "sovereign" right to develop its nuclear programme as it thought best.'

The PM chose to back Kakodkar. 'If Kakodkar is not happy,' Manmohan Singh declared, 'we can't go ahead.... More work is needed on the draft....' He told the officials, 'You must get it modified.'

The group broke for dinner. When they met again, things had 'hotted up'. 'Most in our group felt the "opportunity might get lost because of this fellow (Kakodkar)",' Kakodkar recalled. Some suspected that he was not for the agreement. 'This was not true. But (I felt) it had to be subject to India getting fully satisfied—and ensuring that the principle of separating the civil from the military was fully embedded in the agreement.'

To the prime minister, Kakodkar's reservations indicated the reaction that might greet him back in India. 'He was worried about the Left and Sonia Gandhi,' said Shyam Saran. 'These were political reservations.' As the PM told Natwar Singh later: 'I won't be able to sell it back home.'

'That was his worry,' Natwar Singh said to me.

When the marathon meeting at Blair House finally ended that night, the prime minister was clear. He would not override the reservations of the scientists. He decided that the joint statement by him and George Bush planned for the next day would have to be limited to just a bland, two-line formulation on civil nuclear energy.

'I conveyed this (Manmohan Singh's decision) to Nicholas Burns who was very disappointed,' Shyam Saran said. Burns passed on the information to President Bush and to Condoleezza Rice. Rice then spoke to the president: 'It isn't going to work,' she told her boss. 'Singh just can't make it happen.'

'Too bad,' Bush replied philosophically. He didn't say more.

■

18 July—the day the joint statement was to be released started very early for Natwar Singh. The phone rang at 'an unearthly hour' in his suite at the

Willard Hotel. He was staying there with the Indian delegation. A sleepy Singh picked up the receiver. Condoleezza Rice was on the line. 'I want to see you,' she said. As Natwar Singh was anyway billed to see Rice that day, he was startled by her request at that unusual hour. But he did not show his surprise. He merely said he would come over.

'No, I am going to come and see you now,' she insisted. Natwar Singh guessed Rice wanted to talk about why the draft agreement had run into trouble.

Years later, Rice would provide her version of the events as they unfolded on the morning of 18 July. 'I woke up at 4.30 a.m. and sat (up) straight in bed,' Rice wrote in her book, *No Higher Honour*. 'I am not letting this go down, I thought.'

Manmohan Singh was to meet Bush at the Oval Office at 10 a.m.

Rice first rang Burns. 'I am not prepared to let this fail,' she said. 'Arrange for me to see the prime minister.' Burns called back shortly to say that the prime minister did not want to meet her. 'Get me the foreign minister,' she said. It was then that she spoke to Natwar Singh. She arrived at his hotel very soon after her call—it appeared that she had been ready to move even as she called. 'It must've been around 6.30 a.m., I was still in my dressing gown,' said Singh.

'Why is the prime minister refusing to see me?' Rice asked Natwar Singh.

'He does not want to say "no" to you.'

'Let me see him personally and let him give me a hearing,' she said. 'I want to save the agreement.... The United States wants to take this thirty-year millstone from around your neck, you should do it.... Ask him again,' she added.

Natwar Singh phoned the prime minister. 'Woh aa rahi hain (She is coming),' he told Manmohan Singh, 'aap mil lo (There is no harm in meeting her).'

Manmohan Singh agreed to meet Rice at 8 a.m. at Blair House. 'I joined them a little later,' Natwar Singh said. At the meeting Rice said to the prime minister, 'You tell me what is standing in the way.... What's the problem and let me see if I can resolve it.' Rice had been authorized by President Bush to address India's concerns—before meeting the prime minister she had called Bush to tell him she was making a final effort to salvage the deal.

'Mr Prime Minister...you and President Bush are about to put US–Indian relations on a fundamentally new footing,' Rice told the PM. 'I know it's hard for you, but it's hard for the president too. I didn't come here to negotiate the language, only to ask you to tell your officials to get this done. And let's get it done before you see the president.'

The prime minister, Rice wrote, 'eventually gave his nod to his people to try again.' After the meeting with Manmohan Singh, she drove directly to the White House to tell the president the good news—that they were giving the agreement another shot.

After Condoleezza Rice left, Manmohan Singh asked Anil Kakodkar to come over. The PM asked him straightaway what would be acceptable to him. Natwar Singh was with the PM. Silently, Kakodkar picked up a tissue from a box that was on the table before him. He sat down and scribbled two sentences on it. 'They were words to the effect that the autonomy of our three-stage strategic programme should not be restricted in any way.' He handed the message to the PM. The PM looked at the paper and passed it to Natwar Singh, who put it in his pocket. Then Kakodkar left.

Natwar Singh showed Kakodkar's demand to Rice. She looked at it and said, 'In principle this would be OK.' She said she would have to run it past others, 'But we can go ahead. Broadly speaking, there is a convergence of views.'

'From our point of view, we did not want any ambiguity in the language,' Saran said to me. He and Burns got back to work on the draft once more.

Meanwhile, as planned, Manmohan Singh met Bush at the Oval Office at 10 a.m. Natwar Singh, Prithviraj Chavan, M. K. Narayanan, and Condoleezza Rice awaited the outcome of the meeting. When Bush and Singh came out of the room, they were smiling.

'Ho gaya hai (It had happened), that was obvious,' Natwar Singh recalled.

However, as those working on the agreement were still putting the final touches to the document in a room not far from the Oval Office, 'we stood there chatting and joking', recalled Natwar Singh.

'I told Bush a story about Idi Amin to lighten the moment,' said Natwar Singh. Amin, the Ugandan dictator who had thrown thousands of his countrymen into prison, once told his foreign minister that Uganda should be renamed 'Idi' and that the decision should be conveyed to the UN.

'There is a problem,' the sharp Ugandan foreign minister told his boss. 'The people of Cyprus are called Cypriots. The people of Idi will be called Idiots.'

Idi Amin dropped the idea.

Everyone laughed. There was a let-up in the tension, though the final word had not yet come from the drafting team.

Finally, the two leaders moved towards the room in which a press conference had been scheduled to be held at noon. The plan had been to announce the joint statement at the presser, but as the drafting teams were unable to finalize the document, a non-committal press statement was issued.

After the press conference was over and the last cars in the Indian delegation were about to leave the White House for Foggy Bottom, the office of the State Department where Condoleezza Rice was hosting a lunch for the prime minister, S. Jaishankar, who was then the joint secretary (Americas) in the MEA, came rushing up to the departing Indian delegation, and gave a thumbs up sign. 'It's done,' his voice was jubilant.

It was decided that the joint statement would be released a little later—after the officials had fine-tuned it further at another post-lunch session. Manmohan Singh and Sanjaya Baru, his media advisor, decided that the news of the 'breakthrough' should not miss the next morning's papers in India. By now, it was close to midnight back home. Most dailies would be about to be put to bed.

The PM told his media advisor to brief two mediapersons to have their stories about the agreement ready. They could be rushed into print when they were given the go-ahead. These journalists were N. Ravi of *The Hindu* and C. Raja Mohan of the *Indian Express*. They could 'be relied upon to keep their stories ready, ask their editors in India to delay printing, but not reveal the news till they got the green signal', said Baru.

■

The next morning, Manmohan Singh was scheduled to address a joint session of the US Congress. At the best of times, Singh was considered a poor and dull orator, so soft-spoken that he tended to swallow his words. But that day he was different. He read out his forty-five-minute prepared address to a packed house. 'As Jaishankar and I sat with copies of the speech, pen in hand to mark statements that were applauded,' Sanjaya Baru was to write years later, 'we found him being applauded for every minute of speaking time.' Each round of applause mattered. For Singh knew he was speaking to the very men and women who would be called to approve the nuclear deal.

In the joint statement that was prominently printed in newspapers in India and the US, Bush had promised to lobby his own Congress—and the US allies—to change the American laws which prevented nuclear cooperation with India because it had not signed the Non-Proliferation Treaty. India, in return, had promised to separate its civilian reactors from the military ones, to continue its moratorium on testing, and place only its civilian nuclear reactors under IAEA inspections.

The statement said the US president would 'work to achieve full civil nuclear energy cooperation with India'—and in order to do this, to 'seek agreement from Congress to adjust US laws and policies'. The US would also 'work with friends and allies to adjust international regimes to enable full civil nuclear energy cooperation and trade with India'. This would also include, but not be limited to, an 'expeditious consideration of fuel supplies for safeguarded nuclear reactors at Tarapur'.

On his part, the Indian prime minister said India would be ready to assume the same responsibilities and 'acquire the same benefits and advantages as other leading countries with advanced nuclear technology, such as the United States'.

India's responsibilities, the statement said, would 'consist of identifying and separating civilian and military nuclear facilities and programs in a phased manner'; it would file 'a declaration regarding its [civilian] facilities with the International Atomic Energy Agency (IAEA)'; it would take a decision 'to place voluntarily' its civilian nuclear facilities under IAEA safeguards; it would sign an 'Additional Protocol' with respect to civilian nuclear facilities; it would continue its moratorium on nuclear testing; it would work with the United States for the conclusion of a multilateral Fissile Material Cut Off Treaty; and it would refrain from the 'transfer of enrichment and reprocessing technologies to states that do not have them'.

The Indian prime minister and US president agreed to review the progress made on the agreement when Bush visited India in 2006.

∎

On 19 July 2005, Kakodkar went to say goodbye to Prime Minister Manmohan Singh. He was returning to Mumbai, where he lived. This time, he was not travelling on Air India One, as he had done when coming to the US as part of the PM's team. Having taken a position different from the others, a tense Kakodkar had had a bad night on 17 July. But Manmohan Singh complimented Kakodkar, 'That night you saved the nation.' The prime minister then told Kakodkar, 'I (too) couldn't sleep that whole night. I kept praying.'

III

'Natwar, how could *you* of all the people agree to this?' Sonia Gandhi asked Natwar Singh with some asperity. He was briefing her about what had transpired in Washington DC. Singh was known for taking an anti-American position, hewn as his sensibilities were during Nehru's years of non-alignment and the Cold War.

'You know there is an undercurrent in the country regarding American policy,' she said irritably. 'This deal is not acceptable to most Indians.'

She 'reprimanded' the government for the 18 July 2005 agreement, according to academic Zoya Hasan. Hasan had quoted Natwar Singh in her book—though later Sonia Gandhi was to change her mind about the deal.

Back home in hot and muggy Delhi, the euphoria of Washington DC evaporated. The PM faced divided public opinion—and widespread criticism of the joint statement he had issued with George Bush.

It was not just Sonia Gandhi who was perturbed; many senior Congress leaders were also not convinced. They worried about the impact it could have on the Congress's image as a left-of-centre party and on the country's relations with Russia and China. Close to home, they were concerned about how it would affect the Congress's relationship with the Left parties, which had propped up the Manmohan ministry in power.

A section of the media also seemed unconvinced. 'Nuclear bargain may prove costly in long run,' wrote *The Hindu*. 'India Compromised' screamed the headline in *The Pioneer*, reflecting the BJP's view. But there were others in the media who welcomed the deal as a 'historic breakthrough', a 'paradigm shift', ending the isolation the country had faced for three decades. Yet others took a middle position and called it a 'Grand Bargain'.

The criticism came essentially from four quarters. There was Sonia Gandhi and the Congress leaders who had reservations, as noted. Then there were the Left parties, who scrutinized every word in the joint statement and came out with a detailed critique. A group of scientists, defence analysts, environmentalists, and activists had more fundamental problems with the agreement. Surprisingly, the strongest criticism came from the BJP which had, under Vajpayee as PM, initiated the whole process for a strategic partnership with the US.

It was Vajpayee's strident criticism of the deal which took the prime minister by surprise. Vajpayee slammed Manmohan Singh for having 'given away too much' to the Americans. 'Separating the civil and military would be very difficult, if not impossible,' he said. 'The costs involved will be prohibitive.' Former national security advisor under Vajpayee, Brajesh Mishra, mounted a blistering attack against the prime minister. Since the fissile material from civilian reactors could no longer be used to produce weapons under the agreement, India, Mishra said, '(was) in effect putting a cap on its nuclear weapons capability'. Manmohan Singh, he felt, had made a major concession.

Mishra also rubbished the government's claim that India had been recognized as a NWS by the US or by others in the Nuclear Suppliers Group. US under secretary of state Nicholas Burns had clearly said that India was only a nuclear-weapon power, not a nuclear-weapon state. He revealed that when Vajpayee was in power, the government had offered to put only 'a couple of our existing reactors....and all our future reactors under safeguards'. But these were neither fast breeder reactors, nor reactors under construction, only those being planned. The BJP demanded a vote in parliament on the deal—and for the deal to be renegotiated.

The joint statement had triggered a major debate in the country. Nuclear scientists and defence analysts were sharply divided in their opinion, many expressing 'fears and concerns' about the deal. Among those who opposed it were P. K. Iyengar, former chairman of India's Atomic Energy Commission of India; Dr A. N. Prasad, former director of the Bhabha Atomic Research Centre at Trombay; Dr A. Gopalakrishna from the Atomic

Energy Regulatory Board and strategic expert Bharat Karnad—all known names in the country's nuclear establishment. They dubbed the deal a 'strategic sellout'—that was also the name of the book they were later to author jointly.

Gopalakrishna was scathing in his critique: 'There is no need for India to surrender its indigenous nuclear power programme as a sacrificial offering to please the US, in return for the promise of a broader strategic alliance or a great power status for India.'

P. K. Iyengar said that India's nuclear programme was an integral whole and could not be divided into two separate categories of military and civilian. What it essentially lacked was funds. 'We only want money, not their expertise, technology or science.'

The primary opposition to the deal however came from the Left parties. They were concerned not just about the government having given away too much in return for being able to buy the much-needed uranium for the Indian reactors. The CPI (M), Revolutionary Socialist Party (RSP) and the Forward Bloc criticized the joint statement at length. The politburo of the CPI (M) charged the government of having compromised India's independent foreign policy, making it 'a strategic ally' of the US. It was deeply unhappy at not being consulted about such a vital policy decision, even though it was an ally. Its statement held out a veiled warning—'The CPI (M) expects the government not to undertake unilateral measures which may compromise national interests.'

The deal's supporters however felt that it would do away with the stigma that India had faced after its tests in 1974 and 1998. It would enable the country to do business with the atomic energy industry globally, which sanctions had prevented. But some apprehended the deal would be sabotaged at the American end, by opposition from within the US Congress. But otherwise, they saw it as a step forward in a journey which would bring about a qualitative change in India's relationship with the US. It is what Manmohan Singh wanted— signifying a major shift in the country's foreign policy.

■

On 1 March 2006, George W. Bush arrived in India. The Maurya Sheraton Hotel in Delhi was all geared up to receive the US president; it had specially organized the hotel schedule in such a way that Bush could retire early for the night.

There was an important breakthrough during the Bush visit. And that was the agreement on what was called the 'Separation Plan'. It marked step two of the Indo–US Civil Nuclear Deal. The Americans, as mentioned, had started off from the position of wanting to put all the Indian nuclear reactors under safeguards. The Indian side had resisted. Again, these negotiations 'went down to the wire'. It took hard bargaining by the Indian side to have just the civilian nuclear reactors put under the IAEA's scrutiny, and not the military ones.

Just before Bush arrived, Manmohan Singh had given an interview to the American journalist Charlie Rose. In that interview, the prime minister had admitted that separating the nuclear reactors into civilian and strategic ones—what was in technical jargon called 'islanding'—had been a sticking point between the two sides. Just as Bush had to consider the concerns of the US Congress, Manmohan Singh had to address the concerns of the Indian parliament. 'I have promised our parliament that I will do nothing which will hurt India's strategic programme.'

A prolonged session between the two sides took place at the imposing Hyderabad House in Delhi on 2 March 2006. National Security Advisor M. K. Narayanan and Shyam Saran represented the Indian side. After the joint statement in July 2005, Narayanan—considered close to Sonia Gandhi—had suddenly emerged as a key Indian interlocutor. He became a bridge between the pro-deal negotiating team and the more cautious Department of Atomic Energy, which according to Shyam Saran 'seemed to be convinced that we were about to sell the store to the Americans'.

On the American side, there was Narayanan's counterpart, National Security Advisor Stephen J. Hadley, and Nicholas Burns, the US under secretary of state. The four men were at it till 3 a.m. But no solution seemed to be in sight. The scientists—R. Chidambaram, who was scientific advisor to the PM, and Anil Kakodkar—were close at hand. They sat patiently in a room nearby, in case their advice was needed.

There was deadlock over a couple of points which eluded a solution. The tricky one was the US demand that India put its civilian reactors under safeguards 'permanently'.

The next morning, the working group met again. Prime Minister Singh and President Bush sat in an adjoining room, chatting and waiting, as they had done on 18 July 2005, for the impasse to dissolve. Finally, there was a breakthrough—and it came after Bush intervened personally. The Americans promised to work with India to build fuel reserves to last the lifetime of each civilian reactor, in case there were disruptions, for whatever reasons.

On 3 March 2006, the two leaders announced the joint agreement on civil nuclear cooperation. That evening the two leaders stood together at the spruced up and artistically lit Purana Qila, once Delhi's capital. Standing against the backdrop of the historic fort, the NBC was to write, George Bush projected the landmark nuclear deal as the centrepiece of America's 'new romance with this one-billion-strong democracy'. The normally shy and reserved Manmohan Singh grew effusive when he referred to the part Bush had played to bring the two countries closer to each other. Two years later, at the conclusion of the deal in 2008, he was to tell Bush at a public event, 'The people of India deeply love you'—a comment which provoked controversy.

■

For the remaining part of 2006, the action shifted to the US. President Bush had to fulfil his side of the bargain. He had to amend the US laws to enable nuclear commerce with India which had not yet signed the Nuclear Non-Proliferation Treaty.

First there was the passage of the Hyde Act, which amended the US Atomic Energy Act, 1954—and this was necessary. For the US Atomic Energy Act allowed the US civil nuclear cooperation with a country only under certain conditions—that it was a member of the NPT (which India had not signed), it had not exploded a nuclear device (which India had done in 1974 and in 1998), it had put its ongoing strategic nuclear programme under international safeguards (which India had disallowed). That is why India had to be exempted from these binding legal conditions.

In November 2006, the Henry J. Hyde United States–India Peaceful Atomic Energy Cooperation Act of 2006 (PAEC Act) was passed, amending the relevant portions of the US Atomic Energy Act, 1954. But it sharply polarized political opinion back in India. The Left parties—and other critics—were quick to point out the many restrictive clauses in the Act that impinged on India's sovereignty—even as it provided for a waiver from certain provisions of the US law. These barred India from access to technologies for uranium enrichment, reprocessing of spent fuel, and heavy-water production (at best it permitted these on a case-by-case basis). The Act contained a condition that the US president would make an annual 'certification' to the Congress that India had complied with its non-proliferation—and other—commitments.

After the Separation Plan finalized by the two countries in March 2006, India had thought it would now be a simple matter to change the US law. But 'extraneous' provisions were thrown into the Hyde Act to satisfy the different lobbies and interest groups at work in the US. This led to a furore in India, as it interfered with India's foreign policy, such as its relations with Iran, and obstructed its sovereign right to take its own decisions.

Secretary of State Condoleezza Rice personally intervened by writing a letter to Congress members. She urged them to accommodate India's concerns. Mindful of the new business opportunities that could open up in India, US business groups, the wealthy Indo–American community, and the Indian government lobbied with members of the US Congress.

Barack Obama, then senator and later to become US president, was opposed to the deal. Senator Joe Biden, also to become president some years down the line, was 'supportive'. The Indian ambassador to the US,

Ronen Sen, mobilized the Indian diaspora to lobby the US lawmakers. Eventually some legislative amendments were made by US lawmakers, though they did not satisfy the critics, particularly the Left parties.

■

The Hyde Act paved the way for the next stage in the long and tortuous process of finalizing the deal—the formulation of the 123 Agreement. It was the formal appellation for the Indo–US Civil Nuclear Deal. Despite the many differences between the two sides, this stage was also successfully cleared on 27 July 2007. Before the deal could be ratified by the US Congress—there was no requirement for Indian parliament to vote on it—two more hurdles had to be crossed in the obstacle race that both Manmohan Singh and George W. Bush had resolved to run.

One was for India to go to the IAEA—to secure for itself an India-specific safeguards deal. The IAEA had two sets of safeguards, one for NPT signatories who had to put all their facilities under scrutiny of the international body, and the other for countries which had not opted for the NPT—the latter would voluntarily place specific facilities under the safeguards of the UN body. In India's case, the agreement would be called the India-specific Safeguards Agreement (ISSA), because it was not a signatory to the NPT. 'India had insisted that the safeguards agreement should be India-specific,' Shyam Saran said. Once this hurdle was crossed, the US would work to facilitate a waiver for India from the Nuclear Suppliers Group, to enable it to buy fuel, equipment, material, and sensitive technology for its civil nuclear programme—which it had been denied after its explosions in 1974 and 1998.

Only after this stage was crossed would the 123 Agreement go to the US Congress for adoption. The US president would then sign it into law. India and the US would then formally operationalize the deal and India would finally be able to get the nuclear energy (as opposed to fossil fuel) for its growing energy needs.

While the country could continue with its strategic nuclear weapons programme, placing the civil nuclear reactors under IAEA safeguards 'in perpetuity' had its flipside. It meant that all the spent fuel at these facilities would not be available for the nuclear weapons programme. This could limit the size of the country's nuclear stockpile. On its part, the US would have calculated that this would limit India's nuclear ambitions. But those in charge of the country's nuclear programme were confident they had enough fuel for their strategic needs.

From the beginning, the Indo–US Civil Nuclear Deal was less about clean energy and more about an India–US strategic relationship. US presidents from Carter to Clinton had tried to rein in India's nuclear aspirations. After the 1998 tests, as we've seen earlier, the US had imposed

HOW PRIME MINISTERS DECIDE

punitive sanctions against India. Counterintuitively, the tests by Vajpayee also set the stage for a new phase in the India–US relationship. India had risen in importance in the US's eyes by the start of the new millennium—as it revisited its foreign policy goals in a post-Cold War world. On the Indian side, the deal's chief architect, Prime Minister Manmohan Singh, was to say later that the deal had 'expanded India's foreign policy options'.

It was a risky leap taken by India's cautious and bureaucratic prime minister. According to the journalist Shekhar Gupta, it was then that the 'post cold war India was born'.

IV

'He wants to be the chairperson of the UGC, and I want to make him the finance minister of India,' P. V. Narasimha Rao remarked to Congressman Brij Mohan Bhama about Manmohan Singh.

Manmohan Singh had called on Rao after he took over as Congress president in June 1991, following Rajiv Gandhi's assassination. He had been appointed UGC chairman by Prime Minister Chandra Shekhar. But as the government was on its last legs, and Chandra Shekhar was caretaker prime minister, Singh was worried that he may be left with no accommodation in Delhi if Chandra Shekhar lost, which seemed likely. Bureaucrats had warned him that a caretaker PM did not have the authority to make such an appointment, and it may come unstuck. Manmohan Singh was the chief economic advisor to the prime minister but had asked Chandra Shekhar to make him UGC chairman also.

Manmohan Singh wanted Rao to help regularize his appointment. He was carrying his appointment letter as UGC chairman. According to Bhama, who was close to R. K. Dhawan and Satish Sharma, and was at Rao's residence that day, he wanted Rao's help to do this. 'I know you are going to become PM,' Singh told Rao, according to Bhama. Rao assured Singh of help—and said he would speak to whoever took over as PM after the elections. The poll results were yet to come out.

Rao then turned to Manmohan Singh and asked for his ideas—on how to bring back the gold which had been mortgaged during Chandra Shekhar's premiership and was lying in bank vaults abroad. Manmohan Singh agreed to help him, which he did as finance minister.

Manmohan Singh, later hailed as the author of economic reform in India, was tentative in those early days and weeks as finance minister. It was Rao who made most of the difficult decisions. It was later that Manmohan Singh made his mark.

■

'I can say that the idea of (making) Manmohan Singh finance minister was mine,' R. Venkataraman, who was then the president of India, told me in

2002. Rao had turned to RV, as R. Venkataraman was known, for advice. Venkataraman had held the finance portfolio under Indira Gandhi (1980–82) and was familiar with the demands of the job. 'I suggested two names to PV—I. G. Patel and Manmohan Singh,' Venkataraman said. I. G. Patel, a former governor of the Reserve Bank of India, expressed his inability to take over. Manmohan Singh agreed.

Rao had started looking around for who could head the finance ministry the moment he took over as Congress president—someone who was well connected to multilateral institutions like the IMF and World Bank. The Soviet Union had collapsed. A unipolar world had emerged. He knew which way the winds were blowing internationally. Even though the election results were not yet out, he knew that he had a good chance of becoming PM. By the time he was formally elected leader of the CPP, he had made up his mind on who he wanted.

At this point, Congress leader Captain Satish Sharma came to see him. 'So, who do you have in mind for finance?' Sharma asked casually. Rao knew where this was heading. He replied quickly, 'It will be a technocrat.' He wanted to pre-empt any suggestion that Sharma might have brought from Sonia Gandhi about who should head the Finance Ministry. Rao deputed P. C. Alexander, who was informally assisting him with cabinet formation, to meet Manmohan Singh.

Alexander telephoned Singh at 5 a.m. on 21 June 1991, asking to meet him—and then went to see him with Rao's offer. Manmohan Singh agreed to take the job. P. V. Narasimha Rao was sworn in as prime minister and Manmohan Singh as finance minister around noon that day.

■

Harsh decisions lay ahead for the prime minister and his new finance minister. The first major decisions to be made were the devaluation of the rupee, and the mortgaging of RBI gold. For the first time, India ran the risk of what was called a sovereign default—of not being able to pay the interest on its foreign loans. The economy was tanking. The rate of growth had declined, inflation was up, and foreign exchange reserves were perilously low, down to only three weeks of imports because of the oil crisis caused by the war that was raging in West Asia after Iraq invaded Kuwait.

'We now need to obtain foreign exchange by pledging gold,' S. Venkitaramanan, who was governor of the Reserve Bank of India, told the finance secretary, S. P. Shukla. This was to be the RBI's gold which would be pledged to the Bank of England and Bank of Japan; it had to be shifted to the vaults of these banks before they could give India the foreign exchange. Once the officials had done the necessary paperwork, the prime minister and finance minister had to OK the decision.

S. P. Shukla and Deepak Nayyar took the file to Manmohan Singh.

'We carried the file by hand,' Nayyar recalled.

'Why do I have to sign it?' Manmohan Singh said. 'The PM has to sign it.'

'We told him that since it was the RBI's reserves (of gold) and under the RBI Act, it needed his separate approval.'

He insisted, 'No, it is not necessary.'

The officials took off for 9, Motilal Nehru Marg, where the PM was still staying. He had not yet moved in to the PM House at Race Course Road. They had also seen him a day before he had taken over as PM, poring over lists of Congress MPs to swear in the next day. They had given him a top secret note 'on the state of the economy, on our choices, our chances'. It only needed ratification by him.

Rao heard them out in silence. 'I always knew we were in difficulty,' he said slowly. 'But I did not know it is such a mess.'

This time when he saw Shukla and Nayyar, Rao looked up at the officials enquiringly, 'Gold, Deepak?'

Nayyar replied, 'This is for you to approve.'

'Laaiye,' he said. And he signed it.

Rao showed no hesitation in taking the decision. Chandra Shekhar had baulked, knowing he would be vilified for mortgaging the country's gold. 'Ballia ke log kahenge maine unka sona bech diya (The people of Ballia will charge me of selling their gold),' he had remarked irritably. But Rao knew that at that point it was the only option available to him.

'Once Manmohan Singh heard that PV had signed it, he came running to my room and he (too) signed (it).' Nayyar revealed.

Between 4 and 18 July 1991, the RBI pledged 46.91 tonnes of gold to the Bank of England and Bank of Japan to raise $400 million. These consignments were dispatched in four lots during this period. In May 1991, the State Bank of India had sold 20 tonnes of gold to the Union Bank of Switzerland to raise $200 million.

In the initial weeks after he took over as finance minister, Manmohan Singh came across as 'nervous, hesitant, indecisive', according to Deepak Nayyar. It was later that he came into his own. Rao, though not very familiar with the ways of the Finance Ministry, was, on the other hand, 'quiet, self-effacing but amazingly decisive'. 'Well, that's it. We do it,' he would say.

The structural reforms by Narasimha Rao and Manmohan Singh were initiated with the devaluation of the rupee, a condition which had been imposed by the World Bank and IMF. Devaluation, which made currency cheaper, was supposed to restore some of the imbalance between India's low exports and high imports. It made exports more competitive, thereby helping the balance of payments (BOP) situation. The BOP crisis, the result of imports exceeding the country's exports, had been going on since the 1980s. When it came to devaluation, Prime Minister Rao was more cautious. He knew he was heading a minority government and would have to persuade his coalition partners to go along with the decision which was controversial. Highly cautious, Rao decided to send a delegation comprising Manmohan Singh, Naresh Chandra, S. P. Shukla, and Deepak Nayyar to consult with President R. Venkataraman to get his approval. The president suggested that devaluation be undertaken in several phases.

'Manmohan Singh...told me that if it was done in several lots, people would think that it (the rupee) would devalue more and more,' R. Venkataraman said. '(But) I wanted it done in many goes.' The president felt that an 'overnight decision' would lead to 'bad inflation'.

'If you have to devalue by ₹5, why don't you devalue 25 paise a day for twenty days?' R. Venkataraman asked Manmohan Singh.

Taken aback by this suggestion, the group told him politely that it would not be such a good idea. But the PM did not want to oppose the president, conscious as he was about heading a minority government. 'Abhi rashtrapati keh rahe hain to manana parhega (If the president is saying so, we will have to listen to him),' Rao told the officials.

'We told the prime minister that it would be as unmitigated disaster if we did what RV wanted,' said Deepak Nayyar. Rao eventually agreed.

Finally, devaluation was done in two lots on 1 July and 3 July 1991—first for 9 per cent and then for 11 per cent. The government decided to go in for 20 per cent devaluation of the rupee against the dollar and other currencies; the World Bank had suggested 22 per cent devaluation in its country report. It led to inflation. But greater access to international credit helped the country with its balance of payments crisis.

'The first step of devaluation was done to test the waters,' Manmohan Singh was to reveal years later. 'Prime Minister Narasimha Rao had doubts over the second instalment of this exchange rate adjustment, and told me, in fact, to stop it. But when I called up (C.) Rangarajan (deputy governor of the RBI), he said he'd already shot the goal.'

Congress leader Jairam Ramesh, who had been an advisor to Manmohan Singh, revealed that Singh—though he had been instructed by PM Narasimha Rao in the early hours of 3 July 1991 to call off the second step of devaluation—did so only at 9.30 a.m., when it was too late. The devaluation had already been carried out by 9 a.m.

Jairam Ramesh did not explain why the finance minister waited until 9.30 a.m.; the prime minister had given him instructions in the early hours of that morning. Also, Ramesh did not clarify why Manmohan Singh chose to talk to the deputy governor C. Rangarajan and not to the RBI governor S. Venkitaramanan. Was this part of a deliberate strategy? Was Manmohan Singh the 'real star' of the second stage of devaluation, about which he was convinced—with Rangarajan playing 'along with the Finance Minister's strategy'?

And yet, it would seem out of character for a diffident Manmohan Singh, even as he was set on a two-stage devaluation, to decide to upstage the prime minister so early in his career as finance minister—so as to please the multilateral institutions. Or could it be that Rao, who had his own ways of managing contradictions, wanted to kill two birds with one stone? To have the two-stage devaluation, which he knew he could not avoid, and also signal his critics that he had been outfoxed—and was therefore helpless.

'An economist amongst politicians, and a politician amongst economists'—that is how Manmohan Singh was known in political circles. When he became finance minister—and prime minister in 2004—he was seen as a renowned economist, but a political novice. Later, he was hailed as the author of the economic reforms in India. There was a time, when, as the secretary of the South–South Commission (1987–90), he had implied in a report he had written that India should not go to the IMF because it would be detrimental to its economy. He was to change his opinion when he became finance minister—his turnaround was criticized, among others, by socialist leader George Fernandes, later to become India's defence minister.

Chandra Shekhar, under whom he had served as chief economic advisor, accused him of withholding from him, when he was prime minister, the India country reports that were sent by the World Bank to the government. They contained prescriptions about what India should do about the economic crisis it faced.

In his first years as a minister, Manmohan Singh looked to Rao for advice. In his first Budget speech on 24 July 1991, Singh, who flagged off the structural reforms, had wanted to blame the previous government for the economic mess the country was in. The politically astute Rao told him gently, 'We must not apportion blame.' Fixing the economic crisis was 'a collective responsibility'—especially as theirs was a coalition government. Saddled with running a minority government, Rao did not want to start on the wrong note with the Opposition parties.

'PV ko guru maantae thae Manmohan Singh (Manmohan Singh used to consider PV as his teacher). He used to touch Rao's feet,' recounted Bhuvnesh Chaturvedi, who was MoS in Rao's PMO.

But in the years that followed, Manmohan Singh became his own man; as prime minister he presided over an expanding economy with a high growth trajectory during his first term in office. As finance minister, he had more freedom under Narasimha Rao than he did as prime minister under Congress president Sonia Gandhi.

■

Manmohan Singh was born in 1935 in Gah, a backward village which is now in Pakistan. When India achieved Independence in 1947, and the country was partitioned, his family crossed the border to the Indian side. He lost his mother at a very early age and was brought up by his grandmother, whom he was very attached to. Gah had no electricity, no school, no health facilities, and the young Manmohan had to walk miles to go to his Urdu medium school. At night he studied by a kerosene lamp. He showed promise from an early age—and went on to become an eminent economist.

Manmohan Singh's impressive rise from humble beginnings was credit, he would say, to the 'system of scholarships' for poor students that existed in India at the time.

'I could never have afforded to go to Oxford or Cambridge on the basis of resources at my disposal,' he told American journalist Charlie Rose. 'My parents could not send me, but I did well in the examinations in India, and therefore I was able to win a scholarship. And that is how I went to Cambridge.' He graduated from Cambridge, and then got a DPhil in economics from Nuffield College at Oxford University in 1962. He decided to study economics, he said, in an effort to understand why India was such a poor country.

During his interview to Rose, he was asked how he became a capitalist and such a firm believer in a free market—despite his humble beginnings. The interviewer wanted to know why he had not opted for socialism, a planned economy and statist measures to address inequality in the country. Singh replied that he 'still felt that equity is something which we should worry about'. But, he added, 'I do believe that capitalism has shown a great deal of dynamism.'

Manmohan Singh joined the government in 1971 and went on to hold high civil service positions in the Indian administration. He was secretary in the Ministry of Finance, governor of the Reserve Bank of India, and deputy chairman of the Planning Commission. He became the prime minister in 2004 in an unexpected turn of events—and headed the Congress-led UPA government for ten years.

But he could not win the only Lok Sabha election he contested in 1999, from South Delhi, even though it was an urban constituency. It was a 'low point' in his career which 'depressed' him. More so, as his wife Gursharan Kaur was to say, '...he has been a winner all his life.' Many suspected that some veteran Congress leaders had deliberately worked behind the scenes to get him defeated. Singh was seen as an erudite but colourless politician; the usual line of vehicles outside the PM House or the crowds which normally thronged there to meet the head of government, were missing outside 7, Race Course Road, when he was prime minister. He had himself chosen to underplay his political role.

Yet, whenever his understanding of politics was questioned, Singh would bristle. 'It is not true that I am politically naive,' he said to an interviewer. And then he added: 'I have been in the public system since 1971...(and) dealt with politicians of all shades of opinion. I (have) worked with almost every prime minister...I have, I think, a reasonable appreciation of how to manage the political process....'

This turned out to be not just an idle boast. His ability to 'manage the political process' was on full display in the way he negotiated the Indo–US Civil Nuclear Deal, despite the tortuous process it went through, not for a month or two, but over a period of three and a half years, spanning most of his first term as PM. The terrain he navigated would have been difficult enough for a strong political leader with a brute majority, let alone someone who was a compromise choice to lead the country—and seen as a weak leader. But then, the nuclear deal was the only instance when Singh asserted his authority in a way not otherwise seen during his entire premiership.

Singh showed an understanding of a complex and a knotty situation, a grasp of realpolitik, and a steely determination to achieve his objective no matter what stood in the way. Also, during the time it took to finalize the Indo–US Civil Nuclear Deal, he managed to bring around, or get around, everyone and everything that stood in his way—politicians of every hue, detractors within his own party, critics at home and abroad, and, most of all, the power behind his throne—Sonia Gandhi.

V

The Manmohan Singh story is not complete without looking at the role Sonia Gandhi played in the decision-making processes during his premiership; it is as much about her as about him.

On 13 May 2004, Sonia Gandhi settled herself in front of the TV set at 10, Janpath. It was eight in the morning, when the first results of the general election began to trickle in. She blinked rapidly as the numbers flashed on the screen. She used to say that when she was tense, she had the habit of blinking more frequently. The outcome of the polls, she knew, would reflect on her leadership—this was the first time she had led the Congress Party from the front and thrown herself completely into campaigning.

By 10.30 a.m., the picture had become clear. The Congress was leading. The BJP had been so confident of winning the election that it had advanced the polling dates by six months. Sonia Gandhi's strategy of tying up with regional parties had paid off. The Congress tally was 145 seats, 7 more than that of the BJP. It was Andhra Pradesh which had come to the Congress Party's rescue. The state had added an impressive 34 Lok Sabha seats to the UPA kitty (the Congress got 29 seats and Congress ally, the Telangana Rashtra Samithi 5, out of 42 MPs that Andhra sent to the Lok Sabha). The Congress emerged as the single largest party.

When her daughter Priyanka Gandhi walked in, the normally stoic Sonia hugged her excitedly. 'We have done it,' she said.

As it became clear that the BJP had been shown the door, events began to speed up for Sonia Gandhi. The Congress was in a pole position to form the new government. Even before the results were finally in, leaders of allied parties had come calling on her—all through 13 and 14 May 2004. Before the elections, it was Sonia Gandhi who had reached out to the regional parties—at the time they had given her the runaround. Now they rushed to give her their letters of support.

Along with its pre-poll allies, the Congress had garnered 222 seats. Fifty more were needed to reach the magical midway mark of 272 to form the government. The four Left parties—CPI (M), CPI, RSP, and Forward Bloc—had surprisingly totted up 59 seats—they had fared well in their three bastions of West Bengal, Kerala, and Tripura. They were Sonia Gandhi's first preference as partners. She suddenly felt a rush of relief that she would not have to be at the mercy of the Samajwadi Party, the Bahujan Samaj Party, and the Rashtriya Lok Dal, headed by maverick leaders, to form the government. She knew the problems her husband, Rajiv, before, had faced with the Samajwadi Party. The SP would have demanded its pound of flesh at every turn in return for its support. The SP, which was in power in UP, had spurned the Congress's offer to form an alliance before the (2004) Lok Sabha elections. With UP accounting for 15 per cent of the seats in the Lok Sabha, the SP had hoped to emerge as the kingmaker in Delhi. But now, even though it had won 35 seats, the Congress did not need to depend on them.

Within hours of the results, the top brass of the CPI (M) and CPI were huddled together at A. K. Gopalan Bhavan—the CPI (M)'s newly built headquarters in central Delhi. CPI (M) General Secretary Harkishan Singh Surjeet, famous for sewing up anti-BJP alliances, his party colleagues Sitaram Yechury, and Prakash Karat, and CPI leaders, A. B. Bardhan and D. Raja, took stock of the new situation. The Left had decided even before the elections to support a secular government, if the opportunity arose, to keep the BJP out. When Sonia Gandhi heard that the Left was favourably inclined to supporting the Congress government, she quickly moved to firm up their support. The Left decided not to join the government, which Sonia would have welcomed, but support it from 'outside'.

When CPI leader A. B. Bardhan called for the government to go in for a Common Minimum Programme (CMP), Sonia Gandhi moved with alacrity. She appointed Manmohan Singh to head the group to formulate the CMP; Pranab Mukherjee, Arjun Singh, and Jairam Ramesh were the other members of the committee.

Sonia Gandhi reached out to the Congress's pre-poll allies, and to smaller parties, and invited them to join the United Progressive Alliance (UPA), as the Congress-led alliance came to be called. One of those who backed her early was Sharad Pawar, even though he had broken off from the Congress in 1999, in protest against Sonia's foreign origins—and gone on to form his Nationalist Congress Party (NCP). Others, too, joined the fold.

Even before the results were out, Sonia Gandhi's managers in the Congress had started to project her as the prime ministerial candidate of the UPA. On 7 May, before the results were out, her political secretary Ahmed Patel contacted V. P. Singh. He moved through journalist Santosh Bhartia, who was close to VP. Patel asked for VP's help to make Sonia prime minister—even though it was VP who had dethroned her husband Rajiv Gandhi as PM in 1989. Though out of power, VP was respected by many of the Opposition leaders. On 10 May 2004, VP drove from Apollo Hospital, where he used to undergo dialysis, to 10, Janpath, to meet Sonia Gandhi. In the following hours he spoke to the Left leaders, H. D. Deve Gowda, and DMK chief M. Karunanidhi to lend their support to Sonia Gandhi. He brought around Karunanidhi even though the DMK leader said he had promised support to the Atal Bihari Vajpayee-led NDA.

With the results just out, Ahmed Patel, who normally avoided the media, decided to sit down with a reporter. He spoke at length about why Sonia Gandhi was the best choice for prime minister. The purpose of the 2,000-word interview to Sheela Bhatt was to float the idea—and test the waters.

The Congress managers called a meeting of the CPP on 15 May to elect its leader. Manmohan Singh presided over the meeting. He was to propose Sonia Gandhi's name and Pranab Mukherjee would second it. But an excited Mukherjee, who had been elected to the Lok Sabha for the first time (he had previously been a member of the Rajya Sabha), grabbed the mike, and welcomed the assembled MPs to the CPP meeting as 'the oldest Congress member in the Parliament' and yet 'one of the newest members in the Lok Sabha'. Everyone laughed. He then proposed Sonia Gandhi's name as the leader of the CPP and gave her the mike. In a spirited speech, Sonia Gandhi accepted the position; she called the Congress victory a rejection of the ideology of the BJP and the RSS. It was a vote to create an 'inclusive, secular and united' India.

∎

Sunday, 16 May, was a day which was to change the fortunes of Sonia Gandhi—and of Manmohan Singh. It was the day she had invited leaders of the Congress's pre-poll allies—and the Left parties—to dinner at 10, Janpath. The dinner meet was to give formal shape to the UPA—and to endorse Sonia Gandhi as its prime ministerial candidate. At the end of the evening, there were thirteen parties in the alliance besides the Congress. They were the Rashtriya Janata Dal (with 24 MPs), Dravida Munnetra Kazhagam (16), Nationalist Congress Party (9), Pattali Makkal Katchi (6), Telangana Rashtra Samithi (5), Jharkhand Mukti Morcha (5), Marumalarchi Dravida Munnetra Kazhagam (MDMK) (4), Lok Jan Shakti Party (4), Kerala Congress (1), Indian Union Muslim League (1), Jammu and Kashmir Peoples' Democratic Party (1), Republican Party of India-Athavale (1), and the All India Majlise-e-Ittehadul Muslimeen (1).

Jairam Ramesh read out the final resolution. It proposed Sonia Gandhi's name for prime ministership. Samajwadi Party leader Amar Singh could be heard complaining plaintively that the list of signatories did not include the Samajwadi Party!

Amar Singh had actually not been invited to the dinner. He had tagged along with CPM leader Harkishan Singh Surjeet. Salman Khurshid and Ambika Soni had stood at the gate of 7, Janpath, welcoming leaders for the dinner, when he arrived with Surjeet. When they saw Amar Singh alighting from the car and get into an argument with the Special Protection Group looking after Sonia Gandhi's security, they sent a quick word in to Ahmed Patel. Patel okayed Amar Singh's entry. A few minutes later, the visitors were sent in.

In those days, Amar Singh was the superstar of the Samajwadi Party, which, as we have seen, was in power in Uttar Pradesh, and was supported by the Congress. But Sonia Gandhi did not even look at Amar Singh that evening as he sat down. Other Congress leaders followed Sonia Gandhi's cue; they too were cool towards him. Ambika Soni was later heard saying loudly that he had 'gate-crashed'—which upset him no end, for he saw it as a deliberate snub to him. She had been unhappy with Mulayam Singh Yadav for fielding candidates all over the country in the 2004 elections which had damaged the Congress and helped the BJP come to power in many seats.

Sonia Gandhi was unusually reclusive at the dinner that evening. She sat in a corner, and surprisingly, talked mostly to V. P. Singh. Though VP had politically hurt her husband the most, it was he who would prevail upon Ram Vilas Paswan to join the government and accept the Communications Ministry instead of insisting on the Railways Ministry.

Despite being ignored by Sonia Gandhi, but keen to yoke themselves to power, the SP announced they would give the government 'outside' support. So did the Bahujan Samaj Party and the Rashtriya Lok Dal. The strength of the members of the UPA, plus those providing it outside support, rose to an impressive 317 seats in parliament.

The next day, 17 May, started with the stock exchange crashing. The prospect of a Sonia-led government, which would be supported by the Left parties, was far from reassuring for the markets. The response of the financial sector to the possibility of a UPA government was totally negative, even though the government was to be led by the Congress, the party which had initiated economic reforms in 1991.

Contention had started to build up over Sonia Gandhi's foreign antecedents. While a melancholy Vajpayee, the outgoing PM was to accept the verdict philosophically—'Kuch tajjub to hua ki kaise hogaya yeh (I was somewhat amazed as to how all this happened)'—the BJP trained its guns on Sonia, attacking her foreign antecedents as a way to stop her becoming prime minister.

'I will only wear white, sleep on the bare floor and eat only roasted chana', threatened the firebrand BJP leader Sushma Swaraj, when she heard that Sonia Gandhi would become prime minister. Even more dramatically, the married Swaraj threatened to tonsure her head like a Hindu widow in mourning. Swaraj told the media, 'If after 60 years of independence we coronate another foreigner for the top job, then it would have meant that 100 crore people were incapable.' A foreigner will be 'privy to all the defence secrets', she said. Uma Bharati resigned as chief minister of Madhya Pradesh 'to uphold the dignity and honour of 100 crore Indians', and K. N. Govindacharya launched a nationwide 'swabhiman' (self-respect) movement. Continuing with their dramatic protests, scores of women in Delhi held knives to their wrists to draw out their own blood—so as to corner the Congress. The transition from one government to another, which usually happened without a hitch in India, suddenly did not look smooth. But, then, politics rarely follows a prepared script.

■

Even as the Opposition voices grew hysterical, a sombre meeting was underway at 10, Janpath, in the afternoon on 17 May. It would dramatically change the contours of the UPA government—and its leadership.

'It must have been around 2 p.m. I think it was just before a meeting of the senior leaders was to take place,' Natwar Singh told this writer. 'I was trying to contact Manmohan Singh. They said he is at 10, Janpath.... I went there to find him.... When I arrived, they (the secretaries) said, "Aap andar jaaiye (You can go in)".' As a Gandhi family acolyte, he had easy access to the Gandhi household.

'She (Sonia) was sitting there on the sofa.... Manmohan Singh and Priyanka (were there as well). Suman Dubey came shortly thereafter. Sonia Gandhi was looking distraught.... Then Rahul came in and said in front of all of us, "I will not let you become prime minister. My father was assassinated, my Dadi was assassinated. In six months, you will be killed."'

Rahul threatened to take an extreme step if Sonia did not listen to him. 'This was no ordinary threat,' recalled Natwar Singh, 'Rahul is a strong-willed person. He gave Sonia 24 hours to decide.'

'Sonia was visibly agitated and in tears after Rahul said that he was prepared to "take any possible step to prevent his mother" from taking up the prime ministership.'

There was a shocked silence in the room.

'What could you say? It was a very difficult fifteen to twenty minutes. And they were very tense.' Manmohan Singh was speechless. 'Priyanka did say something like "Rahul is against it, and he is capable of doing anything".'

'We asked Sonia to go inside. And said we would sort out matters,' Natwar Singh recalled.

'It was Rahul's threat to do something drastic that made Sonia Gandhi change her mind. Basically her son made the decision for her.' Natwar Singh said. He added. 'As a mother it was impossible for her to ignore Rahul.'

Atal Bihari Vajpayee had also advised Sonia not to accept the prime ministership. Soon after she was elected as the leader of the CPP, the two of them spoke to each other, and Sonia sought his 'ashirwad'. By now, she was being seen as the next prime minister of India.

Vajpayee congratulated her and said, 'You have my ashirwad in abundance.' And then he added, 'Don't take the prize. You will divide the country and could end up straining the loyalty of the civil services.'

Vajpayee was close enough to Sonia to be able to speak to her so frankly—and at a time when she was riding high, having emerged as the victor. Though they were opponents, they enjoyed a cordial relationship all through. When the parliament building was attacked in December 2001, Sonia had immediately called up Vajpayee to find out if he was safe and all right. He was touched by her gesture—and many saw it as a sign that 'India's democracy was safe'.

That Manmohan Singh had been called to the meeting with Rahul was significant. He was the only person present, besides the immediate family, and Suman Dubey, who was a family friend—until Natwar Singh arrived there accidentally on his mission to find Manmohan Singh. It was clear that Sonia Gandhi wanted all those present to know about her decision and learn about Rahul's feelings directly from him. Manmohan Singh's presence at the meeting showed that by then Sonia had made up her mind to appoint him prime minister.

As things were to turn out, Rahul's fear for his mother's life, which made her give up the country's premiership, having come within grasping distance of it, brought her acceptance in the party and in the country— as nothing else could have done. For all her foreign origins, she was to become the longest serving party chief, the Congress Party's helmswoman for twenty-two years—and the tallest in the party when she stepped down in 2022.

There are many political dynasties around the world. But there was none parallel to the Nehru–Gandhi family, Natwar Singh was to point out years later. Seven members of the family ruled or wielded power and influence of an unprecedented kind over a large country for over a century—Motilal Nehru, Jawaharlal Nehru, Indira Gandhi, Sanjay Gandhi, Rajiv Gandhi, Sonia Gandhi, and Rahul Gandhi, with Priyanka Gandhi Vadra shaping up (at the time of writing) for a political role as well.

Sonia's decision to spurn the country's prime ministership made this Turin-born woman of Italian origin the longest link in that chain, not as executive head of government but as the president of India's grand old party—and as the power behind Manmohan Singh's premiership.

■

Soon after the turbulent exchange with Rahul, Sonia walked out of the room. She was slated to meet senior party leaders whom she had called to 10, Janpath that afternoon. She was accompanied by Manmohan Singh and Natwar Singh. Among those waiting to see her were Pranab Mukherjee, Shivraj Patil, Ghulam Nabi Azad, M. L. Fotedar, Ahmed Patel, and others. 'I have requested Dr Manmohan Singh to take over as prime minister,' she told the assembled group.

There was a stunned silence.

'I am grateful,' Manmohan Singh finally said, feebly. 'But I cannot accept. I don't have the mandate.'

Knowing that Sonia Gandhi's mind was made up, Natwar Singh interjected at this point, 'Manmohan Singhji has no right to say "No" because the person who has the mandate is transferring it to him.'

Natwar Singh added: 'I got dirty looks from Pranab Mukherjee.'

Besides those inside the house, many Congress MPs were waiting outside. Word had got around that Sonia Gandhi might not take up prime ministership. In the 44°C heat, politicians and members of the media had been waiting restlessly for hours. Finally, Pranab Mukherjee and Natwar Singh emerged from the bungalow. They told everyone present that Sonia Gandhi would be meeting the president in Rashtrapati Bhavan the next day. Many sighed with relief; they thought she had decided to stake her claim to form the government.

■

That morning Sonia Gandhi had called Ahmed Patel and Ambika Soni separately to inform them about her decision not to take up the prime ministership. Patel and Soni were her political secretaries, though often at loggerheads. Sonia told Patel that she did not want the new government to get weakened by the fierce opposition to her foreign origins. Patel, who would go on to wield enormous power in the years that followed (Sonia came to depend on him heavily), tried to dissuade her—unsuccessfully. She also informed Janardan Dwivedi, her politically-savvy Hindi speechwriter about her decision.

Ambika Soni spoke in an idiom Sonia could relate to. With her husband in the foreign service Soni had travelled the world before Indira Gandhi spotted her and made her chief of the Youth Congress during the Emergency years. Such was the comfort level that Sonia enjoyed with her, that when they were travelling together, Ambika could walk into Sonia's room even when she had her hair in rollers! Realizing that Sonia could not be persuaded, Soni did not even try to get her to change her mind. 'You must do it in a way that it is remembered by posterity,' she told Sonia.

Sonia had 'drawn up' a 'matter-of-fact' statement with Ahmed Patel, about her decision not to become prime minister. Given the hectic pace of events since the results, she had not had a moment to think of what she would say. 'You should formulate something which will strike an emotional chord with people,' Soni suggested.

I received a call from Sonia Gandhi on the 17th morning—in response to a request to speak to her. As I congratulated her, she began to dwell on the problems the BJP would create for her if she became PM, which could lead to violence in the country. Though her exact words elude me, she said something like, 'They are going to make my functioning very difficult.' When I put down the receiver, it suddenly struck me that she had sounded sombre, not upbeat. And I wondered why she was referring to the difficulties ahead in a moment of victory. The conversation was to come back to me thirty-six hours later when she announced her decision not to accept the prime ministership.

Sonia Gandhi had deputed Congress functionaries to talk to a few prominent leaders about her decision before she made it public. On 17 May, Natwar Singh and M. L. Fotedar had headed to see V. P. Singh and Lalu Prasad Yadav. VP listened quietly when they told him that Sonia now wanted to make Manmohan Singh the prime minister. 'I have no objection,' VP told his visitors. He told me in the course of a conversation not long afterwards, 'Her children did not want her to become prime minister, they feared for her life.'

CPI (M) leader Somnath Chatterjee, confirmed to me what V. P. Singh had said—that Sonia's decision to give up the prime ministership was 'because of her children'. 'We had agreed on her becoming prime minister, what can we do if her children feared for her life and did not want her to become PM?' That evening of 17 May, she invited the leaders of parties supporting the Congress Party to 10, Janpath, to tell them of her decision—and nominate Manmohan Singh as prime minister. She did not give the assembled leaders any reason for her decision.

'It was a very difficult meeting,' Natwar Singh recalled. The leaders were very upset. Rashtriya Janata Dal leader Lalu Yadav went ballistic. 'Why did you not tell us earlier? We have learnt about it from TV,' he stormed. Harkishan Singh Surjeet tried to dissuade Sonia. Ram Vilas Paswan, head of the Bihar-based Lok Jan Shakti Party, said they had given their support to Sonia Gandhi, not to someone else.

By then, the media had picked up the uncertainty that surrounded Sonia Gandhi's elevation as PM. West Bengal chief minister Jyoti Basu, who was in Delhi that day, expressed 'disappointment (with her decision)'.

'The Left expected her to become prime minister,' said Prakash Karat later. 'It was a surprise to us that it would be Manmohan Singh. It was a fait accompli presented to her party, the UPA, and the supporting Left parties.'

Those present at the evening meeting were so upset that it was decided she defer her decision till the next day. However, Sonia Gandhi remained unyielding. The mother in her had overpowered the politician.

■

The morning of 18 May started with a private meeting of the family—Sonia, Priyanka, and Rahul—at 10, Janpath. They discussed 'the most difficult decision of their lives'.

Later that day, accompanied by Manmohan Singh, Sonia Gandhi called on the president, A. P. J. Abdul Kalam. Normally, when the leader of the party that has won the most seats is invited to meet the president, s/he emerges from Rashtrapati Bhavan as the prime minister-designate. However, when Sonia Gandhi and Manmohan Singh came out on to the forecourt of Rashtrapati Bhavan to face the hordes of mediapersons assembled there, she did not say anything about having been invited to form the government. 'I will meet the president again tomorrow to complete the negotiations,' she told a baffled media. The government, she said, would be formed as soon as possible.

Rumours were now flying thick and fast in Delhi—that she might not take over the country's top position. It was said that the president had spiked her claim to form the government because of her foreign origins. Subramanian Swamy (who was then president of the Janata Party) added grist to the mill. He alleged that the president had not invited her to lead the government because her Indian citizenship was 'flawed' and she had given no proof of having given up her Italian citizenship.

The rumour was finally laid to rest eight years later when A. P. J. Abdul Kalam put the record straight in his memoirs. 'Mrs Gandhi came to Rashtrapati Bhavan along with Dr Manmohan Singh.' Kalam wrote. '...After exchanging pleasantries, she showed me the letters of support from various parties.'

Kalam said he told her, 'The Rashtrapati Bhavan is ready for the swearing-in ceremony at the time of your choice.' The letter of invitation to her had already been drafted. 'That is when she told me that she would like to nominate Dr Manmohan Singh....This was definitely a surprise to me and the Rashtrapati Bhavan secretariat had to rework the letter....'

'If she had made any claim for herself, I would have had no option but to appoint her,' Kalam wrote. For there was no law to prevent a naturalized Indian from becoming prime minister, provided s/he had been elected by MPs.

■

That evening, Sonia Gandhi walked into the Central Hall of Parliament to address the Congress MPs who had assembled there. She walked in followed by her son, Rahul, and daughter, Priyanka, who was accompanied by her husband, Robert Vadra. All three looked grave. Sonia took a seat behind the long, polished teak table which had witnessed so many historic moments over the years, including the 'tryst with destiny' speech made by her grandfather-in-law, Jawaharlal Nehru, at midnight on 14 August 1947. Manmohan Singh sat beside her.

MPs lined up to congratulate her—and to garland her. Then she rose to speak. 'I was always certain that if ever I found myself in the position that I am in today, I would follow my own inner voice. Today, that voice tells me I must humbly decline this post.'

'No, no', went up cries from the audience. Some MPs stood up. They started waving their arms. It was to indicate that they did not accept what she was saying.

Sonia Gandhi continued, 'You have unanimously elected me your leader. In doing so, you have reposed your faith in me. It is this faith that has placed me under tremendous pressure to reconsider my decision.' Again, there were protests from the audience. Sonia urged them to sit down. 'I speak to you to understand the force of my conviction. I request you to accept my decision and to recognize that I will not reverse it.... As one of you, and as president of the Congress Party, I pledge myself to work with you and for the country.' When she finished, she was mobbed. Many of those present entreated her to change her mind. But she stood firm.

Her decision was acclaimed all over India. Editorials—in India and abroad—praised her. 'With her decision,' The Hindu wrote, 'Sonia had seized the moral "high ground".' The Nation of Pakistan called it an 'astute' move. India Today described it as a 'strategic renunciation'. The Times of India saw it as a 'well-calculated assessment of the political forces lined up against her'—with her decision to nominate Manmohan Singh as PM, she had 'put forward the one man who could unite the fractious party...reassure the nervous middle class and outside investors'. The Hindustan Times lauded her for being the only person in Indian history to have turned down the prime ministership 'not once but twice'. After Rajiv Gandhi's assassination in 1991, she had refused to take over as Congress president. Had she done so, she would have gone on to become PM, instead of P. V. Narasimha Rao.

(Before her, both Jyoti Basu and V. P. Singh had turned down the country's premiership in 1996.)

The Congress managers went into overdrive to laud her 'sacrifice'. There were stories in the media that Sonia Gandhi had never planned to take up the prime ministership in the first place. And that she had made up her mind in March 2004 itself that, were such a moment to come, she would install Manmohan Singh on the Delhi throne. Privately, party leaders said that she had zeroed in on Manmohan Singh because he was a technocrat with no independent political following, was soft-spoken, self-effacing, and not theatrical in his deportment or actions. Above all, he was not likely to be a threat to her or to her children in the future. Therein lay his acceptability.

A simple Punjabi meal was cooking in the Singh household when word reached Gursharan Kaur that her husband would be the next prime minister. A smiling Gursharan Kaur personally brought water for the visitors when the *Indian Express* team arrived at 19, Safdarjung Road, to interview her—and she opened her family album to them.

After eight days of breathtaking developments, Sonia Gandhi announced on 19 May that Manmohan Singh would be the prime minister. On 22 May 2004, the seventy-one-year-old Singh was sworn in as the thirteenth prime minister of India.

VI

'If I was your daughter would you advise me to come into politics?' Sonia Gandhi had asked P. V. Narasimha Rao, a year after her husband Rajiv was assassinated in 1991.

'If you were my daughter, I would say no,' Rao told her categorically.

'But if you want me to groom your children, I can do so, I can take them with me on trips,' he added.

The Sonia Gandhi of 2004 was a far cry from the carefree, apolitical young woman who had come to India in 1968 to marry Rajiv. They had met as students in Cambridge, UK, and fallen in love. In her early years in Delhi, she was an easy-going, party-loving, politics-shunning housewife. She and Rajiv socialized with the city's jet set, and kept away from the rough and tumble of Indian politics, even though they lived in the prime minister's residence at 1, Safdarjung Road. Politics was left to Indira Gandhi and her younger son, Sanjay. The tragic deaths of her mother-in-law and brother-in-law, and the ascension of her husband to prime ministership, over her strident objections, changed all that. She began taking an interest in politics.

However, after Rajiv was killed, she grew increasingly reclusive. But even during those dark years, she did not rule out a political role for herself. Nor did she dissuade partymen from raising demands from time to time that she enter active politics. It was a way to keep the Congress leaders guessing—and on the right side of the Nehru–Gandhi family, at a time when she held no position. Conscious of the legacy of the family, she may have also wanted to keep the political option open for her children in case they decided to join politics later. She always gave a stock answer whenever asked about their entry into politics: 'It is upto them to decide.'

As she weighed her options, she continued with quasi-political activity. She established the Rajiv Gandhi Foundation and organized international conferences under the auspices of the Indira Gandhi Memorial Trust and Nehru Memorial Fund, both of which she headed after Rajiv's death.

It was in 1995 that she first gave a hint that she might enter active politics. During a visit to Amethi, the constituency that had been represented by her husband, she expressed her unhappiness over the tardy progress made in the Rajiv Gandhi assassination probe. It was (as noted in Chapter 4), an oblique criticism of Rao. This was seen as a sign that she was now looking for a larger political role for herself.

On 8 May 1997, out of the blue, she let it be known that she had become a primary member of the Congress Party. When she took over as president of the Congress in February 1998, Congressmen were deserting the party. Her predecessor, Sitaram Kesri, appeared to be losing his grip over the party, and was unceremoniously ejected from his position in what was a coup backed by her—and she went on to replace him. However, despite the important position she now held, she was still new to the game.

Sonia was keenly aware of her limitations and of her place in the Congress pantheon. Once when she was compared to the other Mrs Gandhi, Indira, she said quietly, 'I am not Nehru's daughter.'

Sometimes her nervousness was palpable—and this was evident at a tea party thrown for her in 1998 by Najma Heptulla, deputy chairperson of the Rajya Sabha. The idea was for Sonia to meet presspersons informally. Tea was laid out for the journalists on the sprawling lawns of Heptulla's residence at 4, Akbar Road. Sonia had asked for black tea with a slice of lemon and this was brought to her. She sat there surrounded by mediapersons. They began to ask her questions. I happened to be standing right behind her, and could actually see her hand shaking as she held the cup, and faced the questions. Equally nervous Congress leaders hung around and prompted her as and when required.

But Sonia was a quick learner. A year later, in 1999, when flying to Bellary from where she contested the Lok Sabha elections against BJP's Sushma Swaraj, a couple of us journalists who were on the same flight went up to speak to her. This time our questions did not ruffle her.

During the flight she had obviously been practising the speech she was to deliver. It lay on the foldout table in front of her—the Hindi speech was printed out in English script in a very large font, it looked like 48 points. The 'th' in the words seemed to be underlined, obviously to indicate where the emphasis was to be placed.

Sonia used to work hard on her speeches. 'Each of Sonia's speeches... would take six to eight hours. Sometimes these agonizing "speech sessions" lasted till midnight....' Natwar Singh recalled. 'She would read the speech aloud and I would time it.' Congress leaders would say that she would relax only after she had delivered her speech. Till then, you could not get her full attention. She generally read out her speeches.

Sonia was a good listener. I had once asked her what she and Mayawati, whom she was courting before the 2004 polls, had talked about for two and a half hours when they met at Mayawati's house on 1 February 2004. Sonia replied, 'I didn't talk much. It is she who talked. She went over the guest house incident in great detail.'

Cautious to a fault, Sonia was also highly pragmatic. When the party lost in the state elections in Madhya Pradesh, Rajasthan, and Chhattisgarh in the winter of 2003, and Congress morale slumped, observers predicted that the Congress would be reduced to double digits in the general elections in mid-2004. Sonia decided to hit the road. She also decided to stitch together alliances with other parties, reversing the Congress's 'go-solo' policy of 6 September 1998, which had been adopted at Pachmarhi.

Once she had decided to go in for alliances, she walked across to see Ram Vilas Paswan who lived at 1, Janpath, just on the other side of the boundary wall of her house—and struck up an alliance with his party, the Lok Jan Shakti. She put aside her antipathy towards Sharad Pawar, who had criticized her foreign origins in 1999 and quit the Congress to launch his regional outfit, the Nationalist Congress Party. It was she who called on him to seek his cooperation and not the other way around, as had been the practice in the past. She made overtures to the DMK, the party the Congress had held responsible for Rajiv Gandhi's assassination. When DMK chief M. Karunanidhi called on Sonia Gandhi before the elections, she waited for him to arrive in the portico of 10, Janpath—and then personally escorted him into the house. This was normally not the drill, except in the case of very special guests. Otherwise, visitors were shown into a small anteroom at the front of the house till they were called into her study. She also tied up with the RJD; its leader, Lalu Prasad Yadav, had been the first non-Congress leader to stand by her when she was being attacked for her foreign antecedents. Her political nous paid off in 2004—she defeated the BJP and led the Congress to victory. She appointed Manmohan Singh as prime minister, but it soon became clear that her role in the new government would not be a passive one. It was Sonia Gandhi who decided who would be in the cabinet in 2004.

'It's no secret,' admitted Montek Singh Ahluwalia, a long-time associate of Manmohan Singh, 'the decision of who (was) going to be in his cabinet was not (going to be) his alone. He was brought in as a technocrat to run the government. The political head of the Congress Party and the UPA coalition was Sonia Gandhi.' Her coterie made no secret of the fact that the PM would get on with 'governance', while she would take all the 'political decisions'. Besides deciding on who would be in the cabinet, she also had a say—and her way—in government appointments. Manmohan Singh mostly went along with what she wanted done. While Sonia Gandhi ceded her claim to prime ministership to Manmohan Singh, she continued to wield power as president of the Congress Party, and chairperson of the ruling UPA.

■

At 9 a.m. on 17 July 2004, a confident Sonia Gandhi breezed into the room at 2, Motilal Nehru Marg, in Delhi. It was to be the office of the newly constituted National Advisory Council (NAC)—and she was all set to preside over its first meeting. As she walked into the room, some of the NAC members assembled there stood up as a sign of respect. Others half rose—not knowing how to respond. The rest sheepishly put their hands on the armrests on their chairs in an attempt to get up but were relieved they did not have to do so. They did not want to come across as being too deferential. But all had suddenly become conscious of Sonia Gandhi's enhanced stature—after she had said 'no' to prime ministership. They were trying to figure out how to respond to the new situation.

The idea to set up the NAC—headed by Sonia Gandhi—had come up during discussions soon after she had declined the prime ministership. The union cabinet decided that the NAC would help it implement the UPA's Common Minimum Programme. It came into existence on 4 June 2004—within two weeks of the PM taking over.

Sonia Gandhi did not need the NAC to get things done by the government. She was powerful enough as the president of the Congress Party, chairperson of the CPP and the chair of the UPA, to get decisions made just by speaking to a minister directly or through one of her aides.

The NAC was really to give her an 'in' into the government's decision-making processes. It gave her an office to work from, staff to assist her—and it gave her the rank of a cabinet minister. And it would enable her to suggest programmes which she could forward to the government for implementation.

At its first meeting, Sonia Gandhi welcomed all the members. There were twelve of them—among them Right to Information (RTI) activist Aruna Roy, former Planning Commission member N. C. Saxena, development economist A. K. Shiv Kumar, and economist Jean Drèze. Others included educationist Mrinal Miti, social activist and entrepreneur Madhav Chavan from Pratham, and writer-economist C. H. Hanumantha Rao. Jairam Ramesh was there as member secretary. Aruna Roy had been leading the Right to Information campaign for several years; Jean Drèze had been working on an employment guarantee scheme based on the programme which had been successful in Maharashtra. The RTI and an employment guarantee scheme were promises included in the UPA's Common Minimum Programme. The employment guarantee scheme later named Mahatma Gandhi National Rural Employment Guarantee Act (MGNREGA) was close to Sonia Gandhi's heart.

'It was a no-brainer that it would come up for discussion at the first meeting of the NAC,' remarked a NAC member. During her tenure as chairperson of the NAC, Sonia Gandhi would preside over several rights-based initiatives. Many of the initiatives she spearheaded at the NAC had grown out of the discussions she had had from 1996 onwards with academics, activists, historians, judges, social scientists, and civil society groups—many of them with left-of-centre leanings who would brief her on national issues. It was at this time she met people like Romila Thapar, Yogendra Yadav, J. N. Dixit, and many others. Mohit Sen of the CPI was a frequent visitor to 10, Janpath. In the months that followed, Sonia's left-of-centre position would help balance the 'reformist' leanings of Manmohan Singh.

■

'The prime minister will see us at 4 p.m. today,' Arun Bhatnagar, the newly appointed NAC secretary, an IAS officer, told the group at its first meeting. Sonia Gandhi had requested a meeting with the prime minister; Manmohan Singh had invited them for tea at his residence at 7, Race Course Road. At 4 p.m., they were ushered into a conference room at the PM House. There was a rectangular conference table and two chairs had been placed at the head of the table. When the prime minister arrived, he invited Sonia Gandhi to take one and he took the other, thereby giving her parity of status.

'Sonia Gandhi was seen like a god at the time,' remarked one of the NAC members later, 'having given up prime ministership and having made Manmohan Singh PM. Mani Shankar Aiyar had called her "Mother Teresa".'

'I am glad you have started (work),' the PM told the group conversationally, asking them about their meeting that morning.

'We discussed NREGA,' one of them replied.

'Yes, it is a good programme and it is in the Common Minimum Programme,' the PM said. Then he suddenly asked, 'How much will it cost?'

'₹35,000 crores,' someone replied.

'Where will we get the money?' the PM asked edgily.

'I thought to myself, what an unfair question,' recalled one of the members afterwards. 'Manmohan Singh had been finance minister, governor of RBI, and now prime minister. Even if he had not been FM or RBI governor, how could a PM be asking such a question?' It was after all not an economic question but a political one and had to do with the allocation of resources for something the government had said would be its priority. As the PM had acknowledged, it was part of the Common Minimum Programme, and the UPA was committed to implementing it. 'If he can't answer that question, how can we do so as outsiders?' thought this member.

Sonia Gandhi said hardly anything at the meeting. It lasted no more than twenty minutes. However, it brought home to some of the NAC members that their initiatives might not be as easy to push through as they had first thought, despite the clout Sonia Gandhi wielded.

In government circles, it quickly became known that Manmohan Singh was not enthused about NREGA (renamed MGNREGA through an amendment in the Act in 2009). 'Being a true monetary economist, he did not support what he believed were non-productive benevolent activities,' wrote Pranab Mukherjee in his book *The Coalition Years*. Sonia Gandhi knew she had to move strategically. She had the support of the Left parties, which were vocal in their defence of the right to work. When NAC members met the Left leaders, a charged CPI leader A. B. Bardhan said repeatedly, 'We must fight.' According to a NAC member, 'he used the word about twenty-five times'. Finally, the Lok Sabha passed NREGA on 23 August 2005. The next day it was cleared by the Rajya Sabha. It aimed at enhancing the 'livelihood security of the households in rural areas of the country by providing at least one hundred days of guaranteed wage employment in every financial year to every household whose adult members volunteer to do unskilled manual work'.

On 5 September 2005, the president gave his assent to it. The right to work had become a statutory right in India. Sonia Gandhi had pulled off one of the biggest coups of her career as a public figure.

Besides NREGA, the NAC provided inputs to the government on policy decisions, and recommended legislations for the Manmohan ministry to enact. No matter what the prime minister, or his senior ministers, might have felt about the NAC's recommendations, they found it difficult to say 'no' to Sonia Gandhi.

The UPA went on to pass several rights-based legislations. The far-reaching Right to Information Bill was passed on 15 June 2005. There was the Right to Education, legislated in 2009, and finally the Right to Food which was cleared in 2013, during UPA-II, after long-drawn-out negotiations.

Sonia Gandhi would often write to ministers as NAC chairperson.

Members of the NAC Secretariat would call up secretaries of ministries asking them to prepare power-point presentations for NAC members or fix up appointments to go and meet them. Dr K. Srinath Reddy from AIIMS came and briefed the group that was working on the constitution of the National Rural Health Mission (NRHM); the NRHM was launched on 12 April 2005 to provide affordable, accessible healthcare to rural populations. Others held meetings with Montek Singh Ahluwalia, deputy chairman of the Planning Commission.

The BJP took swipes at Sonia Gandhi and called her a 'Super Prime Minister'—and her position as NAC chairperson 'unconstitutional', Critics dubbed the NAC as an 'alternative...cabinet'—its existence was not 'in keeping' with the country's Constitution. In government circles, the NAC was 'disparagingly' referred to as 'Sonia's jholawalla crowd', adding yet 'another layer of bureaucracy to decision-making'.

But for the NAC members, it was a never-before opportunity to put in place a rights-based framework in India. Sonia Gandhi, seen at the time as one of the most powerful women in the world, became their 'Brahmastra', making possible what had hitherto seemed impossible. But it was clear, and Rural Development Minister Raghuvansh Prasad Singh openly articulated this reality when he said, 'The NAC is useful only if Soniaji is heading it. Otherwise it has no meaning.'

Reflecting on those years, economist Jean Drèze, a prominent member of the NAC, said to me: 'UPA will be remembered both for the high economic growth and for a rights-based framework.... Economic growth created an opening and Mrs Gandhi stepped in with her commitment to social policy.' Drèze's comment summed up the unprecedented confluence of forces that had come about in 2004 with the advent of the UPA government—a prime minister who believed in high economic growth and an equally powerful leader who wanted to position the ruling Congress as a pro-aam admi (ordinary person) entity. Sonia Gandhi knew she had to take on board the concerns of the Left parties, which ensured the UPA's survival. On their part, the Left parties wanted the government to provide a safety net to the poor—give primacy to the public sector, eschew disinvestment, and not tie itself too closely to American interests. The UPA's Common Minimum Programme had chosen to focus on the 'aam admi'—it did not use the word 'poor', which had socialist connotations from the past.

Sonia Gandhi often acted as a buffer between the Left parties and the prime minister, knowing that the Left thinking was at variance with the economic philosophy of Manmohan Singh. She knew instinctively that the Congress needed to maintain a left-of-centre image in a largely poor country like India. This was also critical for her personally, given her foreign origins. She had not forgotten that the NDA's 2004 'India Shining' poll campaign had not clicked with ordinary people.

Whatever their differences, Manmohan Singh was careful not to take on Sonia Gandhi directly. While he would ask from time to time how the NAC's programmes were going to be funded, he would usually leave it to Finance Minister P. Chidambaram and Planning Commission Deputy Chairman Montek Singh Ahluwalia to express concern about the fiscal implications of the NAC's social welfare initiatives. Ultimately, however, the PM would fall in line.

The other major issue on which Sonia Gandhi and the PM diverged was the Indo–US Civil Nuclear Deal—and the new strategic relationship Manmohan Singh wanted to forge with the US. On this, the prime minister refused to give in.

VII

'So be it'. These three words by Prime Minister Manmohan Singh created an uproar in Delhi's political circles in August 2007. Singh told Manini Chatterjee of The Telegraph that if the Left wanted to withdraw support to his government over the nuclear deal, 'so be it'. The Kolkata-based paper carried the sensational interview on its front page on 13 August 2007.

Party offices in Delhi and Kolkata were abuzz decoding what the PM meant. The CPI (M) leadership was aghast that the PM should speak in this vein. The Congress leadership was riled that Singh should put the UPA government at risk. 'Who is Doctor sahib to decide about alliances, that is the job of the party,' the highly discreet Ahmed Patel, Sonia Gandhi's political secretary, grumbled. After all, the political side of the UPA's governance was the responsibility of Sonia Gandhi and the Congress she headed. Manmohan Singh was supposed to concentrate only on governance and administration. That was the unstated understanding when he became prime minister. 'How can the PM be so irresponsible?' many Congress leaders asked in private.

They saw the interview as a calculated message sent by the PM to the Left parties. They commented on the choice of the paper and the journalist to whom he had given the interview. As noted, The Telegraph was a Kolkata-based paper and West Bengal was considered the Left's fiefdom. Manini Chatterjee was a journalist likely to be taken more seriously by Left leaders, particularly by CPI (M) leader Prakash Karat, who knew her well. Her credibility with senior Left leaders was high, especially as she had worked full-time with the CPI (M) for several years when she had taken a break from the mainstream media.

'In August I called up Sanjaya Baru,' Chatterjee told me. '(I told him) I would like to pay a courtesy call on the PM, now that I have taken over as resident editor of The Telegraph in Delhi.

'I was told to come to his office in Parliament House at 12. If I remember right, (I was being asked to come) the same day.'

She started off by asking the PM about the Left. As he began talking, Chatterjee's pen moved furiously on the pages of her notebook, to capture every word of what he was saying. 'I looked at him and asked, "can I quote you? This is page one story". He was very exercised over what the Left had said.'

'Yes,' he said. 'But show it to Sanjaya first.' Sanjaya Baru, the media advisor to the PM had been a journalist before he moved to the PMO.

'The meeting did not last very long, only 15-20 minutes.'

She sat with Sanjaya Baru in the anteroom, and for the next ten minutes went over her notes with him. 'I thought to myself, I cannot get a single quote wrong.' Baru okayed what she had noted down.

When she walked out of Parliament House she was in a daze.

Manini Chatterjee's piece appeared on the front page of *The Telegraph* the next day. The headline screamed, 'Anguished PM to the Left: If you want to withdraw, so be it'.

The article quoted the prime minister: 'I told them (the Left) it is not possible to renegotiate the deal.... The Cabinet has approved it, we cannot go back on it. I told them (the Left) to do whatever they want to.' He told Chatterjee, 'If they want to withdraw support, so be it.'

Explaining how the events had unfolded, Baru recalled, 'I had been sitting with him (PM) the previous evening.... We were watching TV in RCR.' Prakash Karat was addressing a press conference (on 11 August 2007), along with other Left leaders. His words held a veiled warning to the Manmohan Singh ministry: "The prime minister and the government must realize that the agreement is not acceptable to the majority in Parliament," Karat had warned. "As far as the approach to the government is concerned, we will take our own counsel."'

Karat was referring to the 123 Agreement on Indo–US civil nuclear cooperation that had been finalized by the two governments in July 2007, almost two years to the day after Manmohan Singh and George W. Bush had first decided to enact the nuclear deal. With the finalization of the 123 Agreement, another major step forward had been taken—and the ball was now back in India's court. Prime Minister Manmohan Singh was raring to take the next steps—to go to the IAEA for an 'India-specific safeguard agreement', and then to the NSG for a 'waiver'. Only then would the US Congress formalize the agreement.

Immediately, the Central Committee of the CPI (M) had met, in early August, and decided to stiffen its opposition to 'stop the deal'.

'We should be prepared...to try and thwart the deal,' the CPI (M)'s apex body resolved, 'even to withdraw support.' Karat's statement reflected the hardening of the Left's stand.

As he and the PM watched Karat's press conference, Baru recalled, 'I could see the PM turn red. He was so angry.' It was not known to many that Singh had a short fuse, and often tended to lose his temper in private. In public he maintained a cool and impeccable demeanour.

The interview electrified the political circuit in Delhi. It also made waves in Kolkata—as it was intended to do. Manmohan Singh had consulted no one in his party about the interview. He planned it only with his media advisor, Sanjaya Baru. And once it was out there, he did not take back his words, nor deny them. The situation was headed for a showdown with the Left.

It was at this stage that Sonia Gandhi decided to intervene. She instructed that a committee be set up comprising leaders from the UPA and the Left parties to look into the objections raised by the Left. Committees were a tried and tested way to buy time. More important, it was a move designed to stop the government from taking the next steps. The prime minister, who was impatient to move ahead, would be reined in. It was then that the government and the Left both agreed to press the 'pause' button: 'No stop, no rewind, only pause', said a headline, summing up the situation.

■

On 30 August 2007, Pranab Mukherjee announced the formation of the UPA-Left Coordination Committee on India–US Civil Nuclear Cooperation. Mukherjee, minister of External Affairs, became its convenor. The committee had five members from the Congress, besides Mukherjee, three from UPA allies, and six from the Left parties. The Congress representatives were Pranab Mukherjee, A. K. Antony, P. Chidambaram, Saifuddin Soz, Kapil Sibal, and Prithviraj Chavan. Sharad Pawar, T. R. Baalu, and Lalu Yadav represented the regional parties, NCP, DMK, and RJD. Members of the Left parties on the committee were the CPI (M)'s Prakash Karat and Sitaram Yechury, CPI's A. B. Bardhan and D. Raja, with the Forward Bloc and RSP represented by D. Biswas, and T. J. Chandrachoodan. Manmohan Singh—and Sonia Gandhi—decided not to be part of the committee.

Pranab Mukherjee called the first meeting of the committee at his office in South Block. He asked the UPA's three allies to come a little earlier as he wanted to chat with them informally, to ascertain their views before meeting with the Left leaders.

Sharad Pawar was a worried man that day. 'If the government goes ahead with the nuclear deal,' he warned, 'the CPM will go to the president and withdraw support.' It might even vote alongside the BJP, he felt. 'We have to be ready for elections,' an anxious Pawar told the group.

Pawar's remarks showed that unlike the Left parties, the Congress's allies were not exercised about the nuclear deal. They were concerned more about the Left–Congress impasse bringing on early elections which they were not ready to face.

Sharad Pawar had read the CPI (M) general secretary's mood right. Prakash Karat had put his party's 'fight against imperialism' on a higher pedestal than its 'battle against the BJP's communalism', which the UPA government stood for—and he was ready to let the government go, if push came to shove.

■

'For us, it all started when Pranab Mukherjee went to Washington in June 2005,' Prakash Karat said years later, referring to the ten-year Indo–US Defence Agreement that Defence Minister Mukherjee had signed with the US in June 2005.

'There was no consultation (with us). Nobody was told (about it). Not even the Cabinet Committee on Security.... We were completely shocked.' The Left, Karat said, saw it as a major policy reversal. The moment Pranab Mukherjee returned to India, 'Bardhan and I rushed to meet him,' Karat told me. 'We had a heated discussion (with him).... You have done this secretly, covertly,' a disappointed Karat accused Mukherjee. 'You had told us it was an exploratory visit.' Later, the Left parties held a protest meeting at Delhi's Constitution Club. 'The nuclear deal was a quid pro quo...a lollipop given to India by Bush,' Karat charged.

When Manmohan Singh went in for a joint statement with George Bush on 18 July 2005, the Left protested again. In response, the Congress leadership asked nuclear scientist Raja Ramanna and the national security advisor M. K. Narayanan to brief the Left leaders and allay their fears. When they had decided to support the UPA, the Left had expected to clash with the Congress on economic issues. They had their differences—but it was only up to a point, and took the form mainly of notes they would submit to the government. Up until February 2006, the Left had submitted nineteen notes to the government—on issues like foreign direct investment (FDI) in telecom, insurance, banking, print media, retail, rates on the Employees' Provident Fund, on the privatization of airports, and so on. On his part, the PM would personally call for action on the issues the Left highlighted. He wanted to keep them in good humour. He also appointed people recommended by Left leaders in universities, the Planning Commission, and other important bodies.

What the Left leaders had not expected were sharp differences on foreign policy issues; they were to be the undoing of the partnership. To the Left, the nuclear deal was a keystone of the growing strategic alliance with the US, mainly in defence, which was not acceptable to Prakash Karat.

■

When Manmohan Singh became prime minister, the man he often turned to for help was CPI (M) general secretary Harkishan Singh Surjeet—despite the differences the PM had with the communists. Manmohan Singh had wanted Montek Singh Ahluwalia as finance minister. But Sonia Gandhi ruled that out—and selected P. Chidambaram instead. The resourceful Surjeet helped Manmohan Singh. Ahluwalia became deputy chairman of the Planning Commission and was given cabinet rank. As a result, he could attend cabinet meetings—and be the PM's eyes and ears. Given his proximity to the PM, there would be more cars of politicians and diplomats parked outside Yojana Bhavan than outside the PM's residence. Before he took over as deputy chairman of the Planning Commission, Ahluwalia asked the PM if there was anyone in particular he wanted him to meet. Manmohan Singh told him to call on Surjeet. Ahluwalia met the eighty-eight-year old Comrade Surjeet who 'offered me tea and biscuits'—not 'disapproval'. The CPI (M) leaders were not happy with the appointment of Ahluwalia who had held a position in the IMF. They had asked Surjeet to intervene and stop it but by then it was too late.

The Congress leaders also looked askance at Ahluwalia's appointment and would joke about the 'Sardar to Sardar' bonhomie which had swung the appointment. All three—Manmohan Singh, Montek Singh Ahluwalia, and Harkishan Singh Surjeet—were Bhapa Sikhs, they would say snidely. The Ahluwalias, Montek and his eminent economist wife Isher Judge Ahluwalia, were long-time personal friends of Manmohan Singh and his wife Gursharan Kaur.

Manmohan Singh's troubles with the Left started the moment Prakash Karat replaced Harkishan Singh Surjeet as general secretary of the CPI (M). Surjeet and Jyoti Basu, former chief minister of West Bengal, both top leaders of the CPI (M), had repeatedly assured Manmohan Singh of their support when he became PM in 2004. He would have no trouble from them, they would say—as long as the Congress adhered to the Common Minimum Programme. After Surjeet stepped down from the leadership of the CPI (M), Karat was a thorn in the PM's side. While Karat's public persona was that of an ideologically unyielding tough negotiator, in person he was gentle—and a thorough gentleman. Karat was especially difficult to deal with on the Indo–US strategic relationship. Congress leaders found him the toughest nut to crack. Under his hawk-like vigil, the UPA's Common Minimum Programme had taken the Left's concerns on board—about 'not moving into the American orbit'. When the two sides were discussing the CMP draft, the Congress had initially talked about forging 'a strategic partnership with the US'. 'We cut that sentence out,' Karat revealed. It was replaced by a blander sentiment which called for 'improving relations with the US', following 'an independent foreign policy', and opposing 'all attempts at unilateralism'.

By mid-2007, when the prime minister gave his explosive interview to *The Telegraph*, Prakash Karat was viewed in many quarters as the most powerful man in India. He held the key to the future of the UPA government.

As the Congress tried to patch up with the CPI (M), Pranab Mukherjee became their man of the moment—as neither the PM nor Sonia Gandhi knew quite how to handle the doctrinaire Karat. They left it to Mukherjee to handle the CPI (M) leader both at informal discussions and at meetings of the UPA–Left Committee on India–US Civil Nuclear Cooperation. 'Only Pranab Mukherjee could have done it,' Karat himself admitted. 'He knew the Left and understood it.'

■

Slowly, the prime minister retreated into a shell after his 'so be it' bravado of August 2007—as Pranab Mukherjee tried to salvage the nuclear deal, and the UPA government. Mukherjee held nine sittings of the UPA-Left Coordination Committee. Six of them were on the Hyde Act and the implications it had for India's foreign policy. It exercised the Left the most. 'We said we would be binding ourselves to the US on our foreign policy,' Karat said. 'The preamble of the Hyde Act made it clear that we will work to isolate Iran'. India had a time-tested relationship with Iran. In response to the Left's criticism, the prime minister told parliament that the Hyde Act was not binding on India. The Left, however, remained unconvinced.

Three meetings of the committee were devoted to the IAEA. Not much progress was made in the first four meetings of the committee. Both sides exchanged detailed papers and counter notes. Pranab Mukherjee made a point of keeping Jyoti Basu in the loop. He hoped Basu would exercise a moderating influence on the CPI (M).

In October 2007, the *Hindustan Times* organized a 'summit' in New Delhi on 12 October—it gave a glimpse into the prime minister's thinking. Both Manmohan Singh and Sonia Gandhi were invited to speak at the conference. The PM was watching the event televised live at his residence at RCR. Before he left his residence for the hotel where the event was being held, he wanted to hear what Sonia had to say. The Left's opposition to the nuclear deal, he heard Sonia say on television, was 'not unreasonable'. The government, she promised, would work for a 'consensus'.

The PM left for the function. The lie of the land was now clear. Manmohan Singh now knew he would have to tone down his defiance. The government, he told the *HT* audience, 'will last its full term'. And if the nuclear deal did not go through, he added, 'it will not be the end of life'.

Journalists mobbed him: 'Will you step down if the Left does not agree to the nuclear deal?'

Manmohan Singh smiled slightly. Then he replied, cryptically, 'It is a suggestion for action.'

The prime minister was taking a step back. And yet, he was also signalling to his party, including Sonia Gandhi, that his options were open—whether or not to continue as PM.

An anxious Sonia Gandhi got on the phone to Montek Singh Ahluwalia. Ahluwalia, she knew, had the PM's ear.

'The PM says he is very upset,' a worried Sonia told Ahluwalia, '.... and he wants to resign. It will be a disaster,' she said. 'Please persuade him that this is not the right thing to do.'

Ahluwalia reported the conversation to Manmohan Singh. 'I completely agreed with her,' Ahluwalia was to say later. He was able to prevail upon the PM not to precipitate a crisis.

■

The fifth meeting of the UPA–Left Committee brought about a shift on both sides—after the nail-biting drama of weeks. On 22 October 2007, Pranab Mukherjee told the Left leaders that the government was prepared to go by the 'sense of parliament'. 'Not a vote', he said, 'but (to get) a sense of the House.'

'You have made an important concession,' Bardhan responded to the government's offer.

Pranab Mukherjee then bowled his googly: 'Unless there is an IAEA text, we will not be in a position to agree whether India's concerns are being addressed.' Mukherjee was referring to the IAEA waiver that the government would need to obtain to keep the deal moving forward. He urged the Left to let the government go to the IAEA. The PM's credibility was at stake, he pleaded.

'We are not against the IAEA', Karat countered. 'We are against the 123 (Agreement) and Hyde Act.' Lalu Yadav, chief of RJD, tried to make peace. He was not bothered about the Hyde Act or about '123', he said. 'Kripya jhagrha mat kariye (Please don't fight),' he said. 'You discuss this with the PM and the Congress president and sort it out.' He added: 'This is not an opportune time for elections (if the Left were to withdraw its support to the UPA and the government were to fall).... We have to act politically. We have to stay together.'

A thaw between the two sides was visible at a lunch given by the prime minister for the leaders of the Left a couple of weeks later—on 10 November 2007. Besides the PM, it was attended by Sonia Gandhi, Pranab Mukherjee, Prakash Karat, and A. B. Bardhan. The Left politicians climbed down somewhat. 'We had been opposed to the government going to the IAEA,' Karat said later. 'But we agreed (at that meeting) to let them go (to the IAEA).' It was also agreed by both sides that the text negotiated with the IAEA would be first shown to the (Left–UPA) Coordination Committee. And the plan would be operationalized only if the committee gave its go-ahead.

'This (agreement) was done with an understanding from Pranab Mukherjee, who was the key interlocutor.... It was given to us with Sonia Gandhi's consent, that they would bring back the draft from IAEA and discuss it with us. And that if we said no to it, they would not proceed.... That was the clear understanding worked out,' said Karat. 'That's where they betrayed us.... (What) happened between November 2007 and June 2008 is the real story,' Karat said.

∎

The prime minister became assertive again in February and March 2008— after his brief show of defiance in August 2007, and being reined in by his party in November 2007.

The turning point came in early February 2008. A group of US Congressmen visited India that month. In it were two Democrats, John Kerry, chairman of the US senate committee on Foreign Relations, and Joe Biden, who later became the US president in November 2020. The third person with them was Republican Chuck Hagel. Biden and his colleagues alerted Manmohan Singh that unless he pressed the accelerator, the opportunity to go ahead with the nuclear deal would slip out of his hands.

The deal, they emphasized, was more likely to go through with a Republican president George W. Bush still in office (until early January 2009) and a Republican majority in the Senate. The US elections were scheduled for November of 2008 and if the Democrats won, neither Barack Obama nor Hillary Clinton would be able to stand up to the non-proliferation lobby in the US. Like the US, India, too, would go to the polls soon thereafter, in the summer of 2009, and it was far from certain that the Congress would return to power. 'We were aware of the (tight) timetable,' Montek Singh Ahluwalia said to me.

Karat, however, believed that the Americans had stepped up pressure on the Indian government. 'We believe the Americans put their foot down, the message being, "forget it (the deal) if it can't be done now".'

Whatever the reasons, Manmohan Singh was galvanized into activity. He began to pursue the deal aggressively once more. He made fresh overtures to his predecessor Atal Bihari Vajpayee, for support, as also the former national security advisor Brajesh Mishra. This time, unlike in 2005, Mishra came out in support of Manmohan Singh. Vajpayee, however, had retired from politics and L. K. Advani, who was in charge of the BJP, was opposed to the deal.

It was at this stage that Manmohan Singh reached out to the Samajwadi Party for their support—he contacted Amar Singh, whose word counted with the SP supremo Mulayam Singh Yadav.

∎

'It was M. K. Narayanan who sold PM the idea that he should get the support of the Samajwadi Party,' a senior Congress leader revealed to me. 'The PM fell for it hook, line, and sinker.'

It was 'Mike', as the National Security Advisor M. K. Narayanan was called by colleagues, who advised Manmohan Singh that he need not be held hostage by the Left parties.

'I did play a role in getting Amar Singh on board,' M. K. Narayanan told me. 'He was the way to get Mulayam Singh on board.'

'I never had to arm-twist,' Narayanan said. 'I told Amar Singh, if you help Manmohan Singh, you will go down in history.'

'Getting M. K. Narayanan on board..."not tangentially but centrally".... was a very important strategic decision (by the PM),' Montek Singh Ahluwalia stated.

'As far as I was concerned,' Narayanan went on, 'I knew where all the pieces were on the chessboard.'

In 2005, Narayanan had had reservations about the deal. He was an appointee of Sonia Gandhi's; she was also not convinced about the deal initially. But then he was not particularly enamoured of the Left, and his position would change a little later. As a junior Intelligence officer in 1959, he had been involved in the operation to dismiss the Communist government in Kerala—a decision taken by Indira. The lore was that he was then noticed by Indira Gandhi, who was president of the Congress at the time—and there was no looking back for him after that. Sonia Gandhi had been instrumental in Narayanan's appointment as NSA after J. N. Dixit's sudden death. When Manmohan Singh opted for Dixit as his NSA in 2004, Narayanan too had made a bid for the position. But the prime minister preferred Dixit.

'Mike' was instead appointed secretary, Security, in the PMO. Internal security was 'hived off' from the NSA and given to him as his responsibility. It was a position specially created for him, at the instance of Sonia Gandhi. He was pulled out of hibernation twelve years after he had retired.

'In 2004, I had suggested his name to Sonia Gandhi, drawing her attention to his proximity to the Gandhi family,' Natwar Singh recalled.

In 2005, on the eve of Republic Day, Narayanan became the national security advisor. The next morning at the Republic Day Parade, he was seen making his way to where Sonia Gandhi sat and 'doing an elaborate namaste to her', recalled Sanjaya Baru.

Soon after their return from Washington DC, a committee suddenly came into existence to take forward the process. It had Narayanan on it, and eminent figures from the Department of Atomic Energy. To his surprise, Foreign Secretary Shyam Saran found he was excluded from the committee. For till then he had been the nodal person negotiating with the Americans. An upset Saran met the prime minister; he wanted to know why he had been pushed out—and requested he be included in the committee.

The prime minister listened to Saran. He appeared sympathetic. But he did nothing. Saran suspected that the committee was 'convinced that we were about to sell the store to the Americans.' Clearly, Sonia Gandhi may have wanted to rein in the prime minister.

'Narayanan made himself the principal interlocutor at a certain stage,' Montek Singh Ahluwalia revealed. Despite his initial reservations, somewhere down the line, Narayanan made himself indispensable to the PM—emerging as the pointsperson in operationalizing the nuclear deal. Narayanan also emerged as the interlocutor between the negotiating team and the DAE. 'The Department of Atomic Energy had faith in me,' Narayanan said. 'If I wanted them to make a change, they'd trust me.'

'Mike' also assisted the PM to mount the operation politically. Although as NSA, his remit was national and international security, it was he who helped to bring around the dramatis personae in the show as it unfolded between 2005–08.

When George W. Bush came to India on 2 March 2006, and as he was getting into his car at the airport, Bush turned to Narayanan who was standing near the prime minister. Placing his hands on Narayanan's shoulders, he said loudly so that everyone around could hear, 'I want that deal.' The message was clear for the negotiating teams. But it was also meant for Sonia Gandhi. By then Sonia's reservations about the deal were known in the inner circles. So was Narayanan's proximity to her. Sometimes President Bush would ask his NSA Stephen Hadley, 'How is it all going Steve?' Hadley, according to 'Mike', would reply, 'All right, except my counterpart (Narayanan) has very powerful friends—he has communion with God almighty every day.' He would be referring to the daily ritual Narayanan would adhere to, no matter what else was going on—of a one-hour prayer before dinner every night.

Having closely watched the twists and turns the process went through, Narayanan was convinced that the 'deal could not be repeated without George Bush and Manmohan Singh' at the heart of it.

Bush would often ask his officials, 'What does Manmohan Singh want? I am committed to him. Help him out.'

It was Manmohan Singh's 'integrity, intelligence and self-deprecating ways' which had impressed Bush. The success of any negotiation depends on give and take. 'But...the PM and the President were on the same wave length, (and) it became easier to deal with (a difficult) situation.'

VIII

On 22 May 2008, Prime Minister Manmohan Singh hosted a dinner at 7, Race Course Road, to celebrate the fourth anniversary of the UPA government. Present at the event were senior Congress leaders. Many regional satraps supporting the UPA had come from their state capitals. Journalists were present in large numbers. All the attendees milled around the sprawling lawns of the PM's official residence. It was a warm summer evening. The political temperature had also been hotting up all through May. Given the serious differences that had developed between the Congress and the Left parties over the nuclear deal, there was even talk of a mid-term poll if the Left withdrew its support to the UPA.

The function started at 7 p.m. with a welcome speech by Prithviraj Chavan, MoS in the PMO. He invited the prime minister to speak. To the PM's left sat Sonia Gandhi, dressed in a deep blue sari, adding the only splash of colour to an otherwise drab stage. Others on the dais, flanking the PM and the chairperson of the UPA, included powerful regional chieftains Lalu Yadav, Sharad Pawar, T. R. Balu, Ram Vilas Paswan, and Mufti Mohammad Sayeed.

The UPA's anniversary celebrations during the previous three years had followed exactly the same drill. Except, this time, the prime minister had invited leaders of the Samajwadi Party to the dinner. He also made a point of playing down the differences between the UPA and the Left. In the course of his speech, the PM spoke of issues which he knew would please them, like the universalization of the employment guarantee scheme, which his government had introduced. Present that evening were CPI (M) and CPI leaders Sitaram Yechury, Prakash Karat, A. B. Bardhan, and D. Raja. But the two smaller partners in the Left Front, Forward Bloc, and RSP, had boycotted the function.

To the surprise of many, the prime minister did not utter one word about his pet project—the Indo–US nuclear deal. Clearly, he did not want to strike a discordant note that day. Ending his speech, Manmohan Singh called on Sonia Gandhi to do the honours—and release the UPA's Report Card. Moving to the centre of the dais, he handed her the green coloured booklet. There was the customary group photograph of all those on the stage holding aloft the report card. It was now Sonia Gandhi's turn to speak. She, too, surprised those present by heaping lavish praise on the prime minister. Differences between the two on the nuclear deal, it was known, had strained their relationship for almost a year. 'Oh, the PM and his nuclear deal,' she had once exclaimed exasperatedly. 'He is so obsessed with it.' Taking their cue from her, others in the Congress would express similar sentiments. 'The PM tends to get carried away,' they would say.

The differences between the two, it was said in Congress circles, had escalated to such an extent that Congressmen were not sure how long Manmohan Singh would continue as prime minister. Sensing an opportunity, the BJP had dubbed Singh a 'lame duck' prime minister.

At the function that evening, several Congressmen talked in undertones about the possibility of Rahul Gandhi 'taking over as prime minister soon'.

Yet, on this occasion, Sonia Gandhi sent a clear message to her partymen. There would be no change in leadership. 'His (PM's) style of functioning is such that it takes a little time to understand (him),' she said. Her tone was conciliatory. '[But] time tells how effective is his leadership.' It was clear to observers that differences apart, nobody else suited her for the top job as much as Manmohan Singh did. Of course, there was the experienced Pranab Mukherjee at hand. He had been waiting in the wings, having been number two in government since the days of Indira Gandhi. But she did not trust him. He would 'informally criticize her functioning' as a senior Congress leader put it. 'But Dr Manmohan Singh never uttered one word against her.' Sonia knew that he did not have an agenda of his own. That is why she had chosen him as prime minister in 2004.

Speeches out of the way, Prithviraj Chavan announced that mediapersons could pick up their copies of the report at the exit gate. And he invited everyone to 'proceed for dinner'. The formal part of the evening was over. Journalists now looked forward to chatting with the politicians present. This was just the kind of function to pick up the juicy titbits. And a lot had been happening. Slowly, everyone made their way to the buffet dinner laid out on the lawns, and then gravitated to the tables which had been set up in what was a free seating arrangement. Except at the PM's table.

Manmohan Singh took his place at the high table. There were name cards on it. All the guests took their seats. Only the place next to the PM remained empty. The Samajwadi Party leader Amar Singh was to sit there but he had not yet made an appearance. That evening, Manmohan Singh wanted to make public the growing amity between his government, Amar Singh, and the Samajwadi Party—intended for the benefit of those present, including the leaders of the Left parties. The prime minister looked around uncertainly. But there was no sign of Amar Singh. After a few minutes, Karan Singh joined the PM's table and took the empty seat. A vacancy at the PM's table would have attracted notice with so many journalists present.

Meanwhile, Amar Singh sat peacefully at his home in Lodi Road. He had called all thirty-nine SP MPs to his residence at 6.45 p.m. and told them that they would go to the PM's dinner together. As the evening wore on, the MPs began to grow restive. But Amar Singh was in no hurry. 'We will go soon,' he told them. By the time they arrived at 7, Race Course Road, it was almost 8 p.m.

Amar Singh had deliberately delayed their entry to the PM House, as he wanted to emphasize the importance of the SP. And he wanted to make the Congress fret. After all, it had ignored the Samajwadi Party for the past four years. Even though Amar Singh had planned to make a grand entrance and take his place at the top table, his face fell when he realized that all the seats at the PM's table were taken. Disappointed, he quickly turned towards another table where there was an empty seat and sat down there. But the prime minister had seen him. Manmohan Singh quickly got up from his table and went across to where Amar Singh sat—even though the SP leader had given him anxious moments. The PM greeted him warmly and sat down beside him.

In May 2008, there was no other man as important as Amar Singh as far as the prime minister of India was concerned. Prakash Karat and the Left thought they would get the better of him.

But they had 'underestimated Manmohan Singh's wiliness'.

■

'Amar Singh used to keep us informed about what was going on,' said Prakash Karat. 'He would tell us how the PM was "wooing" him.' He told the CPI (M) leader he was seeing Manmohan Singh quietly but regularly. The PM had tried to convince him that 'the nuclear deal was in the national interest'. And he, Amar Singh, must get the SP to support it.

'It was sometime at the end of April that he (Amar Singh) started to alert me,' Karat recalled. 'And he hinted that they might move off' (away from the Left).

When the PM began wooing the SP, he would see Amar Singh more often than he would have normally done. The PM also would often pass him to a junior in the PMO, who would try and accommodate what Amar Singh wanted done for his powerful friends.

In 2008, for Manmohan Singh to seek the SP's support could not have been easy. He knew that Sonia Gandhi had kept the SP at arm's length—even as it supported the government from outside till 2007. When the SP was still an ally of the government, the Congress brass had given standing instructions to those in government—oblige them with favours they seek, go easy on the cases against them, but keep the sword hanging over their heads. In other words, keep them on board, but don't get too close to them.

The SP broke ranks with the Congress in 2007. The differences arose during the UP elections in the middle of that year. As a result, the SP lost UP to its arch-rival, Mayawati's Bahujan Samaj Party. In 2008, the SP was leading a 'third front' in parliament, cobbled together with regional groupings like the Telugu Desam Party—this grouping was called the UNPA. After it broke off with the UPA, the SP began to oppose the nuclear deal. It was an old ally of the Left, and the CPI (M) and CPI had supported Mulayam Singh Yadav at critical junctures in his political career. When the prime minister decided that he needed the support of the SP's thirty-nine MPs to save his government and facilitate the nuclear deal, he was on shaky ground. And while Amar Singh was responsive to the prime minister's overtures, he had not given Manmohan Singh the final assurance the prime minister was looking for—that the SP would support the deal and bail out his government, if the Left withdrew support to it.

'Who do you think are the architects of the nuclear deal?' Amar Singh asked this question with a rhetorical flourish.

'You will say George Bush and Manmohan Singh,' he smiled, anticipating the answer. 'Let me tell you it was George Bush and Amar Singh.' He was in a hospital in Singapore, undergoing treatment for kidney failure in 2009. The Indo–US deal had been concluded by then. Amar Singh was not making the comment in jest. He was dead serious—and he was partially right. For he had played a key role in saving Manmohan Singh's government—this had enabled the prime minister to conclude the Indo–US Civil Nuclear Deal. Otherwise, with the way the political forces were massed against him, his government would have either fallen or he would have had to give up on the deal.

■

Amar Singh was cast in the mould of a political fixer. But he was not like the usual fixers who stay in the shadows in the corridors of power, and lobby discreetly on behalf of pressure groups to get what they want. They are part of the political underbelly of every capital in the world. But Amar Singh hated being called a fixer and considered himself a class above them. This was true on more than one count—not only was he an MP himself, and an influential one at that, he liked to flaunt his connections and also bragged about what he was doing.

The story of the Indo–US nuke deal will be incomplete without looking at the role influencers and lobbyists like Amar Singh—and Sant Chatwal in the US—played in making it go through. An influential hotelier in New York, Chatwal was another colourful personality like Amar Singh, who helped to mobilize American Congressmen and senators to support the deal—and worked with Amar Singh, using every trick in the book, to cross the hurdles that threatened to thwart the Manmohan Singh government's efforts. On his part, the erudite Manmohan Singh, otherwise so cautious about preserving his clean image, did not hesitate to utilize their services to get his project through—just as other prime ministers before him had done.

Amar Singh's success lay in trading favours. The secret of his networking was to identify what people needed—and then go on to provide it.

'When you meet people,' he once remarked, 'you have to think of what you can give them, not what you can get from them.' The 'get' came later.

He was first noticed on the political stage when Chandra Shekhar was prime minister. 'I first took him to meet Chandra Shekhar,' said Congress leader Harikesh Bahadur. 'We met Chandra Shekhar at his ashram at Bhondsi (on the outskirts of Delhi).' When Chandra Shekhar came out to see them off after the meeting, he described the activities that took place at the ashram, and told them how there was often a shortage of chairs when many people turned up for the meetings. Two days later, Amar Singh had delivered a large number of chairs to Bhondsi. Amar Singh would later persuade Chandra Shekhar to withdraw the cases against Amitabh Bachchan that had been instituted during V. P. Singh's premiership.

When Narasimha Rao became prime minister, Madhav Sinh Solanki and Madhavrao Scindia, both ministers in his government, tried hard to get Rao to give Amar Singh a post in the party.

'No way,' Rao told them. 'Brokering will then start in the party.' Rao had his own fixers he relied on. But he did not want to alienate Amar Singh, knowing the damage he could cause. So, from time to time, he would help him out. On one occasion, Amar Singh was trying to help Amitabh Bachchan. Rao told his media advisor P. V. R. K. Prasada to help Bachchan 'if it is feasible' and 'if it can be resolved at the level of the Secretary to the Department of Information'. But Rao did not meet Amar Singh.

Amar Singh became a prominent political figure during H. D. Deve Gowda's tenure as PM, and would be in and out of South Block. Another prime minister he dealt with was Atal Bihari Vajpayee. On one occasion, he took industrialist Subroto Roy (before his fall from grace) to meet Vajpayee. Roy wanted to invite the PM to the wedding of his two sons. Initially uncertain, Vajpayee decided to go. However, when Vajpayee arrived at the Rajasansi airport in Lucknow, there was no Subroto Roy to receive him; he had sent his brother instead. Vajpayee was very annoyed.

Although Amar Singh had friends and contacts across the political spectrum, it was his proximity to Samajwadi Party chief Mulayam Singh Yadav which gave him the unfettered power and authority he came to wield. Senior SP leaders—Azam Khan, Raj Babbar, Shahid Siddiqui—left the party because of him. Amar Singh brought the world of riches and glamour to Mulayam Singh Yadav's universe. The earthy Mulayam Singh took to throwing five-star parties in Delhi—it was an incongruous sight to see the diminutive wrestler-turned neta Mulayam in his dhoti and kurta, who had risen through the ranks to become a mass leader, trying to ingratiate himself to the rich and powerful amongst the capital's jet set.

Such was Amar Singh's clout with the rich and the successful that when he underwent a kidney transplant in the middle of July 2009 in a hospital in Singapore, the hospital saw the arrival of well-known actors, industrialists, and politicians who had come to visit their ailing friend. Among them were actors Abhishek Bachchan and Aishwarya Rai Bachchan, industrialist Anil Ambani and his wife Tina Ambani, and actor friend Sanjay Dutt's wife Manyata Dutt. Mulayam Singh Yadav came, as did his son Akhilesh. Hillary Clinton sent a message from Washington DC, asking for updates on the state of his health. The iconic actor Amitabh Bachchan spent three months in Singapore with his friend Amar Singh, according to Jaya Bachchan, and took a flat to be with Singh while he recuperated—like 'bade bhaiya' taking care of 'chote bhaiya'.

Over time, as the ambitions of this one-time liaison officer (with the KK Birla group) soared higher than the world of Indian celebrities. He set his sights on, arguably, the most prominent power couple in the US in the early 2000s—Bill and Hillary Clinton.

In 2005, Amar Singh had telephoned Prakash Karat, and told him that he was going to invite Bill Clinton to dinner in Lucknow.

'It is Bush who is your enemy, isn't it?' he asked Karat. 'You have no problem with Clinton?'

'It was quite hilarious,' recalled Karat.

Amar Singh moved through the hotelier Sant Chatwal to invite Clinton to Lucknow in September 2005. When Clinton came, UP chief minister Mulayam Singh Yadav invited a few hundred people to meet him at his residence at 5, Kalidas Marg. 'It was a sit-down dinner in the open, there was a dance performance by Shiamak Davar's team,' recalled journalist Sunita Aron who attended the evening function. The dancers moved to the beat of the hit song, 'Sexy Rocksy Chicago Girl'. Before the festivities began, Clinton joined Chatwal, who had flown into Lucknow with him, for a private chat, 'where he was introduced to an obscure member of Indian Parliament named Amar Singh'. They met for about an hour but it was the start of a 'close collaboration' between Amar Singh and the Clintons. When Hillary Clinton won her Senate seat in 2006, if there was one man in India who 'almost did a jig' and celebrated as hard as the Democrats in the US, it was Amar Singh. Even before she had finished 'brushing the confetti off her jacket', Amar Singh had announced that he would invite her to India if she won the US presidency in 2008.

Amar Singh would go on to rescue the Manmohan government in the 'cash for vote case' in July 2008—as we will soon see—for which he was arrested in 2011. Till the end of his life, he lamented that the Congress had not helped him when he was in jail—even though he had rescued the Manmohan Singh government. A Congress minister told him they could not do anything because he was tainted. 'I was not tainted when I bailed you out in 2008,' Amar Singh shouted and said that it was the UPA government that was tainted.

A month before he died on 1 August 2020, he rang up Sanjaya Baru, and told him he had seen the film based on Baru's book on Manmohan Singh—*The Accidental Prime Minister*. 'You know, I could have acted my own role better in that film than the person who you had (in it)…. (Instead) Kisi actor ko Amar Singh bana diya aapne (Instead you made someone else Amar Singh).'

■

Sant Chatwal was not always persona grata in the Manmohan Singh durbar—and this became evident at a wedding in Delhi in October 2004 which was attended by Prime Minister Singh. It was a beautiful time of year in the nation's capital. The weather had started to change, the hot and humid air giving way to a cool freshness in the mornings and evenings. Bougainvillea carpeted the roundabouts and bungalows of Lutyens' Delhi in rich white, pink, and red, and the fragrance of the scholar tree (milkwood or devil's tree) called the 'winter smell of Delhi' filled the air.

Satish Sharma, an influential Congressman who had been close to two of India's prime ministers—Rajiv Gandhi and P. V. Narasimha Rao— was hosting the wedding reception of his daughter Sarika on 28 October 2004. Captain Sharma, who had been a minister in Narasimha Rao's government, had invited the who's who from around the country and from the Indian community overseas to the event. It was being held at his sprawling farmhouse in Chhatarpur on the outskirts of Delhi.

The stars at the wedding ceremony in the morning were the four generations of Sonia Gandhi's family. Her mother, Paola Maino, had flown in from Orbassano in Italy. Her daughter, Priyanka, dressed in a gorgeous pink Banarasi silk sari was with husband Robert Vadra—and their daughter, Maira, kept both her proud grandmother and great-grand-mother busy. The normally reticent Rahul Gandhi allowed someone to tie a multicoloured safa (turban) on his head. The cynosure of all eyes, however, was Sonia Gandhi herself, dressed in a pale blue silk sari, and wearing jewellery which was normally not seen on her person. Sonia Gandhi who usually dressed elegantly was given to wearing handlooms. She looked relaxed that day—and obliged people by posing with them for photographs. It was only four months earlier that the Congress-led UPA government had come to power in Delhi, making Sonia Gandhi the most powerful figure in the country, after she had renounced prime ministership.

Prime Minister Manmohan Singh came for the wedding reception in the evening and was welcomed by Captain Sharma and his wife, Sterre, at the entrance. Leading honchos from the world of business and politics greeted the PM. Suddenly it started to rain, and people rushed to find shelter. The PM was brought into the Sharmas' drawing room. There were around eight people in the room—the PM and his wife, Gursharan Kaur, Satish Sharma and his wife, their daughter and son-in-law, and persons from the SPG, according to the senior politician B. M. Bhama. 'I happened to be in the room at the time, and saw with my own eyes what happened next,' recalled Bhama who was close to Captain Sharma at the time. At that point, Sant Chatwal walked into the room—and made a beeline for the PM. 'I saw one of the men in the PM's security group whisper something in the PM's ear,' recalled Bhama. The PM looked towards Chatwal. Within seconds the SPG sprang into action. 'With great respect and politeness, they went up to Chatwal and said, "Sir, you come this way", and before he knew what was happening, they had deftly escorted him out of the room.'

The PM must have known that there were photographers about and must have done some quick thinking. If the cameras caught him chatting with Chatwal—he had CBI cases against him in India—some in the Opposition could have given a different spin to the 'meeting'. And it might not have looked good for the PM. While the PM gave a wide berth to Sant Chatwal that day, eighteen months later, on 19 February 2006, and ten days before George W. Bush arrived in India, he attended the wedding of the hotelier's son, Vikram, in Delhi. The 'big, fat Sikh wedding', as it was described, was celebrated on a grand scale. Fifty thousand kilograms of flowers were shipped in from Holland, Bangkok, and Calcutta; the food, drink, and other decorations were lavish. The festivities continued for ten days. Normally, Manmohan Singh was not given to attending wedding receptions, particularly of those he did not know well. On this occasion, he had decided to come, though he was 'advised' by an aide that it might be prudent to stay away. But the prime minister did not pay any heed to the advice—and he came armed with a bouquet of beautiful yellow flowers. By now, Chatwal had gained entry to the Manmohan Singh durbar. As a former MP from the Congress told me: 'There were few well-known Sikhs the prime minister did not give an appointment to when they visited Delhi (and asked to see him).'

From a family of small-time merchants in Faridkot in Punjab, Chatwal had made his way to the US and become a wealthy hotelier in New York. Indeed, there were few influential Indian visitors to New York who had not been entertained by Chatwal in his penthouse with its floor to ceiling glass windows in Manhattan. The visitors included politicians of all hues, media personalities, judges, senior bureaucrats. He acted as the bridge between them and the contacts he had cultivated in the American establishment. He knew people in the Indian consulate in New York and would get prior information about who was coming when, and for what purpose. His proximity to Bill and Hillary Clinton was widely known.

In 2007–08, he helped with the nuclear deal. And, in return, Manmohan Singh did not hide the role that Sant Chatwal had played in bringing the Indo–US deal to fruition. The Indian government would go on to drop the legal cases against Sant Chatwal—he had spent a brief stint in jail in 1997, had two chargesheets against him, and a case of bank fraud—and he would even be awarded one of the country's highest civilian honours, the Padma Bhushan, in 2010 for 'his services'. The prestigious civilian award was given to Sant Chatwal at the instance of the prime minister despite the ruling Congress Party's reservations. A Congress spokesperson at the time publicly voiced his party's displeasure with the centre's decision. 'The Congress wants the Padma awards to be given to people who enhance the prestige of the award as well as their own,' party spokesman Shakeel Ahmed said. 'No tainted person should be given this award.' The ruling party's oblique criticism obviously reflected Sonia Gandhi's own unhappiness at the decision.

The Indian embassy in the US had also opposed the move. '(The Indian ambassador to the US) Ronen Sen had told the PMO it would not be appropriate to bestow a Padma award on Mr Chatwal because of the controversy surrounding his financial dealings in India and America.' The embassy had refused to nominate Mr Chatwal, 'when asked by the Prime Minister's Office to do so.' But Prime Minister Manmohan Singh, in this instance, overruled both his party and the Indian mission in Washington DC. He must have felt so indebted to Chatwal that he decided to go ahead and honour the controversial hotelier. In November 2008, weeks after the culmination of the Indo–US deal, Manmohan Singh wrote Sant Chatwal a personal letter. He expressed his 'sincere appreciation' to Chatwal for his 'personal efforts' to bring the Indo–US nuclear deal to fruition. Six years later, in April 2014, Sant Chatwal used this note as one of 300 letters of appreciation he had received to plead for leniency in his sentencing. This was after he had been charged with conspiring to make illegal campaign contributions—and he pleaded guilty of violating US federal election law.

When he received the Padma Bhushan, an ecstatic Chatwal said, 'I am very proud of the work I have done in putting the nuclear deal together,' he said. 'There is only one person in the history of America who could put 18 senators and 50 Congressmen in a room in the US senate building...I had four presidential candidates there. It took me four years and millions of dollars, which I paid out of my own pocket.' He had brought together the US Congressmen on 17 May 2008 'to raise awareness about the Indo–US nuclear deal'. However, before Chatwal could bask in the reflected glory of a successfully concluded story, there were many twists and turns in the plot that needed to be navigated.

IX

It was in the third week of June 2008 that Manmohan Singh played his trump card. He threatened to resign again—if he could not make headway on the deal. On 17 June, in the evening, the prime minister called up Sonia Gandhi. He told her he would like to put in his papers. This brought Sonia rushing to 7, Race Course Road, on the morning of 18 June. She asked Pranab Mukherjee to join them.

'It has become untenable for me to continue,' a downcast PM told them. The government was all set to go to the IAEA to negotiate the India specific safeguards agreement. But the Left, he said, insisted that the draft agreement worked out with the IAEA (secretariat) be shown to them first. This had been the understanding worked out at the PM's lunch for the Left leaders on 10 November 2007—but the PM was now backtracking.

'What the Left wants is not possible,' the PM suddenly sprung this on Sonia Gandhi. A secret document could not be shown to those outside the government, he said. If the government cannot go to the IAEA 'immediately', he would resign. With his threat to resign, Manmohan Singh put Sonia Gandhi on the spot. She could either keep him on as PM—and he came with the nuke deal—or she would have to do without him. In that case, there would be no nuke deal. He would have calculated that she would be averse to elevating Pranab Mukherjee as PM. It was a well thought out move by Manmohan Singh. A desperate Sonia Gandhi turned to Montek Singh Ahluwalia again for help. This time, Ahluwalia expressed his helplessness.

'I agreed earlier he shouldn't resign,' he told her. 'But frankly, one can't say to him now you can't, because the position he is taking is very reasonable.' However, he promised to speak to the PM.

'My mind is made up,' Manmohan Singh told Ahluwalia. 'Either I get this done, or I don't get this done.' The media had got word that the PM might resign. Would the government survive? Delhi was rife with suspense about the fate of the government.

Pranab Mukherjee met with the Left leaders again. He tried to persuade them to let the government go to the IAEA board of governors without any preconditions. 'After that, we will see,' he told them. Karat found that too 'vague' for comfort.

Mukherjee may well have secretly hoped that Sonia Gandhi would choose him and let Manmohan Singh go. Mukherjee would have been able to paper over any differences with the Left (among other things, he had won his Lok Sabha election from Jangipur, West Bengal, in 2004 with their support). He was anyway running much of the government, heading scores of GOMs and eGOMs.

'We cannot make him (Manmohan Singh) change his mind,' Congress leaders privately told the Left leaders.

'(What you are witnessing) is the fury of a silent man,' a senior Congress minister told the Left leaders, by way of an explanation.

'Resignation' was a weapon Manmohan Singh had deployed several times in the past. The first time it happened was in the 1980s when he was the chairman of the Planning Commission and Rajiv Gandhi, then PM, had called the Planning Commission members 'a bunch of jokers'. Then, he had threatened to quit as finance minister after the Harshad Mehta scam erupted during P. V. Narasimha Rao's premiership. When there was pressure on him to roll back fertilizer prices during Rao's regime, he had offered to quit again. As PM, he had threatened to resign when the Left tried to block Indo–US military exercises in November 2005. And, of course, he had already threatened to quit once over the nuclear deal.

In the end, Manmohan Singh played his cards right. Sonia Gandhi chose not to jettison him. And then the PM got his lifeline. He received the message he had been waiting for. On 21 June 2008, Amar Singh gave the green signal to the PM—the Samajwadi Party would support his government in parliament. The PM's media advisor, Sanjaya Baru, received a call that day from the US. The voice on the other end of the phone said he was a 'friend' of Amar Singh's. Those who knew Amar Singh believed that the caller could have been Amar Singh himself. 'My friend Amar Singh is in a hospital in Colorado,' the friend said to Baru. 'He wants you to tell the prime minister that American doctors are very warm and friendly people.' They had been taking good care of him. He went on to praise them in effusive terms. The 'friend' asked the message to be conveyed to the PM 'as soon as possible'. Maybe, he suggested, the PM might want to speak to Amar Singh and wish him a 'speedy recovery'. Baru immediately conveyed the message to the PM. The curiously worded message was decoded by the PM to mean that it was a 'final yes' (on the SP's support to the government and the nuclear deal) by Amar Singh.

Frenetic activity followed in Delhi. Within a couple of days, articles began to appear in the media that Mulayam Singh Yadav was having second thoughts about his opposition to the nuclear deal. Karat got so worried that he met Yadav, who had been a tried and tested ally of the Left for years. He wanted Yadav to reaffirm his support to the Left's position. 'I am not committing (myself) on anything,' Yadav told Karat evasively. 'I can't say anything till Amar Singh comes back from the US.' Karat met Yadav again on 1 July 2008. When Amar Singh came back from the US, he told the media that the situation called for all the 'secular forces' to unite. The signs were clear. He was making a case for the SP and the Congress to join hands. The prime minister signalled to the NSA M. K. Narayanan to move in for the kill.

On 2 July, the NSA met Mulayam Singh Yadav and Amar Singh. He 'briefed them on the nuclear deal'. Mulayam Singh Yadav had to find a face-saver to justify his turnaround. On 3 July, Yadav called a meeting of the United National Progressive Alliance (UNPA), the parliamentary grouping the SP was part of, with members who were neither a part of the UPA nor of the NDA. They were to take a final view on whether to support the nuclear deal or not. Soon after the UNPA meet, Mulayam Singh Yadav and Amar Singh sped off to see A. P. J. Abdul Kalam, the former president, who was still heard on matters relating to national security. Kalam had been briefed in advance. He immediately issued a statement. The Indo–US Civil Nuclear Deal, he stated, was in the national interest. He urged Mulayam Singh Yadav to support the government.

It was M. K. Narayanan's idea to get former president A. P. J. Abdul Kalam to issue a statement in favour of the deal, a Congress leader told me, which made it easier for Mulayam Singh Yadav to support the government. It was a fig leaf the SP latched on to. For all of Amar Singh's persuasive powers, Mulayam Singh Yadav was worried about the impact his support to the deal could have on the Muslims who formed the backbone of the SP's base. The deal was synonymous with India moving closer to the US and the Muslims were wary of this.

Everything was now moving to a script. Later that day, M. K. Narayanan had another meeting with Amar Singh at a safe guest house of the IB in Delhi. This time Amar Singh was accompanied by Mulayam Singh Yadav's cousin, Ram Gopal Yadav, who was a professor and wanted to ask many more questions. Narayanan went over the provisions of the deal in detail with him. Together they formulated the statement that the Prime Minister's Office would issue by way of assurances that the SP MPs insisted on.

Narayanan then rushed across to South Block. He hurried into Sanjaya Baru's room and handed him a statement which had to be issued immediately to the media—with words by the prime minister that India would not compromise its independent foreign policy, nor disturb its relations with Iran. These pledges were intended to reassure the Muslims. Having now tied up the loose ends, the prime minister gave officials the go-ahead on 7 July 2008 to submit the draft of the safeguards agreement to the IAEA. This was just before he flew to Japan to participate in a meeting of G8 where he was to meet with Bush on the sidelines. 'I learnt about this (IAEA) aboard the PM's flight on our way to Japan,' recalled journalist Manini Chatterjee. 'I told Joydeep Sarkar (the PM's secretary) that the Left parties will now withdraw their support.' This is precisely what happened. Hours later, on 8 July, the four Left parties announced that they were withdrawing their support to the government of Manmohan Singh. By then Singh did not care. He had lined up alternative support.

Even as Manmohan Singh decided to press ahead, Pranab Mukherjee announced that the government would go to the IAEA only after it had proved its majority on the floor of parliament. But the PM was in no mood to wait till the confidence vote on 21 July. Even if he did not manage a majority, he could always argue that he had gone to the IAEA when his government still enjoyed a majority! Pranab Mukherjee, insiders speculated, may have hoped that in the event of a last-minute upset during the trust vote—which anyway turned out to be close enough—there could be the possibility of a new prime minister being nominated. The fall of the government would have meant the failure of the deal. If that had happened, the Left might have kept the UPA government going with another prime minister at the helm. But that wish died stillborn. Manmohan Singh forged ahead with his plan, as all around him chaos rose and fell.

The BJP suddenly reached out to the Samajwadi Party, offering it the prime ministership if it would reconsider its support to Manmohan Singh's UPA. It said it would be willing to back a UNPA-led government. In other words, they would back Mulayam Singh Yadav as prime minister. The effort was being spearheaded by L. K. Advani, given his opposition to the nuclear deal. But the SP remained steadfast in its support for Manmohan Singh.

Amar Singh did more than his call of duty. He bent over backwards to make sure that all the SP MPs voted for the government. He also won over some others—from the BJP and the RLD. By this time, the Congress managers had swung into action. It was no longer just the PM's project. There were senior Congressmen entrusted with the responsibility of ensuring that the government survived. Ahmed Patel, B. S. Hooda, R. K. Dhawan, and Satish Sharma handled the operation. Wikileaks cables leaked in 2011 were to reveal that massive sums of money, from ₹10 crores to more, were paid to several MPs to vote with the government. CPI leader A. B. Bardhan had addressed a meeting on the lawns of the Constitution Club at Vithalbhai Patel House, not far from Parliament House. He alleged publicly that ₹25 crore was being offered to MPs willing to support the government. In a sting operation carried out by journalist Rajdeep Sardesai, BJP MPs walked into the Lok Sabha on 22 July, waving wads of notes they had been offered to switch sides. The sting, it was said at the time, was the brainchild of Arun Jaitley, leader of the Opposition in the Rajya Sabha.

The allegations notwithstanding, Manmohan Singh's government won the motion of confidence in parliament on 22 July. Its four-year marriage with the Left was over. It had found a new partner in the SP. But Mulayam Singh Yadav had put forth certain conditions for the SP's support. One, that the cases against him—charging him with accumulating wealth disproportionate to his income—would 'not be pursued'. They were not.

Mulayam Singh Yadav had also hoped that SP leaders would be given ministerial berths. The morning after Manmohan Singh had won the confidence motion, Mulayam Singh and Amar Singh arrived at 7, Race Course Road. They were ushered in to see the prime minister. When they came out of his room, both looked visibly angry. 'I was standing there and saw them as they got into their big white Mercedes,' Sanjaya Baru recalled. They had obviously been told that cabinet berths for the SP members were not possible. Sonia Gandhi, it was said, had put her foot down. Even though Manmohan Singh did manage to hang on, the nuclear deal was still some way from becoming a reality. The prime minister continued to give it priority in the remaining months of 2008. For, if India did not go to the IAEA in July 2008, the chair of the secretariat was scheduled to change. The next country to head the organization—Austria was slated to take over—was expected to be not as sympathetic to the Indian proposal. This could have created problems for the clearance of the India-specific safeguards agreement.

X

Vienna—that is where the scene of action now shifted. It was in this peaceful capital of Austria, surrounded by mountains and forests and with the blue Danube running through the city, that the last two hurdles of the marathon race would need to be cleared—before George W. Bush took the Indo–US Civil Nuclear Deal to the US Congress to get its approval. The India-specific safeguards agreement that was to be cleared by the IAEA was the first of these—and it was negotiated without any difficulty. Of the factors working in India's favour, the most important was Mohamed ElBaradei. The Egyptian-born ElBaradei headed the IAEA secretariat and was a friend of India. More important, he had been convinced by the Americans of the need for a clean waiver for India. The IAEA secretariat processed the paperwork. The documents were sent on to the IAEA Board of Governors for approval. ElBaradei had ensured that everything was in order. The IAEA gave its go-ahead to the ISSA on 1 August 2008.

Next came the tough part of the journey—the waiver that would need to be granted to India by the forty-five-member Nuclear Suppliers Group. It would enable it to buy civil nuclear technology and fuel from other countries, despite possessing nuclear weapons and not signing the Non-Proliferation Treaty. If the NSG granted the waiver, it would be the first time it had done so. Though the Americans were facilitating the ride for India, they realized, soon enough, that even the last lap was not going to be easy. They ran into problems from the moment they had submitted a paper for exemptions for India. The NSG met on 21 and 22 August. But there was an impasse. The smaller European countries saw themselves as the 'Ayatollahs of non-proliferation'. They wanted to introduce conditions into the waiver, like terminating fuel and technology supplies, if India were to conduct a nuclear test again. Another meeting of the NSG was fixed for 5 September 2008. This meeting took place in the German Mission in Vienna with Germany in the chair. The Americans submitted their second draft for the waiver. Suspense mounted at the Vienna Intercontinental Hotel where the Indian delegation was staying. The delegation would meet in the Indian embassy during the day. At night they would move to the hotel where facilities and conference rooms had been readied for them to follow the deliberations that were taking place remotely. India could not be physically presence at the NSG meet because it was not a member.

As the shadows lengthened that evening, Foreign Secretary Shiv Shankar Menon paced up and down the conference room in the hotel. Sometimes he would go out to take a call from his minister, Pranab Mukherjee, in New Delhi. At other times, he would be speaking to members of the American delegation. They were inside the NSG meeting, pushing, nudging, and arm-twisting those who were holding out.

In Delhi, the prime minister was closely tracking events. As the meeting progressed, the Indian observers kept a wary eye on China. It hadn't made its stance clear yet. The Chinese had previously objected to India getting parity of status with nuclear weapon states without signing the NPT. They were now shooting off the shoulders of the 'Group of Six', instead of coming upfront. These were Ireland, New Zealand, Austria, Switzerland, Norway, and the Netherlands.

Up until now the Chinese had been hoping the deal would not go through, given the reservations that existed in India, with Sonia Gandhi and the Left opposed to it.

Back in October 2007, the Communist Party of China had laid out the red carpet for Sonia Gandhi in Beijing. She had led a delegation of the Congress Party comprising Rahul Gandhi, Karan Singh, Anand Sharma, and Prithviraj Chavan—in response to what was a party-to-party invitation by the Chinese. Manmohan Singh was unhappy that his permission was not taken for including Chavan, MoS in his PMO, in the delegation. The Chinese President Hu Jintao received the delegation, and a fifty-car cavalcade would accompany them wherever they went. Meetings were arranged with the top leadership—along with twenty-one-course banquets, and sightseeing trips, including a visit to Xian where the terracotta army stands. A special state plane flew them to various places on their itinerary. The Chinese even made a half hour film of the visit. 'It was treated at par with a state visit,' said one of the members who went.

The Chinese had been trying to soften the Indian side for over a year—doing their best to stiffen the opposition to the deal within the Congress. They had also been working on the Left parties, knowing their 'fundamental concerns' about the Indo–US deal. But a year later, in 2008, Sonia Gandhi was no longer opposed to the deal and the Left was not a factor any more. The only card left for China to play at Vienna was to somehow stall a 'clean waiver' for India from the NSG.

As the night of 5 September 2008 wore on, the Indian ambassador to Austria had biryani cooked and packed at the embassy—twenty-one parcels were sent across to the Indian delegation stationed at the Vienna Intercontinental. Slowly, the Americans picked off countries opposed to the waiver one by one and brought them around. Those who caved in were too dependent on the US to continue with their opposition for too long. Only the Chinese were left standing alone that night. They had threatened to withdraw from the negotiations. This would have meant finis to the deal, for the NSG took such decisions by consensus.

Manmohan Singh had spoken to Bush about the growing—but behind the scenes—opposition of the Chinese that was building up. 'You should speak to Hu Jintao directly,' Bush advised him. Singh asked his office to set up a telephone conversation with the Chinese president to request his cooperation. The Chinese side was 'cold' to the idea. The PMO tried once again. Again, it was no go. A couple of months earlier, the Chinese had appeared to be more flexible, 'Back in July 2008, the Chinese had told me—I had gone there—we will not be the last ones standing (against the waiver) if others drop off,' Shivshankar Menon revealed.

That day, on 5 September, Pranab Mukherjee tried to talk to his counterpart in Beijing. The Chinese prevaricated. Finally, late that night, the PM spoke to President Bush again about his difficulty, sources told me. Bush then called up Hu Jintao personally.

Uncertainty continued about the outcome. In Delhi, the prime minister stayed awake at 3, Race Course Road. At midnight in Vienna, it was going down to the wire again. It was going to be a long night. The Americans then suggested that the Indian minister of External Affairs make a statement to reassure the NSG about India's moratorium on testing. This would dissolve the last vestiges of opposition. Pranab Mukherjee issued a statement. He reiterated India's voluntary moratorium on testing. India had announced this soon after it had conducted the nuclear tests in May 1998 when Atal Bihari Vajpayee was the prime minister. But with Mukherjee's statement this time, India was making the commitment before a global community.

At 3 a.m.—it was now the early hours of 6 September—the MEA decided to step up pressure and, woke up the Chinese ambassador in Delhi. India's message was now very clear: if China did not cooperate and stood alone, 'it would affect the overall India-China relations'.

In the early hours of 6 September, the phone rang in Foreign Secretary Shivshankar Menon's room in Vienna. He was still asleep. The Indian delegation had gone to bed in the wee hours. The call was from the Chinese mission in Vienna. 'We have decided to support you,' they said. The Chinese 'abstained' in the vote, allowing for a consensus to prevail. A few hours later, on 6 September, the gavel came down on the table at the NSG meeting. Its bang marked the NSG's formal adoption of the waiver for India on 6 September 2008.

Menon's phone rang again. It was the leader of the American delegation to the NSG, John Rood. 'Congratulations,' he said. 'We have done it.'

'It was a clean waiver,' asserted Shivshankar Menon, 'there were no caveats or review provided in it.'

However, despite Menon's assertion, the waiver was not completely 'clean' as some pointed out later—it retained the restrictions on the export of sensitive technologies. The NSG's 'Statement on Civil Nuclear Cooperation with India' waived the full-scope safeguards required in para 4, and expressly allowed the export of technologies and equipment but 'subject to para 6 and 7'. Under these two paras, suppliers were asked to 'exercise restraint' in the transfer of these sensitive ENR (enrichment of uranium and reprocessing of spent fuel) technologies and equipment. India chose to interpret this in its own way. Menon said the text was ambiguous about the transfer of ENR technologies, and 'did not include or exclude anything'.

According to Anil Kakodkar, individual countries would be left to take the call on the transfer of ENR technology. 'There are very few instances of (the transfer of) ENR technologies between countries,' said Kakodkar. 'Each country would decide its own issue and act according to its own laws. We negotiated separately with each country.'

India went in for agreements with the US, Russia, and France. The timing worked in India's favour as, in June 2011, the NSG was to 'strengthen' its guidelines and make the transfer of ENR technologies contingent on the signing of the NPT.

With the NSG waiver and the India-specific IAEA safeguards in place, which were prerequisites for the US Congress to take up the 123 Agreement for consideration, the stage was now set for the last act of the drama.

■

Manmohan Singh was now taking no chances—as the focus moved to the US Congress which had to ratify the 123 Agreement. The PM wanted to be in the US in those critical days leading up to the vote in the House of Representatives and the Senate. It was due end September. There were loose ends to tie up. Manmohan Singh had mobilized his 'racehorses'. There were also other groups working for Indo–US friendship, and for promoting business between the two countries—lobbying for the deal to go through. Besides the Indian Embassy in the US, Amar Singh was in constant touch with his friend, Sant Singh Chatwal, who had been lobbying with the Democrats.

Manmohan Singh was billed to address the United Nations General Assembly in New York on 27 September 2008. He and President George W. Bush hoped to ink the nuclear deal while Dr Singh was in the US. But the timetable went awry by a few days as Bush was preoccupied with dealing with the global financial crisis that had just taken place. Yet, the US president made time for a meeting with the Indian prime minister.

On 25 September, Bush and Singh met in the Oval Office in the evening. They took stock of the progress made on the Indo–US nuclear deal. Although a lot of work had been done, and it had got to the final stage, it was yet to be formally passed by the US Congress. The leaders were pleased with the role each had played to forge a strategic partnership between the two countries.

'This has taken a lot of work on both our parts,' Bush told Singh, '[and] a lot of courage on your part.' On his part, Manmohan Singh expressed satisfaction at the 'massive' transformation that had taken place in India–US relations during the four and a half years of his premiership. He complimented President Bush for playing the 'most important role'. 'History', he said, would 'record' it.

The meeting was followed by a dinner at the Old Family Dining Room at the White House hosted by Bush. It was billed as a 'family' affair. Besides Bush, ten others were present. The Americans at the dinner, aside from the host, were Vice President Dick Cheney, Secretary of State Condoleezza Rice, NSA Steve Hadley, and Deputy Secretary of State Will Burns. Besides Manmohan Singh, the Indian side comprised External Affairs Minister Pranab Mukherjee, Foreign Secretary Shivshankar Menon, Shyam Saran—who was now the prime minister's special envoy for the Indo–US nuclear deal—Montek Singh Ahluwalia, and NSA M. K. Narayanan.

Manmohan Singh thanked the US president for hosting them despite the unprecedented economic crisis he was grappling with. 'It's a pleasure,' Bush replied graciously. And then he added, 'You are a calming influence on me.' At one point during the dinner, Condoleezza Rice turned to Manmohan Singh and said, 'Mr Prime Minister, we have done some heavy lifting (for you) to get this deal through.... I hope India will fulfil its side of the commitment and buy nuclear reactors from the US....' Before she had completed her sentence, Bush cut her short. 'I don't care if we sell a reactor or not. This is above selling reactors. This is about the relationship between our two countries.'

At the end of the dinner, Bush came out on the porch of the White House to see off the prime minister. The cars were all lined up there, ready and waiting to move. 'The prime minister was already seated in his car,' Shyam Saran recalled. 'I rushed towards mine. Suddenly, President Bush caught me by my shoulder. He said, "This man is my friend. You take good care of him".'

The US House of Representatives approved the Indo–US nuclear deal on 27 September 2008. The US Senate cleared it on 1 October 2008, ending the three-decade ban on the US's nuclear trade with India. President George W. Bush signed the piece of legislation called the US–India Nuclear Cooperation Approval and Non-Proliferation Enhancement Act on 8 October 2008.

THE UNDERRATED PRIME MINISTER WHO TRIUMPHED

Signing the Act, Bush said, 'This is a—it's a big deal.'

On 10 October 2008, Pranab Mukherjee and Condoleezza Rice signed the accord on behalf of the two countries in the Benjamin Franklin Room in the US State Department. It was 1.40 a.m. in India. George W. Bush saw the strategic partnership with India that arose out of the civil nuclear deal as part of his legacy. Manmohan Singh saw the deal as one of the most important decisions of his tenure as prime minister.

XI

In the 2009 elections, the Congress Party came back to power with an increased majority. Ensuring the 'Right to Work' and a loan waiver to farmers worth ₹75,000 crores had helped it beat back the anti-incumbency against the government. It managed to get 206 seats in the Lok Sabha, increasing its 2004 tally by 61 seats. The Indo–US nuclear deal was not an issue in the polls which attracted voters. Few understood—or cared about it. But urban Indians approved of the way in which it had brought India closer to the US, which was a destination for many Indians. Manmohan Singh, who would go on to head the UPA for five more years, was admired for the way in which he had resolutely pursued the deal. His handling of the global financial crisis of 2007–09, and the rapid growth of the economy since 2004, had come in for acclaim by middle class Indians who had made good.

Electoral implications apart, the Indo–US Civil Nuclear Deal ended the 'nuclear apartheid' India had been subjected to for thirty years. There were not just the restrictions on nuclear commerce globally but also the 'technological apartheid' which had kicked into place as a result of sanctions. The deal enabled India to buy fuel, reactors, equipment, and technology from other countries. There was a shortage of uranium in the country and many of the nuclear reactors were running at 40–55 per cent capacity. The opening up of nuclear trade helped India stockpile uranium for each of the civilian reactors that were put under the IAEA's safeguards. After the deal, India has been able to buy uranium from Russia, Canada, Kazakhstan, and other countries. According to the scientists, this has made the situation comfortable for India's nuclear programme, both civilian and strategic. Since 2008, India has also acquired four nuclear reactors from Russia.

Despite Condoleezza Rice's plea at the dinner at the White House in 2008, India did not buy any nuclear reactors from the US. This was partly because they were not priced competitively enough but also because US companies found the nuclear civil liability law passed by India too 'tough' for comfort; it put the onus of liability on the companies selling nuclear energy. The deal also had a demonstrable effect on India's other relationships. It had managed to claim that it was special and thus change the non-proliferation order in its favour. Other countries began to look at India differently. India was recognized as a de facto NWS, even though it had not signed the Non-Proliferation Treaty, and refused to sign the CTBT.

George W. Bush saw India as a countervailing influence against China in the Asia-Pacific region. That notion has continued as India became a part of the Quadrilateral Security Dialogue (also known as the Quad), a strategic 'grouping' between the US, Australia, Japan, and India, started in 2007. It engaged in several diplomatic and military initiatives, prompted by China's growing assertion of its military and economic power in the region, and its belligerence on India's borders.

Manmohan Singh's government was unlike any other that existed before or after. No full-term, rather two-term, prime minister was as hemmed in as he was. Sonia Gandhi took the political decisions and had a say in major policy initiatives. The PM let Pranab Mukherjee, another powerful figure in the government, run much of the administration through key decision-making bodies like scores of GOMs. As a result, Manmohan Singh's authority was severely curtailed, and he worked under constraints.

Could Manmohan Singh have asserted himself more as prime minister despite the fact that he owed his position to Sonia Gandhi, and the model of coalition that called for power sharing with her? For Sonia needed him as much as he needed her.

That however was not his persona. He preferred to be a blade of grass which bends when the storm comes, rather than the tree which stands up straight and falls. That is why he lasted for ten years. But in the process, the authority of the prime minister took a beating—and though upright and sincere, he was seen as among the weak prime ministers India has had. And yet, the resourcefulness, tenacity, and determination Manmohan Singh displayed in pursuing the Indo–US Civil Nuclear Deal revealed a new side to him. Over the more than three years it took to conclude the deal, he displayed traits and political savvy that few imagined he possessed. He took on formidable opponents across the political spectrum—and managed to best them, or win them over to his side. He took enormous risks, putting his government in jeopardy, showed an understanding of the political system in India, displayed a keen knowledge of geopolitics and foreign policy—and demonstrated that he could get his way. This underrated prime minister managed to pull off the unlikeliest of triumphs. And he had the backing of the most powerful man in the world—US President George W. Bush. If it had not been Bush and Manmohan Singh as the main protagonists in the saga, the Indo–US deal may not have had a successful ending.

The Indo–US nuclear deal was not only about the need for clean energy in India. Or even about the strategic partnership India began to forge with the US in the context of changing global dynamics with an ascendant China on the horizon. It was all of these. But at an intangible level, it was about something more—it was a proclamation by Prime Minister Manmohan Singh that he could be his own man.

EPILOGUE

'If there's a prime minister Narendra Modi can be compared with, it is Jawaharlal Nehru,' Karan Singh, who has worked with all the prime ministers of India, told me. '(I suspect) he will never admit this but he would like to be another Nehru and to surpass him.'

How Modi and his supporters would respond to Dr Singh's observation is anybody's guess. For if there is a leader the BJP and the RSS love to run down, it is Nehru.

And yet, for all the differences inherent in their contrasting visions, they are similarities in their popularity and the influence they wielded—the congruence captured momentarily at the Prime Ministers' Museum at Teen Murti Bhavan in Delhi, a project close to Modi's heart. It is striking to find two pictures side by side on the wall above the entrance the reception: Nehru and Modi.

As I mentioned in the introduction, I decided, in the interest of fairness and accuracy, not to include the incumbent prime minister in this book. For one, his term is a work in progress as he works towards a third stint. And, two, unlike with other prime ministers, what would have been missing with Modi would have been the power of hindsight, the journalist's sole beacon to illuminate the inner workings of a prime minister's tenure and the Prime Minister's Office.

At the same time, this book will be incomplete without a word about India's fourteenth and, arguably, its most powerful prime minister—seen in the context of his predecessors. What aspect of which prime minister compare with Modi, making him part of an unbroken chain? And what are the areas in which Modi is his own person, alone and unique, almost sui generis?

Ideologically, Nehru and Modi are poles apart. Modi is steeped in the ideology of the RSS and would like to fulfil its core agenda, to fine-tune the architecture of a 'civilizational state', a Hindu Rashtra within the rubric of the Constitution. Nehru, with his Left and liberal views, championed secularism to make minorities feel secure in an independent, post-Partition India.

The erudite, cerebral, aristocratic, Harrow-Cambridge-educated Nehru was brought up in luxury in the palatial Anand Bhavan in Allahabad which was the hub of the freedom movement. His appeal lay in a handsome, prince-like figure deciding to give up his comforts for the rough and tumble of the freedom struggle.

At the other end is Modi who, by his own admission, helped his father sell tea at Vadnagar railway station as a child. By the time he took over as prime minister in 2014, India's democracy had evolved and devolved—and Modi's appeal lay in his humble beginnings and his rise through the ranks to reach the pinnacle of power.

Modi has had the most powerful Prime Minister's Office of any PM. Nehru's PMO was not powerful; only a joint secretary headed it. And, as already mentioned, Nehru ruled through his ministers, powerful figures in their own right, who, having come through the freedom movement, were able to win elections on their own, though the charismatic Nehru won polls for his party. Many ministers in the Modi government, however, depended on the prime minister to win their elections for them and ceded ground to him. Often, they were informed by the PMO about the decisions they should take.

Both Nehru and Modi had a mass following, one was a Kashmiri Pandit whose family had migrated to the plains of Uttar Pradesh which became the karmabhoomi of the Nehrus. And the other was from an oil presser's family of the Modi Ghanchis—one of the Other Backward Classes in Gujarat. Modi also made Uttar Pradesh his electoral akhara, and it was really UP which catapulted him to power in 2014 and 2019.

India asserted itself on the global stage under both Nehru and Modi. In the 1950s and 1960s, it was as a leader of the non-aligned third world. Today, India is asserting itself as a growing market and an important player in the balancing of powers in an increasingly uncertain global geopolitical scenario.

Nehru, the quintessential educator, would use his public meetings to educate citizens on a host of subjects. Modi, too, tries to play the role of a social reformer through his monthly radio talk, 'Mann ki Baat'. Men and women gather around their radio sets and listen to what he had to say—from the role of anganwadi workers to how to cope with exam stress (his Exam Warrior sessions were rather like Chacha Nehru's homilies), or end the use of single-use plastics.

■

As with her father, so does Modi share many parallels with Indira Gandhi: they are both among the strongest leaders any PMO has seen, power concentrated in their hands. Like her, Modi, too, became larger than the party he leads. Like her famous riposte—'They say Indira hatao, I say garibi hatao'—he, too, underlined the refrain that the Opposition was single-minded in its focus to defeat him, even 'bury' him in a 'kabr' (grave). In parliament, he minced few words: 'Ek akela kitno par bhari pada, desh dekh raha hai (One alone got the better of many, the country is watching).' Like the Indira Gandhi set-up, the Modi establishment has also been sensitive about criticism from the Opposition.

While Indira had to fight for years to marginalize her opponents—inside and outside the party, stalwarts all—Modi, since 2014, has encountered no resistance from within the BJP. Today, he is supreme and unchallenged—there is no moderate vs hardline divide, old vs new in the party. His decision to demonetize ₹1,000 and ₹500 currency notes in his first term in office and abrogate Article 370 of the Constitution, which had accorded a special status to Jammu and Kashmir, in his second term, were closely guarded decisions. He took few political colleagues into confidence.

Every decision carries his imprimatur—like his photo on the Covid vaccine certificates, or free foodgrain bags or flagging off each Vande Bharat train. Never has image politics been so compelling or a prime minister been so ubiquitous in the reach of his image—with his appeal undiminished since he first assumed office in 2014.

From V. P. Singh, Modi has taken many a leaf from the Mandal book, calibrating social justice to the next level, reshaping his 'new BJP'—a far cry from the Brahmin–Bania entity it used to be. He stitched the OBCs and the extremely backward castes into a new national tapestry. He reached out similarly to the Dalits and tribals by restoring the SC and ST Act diluted by the court and with steps like the elevation of a tribal woman Droupudi Murmu as the republic's president.

While Modi continued with the economic reforms initiated by P. V. Narasimha Rao in 1991, he brought in his brand of welfarism to provide a safety net for the poor (like Indira Gandhi did with her 'garibi hatao' slogan, and Manmohan Singh did with the right to food, work, education, and information.)

In the world of strategic affairs, Modi has taken the next steps in the journey Atal Bihari Vajpayee embarked on, and Manmohan Singh followed, to fashion a strategic relationship with the USA—an upshot of Singh's dogged determination to forge ahead with the Indo–US Civil Nuclear Deal in 2008 at all costs.

•

Where does Modi stand out as different from his predecessors? At the time of writing, he is already the longest serving non-Congress prime minister, having completed more than nine years in office, and holding his own in the popularity charts—which can be said about few world leaders today.

Rajiv Gandhi was also known to be tech-savvy, his rise coinciding with the age of the personal computer. But more than any other PM, Modi has effectively used social media, free data, the latest technology and communication tools, and the best that was available to him from around the world by way of PR companies and lobbyists to cultify his leadership and magnify his message. He knows the value of optics today, the need to be messaging 24 by 7 by 365.

His style is to do big and dramatic things—and to spring a surprise. If there is one word that sums up this style, it is 'bhavya' (grand). Once an official had asked him how he wanted a particular building to be done. 'Whatever you do,' he told the official, 'it has to be bhavya.' He has chafed against what he called a 'kalpanik daridrata (lack of imagination to do big things)' in the country.

This penchant for the big and the bold reflects in his vision of national iconography, as well. So, the new Parliament and the Central Vista had to signify an end to the country's colonial past, and identify him with the new structure. Sardar Vallabhbhai Patel's statue had to be the tallest in the world, the Madison Square Garden meeting in New York for the Indian diaspora had to be the grandest such event ever held. Black money had to be eliminated by a fiat delivered on national TV at 8 p.m.

Nehru took the Congress Party to victory in national elections in 1952, 1957, 1962. Indira Gandhi also won three elections, in 1967, 1971, and 1980—but lost in 1977. Vajpayee took his party to victory in three Lok Sabha elections in 1996, 1998 and 1999, but in none of those general elections did the BJP get a majority on its own. However, Vajpayee won as many as ten Lok Sabha elections individually—no small record.

Modi has never lost an election he contested. And he only fought his first election as late as 2002—after he became the chief minister of Gujarat.

In fact, there is no other prime minister who has won as many elections for his party as has Narendra Modi. He contested five elections and took his party to victory in all—three of them in Gujarat, in 2002, 2007, and 2012, and two national wins, in 2014 and 2019, when he became prime minister. The sixth election he contested was a by-poll which he won in early 2002 to get into the Gujarat state assembly to remain as chief minister. He has been the main vote-getter for the BJP in virtually every state election held since 2014.

RSS–BJP ideologue K. N. Govindacharya used to say about Modi's electoral successes, 'Narendra's forte is political marketing....' Politics is equal to power. Power stems from elections. Elections are a battle of images. And therefore politics revolves around images, messages and signalling.'

∎

The Modi phenomenon is seen as a heady mix of Hindutva, nationalism and national pride, OBC empowerment, and social welfarism that provided benefits directly to the poor and the marginalized by way of their newly created bank accounts. Adding to his appeal is the image of a strong and charismatic leader who works hard, and has no family in tow.

It is however, Modi's cultural project for Hindu unity, viewing everything through the prism of India as a civilizational entity, which holds a central place in his scheme of things. At the heart of it is the construction of the

Ram temple in Ayodhya, where he himself laid the foundation stone, the impressive corridor he built in Kashi (Varanasi), and the plans that are afoot to revitalize Mathura. These and other initiatives resonate with many younger Indians, several million of whom were born after the demolition of the Babri Masjid and economic reforms.

In 2014, a BJP government came to power with a majority on its own for the first time in its history—replacing the Congress which had ruled the country for forty-five years after Independence. The BJP went on to improve its tally in the Lok Sabha five years later in 2019. It was more than a transition of power made from one mainline party, the Congress, to another, the BJP.

In 1947, India had opted for a Nehru—and not a Jinnah—and rejected religion as the basis of a modern nation state. In 2023, it was moving towards becoming a Hindu Rashtra—leaving the minorities, no small number in absolute terms—feeling increasingly insecure and beleaguered in a country that became highly polarized.

The Opposition parties found it difficult to figure out how to politically counter the challenge posed by Modi. Concerned about the 'erosion in democratic institutions', they chafed against the use of government agencies like the CBI, Enforcement Directorate, or the Income Tax authorities to bring them in line and to 'harass' them.

As a non-elite, non-English speaking, OBC prime minister, Modi represents the subalternization of Indian politics which had so far been dominated by elites; this has an aspirational appeal for small town and big village India. Modi has attacked the elites by running down Lutyens' Delhi, Khan Market, and political dynasties who rule through a sense of entitlement. Bringing together religion, class, and caste, he has been able to play on existing fault lines—Hindu–Muslim, rich–poor, upper castes–lower castes, and the entitled versus the excluded.

■

There were two broad takeaways for me, as I came to the end of this prime-ministerial story. The first striking aspect about prime ministerial decision-making was how ad hoc, in-the-moment these decisions were irrespective of who the prime minister was or the party to which s/he belonged. Most of the decisions, which were to impact millions were taken not with a fifty- twenty- or even a ten-year perspective. They were made largely with an eye on the immediate: firefighting, responding to a crisis, political exigencies. The goal: to resolve an issue, to come back to power, or to stay in power. If the decisions were usually determined by the need for political survival, the way in which they were taken—influenced by powerful lobbies, characterized by all manner of machinations and deceit, colliding ambitions and cut-throat competition—made for nail-biting suspense and drama.

With growing contention in politics, decision-making in India has become increasingly complex. As the consensus by which the country was run in the first fifteen years after Independence began to break down, sectional interests overtook other considerations. Till the mid-1960s, building institutions for a modern nation, removing poverty, illiteracy, ill health, malnutrition, and working for the larger collective were still the dominant themes—for all the mistakes that were made.

As power for the sake of power became the overarching consideration, narrower interests began to prevail. Indira Gandhi made an art and science of realpolitik—of 'saam daam dand bhed' to get power. She was emulated by generations of politicians, who came after her—cutting across party lines.

Politics is about power. Unless politicians win elections, there is no prime-ministerial story to tell. But where does the Lakshman rekha get drawn, where do vision—and pragmatism—come together for the larger good than just for perpetuating power? That distinguishing line is blurred and almost gone.

My second key takeaway, which hit me with renewed force as I wrote this book, was the realization that India is essentially a coalition—and it should be ruled like a coalition, by consensus, whether there is a single party at the helm or an alliance of parties, whether headed by a strong leader or a weak one.

The intervening years between India's two most powerful leaders—Indira Gandhi and Narendra Modi—spawned a coalition era in the country (barring the five years when Rajiv Gandhi ruled). It lasted for a quarter century—led by V. P. Singh, Chandra Shekhar, P. V. Narasimha Rao, H. D. Deve Gowda, I. K. Gujral, Atal Bihari Vajpayee, and Manmohan Singh. No one party acquired a majority on its own—they had to join hands with other groups to form a government. Or the single largest party broke other groups to lead a government—as happened in the case of Narasimha Rao. The Congress was ceding ground to other political forces, which were jostling to take its place. The BJP was in the forefront of that race.

Paradoxically, it was decisions taken by the Congress prime ministers which hastened the decline of the Congress Party—and led to the rapid rise of the BJP. These decisions included Rajiv Gandhi's move to enact the Muslim Women's Bill and open the locks at the disputed structure of the Babri Masjid in Ayodhya—which alienated both the Hindus and the Muslims. Or P. V. Narasimha Rao's non-decision which brought down the Babri Masjid—it put the temple issue on the back-burner during his tenure, but fuelled Hindu nationalism, with the BJP having tasted blood—and it eroded the faith of the Muslims in Constitutional guarantees. Also, the controversial decision of V. P. Singh, a Congressman who broke ranks with the party, to implement the Mandal Commission Report for empowering the OBCs inflicted a body blow on the Congress Party.

The 1990s was a decade which ended the domination of the Congress. Yet the coalition governments which came to power thereafter did go on to make far-reaching decisions—like the opening up of the economy, affirmative action for the socially and educationally backward classes (Mandal), which changed the politics of North India, the testing of nuclear weapons which took India to the global high table, and reshaped the country's foreign policy.

It goes without saying that the stronger the prime minister, like Indira Gandhi or Narendra Modi, the greater the concentration of power in the PMO—and more likely the possibility of an onslaught on democratic institutions. A weaker PM and a coalition arrangement, and this is ironic, provides more safeguards for democratic functioning, given the multiple interests that kick into play—and act as a check on the excessive use of power.

Undoubtedly, a coalition arrangement can throw up its own set of problems—the buffeting around of the prime minister, the possibility of fragmentation and instability—and corruption by many more players engaging in malfeasance, though this is not to say that single-party-rule is less corrupt.

After seventy-five years of Independence, India has proved all those wrong who felt that a poor, backward and highly diverse nation would not be able to hang together as a parliamentary democracy. It has so far defied doomsayers who predicted the break-up of the nation.

India remains a democracy—but it is a flawed one today, with the steady erosion of institutions, such as parliament, the judiciary, the media, and the Election Commission. Political parties are run like fiefdoms, ministers, for instance, do not speak up freely in the cabinet because they are dependent on the prime minister, or the chief minister, to continue in power.

At the end of the day, it is strong institutions which anchor democracy—and can deliver to the last child. We can have good or bad rulers, but it is these institutions which are the sentinels of a vibrant democratic order—and can exercise a check on the abuse of power.

■

I want to end this narrative with a story about Jawaharlal Nehru and Sardar Vallabhbhai Patel—the iconic, but controversial, first 'jodi' of independent India because it illustrates what leadership is all about. They belong to an age gone by, but have relevance for today's India. They could not have been more different—Nehru, Left and liberal, and a man of ideas, Patel, Right and pragmatic, and a man of action.

It is well known that Jawaharlal Nehru was not the choice of the Congress Party to become the Congress president in April 1946. Nehru was the choice of Mahatma Gandhi. As Congress president, he became the prime minister (vice president of the executive council) in the interim government in September 1946—and again in 1947.

It was at Gandhi's instance that Sardar Patel withdrew in Nehru's favour, a decision that could not have been easy for the hero of the Quit India movement—and one that excites controversy many decades down the line. For Gandhi, Nehru and Patel were 'two oxen yoked to the government cart'. 'One will need the other,' he felt, 'and both will pull together.'

When the transfer of power took place on 15 August 1947, Patel agreed to work under Nehru as deputy prime minister and home minister. But within five months of Independence, they lost Gandhi's unifying presence to an assassin's bullet on 30 January 1948. Just over an hour before Gandhi died, Patel was with Gandhi. They were having a heart-to-heart talk at Birla House in Delhi, and this is a story told by Rajmohan Gandhi in his biography on Patel. The Sardar spoke. Bapu listened, as he spun the charkha. He then ate his evening meal, and continued to listen to an agitated Patel. In the end, Gandhi told Patel calmly that his presence in the cabinet—and that of Nehru—was 'indispensable'. Any breach between the two would be disastrous for the country. They decided to meet with Nehru the next day. Bapu, late for his 5 p.m. meeting, walked out on to the lawns where the prayers were to be held. Patel headed home. Within minutes, Patel and his daughter Maniben were back at Birla House. They were told that Bapu had been shot dead.

Nehru arrived a couple of minutes after Vallabhbhai. He went down on his knees, put his head next to Gandhi's, and cried like a child. 'Then he put his grieving head in the Sardar's lap.' India's last viceroy, Lord Mountbatten, recalled what Gandhi had told him—that his dearest wish was to bring about a full reconciliation between Nehru and Patel. Both men embraced each other. That night, on 30 January 1948, they addressed the nation together, Nehru in English and Hindi and Patel in Hindi.

Three days later, on 3 February 1948, *The Statesman* published an article seeking Home Minister Patel's resignation for his inability to protect Gandhi. Jayaprakash Narayan and other socialists led the attack on Patel. Patel wrote out his resignation letter to the prime minister. However, the letter was not sent. Patel's private secretary, Vidya Shankar, persuaded him to hold it back—as he would be depriving the country of the joint leadership (by Nehru and Patel) that was Gandhi's wish.

As it happened, Nehru also wrote to Patel the same day. 'With Bapu's death, everything is changed and we have to face a different and more difficult world....I think it is my duty and, if I may venture to say, yours also for us to face it together as friends and colleagues. Not merely superficially but in full loyalty to one another... I can assure you that you will have that from me.'

On 4 February, for the first time, Sardar Patel called Nehru, 'my leader'.

'I am deeply touched,' Patel wrote to Nehru the next day, 'we both have been lifelong comrades in a common cause. I had the good fortune to have a last talk with Bapu. His opinion also binds us both and I can assure you that I am fully resolved to approach my responsibilities...in this spirit.'

The new government headed by Nehru and Patel had to oversee one of the largest migrations in human history that displaced 15 million people on the subcontinent. It had to rehabilitate millions of refugees who had come over from Pakistan—and to craft a Constitution based on adult franchise and liberal principles. It had to politically integrate what was British India and the 565 princely states, headed by rulers, used to enforcing their writ, to become a sovereign, independent nation—which was ably done by Sardar Patel, the Iron Man of India. Together they had to stabilize the new country. The British had not handed India a readymade nation.

It is not as if Patel allowed Nehru to get his way always in the months that followed. In the three years after Independence, and till he died in 1950, Patel had his way in many decisions, like the appointment of Rajendra Prasad, a devout Hindu, as India's first president instead of C. Rajagopalachari, whom Nehru wanted. He also got his nominee Purushottam Das Tandon elected as Congress president in 1950 instead of J. B. Kripalani, who was backed by Nehru.

When Patel was canvassing for support for Tandon, and asked Assam minister Fakhruddin Ali Ahmed, later to become president of India, to back him, Fakhruddin replied he would do only 'as Panditji wants'. Patel shot back, 'Fakhruddin, do exactly what you like. But remember Jawaharlal can never help a friend nor ever harm an enemy. I never forget a friend and never forgive an enemy.'

Nehru and Patel differed on many issues—as on their assessment of an organization like the RSS. Nehru believed it was a fascist organization. Patel saw it as courageous but misguided, and banned it for a year and half after Gandhi's assassination.

Patel passed away in December 1950. After his death, Nehru consolidated his hold on both the government and the party. Nehru and Patel were not flawless men. By accepting to be number two, Patel made the greater sacrifice of the two. It must have also been difficult for Nehru to submit to Patel whenever he was outmanoeuvred by his deputy. But they displayed sagacity—and restraint—in those early years of Independence. They held together, despite deep differences, to hold together the new entity called India which had been given in their custody.

Gandhi had known—and Nehru and Patel knew—that they would need to move in step to steer a vast, vibrant, and diverse nation like India, with ethnic, religious, caste, and linguistic differences of a kind that did not exist anywhere else in the world—a challenge that remains as formidable today as it was in their time.

Personifying India's plural ethos, Nehru and Patel showed that it was possible for two divergent strands of thinking to coexist and collaborate for a national cause. They discovered that power is most secure when it is shared, especially with those who act as a sounding board rather than an echo chamber. It is a lesson that India, and its leadership, should not forget.

ACKNOWLEDGEMENTS

When I set about doing this book, I had little idea about the work it would entail. This project would not have been possible without the help and support of many people and I don't know where to start to thank them.

First of all, my thanks to the main players in the book—prime ministers, political leaders, bureaucrats, scientists, my colleagues in the media—who trusted me and gave me information and valuable insights. They straddle the pages of the book.

The hours I was able to spend with V. P. Singh when he underwent dialysis at Delhi's Apollo Hospital, after demitting office, and whose rise to the top I had covered on a daily basis, the many conversations I had with P. V. Narasimha Rao, interviews during the course of my career with Manmohan Singh, Atal Bihari Vajpayee and H. D. Deve Gowda, the many frank conversations with Chandra Shekhar and I. K. Gujral, and meetings with Sonia Gandhi and L. K. Advani—these helped me understand how decisions were made which shaped the country's destiny.

Many of those who spoke to me over the years—most of them with candour—are no longer around—like R. Venkataraman, Krishan Kant, P. Shiv Shankar, Jaswant Singh, Harkishan Singh Surjeet, H. N. Bahuguna, Bhuvnesh Chaturvedi, Sharad Yadav, Ram Vilas Paswan, S. Jaipal Reddy, Devendra Dwivedi, Arun Nehru, H. R. Bhardwaj, M. L. Fotedar, R. K. Dhawan, Yunus Saleem, D. P. Tripathi, Brajesh Mishra, K. Subrahmanyam, S. K. Singh, Naresh Chandra, K. Santhanam, and many more—and it will be my abiding regret that they will not see the book, which their inputs have helped shape.

I learnt a great deal about politics from the late Krishan Kant whom I had first met during the Emergency years when I was working with *Himmat Weekly* and who, over the years, would talk to me in confidence about events as they unfolded, from the V. P. Singh to the Vajpayee years.

I also valued my discussions on different aspects of the VP premiership with Som Pal.

My thanks to Raj Kamal Jha, chief editor of the *Indian Express*, who, despite his busy schedule, gave me valuable steers on the book. I really appreciated the way Kalpana Sharma, former deputy editor of *The Hindu*, and a friend of long years, made time to read the draft of the book and gave me very useful suggestions. Many of my colleagues in the media shared with me their experiences of various prime ministers, they figure in the book, and I am grateful to them.

Books need a support structure to come to fruition. It was my friends—and family—who provided that support system, and constantly held out a helping hand. Sherna Ghyara Chatterjee, though a psychotherapist by profession based in the UK and India, helped with whatever needed doing, transcribing interviews, putting them in order, looking for references—all as a labour of love. So did Aparna Khatri in transcribing many interviews, even typing out some Hindi interviews in the Roman script! Kartik Kant helped with research, and systematizing the material, and had an eye for detail. My thanks to Dr Ravi Rao, Siddharth Singh, and their colleagues at Asia Plateau (Initiatives of Change), a conference centre in Panchgani, for their support to me while I was writing the book.

Above all, to my parents, Saundarya and Gurudutt Chowdhury, who went too soon but were always there for me. My aunt, Vijalakshmi Wadhwa, an academic by profession, made her home available to me in Mumbai whenever I could get away from the hurly-burly of Delhi life to do quiet writing. She wanted to be—and was—the first to be told that I had finished writing the book, and to see the design of the cover. Days after I had submitted the manuscript to the publishers, she was to pass away. While a cousin, Narendra Murkumbi, provided all manner of logistical support and critiqued a chapter, another cousin, Jyoti Narula, offered me the use of his office. My US-based brother-in-law Ravindra Koka always had an encouraging word to say, when it looked like an unending exercise. Many like my sister, Rajni Khanna, and nephew, Amit Khanna, constantly spurred me on to finish the book as a priority.

My special thanks to my publisher David Davidar who believed in the book from day one—and kept up a punishing schedule. My appreciation to him and his proficient team—Aienla Ozukum and Kanika Praharaj—for their hard work and painstaking effort on the book. It was thanks to the Covid years that this book got completed.

And, finally, to the two men in my life—my husband Arun who has for at least two decades been urging me to write a book—and was around with all manner of support, including dealing with computer/tech problems that would crop up, and my musician son Nakul who chafed against my 'being preoccupied' all the time. His constant refrain: 'When will this be over?'

It's finally over.

NOTES

INTRODUCTION

ix 'The final responsibility is yours...that can be awesome': V. P. Singh to author, October 1999, Apollo Hospital, New Delhi.

ix 'The higher the responsibility, the lesser the freedom': Ibid.

ix 'Yes, the top is lonely': Chandra Shekhar to author.

ix 'The space to yourself is just not there': I. K. Gujral to author.

ix 'The higher you go, the more lonely you are': Atal Bihari Vajpayee, quoted in N. K. Singh, 'A Dove Among Hawks', *India Today*, 31 May 1996.

ix When the scams tumbled out against Manmohan Singh's government: 'UPA report card: Nine years, nine scams', *India Today*, 22 May 2013.

ix Rajiv Gandhi, who had enjoyed an unprecedented majority of 414 members: 'Statistical Report on General Elections, 1985 to the Eight Lok Sabha: Volume II', Delhi: Election Commission of India, 1986, available at <https://eci.gov.in/files/file/4119-general-election-1985-vol-i-ii/>.

ix 'The moment someone enters my room': Indira Gandhi to Krishan Kant.

x last days he spent in Dehradun in May 1964: Raj Kanwar, 'Nehru's Last Days in Dehra Dun: Nehru kept the Final Appointment', *The Citizen*, 26 May 2020.

x By his bedside lay a book of poems: Gopalkrishna Gandhi, 'Nehru was a leader of shining veracity', *Hindustan Times*, 26 May 2016.

x His PR machinery constantly put out photos: Kavita Upadhyay, 'PM Modi spends night in meditation cave near Kedarnath', *Indian Express*, 19 May 2019; Mahesh Langa, 'Narendra Modi dedicates Sardar Patel's 182-metre-tall "Statue of Unity" to nation', *The Hindu*, 31 October 2018; 'PM retraces Mahatma Gandhi's train journey in South Africa', *The Tribune*, 9 July 2016; Arjit Garg, 'PM Modi Takes His First International Flight on New Air India One: All You Need Know About the Plane', *News18*, 26 March 2021; 'PM Modi's characteristic hand wave inside seemingly empty Atal Tunnel is cracking up social media', *Scroll.in*, 4 October 2020.

xi 'the only man in the Cabinet': This phrase was first used by Piloo Mody, founder of the Swatantara Party, to describe Indira Gandhi, cited in 'Kissinger salute to "strong" man in Indira', *The Telegraph*, 25 December 2007. According to declassified American documents, Henry Kissinger told Afghan head of state Muhammad Daoud in 1976 that he wished the American establishment had a man as strong as the Indian PM Indira Gandhi.

xi 'web of larger interests, petty approaches and genuine views': P. V. Narasimha Rao to author, in a written Q and A, after he demitted office. The Q and A is undated and was also found in his personal papers and was referred to in Vinay Sitapati, *Half Lion: How P.V. Narasimha Rao Transformed India*, Gurgaon: Penguin Random House, 2016, p. 338.

xvii The Congress, which till 1989 had ruled the country for thirty-nine years out of the forty-two years: See www.pmindia.gov.in/en/former-prime-ministers/.

xiii On both occasions, he ruled the country for thirteen days: Sumantra Bose, *Transforming India: Challenges to the World's Largest Democracy*, Cambridge, Massachusetts, and London, England: Harvard University Press, 2013, p. 79.

xiii It is this norm which Pranab Mukherjee cited: Pranab Mukherjee, *The Turbulent Years: 1980–1996*, Delhi: Rupa Publications, 2016, p. 70.

xiii Nanda is also remembered for converting the 27.5-hectare mansion: Janardan Thakur, *All the Prime Minister's Men*, New Delhi: Vikas Publishing House, 1977.

xiii Nehru was chosen by Mahatma Gandhi: Raj Singh, 'Why Gandhi opted for Nehru and not Sardar Patel for PM?', *India TV*, 31 October 2015.

xiv 'Think deeply about the right course': C. P. Srivastava, *Lal Bahadur Shastri: A Life of Truth in Politics*, Delhi: Oxford University Press, 1995, p. 33.

xiv he was often called the 'little sparrow': Janardan Thakur, *Prime Ministers: Nehru to Vajpayee*, Mumbai: Eeshwar, 1999, p. 64.

xiv The 'homespun' prime minister became a national hero: Welles Hangen, *After Nehru, Who?*, New York: Harcourt, Brace and World, 1963, p. 108.

xiv 'goongi gudiya': 'A Fitful Improvisation', *Thought*, 22 January 1966.

xiv 'this chokri': Bipan Chandra, Mridula Mukherjee, and Aditya Mukherjee, *India Since Independence: Revised and Updated*, Delhi: Penguin Books, 2008.

xiv 'the old witch': '"[Indira Gandhi] Is A Bitch ... The Indians Are Bastards"', *Outlook*, 3 February 2022.

xiv 'Durga': Pupul Jayakar, *Indira Gandhi: A Biography*, New Delhi: Penguin Books, 1995, p. 235.

xiv this surge led to the formation of nine state governments: In 1967, the Congress lost in Punjab, Delhi, UP, Bihar, West Bengal, Orissa, Goa, Kerala, and Madras, now Tamil Nadu. In Rajasthan, it did not get a majority but formed a government with the help of others.

xv   'Mummy has to be helped somehow': Steven R. Weisman, 'Assassination in India; Rajiv Gandhi : A son who won, lost and tried a comeback', *The New York Times*, 27 May 1991.

xv   specifically the alleged payment of illegal kickbacks: 'What is the Bofors scam case?', *Indian Express*, 3 February 2018.

xv   The 'PM India remained deprived of': Muchkund Dubey, quoted in *Chandra Shekhar – The Last Icon Of Ideological Politics*, Delhi: Rupa Publications, 2019.

xv   But he parted company with her during the Emergency: Harivansh and Ravi Dutt Bajpai, 'Emergency chronicles: The party Chandra Shekhar brought to power, sent him to jail', *Indian Express*, 25 June 2019.

xv   walking 4,260 kilometres on foot in his chappals: Venkitesh Ramakrishnan, 'A Rebel's Journey', *Frontline*, 27 July 2007.

xv   Women would wait for him by the wayside: As seen by the author, when she covered the yatra for two days in Tamil Nadu in 1983.

xvi   'charisma of a dead fish': Jairam Ramesh, quoted in Sitapati, *Half Lion*, p. 98.

xvi   Vajpayee formed a government at the head of a twenty-four-party coalition: Keith Jones, 'Hindu chauvinist-led coalition to form India's next government', World Socialist Web Site, 9 October 1999.

xvi   Vokkaligas, an agrarian community, are categorized as a 'backward class': 'Central List of OBCs', National Commission for Backward Classes, available at ncbc.nic.in.

xvi   'government of chief ministers': Neerja Chowdhury, 'Keeping Confidences: Political Reporting', in V. Eshwar Anand and K. Jayanthi (eds.), *A Handbook of Journalism: Media in the Information Age*, Delhi: Sage Publications, 2018, p. 129.

xvii Nehru 'riding a white stallion through the crowded streets of Lahore': I. K. Gujral, *Matters of Discretion: An Autobiography*, New Delhi: Hay House Publishers, 2011, p. 27.

xvii 'kitchen cabinet': Katherine Frank, *Indira: The Life of Indira Nehru Gandhi*, London: HarperCollins Publishers, 2001, p. 299.

xvii The 'Gujral doctrine' he espoused: Kanwal Sibal, 'The Enduring Relevance of the 'Gujral Doctrine', *India Today*, 16 December 2019.

xvii 'I am what I am,' he used to say, 'because of education': PTI, 'I am what I am today because of education: PM', *Times of India*, 1 April 2010.

xvii 303 seats, up from 282: 'From 2 to 303 seats: How BJP has grown over the years', *Times of India*, 30 May 2019.

xvii A polarizing PM, Narendra Modi shaped a 'new BJP': Niranjan Sahoo, 'Mounting Majoritarianism and Political Polarization in India', Thomas Carothers and Andrew O'Donohue (eds.), *Political Polarization in South and Southeast Asia: Old Divisions, New Dangers*, Carnegie Endowment for International Peace, pp. 9–23.

xvii He pursued the BJP's core, pro-Hindu agenda: Azeem Ibrahim, 'Modi's Slide Toward Autocracy', *Foreign Policy*, 13 July 2020.

xviii Modi was the second OBC (Other Backward Classes), after Deve Gowda: Sowmya Aji, 'I was India's first OBC PM, not Narendra Modi: H D Deve Gowda', *Economic Times*, 13 July 2015.

xviii 'I am...born in a Jat family': Thakur, *Nehru to Vajpayee*, p. 155. There are different theories about whether the Jats are Rajputs, Vaishyas, or Shudras; they are now considered OBCs in nine states of India. The Vokkaligas were also categorized as backward classes in Karnataka since 1974. Narendra Modi, as already mentioned, belongs to the Ghanchi caste (of oil millers), also OBCs in Gujarat.

xix   J. R. Jayewardene, a former president of Sri Lanka, had once said: Nirupama Subramanian, 'Explained: Sri Lanka's coming constitutional changes and why its Tamil polity is worried', *Indian Express*, 13 September 2020.

xx   'Actually it is the PM who makes the appointments': Bhuvnesh Chaturvedi to author.

xx   only the prime minister and home minister remain on it: Bharti Jain, 'PMO wields full control over bureaucratic appointments', *Times of India*, 14 August 2014.

xx   thanks to guidelines framed at the instance of the Supreme Court: Prashant Bhushan, 'Centre's Move to Subvert CBI and ED Undoes Years of Effort to Secure Their Independence', *The Wire*, 24 November 2021.

xx   'At the informal level a lot of things are made possible': Bhuvnesh Chaturvedi to author.

xx   In May 2013, the Supreme Court had sharply indicted the government by calling the CBI a 'caged parrot' and 'its master's voice': Ross Colvin and Satarupa Bhattacharjya, 'A "caged parrot" - Supreme Court describes CBI', *Reuters*, 10 May 2013.

xx   the Modi government added the Enforcement Directorate (ED) as an additional instrument: Supriya Sharma and Arunabh Saikia, 'How the Modi government has weaponised the ED to go after India's Opposition', *Scroll.in*, 5 July 2022.

xxi   The Constitution also provides for the invocation of a state of emergency: Article 352 of the Constitution provides for a national emergency in an extraordinary situation—like war, external aggression, or internal rebellion—which may threaten the security, peace, and stability of the country.

xxi   dismissed nine state governments run by the Congress: Arul B. Louis and Prabhu Chawla, 'PM Indira Gandhi dismisses governments in nine states, looks to put Congress in power', *India Today*, 15 March 1980.

xxi   interpreted 'consultation' to mean 'concurrence': Suhrith Parthasarathy, 'An anti-constitutional judgment', *The Hindu*, 30 October 2015.

xxi   This was struck down in 2015: Rahel Philipose, 'Collegium vs NJAC: What is the renewed debate over appointment of judges?', *Indian Express*, 17 December 2022.

xxi   '360 degree' process of doing 'due diligence': Pranab Dhal Samanta, 'View: A new CJI provides GoI the chance to have another go at judicial reforms, *Economic Times*, 18 November 2019; Sourav Roy Barman, 'Govt "never deliberately" delayed appointments of judges: Rijiju', *Indian Express*, 4 February 2022.

xxii   with the government seeking a direct role in the appointment of judges: Rupam Jain and Arpan Chaturvedi, 'Indian judges concerned as government seeks bigger role in judicial appointments', *Reuters*, 19 January 2023.

xxii   wrote a sensational tell-all book about the family: The book was titled *Reminiscences of the Nehru Age*. Chand Joshi, 'Book review: Reminiscences of the Nehru Age by M.O. Mathai', 28 February 1978, *India Today*.

xxiii Mishra, also the national security advisor, was often called the de facto head: K. P. Nayar, 'Shakti Sinha was a politician by instinct, and a street fighter for causes he believed in', *moneycontrol.com*, 8 October 2021.

xxiii Manmohan Singh's PMO was 'unpretentious' and 'subdued': Vijayraj Singh, 'How Modi changed the PMO', *The Statesman*, 14 March 2019.

xxiii Narendra Modi governs through his PMO: Ashok Upadhyay, 'How many people work at PM Modi's office? This is what PMO said in RTI reply', *India Today*, 6 August 2021.

xxiii 'Yes, there are dossiers': Chandra Shekhar to author, 12 February 2000.

xxiii 'There are...files in the PMO on politicians': Bhuvnesh Chaturvedi to author, 30 November 1999.

xxv   Indira Gandhi used saam, daam, dand, bhed: Syed Mubin Zehra, 'Eternal Wisdom', The *Week*, 27 December 2015.

xxv   He enabled the opening of the locks: Sanaya Chandar, 'Rajiv Gandhi: The man who opened a can of worms at the Babri mosque', *Quartz*, 9 November 2019.

xxv   'king of Hindu hearts': Saisuresh Sivaswamy, 'Ram temple crowns Modi as first Hindu Hriday Samrat', *Rediff.com*, 4 August 2020.

xxv   made a case for reserving 27 per cent of jobs in government: 'Report of the Second Backward Classes Commission', First Part, Vol. I, 1980, Government of India.

xxv   The OBCs comprised 52 per cent of India's population: Ibid.

xxvi   Did Narasimha Rao collude with the BJP to bring down the Babri Masjid, as some believe: Jeevan Prakash Sharma, 'PM Narasimha Rao, Udupi Math Chief Conspired During Demolition Of Babri Masjid: BJP MP Sakshi Maharaj', *Outlook*, 10 November 2019; Sitapati, 'The Fall of Babri Masjid', *Half Lion*.

xxvi   the longest prime minister-in-waiting in India: A. B. Vajpayee to Krishan Kant, Rashmi Kant to author, March 2021.

xxvi   turned a dove in 1979: 'Vajpayee Opposed Nuclear Option In 79', *Financial Express*, 20 January 2004.

xxvii 'anchor of stability in Asia': Aziz Haniffa, 'India is anchor of stability in Asia: US lawmaker', *Rediff.com*, 26 July 2009.

xxvii 'Doctor sahib': IANS, 'Modi attacks Manmohan Singh in Parl, says note ban unparalleled in world', *Business Standard*, 9 February 2017.

xxvii 'half prime minister': Tavleen Singh, 'Caste in class', *Indian Express*, 15 January 2006.

xxvii Even a PM at the head of a coalition government is very powerful: 'Gujral Says He Wants To Keep His Reputation Intact', *Business Standard*, 27 January 2013.

CHAPTER 1: THE PRIME MINISTER WHO ROSE FROM THE ASHES: INDIRA GANDHI STAGES A COMEBACK

1   'I think I will just go to the hills and retire there': Anil Bali to author.

1   'After all, what are my needs?': Ibid.

1   She had even lost in her own constituency of Raebareli: Her constituency, Raebareli, was located in the heart of UP.

1   'empress of India': Diego Maiorano, 'The Empress's long-term legacies', *The Hindu*, 31 October 2014.

1   winning all 345 seats in the northern states: S. Venkat Narayan, 'Janata party in power', *India Today*, 21 December 2015.

1   On 22 March 1977, Indira Gandhi had resigned as prime minister: Henry Kamm, 'Ms. Gandhi Resigns as Premier after Her Party Loses Majority; Rivals Give a Pledge of Liberties', *New York Times*, 22 March 1977.

2   'Maybe, but then who will want to read my memoirs': Anil Bali to author

2   'We are winning 70 seats (out of 85) here': Akbar Ahmad 'Dumpy' to author.

2   'I couldn't sense the enthusiasm that used to be there earlier': Anil Bali to author, 24 November 2021, New Delhi.

2   On one occasion, when Dilip Kumar had come to campaign: Ravi Nair to author, 23 December 2021.

2   She had become 'paranoid': Anil Bali to author.

2   'contraption installed on the roof to prevent satellite surveillance of the house': Ibid.

3   'I don't know what to do about these carpets of mine': Ibid.

3   'It is not a courtesy they will extend to a former PM': Ibid.

3   The Janata government did not object: Ravi Nair to author, 1 January 2023.

3   'I am worried about Sanjay and his safety': Anil Bali to author.

3   'They will not allow him to live': Ibid.

3   There was no office car, no staff car: Debarghya Sanyal, 'Indira Gandhi in glimpses', Business Standard, 31 May 2016, citing K. P. Mathur, *The Unseen Indira Gandhi: Through Her Physicians Eyes*, New Delhi: Konark Publishers, 2015.

4   'Pupul, I have lost': Pupul Jayakar, *Indira Gandhi: A Biography*, New Delhi: Penguin Books, 1995, p. 320.

4 'a night of wild rejoicing': Ibid., p. 325.

4 Pande got the note approved by Indira: B. D. Pande, *In the Service of Free India: Memoir of a Civil Servant*, New Delhi: Speaking Tiger, 2021.

5 'I have done what I could. Now I want to live in peace': Kamal Nath to author.

5 'Yes, yes, yes,' Jatti said: P. N. Dhar, *Indira Gandhi, the 'Emergency', and Indian Democracy*, Delhi: Oxford University Press, 2000, p. 356.

5 'My colleagues and I accept the people's verdict unreservedly': Inder Malhotra, 'From the archive, 23 March 1977: Indira Gandhi loses election', *The Guardian*, 23 March 2015.

5 'Sanjay to quit active politics': A. N. Dhar, 'Mrs Gandhi Resigns', *Indian Express*, 23 March 1977.

5 'sorry if what I did in my personal capacity': Malhotra, 'From the archive, 23 March 1977: Indira Gandhi loses election', *The Guardian*.

5 'I heard this from Nagarkar himself': Ravi Nair to author, 23 December 2021.

6 'this had to be handled with care': Ibid.

6 'JP and the PM met Indira Gandhi': Ravi Nair to author, 13 December 2021.

6 'I want to retire to the Himalayas': Anil Bali to author.

6 'A gardener told us that the sandooks [trunks]': Ravi Nair to author, 13 December 2021.

6 decided to dismiss the Congress governments in nine states: Bhagwan D. Dua, 'Presidential Rule in India: A Study in Crisis Politics', *Asian Survey*, Vol. 19, No. 6, 1979, pp. 611–26; Ravi Nair, 'The Coup in India That Was or Never Was', *The Leaflet*, 12 January 2021.

6 Jatti decided to withhold his consent, not once but twice: Nair, 'The Coup in India That Was or Never Was'.

6 He let it be known to the government: William Borders, 'Constitutional Conflict Ends in India as Acting President Accepts Order Dissolving Nine State Legislatures', *New York Times*, 1 May 1977.

7 'bring troops to New Delhi to protect her in case she lost the elections': Javier Moro, *The Red Sari: A Dramatized Biography of Sonia Gandhi*, New Delhi: Lotus, 2015, p. 182.

7 'I have many armed paramilitary forces': Jayakar, *Indira Gandhi*, p. 318.

7 several ministers were left with a 'spooky' feeling that day: Ravi Nair to author, 13 December 2021.

7 He did not know what was being planned but wanted George 'to be careful': Nair, 'The Coup in India That Was or Never Was'.

7 George Fernandes sent Ravi Nair to take a 'chakkar' (round) of the 'security' areas of New Delhi: Ibid.

8 He came back and reported the 'all clear' to George Fernandes: Ibid.

8 'George got 200–300 of us socialist youth': Ibid.

8 The Janata Party came to power in seven of them: 'Janata Voted to Power in Seven States', *Indian Express*, 16 June 1977.

8 Desai was reluctant to prosecute her for the Emergency and its excesses: Ravi Nair to author, 23 December 2021.

8 By April 1977, the Janata government decided to set up eight commissions of enquiry: Christophe Jaffrelot and Pratinav Anil, *India's First Dictatorship; The Emergency, 1975–77*, New Delhi: Harper Collins Publishers, 2021, p. 432.

8 'excesses, malpractices and abuse of authority': William Borders, 'India Planning Court to Investigate All Charges Against Ousted Regime', *New York Times*, 8 April 1977.

9 she said it was the collective responsibility of the cabinet: Jaffrelot and Anil, *India's First Dictatorship*, pp. 434–35.

9 'information is power': Anil Bali to author, 13 September 2020.

9 Sanjay liked vegetarian food: Anil Bali to author.

9 It was a different Sanjay from the teenager who had been known for his wild and wayward ways: Jayakar, *Indira Gandhi*, p. 294.

9 'Do you know how to play the piano?': Ibid.

9 The rooms inside the green and white cottage: Ashok Mehrotra at the guest house, who had been with Mohan Meakin for fifty-seven years, to author om 26 September 2022, at Solan.

9 'I got him a monkey cap, so people would not recognize him': Anil Bali to author, 6 November 2020.

9 'Log maarne ke liye taiyyar thae': Anil Bali to author, 6 November 2011.

10 'If the Janata Party had left Sanjay alone': Kamal Nath to Neerja, 3 August 2021, New Delhi.

10 'Take that crying look off your face': Ambika Soni to author, 26 September 2020.

10 the 'sarkari sant' as he was called by the media: Ashok K. Singh, 'Demonetisation: Modi should know people might just vote him out', *dailyO*, 14 November 2016. Jaffrelot and Anil, *India's First Dictatorship*, p. 26.

10 He had called the Emergency an 'anushasan parva': Jaffrelot and Anil, *India's First Dictatorship*, p. 26.

10 'I never came for talks': 'Forty Years Ago, July 27, 1977: Morarji's Apology', *Indian Express*, 27 July 2017.

10 'Morarji Desai, Charan Singh, and Jagjivan Ram are big egoists': Anil Bali to author.

11 He challenged her victory in the Allahabad High Court: 'Raj Narain; the Only Politician to Defeat India's Indira Gandhi', *Los Angeles Times*, 2 January 1987.

11 hailed as a giant killer: Janardan Thakur, *Prime Ministers: Nehru to Vajpayee*, Mumbai: Eeshwar Publications, 1999, p. 187.

11 'Sanjay had matured after Mrs Gandhi went out of power': Jagmohan Malhotra to author.

11 In this, as with other moves Indira Gandhi made, Sanjay was the key architect: Anil Bali to author.

11 She could not forget that his exit from the Congress on 2 February 1977: William Borders,

11 Jayaprakash Narayan who had called her a 'dictator': 'Indira Gandhi meets Jayaprakash Narayan', *India Today*, 15 September 1977.

11 This was the man she had thrown into prison on 25 June 1975: Sandhya Ravishankar and ET Bureau, 'Sunday ET: 'A look at some unique letters that Jayaprakash Narayan wrote to Indira Gandhi when he was being kept in solitary confinement in prison', *Economic Times*, 29 June 2015.

12 Some RSS leaders had reached out to Sanjay through Kapil Mohan: Anil Bali to author; Subhas Arya to author.

12 There were five men who influenced Indira Gandhi's life: Ramachandra Guha, 'The Men in Indira's Life', *Times of India*, 13 May 2007.

12 But, it was her son, Sanjay Gandhi, who wielded the maximum power over his mother: B. N. Tandon, *PMO Diary*.

12 He was her 'blind spot': Dhar, *Indira Gandhi, the 'Emergency', and Indian Democracy*, p. 341.

12 she had 'very little control over him': Ibid., p. 329 and p. 341.

12 In the late 1950s, she tilted rightwards under the influence of Congress heavyweights: Ravi Visvesvaraya.

13 the rabidly anti-communist Sanjay Gandhi: 'From the archives | If Sanjay Gandhi had lived', *India Today*, 25 June 2018.

13 'Regulations, whose only virtue is restriction on production, do not make us more socialist': Lok Sabha Debates (English Version): Eighth Session (Seventh Lok Sabha)', Vol. XXIV, No. 8, New Delhi: Lok Sabha Secretariat, 1 March 1982, p. 382, available at <https://eparlib.nic.in/bitstream/123456789/3447/1/lsd_07_08_01-03-1982.pdf>.

13 'I don't really have a political philosophy. I can't say I believe in any ism': Welles Hangen, *After Nehru, Who?*, London: Rupert Hart-Davis, 1973, p. 181.

13 'religiosity and nationalism' were to become 'guiding tenets' of her premiership: Jaffrelot and Anil, *India's First Dictatorship, The Emergency*, p. 278.

13 'Hindu philosophy and a deep commitment to India': Ibid.

13 Though a 'de-ideologized' leader: Ibid., p. 284.

13 'Deeply ashamed, Indira never again panicked in the face of danger': Indira Gandhi, *Anand Bhavan Memories*, New Delhi: Indira Gandhi Memorial Trust, 2006, p. 71.

14 the three-year-old Indira sat on his lap as he refused to defend himself in court: Katherine Frank, *Indira: The Life of Indira Nehru Gandhi*, London: HarperCollins Publishers, 2001, p. 21.

14 'We believe that it is the inalienable right of the Indian people': Jawaharlal Nehru, *An Autobiography*, New Delhi: Jawaharlal Nehru Memorial Fund and Oxford University Press, p. 612, available at <https://archive.org/details/in.ernet.dli.2015.98834>.

14 Indira grew conscious of the many slights her mother had to suffer in the Nehru household: Sagarika Ghose, 'Revolution's Child', *Indira: India's Most Powerful Prime Minister*, New Delhi: Juggernaut, 2018.

14 'It was an extremely insecure childhood': Jayakar, *Indira Gandhi*, p. 36.

14 'I was part of the processions and meetings and everything that took place': Ibid.

14 'made possible a woman prime minister thirty-six years later': Ibid., p. 35.

15 'shadow of her husband': Promilla Kalhan, 'A New Relationship', *Kamala Nehru: An Intimate Biography*, Delhi: Vikas Publishing House, 1973, p. 45.

15 'he was unstable': Frank, *Indira: The Life of Indira Nehru Gandhi*, p. 111.

15 'was always there for me ': Ibid., p. 114.

15 Feroze was 'loud, boisterous and a great user of expletives. Nehru was soft-spoken, subtle and did not swear even when enraged': Frank, *Indira: The Life of Indira Nehru Gandhi*, p. 169.

15 'Only for my or Nehru's eyes': Aflatoon Desai, Narayan Desai's son, to author, telephonic interview from Varanasi, 17 July 2021.

15 'Meet me at Baroda station': Ibid.

16 'It was my moral responsibility to reach this to you': Ibid.

16 Indira and Feroze were married on Ram Navmi day on 26 March 1942: Frank, *Indira*, p. 176.

16 Gandhi called the proposal 'a post-dated cheque on a failing bank': Ibid., p. 79.

16 'show them his garden, his hunting trophies, his fishing tackle': Bertil Falk, *Feroze Gandhi: The Forgotten Gandhi*, Roli Books, 2016.

17 'Sanjay and Rajiv...counted their grandfather among the major factors in the breakup of their family life': Vinod Mehta, *The Sanjay Story: From Anand Bhavan To Amethi*, New Delhi: HarperCollins, 2012, p. 55.

17 he blamed his mother for the 'neglect and death of his father': Jayakar, *Indira Gandhi*, p. 293.

17 'People do not realize how much Papu depended on me': Ibid., p. 168.

17 Many saw Indira as a convenient conduit to her father: Frank, *Indira*, pp. 236–37.

17 It was also the first display of Indira's 'ruthlessness': Ibid., p. 253.

17 'The unrest in Kerala...touched a raw nerve in her': Ibid.

17 Indira had clashed with him over the bifurcation of the state of Bombay: Ibid., p. 256.

18 'a saint who had strayed into politics': Thakur, *Prime Ministers*, p. 104.

18 She saw herself as a 'tough politician': Ibid.

18 'Mera baap sant thaa, main nahin hoon': Related by I. K. Gujral, part of Indira Gandhi's 'kitchen cabinet' at the time, to journalist Qurban Ali, who told the author in a telephonic interview, 12 June 2022.

18 joined hands with the 'Syndicate' of leaders opposed to her: The Syndicate was a term used for a group of leaders in the Congress who exercised an unyielding grip over the party after Nehru's death and controlled many of the state Congress committees. It included K. Kamaraj from Tamil Nadu, S. K. Patil from Maharashtra, Atulya Ghosh from West Bengal, Biju Patnaik from Odisha, and S. Nijalingappa from Karnataka.

18 Nehru was mildly 'disapproving': Frank, *Indira*, p. 250.

18 'Do you think this government can survive': Ibid., p. 281.
18 'Lal Bahadur Shastri has died of a massive heart attack': I. K. Gujral, *Matters of Discretion: An Autobiography*, New Delhi: Hay House, 2017, p. 38.
18 'Mrs Gandhi wants you to come over immediately': Ibid., p. 39.
19 'Mrs Gandhi was quite excited': Ibid.
19 They told her she could be 'elected the prime minister': Ibid.
19 there sat 'the hat trick' from Allahabad: A political wag present there pointed to Indira Gandhi, and remarked to journalist Nikhil Chakravartty that there is 'the hat trick' from Allahabad. Also in Frank, *Indira*, p. 285.
19 She won 355 votes against Desai's 169 votes: Frank, *Indira*, p. 292.
19 'It was a brilliant public relations exercise': Natwar Singh.
19 'this chokri': Chandra, Mukherjee, and Mukherjee, *India Since Independence: Revised and Updated*.
19 'goongi gudiya': Frank, *Indira*, p. 296.
19 'an innocuous person': '1966: India's food production went down again due to monsoon failure', 2 July 2007, *India Today*.
20 'get both food and foreign exchange without appearing to ask for them': Frank, *Indira*, p. 296.
20 'new, bouffant hairstyle, full make-up and jewellery': Ibid., pp. 296–97.
20 Johnson had said he wanted to ensure that 'no harm comes to this girl': Ibid., p. 297.
20 'whirl around the dance floor with the American president at a White House banquet': Ibid.
20 'It was L. K. Jha, her principal secretary, who...influenced her decision on devaluation': Natwar Singh to author.
20 'A big man's daughter, a small man's mistake': Frank, *Indira*, p. 299.
20 She started to attack the US's Vietnam policy as 'imperialist aggression': Ibid.
20 He put the wheat supply to India under the PL 480 programme: In 1954, US President Dwight D. Eisenhower had signed into law the Agricultural Trade Development and Assistance Act, popularly known as Public Law 480 or Food for Peace programme. PL 480 enabled 'friendly countries' to buy food from the US with their own currency, saving their foreign exchange. It enabled the US, which used the programme as a foreign policy tool, also to get rid of its surplus grain.
21 'New Indian leader comes begging': '1966: India's food production went down again due to monsoon failure', *India Today*.
21 This eventually led to the Green Revolution: The green revolution in India led to increased food production, using high yielding varieties of seeds, particularly for rice and wheat, double cropping annually, and the use of chemical fertilisers and pesticides.
21 'Yes, of course, yes,' P. N. Haksar replied: Ramesh, *Intertwined Lives*.
21 he was a local guardian to her sons: Ibid.
21 'most powerful bureaucrat in the country post-independence': Vasudha Venugopal, 'Indira Gandhi was the leader but sootradhar of 1971 was PN Haksar: Jairam Ramesh', *Economic Times*, 15 June 2018.
21 considered the 'father of the prime minister's office': Bhuvnesh Chaturvedi to author.
21 She circulated a note at the All India Congress Committee (AICC): Ramesh, *Intertwined Lives*, p. 139.
21 'one of the best kept secrets of the Government of India': Natwar Singh quoted in Ghose, *Indira*, p. 109.
22 'a vote of conscience': Ramachandra Guha, *India after Gandhi: The History of the World's Largest Democracy*, London: Pan Books, 2012, p. 438.
22 'indiscipline': Frank, *Indira*, pp. 316–17.
22 These were tax free privileges and allowances made to 278 princes: Ibid., p. 323.
22 It was Haksar who devised the nuts and bolts of the strategy: Ramesh, *Intertwined Lives*, pp. 206–207; Natwar Singh to author, 29 May 2022.
22 India trained and supported the Mukti Bahini: Ramesh, *Intertwined Lives*, p. 209.
22 'Kashmir mafia': Natwar Singh to author, 29 May 2022.
23 She was at her 'combative... best' and 'did all the talking with Nixon': Ramesh, *Intertwined Lives*, p. 228.
23 Atal Bihari Vajpayee hailed her as 'Durga': Vajpayee later denied it though Congress leader Bhuvnesh Chaturvedi disclosed during the course of a conversation in New Delhi with me that he had been at the meeting where Vajpayee had called Indira Gandhi 'Durga'.
23 the equation between 'Induji' and 'Babooji': Ramesh, *Intertwined Lives*, pp. 78, 82, 83.
23 he headed Maruti, a project to build a small 'people's car': Sharmistha Mukherjee, '40 Years Ago... and now: How the people's car was born, and how it stayed that way', *Business Standard*, 19 November 2014.
23 'You will have to make up your mind': Natwar Singh to author.
23 The rift had been in the making for a while: Ramesh, *Intertwined Lives*, p. 381.
23 'He used to say that the communists should be thrown in the sea': Anil Bali to author.
23 'silent critic': Ramesh, *Intertwined Lives*.
23 'ideological compass': Ibid.
24 'As in war, so in peace, the art always lies in either winning over the enemy': Ibid., p. 387.
24 And she signed the letter 'Indira Gandhi': Ibid., p. 388.
24 She had actually wanted a girl when she was pregnant with Sanjay: Anil Bali to author.
24 he used to break flower pots in his grandfather's house: Ibid.
24 'Rajiv was courteous, well behaved, a fair student; Sanjay was rebellious, destructive': Jayakar, *Indira Gandhi*, p. 294.
25 However, her did not complete the three-year training programme: Mehta, *The Sanjay Story*, p. 65.
25 The chief minister of Haryana, Bansi Lal, helped with 297 acres of land: J. Anthony Lukas, 'India is as Indira does', *New York Times*, 4 April 1976.

25   Fifty thousand cars were to be produced—10,000 by October 1973, 25,000 by 1974: Michael Henderson, *Experiment with Untruth: India under Emergency*, Delhi, Bombay, Calcutta, Madras: The Macmillan Company of India, 1977, p. 14.

25   On 14 December 1983, when a little white Maruti 800 rolled out of a factory in Gurgaon: Anil Sasi, 'Maruti Suzuki 800: The Car With No Name', *Financial Express*, 23 February 2014.

25   A little after 6 a.m., she got word that D. P. Dhar had died: Dhar, *Indira Gandhi, the `Emergency', and Indian Democracy*, p. 300.

26   'The Allahabad judgment has come and the Prime Minister has been unseated': Ibid.

26   The court held her guilty under the Representation of the People Act, 1951: Satya Prakash, 'The court verdict that prompted Indira Gandhi to declare Emergency', *Hindustan Times*, 26 June 2015.

26   Indira Gandhi moved between the two groups, looking 'uncommunicative and withdrawn': Ibid., p. 301.

26   'The day the Allahabad judgment came': Karan Singh to author.

26   'She did not say a word': Ibid.

26   There were two groups who did not want her to resign: Ibid.

27   'However, Justice Sinha's strong conscience did not permit him to take the bait': Prakash, 'The court verdict that prompted Indira Gandhi to declare Emergency'.

27   The Congress was trounced by the Janata Morcha: Ravi Visvesvaraya Sharada Prasad, '12 June 1975: The Day That Changed India, Shook Indira', *OPEN*, 13 June 2022.

27   The president signed the Emergency decree at 11.45 p.m.: Coomi Kapoor, 'Ruler alone is not accountable, everyone who succumbs to authority is no less guilty', *Indian Express*, 25 June 2020.

27   The meeting was held at '5 or 6 a.m.': Pande, *In the Service of Free India*, p. 140.

27   The cabinet ratified it the next morning: Technically speaking, the business rules, to govern the functioning of the government and its various departments, allowed the prime minister to take a decision and get it ratified by the cabinet afterwards. According to Rule 7 of the Government of India (Transaction of Business) rules, cases listed under the second schedule, including those relating to a proclamation of emergency, must be approved by the cabinet. However, rule 12 of TOB states that the 'PM may, in any case or classes of cases, permit or condone a departure from these rules to the extent he deems necessary.' The PM can take a decision on behalf of the Cabinet subject to post facto approval. See Montek Singh Ahluwalia, 'IN THE SERVICE OF FREE INDIA: MEMOIR OF A CIVIL SERVANT by Late B. D. Pande', IIC Programmes, 15 March 2022, available on YouTube at <https://youtu.be/qu8vAQKyuwg>.

27   'Sanjay was an important influence in her decision to opt for the Emergency': Karan Singh to author.

28   'Simhasan khali karo ki janata aati hai': '"Singhasan Khali Karo ki janata aati hai"- Dinkar and JP's call for "Total Revolution"', *The Leaflet*, 26 June 2020.

28   'illegal and immoral' orders of the government: Amrith Lal, '40 years on, those 21 months of Emergency', *The Indian Express*, 20 July 2015.

28   'Vinash kale vipreet buddhi': Thakur, *Nehru to Vajpayee*, p. 105.

28 . 'You have been calling me a dictator when I was not. Now, yes, I am.': Henderson, *Experiment with Untruth*, p. 7.

29   Mukherjee, however, was to say later that the Emergency 'could have been avoided': PTI, 'Emergency could have been avoided: Pranab Mukherjee', *Economic Times*, 21 May 2019.

29   'The All India Radio is not projecting Indira Gandhi enough': I. K. Gujral to author, New Delhi, 2 July 2003.

29   'The I&B is no more your cup of tea': Ibid.

29   'Sanjay wants to send you as ambassador to Australia': B. N. Uniyal to author.

29   'Youth Congress chala sakoge kya?': Tariq Anwar to author.

29   'Which way do we go now?': Santosh Bharatiya to author.

30   'Talk less and work more': 'July 6, Forty Years Ago: Talk less, work more', *Indian Express*, 6 July 2015.

30   He embarked on pitiless 'beautification drives': John Dayal and Ajoy Bose, 'The Bulldozers', *For Reasons of State: Delhi Under Emergency*, New Delhi: Penguin Random House, 2018.

30   Bulldozers razed 150 pukka houses: Ibid.

30   They were relocated 24 kilometres away: Ibid.

30   According to government figures, more than 7 million men were sterilized: Lynn C. Landman, 'Birth Control in India: The Carrot and the Rod?', *Family Planning Perspectives*, Vol. 9, No. 3, 1977, pp. 101–10.

30   There were cases of farmers being sterilized under duress: Dayal and Bose, 'The Days of the Long Knives', *For Reasons of State: Delhi Under Emergency*.

31   'What a mistake it has been to go in for elections': Akbar Ahmad 'Dumpy' to author, 22 January 2021.

31   'Sanjay was driving a Matador and I was sitting': Ibid.

31   'But Indira Gandhi was adamant': Ibid.

31   'I don't give the Janata government three years': Ibid.

32   despite being told by the IB that she would win 340 seats, she knew she would lose: Ravi Visvesvaraya Sharada Prasad, 'Why Did Indira Gandhi Call for Elections in January 1977?', *OPEN*, 23 January 2022.

32   'obliquely hinted to my father': Ibid.

32   'lose the elections badly, and that she was worried about her son Sanjay Gandhi': Ravi Visvesvaraya Sharada Prasad, 'The inside story of why Indira Gandhi called the 1977 elections', *Hindustan Times*, 19 March 2021.

32   'Yeh gore logon se likhwao': Mohan Guruswamy, who worked closely with Chandra Shekhar in the Janata Party, to author, telephonic interview, 23 May 2022.

32   The World Bank was impressed by her handling of industrial relations: Jaffrelot and Anil, *India's First Dictatorship, The Emergency*, p. 415.

32	'Right action is necessary': Jayakar, *Indira Gandhi*, p. 312.
32	'It was on October 28, (1976) that a frail movement': Ibid.
33	'Will you hold the elections ultimately by February 1977?': Gautam Bajaj to author, Paunar Ashram, Wardha, Maharashtra, 8 November 2022. Gautam Bajaj was the son of veteran Gandhian Radhakrishna Bajaj, related to Jamnalal Bajaj who Gandhi used to look upon as his fifth son.
33	'Indira Gandhi had respect and affection for Vinobaji': Ibid.
33	'It was a daring attempt (by Sanjay) to bypass the Prime Minister: Dhar, *Indira Gandhi, the 'Emergency', and Indian Democracy*, p. 329.
33	'impatient for the driver's seat': Ibid.
33	'It was apparent to me...that Indira Gandhi was...afraid of her son': Ibid.
34	'hear a single word critical of him': Inder Malhotra, 'The abrupt end of Emergency', *Indian Express*, 4 August 2014.
34	'Get rid of this election nonsense...just make our sister (Indira) president for life': 'From the archives I If Sanjay Gandhi had lived', *India Today*.
34	This was on 5 November 1976: Malhotra, 'The abrupt end of Emergency'.
35	'one party dictatorship under the cover of Constitution': Samar Mukherji, speaking in the Lok Sabha on 1 September 1976, quoted in Michael Henderson, *Experiments with Untruth: India under Emergency*, Delhi: Macmillan, 1977, p. 181.
35	'That is when she started thinking of elections': Malhotra, 'The abrupt end of Emergency'.
35	'You are going to be put in the cell next to Charan Singh': Satyapal Malik to author.
35	'He was not averse to the idea': Ibid.
35	'So, others like Biju Patnaik, Piloo Mody, Radhakrishnan': Ibid.
35	Only on one occasion, did he get carried away and gave a 'teevra bhashan': Ibid. The original speech is available as part of the Charan Singh Archives, <www.charansingh.org/archives/historical-speech-hindi-uttar-pradesh-vidhan-sabha>.
36	Besides Charan Singh and him, there were Om Mehta and Mohammed Yunus: C.G.K. Reddy, 'Appendix 5', *Baroda Dynamite Conspiracy: The Right to Rebel*, New Delhi: Vikas Books, 1977.
36	They agreed to 'behave responsibly': Satyapal Malik to author.
36	He was able to move out occasionally under watch: Ram Bahadur Rai to author, 4 July 2022.
37	'There is no question of expressing regret': Ibid.
37	JP had repeatedly called upon Opposition leaders to form a unified party: Ibid.
37	By this time, the RSS had offered to cooperate with the government: A. G. Noorani, *The RSS: A Menace to India*, New Delhi: LeftWord Books, 2019, pp. 488–98.
37	'Let's be clear, Indira Gandhi opted for elections': Natwar Singh to author.
37	On 1 January 1977, Dhar invited Swaminathan home: Dhar, *Indira Gandhi, the 'Emergency', and Indian Democracy*, p. 349.
37	That evening he sent Dhar a bottle of whisky: Ibid., p. 350.
37	The date for the election, however, was decided 'by the Prime Minister's astrologers': Malhotra, 'The abrupt end of Emergency'.
38	'Om Mehta told me that Indira Gandhi wanted to legitimize the Emergency': Satyapal Malik.
38	She also wanted him to 'serve a period of apprenticeship': Dhar, *Indira Gandhi, the 'Emergency', and Indian Democracy*, p. 329.
38	She wanted to project him as 'the rising son of India': Thakur, *Prime Ministers*, p. 119.
38	'Our thunder has been stolen': Dhar, *Indira Gandhi, the 'Emergency', and Indian Democracy*, p. 345.
38	Leaders of the four largest outfits of the Opposition: Ravi Visvesvaraya Sharada Prasad, 'How Morarji Desai Became Prime Minister in 1977', *OPEN*, 24 April 2022.
39	'Jab se election announce hua hai, chaprasi theek se paani tak nahin pila rahe hain': Pran Sabharwal to Qurban Ali, who shared this with the author, 12 June 2021, New Delhi.
39	'When you stifle the flow of information to the people': K. S. Komireddi, *Malevolent Republic: A Short History of the New India*, Chennai: Context, 2019, p. 22.
39	'No DA, no vote': Dayal and Bose, 'The Denouement', *For Reasons of State: Delhi Under Emergency*.
39	'Where is your son?': Ibid.
39	The Janata Party, as already noted, won 298 Lok Sabha seats: 'Statistical Report on General Elections, 1977 to the Sixth Lok Sabha: Volume I', Delhi: Election Commission of India, 1978, available at <https://eci.gov.in/files/file/4116-general-election-1977-vol-i-ii/>.
39	Jagjivan Ram's Congress for Democracy (CFD), which notched up 28 seats: Ravi Visvesvaraya Sharada Prasad, 'How Morarji Desai outwitted Jagjivan Ram and Charan Singh', *OPEN*, 22 March 2021.
39	The Indira Congress won 154 seats: 'Statistical Report on General Elections, 1977 to the Sixth Lok Sabha: Volume I'.
41	JP might not 'survive for more than two months': Sandhya Ravishankar, 'Sunday ET: A look at some unique letters that Jayaprakash Narayan wrote to Indira Gandhi when he was being kept in solitary confinement in prison', *Economic Times*, 29 June 2015.
41	When his health continued to worsen, his detention order was revoked: Henderson, *Experiment with Untruth*, p. 31.
41	'A number of my friends have expressed a doubt, which I share': Rama Goyal (ed.), *Saving India from Indira: Untold Story of the Emergency: Memoirs of J. P. Goyal*, New Delhi: Rupa Publications, 2019.
41	'total revolution': Lalan Tiwari, Democracy and Dissent: (a Case Study of the Bihar Movement—1974–75), Delhi: Mittal Publications, 1987, p. 260.

41   It had started as the Nav Nirman Andolan by students in Gujarat: Henderson, *Experiment with Untruth*, p. 3.
41   'What, now?': Quoted in an unpublished study on the Chattra Yuva Sangharsh Vahini, by Neerja Chowdhury, for Vishwa Yuvak Kendra, 1980.
42   'Suddenly we came across this potli': Kumar Prashant to author, 16 January 2021, telephonic conversation.
42   'I remember lines like "kuchh log apne aapko bahut superior samajhte hain"': Ibid.
42   'Tum bhagyashali ho ki tum se barabari se baat karte hain: Ibid.
43   She was trying to show her complete unconcern about the matter: Ibid.
43   At this meeting, Indira Gandhi asked JP to 'help (her)': Ibid.
44   'Kaise aana hua?': Kumar Prashant to author, 16 January 2021, telephonic conversation.
44   'It's nonsense to say that he did not want office': Jayakar, *Indira Gandhi*, p. 391.
44   'The PM told Mr Narayan…that he needed somebody to point out where he was going wrong': Ravi Visvesvaraya Sharada Prasad, 'Nehru wanted Jayaprakash Narayan as his political successor, not Indira Gandhi', *The Print*, 27 May 2020.
44   'The Prime Minister asked Mr Narayan, cajoled him, then begged him': Ibid.
45   The Praja Socialist Party (PSP) discussed the proposal: Ibid.
45   At a meeting of the PSP at Betul—where he was accused of being power hungry: Qurban Ali to author.
45   'right aims and the right means to achieve them': Dhar, *Indira Gandhi, the 'Emergency', and Indian Democracy*, p. 246.
45   'confused': Jayakar, *Indira Gandhi*, p. 391.
45   'But Indira Gandhi had also tapped the phones of all the Opposition leaders': Kumar Prashant to author.
45   a 'personal' visit: 'August 15, 1977, Forty Years Ago: Indira Calls On JP', *Indian Express*, 15 August 2017.
45   'Jitna tumhara bhootkaal ujjwal raha hai, utna hee tumhara bhavishya bhee ujjwal ho': Ibid.
45   'Ghar aye ko dua dee jaati hai ya bad-dua deni chahiye': Kumar Prashant to author.
45   He had given the Janata government one year to perform: Ajay Singh, 'I am completely disappointed with the Janata Party's performance: Jayaprakash Narayan', *India Today*, 31 March 1978.
46   'I am now not fighting a political battle': Kumar Prashant to author, telephonic interview, 16 January 2021.
46   'I saw him put his hand on her shoulder': Kumar Prashant to author, 27 January 2021.
46   'Safalta aur vifalta ki paribhashayen bhinn hain meri': From 'Shodh ki manzilaen', a poem written by Jayaprakash Narayan in Chandigarh while in jail, in August 1975.
46   'Sanjay, I, and Surendra Singh were playing badminton': Akbar Ahmad 'Dumpy' to author.
47   She had been tipped off that she was going to be arrested: Ravi Nair to author, December 2021.
47   'Nuremberg-style trial': Thakur, *Prime Ministers*, p. 158.
47   'We must take action only according to the law': 'Operation blunder? (Oct 31, 1977)', *India Today*, 21 May 2013.
47   'Handcuff me,' she shouted at Superintendent of Police: Thakur, *Prime Ministers*, p. 175.
47   'King five to queen four, king five to queen four': 'Indira Gandhi's arrest seen as Janata Party's first major political blunder', *India Today*, 2 April 2015.
47   'Madam…it is not necessary for the CBI to serve a copy of the warrant': Thakur, *Prime Ministers*, p. 175.
47   N. K. Singh had been chosen personally by Home Minister Charan Singh: 'Indira Gandhi's arrest seen as Janata Party's first major political blunder'.
48   'Why should I?' she countered: Thakur, *Prime Ministers*, p. 175.
48   Then suddenly, her muscular, moustachioed bodyguard lay down in front of the jeep: Ibid., p. 176.
48   'The CBI were taking her towards Bhatkal (Lake) in Haryana': Akbar Ahmad 'Dumpy' to author.
48   'they have sabotaged me once again': 'Indira Gandhi's arrest seen as Janata Party's first major political blunder'.
48   'These are not the cases on which we should have taken action now': Ibid.
49   By arresting her, Charan Singh thought he would become the hero: Thakur, *Prime Ministers*, p. 174.
49   'Ab aap Raj Narain se mil lo': Anil Bali to author.
49   'Sanjay had become very close to Kapil Mohan': Kamal Nath to author.
49   he often called himself Hanuman to Charan Singh's Ram: Chandan Mitra, '"Revolving door politics became the hallmark of Indian democracy"', *India Today*, 26 December 2005.
49   'he was seen as a terror by the British in the 1942 Quit India movement': Anand Kumar to author, telephonic interview, 22 June 2022.
49   'Follow Chaudhary sahib': Sunil Sethi, 'The importance of being Raj Narain', *India Today*, 31 August 1979.
49   implementing the recommendations of the state appointed Mungeri Lal Commission: The Mungeri Lal Commission in Bihar, which gave its report in 1977, had suggested that OBCs be divided in two categories: Extremely Backward Classes (EBCs), which also included weaker sections amongst the Muslims, and the Backward Classes.
50   'a collection of impotent men': Inder Malhotra, 'The Disintegration of Janata', *Indian Express*, 15 September 2014.
50   'They were like brothers': Pushpa Mohan to author.
50   'Raj Narain used to often phone me and say': Ibid.
51   'What does the future hold for me?': Qurban Ali to author, telephonic interview, 22 April 2022.
51   He deliberately cultivated a rustic image to 'declass' himself: Dr Anand Kumar, former professor of Sociology at JNU, to author, 22 June 2022, telephonic conversation.

51 'Bol dena hum Raja Balwant Singh ke khaandan se hain': Dr Anand Kumar to author, telephonic interview, 22 June 2022. He was at a meeting in Varanasi on 1 April 1980 when Raj Narain said this after he was given the news that he had been expelled from the BLD by Charan Singh.

51 'You put ittar but spread bad odour about me': Qurban Ali to author, New Delhi, 7 February 2023.

51 'I would often sit outside the room along with Kapil Mohan': Akbar Ahmad 'Dumpy' to author.

52 'Kapilji would meet his guests and leave them alone to talk in his study room': Pushpa Mohan to author.

52 'Once we had the annaparashan (first food given a child) ceremony of our nephew': Ibid.

52 'a Bolshevik move': Thakur, Prime Ministers, p. 156.

52 'wicked as Cleopatra': David Selbourne, 'Charan Singh and Cleopatra', Sunday, Vol. 7, Issue 15, 2 September 1979.

52 'He used to hate her': Satyapal Malik to author.

53 'Colonel (V. R. Mohan) bahut pareshan thae': Pushpa Mohan to author.

53 The 'all powerful Sanjay' had helped Kapil Mohan in 'so many ways': Subhash Arya to author.

53 'I don't want to spell this out': Ibid.

53 'I brought the car to Kapil Mohan myself': Anil Bali to author.

53 'Shri Indira Gandhi maen mati nahin hai': Anil Bali to author.

54 'He will have the support of the Congress (I)': Jayakar, Indira Gandhi, p. 384.

54 'Aap bhi ban sakte ho PM,' Sanjay had held out a carrot: Anil Bali to author.

54 'No one is above the law': 'Pride and Punishment, New York Times, 20 December 1978.

55 'I want you to give your time to it, now that you are back': Anand Kumar to author.

55 Then he introduced Anand Kumar to them as having just 'returned from America': Ibid.

55 'He called on me twice.... But I did not discuss politics with him': Madhu Limaye, Janata Party Experiment: An Insider's Account of Opposition Politics, 1977-80, B. R. Publishing Corporation, 1994, p. 498.

56 'Sir give this man a licence to manufacture small cars because he learnt it in his mother's womb': Jaffrelot and Anil, India's First Dictatorship, p. 61.

56 it charged Sanjay and Information and Broadcasting minister V. C. Shukla: Dilip Bobb, 'Kissa Kursi Ka case: Supreme Court sends Sanjay Gandhi to 30 days judicial custody', India Today, 31 May 1978.

56 The Supreme Court was to acquit Sanjay and Shukla of the charges in April 1980: Stuart Auerbach, 'Indian Supreme Court Acquits Gandhi's Son Of Criminal Charges', Washington Post, 12 April 1980.

56 'Babuji dekh laenge garhi ko': Anil Bali to author.

57 The FIR Suresh Ram filed that day in the Kashmere Gate police station: Farzand Ahmed, Arul B. Louis, and Prabhu Chawla, '"Abduction" of Defence Minister Jagjivan Ram's son and his girl friend rocks the nation', India Today, 15 September 1978.

57 Suresh Ram because he was involved in all kinds of 'nefarious activities': Anil Bali to author.

57 They knew he used to take photographs with a 'Polaroid camera': K. C. Tyagi to author, 4 August 2020, New Delhi.

57 They wanted to lay their hands on the photos: Anil Bali to author.

57 As soon as Narain's boys managed to lay their hands on photographs: Editor Khushwant Singh would say of India's first politico-sex scam—if 'Kamasutra contained 64 poses then this one includes nine of them'. See G. Pramod Kumar, '38 Years After Maneka Gandhi Published India's First Sex Scandal Photos, A Similar Fate Has Befallen Her Son Varun', HuffPost, 24 October 2016.

57 'Babuji Raj Narain ko manane aaye thae': Anil Bali to author.

57 Jagjivan Ram obviously 'wanted to strike a bargain': Ibid.

57 Jagjivan Ram and Narain were inside for 'about twenty minutes': Ibid.

57 'Main PM banane wala hoon, kisi ko mantri banana ho toh batana?': Ibid.

58 'Take these photographs to Sanjay. Now. Immediately': Ibid.

58 'I told him about the accident and handed him the photographs': Ibid.

58 'And you tell Kapil Mohan to keep Raj Narain under control': Ibid.

58 'Ek aur bete nae apne baap ko duba diya.': Rashmi Kant to author, 6 August 2020, New Delhi.

58 'Ab meri izzat apke haathon maen hai': Ibid.

59 'They used to hold secret meetings at 6, Krishna Menon Marg': Ibid.

59 'They would decide the time of the rendezvous at their previous meeting': Ibid.

59 'It was later that he told me the whole story': Ibid.

60 'I know you are doing your job, I will tell you what we discussed': Rashmi Kant to author.

60 'Ram was crying copiously': Saeed Naqvi to author, 23 May 2022, telephonic conversation.

60 The article was headlined, 'The Real Story': Dilip Bobb, 'Surya magazine's "expose" on the sex scandal involving Jagjivan Ram's errant son', India Today, 31 October 1978.

60 The court was finally to acquit Om Pal Singh and Tyagi: Samarpal Singh, who worked closely with Charan Singh and was rooming with Om Pal Singh at the time, to author, 9 August 2020.

60 a plan by 'Charan Singh and his henchman (Raj Narain)' to entrap Jagjivan Ram's only son, Suresh Ram in a 'sordid sex scandal': Ajoy Bose, 'The Unhappy Medium', India Today, 5 February 2022.

61 For six days Indira Gandhi's position had looked 'precarious': Jaffrelot and Anil, India's First Dictatorship, The Emergency, p. 301.

61 The IB had told her that she enjoyed the support of only 191 of the 350 Congress members: Ibid.

61 'The idea was to prevent a split in the Janata Party': Rajmohan Gandhi to author.

61 'A Chamar can never be the prime minister of this country': Thakur, Prime Ministers, p. 132.

61 'Kissi bhi keemat par Jagjivan Ram pradhan mantri nahin banane chahiye': Anil Bali to author.

62   'Main toot gaya hoon': Rashmi Kant to author, 12 September 2020, New Delhi. He had heard this from
      his father Krishan Kant, who had been told this by Jagjivan Ram.
62   'My sense was that Indira Gandhi turned to this dharamkaram (religion) really for Sanjay': Anil Bali to
      author.
62   astrologers had warned her that Sanjay's horoscope showed 'a lifeline cut short': Ibid.
62   In 1980, she did it in the name of God: Jayakar, *Indira Gandhi*, p. 399.
62   But politicians and religious leaders convinced her: Frank, *Indira*, p. 276.
62   'seen as a Hindu first and a Hindu last': Anil Bali to author.
62   After she lost power, she visited temples, big and small: Jayakar, *Indira Gandhi*, p. 359; Frank, *Indira*, pp.
      430–31.
62   In October 1977, she went to the Ambaji temple in Gujarat: Ghose, *Indira*.
62   She went to Vaishno Devi: 'December 18, 1977, Forty Years Ago: Maruti probe', *Indian Express*, 18
      December 2017.
62   she took part in the Kumbh Mela in 1977: Shyamlal Yadav and Seema Chishti, 'Explained: What's in
      Allahabad's name', *Indian Express*, 16 October 2018.
62   She visited the parmacharya, the most senior shankaracharya of Kanchi: Nambi Marthandam, 'Indira
      Gandhi's two-day tour of Tamil Nadu ends in a grand fiasco', *India Today*, 30 November 1977.
63   'My family is in distress,' Indira Gandhi told him: Ibid.
63   Those in Kanchipuram believed that Indira Gandhi decided on the hand as the Congress symbol because
      the Parmacharya: Geetha Venkataramanan, 'Time stands still here', *Times of India*, 26 March 2015.
63   Others feel she changed her party's symbol from the cow and calf to the hand: Arjumand Bano, 'Deoria
      voters credit Deoraha Baba's blessings for Indira's win in 1980', *Times of India*, 29 March 2019.
63   Anandamayi Ma gave her a rare ekmukhi rudraksh: Jayakar, *Indira Gandhi*, p. 341.
63   Every day, 'there would be an offering of 108 flowers': Anil Bali to author.
63   Her friend Pupul Jayakar was disturbed to see her become more and more superstitious: Jayakar, *Indira
      Gandhi*, p. 418.
63   Indira asked a pregnant Maneka to retire to her room: Jayakar, *Indira Gandhi*, p. 399.
63   'Mrs Gandhi conducted a mahamrityunjay paath at her home for a month': Satyapal Malik to author.
63   'Mrs Gandhi was very religious': Karan Singh to author.
64   'Indira Gandhi bahut badi Hindu hai': Anil Bali to author. Bali had heard this from Deoras.
64   'Balasaheb Deoras and his brother saw in Indira Gandhi a potential leader of the Hindus': Ibid.
64   'The biggest measure of credit for this achievement goes to you': A. G. Noorani, *The RSS and the BJP: A
      Division of Labour*, Vol. 3, New Delhi: LeftWord Books, 2000, p. 40.
64   In 1974, she won the RSS's admiration again for exploding the nuclear device: Bernard Weinraub, 'India
      Becomes 6th Nation to Set Off Nuclear Device', *New York Times*, 19 May 1974.
64   he would often refer to himself as 'a communist within the RSS': Nilanjan Mukhopadhyay, *The RSS: Icons
      of the Indian Right*, New Delhi: Tranquebar, 10 April 2019, p. 258.
64   Balasaheb Deoras was impressed, initially, with the 'discipline' it sought to inculcate: 'RSS backed Indira
      Gandhi's Emergency: Ex-IB chief', *India Today*, 21 September 2015.
64   Five days after the Emergency, Mrs Gandhi jailed Balasaheb Deoras: A. G. Noorani, 'RSS & Emergency',
      Frontline, 3 August 2018.
64   she banned the RSS and twenty-three other organizations on 4 July 1975: 'Imposition of Emergency, 1975:
      The Build up', *Indian Express*, 20 July 2015.
65   it would try and effect 'a compromise' with Indira Gandhi: Ravi Visvesvaraya, 'The story of how RSS
      leaders deserted Jayaprakash and the resistance during Indira's Emergency', *The Print*, 25 June 2020.
65   'Your address (on 15 August 1975 from Red Fort) was timely and balanced': Madhukar Dattatraya
      Deoras, *Hindu Sangathan aur Sattavaadi Rajneeti*, Noida: Jagriti Prakashan, 1997, p. 270, cited in Shamsul
      Islam, 'On 45th Anniversary of The Emergency In India: Contemporary Documents Prove RSS Leadership
      Kowtowed To Indira Gandhi', *Frontier Weekly*, 26 June 2020.
65   '(The) Sangh has no relation with these (Bihar and Gujarat) movements': Ibid.
65   'I beg you to try to remove the wrong assumptions of the PM about RSS': Ibid.
65   'detrimental to internal security and public peace': Noorani, 'RSS & Emergency'.
65   'it was also Bal Thackeray who persuaded the RSS to support the Emergency': Kamal Nath to author, 4
      August 2021.
65   'Once the law and order situation improves, the Emergency can be lifted': Ibid.
65   The controversy continues to resurface from time to time: Balasaheb Deoras's letters to S. B. Chavan, the
      chief minister of Maharashtra, urging him to get the ban on the RSS lifted, were tabled in the Maharashtra
      assembly on 18 October 1977, after the Emergency was lifted.
66   'But Mrs Gandhi refused': 'RSS backed Indira Gandhi's Emergency: Ex-IB chief', *India Today*, 21
      September 2015. This was also confirmed by Anil Bali to author, New Delhi, 12 July 2021.
66   *Panchjanya*, the RSS mouthpiece praised him: Noorani, 'RSS & Emergency'.
66   'Sanjay Gandhi Special Number': Ibid.
66   'quietly establish a link with the PM house': 'RSS backed Indira Gandhi's Emergency: Ex-IB chief'.
66   'Chunav se Sangh alag ho jaye': K. N. Govindacharya to author, 8 December 2020.
66   'We cannot leave them (Janata Party) midstream': Ibid.
66   'The line of communication was from Eknath Ranade to Moropant Pingle to Balasaheb Deoras': Ibid.
67   'The RSS helped Indira Gandhi come to power in 1980': Anil Bali to author.
67   'She used to admit privately that had it not been for the support by the RSS': Ibid.

67 'maybe she was in touch with the RSS': Karan Singh to author, 4 January 2021.
67 '(The) RSS,' Rajeswar said, 'had specifically conveyed its support to the Congress in the post Emergency elections': 'RSS backed Indira Gandhi's Emergency: Ex-IB chief'.
67 'Even before the 1989 elections...R. K. Dhawan had sent word, seeking our (RSS) help': K. N. Govindacharya to author, 19 June 2022.
67 Before the 1984 elections, RSS leader Nanaji Deshmukh had exhorted people to vote for the Congress: Noorani, 'RSS & Emergency'.
68 'Why does it (RSS) not open its doors to non-Hindus?': A. G. Noorani, 'Vajpayee's two faces', Frontline, 19 February 2000.
68 Around 800,000 farmers had gathered at Delhi's Boat Club to celebrate: Arul B. Louis, 'Kisan Rally: Farmers Throng the Capital with Festive Gaiety', India Today, 15 January 1979.
68 'The kisan will demand no more': Janardan Thakur, 'Was the Kisan Rally organised merely to boost the bruised ego of Charan Singh?', India Today, 15 January 1979.
68 'I had a good rest': William Borders, Mrs. Gandhi Is Let Out of Prison, New York Times, 27 December 1978.
68 The child, Jayant, had been born in America: Jayant Chaudhary, son of Ajit Singh was to take over as the president of the Rashtriya Lok Dal, after his father's death in 2021.
68 'Mrs Gandhi chai pee laengi, toh Morarji theek ho jayenge': Satyapal Malik to author. Malik was a lieutenant of Singh, and had been instrumental in getting Chaudhary sahib released from Jail in March 1976, as we saw.
69 On 24 January 1979, he made him deputy prime minister, and gave him the finance portfolio: 'HT This Day: Jan 24, 1979 - Charan Singh, J. Ram become Dy PMs today', Hindustan Times, 23 January 2022.
69 'dual membership': Pranab Mukherjee, The Dramatic Decade: The Indira Gandhi Years, New Delhi: Rupa Publications, 2015, p. 213.
69 'If the RSS is fascist, so am I': Vinod Kumar, 'How Jayaprakash Narayan's historic blunder paved the way for BJP's rise', The Print, 6 October 2019.
70 'North India has seen two powerful mass leaders in the post Nehru era—Indira Gandhi and Charan Singh': Jaipal Reddy to author during a conversation, New Delhi, 20 October 2001.
70 'I want this government and the party to stay': 'Battle-scarred leaders of Janata Party pull out their faded olive branches', India Today, 31 May 1979.
70 'He will create problems for only one ministry': Ibid.
70 'This is not the time (to strike),' Charan Singh told Nath evasively: Kamal Nath to author.
71 Indira had ensured that no further proceedings could take place in the Special Courts: Jayakar, Indira Gandhi, p. 385.
72 'Urs...has left...and...I'll be convicted by the end of October': Thakur, Prime Ministers, p. 149. The Indian National Congress (Requisitionists) of Indira Gandhi, formed in 1969, split into two on 2 January 1978 at her initiative. Out of power in 1977, she had been trying to become the president of the party, without success. On 1 January 1978, her supporters organised a 'national convention of Congressmen' and passed a resolution electing her as the Congress President. K Brahmanand Reddy was heading the party at the time. Fifty-four of the Congress MPs moved away with her. Almost 100 others stayed on the other side with Brahmanand Reddy and YB Chavan, who was then the party's leader in Parliament. Her group came to be known as Congress (Indira). Given that many senior Congress leaders, deposing before the Shah Commission had blamed Indira Gandhi for the excesses of the Emergency, Brahamananda Reddy, expelled her from the party. Devraj Urs had stayed with Indira Gandhi in 1978, but broke ranks with her in 1979 to form the Congress (Urs), which became Congress (S).
72 politics was in a state of 'restless motion': Madhu Limaye, Janata Party Experiment: An Insider's Account of Opposition Politics – 1977–1980, Volume II, New Delhi: B.R. Publishing, 1994, p. 456.
72 'I managed to persuade him': Kamal Nath to author.
72 'It was during those critical days': Jayakar, Indira Gandhi, p. 386.
73 It paused against only one name—George Fernandes: Anil Bali to author.
73 It was Fernandes's socialist colleague, Madhu Limaye: Leila Kabir Fernandes to author, 1979.
73 '(the) total break-up of the Janata Party is the historic necessity (today)': The author was in attendance.
73 'Do all our years of friendship mean nothing to you?': Jaya Jaitly, Life Among the Scorpions: Memoirs of a Woman in Indian Politics, New Delhi: Rupa Publications, 2017, p. 252.
73 'George knew he was committing hara-kiri': Ravi Nair to author.
73 Morarji Desai was left with only 214 MPs: Michael T. Kaufman, 'Indian Leader Quits after Many Defect from Ruling Party', New York Times, 16 July 1979.
74 'Step down from the leadership of the Janata Parliamentary Party': I. V. Chalapati Rao and P. Audinarayana Reddy, Farm House to Rashtrapati Bhavan, Hyderabad: Booklinks Corporation, 1989. Relevant extract available at www.rediff.com/news/apr/12cong7.htm.
74 thanked her for her 'unconditional support': Sunita Aron, 'Charan Singh — the only Indian PM who did not face Parliament even once', The Print, 20 July 2019.
74 'My life's ambition is fulfilled': Thakur, Prime Ministers, p. 179.
75 'Why should you go to her, you are PM now?': Satyapal Malik to author.
75 'She threw away the bouquet and went inside the house': Ibid.
75 'If Indiraji wants to support me, there can be no bargain': Thakur, Prime Ministers, p. 183.
76 'Do you think we can tolerate a man who called Indiraji a liar?': Ibid., p. 179.
76 'Sanjay Gandhi had a Machiavellian mind nobody on the Janata side could match': Ravi Nair to author, 23 December 2021.

76   could not prove his majority on the floor of parliament: Aron, 'Charan Singh — the only Indian PM who did not face Parliament even once'.

76   'Your mataji (mother) came in my dreams': Anil Bali to author.

77   Indira Gandhi hit the road in September 1979: S. Venkat Narayan, 'Indira Gandhi hits the campaign trail', *India Today*, 31 December 1979.

77   'I am the issue,' she had replied: Inder Malhotra, *Indira Gandhi: A Personal and Political Biography*, India: Hay House, 2014, p. 128.

77   She only asked people to elect a 'government that works': Inder Malhotra, 'The Return of Indira', *Indian Express*, 29 September 2014.

77   Darshan was all they wanted: Narayan, 'Indira Gandhi hits the campaign trail'.

78   'If Mrs Gandhi returns to power next month, it will certainly be the quickest comeback in recent political history': Ibid.

78   'Venkatji, namaskar. Main Yashpal Kapoor bol raha hoon': S. Venkat Narayan to author, 3 August 2021.

78   'If you come to power, what will be the role of V. C. Shukla and Sanjay Gandhi?': Ibid.

78   'I am going to jump, you people come when the ladder arrives': Ibid.

79   20 per cent from February 1979 to the end of year: Stuart Auerbach, 'Gandhi's Resounding Victory Has Wiped Out Her Opposition', *Washington Post*, 12 January 1980.

79   helped her take the 'Hindu-first' card away from the BJP: J. Manor, 'Parties and the Party System', Atul Kohli (ed.), *India's Democracy—An Analysis of Changing State-Society Relations*, Princeton University Press, 1990, p. 82.

79   'Don't you know, you cannot go off centre-stage?': Ambika Soni to author, 26 September 2020.

79   And 150 of them were 'staunch Sanjay supporters': Malhotra, 'The Return of Indira'.

80   The victory had given him legitimacy as the 'crown prince': Ibid.

80   'He can't be made CM': Ahmad Akbar 'Dumpy' to author.

81   'Tell him that if he insists, I will resign': H. R. Bhardwaj to author.

81   'She would put money in a lifafa (envelope) and give it to me': Anil Bali to author.

82   'Madam, you have to go to Chamunda Devi': Ibid.

82   'You tell Indira Gandhi, this is Chamunda': Ibid.

82   'In the plane I screamed and screamed for, I think, two hours': SimiGarewalOfficial, 'Rendezvous with Maneka Gandhi Part 1 & 2', YouTube, accessed April 2022.

83   'I don't know who cancelled my programme': Anil Bali to author.

83   Later, Indira confided to Pupul Jayakar that Sanjay's death was her fault: Jayakar, *Indira Gandhi*, p. 418.

83   'The prime minister wants to see you': Anil Bali to author.

83   'As she performed the puja, the pandit's hands shook': Ibid.

84   'I have never seen such a beautiful place': Ibid.

CHAPTER 2: THE SECULAR PRIME MINISTER WHO UNDERMINED SECULARISM: RAJIV GANDHI'S WAFFLING OVER SHAH BANO

85   'This Sonia said in my presence': D. P. Tripathi to author, March 2018, on tape.

85   'You will lose your credibility': Ibid.

86   If Rajiv went ahead, it would become 'very difficult' to stop the march of the 'Hindu fanatical forces': D. P. Tripathi to author, 19 April, 2018, New Delhi.

86   For the bill was followed by the 'equally disastrous...decision': Ibid.

86   The media had dubbed 1985 as the 'Year of Hope': Thakur, *Prime Ministers*, p. 222.

87   To assuage irate Hindu sentiment, Rajiv Gandhi went in for what was a typical 'management solution': D. P. Tripathi to author, March 2018.

87   And that was to open an enclosure within the Babri Masjid: One of the largest mosques in the state of Uttar Pradesh, the Babri Masjid was built in the Tughluq, Lodi, and Sharqi style, and replicated the architecture of other mosques of the Delhi Sultanate. According to Farsi inscriptions on the entrance to the sandstone mosque, it was constructed in the sixteenth century on the orders of the first Mughal emperor, Babur. The mosque consisted of a liwan (prayer chamber) to the west divided into three, a central, larger nave flanked by two aisles with arched entrances and topped with domes. The interior's acoustics were apparently something unique—'A whisper from the Babri Masjid Mihrab could be heard clearly at the other end, 200 feet away and through the length and breadth of the central court'. The masjid was considered as a 'passive environmental control system' which employed a variety of Islamic architectural elements such as the high ceiling, domes, vaults, and its six large grille windows to keep the allow natural ventilation and daylight while keeping it cool inside. (Radhika Ravi Ranjan, 'Babri Masjid: Echoes of a bygone era', *SpeakingTree.in*, 6 December 2012)
'The Babri Masjid was situated on high ground. It had a steep slope on the west—the side facing Mecca which is always at the rear of a mosque, a gradient on the north and south, and level ground on the east, which is the entrance of the mosque.' (Valay Singh, *Ayodhya: City of Faith, City of Discord*, New Delhi: Aleph Book Company, 2018) The entrance had a main gate that was locked by an executive order in December 1949. There was a second smaller gate that, according to sources, was used surreptitiously by pujaris who conducted rituals within the mosque from time to time. This was the gate Rajiv Gandhi had 'managed' to unlock in 1986. Within the Babri Masjid compound but separated from the inner courtyard by a high stone wall was the Ramachabutara, a 17x21x6 feet raised platform in the south-eastern corner of

the complex. Until the appearance of Ram Lalla in the central nave of the mosque, this is where Lord Ram was worshipped. There were iron railings towards the west and a wide open space to the north, which would be cordoned off by the Ram Deewar erected in 1991. Also to the north was the raised concrete platform for the Singh Dwar, lion gate, constructed in July 1992 as the proposed site of the Ram Temple. The eastern wall had a gate, a few steps north of the chabutara, opening to a straight narrow lane that took one to the town. 'The Ram Janmabhoomi–Babri Masjid complex was surrounded on three sides by Hindu temples, which had been built on graveyards.' (*Ayodhya*, p. 235) These temples formed part of the 2.77 acres of land surrounding the disputed area 'acquired by the Kalyan Singh government in 1991' (Utkarsh Anand, 'Ayodhya Verdict: India's Biggest Legal Battle Was About Just 0.3 Acre Land, Not 2.77 Acres', *News18*, 10 November 2019) and given to the VHP's Ram Janmabhoomi Trust; they would be demolished in October 1991. Only a few hundred metres away from the mosque complex was the Ram Katha Kunj.

88 In December 1949, a group of Hindus surreptitiously placed an idol of the deity Ram Lalla: Krishna Jha and Dhirendra K. Jha, 'The Untold Story of How the Rama Idol Surfaced Inside Babri Masjid', *The Wire*, 6 December 2021.

88 But a court judgment allowed Hindus to worship the idol from behind a locked grille: Singh, *Ayodhya*, p. 205.

88 'This was the sum total of Rajiv Gandhi's thinking': D. P. Tripathi to author, March 2018.

88 'Rajiv Gandhi's impressive majority in parliament slumped from 414 to 197': Shubhodeep Chakravarty, 'INKredible India: The story of 1989 Lok Sabha election - All you need to know', *Zee News*, 7 April 2019.

88 'Indira Gandhi assaulted, return to Delhi immediately': Mukherjee, *The Turbulent Years*, p. 68.

89 'Did she deserve all these bullets?': Ibid., p. 69.

89 'She is dead': Ibid., p. 70.

89 'I cited precedents': Ibid.

89 'Do you think I can manage?': Ibid., p. 71.

90 'We couldn't really talk about it': T. N. Ninan, 'I'm sure the people in Punjab want peace: Rajiv Gandhi', *India Today*, 31 May 1986.

90 He wanted to ensure that it was Rajiv, not Pranab Mukherjee, who was sworn in: Arun Nehru to author.

90 Nehru had convinced many Congress leaders: P. C. Alexander, *Through the Corridors of Power: An Insider's Story*, New Delhi: HarperCollins, 2004, p. 217.

91 'No risk can be taken,' Nehru told him: Ibid., p. 219.

91 'no choice…he would be killed anyway': Sonia Gandhi, *Rajiv*, Delhi: Viking/Penguin India, 1992, p. 9.

91 It is there that the cabinet secretary had a quiet word with Rajiv: P. C. Alexander, *My Years with Indira Gandhi*, New Delhi: Vision Books, 1991, p. 155.

91 He agreed that they should wait for the president to return: Alexander, *Through the Corridors of Power*, p. 220.

92 Nehru had died at 2 p.m. and Gulzari Lal Nanda was in place by 4 p.m.: Sumit Mitra and Prabhu Chawla, 'Indira Gandhi assassination places India at a crucial crossroads in its history', *India Today*, 30 November 1984.

92 Mrs Indira Gandhi's death should not be officially announced: Mukherjee, *The Turbulent Years*, p. 71.

92 Mukherjee suggested that instead, the Congress Parliamentary Board (CPB) should be called immediately: Ibid., p. 72.

92 The CPB met at 5 p.m. that day: Frank, *Indira*, p. 496.

92 G. K. Moopanar, who was secretary of the CWC, wrote a formal letter: Mukherjee, *The Turbulent Years*, p. 73.

93 suspected P. V. Narasimha Rao of spreading the canard that Mukherjee wanted to become the interim PM: A senior Bengali journalist who was close to Pranab Mukherjee to author, New Delhi.

93 'That day, when I administered the oath to Rajiv as PM': H. S. Hanspal, former MP and chief of the Congress in Punjab, 12 September 2022, telephonic interview.

93 An 'eerie silence' hung over the ceremony: Mitra and Chawla, 'Indira Gandhi assassination places India at a crucial crossroads in its history'.

94 'I, Rajiv Gandhi, do solemnly affirm': Ibid.

94 'peace, communal harmony and unity': Mukherjee, *The Turbulent Years*, p. 76.

94 'We have received Intelligence reports that there will be widespread violence in the city tomorrow': Vinay Sitapati to author, 22 March 2022, on phone from Princeton, USA.

95 'The PMO will coordinate a single response to the violence': Ibid. Also Vinay Sitapati, *Half Lion: How P. V. Narasimha Rao Transformed India*, Delhi: Penguin Viking, 2016, p. 63. Sitapati refers to the phone call in his book without taking the name of the 'young Congress leader' who had called Rao.

95 The day after the assassination, an agitated Pupul Jayakar, Indira Gandhi's close friend, called up Rao: Jayakar, *Indira Gandhi*, pp. 490–91.

95 Rajiv as prime minister 'was an unknown quantity to him': Vinay Sitapati to author, 22 March 2022, on phone from Princeton, USA.

96 'Rao's concern at the time would have been what will happen to him': Ibid.

96 'It was his vilest hour': Vinay Sitapati, *Half Lion: How P. V. Narasimha Rao Transformed India*, Delhi: Penguin Books, 2016, p. 65.

96 absolved Rao of any role in the violence: Ibid., p. 64.

96 'Choorhiya pehen rakhi hain kya? Maa ko maara hai': Shahid Siddiqui to author, 19 August 2021.

96 Delhi Metropolitan Council: Delhi Metropolitan Council administered the Union Territory of Delhi between 1966–90, and was headed by a chief executive councillor.

96   Lalit Maken, H. K. L. Bhagat, Sajjan Kumar, Jagdish Tytler, Kamal Nath: Sunil Sharan, 'The wounds of 1984', *Times of India*, 13 May 2019.

97   'When we were collating material to present': Hartosh Singh Bal, 'The Shattered Dome', *The Caravan*, 1 May 2014.

97   'detailed information about the community had been gathered by the Government': Ibid.

97   The government estimated that about 2,733 Sikhs were killed in Delhi over the next three days and 3,350 nationwide: Gaurav Vivek Bhatnagar, 'What Delhi HC Order On 1984 Anti-Sikh Pogrom Says About 2002 Gujarat Riots', *The Wire*, 17 December 2018.

97   8,000 to 17,000 were killed across forty cities in the country: 'Sikh leaders welcome death penalty to 1984 anti-Sikh riots case convict', *DNA*, 21 November 2018; 'Take up Gujarat riots also', *Hans India*, 19 December 2018.

98   Rajiv Gandhi took the leap into politics to 'help Mummy': Thakur, *Prime Ministers*, p. 220.

98   'We were sitting at the lunch table at 12, Willingdon Crescent': Akbar Ahmad 'Dumpy' to author, 22 January 2021, telephonic conversation.

98   But US President Ronald Reagan had personally signed an order: Wajahat Habibullah, *My Years with Rajiv: Triumph and Tragedy*, Delhi: Westland, 2020, p. 43.

98   'Sanjay immediately asked R. K. Dhawan to get in touch with Arun Nehru': Akbar Ahmad 'Dumpy' to author, 22 January 2021, telephonic conversation.

99   'On second thoughts, it will be better to buy material and get your kurtas stitched': Ibid.

99   'Whenever you see colour, think of us': 'Arun Nehru and Arun Singh: Rajiv Gandhi's power-brokers', *India Today*, 15 December 1984.

99   They had their own circle of friends among the elite of Lutyens' Delhi: Tavleen Singh, *Durbar*, Delhi: Hachette, 2013.

99   'I will never forgive Sanjay for having brought Mummy to this position': Jayakar, *Indira Gandhi*, p. 321.

99   Fotedar came back to her and said he had found the reaction to all three names 'unsuitable': M. L. Fotedar to author, 1 January 2005, Gurgaon.

99   'she used to discuss with me the pros and cons of Rajivji entering politics': M. L. Fotedar to author, 1 January 2005, Gurgaon. Also M. L. Fotedar, 'Political Secretary, 1980–87', *The Chinar Leaves: A Political Memoir*, New Delhi: HarperCollins, 2015.

99   Arun Nehru organized a group of around fifty MPs: Rasheed Kidwai, 'Death bridges a bitter family divide', *The Telegraph Online*, 27 July 2013.

100   Maneka left the PM House in the middle of the night on 29 March 1982: Chingkheinganbi Mayengbam, 'Why did Maneka Gandhi leave Indira Gandhi's residence with son Varun in the middle of the night?', *India Today*, 20 January 2023.

100   'She (Sonia) is dead against the idea of (my) getting into politics': Dilip Bobb, 'Sonia is dead against the idea of getting into politics', *India Today*, 31 August 1980.

100   'One afternoon, in late 1980, Rajiv told me quietly': Suman Dubey, 'Rajiv Gandhi enters into the Lok Sabha from Amethi in 1981', *India Today*, 26 December 2005.

100   'The way I look at it,' Rajiv had said, 'is that mummy has to be helped somehow': Ibid.

100   'Rajiv makes debut': 'May 12, 1981, Forty Years Ago: Rajiv in Amethi', *Indian Express*, 12 May 2021.

100   'Sari pehenna, teeka lagana': Habibullah, *My Years with Rajiv*, p. 45.

101   'I had arranged for lunch Dussehri mangoes, lemon chicken and arhar dal without any masala': Anil Bali to author, 13 September 2020, New Delhi.

101   Rajiv Ratna Birjees Gandhi: Rajiv's name was chosen carefully for him. Rajiv meant lotus, named after his grandmother Kamla, Ratna, a jewel after his grandfather Jawahar, and Birjees came from the Parsi side of the father and meant 'Jupiter' or 'auspicious' in Persian.

101   'I am having the privilege of travelling with the next prime minister of India': Ibid.

101   The inaugural on 19 November 1982—it happened to be Indira Gandhi's birthday—was a gala affair: Sahil Bhalla, 'Flashback 1982: The Asian Games that transformed Delhi', *Scroll.in*, 25 September 2015.

102   Unlike other party offices at the time, Rajiv's office had a computer: Frank, *Indira*, p. 473.

102   'English-speaking, Doon School-educated Indians': Singh, *Durbar*.

103   'If there is no order and the whole thing is not over in fifteen minutes, I will go back': Amarnath K. Menon, 'Rajiv Gandhi gives Andhra CM T.M. Anjiah a piece of his mind for flouting airport rules', *India Today*, 28 February 1982.

103   His peremptory behaviour drew 'howls of protest': Ibid.

104   He won 201 out of 294 seats in elections that were held in January 1983: 'Andhra Pradesh Assembly Election Results in 1983', available at <www.elections.in/andhra-pradesh/assembly-constituencies/1983-election-results.html>.

104   She knew that Rajiv was both gullible and trusting: Mani Shankar Aiyar to author, 16 February 2021, telephonic conversation.

104   Industrialists called him a 'one window clearance': Inderjit Badhwar and Prabhu Chawla, 'Mystery surrounds circumstances under which Arun Nehru was ousted from power', *India Today*, 30 November 1986.

104   'Arun Nehru was sitting on a chair, with legs stretched': Shahid Siddiqui to author.

105   'Acha, toh tu mujhe national interest sikhayega?': Ibid.

105   'Main usko toh theek kar doonga': G. S. Chawla to author.

105   The key members were Mrs Gandhi's aide M. L. Fotedar: G. S. Chawla, 'The Gang Who Created Unrest In Punjab', *Outlook*, 4 February 2022.

105   dissuaded Indira from signing an agreement with the Akali Dal: Ibid.
105   Zail Singh had even paid the bill for a press conference that he had organized for Bhindranwale: Mark Tully and Satish Jacob, *Amritsar: Mrs Gandhi's Last Battle*, Calcutta: Rupa & Co., 1985, p. 60.
106   'radical devolution of power': Swapnajit Kundu, 'Khalistan movement: How it started, who supported it and other developments over the years', *News9*, 12 May 2022.
106   Zail Singh, who had by now become president—and was helping Arun Nehru: G. S. Chawla, *Bloodshed in Punjab: Untold Saga of Deceit and Sabotage*, Delhi: Har-Anand publications, 2016.
106   'I've told Mummy so many times': Singh, *Durbar*, p. 144.
106   the 'baba log' or 'computer boys' as they were called: Sunil Sethi, 'Rajiv Gandhi and the "baba log" years', *Business Standard*, 24 August 2019; S. Balakrishnan, 'The Angry Loyalist', *The Illustrated Weekly of India*, 19 November 1989, p. 42.
106   plan to ready an 'invasion blueprint': Frank, *Indira*, p. 478.
107   'delayed and resisted': Ibid.
107   'She was scared of attacking a house of God': Ibid.
107   the Congress's baba log went on to destabilize the duly elected opposition governments: Bhabani Sen Gupta, 'As LS polls loom, Cong(I) unleashes nation-wide "operation topple" against four states', *India Today*, 15 February 1984.
107   'In 1984, after Indira Gandhi's death, I was doing the planning for the Congress': Arun Nehru to author, 16 May 2001.
108   'She was killed by people who hoped to break India into fragments': Sunil Sethi, 'Rajiv Gandhi goes on a gruelling campaigning spree, covers 19,000 km in 12 days', *India Today*, 31 December 1984.
108   'When a big tree falls': 'Watch Rajiv Gandhi make his infamous "big tree falls" speech justifying the 1984 anti-Sikh riots', *Scroll.in*, 20 November 2015.
108   'Rajiv Gandhi ka ailan/nahi banega Khalistan': Raghav Bikhchandani, 'When ad agency helped Congress score big 1984 win', *The Print*, 20 March 2022.
108   'the campaign depicted Sikhs as enemy': Raghunath AS (asraghunath), Tweet, 5 May 2019, <https://twitter.com/asraghunath/status/1124997320251138048?s=20>. A former journalist, Raghunath A. S. documented the ads that had been used in 1984 in a Twitter thread in 2019.
108   'the cheapest election we fought': Arun Nehru to author, 16 May 2001.
108   'Gone is the comfortable slouch': Sethi, 'Rajiv Gandhi goes on a gruelling campaigning spree, covers 19,000 km in 12 days'.
109   The Congress won 84 out of 85 seats in UP.: 'Statistical Report on General Elections, 1984 to the Eight Lok Sabha: Volume I', Delhi: Election Commission of India, 1985, available at <https://eci.gov.in/files/file/4119-general-election-1985-vol-i-ii/>.
109   The party came to power with an unprecedented majority of 404 Lok Sabha seats: Ibid.
109   This tally went up to 414: 'Statistical Report on General Elections, 1985 to the Eight Lok Sabha: Volume II', Delhi: Election Commission of India, 1986, available at <https://eci.gov.in/files/file/4119-general-election-1985-vol-i-ii/>.
109   'What can I say?': T. N. Ninan, 'Prime Minister Rajiv Gandhi leads Congress(I) to a brute majority in eighth Lok Sabha', *India Today*, 15 January 1985.
110   'toppled the dignified former Foreign Ministry official Natwar Singh to the ground': Mary Anne Weaver, 'Rajiv Gandhi and the "two Aruns in waiting"—a new way of running India', *The Christian Science Monitor*, 7 January 1985.
110   'I don't remember seeing him at the PM House coming to meet Rajiv': Vivek Bharat Ram to author.
110   'Arun Singh was deferential to Rajiv as prime minister, but Arun Nehru was far from deferential': B. N. Uniyal to author, 27 February 2021, telephonic conversation, New Delhi.
110   'Arunji, kuch toh umar ka lihaz kariye': Ibid.
110   'I kept waiting for the call': Mukherjee, *The Turbulent Years*, p. 88.
111   On 1 January 1985, R. K. Dhawan drove to 1 Safdarjung Road: Pankaj Vohra to author, 1 August 2022, New Delhi, telephonic interview.
112   'It was Sonia Gandhi who decided that they wielded too much power': Ibid.
112   'this government is not going to last very long': Rashmi Kant to author, 3 April 2018, New Delhi. He had heard this from his father, Krishan Kant.
112   'There can never be anyone as powerful as R. K. Dhawan': Pankaj Vohra to author, 1 August 2022, New Delhi, telephonic interview.
113   'Aya Ram, Gaya Ram': Chitleen K. Sethi, 'As turncoats grab headlines, a look back at the original "Aaya Ram, Gaya Ram"', *The Print*, 19 May 2018.
113   Over the course of 1985, Rajiv Gandhi would sign two accords: 'A Different Accord', *The Print*, 21 August 2010.
113   Rajiv Gandhi went on to set up six technology missions: Kumar Shakti Shekhar, '5 ways how Rajiv Gandhi changed India forever', *India Today*, 20 August 2018.
113   In 1988, Rajiv Gandhi lowered the voting age from twenty-one to eighteen: Ibid.
114   it was the overspending during his term that led to a balance of payment crisis: Ankit Mittal, 'The long road to the 1991 economic crisis', *Mint*, 8 July 2016.
114   The second was the Bofors gun deal in mid-1987: There had been charges of commissions and bribery in the purchase of the 155 mm howitzer gun from the Swedish arms manufacturer AB Bofors for the payment of kickbacks worth Rs 64 crores in the gun deal.
115   'Come and have a cup of coffee with me': Arun Nehru to author, 16 May 2001, New Delhi.

115 'What is your opinion on Shah Bano': Arif Mohammad Khan to author, 21 August 2018, New Delhi.

115 In 1937, the British had enacted a law called the Muslim Personal Law (Shariat) Application Act: Razia Patel, 'Indian Muslim Women, Politics of Muslim Personal Law and Struggle for Life with Dignity and Justice', *Economic and Political Weekly*, Vol. 44, No. 44, 2009, p. 45.

116 Muslims in India followed local and religious customs in the way they organized their personal lives: Shoaib Daniyal, 'A short history of Muslim personal law in India', *Scroll.in*, 4 September 2017; Qazi Sarah Rasheed and A. K. Sharma, 'Muslim Women's Rights in India: Codified Personal Laws Needed', *Economic and Political Weekly*, Vol. 51, No. 37, 2016, p. 22.

116 All who spoke on the issue happened to be Muslims, except for one Janata Party MP: Mani Shankar Aiyar to author, 16 February 2021, telephonic interview.

116 'What Banatwalla is saying is all wrong': Arif Mohammad Khan to author, 21 August 2018, New Delhi.

116 'It has nothing to do with personal law, as is being made out by the Muslim Personal Law Board': Ibid.

116 'even on the occasion of divorce, which announces the annulment of the relationship': Arif Mohammad Khan to author, 21 August 2018, New Delhi; Arif Mohammad Khan, *Text and Context: Quran and Contemporary Challenges*, New Delhi: Rupa Publications, 2010, pp. 1–2.

117 It was 'blasphemy for anyone to object to money being given to a destitute': Ajaz Ashraf, 'Arif Mohammad Khan on Shah Bano case: "Najma Heptullah was key influence on Rajiv Gandhi"', *Scroll.in*, 30 May 2015.

117 'We did not know this': Arif Mohammad Khan to author, 21 August 2018, New Delhi.

117 'Baat toh sahi hai': Ibid.

117 'No, no, we cannot agree to what these people are saying': Ibid.

117 'File pe toh Rajivji ne aur bhi sakht likha hai': Ibid.

117 He was a 'modern' leader: Ashraf, 'Arif Mohammad Khan on Shah Bano case: "Najma Heptullah was key influence on Rajiv Gandhi"'.

117 'Arif will intervene first in the discussion': Arif Mohammad Khan to author, 21 August 2018, New Delhi.

117 'We should have better practices these days': 'Lok Sabha Debates (English Version): Third Session (Eighth Lok Sabha)', Vol. IX, No. 23, New Delhi: Lok Sabha Secretariat, 23 August 1985, p. 453, available at <https://eparlib.nic.in/bitstream/123456789/3598/1/lsd_08_03_23-08-1985.pdf>.

117 'Rajiv praised me generously for what I had said in the Lok Sabha': Arif Mohammad Khan to author, 21 August 2018, New Delhi.

118 'Something happened in my family—extended family': Arif Mohammad Khan to author, 21 August 2018, New Delhi.

118 The upshot of it all was that the woman had to marry someone else: This was according to 'Nikah Halala', a traditional practice amongst orthodox Muslims, which requires a woman to marry and consummate the marriage before she can return to her first husband. 'Halala is a practice by which, to remarry her husband, a Muslim woman is required to marry another man, consummate that marriage, and get a divorce from this temporary husband. There have been incidents of disreputable mullahs offering to temporarily marry women for this.' (See Ghazala Wahab, *Born a Muslim*, p. 129.)

118 'I never forgot this incident': Arif Mohammad Khan to author, 21 August 2018, New Delhi.

118 Following Arif Mohammad Khan's intervention in parliament: Vasudha Dhagamwar, 'After the Shah Bano Judgement – II', *Times of India*, 11 February 1986.

118 Ali Mian, as Maulana Abul Hasan Ali Nadwi was popularly called, had handed Rajiv a memorandum: Fasihur Rahman, 'Triple Talaaq and Shah Bano Case', *Mainstream*, Vol. LVII, No. 34, 11 August 2019.

119 Ali Mian was 'backed by the entire Islamic world': Shahid Siddiqui to author, 25 March 2019, New Delhi.

119 'So, she could not be taking money from him every month': Ibid.

119 came out 'very strongly' against the judgment: Ibid.

119 This also exerted its own pressure on the AIMPLB: Rahman, 'Triple Talaaq and Shah Bano Case'.

119 Though a local initiative, it attracted three lakh people: Ashraf, 'Arif Mohammad Khan on Shah Bano case: "Najma Heptullah was key influence on Rajiv Gandhi"'.

119 Like Muslims elsewhere in the world, they had protested when the holy Al-Aqsa Mosque in Jerusalem was attacked: Abdel Raouf Arnaout, 'Fires still engulfing Al-Aqsa Mosque: Palestinians', Anadolu Agency, 21 August 2019.

119 'We used to mostly express our power through the exercise of the vote': Shahid Siddiqui to author, 25 March 2019, New Delhi.

119 Ali Mian gave her full credit for the role she had played: Maulana Abul Hasan Ali Nadwi, *Karwan-e-Zindagi*.

120 'Najma Heptulla pays more money to her hairdresser than what the court has allocated to Shah Bano!': Arif Mohammad Khan to author, 21 August 2018, New Delhi.

120 'If Arif Mohammed Khan, who is a minister, can speak in a debate on a private members' bill, why can't I speak?': Fasihur Rahman, *Wings of Destiny: Ziaur Rahman Ansari – A Life*, New Delhi: Highbrow Scribes Publications, 2018.

120 Ansari was a senior Muslim minister in Rajiv's cabinet: Mani Shankar Aiyar to author, 16 February 2021, telephonic interview.

120 'Rajiv took the resignation letter, tore it and threw it in the dustbin': Aziz Qureshi to author.

120 He lambasted the Shah Bano judgment as 'prejudiced': Rahman, 'Triple Talaaq and Shah Bano Case'.

120 'It is clear beyond doubt,' the *Times of India* wrote in an editorial: Girilal Jain, 'EDITORIAL: Unanswered Questions', *Times of India*, 6 March 1986.

120 Pulled in two directions, till mid-November 1985, Rajiv Gandhi was still uncertain: Arif Mohammad Khan to author, 21 August 2018, New Delhi.

120 'There was a phone call from the PM house': Ibid.
121 'Soon after I boarded the flight, an officer told me': Ibid.
121 'It is not as if some way cannot be found out of this impasse': Ibid.
121 'Nahi, koi sawaal hi nahin inke saath samjhauta karne ka': Ibid.
121 'If I am not included in these negotiations, it means the government has agreed to their condition': Ibid.
122 M. J. Akbar was an educated and articulate Muslim, and a leading journalist who had established a rapport with the prime minister: Wajahat Habibullah to author; Habibullah, *My Years with Rajiv*, 2020.
122 'I was looking after minority matters': Wajahat Habibullah to author, 26 April 2019, New Delhi.
122 'the whole question of personal law and its application in India': Ibid.
122 The maximum the government should do, he felt, was 'not to intervene in the matter': Ibid.
122 'I sent out a single note...it must still be there': Ibid.
123 'Will you come over?' he asked without preamble: Ibid.
123 'You are one of us': Ibid.
123 'They might feel that they are not one of my own': Ibid.
123 they would conclude that Rajiv did not 'really think of them as part of his family': Ibid.
123 'I and (or for that matter) Akbar—had both made an "error" of judgment in 1985': Ibid.
124 Ever since the uprising of 1857, Islamic clerics had taken it upon themselves to represent the community: Ibid.
124 The matter was out of his hands: Ibid.
124 The debate over the Shah Bano judgment divided the Congress Party right down the middle: Wajahat Habibullah to author; D. P. Tripathi to author, March 2018, on tape.
124 P. V. Narasimha Rao, Arjun Singh, N. D. Tiwari, and S. B. Chavan: D. P. Tripathi to author, 19 April 2018, New Delhi; Arif Mohammad Khan to author, 21 August 2018, New Delhi.
124 he consulted them on how to handle the snowballing Muslim reaction: Arif Mohammad Khan to author, 21 August 2018, New Delhi; Wajahat Habibullah to author, 26 April 2019, New Delhi.
124 Rao told Rajiv that 'prolonging this affair': Arif Mohammad Khan to author, 21 August 2018, New Delhi.
124 'Though Rajiv had asked me at PMH to speak in parliament': Ibid.
125 'I knew that Rajivji would not have changed his mind': Ibid.
125 Rajiv Gandhi was also mindful of international Islamic opinion: Shahid Siddiqui to author, 25 March 2019, New Delhi.
125 'Though I kept my campaign very secular': Farzand Ahmed and Ajay Kumar, 'By-elections to seven Lok Sabha and nine Assembly seats leave Congress(I) badly bruised', *India Today*, 15 January 1986.
125 'This young, nice prime minister, who wants to be good to everyone, is destroying his party in its 100th year': Shekhar Gupta, 'Victory of Asom Gana Parishad ushers in new era of hope and change in Assam', *India Today*, 15 January 1986.
125 He convinced Rajiv about the rightness of going in for a bill to undo the judgment: Ajay Kumar, 'Muslim Women's Bill sparks off heated debate, puts Rajiv Gandhi govt in a tight corner', *India Today*, 31 March 1986.
126 Rajiv urged Najma Heptulla to check this out: Ibid.
126 He instructed Ashoke Sen to frame a law and take the help of Ziaur Rahman and other Muslim leaders: Shahid Siddiqui to author, 25 March 2019, New Delhi.
126 'You didn't become Prime Minister just like that': Ibid. Siddiqui said he had been told this by Rajiv Gandhi himself.
127 The three issues had come to be identified with the BJP as its 'core issues': Article 44 of the Constitution laid down that the State shall endeavour to have a Uniform Civil Code all over India which would have a uniform law applicable to all religious communities in matters such as marriage, divorce, inheritance, adoption. Article 370 of the Constitution guaranteed special status to the state of Jammu and Kashmir. The VHP and the RSS had been committed to building a Ram temple in Ayodhya, seen as the birthplace of Lord Ram.
127 'What does Rajiv think he is doing?': Wajahat Habibullah to author, 26 April 2019, New Delhi. Habibullah had heard Nehru say this.
127 How could Rajiv forget the 'Hindu vote bank': Neerja Chowdhury, 'The Political Fallout', *The Statesman*, 20 April 1986.
127 Some discussed, in undertones, whether the Muslim Women's Bill could be defeated on the floor: Author in conversation with some of the MPs at the time.
127 It could be against his leadership: Shahid Siddiqui to author, 25 March 2019, New Delhi. Siddiqui was told this by Rajiv Gandhi.
127 'The draft of the Bill is ready, please go and see the Law Minister now': Arif Mohammad Khan to author, 21 August 2018, New Delhi.
128 'Have they (the AIMPLB and others involved) agreed to this?': Ibid.
128 'Arif, I am pleading with you to keep quiet': Ibid.
128 'He did not say please don't share it with the Muslim leaders': Arif Mohammad Khan to author, 19 August 2021, telephonic interview.
128 Among its advisors, as already noted, were the Congress minister Salman Khurshid: Ashraf, 'Arif Mohammad Khan on Shah Bano case: "Najma Heptullah was key influence on Rajiv Gandhi"'.
128 But by then, the government let it be known that if anyone pressed: Arif Mohammad Khan to author, 19 August 2021, telephonic interview.
128 The AIMPLB had no problem with enhancing the financial settlement for the divorced woman: Kumar, 'Muslim Women's Bill sparks off heated debate, puts Rajiv Gandhi govt in a tight corner'.

129   Congress leader Mani Shankar Aiyar was to say years later that the 'cleverly worded section': Mani
      Shankar Aiyar, 'Shooting from the lip', *The Week*, 27 September 2020.
129   'Rajiv Gandhi and his legal advisers' had 'resolved the dilemma': Mani Shankar Aiyar, 'Rajiv Gandhi Was
      Attacked For This Decision. I Believe It Was Genius.', NDTV, 2 August 2016.
129   'Ashoke Sen did not inform Rajiv Gandhi about it': Arif Mohammad Khan to author, 19 August 2021,
      telephonic interview.
129   He was speaking at a public meeting at Delhi's Siri Fort Auditorium: Hemant Sharma, *Yuddha Mein
      Ayodhya*, Delhi: Prabhat Prakashan, 1 January 2018.
129   It had to look for ways to deflect attention from the bill and find 'a balancing act': Arif Mohammad Khan,
      'Looking back: When another Muslim women bill sparked competitive communalism', *Hindustan Times*,
      31 July 2019.
129   He acknowledged that the Shah Bano judgment had caused uncertainties in the minds of 'certain
      communities': Kumar, 'Muslim Women's Bill sparks off heated debate, puts Rajiv Gandhi govt in a tight
      corner'.
129   The CrPC gave women only a pittance: Ibid.
129   'Muslims (generally) do not accept parliament's right to amend their laws': Shahid Siddiqui to author, 25
      March 2019, New Delhi.
129   that it would awaken 'the sleeping Hindu giant': Khan, 'Looking back: When another Muslim women bill
      sparked competitive communalism'.
130   'I have been looking for you,' Singh said: Arif Mohammad Khan to author.
130   'For one and a half hours,' Khan recalled, 'he put a lot of pressure on me': Ibid.
130   'I was in parliament and I saw Arif in the House visibly upset': Arun Nehru to author in exclusive, hitherto
      unused interview, 16 May 2001, New Delhi.
130   'What are you doing?' he asked the PM: Ibid.
131   'Rajiv, you had said this before Arif': Ibid.
131   'Arif is going to be physically attacked': Ibid.
131   'You can't ditch people like this': Ibid.
131   'Mujhe jahaan tak yaad hai': Arif Mohammad Khan to author, 21 August 2018, New Delhi.
131   'Rajivji ghabraye toh usi se thae': Ibid.
131   'I am telling you the exact words...he said': Ibid.
131   'If the Muslims don't want social reform': Ibid.
131   'Even Shah Bano has now said that she will give up the maintenance allowed her': Ibid.
132   'Prominent Muslim leader Syed Shahabuddin visited our house': Saeed Khan, '"My mother was wronged,
      gravely wronged"', *Hindustan Times*, 12 November 2011.
132   'Even in Indore there was a lakh strong rally which passed in front of our house': Ibid.
132   The PM told them the situation was 'very critical': Ibid.
132   'Rajiv asked us to announce that we were refusing the maintenance': Ibid.
132   She announced she was not taking the maintenance ordered by the court: Tavleen Singh, 'Shah Bano makes a
      dramatic turnaround, requests Supreme Court to withdraw its judgement', *India Today*, 15 December 1985.
132   'I thought my mother will live for another two, five, ten years': Khan, '"My mother was wronged, gravely
      wronged"'.
133   'Taala khulwa do,' Arun Nehru advised the prime minister: Arif Mohammad Khan to author, 21 August
      2018, New Delhi. He had been told this by Arun Nehru himself.
133   A worried Rajiv had called his cousin over to get his advice: Sharma, *Yuddh Maen Ayodhya*, p. 263.
133   'Hindus khush ho jayengae,' Nehru told Rajiv: Shahid Siddiqui to author. Siddiqui had heard this from
      Rajiv Gandhi.
134   The editor of the *Times of India*, Girilal Jain, had penned a blistering piece against Rajiv Gandhi: Jain,
      'EDITORIAL: Unanswered Questions'.
134   Another eminent editor, Arun Shourie had written two equally critical pieces in the same paper: Mentioned
      in Kumar, 'Muslim Women's Bill sparks off heated debate, puts Rajiv Gandhi govt in a tight corner'.
134   'I found Rajiv completely innocent of Muslim Personal Law': Arun Shourie to author, 12 September 2022,
      in a telephonic conversation in New Delhi.
134   'How could paying `179.20 a month to a seventy-three-year-old destitute woman endanger Islam?': Ibid.
134   'Taala khul sakta hai kya?': Arif Mohammad Khan to author, 21 August 2018, New Delhi. He said that
      Arun Nehru had himself told him this.
134   He 'reportedly found no specific court order regarding its closure': Farzand Ahmed, 'Order to reopen Ram
      Janmabhoomi temple complex in Ayodhya sees tensions come to the boil', *India Today*, 28 February 1986.
135   On 18 September 1985, UP chief minister N. D. Tiwari had suddenly written to Rajiv Gandhi: Prabhu
      Chawla, 'N. D. Tiwari happily leaves his chief ministership for Vir Bahadur Singh in UP', *India Today*, 15
      October 1985.
135   The next morning Tiwari took a flight to Delhi to be sworn in: Ibid.
135   When Indira Gandhi was alive, she had shot down Arun Nehru's idea: Wajahat Habibullah to author, 12
      September 2022, in a telephonic conversation.
135   'I did not want it said later that Arun Nehru had given instructions to Vir Bahadur Singh': Arif
      Mohammad Khan to author, 21 August 2018, New Delhi. He said that Arun Nehru had himself told him
      this.
135   'I don't know whether what Arun Nehru told me was correct or incorrect': Ibid.
135   'All I can say is that Arun Nehru was managing the whole affair': Sharma, *Yuddh Maen Ayodhya*, p. 255.

135 Singh sent a message to the VHP: Ibid., p. 258; K. R. Malkani, *The Politics of Ayodhya & Hindu-Muslim Relations*, New Delhi: Har-Anand Publications, 1993, p. 27.

135 'The authorities (the allusion was to the district magistrate and superintendent of police) informally asked the VHP to move an application': Ibid.

136 'The VHP…was interested in unlocking but not in going to court': Ibid.

136 one of his links to the VHP was B. P. Singhal: G. S. Chawla to author, 21 August 2021, telephonic interview.

136 In 1986, B. P. Singhal was additional secretary: Later both Nehru and B. P. Singhal were charged for misdoing in the deal to purchase the Czech pistols, and the case was to go on until Nehru's death.

136 'Arun Nehru masterminded this coup': Chowdhury, 'The Political Fallout'.

136 'Rajiv Gandhi had indicated in no uncertain terms that the gates of the Ram Janmabhoomi must open': Ibid.

136 It was the RSS which had sent her word that Karan Singh was the best Hindu face the Congress should project: Anil Bali to author, 8 August 2019, New Delhi.

137 Though there had hardly been any contact between Indira Gandhi and Karan Singh: *Kashmir and Beyond 1966-84: Select Correspondence between Indira Gandhi & Karan Singh*, Jawaid Alam (ed.), New Delhi: Penguin India, 2011, pp. 286–87.

137 she decided to patch up with him after 1980: Karan Singh to author.

137 Karan Singh organized virat Hindu sammelans (mega Hindu conventions) all over the country: 'Ashok Singhal: The man who shaped the concept of Hindu vote bank', *DNA*, 18 November 2015.

137 'being the canny politician that she was, she used these sammelans' to her advantage: Karan Singh to author, 4 January 2021.

137 VHP undertook yatras to touch 3 lakh villages to 'unite Hindu society': Sumit Mitra, 'VHP-organised Ekaimata Yagna to roll across India with 92 religious caravans', *India Today*, 30 November 1983.

137 'Hinduism in danger', and the 'pampering of Muslims as a vote bank': Ibid.

137 'The Ekatmata Yatra in 1983 by the VHP was funded by Indira Gandhi': Anil Bali to author.

137 She knew how to play the game both ways: Manjari Katju, *Vishva Hindu Parishad and Indian Politics*, New Delhi: Orient Longman, 2003, p. 40.

137 She had also been quietly encouraging new Hindu organizations that had suddenly mushroomed: Neerja Chowdhury, 'Short-sighted Move to Appease Communities', *The Statesman*, 1 May 1986.

137 The meeting, which could not have been held without a clearance at the top: Mitra, 'VHP-organised Ekaimata Yagna to roll across India with 92 religious caravans'.

138 'Ayodhya as an electoral issue' at an 'appropriate moment': Ashok Singhal to author; also alluded to in author's three pieces in *The Statesman* dated 20 April and 1 May 1986.

138 she had become more mindful of the sensibilities of the Hindus than about the sensitivities of the Muslims or the Sikhs: Frank, *Indira*; Jayakar, *Indira Gandhi*; S. S. Gill, *The Dynasty: A Political Biography of the Premier Ruling Family of Modern India*, New Delhi: HarperCollins, 1996.

138 Each time she 'backed out': Harkishan Singh Surjeet to Mark Tully and Satish Jacob, cited by Rasheed Kidwai, 'Opinion | Indira Gandhi and Her Reluctance in Carving Out Punjabi-Speaking Punjab', News18, 31 October 2018.

138 Rajiv met Bhaurao thrice between 1982–84, when Indira Gandhi was still PM, and once in early 1991: Subhash Arya to author, 24 July 2020, telephonic interview. Also confirmed by Anil Bali to author, 7 March 2018, New Delhi.

138 Bhaurao and Rajiv hit it off well and talked about all manner of subjects: Ibid.

139 'Bhaurao used to feel that Hinduism would be safe with Rajiv': Anil Bali to author, 7 March 2018, New Delhi.

139 'I am an eyewitness to Rajiv Gandhi doing charan sparsh': Banwarilal Purohit to author.

139 'He said it was like his meeting with JP when he was underground': K. N. Govindacharya to author, 3 July 2018, New Delhi.

139 'We would make a point of getting fresh jamun juice for him': Pushpa Mohan, wife of Kapil Mohan, to author, 4 November 2020, telephonic interview, New Delhi.

139 Anil Bali would take the jamun juice to Jhandewalan 'whenever I went to meet him there': Anil Bali to author, 7 March 2018, New Delhi.

139 'so that Dhawan didn't get to know anything': Ibid.

139 'If there was one person who was a Hinduizing influence on Rajiv Gandhi between 1985–89': Ibid.

139 'Tell Rajiv not to talk of this (his talks with the RSS) on the dining table': M. L. Fotedar to author.

139 'She knew that Sonia was dead against the RSS': Anil Bali to author, 7 March 2018, New Delhi.

139 'I even remember the colour of the car—it was chocolate in colour: Pankaj Vohra to author, 1 August 2022, New Delhi.

139 'Chiranjeevi Rajiv, Ramayana agar Bharat men nahin dekhi jayegi': Anil Bali to author, 7 March 2018, New Delhi.

140 'Bhaurao sent the message through me to Rajiv in January 1989': Anil Bali to author, 7 March 2018, New Delhi.

140 The IB had assured him that the party would win 300 seats: Pankaj Vohra to author, 1 August 2022, New Delhi.

140 'secret pact' between the RSS and Rajiv Gandhi, on the 'shilanyas': 'Cong ex-MP alleges secret pact between Rajiv & RSS', *Times of India*, 26 April 2007.

140 'As the Congress pointsman at that time, I facilitated a meeting between then RSS': Ibid.

140 'Soon after that, Deoras had a meeting with the then Union Home minister Buta Singh': Ibid.

140 'I remember Singh used to often come to Jhandewalan in those days': Subhash Arya to author, 24 July 2020, telephonic interview, New Delhi.
140 Rajiv Gandhi was to tell Syed Shahabuddin that Buta Singh and N. D. Tiwari had 'misled' him: Syed Shahabuddin to author, 20 July 2005, New Delhi.
140 'I will tell you what RG told me in 1991 March, two months before he died': Ibid.
140 'Shahabuddin Saab, you are right': Ibid.
141 'He (Rajiv) admitted (that day) that the shilanyas was done in violation of the court order': Ibid.
141 Rajiv requested Bhaurao to reject the formula evolved by Chandra Shekhar: Anil Bali to author, 7 March 2018, New Delhi.
141 'He served them each a piece of the apple he had cut': Ibid.
141 'Bahut shaleen ladka hai': Ibid.
141 'You don't know what is bugged and what is not': Ibid.
141 'Three times he put his hand on my back': Ibid.
142 The Deoras brothers, Balasaheb and Bhaurao, found Rajiv 'innocent', who could be 'moulded': Pankaj Vohra to author, 1 August 2022, New Delhi.
142 He represented political stability which the RSS found alluring: Anil Bali to author, 12 September 2020, interview on phone. Subhash Arya to author confirming it, 24 July 2020, telephonic interview.
142 'Not a word to Arun Nehru,' she emphasized: Anil Bali to author, 7 March 2018, New Delhi.
142 'Bhaurao felt the lock-opening would create a national consensus': Govindacharya to author, 3 July 2018, New Delhi. Confirmed by Anil Bali to author, 12 September 2020, telephonic interview, New Delhi.
143 'You have taken a historical step. Hindu Hridaya samrat bano aur rajya karo': Anil Bali to author, 7 March 2018, New Delhi.
144 Umesh Chandra Pandey immediately filed an appeal in the Faizabad district court on 31 January: Malkani, *The Politics of Ayodhya*, p. 27.
144 It was rumoured that a senior judge of the Supreme Court had spoken to Judge Krishna Mohan Pandey: Ilyas Azmi, 'I Would Have Sentenced Rajiv Gandhi and Veer Bahadur Singh to Death', *Urdu Media Monitor*, 11 April 2015.
144 The structure, he argued, had been locked by the court in 1949 by an administrative, and not a judicial, order: Kumar Anshuman, 'SC tried to create a balance between parties, says the man on whose petition locks were opened in 1986', *Economic Times*, 9 November 2019.
144 'The DM and SSP came to the court personally': Sharma, *Yuddh Maen Ayodhya*, p. 252; Also told by Judge Krishna Mohan Pandey to Arif Mohammed Khan, and Khan to author, 21 August 2018, New Delhi.
144 at the instance of the district administration then, as action under Section 144 of the CrPC: District administrations takes action under (Section 144), Criminal Procedure Code when there is a threat to law and under, prohibiting the gathering of more than five people, so that the public peace is not disturbed.
144 'We are the government on the spot, and we will manage the law and order': Sharma, *Yuddh Maen Ayodhya*, p. 252.
144 'We told the district judge we will be able to handle the situation': Indu Kumar Pandey to author, 5 August 2021.
145 'who will send a Doordarshan team here?': Judge Krishna Mohan Pandey to Arif Mohammed Khan, and Khan to author, 21 August 2018, New Delhi.
145 'Then I felt reassured that the government wanted this': Ibid.
145 Judge Pandey relied on the assurances given by the district officials to allow direct 'darshan' of 'Ram Lalla': Sharma, *Yuddh Maen Ayodhya*, p. 251.
145 'Heavens are not going to fall by opening the locks at gates "O" and "P"': Ibid.
145 After that, the DM and the SSP made a point of personally escorting the district judge to his residence: Ibid., p. 246.
145 The rusty locks were broken open at 5.19 p.m.: Chowdhury, 'The Political Fallout'.
145 'I was told this by a Congress leader from UP who sat in the anteroom': Wajahat Habibullah to author, 12 September 2022, telephonic interview.
145 neither the munsif nor the district judge had the right to take a view in the matter: Sharma, *Yuddh Maen Ayodhya*, p. 254.
145 The VHP took the credit for the lock opening: Chowdhury, 'The Political Fallout'.
146 'Shah Bano will now take a back seat': Arif Mohammad Khan to author in 21 August 2018, reconfirmed in 19 August 2021.
146 'I have no such fears': Ibid.; Khan, *Text and Context*, p. 4.
146 'I had alerted the concerned parties on the other side': Ibid.
146 'Aur bhi bahut si masjidon par gairon ka kabza hai': Ibid.
146 'Everything was pre-planned,' remarked advocate Abdul Mannan: Ahmed, 'Order to reopen Ram Janmabhoomi temple complex in Ayodhya sees tensions come to the boil'.
146 They decided to form the Babri Masjid Movement Coordination Committee: Anshuman Kumar, 'Ayodhya case: A brief history of India's longest running property dispute', *Economic Times*, 10 November 2019.
146 'eroded' their 'faith in secularism': Ahmed, 'Order to reopen Ram Janmabhoomi temple complex in Ayodhya sees tensions come to the boil'.
147 'If the Babri Masjid is not restored to the Muslims, they will begin to hate the Congress(I)': Neerja Chowdhury, in a three-part series, *The Statesman*, 20 April 1986.
147 'He was presented with a fait accompli': Wajahat Habibullah to author, 12 September 2022, in a telephonic conversation, New Delhi.

147 Though he was still in the PMO, Habibullah had not been involved in the decision to open the locks: Wajahat Habibullah, 26 April 2019, New Delhi.

147 'interfering with places of worship of any religion is wrong and should never be done': Ibid.

147 'Yes, but I don't know yet who ordered it,' Rajiv said: Wajahat Habibullah, 26 April 2022, New Delhi.

147 'And when I find out I am afraid I will have to take action': Wajahat Habibullah, 26 April 2019, New Delhi; Habibullah, *My Years with Rajiv*.

147 'Yes, Rajiv Gandhi also told me that he had not given the order': Shahid Siddiqui to author, 7 March 2020, in a clarificatory phone call made from Mumbai.

147 'I don't think Rajiv Gandhi was aware of the opening of the locks': M. K. Narayanan to author, 8 August 2022, telephonic interview, Chennai.

147 'It is not possible that Rajiv Gandhi did not know about the opening of the locks': Anonymous senior Congress leader to author, 3 August 2021, New Delhi.

148 'In July 1985, Rajiv Gandhi told me not to bother further about the Swedes': R.O. & A.C. before author, Signed, Signature, 18-3-97, Keshav Mishra, Dy SP/CBI/SPE/SIG New Delhi.

148 Nehru had got into a wrangle with the Swedish government: Ibid.

148 'I was forced into it': Arun Nehru to author, 16 May 2001, New Delhi.

148 'We started scrapping from Day One': Ibid.

148 'It is my team now': Ibid.

149 'When I became the minister of Internal Security': Arun Nehru's deposition to the CBI in March 1997, New Delhi.

149 'Rajiv Gandhi did not have time to meet them, so they met me': Ibid.

149 'It was inconceivable for the intelligence chiefs not to report to the prime minister': M. K. Narayanan to author, 16 August 2022, telephonic interview, Chennai.

149 The intelligence agencies at the time 'still stuck to form, even if the substance of their role had been diluted': B. N. Uniyal to author, 27 February 2021, telephonic conversation, New Delhi.

149 'Sometimes he would invite me for lunch, and chat': M. K. Narayanan to author, 16 August 2022, telephonic interview, Chennai.

149 'he was overstepping his boundaries, and that was the main problem': Ibid.

149 'But sometimes Arun Nehru would drop in to see Rajiv': B. N. Uniyal to author, 27 February 2021, telephonic conversation, New Delhi.

149 'It was a way to bring opponents, inside and outside the party, "in line"': Ibid.

149 'Rajiv Gandhi was upset over this (state of affairs)': Arun Nehru's deposition to the CBI, 16 March 1997.

149 'So, they used to give verbal reports to me': Ibid.

149 'My working style was so aggressive': Arun Nehru to author, 16 May 2001, New Delhi.

150 'He used to ask me what good is your sense of history': Ibid.

150 'He reversed everything she had done': Ibid.

150 'I opposed him': Ibid.

150 '(The trouble is) you want confrontation, I want conciliation': Ibid.

150 'Then she became the maharani': Ibid.

150 'I could not care less for the domestic lobby or the kitchen cabinet': Ibid.

150 Sonia suspected that Arun Nehru was keeping surveillance on Rajiv and the family: Shahid Siddiqui to author, 25 March 2019, New Delhi. Also a senior Congress leader who was close to Arun Nehru to author, 3 August 2021, New Delhi.

150 'Sonia Gandhi had told Rajiv, that I was holding them under surveillance': Arun Nehru to author, 16 May 2001, New Delhi.

150 'the security of the PM's house was (now) my business': Ibid.

150 He was insolent, could be dismissive of him and even snap at Rajiv: B. N. Uniyal to author, 27 February 2021, telephonic conversation, New Delhi.

151 'Mitra bhi agar Raja ho jaye toh aap usko "hey rajan" bulate hain': Ibid.

151 'Arun Nehru never liked the family's proximity to Quattrochi': Dinesh Trivedi to author, 5 May 2001, New Delhi.

151 'Sonia might not have forgotten about it': Anonymous source to author.

151 'Shah Bano was not just about Shah Bano': Shahid Siddiqui to author.

151 '(Arun Nehru) felt that he was the "real" blue blooded Nehru': Anonymous member of Congress to author, 3 August 2021, New Delhi.

151 'Rajiv Arun Nehru se bahut ghabrate thae': G. S. Chawla to author, 21 August, 2021, telephonic conversation, New Delhi.

152 'Who does not position himself?': Arun Nehru to author in an as yet unpublished interview, 16 May 2001, New Delhi.

152 Rajiv had a showdown with Arun Nehru in early May 1986: G. S. Chawla, *Bloodshed in Punjab: Untold Saga of Deceit and Sabotage*, New Delhi: Har-Anand Publications, 2016.

152 At 3 a.m. on 31 May 1986, he suffered a heart attack: Prabhu Chawla, 'Arun Nehru suffers heart attack, speculation rife about break from active political life', *India Today*, 30 June 1986.

152 'He came through the bathroom door, not from the front entrance': G. S. Chawla to author, 21 August 2021, telephonic conversation, New Delhi.

153 He had said as much to Natwar Singh in July 1986: Natwar Singh to author, 21 June 2018, New Delhi. Also Wajahat Habibullah to author, 26 April 2019, New Delhi.

153 'He offered to send me as high commissioner to UK': Arun Nehru to author, 16 May 2001, New Delhi.

153 'We had a very bad meeting': Ibid.

153 The meeting ended with Rajiv asking Nehru to resign: Fotedar, 'The 1985 Centenary Session', *The Chinar Leaves*.

153 'I thank you for the opportunity you have given me to work with you': Prabhu Chawla, 'Cabinet reshuffle: Rajiv Gandhi cuts to size powerful men like Arjun Singh, Arun Nehru', *India Today*, 15 November 1986.

153 'We should wait for the repercussions': M. L. Fotedar to author. 1 January 2005, Gurgaon.

154 'Rajivji was tense': Ibid.

154 Sonia had a wide smile on her face: Fotedar, 'The 1985 Centenary Session', *The Chinar Leaves*; Pankaj Vora to author, 11 March 2021, New Delhi.

154 'I understood then why Arun Nehru had been dropped': M. L. Fotedar to author.

154 'From then on, VP realized that things were up for him also': Arun Nehru to author, 16 May 2001, New Delhi.

154 Bofors had paid bribes to Indian politicians: Jack Cinamon and Devan van der Poel, 'The Bofors Scandal', *Corruption Tracker*, 7 March 2023.

154 'It was Arun Nehru who leaked the Bofors story to the Swedish Radio': H. R. Bhardwaj to author, 26 February 2018, New Delhi.

154 'What they are telling you is all wrong': Qurban Ali to author, 15 June 2021, New Delhi.

155 'It was Arun Nehru': Ibid.

155 'At the time of the shilanyas also, there was a formal agreement': Ibid.

155 'Rajiv was no longer as naive as people thought': H. R. Bhardwaj to author, 20 August 2003, New Delhi.

155 Once again, Rajiv wilted under pressure, this time from the Hindu groups: Chowdhury, 'The Political Fallout'.

155 His Westernized thinking led him to make the biggest miscalculations of his career: Wajahat Habibullah to author, 26 April 2019, New Delhi.

156 It was that 'courts did not matter. Political agitations did. So did electoral vote banks': Chowdhury, 'The Political Fallout'.

CHAPTER 3: THE CRAFTY PRIME MINISTER WHO REMADE INDIAN POLITICS: V. P. SINGH'S MANDAL GAMBIT

157 The reporter dashed out of the Central Hall: It had acquired its name for its location between the Lok Sabha, the Rajya Sabha, and the house of the princely states (reading room) adorned with symbols announcing its merger into the Union of India after 1947. (Sitaram Yechury, 'Central Hall of Parliament: The Unsung Tales', *Deccan Herald*, 21 August 2022.)

157 But, after the polls, he decided to make a bid for the top job himself: Harinder Baweja, 'Jat leader Devi lal seems to be unstoppable', *India Today*, 30 November 1989.

157 'Even Rajiv Gandhi did not humiliate Raja sahib (V. P. Singh) like this': S. N. Singh to author, 1 December 1989 at 28, Lodi Estate, New Delhi.

158 until Rajiv Gandhi sacked him: 'Gandhi Expels Three Former Ministers From Party', 16 July 1987, *The Associated Press*.

158 helped craft the Janata Dal: The parties which merged to form the Janata Dal on 11 October, 1988 were the Janata Party (including Lok Dal (A) which had by then merged into it), Congress (Secular), Lok Dal (B) and Jan Morcha).

158 'I told VP two...days before the election (of the leader), leave this to me and you stay out of it': Arun Nehru to author, 16 May 2001, New Delhi.

158 It had lost 217 seats of the record majority of 414 seats: 'Statistical Report on General Elections, 1989 to the Ninth Lok Sabha: Volume I', Delhi: Election Commission of India, 1990, available at <eci.gov.in/files/file/4120-general-election-1989-vol-i-ii>.

158 resignation to President Venkataraman on 29 November: Nooruddin Inamdar, 'November 29 - The day Rajiv Gandhi resigned as Prime Minister of India', *Free Press Journal*, 28 November 2022.

158 Rajiv was clear that he did not have the stomach to run a coalition government: H. R. Bhardwaj to author, 20 August 2003, New Delhi.

159 The Janata Dal that V. P. Singh had put together in 1988 had been victorious in 143 Lok Sabha constituencies: 'Statistical Report on General Elections, 1989 to the Ninth Lok Sabha: Volume I'.

159 The party had won 54 of 85 seats in UP and got 32 out of 54 seats in Bihar: Ibid.

159 the Left parties had together mopped up 52 seats between them: CPI (M) got 33, CPI 12, Revolutionary Socialist Party 4, and the All India Forward Bloc 3. In this election Assam did not go to the polls: Richard Sisson, 'India in 1989: A Year of Elections in a Culture of Change', *Asian Survey*, Vol. 30, No. 2, 1990, p. 117.

159 'Vishwanath if you contest, I will also contest': Chandra Shekhar to author.

160 'I propose Devi Lal's name': V. P. Singh to author, 16 October 1999, Apollo Hospital, New Delhi.

160 'VP ho gaya': Ibid.

160 'Kill, kill, kill, earlier story': Inderjit Badhwar and Prabhu Chawla, 'V.P. Singh becomes new prime minister of India, National Front comes to power', *India Today*, 15 December 1989.

161 'Iska anjam acha nahin hoga': Chandra Shekhar to author, 1 December 1989, Central Hall, Parliament House.

161 'Biju had called me to Orissa Bhavan and told me that VP': Chandra Shekhar to author, 20 November 2002.

161 'Biju came to see me and offered me the deputy PMship': Ibid.
161 'Arrey Ballia, if I had known you would run a government like this': Ibid. Such was the relationship between the two that Biju Patnaik would affectionately call Chandra Shekhar 'Ballia' (the place he was born in eastern UP) and Chandra Shekhar would address him as 'Odia' (resident of Odisha.)
162 'What is the Janata Dal without me?': Som Pal to author, New Delhi.
162 Devi Lal would be ready to support the BJP's demand for a Hindu Rashtra: Badhwar and Chawla, 'V.P. Singh becomes new prime minister of India, National Front comes to power'.
162 'Mamaji, all through the campaign, you had said again and again that V. P. Singh will be prime minister': Som Pal to author, New Delhi.
162 'The numbers are stacked heavily against Chandra Shekhar': Ibid.
162 Industrialists had sent their representatives to Delhi within hours of the results: Badhwar and Chawla, 'V.P. Singh becomes new prime minister of India, National Front comes to power'.
163 'Mamaji, running the central government is not like running the Haryana ministry': Ibid.
163 'If you support VP as PM...you can become the deputy prime minister': Ibid.
163 '(However) I was advised by P. Upendra of TDP that I would be inviting trouble': V. P. Singh to author.
163 'Send Arun Nehru to me': Som Pal to author.
163 'Did we fight Rajiv Gandhi to create a mess like this?': Kuldip Nayar to author.
164 'Raja ki jaan tote maen hoti hai': Ashwini Kumar Chopra to author.
164 Nayar, Sethi, and Chopra walked out of Haryana Bhavan together: Kuldip Nayar to author.
164 'I used to give it back to Devi Lal,' Nehru said later: Arun Nehru to author, 1 June 2001, New Delhi.
164 'We don't care about Devi Lal,' Arun Nehru told the group: Ibid.
165 'Are you a doctor or what?': Som Pal to author.
165 'Chandra Shekhar will contest.': Arun Nehru to author, 16 May 2001, New Delhi.
165 'Only Biju could have...persuaded Devi Lal': Chandra Shekhar to author.
165 'Somehow find a way out': Arun Nehru to author, 16 May 2001, New Delhi.
165 'Arun don't push things so hard that the party breaks': Ibid.
165 'Devi Lal was aggressive and unreasonable': Arun Nehru to author, 1 June 2001, New Delhi.
166 'I think it was Devi Lal's own idea that his name be proposed first': V. P. Singh to author.
166 'Hum aap ke liye kuchh bhi kar sakte hain': Ibid.
166 'Us (Chandra Shekhar) se vaada kiya hai ki main banoonga': Arun Nehru to author, 1 June 2001, New Delhi.
166 'It was not (previously) thought out': Ibid.
166 'It was Arun Nehru's idea': S. P. Shukla to Neerja, 25 October 2002, New Delhi.
166 Arun Nehru finally convinced Biju Patnaik that it was the only way out of the impasse: Santosh Bhartiya to author.
166 'We told Devi Lal that he should tell Chandra Shekhar what the samjhauta (deal) was': Arun Nehru to author, 1 June 2001, New Delhi.
167 'You also tell some MPs about this quietly,' Patnaik told Jena: Srikant Jena to author.
167 'VP ko banana hai': Ibid.
167 At 12 noon, on 2 December 1989, President R. Venkataraman administered the oath of office: R. Venkataraman, *My Presidential Years*, New Delhi: Indus (HarperCollins), 1994, pp. 324–25.
167 'South Block is the PM's office. You have not yet been given a portfolio': Ashwini Kumar Chopra to author.
168 Suddenly Devi Lal interrupted them, 'Woh oop bhi uttar jayega': Kuldip Nayar to author, 7 June 2002, New Delhi.
168 'It is because of me that he is prime minister today': Som Pal to author, New Delhi, 2 March 2022.
168 'You became the prime minister because I told a lie': *Sunday*, 18–24 March, 1990, quoted in Thakur, *Prime Ministers*, p. 276.
168 They were JKLF 'area commander' Sheikh Abdul Hameed: Barbara Crossette, 'Abducted Woman Freed in Kashmir', *New York Times*, 14 December 1989.
168 'I did not go to the press or to the cabinet (about it)': V. P. Singh to author, New Delhi.
169 Janata Dal victory in the state elections in UP in November 1989: Debashish Mukerji, *The Disruptor: How Vishwanath Pratap Singh Shook India*, New Delhi: Harper Collins, p. 333.
169 'Aap UP ke pachrhe maen mat parho': Som Pal to author, 13 March 2022.
169 'If Mulayam Singh is not allowed to become CM': Som Pal to author, 3 March 2022.
169 'Mayhem in Meham': Harinder Baweja, 'Haryana CM Om Prakash Chautala rigs his own political future', *India Today*, 31 March 1990.
169 'a cross between a horror movie and burlesque theatre': S. Nihal Singh, 'A Shameful Episode', *India Today*, 15 March 1990.
169 Chief Minister Chautala allegedly used open intimidation and booth capturing: Baweja, 'Haryana CM Om Prakash Chautala rigs his own political future'.
169 Chautala himself allegedly led groups of hoodlums through the villages of Meham: Ibid.
170 'The entire election process was vitiated': 'By-Election, marred by violence, vote fraud, countermanded', *AP News*, 8 March 1990.
170 Several Janata Dal leaders—Ajit Singh, George Fernandes, Madhu Dandavate, and Nathuram Mirdha: Baweja, 'Haryana CM Om Prakash Chautala rigs his own political future'.
170 'Who asked Ajit Singh to go to Meham?': V. P. Singh to author, 18 October 1999, Apollo Hospital, New Delhi.
170 'Ae Pande tujhe kya pata hai iske bare maen?': Ibid.

170   'Your first instincts are often right. I was trained under Indira Gandhi': Ibid.
171   'In April (after Meham), I wanted to go in for parliamentary elections': Ibid.
171   'He is likely to give the Congress a chance to form the government': Ibid.
171   'Devi Lal was a divine gift to us': M. L. Fotedar to author, 1 January 2005, New Delhi.
171   'Even RV (President R. Venkatraman) was privately against VP at the time': Ibid.
171   'Dethrone the VP government,' Sharma advised Rajiv: N. K. Sharma to author, 25 January 2000, New Delhi.
171   'Devi Lal had already told me that the PM was not listening to him on issues concerning the farmers': Ibid.
172   He had been tipped off by the IB; some officers had remained in touch with Gandhi: Ibid.
172   'We have to talk to Chaudhary sahib (Devi Lal)': Ibid.
172   'Panditji, will you repeat what you told me last night': Ibid.
172   By now, the BJP also joined the ranks of those who were demanding Chautala's resignation: Inderjit Badhwar and Prabhu Chawla, 'V.P. Singh asserts himself by forcing Chautala's resignation and Jagmohan's removal', *India Today*, 15 June 1990.
172   All through this period, the distance between Devi Lal and V. P. Singh had been growing: N. K. Sharma to author.
172   'I took with me the draft of a letter': Ibid.
173   'I was told that somebody would meet me at the Mumbai airport with my boarding card': Ibid.
173   'As soon as I came down the aircraft stairs, there was a person waiting there with my boarding card': Ibid.
173   'VP is neglecting me': Som Pal to author.
174   'Devi Lal phoned this morning and said he was very happy with the dinner': Ibid.
174   'V. P. Singh is a fantastic person': Devi Lal to Som Pal who shared this with the author.
174   'When I arrived, he handed me a two page statement by Banarasi Das Gupta': Som Pal to author.
175   'We had gathered at Arun Nehru's house in the evening': Satyapal Malik to author.
175   The PM asked them to come: Seema Mustafa and H. Baweja, 'Dramatic developments that almost led to the fall of the National front Government', *India Today*, 15 August 1990.
175   'We went to VP's house around 11 p.m.': Satyapal Malik to author.
176   'VP is a self consuming target': Surendra Mohan to author, 12 September 2003, New Delhi. He had been told this by Kuldip Nayar.
176   'In other words, the way would be cleared for Nehru for the top job': Ibid.
176   'He (Arun Nehru) was constantly giving Rajiv information (about what was going on in the Janata Dal)': M. L. Fotedar to author.
176   'I had asked VP why the Janata Dal had collapsed so quickly': Dinesh Trivedi to author.
176   'When Rajiv realized that the government could collapse, he hurried (up) the process': Ibid.
176   'I had the feeling that Rajiv Gandhi was behind the resignations of Arun Nehru and Arif Khan': H. R. Bhardwaj to Neerja, 20 August 2003, New Delhi.
176   'He was not so worried about what Rajiv Gandhi would do': Govindacharya to author, 3 July 2018, New Delhi.
176   'The PMO had got this information—that they (BJP) may bring down the government at the end of the Rath Yatra': Prem Shankar Jha to author, 1 September 2021.
177   In June 1990, at its meeting in Haridwar, the Vishwa Hindu Parishad had already upped the ante and called for kar seva: A term used for those performing selfless service—usually with spiritual connotations.
177   'When I took over, I had thought that the BJP will take two years before it pulled the plug': V. P. Singh to author, New Delhi.
177   'I was in favour of asking him to resign': Ibid.
177   'You could have managed it differently': Ibid., October 1990.
177   'there is no need to go in for Mandal': Som Pal to author, 13 March 2022.
177   'If you go in for Mandal, it will be others, not you, who will benefit': Ibid.
178   'I had (once) asked him about his views on reservations': Dinesh Trivedi to author.
178   'Mandal was the realization of the Janata Dal politically': V. P. Singh to author, 20 October 1999, Apollo Hospital, New Delhi.
178   The secure RAX phone in Sharad Yadav's bedroom rang late at night: Secure RAX telephone sets were given to ministers and senior bureaucrats to prevent interception of phone calls by intelligence agencies of foreign countries.
178   'Sharad bhai, ab toh Devi Lalji ke saath kaam karna mushkil ho gaya hai': Sharad Yadav to author, 27 December 2005, New Delhi.
179   'Jo Devi Lalji ki sthiti thee woh ab aapki rahegi': Ibid.
179   'It's quite late, Sharad bhai, I will call you in the morning': Ibid.
179   Having made that decision, he started calling up prominent OBC leaders: Ibid.
180   Their meeting lasted 'for two hours': Ibid.
180   'This had been signal enough for me that the PM was in no hurry to bring in Mandal': Ibid.
180   Ram Pujan Patel, a prominent Kurmi leader from UP, who later joined VP's cabinet, shot off a letter to the prime minister: Ram Pujan Patel to author, New Delhi, 28 February 2003.
180   'You should announce the decision to implement the Mandal Commission Report': Sharad Yadav to author.
181   'For long term survival,' VP would say, 'it is the poor who give stability, whichever the party': V. P. Singh to author, 20 October 1999, Apollo Hospital, New Delhi.
181   At the time, twelve out of twenty-five states already had quotas for the OBCs: Mukerji, *The Disruptor*, p. 396.

181 'The idea,' he told the assembled group, 'is to remove these discrepancies.': Som Pal to author.

182 Around two dozen MPs spoke at the meeting: Som Pal to author, 11 February 2022, New Delhi.

182 'No legislation is required to do this': Som Pal to author, 16 February 2000, New Delhi.

182 'As long as a savarna (upper caste) is a prime minister, the Mandal report will never be implemented': Ibid.

182 'We should announce it on the first day of the parliament session': Ibid.

182 It was ten years earlier that Bindeshwari Prasad Mandal: B. P. Mandal was the former chief minister of Bihar and the chairman of the five-member civil rights commission, popularly known as the Mandal Commission, appointed by Morarji Desai in December 1978.

182 But he told his secretary to make sure that the 'official' dealing with the 'backward issue' was present: B. G. Deshmukh was additional secretary home at the time, later to be principal secretary to V. P. Singh when Mandal was adopted. He had been overseeing everything to do with the Mandal Commission from the time it was set up on 1 January 1979.

183 'Saab, aap ne report par bahut mehnat ki hai. Par aaj hum iskaa visarjan kar aaye hain': S. S. Gill to author, 26 July 2004, New Delhi.

183 'This government won't have the same commitment to the idea': Ibid.

183 'Every word of the report was written by me,' Gill said: Ibid.

184 'if you don't understand caste you can't really understand...its ramifications': Ibid.

184 'those who implemented it had not read the report': Ibid.

184 in the final analysis, it relied more on 'social backwardness': 'Report of the Second Backward Classes Commission', First Part, Vol. I, 1980, Government of India.

184 the OBC quota, to be safe, had to be fixed at 27 per cent: 'Report of the Second Backward Classes Commission'.

185 the caste system that inheres among Hindus: 'Origin of Caste System in India', *Hindustan Times*, 3 June 2003.

186 'I don't think Nehru really understood caste': S. S. Gill to author, New Delhi.

186 He listed 2,399 castes as backward, entitled for help: Nomita Yadav, 'Other Backward Classes: Then and Now', *Economic and Political Weekly*, Vol. 37, Vo. 44/45, 2002, p. 4495.

186 'We got the impression that he wanted to implement it (Kalelkar Report), but he did not say so directly': Shiv Shankar to author.

186 'We went to see Pantji in his office': Ibid.

186 Interestingly, even though the report's author, Kalelkar, was sympathetic: S. S. Gill to author.

186 In 1961, however, it decided it would leave it to state governments to decide: Mukerji, *The Disruptor*, p. 384.

186 The state governments set up their own commissions: 'Report of the Second Backward Classes Commission', pp. 5–11, in Mukerji, *The Disruptor*, p. 385.

187 It was in 1959, that socialist icon Ram Manohar Lohia had first flagged the idea of reserving 60 per cent: P. R. Ramesh, 'Bihar: Land without Justice', *Open*, 6 August 2015.

187 'Sasopa ne bandhi gaanth, pichde paanve sau maen saath': Akshaya Mukul, 'Ram Manohar Lohia: The Quota Marshall', *TOI Crest*, 3 April 2010.

187 This effectively reduced the quantum of OBC reservations to 20 per cent: Shyama Nand Singh, 'Anti Reservation Agitations in Bihar', *The Indian Journal of Political Science*, Vol. 52, Issue 1, January–March 1991, pp. 24–42.

187 This had the pro-reservationists up in arms and divided the Janata Party: Govindacharya to author, July 2018.

188 'I once went to Charan Singh for some work when he was Home Minister': Shiv Shankar to author.

188 it was Shiv Shankar who had quietly advised the commission not to adopt economic criteria: B. G. Deshmukh, *A Cabinet Secretary Looks Back: From Poona to the Prime Minister's Office*, New Delhi: HarperCollins India, 2004, p. 287.

188 'Shiv Shankarji, kya karaen?': Shiv Shankar to author, 6 June 2007, New Delhi.

188 'Aisa ATR likhiye ki saamp bhi mar jaye aur laathi bhi naa toote': Ibid.

189 'Who will head the committee of ministers?': Ibid.

189 'Shiv Shankarji, what's going on in the committee?': Ibid.

189 The South had gone in for reservations long before the northern states did so: Mukerji, *The Disruptor*, p. 383.

189 26 out of 28 Lok Sabha seats: 'Statistical Report on General Elections, 1977 to the Sixth Lok Sabha: Volume I', Delhi: Election Commission of India, 1978, available at <eci.gov.in/files/file/4116-general-election-1977-vol-i-ii>.

190 Rajiv felt that 'other steps' should be taken to improve the lot of the backward classes: Deshmukh, *A Cabinet Secretary Looks Back*, p. 282.

190 'The Mandal Commission's Report is a can of worms': Inder Malhotra, 'Mandal vs Mandir', *Indian Express*, 23 March 2015.

190 He had also shot down the proposal to go for reservations for OBCs in panchayati raj institutions: Shiv Shankar to author, June 2007; Deshmukh, *A Cabinet Secretary Looks Back*, p. 287.

190 Rajiv still spoke critically of them: 'Lok Sabha Debates (English Version): Third Session (Ninth Lok Sabha)', New Delhi: Lok Sabha Secretariat, 6 September 1990, available at <eparlib.nic.in/bitstream/123456789/3295/1/lsd_09_03_06-09-1990.pdf>.

190 He spoke for two and half hours—in the longest ever speech delivered in the Lok Sabha: L. K. Advani, *My Country, My Life*, New Delhi: Rupa & Co., 2008, p. 448.

190 'Ministers are provoking caste wars': 'Lok Sabha Debates (English Version): Third Session (Ninth Lok Sabha)', p. 532.
190 The ministers had trickled in for the meeting earlier in the afternoon: Mukerji, *The Disruptor*, p. 222.
191 a message to the bureaucracy that he was not going to be vindictive: V. P. Singh to author.
191 'I never had problems in my cabinet': Ibid.
191 'We will first discuss the implementation of the Mandal Commission report': Deshmukh, *A Cabinet Secretary Looks Back*, p. 280.
191 He turned to the PM and said flatly that he 'had no notice': Ibid.
191 He asked his minister for Social Welfare to go ahead and make his presentation: Ibid; confirmed by Ram Vilas Paswan to author.
192 The work was done essentially by the Ministry of Social Welfare, and its secretary, P. S. Krishna: V. P. Singh to author.
192 'I had called Ram Vilas Paswan and told him that irrespective of the (party) committee': Ibid.
192 As he warmed up, Paswan made a case for the implementation of the Mandal Commission Report: Deshmukh, *A Cabinet Secretary Looks Back*, p. 280.
192 Yadav also spoke in favour of the proposal: Ibid.
192 Ajit Singh, minister for Industries, was for going ahead: Ibid.
192 Mufti Mohammed Sayeed, India's first Muslim home minister, pleaded for more time: Ibid.
192 Two people had expressed themselves clearly against the proposal: V. P. Singh to author; confirmed by Arun Nehru.
192 hiking of the OBC quota from 10 per cent to 28 per cent in technical and medical colleges: Parmanand Singh, 'Reservations, Reality and the Constitution: Current crisis in India', *Cochin University Law Review*, Vol. 11, 1987, p. 290.
192 'Sir, don't do it. We did it in Gujarat. It will create many problems': Chimanbhai Mehta to author.
192 'Vishwanath, politics is not arithmetic': Arun Nehru to author, 1 June 2001, New Delhi.
193 But Dandavate, a socialist, was a long-standing supporter of Mandal: Ibid.; Deshmukh, *A Cabinet Secretary Looks Back*, p. 280.
193 'I supported the (VP) move 100 per cent': Madhu Dandavate to author.
193 Deepak Nayyar had pored over the Mandal Commission Report: Deepak Nayyar, 16 February 2000.
193 'Deepak, you leave politics to me': Ibid.
193 'I have not gone the whole hog': Ram Vilas Paswan to author.
193 was to apply only to central government jobs and to public sector units: Ibid.
193 VP heard his colleagues out: Deepak Nayyar to author. Nayyar, chief economic adviser to the VP government, was present in the meeting.
193 'No one really resisted it in the cabinet': V. P. Singh to author.
193 'This, then, is the consensus': Deshmukh, *A Cabinet Secretary Looks Back*, p. 281.
194 'Can you prepare a note for me so that I can announce the decision in parliament tomorrow?': Ibid.
194 Deshmukh was surprised: Ibid.
194 But he became disenchanted with Rajiv Gandhi: Shiv Shankar to author; M. L. Fotedar to author.
194 'Shiv Shankar advised VP to go in for Mandal': H. R. Bhardwaj to author, New Delhi.
194 'It was such a mundane type of writing that it couldn't fit the description of social justice': Shiv Shankar to author, 6 June 2007, New Delhi.
194 VP went over with him the points he would make in parliament the next day: Mukerji, *The Disruptor*, p. 396.
195 'It's the one time I did not consult them,' VP admitted: V. P. Singh to author.
195 'If the Janata Dal is bent upon playing the Mandal card': Som Pal to author, 16 February 2000.
196 'Devendra, which one of them is the "chaiin" (the crafty one)?': Devendra Dwivedy to author, 2 February 2001, New Delhi. Dwivedy was a close friend of Sant Bux Singh.
196 given in adoption to the childless raja of Manda: Mukerji, *The Disruptor*, p. 8.
196 VP's horoscope that 'matched' the requirements of the raja of Manda: Devendra Dwivedy to author, 2 February 2001, New Delhi; Ibid., p. 19.
197 VP recalled years later that he could still remember its flavour: V. P. Singh to author.
197 Sant Bux and his other brother, Har Bux Singh, would sometimes surreptitiously accompany him in the 'buggy': Seema Mustafa, *The Lonely Prophet: V.P. Singh, a Political Biography*, New Delhi: New Age International, 1995; V. P. Singh to author.
197 A year after VP's move to Allahabad, his adoptive father died: Mukerji, *The Disruptor*, p. 3.
197 'I was insecure, very insecure': Ibid., p. 19.
198 'erudite and articulate': Ibid., p. 112.
198 VP donated 200 bighas of his own lands to the Vinoba Bhave-led Bhoodan movement: Indra Shekhar Singh, 'A grandson's tribute: The forgotten idealism of VP Singh' *Scroll.in*, 25 June 2016.
198 They would go to the villages at night, each one pretending to be the candidate: Mukerji, *The Disruptor*, p. 68.
198 He was so moved by the gesture that he declared VP would be his fifth son: V. P. Singh to author.
199 Later VP admitted that a desire for recognition and to leave a mark: Mukerji, *The Disruptor*, p. 62.
199 He managed to get a Dalit candidate to withdraw in his favour: Ibid., p. 84.
199 'My jeep used to be loaded mostly with Dalits': V. P. Singh to author, 20 October 1999.
199 'My own election gave me insight of the fire burning below': Ibid.
199 'As I entered...Bahuguna told me, "Inko andar lekar jao"': Devendra Dwivedy to author.

200 'We are going to be giving `1 lakh to each candidate': Ibid.
200 When Mrs Gandhi was arrested in December 1978, he was one of those who went to jail in protest: V. P. Singh to author.
200 He was pragmatic, discreet, and known for a quiet efficiency: Devendra Dwivedy to author, 12 February 2001, NCP office, BD Road, New Delhi.
200 'We are going from Lucknow right up to Bullandshahr': V. P. Singh to author, October 1999.
200 'If you can correct the situation, come': Ibid.
201 His brother had paid the price for his office: Anand Sagar, 'Senior judge of Allahabad High Court, 15-year-old son killed by dacoits', India Today, 15 April 1982.
201 In the forty-one days that followed, 299 'dacoits' were eliminated in 'encounters': Chaitanya Kalbag, 'Dacoit menace continues to dog Uttar Pradesh', India Today, 31 January 1982.
203 'Both of them lay down on it in their kachcha-banians after bathing': H. R. Bhardwaj to author, 26 February 2018, New Delhi.
203 Indira Gandhi had expressed the hope that V. P. Singh would be part of Rajiv's core team: M. L. Fotedar to author; H. R. Bhardwaj to author; Devendra Dwivedy to author.
203 'One day at midnight—this was just before the 1984 elections': Ibid.
203 'the poet and the poem': Suruchi Mazumdar, 'The poet's poem', The Indian Express, 22 December 2007.
203 At this time, the Bachchans were living at 13, Willingdon Crescent: Jaya Bachchan to author, 2001, New Delhi.
203 The Gandhis lived in 1, Safdarjung Road and the two houses were near enough: 'What went wrong with Dosti No1?', Times of India, 17 October 2004.
203 The Bachchan and Gandhi boys would swim together in the pool in Rashtrapati Bhavan: Jaya Bachchan to author, 2001, New Delhi.
204 'But you have to do it quietly. No one should know': H. R. Bhardwaj to author.
204 'I don't know the "p" of politics': 'What went wrong with Dosti No1?'
204 'There's no problem,' he told Rajiv Gandhi politely: H. R. Bhardwaj to author.
204 escorted Amitabh and Jaya Bachchan to Lucknow: Jaya Bachchan to author, August 2021.
204 'It was decided that the Bachchans would then go onto Allahabad incognito': H. R. Bhardwaj to author.
204 'There were 1,785 chunnis thrown': D. P. Tripathi to author.
205 VP was not alone in feeling threatened by Bachchan: Mukerji, The Disruptor, p. 248.
205 He agreed to be present only when Rajiv came to Allahabad to campaign: D. P. Tripathi, New Delhi.
205 VP felt that he had been 'exiled from Allahabad': V. P. Singh to author.
205 'We have to defeat these (Opposition) people first': Arun Nehru to author, 16 May 2001, New Delhi.
205 A few years later, in mid-1987, he resigned as MP: T. N. Ninan and Brij Khindaria, 'Amitabh Bachchan resigns from Lok Sabha, Ajitabh lands in Swiss trouble', India Today, 15 August 1987.
205 'The finance minister has to be very tough': M. J. Akbar, interview with Rajiv Gandhi, 'The Assassination Was Done not to Kill Mrs Gandhi, It Was Done for the Reaction', Sunday, 10–16 March 1985.
205 Some corporate leaders hailed it as the 'best ever in independent India': Suman Dubey, 'Vishwanath Pratap Singh's Budget Makes a Clean Break with the Past', India Today, 15 April 1985.
206 He would repeatedly urge Vinod Pande to 'catch the bigger fish': S. P. Shukla to author, 25 December 2002.
206 'I have only turned the ignition': T. N. Ninan, 'From tax raids to price rise, V.P. Singh is at the centre of several converging storms', India Today, 15 September 1985.
206 Bhure Lal and his team raided the home of the eighty-two-year-old industry doyen S. L. Kirloskar: Mukerji, The Disruptor, p. 227.
206 Lalit Thapar, chairman of Thapar Industries, was arrested at 1 a.m.: Ibid., p. 228.
206 Thapar apologized and accepted most of the charges levelled against him: Ibid.
206 Other prominent industrial houses which were hauled up included Bajaj Auto, Voltas, and Bata: Ibid., p. 226.
207 'all conversion of non-convertible debentures into shares': Ibid., p. 231.
207 'Aisa shaneechar bitha diya hai sir par': Som Pal to author.
207 'was holding a huge amount of funds on behalf of Rajiv's late mother and wanted to know what to do with the money': Mukerji, The Disruptor, p. 238.
207 They called VP a traitor and a CIA agent: Ibid., p. 267.
207 The document turned out to be a forgery: Mayank Chhaya, 'Remembering former Indian PM V P Singh and the St Kitts saga', South Asia Monitor, 26 June 2021.
208 'Yeh jail maen nahin hain, kya itna kam soft hai?': V. P. Singh to author.
208 a 'raid raj' had been unleashed in the country: Mukerji, The Disruptor, p. 245.
208 'It was in 1985 that VP Singh began to see the possibility of becoming prime minister': Som Pal to author.
208 'I think the possibility had occurred to him even when he was chief minister of UP': Devendra Dwivedy to author, 27 March 2001.
208 'The composure, composition, and expression were just right': Som Pal to author, 25 January 2000.
209 'This was VP's first exercise in PR. What came later was not an accident': Ibid.
209 VP was now replacing Rajiv as the Mr Clean of Indian politics: Prabhu Chawla, 'Finance to defence: PM Rajiv Gandhi removes V.P. Singh from the limelight', India Today, 15 February 1987; Som Pal to author, 25 January 2000.
209 'It was Quattrochi who was one of the reasons for my differences with Rajiv': V. P. Singh to author, 18 October 1999, New Delhi.
209 'Or there is no point in my staying on': Ibid.

210   'I am a disciplined soldier of the party': Som Pal to author.
210   'I need a responsible person to head the defence ministry': V. P. to Neerja, 18 October 1999, New Delhi.
210   At this time, Rajiv was also unhappy with the role played by the chief of army staff, General K. Sundarji: Ibid.
210   'Dekhaenge. Abhi to hum machine ko study kar rahen hain': V. P. Singh to author.
211   VP put all the information on file and ordered a departmental enquiry: V. P. Singh to author, 22 October 1999, New Delhi.
211   'What will be the result of the enquiry?': V. P. Singh to author, 29 May 2003.
211   Rajiv ordered that from then on the government would directly negotiate the arms deals: Hamish McDonald, *Ambani and Sons*, cited in Mukerji, *The Disruptor*, p. 257.
211   All day VP had left messages at the PM House: V. P. Singh to author, 22 October 1999, New Delhi; M. L. Fotedar to author.
212   Abhay, a physician, took him there in his Maruti 800 Omni: V. P. Singh to author, 22 October 1999, Apollo Hospital, New Delhi.
212   VP left his resignation letter with M. L. Fotedar: M. L. Fotedar to author.
212   'My mother said to me, "You must stay with V. P. Singh"': Som Pal to author, 29 January 2000, 28, Lodi Estate, New Delhi.
212   'You were doing such good work': Ibid.
212   'If you wanted to work under Rajiv's leadership, why did you resign?': Ibid.
212   'Come if you can': Ibid.
213   'Som Palji, you are asking me to leave the organization in which I have spent twenty years': Ibid.
213   'What is to be done now?': Ibid.
213   'And, both parties realize they cannot come to power at the centre on their own': Ibid.
213   The Swedish broadcaster announced that the Swedish armament company had paid commissions: Ramesh Chandran, 'Something is very rotten in the Indian gun deal: Sverige Radio', *India Today*, 15 May 1987.
214   The signal that went out after the evening was that V. P. Singh had joined hands with Arun Nehru against Rajiv Gandhi: Arif Mohammad Khan to author, New Delhi, 21 August 2018.
214   The event had been crafted to get a sense of 'kaun kitne paani maen hai': Satyapal Malik, 5 May 2001, New Delhi. Attribution check
214   'I was told, you must come to the tea party': Satyapal Malik to author.
215   'The first time he called me, I went, thinking that perhaps he wanted to smoothen things out': V. P. Singh to author.
215   'I have run this machine with your mother': Ibid.
215   'We used to go and see Indiraji at her Willingdon Crescent house': Ibid.
215   'Rajivji, if I can stand firm for three months toh main kharha reh jaunga': Ibid.
216   'aar paar ki larhai': V. P. Singh to author.
216   'I am sticking with you,' he said: Ibid.
216   He first made the announcement to the press in Haridwar: Mukerji, *The Disruptor*, p. 274.
216   the *Indian Express* carried an exposé against Ajitabh Bachchan: Ninan and Khindaria, 'Amitabh Bachchan resigns from Lok Sabha, Ajitabh lands in Swiss trouble'.
216   VP immediately wrote to the prime minister urging Rajiv to 'unturn this stone': V. P. Singh to author, October 1999.
217   'There is no question of meeting him': Ibid.
217   'I was at (Ramakrishna) Hegde's house when the news came': Ibid.
217   a week after his expulsion from the Congress Party: Though expelled from the party he had not yet moved house. Soon thereafter he moved to a much smaller house, 28 Lodi Estate, allocated to MPs.
217   Groups of people standing by the roadside would raise full-throated slogans: Inderjit Badhwar and Prabhu Chawla, 'Expulsion of V.P. Singh, other dissidents from Congress(I) threatens to snowball into a major political movement', *India Today*, 15 August 1987.
218   'VP Singh aur bhanda phorho, aur bhanda phorho': Ibid.
218   The slogan, 'Takht badal do, taj badal do, beimaano ka raaj badal do': Ibid.
219   had won 60 seats on its own, and its ally, the BJP, had got 16: 'Statistical Report on General Elections, 1987 to the Legislative Assembly of Haryana', New Delhi: Election Commission of India, 1987, available at <eci.gov.in/files/file/3821-haryana-1987/>.
219   'Haryana has shown the way to the country': Som Pal to author.
219   'Mamaji, what has made you change your mind in such a short time?': Ibid.
219   'I was called inside. I was told that a meeting should be arranged somewhere in UP': Ibid.
220   'It was when I started to get such a strong and wide response': V. P. Singh to author, 18 October 1999.
220   'Personally I would have opted for continuing as a front': Ibid.
220   'Every party in the Opposition would have been split': V. P. Singh to author, 16 October 1999, Apollo Hospital, New Delhi.
220   'At that time Atal Bihari Vajpayee, Jaswant Singh, and Bhairon Singh Shekhawat': Ibid.
220   Vajpayee would later deny this: Kingshuk Nag, *Atal Bihari Vajpayee: A Man for All Seasons*, New Delhi: Rupa Publications, 2015, p. 103.
220   BJP leader Jaswant Singh warned VP not to bring together existing parties: V. P. Singh to author, 16 October 1999, Apollo Hospital, New Delhi.
221   'Vishwanath, cement can join one boulder with another, but (it) cannot join a boulder with a piece of wood': V. P. Singh to author, 18 October 1999.

221 'Managing contradictions is an art': Ibid.
221 VP defeated the might of the Congress—and won handsomely: Dilip Awasthi, 'Jan Morcha leader V.P. Singh delivers a crushing blow to Congress(I) in Allahabad', *India Today*, 15 July 1988.
221 'Rajiv, he rammed his bicycle into mine and drove away': Ibid.
222 'The National Front is a chariot of God Aditya (sun)': Prabhu Chawla, 'Seven party National Front formally launched in Madras', *India Today*, 15 October 1988.
222 'Not a hero but a zero', Devi Lal lashed out at Bahuguna: Ibid.
222 The JPC in April 1988 exonerated the government of any wrongdoing: T. N. Ninan, Prabhu Chawla, 'Bofors inquiry: Joint Parliamentary Committee report reveals more than it conceals', India Today, 15 May 1988.
222 The CAG report was for Rajiv Gandhi what the Allahabad judgment had been for his mother: Shekhar Gupta, Bhaskar Roy, 'CAG report on Bofors gun deal revitalises Opposition, puts Congress(I) on the defensive', *India Today*, 15 August 1989.
223 'The CAG report has ended the 1984 mandate for Rajiv,' V. P. Singh thundered: Ibid.
223 The MPs agreed to go along with his plan: Ibid.
223 With this move, VP had managed to unsettle the Congress: Inder Malhotra, 'Rear view: Rajiv's resounding defeat in 1989', *Indian Express*, 2 February 2015.
223 'From Left to Right we have now all come together to defeat a common enemy': Gupta and Roy, 'CAG report on Bofors gun deal revitalises Opposition, puts Congress(I) on the defensive'.
223 'Now we need Comrade Vajpayee and Pandit Namboodiripad to work together to oust Rajiv!': Ibid.
223 'Gali gali maen shor hai, Rajiv Gandhi chor hai': Tehseen Poonawalla, 'In my childhood, I heard "Gali Gali Mein Shor Hai, Rajiv Gandhi Chor Hai" but no one was jailed. Then why is it happening now?', Discussion with Times Now, available at www.facebook.com/watch/?v=757301959372053.
224 to get a glimpse of the 'raja turned faqir': As seen by author on the campaign trail with V. P. Singh.
224 V. P. Singh's poll strategy was simple: strike at Rajiv and demolish the Congress: Inderjit Badhwar and Prabhu Chawla, 'Rajiv Gandhi loses his charismatic touch, V.P. Singh proves to be a formidable campaigner', *India Today*, 30 November 1989.
224 And, at every rally, he would ask, 'Bofors ka dalaal kaun hai?': Inderjit Badhwar, 'General Elections '89: V.P. Singh cuts tireless electoral swathe through Hindi heartland', *India Today*, 30 November 1989.
224 described the Opposition as 'scorpions and fighting roosters': Badhwar and Chawla, 'Rajiv Gandhi loses his charismatic touch, V.P. Singh proves to be a formidable campaigner'.
224 Ram Rajya in the country: Tapan Kumar Banerjee, 'Rajiv would have built temple, saved Congress', *The Statesman*, 18 October 2020; Hardeep Singh Puri, @HardeepSPuri, 'In 1989, Rajiv Gandhi started his campaign from Faizabad & promised Ram Rajya. A case of Congress and selective amnesia', 9:25 pm, 5 May 2014, twitter.com/HardeepSPuri/status/463346239598129152.
224 'It was that day…for the first time…that I felt we had a chance': V. P. Singh to author.
225 Whether he himself decided at the last moment to pour kerosene all over his entire body: Janata Dal anonymous sources to author.
225 Rajeev had told his mother the night before, 'Hum sirf tamasha karne jaa rahe hain': Nonita Kalra, 'Rajeev Goswami's tragedy provides agitation a rallying point', *India Today*, 15 October 1990.
225 'As I got to the spot where he was…I saw an image I will never forget': Parag Vohra, 'The Last Refuge', *Outlook*, 3 February 2022.
225 Rajeev Goswami survived, only to die fourteen years later: Dalip Singh, 'Burnout in obscurity - Forgotten anti-Mandal face fades', *The Telegraph*, 24 February 2004.
226 'I had expected opposition to Mandal': V. P. Singh to author, 16 October 1999, Apollo Hospital, New Delhi.
226 'But,' he said again and again, 'not…immolations': Ibid.
226 The politically affiliated students' unions, the Congress-aligned National Students Union of India (NSUI) and the pro-BJP Akhil Bharatiya Vidyarthi Parishad (ABVP): Vohra, 'The Last Refuge'.
226 Sixty-three youngsters died by immolating themselves: Christophe Jaffrelot, *India's Silent Revolution: The Rise of the Lower Castes in North India*, London: Hurst & Company, 2003, p. 346.
226 Ultimately, the figure went up to 200: Guha, 'Rights', *India after Gandhi*.
227 'Mandal toh aapke manifesto maen bhi thaa, usi se prerna lee hai': V. P. Singh to author, 16 October 1999, Apollo Hospital, New Delhi.
227 'I was clear because BJP was the aspirant for the same chair': Ibid.
227 'Our fight is ultimately going to be against VP Singh': K. N. Govindacharya, 2 December 1989, BJP Office, Ashoka Road, Delhi.
228 'But I can't share a platform with you, please don't feel bad about that': K. N. Govindacharya to author, 2018.
228 'Please, talk to your people and get the BJP flags down': Ibid.
228 'We will see later who gets the better of whom': Ibid.
228 'The decision to hold the (Somnath to Ayodhya) Rath Yatra was made (as early as) on 29 June 1990': Ibid.
228 'The idea for the Rath Yatra was mine': Ibid.
229 'When she referred to the Ram Janmabhoomi movement, the crowd was silent': Ibid.
229 'What's the hurry?': Ibid.
229 'Though I was young, Advaniji used to listen to me and give weight to what I had to say': Ibid.
229 'The idea was for Advani to set out from Kanyakumari or Kalady': Ibid. Kalady is the birth place of the eighth-century philosopher Adi Shankara.

230   'I don't believe in this nautanki': Ibid.
230   'You leave all that to me,' Mahajan said: Ibid.
230   'The Rath Yatra was decided much before (the Mandal decision)': Ibid.
230   the BJP billed the Rath Yatra as a response to his decision: Ibid.
231   'There was a lot of politics behind Mandal': V. P. Singh to author.
231   'If you don't, you have a temple next door': V. P. Singh to author, New Delhi, 22 October 1999.
231   'If you will do kar seva, what will there be left for us to do!': Ibid.
232   'Not even a sparrow will enter Ayodhya': Neerja Chowdhury, 'How Oct 1990 shaped Mulayam's M-Y politics', *Indian Express*, 16 October 2022.
232   'The same day I rang up Lalu (Yadav) at 9 p.m. and told him to arrest Advani': V. P. Singh to author.
232   'Aapne Mandal kiya, toh humne Kamandal kar diya': Ibid.
232   'Rajiv was not as naive as people believed': H. R. Bhardwaj.
232   Arun Nehru sent a message to Rajiv Gandhi: Dinesh Trivedi to author.
232   'Even the neighbouring countries...had been alerted...': Ibid.
232   'I think it was (just) before the confidence motion in the first week of November': Ibid.
233   'they really apprehended Nehru's return to the Congress': Ibid.
233   It was President R. Venkataraman who torpedoed the proposal to make Rajiv Gandhi prime minister: M. L. Fotedar to author. Also Fotedar, 'The 1989 Lok Sabha Elections—The Politics of Mandal and Kamandal', *The Chinar Leaves*.
233   'RV (Venkataraman) was personally against Rajiv': H. R. Bhardwaj to author.
233   'But he did not say anything': M. L. Fotedar to author.
233   'This man (VP Singh) has tried to finish us': Anonymous source in the VP government, who wished to remain unidentified, 1 September 2021.
234   supported from the 'outside' by the Congress led by Rajiv Gandhi: Fotedar, 'The 1989 Lok Sabha Elections—The Politics of Mandal and Kamandal', *The Chinar Leaves*.
234   'Jab tak samaj maen vishamta hai, tab tak samajik nyay ki avashyakata hai': V. P. Singh to author.
234   On 1 October 1990, the court put the decision 'in abeyance': 'Effective Stay on Quota Order', *Hindustan Times*, 2 October 1990.
234   Two years later, in 1992, the highest court in the land upheld the validity of the government's decision: Abhay Singh Yadav, 'OBC reservation', *Times of India*, 16 October 2022.
235   The RSS had attempted to question reservations during the 2015 Bihar elections: Row erupts over RSS chief's remarks on quota, *Times of India*, 22 September 2015.
235   And as many as 983 OBC communities, out of 2,600, had got no representation at all in jobs: 'Understanding sub-categorisation of OBCs and Justice G Rohini Commission', *Business Standard*, 8 July 2022.
235   Instead, till September 2022, it had got as many as ten extensions: Ibid.
235   'Mandal changed the grammar of politics': V. P. Singh to author.
235   These groups began to demand patronage on the basis of their numbers: James Manor, Rajni Kothari, *Caste in Indian Politics*, 2nd edn, Orient BlackSwan, 2010.
235   Caste-based regional parties grew in North India: Regional parties had been around for much longer in the South and the West of the country. Some of them had derived their strength more from sub-nationalism, the Shiv Sena in Maharashtra from 'Marathi asmita' (Maharashtrian identity), Telangana Rashtra Samithi from Telugu nationalism, and the YSR Congress in Andhra Pradesh from Andhra pride. However, the Dravidian parties, the DMK and AIADMK, of Tamil Nadu had grown out of the anti-Brahmin movement for self-respect from 1930s onwards under the stewardship of 'Periyar' E. V. Ramaswamy Naicker. He had formed the Dravida Kazhagam which later split into DMK and AIADMK.
236   'Tilak, Tarazu, aur Talwar, Inko maro joote chaar': Amit Verma, 'For Maya, no looking back', *Deccan Chronicle*, 24 July 2016.
236   'Make up your mind, do you want social justice or do you want a Yadav raj?': A Janata Dal leader to author, 5 July 1991, New Delhi.
236   he became the first MBC—he belongs to the Ghanchi or the oil-presser's caste: 'Narendra Modi belongs to Modh-Ghanchi caste, which was added to OBCs categories in 1994, says Gujarat government', *DNA*, 9 May 2014.
236   VP would repeatedly say that Mandal meant 'satta maen shirkat': V. P. Singh to author.
237   V. P. Singh read out to me a couple of poems he had written: VP's poems were published in a book, *Everytime I Wake Up*, Penguin, 2006.
237   'You come to a stage when you ask what is the meaning of all this?': V. P. Singh to author, August 2003.
237   'I used to play with paper boats in my childhood': Ibid.
238   VP was a contradiction in many ways: Devendra Dwivedy to author, 2 February 2001.
238   'no such thing as loyalty in politics': V. P. Singh to author.
238   'The idea was that once they start to participate in the management of the country, there would be no fissiparous tendencies': V. P. Singh to author, October 1999.
238   P.V. Narasimha Rao came to power in 1991: PV Narasimha Rao acquired a majority by breaking other parties.
239   'I ran history. It will define governments and coalitions in the time to come': V. P. Singh to author, 16 October 1999, Apollo Hospital, New Delhi.

CHAPTER 4: THE PRIME MINISTER WHO REFUSED TO DECIDE: P. V. NARASIMHA RAO AND THE DEMOLITION OF THE BABRI MASJID

240 'I heard you were doing puja after twelve o'clock': Ram Bahadur Rai to author.
240 'Dada, you think I don't know politics. I was born in rajniti': Ram Bahadur Rai to author 18 February 2019, New Delhi, confirmed on 24 June 2020 on the phone.
240 He was accompanied by three other journalists: Ibid.
241 'They used to meet Rao frequently': Ibid.
241 After the first dome collapsed, President Shankar Dayal Sharma shot off a letter to the prime minister: Shahid Siddiqui to author, 25 March 2019, New Delhi. Siddiqui was shown the written letter.
241 council of ministers: The council of ministers comprises all the ministers, senior and junior, in the government as opposed to the Cabinet which comprises senior ministers with Cabinet rank.
241 Rao expressed similar sentiments to another visitor: Rashmi Kant to author, 13 June 2020, New Delhi, telephonic interview.
242 'I started off by asking him about Ayodhya': Ibid.
242 'Yeh tho hona hee thaa': Ibid.
242 'Kya karoon, saari umar clerk hee tho raha hoon': Ibid.
242 'I don't know whether he was happy or unhappy': Ibid.
242 'he said unse baat ho gayee thee ki 6 December ko aisa karenge': Som Pal to author, 15 February 2021, New Delhi. Reconfirmed 11 September 2021.
243 'RSS chief K. Sudarshan also confirmed this to me': Ibid.
243 Having ridden the Babri storm, he was consulting political leaders: Ibid.
243 'Maybe history will judge you differently in the future': Ibid.
243 'And that he approved of what had happened': Ibid.
243 Despite their diverse views, they were expected to act 'in harmony' for 'the national good': P. V. Narasimha Rao, *Ayodhya: 6 December 1992*, New Delhi: Penguin Books, 2006, p. 2.
243 'good faith in a federal structure': Ibid.
243 'sarvadharma sambhav': Ibid., p. 48.
243 pitchforked the country's politics 'right into the religious ambit': Ibid., p. 188.
243 'if only to counter' the challenge posed by it: Ibid.
244 'Khayal rakhna. Keep in mind a Rajya Sabha seat for me, should the opportunity arise': Janardhan Reddy to Krishan Kant to author, Hyderabad, 25 December 1995.
245 'We will form the government': M. L. Fotedar to author.
245 'He had never used that word earlier': Ibid.
245 Then she clearly heard him say, 'I am telling you to go': Jayanthi Natarajan to author, 16 March 2021, telephonic interview.
245 'Several guys bundled him up, and (G. K.) Moopanar and I and some others took him to the general hospital': Ibid.
245 'Everyone is important,' Natarajan said irritably: Ibid.
246 'She did not speak with anyone': Ibid.
246 'Who will lead the Congress Party now?': P. V. Narasimha Rao to Bhuvnesh Chaturvedi to author; Vinay Sitapati, *Half Lion: How P. V. Narasimha Rao Transformed India*, New Delhi: Penguin Books, 2016, p. 90.
246 'People will say, you are playing politics': Bhuvnesh Chaturvedi to author, 1999, New Delhi.
246 He did not really trust Mukherjee: Ibid.
246 Mani Shankar Aiyar sat alone in a corner: As seen by author on the day at Teen Murti House.
247 'This was enough indication (to me) that he was willing': Bhuvnesh Chaturvedi to author, 7 October 1999, New Delhi.
247 'George, Arjun Singh, and I had decided we should make Sonia Gandhi president of the Congress': M. L. Fotedar to author, 1 July 2005, Gurgaon.
247 'Arjun Singh, G. K. Moopanar, Sitaram Kesri, and I went to see PV': Ibid.
247 'Sir, I will propose her name': Ibid.
247 'Fotedarji, the atmosphere is favourable for Sonia Gandhi': Ibid.
247 Pawar agreed to support the resolution: Ibid.
247 But Pawar upstaged him: Rajeev Deshpande, 'Rajiv Gandhi wanted to oust me from Maharashtra CM's chair: Sharad Pawar', *Times of India*, 13 December 2015.
248 'Let's pass the resolution first': Ibid.
248 'They thought they would be able to control Sonia': Bhuvnesh Chaturvedi to author.
248 He requested George to send in a note to Sonia Gandhi: M. L. Fotedar to author, New Delhi.
248 'She will be a leader in reserve': Ibid.
248 'you must decide who should be the next prime minister': Natwar Singh to author; K. Natwar Singh, *One Life Is Not Enough: An Autobiography*, New Delhi: Rupa & Co., 2014, pp. 288–89.
248 'Why don't you consult P. N. Haksar?': Ibid.
249 'and tell him that Soniaji has requested him to become Congress president and prime minister': Ibid.
249 'You (should) send Aruna Asif Ali and Natwar to Shankar Dayal Sharma': Ibid.
249 'It is very gracious of Soniaji to make the offer': Natwar Singh to author, 21 June 2018, New Delhi; Singh, *One Life Is Not Enough*, p. 289.
249 'Send now for P. V. Narasimha Rao,' advised Haksar: Ibid.

249   It was Sonia Gandhi's nod for Rao which came as a clincher: Rajesh Ramachandran, 'Sonia Gandhi did not choose Narasimha Rao as PM in 1991: R. D. Pradhan former home secretary', *The Economic Times*, 4 August 2014.

250   'The slogans erupted when Narayan Dutt Tiwari was introducing PV to UP': Bhuvnesh Chaturvedi to author, 26 April 2000, New Delhi.

250   'Maa bete ka balidan, yaad karega Hindustan': 'Reports from states suggest sympathy factor likely to help Congress(I) in coming elections', *India Today*, 15 June 1991.

250   it won 20 out of 27 seats in the second phase compared to 5 out 15 seats in the first phase: Mukherjee, *The Turbulent Years*, p. 135.

250   sharp decline from the 171 the Congress had won from these states in the 1984 general elections: Thakur, *Prime Ministers*, p. 322.

250   Congress had won the most seats—232—though it was short of an absolute majority in parliament: 'Statistical Report on General Elections, 1991 to the Tenth Lok Sabha: Volume I', Delhi: Election Commission of India, 1992, available at <eci.gov.in/files/file/4121-general-election-1991-vol-i-ii>.

250   'except for Shiv Shankar': Bhuvnesh Chaturvedi to author.

250   It was Sharad Pawar, the Maharashtra strongman, who emerged as the serious challenger: Prithviraj Chavan to author, 19 July 2019, Mumbai.

250   Under his leadership, the Congress had won 38 out of 48 Lok Sabha MPs in Maharashtra: 'Statistical Report on General Elections, 1991 to the Tenth Lok Sabha: Volume I'.

250   He had also funded many Congress candidates across the country : Prithviraj Chavan to author, 19 July 2019, Mumbai.

251   Salve and Najma Heptulla and Suresh Kalmadi were mobilizing support for their leader: Ibid.

251   they passed a resolution for a 'conscience vote' to select the leader: Ibid.

251   announced a press conference, and let it be known that he would expose Pawar's involvement in a land scam: N. K. Sharma to author, 12 July 1999, Delhi.

251   'Sonia Gandhi would not have brooked an independent minded PM': Deshpande, 'Rajiv Gandhi wanted to oust me from Maharashtra CM's chair'.

251   'Please go to Salve's house and bring Sharad Pawar to PV's residence at 9, Moti Lal Nehru Marg': N. K. Sharma to author.

251   'I am an old man...you are much younger, you have your whole life ahead of you, your chance will come': A. G. Kulkarni, who was close to Pawar, to author, winter of 1991, New Delhi; Bhuvnesh Chaturvedi, who heard it from P. V. Rao, to author, New Delhi.

252   At 10, Janpath, when Rao was inside with Sonia, 'a group of us were sitting (outside) in George's room': N. K. Sharma to author, New Delhi.

252   On 21 June 1991, P. V. Narasimha Rao was sworn in as the ninth prime minister: See also p. xiii on how this book counts the number of prime ministers there have been in the country since Independence.

252   'I am a Brahmin. I know how to deal with these people': Ved Aitharaju, 'A Tribute to PV Narasimha Rao: "The Brahmin and Telengana in him need to be acknowledged"', 28 June 2020, available at vedaitharaju. medium.com.

252   Telugu Brahmins were divided into two major groups: K. S. Singh, *People of India Vol.6: The India's Communities (N-Z)*, Delhi: Oxford University Press, 1998.

253   'geographically a bridge between the North and the South': P. V. Narasimha Rao in his convocation address at Telugu University, Hyderabad on 7 July, 1991. Quoted in *P. V. Narasimha Rao: Selected Speeches 1991-92*, Ministry of Information and Broadcasting, 1991, p. 239, cited in Sitapati, *Half Lion*, p. 12.

253   The residents of this small inhabitation spoke Telugu, Hindi, Marathi, Kannada, and even a smattering of Odia: Sitapati, *Half Lion*, p. 12.

253   Having spent many years in Nagpur for study, he spoke Marathi fluently: Ibid., p. 27.

253   Once asked if he had read Gabriel García Márquez's Love in the Time of Cholera: Sagarika Ghosh, 'Now, Meet PV The Novelist', *Outlook*, 18 October 1999.

253   Rao on the other hand went on to join the Congress Party: Sitapati, *Half Lion*, p. 16.

254   For a year, he was based in a camp in Chanda in Maharashtra and would ferry arms to groups: Ibid., p. 21.

254   But it was marked by violence, and around 40,000 Muslims were killed: Ibid.

254   The anti-nizam movement had brought together three diverse religio-political streams: Ibid., p. 20.

255   Somehow, Rao managed to avoid taking sides and did it without alienating either: Sitapati, *Half Lion*, p. 22.

255   Rao also learnt in those days the importance of staying on the right side of the High Command: High Command is a popular term used for leadership of a party which takes the ultimate decisions, and was used for the Nehru–Gandhi family in the Indian National Congress.

255   as charismatic as a 'dead fish', in the words of a Congressman, Jairam Ramesh: Ibid., p. 98.

256   At one time, she had even contemplated sending him to the Rashtrapati Bhavan: Fotedar, 'Political Secretary, 1980–887', *The Chinar Leaves*.

256   would write under a pseudonym, for the magazine *Mainstream*: Sitapati, *Half Lion*, p. 77.

256   'Indira Gandhi will never, repeat never, get over her...very complex...feeling of inferiority': P. V. Narasimha Rao, 'Chapter 41', *The Insider*, New Delhi: Penguin Books, 2014.

256   He was even more critical of Rajiv Gandhi's capabilities: Though it used to be said that 'no one really knows what goes on in Narasimha Rao's mind', it was Nikhil-da that PV sometimes opened up to. 'There was hardly any topic that he did not discuss with me during our long association', Rao had said about Nikhil. P. V. Narasimha Rao, 'Nikhilda: Some Nostalgic Reflections', Vol. XLVII, No. 46, *Mainstream*, 31 October 2009.

257 'Kya stand loon?': Nikhil Chakravartty to Krishan Kant to author.

257 Entitled 'The Great Suicide', and penned under a pseudonym, 'Congressman': Congressman, 'The Great Suicide', Vol. LIII, No. 6, *Mainstream*, 31 January 2015.

257 '(Vincent) George says this is Sonia Gandhi's choice and adds more names': Bhuvnesh Chaturvedi to author, 30 November 1999, New Delhi.

257 keep her briefed about what the government was doing: Ibid.

258 'I will groom them. I will take them with me on some of my tours': P. V. Narasimha Rao to author, informal chat, New Delhi.

258 'except those files he did not want to clear': Anonymous sources close to P. V. Narasimha Rao to author.

259 'Can't you people even handle a simple matter?': Ibid.

259 'No decision is also a decision': Ravish Tiwari, 'PV Narasimha Rao was a master tactician, a "fox" who "was remarkably decisive": Jairam Ramesh', *Economic Times*, 29 August 2015.

259 'PV thanda karke khate hain': Bhuvnesh Chaturvedi to author.

259 Pout—a nickname the media gave Rao: Sanjaya Baru, 'How PV Narasimha Rao, India's first "accidental" prime minister, earned his place in history', *Indian Express*, 28 June 2021.

259 'It was only when he did not want to take a decision that he would postpone it': Anonymous source to author, 9 September 2019.

260 He had given instructions to the PMO that if they asked for any 'work to be done': Bhuvnesh Chaturvedi to author.

260 'Na jaane kis bhesh main Narayan mil jaye': Ibid.

260 90 per cent of those who cast their vote opted for him: Srinivasa Prasad, 'A reporters diary from Nandyal: From AK 477s and crude bombs in 1991 to outpouring of venom in 2017', *Firstpost*, 31 August 2017.

260 'PV bahut zaalim hain': Bhuvnesh Chaturvedi to author.

260 Mukherjee was hoping to get the finance portfolio: Bhuvnesh Chaturvedi to author, New Delhi; Mukherjee, *The Turbulent Years*, p. 138.

260 'It will be problematic': Bhuvnesh Chaturvedi to author, October 1999.

261 'Perhaps a day will come when I can speak to you about it': Mukherjee, *The Turbulent Years*, p. 138.

261 'I will leave the post in forty-five days': M. L. Fotedar to author; Fotedar, 'The Rao Years', *The Chinar Leaves*.

261 'As soon as there is a consensus on some name, I will step down': M. L. Fotedar to author.

261 'Unki meherbaani hai ki mujhe leader banaya, rakhenge tho bhi theek': Arjun Singh to Bhuvnesh Chaturvedi who told author, 7 October 1999, New Delhi.

261 When he and Sharad Pawar won convincingly in the election to the Congress Working Committee at Tirupati: The author was present at this session

262 In those days, Rao lived in 'a one-room quarter in Sona Gali': R. K. Khandekar to author, 23 December 2020.

262 'The Sangh has this speciality of befriending people, meeting them over a cup of tea': Govindacharya to author, 2 August 2020, on the phone.

262 The Sangh (RSS) had also got to know R. K. Khandekar during this period: Govindacharya to author, 4 August 2020, on the phone.

262 'I had been a swayamsevak since I was six and used to attend the RSS shakhas': R. K. Khandekar to author, 23 December 2020.

262 Khandekar also took care of the money that came to Race Course Road for Rao's political activity: Bhuvnesh Chaturvedi to author, 27 October 1999, New Delhi.

263 He used to carry an extra set of clothes for Rao, 'even a pair of goggles': R. K. Khandekar to author, 6 September 2020.

263 Khandekar was a go-between Rao and BJP–RSS leaders: K. N. Govindacharya to author.

263 Bhaurao Deoras had kept in touch with Rao even after he became prime minister: Subhash Arya, right-hand man of Bhaurao, to author; R. K. Khandekar to author.

263 'Give me a warning if you ever decide to bring down the Babri mosque': Malkani, *The Politics of Ayodhya*.

263 'PV would have actually finished the BJP if he had continued in power a little longer': Bhuvnesh Chaturvedi to author.

263 Vajpayee immediately shot back, calling Rao, 'gurughantal': Sidharth Mishra, 'When dialogue turns curt', *Millenium Post*, 31 October 2013.

263 'most scholarly prime minister': Advani, *My Country, My Life*, p. 391.

263 one who understood 'the trials and tribulations of Hindus': Ibid.

264 With the Ekta Yatra, Joshi hoped 'to divert attention from the temple issue': Zafar Agha and N. K. Singh, 'BJP discovers national unity', *India Today*, 15 December 1991.

264 He manoeuvred the situation in such a way so as to 'create doubts about its motives': Bhuvnesh Chaturvedi to author.

264 The banned militant organizations, Jammu and Kashmir Liberation Front (JKLF) and Hizbul Mujahideen: Philip Oldenburg (ed.), *India Briefing, 1993*, New York and Oxon: Routledge, 2018.

264 An event which was meant to be witnessed by thousands had only sixty-seven BJP members: Kaveree Bamzai, Harinder Baweja, and Dilip Awasthi, 'BJP flag-hoisting ceremony in Srinagar turns out to be a damp squib, militancy gets a boost', *India Today*, 15 February 1992.

265 'Had Rajiv been alive, he would have stopped the Ekta Yatra': Bhuvnesh Chaturvedi to author.

265 Rao's strategy all along had been to make the BJP look like 'another Congress'—and not 'a party with a difference': Ibid.

265 'We could always hold it high. We cannot do it any longer': N. K. Singh, 'Gujarat Chief Minister Keshubhai Patel's government held to ransom by group of 47 BJP MLAs', *India Today*, 31 October 1995.

265 The 'master puppeteer' behind the scenes was none other than P. V. Narasimha Rao: Bhuvnesh Chaturvedi to author, 30 November 1999, New Delhi.

265 Naresh Chandra, governor of Gujarat, was never in touch with the PM directly: Ibid. Also confirmed by Naresh Chandra.

265 'It was done in a planned manner by P. V. Narasimha Rao': Ibid.

265 The RSS mouthpiece, *Panchjanya*, wrote in PV's favour: *Panchjanya*, 7 December 1991.

265 RSS chief Balasaheb Deoras had good things to say about him: N. K. Sharma to author, 25 January 2000, New Delhi.

266 The sants told the PM they had come to personally apprise him of their proposed kar seva: Hemant Sharma, *Yuddha Mein Ayodhya*, Delhi: Prabhat Prakashan, 1 January 2018, p. 85.

266 'Moonh jo band rakha hai': Rao to Bhuvnesh Chaturvedi who told author, 27 October 1999, New Delhi.

267 Documents had been exchanged between both sides to support their respective claims: L. K. Advani, *My Country, My Life*, New Delhi: Rupa & Co., 2008, p. 388.

267 The All India Babri Masjid Action Committee (AIBMAC) had built a case that the story of Ramayana was mythological and not historical: Ibid., p. 387.

267 Rao assured them he would pick up from where Chandra Shekhar had left off: Ibid., p. 392.

267 'Kaho, Devendra, kaise ho': Devendra Dwivedy to author, 28 February 2001, Parliament House, New Delhi.

267 He had made 3,000 photocopies of one of his vitriolic missives and sent them to party leaders: Thakur, *Prime Ministers*, p. 322.

268 'I think you should talk to the BJP': Devendra Dwivedy to author, 28 February 2001, Parliament House, New Delhi.

268 'You are the best person to talk to the BJP, you have a good relationship with them': Ibid.

268 'I remember I reached there at 10.07': Ibid.

268 'The PM spoke to both Vajpayee and me to prevail upon the leaders of the temple movement to give him some time': Advani, *My Country, My Life*, p. 392.

269 It stopped the kar seva on 26 July and decided to give Rao three months: Ved Pratap Vaidik to author, 14 September 2018, Gurgaon.

269 'He is a cold man, but he got up and caught me by both my shoulders: Devendra Dwivedy to author, 28 February 2001, Parliament House, New Delhi.

269 The PM agreed. 'I am going to Ballia the day after': Ibid. The PM was going to Ballia (in UP) to attend a function organized by former PM Chandra Shekhar to honour the memory of Jayaprakash Narayan. As noted, Rao used to go out of his way to keep Opposition leaders happy.)

270 'After this, PV started to avoid me': Ibid.

270 'It is not a problem of my making': Naresh Chandra to author about what P. V. Rao had told him, 25 December 2001, New Delhi.

270 'I was officially neither a secretary to the Government of India': Ibid.

270 'In the way he designed the post, and this was typical of the way Rao functioned': Ibid.

270 'could not call me for questioning': Ibid.

270 'larger national interest': Ibid.

270 Rao told Chandra to collect all the papers about the dispute: Ibid.

270 'Not one of my successors had talked to me even for five minutes about what I had done on Ayodhya': Chandra Shekhar to author, 12 August 2003, New Delhi.

271 Murthy had prophesied that Rao would become prime minister: Krishan Kant to author, 25 December 1995, Hyderabad. Confirmed by Rashmi Kant to author, 3 April 2018, New Delhi.

271 'From then on, I think somewhere inside him': Anonymous senior government official to author.

271 'over and over again' with Naresh Chandra the major milestones: Naresh Chandra to author, 31 March 2017, New Delhi.

271 constructed by the Mughal general, Mir Baqi, in 1528 on the orders of Emperor Babur: Singh, *Ayodhya*, p. 28.

272 There were a few clashes between the two communities in the nineteenth century: Copies of the East India company records available in the national archives, quoted in Rao, *Ayodhya*, p. 4.

272 In 1934, Hindu rioters demolished a portion of the mosque; it was rebuilt by the British: Kumar Anshuman, 'Ayodhya case: A brief history of India's longest running property dispute', *Economic Times*, 10 November 2019.

272 The action in 1949 took place in the dead of night on 22 December: Singh, *Ayodhya*, p. 188; Report of the Liberhan Commission of Inquiry; Sharma, *Yuddha Mein Ayodhya*; Ram Bahadur Rai to author.

272 started chanting prayers to the chimes of bells, cymbals, and conches: Based on the testimony of Bhaskar Das, in Singh, *Ayodhya*, p. 194.

272 Hindu Mahasabha, which was the precursor of the Bharatiya Jan Sangh: Ram Bahadur Rai to author, 18 February 2019, Indira Gandhi Centre of Arts, New Delhi; Sharma, *Yuddha Mein Ayodhya*; Singh, *Ayodhya*, p. 187.

273 It is not so known that Nanaji Deshmukh, a senior RSS leader: Ram Bahadur Rai to author, 18 February 2019, New Delhi.

273 'One day I had gone to meet Nanaji Deshmukh at the Deen Dayal Shodh Sansthan': Ibid.

273 'Abhiram Das, Bhaiji Hanuman Prasad Poddar, Mahant Ramchandra Paramhans, and Shakuntala Nair': Ibid.

273 'And it was found at 5 a.m.': Ibid.
274 The City magistrate Guru Datt Singh, working under Nair, 'attached' the structure: Attachment is a legal process by which the court designates a property owned by a debtor to be transferred to a creditor.
274 On 14 August 1949, it had vowed to free all the temples where Muslims had constructed mosques: Ram Bahadur Rai to author, Indira Gandhi Centre of Arts, New Delhi, 19 February 2019. Also Sharma, *Yuddh Mein Ayodhya* and Singh, *Ayodhya*.
274 'communally vitriolic attack against Dev': Krishna Jha and Dhirendra K. Jha, *Ayodhya: The Dark Night: The Secret History of Rama's Appearance in Babri Masjid,* New Delhi: Harper Collins Publishers India, 2016.
274 He even distributed tulsi leaves during his campaign to win people over: Singh, *Ayodhya*, p. 186.
274 to marginalize Narendra Dev who was his rival in UP and enjoyed Nehru's confidence: Ibid., p. 185.
274 They decided to place the Ram idol in the Babri Masjid to arouse Hindu sentiment in their favour: Jha and Jha, *Ayodhya: The Dark Night*.
274 'the Congress leaders had to appeal to the Hindu feeling of voters': Ibid.
275 Kalyan Singh allowed the demolition to take place: Ravi Singh Sisodiya, 'Babri demolition case: Kalyan Singh charged with criminal conspiracy', *Times of India*, 28 September 2019; 'And It All Came Crashing Down: How Babri Masjid Demolition Brought Down Kalyan Singh Govt', *News18*, 29 September 2020.
275 all over just 1,500 square yards of land: *M Siddiq (D) Thr Lrs vs Mahant Suresh Das & Ors*, 9 November 2019, available at <indiankanoon.org/doc/107745042/>.
276 'liberate' the sites in Mathura and Varanasi: 'Right-Wing Groups Want to "Liberate" Kashi and Mathura Temples; RSS Says Won't Push', *The Wire*, 9 September 2020.
276 The first legal suit over the Babri Masjid was filed by Mahant Raghubir Das in 1885: Singh, *Ayodhya*, p. 28.
276 In 1959, the Nirmohi Akhara filed a 'title suit' for the ownership of the disputed land: Rao, *Ayodhya*, p. 9.
276 he acquired '2.77 acres' of disputed land around the mosque: 'Ayodhya Verdict: India's Biggest Legal Battle Was About Just 0.3 Acre Land, Not 2.77 Acres', News18, 10 November 2019.
277 They informed VP about what they were doing—and he endorsed their efforts: Krishan Kant to author, 25 December 1995, Hyderabad in a confidential conversation, confirmed by his son Rashmi Kant to author, 3 April 2018, New Delhi.
277 'I went to (meet) Krishan Kant at his house at Telegraph Lane': Yunus Saleem to author, 9 July 2003, New Delhi.
277 'I have suggested your name and that of Ali Mian (for the talks)': Ibid.
277 'You fix a meeting with the Shankaracharya and we will go to him together': Ibid.
277 'If we were to go to Madras to meet the Shankaracharya of Kanchi, the president would have wondered': Krishan Kant to author, 25 December 1995, Hyderabad, confidential conversation.
278 'it will be the greatest event of this century': Ibid.
278 Krishan Kant saw the Shankaracharya of Kanchi 'at least a dozen times': Ibid.
278 'When Mohammed Yunus Saleem and Krishan Kant met me and informed me that the shankaracharyas': Yunus Saleem to author, translating what Ali Mian had written, 9 July 2003, New Delhi.
278 'I remember he was lying curled up on a cemented platform': Krishan Kant to author, 25 December 1995, Hyderabad.
278 'He did not say anything but just nodded his approval': Yunus Saleem to author, 9 July 2003, New Delhi.
278 On the verge of a breakthrough, the talks were sabotaged: Yunus Saleem and Krishan Kant to author during separate conversations.
279 'You leave the VHP to me': Ibid.
279 He knew the BJP would have to approve any solution that was worked out: Krishan Kant to author, 25 December 1995, Hyderabad.
279 'Come and meet me at the PM house': Chandra Shekhar, 12 August 2003, New Delhi.
279 Chandra Shekhar decided to negotiate directly with the VHP: Ibid.
279 For his sixty-three member Janata Dal (S) was being supported by Rajiv Gandhi's Congress party: Mukerji, *The Disruptor*, p. 418.
279 'I won't let one brick fall,' Chandra Shekhar told them: Ibid.
280 'Are you ready?': Ibid.
280 Bhairon Singh Shekhawat, Sharad Pawar, and, later, Mulayam Singh Yadav to find 'a way out': Ibid.
280 On 1 and 4 December 1990, meetings were held between the VHP and Babri Masjid leaders: Rao, *Ayodhya*, p. 82.
280 'Tantric-godman' Chandraswami also helped to 'get the sadhus together': Chandra Shekhar to author, 12 August 2003, New Delhi.
280 He 'reached out to 200 sadhus,' including Nritya Gopal Das: Ibid.
280 'Kaun mahatma hai aur kaun duratma hai, kaam zaroori hai': Ibid.
280 Chandra Shekar told Om Prakash Chautala to keep the sadhus 'happy': Ibid.
280 'There was a readiness on both sides to find a solution': Ibid.
280 'then we could build a grand temple on the banks of Bhagirathi and Sarayu': Ibid.
281 led the Babri Masjid Movement Coordination Committee (BMMCC): In February, 1986, Syed Shahabuddin had formed the Babri Masjid Movement Coordination Committee. By December 1988, it had split into two—the BMMCC, and the All India Babri Masjid Conference (AIBMC), a group opposed to Shahabuddin. (Pankaj Pachauri, 'Babri Masjid Movement Coordination Committee jockey for leadership', *India Today*, 31 December 1988).
281 'But I will not accept you as a judge and arbitrator': Syed Shahabuddin to author, 20 July 2005, New Delhi.

281 'He wanted to build his political future on this action': Ibid.
281 'agree to leave (aside) their claim on Kashi and Mathura—if an agreement took place on Ayodhya': Chandra Shekhar to author, 12 August 2003, New Delhi.
282 'Vishnu Hari Dalmia...told me that Chandra Shekhar had pleaded with him to give up Varanasi and Mathura': Romesh Bhandari to author, 22 October 2003, New Delhi.
282 However, both sides agreed to abide by the court verdict: Chandra Shekhar to author, 12 August 2003, New Delhi.
282 'it will have to be mandatory, not recommendatory': Ibid.
282 'The crown prince was involved, his help was taken, and through him the religious heads were spoken to': A member of the three-member interlocutor committee to author, 28 February 2003, Ibid.
282 'We were briefed by the top Muslim leaders (in India) that this could be a way out, and the fight would end': Ibid.
282 The VHP had even decided to call the AIBMAC leaders for dinner: Chandra Shekhar to author, 12 August 2003, New Delhi.
282 He did it 'in good faith', he said later: Sharad Pawar to author; Sharad Pawar, On My Terms: From the Grassroots to the Corridors of Power, New Delhi: Speaking Tiger Books, 2015.
282 'Who is going to look after the state?': Source close to Sharad Pawar, to author, 28 February 2003, New Delhi.
282 the rebels were finally left with the backing of only 11 out of the 210 MLAs: Sharad Pawar to author, 28 February 2003, New Delhi; also in On My Terms.
282 But whispers grew in Delhi's power circles that Chandra Shekhar 'was gaining ground': Chandra Shekhar to author, 12 August 2003, New Delhi.
283 The coterie feared that Sharad Pawar may join hands with Chandra Shekhar: Ibid.
283 But he got cold feet at the last moment: Bhuvnesh Chaturvedi to author, New Delhi.
283 'I can't say if it (resolution of the problem) would have happened': Chandra Shekhar to author, 13 August 2003, New Delhi.
283 'This...he...discussed in great detail with me': Naresh Chandra to author, 31 March 2017, New Delhi.
283 He had arrested more than 1.5 lakh kar sevaks in UP: PTI, 'Mulayam Singh Yadav justifies police firing on kar sevaks in 1990', Times of India, 20 November 2017.
284 But on 30 October, the personnel of the UP Provincial Armed Constabulary (PAC) guarding the structure allowed a security breach to take place: Suman Chattopadhyay, 'A blow-by-blow account of how they demolished Babri Masjid', DailyO, 15 February 2018.
284 It was filmed by the IB and the film was sent to the Home Ministry in Delhi: Naresh Chandra to author, 31 March 2017, New Delhi.
284 'I was monitoring the situation hour by hour': Ibid.
284 'I gave strict instructions to the senior police officers that the UP PAC must act': Ibid.
284 'The official figure of the dead was twelve but really eighteen were killed': Ibid.
284 Later Mulayam Singh Yadav disclosed that twenty-eight people had died: PTI, 'Mulayam Singh Yadav justifies police firing on kar sevaks in 1990'.
284 Once the crowd collects (and becomes unruly), you will have to shoot: Naresh Chandra to author, 31 March 2017, New Delhi.
285 He had declared that not a parinda (bird) would be able to enter the structure on that day: Singh, Ayodhya, p. 220.
285 earned him the title of 'Mullah Mulayam': Naresh Chandra to author, New Delhi.
285 'he would not have allowed this to happen': Ibid.
285 to deploy such a massive force 'to seal the borders between states was impossible': Naresh Chandra to author, 31 March 2017, New Delhi.
285 Much later, in 2007, Rahul Gandhi had claimed that Babri Masjid would not have fallen: TNN, 'Babri wouldn't have fallen if a Gandhi was PM: Rahul', Times of India, 20 March 2007.
285 'Agar main hota, toh 2,000 log bhi mar jaate na, I would have protected the (Babri Masjid) structure': Chandra Shekhar to author.
285 'No journalist can be a friend, though a friend can be a journalist': P. V. Narasimha Rao to Krishan Kant, who told author.
286 Prime Minister Rao told parliament he wanted to 'defuse the situation', 'avoid a confrontation', 'bring about a reconciliation': Rao, Ayodhya, p. 199.
286 PV 'should have entrusted the task of tough negotiations with other political parties to': Mukherjee, The Turbulent Years, p. 154.
287 'It was this mobilization (by the PM) that created a panic in the VHP': Anonymous source who had worked closely with P. V. Narasimha Rao to author, 25 September 2019, New Delhi.
287 Though Rao was to disclose his plans to build the temple to his trusted aide P. V. R. K. Prasad: Bhuvnesh Chaturvedi to author.
287 'PV's talks with Hindu Sant and Muslim Fakirs was to finish the BJP's hold on them': Bhuvnesh Chaturvedi to author, 26 April 2000, New Delhi.
287 'PV had once talked to K. K. Birla about (the latter donating) `2 crores for building the temple': Ibid.
287 Some feared that Narasimha Rao wanted to create 'some kind of a confederation of Hindu churches': Anonymous source who had worked closely with P. V. Narasimha Rao to author, 25 September 2019, New Delhi.
287 'The day the kar seva was announced, PV got a sense that "dal maen kuch kaala hai"': R. K. Khandekar to

author, 23 December 2020, telephonic conversation, Nagpur.
288 'It was then that Rao sahib began to feel it may not be possible to save the Babri Masjid': Ibid.
288 'Arjun Singh had come to see me at 6, Kushak Road': M. L. Fotedar to author, 1 January 2005, Gurgaon.
288 'You can even take my resignation now and you can send it on afterwards': Ibid.
288 'Ab toh yudh hone wala hai': Kishore Kunal to author, Patna.
288 'This time it is not me who has called you': Ibid.
289 'Jo VHP ke saath log jude hue hain, unko kuch udhar se tod karke idhar mila dijiye': Ibid.
289 'Yeh kaam maine zindagi bhar nahi kiya hai': Ibid.
289 'I am not going to sack the UP government. Kalyan Singh's is a duly elected government': Ibid.
289 'You make Ayodhya, Faizabad, and Nandigram into a union territory': Ibid.
289 'It is a good suggestion,' Rao said: Ibid.
290 'I told him, sir, please get this circulated, it will be accepted': Ibid.
290 Their plan recommended kar seva on the 2.77-acre-plot around the disputed area: K. R. Malkani, *The Politics of Ayodhya & Hindu-Muslim Relations*, Ayodhya: Har-Anand Publications, 1993, p. 34.
290 suggested he acquire rubber bullets to be used in Ayodhya: Ved Pratap Vaidik to author, 14 September 2018, Gurgaon.
290 'Why are you getting so worried?': Ibid.
290 'the PM finally gave clearance for moving central forces into UP': Madhav Godbole to author.
291 Not unexpectedly, the UP chief minister protested vehemently: Kalyan Singh to author.
291 'Whatever the judgement, it will help': L. K. Advani to Kamal Nath, to author.
291 Kalyan Singh had helped the Nyas acquire a large swathe of 42 acres of land around the structure: Rao, *Ayodhya*, p. 91.
292 'I did not hesitate even for a minute to state that the proposal would be acceptable': Advani, *My Country, My Life*, p. 394.
292 'There is no such proposal': Advani, *My Country, My Life*, p. 394.
292 PV dismissively referred to his ministers as 'har-fan-maula': Malkani, *The Politics of Ayodhya*, p. 32.
292 'What Advani said was correct': Kamal Nath to author, 3 August 2021, New Delhi.
292 'The prime minister's refusal to get the court to expedite its verdict was one of the reasons for the breakdown of the talks': Kishore Kunal to author, 25 April 2017, Patna.
292 'We would have followed a different course': Advani, *My Country, My Life*, p. 398.
292 It had reserved its judgement on 4 November 1992: Ibid., p. 396.
292 This had earlier been 'privately hinted (to Singhal) by the PM': Malkani, *The Politics of Ayodhya*, p. 24.
292 'PM's advisors—in the PMO, Ayodhya cell or Intelligence Bureau—had advised him that a showdown was (now) inevitable': Ibid.
293 '"Let's see"—what she actually means is "no"': Madhav Godbole to author, 3 February 2019, Pune.
293 Godbole claimed his plan had the backing of his boss, Home Minister Chavan: Ibid.
293 It would give the security forces enough 'lead time' to take over the complex immediately: Madhav Godbole, *Unfinished Innings: Recollections and Reflections of a Civil Servant*, Hyderabad: Orient BlackSwan, 1996, p. 356.
293 He knew that the Opposition would corner the prime minister on Ayodhya: Ibid., p. 364.
293 But Rao did not think much of the plan: P. V. Narasimha Rao to Karan Thapar, 10 December 1992, 'Babri Masjid demolition: The most comprehensive video coverage from 1992' (video credit: Eyewitness, January 1993); Report of the Liberhan Commission of Inquiry, available at <www.mha.gov.in/about-us/commissions-committees/liberhan-ayodhya-commission>; and M. D. Nalapat, 'Interview with former Prime Minister P V Narasimha Rao', *Roots of Power: An Indian Eye on the World*, 28 June 2017, available at <blog.mdnalapat.com/interview-with-former-prime-minister-p-v-narasimha-rao-2f6997d2f03a>.
293 'I mentioned to the PM that...the governor's report could be dispensed with': Madhav Godbole to author, 3 February 2019, Pune.
293 Chandra Shekhar had told me he had imposed President's Rule: Chandra Shekhar to author, 15 February 2000, New Delhi.
293 'I still have that letter somewhere in my almirah': Naresh Chandra to author, 31 March 2017, New Delhi.
294 It was said of him that he would do 'nothing without the go-ahead of PV': Anonymous high level sources to the author. They had been in Andhra Pradesh at the time and were in the know.
294 'During his discussion with the home minister, he had agreed to send his report': Godbole, *Unfinished Innings*.
294 He went to the extent of stating that President's Rule would endanger the disputed structure: Rao, *Ayodhya*, pp. 150.
294 'Satya Narayan Reddy would not have put down an alphabet, a comma, a full stop without asking Rao': Anonymous high level sources to the author.
294 The president had told him this when Fotedar met him on 6 December 1992: M. L. Fotedar to author, 1 January 2005, Gurgaon.
294 Rao did act politically and replaced Janardhan Reddy in October 1992: Krishan Kant to author, 25 December 1995, Hyderabad.
295 'Kalyan Singh has refused to accept action under Article 138(2)': Godbole, *Unfinished Innings*, p. 372.
295 'President's Rule has now become inevitable': Ibid.; M. L. Fotedar to author, 1 January 2005, Gurgaon. Fotedar had been told this by those present at the meeting.
295 He prepared forty-five copies of it: Madhav Godbole to author, 3 February 2019.
295 Rao backed off—and relied on 'procedure' to do so: Ibid.
295 Legal strictures would have given his colleagues in the Congress: Naresh Chandra, reflecting Rao's

thinking, to author, 31 March 2017, New Delhi.
296   'According to conservative estimates, at least 50 to 100 people would have been killed in Ayodhya': Ibid.
296   It is another matter that the failure to protect the mosque led to around 1,000 people being killed: 'Bloody aftermath of Babri Masjid demolition across India', *India Today*, 5 December 2011.
296   'Suppose P. V. Narasimha Rao had given a free reign to munshis (managers) like me': Naresh Chandra to author, 31 March 2017, New Delhi.
296   Former West Bengal Governor Gopalkrishna Gandhi once called the CBI the 'Department of Dirty Tricks': PTI, '"CBI is often called Department of Dirty tricks": ex Bengal Governor Gopal Krishna Gandhi', *NDTV*, 15 April 2014.
296   'Because it's a slippery slope': Naresh Chandra to author, 31 March 2017, New Delhi.
296   'he didn't share it with anybody, not even with me': Ibid.
297   In a tear-choked voice, he expressed his helplessness about the rising tensions in Ayodhya: Mani Shankar Aiyar, '"India Is A Hindu Nation," PV Narasimha Rao Told Me', *NDTV*, 7 July 2016.
297   But the counsel for the Centre did not show up in court: Advani, *My Country, My Life*, p. 397.
297   Singh came back and informed the PM that the situation was 'under control': Bhuvnesh Chaturvedi to author, 27 October 1999, New Delhi.
297   Kalyan Singh told him it would agitate the kar sevaks gathered there: Arjun Singh with Ashok Chopra, *A Grain Of Sand In The Hourglass of Time: An Autobiography*, New Delhi: Hay House, 2012, p. 273.
297   Godbole, a straightforward civil servant, 'didn't realize what...was going on': Naresh Chandra to author, 31 March 2017, New Delhi.
298   'The UP CM was saying that everything is under control': Ibid.
298   'what will happen the day after tomorrow?': Kishore Kunal to author, 25 April 2017, Patna.
298   'Jaisa Supreme Court ka direction hoga, waisa hi karna hai': Ibid.
298   All that the Supreme Court did was to appoint a district judge of Meerut: Rao, *Ayodhya*.
298   'The state has abdicated its authority': Kishore Kunal to author, 25 April 2017, Patna.
298   'There is such a large force stationed there': Ibid.
299   'Hum log usko gira karke, leepa-pothi karke, sab baraabar kar denge zameen ko': Ibid.
299   It would be remembered afterwards as a 'Black Sunday': PTI, 'Babri mosque anniversary: "Day of victory" vs "day of sorrow"', *Deccan Herald*, 6 December 2015.
299   'Narasimha Rao is my closest friend,' he would claim: Ved Pratap Vaidik to author, 14 September 2018, Gurgaon.
299   senior officials in the PM's establishment vouched for his proximity to Rao: Naresh Chandra to author.
299   That morning, before he left for the office, Vaidik called Rao: Ved Pratap Vaidik to author, 14 September 2018, Gurgaon.
299   Rajendra Singh: Singh was number two at the time but the de facto head with the RSS sarsanghchalak Balasaheb Deoras keeping ill health.
299   'PTI picked it up from us': Ibid.
299   'My phone is yours': Ibid.
300   'The kar seva will only be symbolic, as we had decided': Sharma, *Yuddha Mein Ayodhya*, p. 58.
300   It was only after calling Katiyar that the PM spoke to the chief of the Intelligence Bureau, V. G. Vaidya: R. K. Khandekar to author.
300   'Preparations are going on for the kar seva': V. G. Vaidya to author.
300   The prime minister then went through his usual morning drill: Sitapati, *Half-Lion*, p. 225.
300   'Arjun Singh is angry,' Sharma told him. 'Your loyalists have been attacking him': N. K. Sharma to author.
300   that the 'old guard in my party will not understand ' his desire to import computers: Sitapati, *Half Lion*, p. 67.
300   Being a Sunday, the PM had no official engagements: R. K. Khandekar to author, 6 September 2019, telephonic conversation.
300   'He had only one thing on his mind and that was (the) Babri Masjid': R. K. Khandekar to author, 2020.
300   'What's happening?': S. Rajgopal to author, 10 March 2019, Mumbai.
300   'I was about to leave and go and see her but then decided to go to office instead': Ibid.
301   The Ayodhya cell was expected 'to guide the home secretary': Naresh Chandra to author, 31 March 2017, New Delhi.
301   Madhav Godbole 'was an upright officer, and the best you could get', but found him 'opinionated and obstinate': Ibid.
301   'Pehla dome gir gaya hai': V. G. Vaidik to author.
301   Babri Masjid: The mosque consisted of a central nave—it is here the idol of Ram Lalla was placed in 1949—and the mosque was topped with three domes. Within the Babri Masjid compound but separated from the inner courtyard by a high stone wall was the Ramachabutara, a 17x21x6 feet raised platform in the south-eastern corner of the complex. It was the gate at the entrance of the mosque. which Rajiv Gandhi had got unlocked in 1986. To the north was the raised concrete platform for the Singh Dwar, or lion gate, constructed during the kar seva in July 1992 as the proposed site of the Ram Temple.
301   The kar sevaks had washed the Ram Chabutra that morning: Business Standard, 'Babri Masjid demolition: The most comprehensive video coverage from 1992' (video credit: Eyewitness, January 1993), YouTube, available at <www.youtube.com/watch?v=k-bhAFsnv2s>, accessed May 2022.
301   By 12.20 p.m., around eighty members of the mob had managed to climb atop the domes: Ibid.
301   'Then began a frenzied demolition with shovels, iron rods and pickaxes': Rao, *Ayodhya*, p. 154.
301   'As the kar sevaks chipped away at the structure': Rao, *Ayodhya*, p. 157.
301   By 4.55 p.m., it was all over: Business Standard, 'Babri Masjid demolition: The most comprehensive video

coverage from 1992'.

302 'I had known him since the days he used to come to the *Indian Express* in Delhi': Praveen Jain to author, 2 August 2019.

302 'He gave me a (ID) card of the VHP...and a yellow kar sevak scarf': Ibid.

302 'At the time, no one really believed that the Babri Masjid could be destroyed the next day': Ibid.

302 On the night of 5 December, there was a secret meeting held in Ayodhya: Hemant Sharma, *Ayodhya Ka Chashmadeed* and *Yuddha Mein Ayodhya*, Delhi: Prabhat Prakashan, 1 January 2018. Sharma had covered the events for *Jansatta* and written in the paper *Prabhat Prakashan*.

302 The VHP's secret plan was being fine-tuned till the early hours of the morning: Sharma, *Yuddha Mein Ayodhya*.

303 'I first ran towards the platform from where the BJP leaders had addressed the crowds': Praveen Jain to author; also Praveen Jain, 'My camera had "evidence" masjid demolition, but it was consigned to bin of history', *The Print*, 3 October 2020.

303 when he had to give evidence in one of the Babri Masjid demolition cases: In December 1993, two FIRs were filed in the Babri Masjid demolition case, one against eminent BJP leaders for allegedly giving inflammatory speeches before the destruction of the mosque. And the other against unknown kar sevaks for demolishing the sixteenth century mosque. See 'Babri demolition case: A tale of two FIRs', *Times of India*, 30 September 2020.

303 'The sun was as sweetly warm as the nip in the air was refreshing': Malkani, *The Politics of Ayodhya & Hindu-Muslim Relations*, p. 1.

303 The Kendriya Marg Darshak Mandal, the highest decision making body of the Vishwa Hindu Parishad: 'VHP's "Margdarshak Mandal" endorses decision on temple construction', Zee News, 27 January 2002.

303 'We won't need the press note now': Malkani, *The Politics of Ayodhya & Hindu-Muslim Relations*, p. 1.

303 Malkani was to describe the day's events as 'unfortunate': Ibid.

303 'but... we wanted it gone through a due process of law': Ibid.

303 The party took 'moral responsibility' for what had happened: Rao, *Ayodhya*, p. 156.

304 'For about ten minutes, the prime minister sat in his chair motionless': P. V. Narasimha Rao's friend, who was with him that day, to author, April 2019.

304 was at it 'for the next two hours': Rao's friend, who was with him that morning, to author, 1 October 2022, New Delhi.

304 He spoke only to Home Minister S. B. Chavan: Madhav Godbole to author, 3 February 2019, Pune. Godbole said that the home minister had told him that he had spoken to the PM.

305 they had directions that the PM 'was not to be disturbed': Singh with Chopra, *A Grain Of Sand In The Hourglass of Time: An Autobiography*, p. 277; P. R. Kumaramangalam to author.

305 The inability to reach Rao at the peak of the crisis led to the rumour: 'Was Narasimha Rao responsible for Babri masjid?', *India Legal*, 14 July 2016.

305 'Apne buddhe premi se baat hui kya?': Ved Pratap Vaidik to author, 14 September 2018, Gurgaon.

305 'Kya chal raha hai?': Ibid.

305 'I spoke to Narasimha Rao at 1.40 p.m.': M. L. Fotedar to author, 1 January 2005, Gurgaon.

305 'the Congress will be finished': Ibid.

305 'Should we hold a cabinet meeting?': Ibid.

305 But, like his other colleagues, he felt uneasy instead towards North Block: Madhav Godbole, *Unfinished Innings: Recollections and Reflections of a Civil Servant*, Hyderabad: Orient BlackSwan, 1996, p. 382.

305 'We were monitoring the situation from my office in North Block': Madhav Godbole to author, 3 February 2019, Pune.

306 the central government had dispatched around '20,000' men: Rao, *Ayodhya*, p. 174.

306 They were stationed at nearby Faizabad, ready to assist the state government: C. Pal Singh, 'Babri Masjid Demolition—Non-effectiveness of enforcement agencies- Constitutional limitations, *Law Street Journal*, 26 June 2016.

306 They were equipped with an array of 'soft' weapons: W. P. S. Sidhu and Dilip Awasthi, 'Babri Masjid demolition: Law enforcers remained mute spectators as kar sevaks broke the law', *India Today*, 31 December 1992.

306 'Don't waste any time,' he said again and again: Madhav Godbole to author, Pune.

306 Till 11 a.m. 'everything seemed to be okay': V. G. Vaidya to author.

306 'A group of kar sevaks have entered the masjid and got on top of the dome': V. G. Vaidya, March 2019, Pune.

306 'The PM had so many political sources, and he would have known immediately': Ibid.

306 Vaidya had also informed the home minister, S. B. Chavan: Madhav Godbole to author.

306 'Oh my God,' exclaimed Rajgopal. 'This can't be happening': S. Rajgopal to author, 10 March 2019, Mumbai.

306 'Yeh tho nahin ho sakta': Madhav Godbole to author.

306 'I hadn't thought that they would go to the extent of going to the top of the mosque': Ibid.

306 He also believed that the RSS and the VHP would not destroy the structure because it had been used as a temple: Naresh Chandra to author; Madhav Godbole to author.

307 Kalyan Singh had given a solemn promise to the Supreme Court only ten days earlier: Manoj Mitta, 'When Even the Supreme Court Let Down the Nation', *The Wire*, 6 December 2017. The Kalyan Singh government had given an affidavit to the Supreme Court on 27 November 1992, in the run up to the demolition of the Babri Masjid, which promised to 'safeguard and protect' the mosque and maintained

that it had an 'enviable' record, of 'maintaining law and order' and 'communal harmony'. The affidavit had also cited a letter from BJP MP Swami Chinmayanand, who was one of the organizers of the proposed kar seva on 6 December that the kar sevaks would not violate an order of the High Court, given earlier, against any construction at the disputed site. It was on the basis of Kalyan Singh government's affidavit that the Supreme Court gave its go ahead for a 'symbolic' kar seva to be held on 6 December, performing some rituals.

307   'We will have to get the CM's permission: Madhav Godbole to author, 3 February 2019, Pune.

307   By around 1 p.m., the five top officers of the Indian government were in North Block: Ibid.

307   'We felt our options had closed': Ibid.

307   'Aap Shankar Raoji (S. B. Chavan) se baat kar lo': Ved Pratap Vaidik to author, 14 September 2018, Gurgaon.

307   He took off for the ashram of the controversial godman: Prithviraj Chavan to author.

307   'Chavan was really a dummy home minister': R. K. Khandekar to author, 23 December 2020, in a telephonic interview from Nagpur.

307   'Please tell him bahut bada sankat paida ho gaya ahi': Ved Pratap Vaidik to author.

308   Chavan had also spoken to Kalyan Singh at 12.25 p.m.: Sharma, *Yuddha Mein Ayodhya*, p. 61.

308   Both had gone to jail in 1965 for taking part in a Bharat bandh: Ved Pratap Vaidik to author, 14 September 2018, Gurgaon.

308   'Doctor saab, Kalyan Singh meri jaan kha raha hai': Ibid.

308   'Mera phone hi nahi le rahein. Aap unse baat keejiye': Ibid.

308   'Ab itna galat kaam kar diya': Ibid.

308   'Mere saath bahut bada dhokha hua hai': Ibid.

308   'Rao saab, Raja ko kabhi nahin kehna chahiye ke mere saath dhokha hua hai': Ibid.

309   At around 3 p.m., the prime minister met Home Secretary Godbole: Madhav Godbole to author, 3 February 2019, Pune.

309   After that Rao separately met Naresh Chandra: Naresh Chandra to author, 31 March 2017, New Delhi.

309   'Instead, Kalyan Singh put it down in writing that the police will not open fire on the kar sevaks': Prabhat Kumar to author, 18 October 2022, Panchgani.

309   'he knew all about' what he was being told: Madhav Godbole to author, 3 February 2019, Pune.

309   'We should first impose President's Rule before accepting his resignation': Ibid.

309   The cabinet would meet at 6 p.m. and take a view on the dismissal of the government: Godbole, *Unfinished Innings*, p. 384.

309   Cabinet Secretary Rajgopal's office got a call from the PMO 'in the afternoon': S. Rajgopal to author.

309   The PMO instructed the cabinet secretariat to fix the cabinet meeting: Ibid.

310   Fotedar got word about the cabinet meeting around 5 p.m.: M. L. Fotedar to author.

310   'It took us time to get him back here.... Narasimha Rao did not want to start (the meeting) in his absence': Naresh Chandra to author.

310   Naresh Chandra arrived at 7, Race Course Road, 'around 4.30 pm': Ibid.

310   'But I got a mouthful from him': Ibid.

310   'He was very angry, I got a bit of a shock (seeing him)': Ibid.

310   'Everyone (and he was including the PM in this) knew the situation could spin out of control': Ved Pratap Vaidik to author, Pune.

311   'The moment the cabinet okayed President's Rule, we would rush the papers to the President for him to sign': Naresh Chandra to author.

311   'I received a phone call from the Ayodhya police control room': Kalyan Singh to author, 3 September 2018, Lucknow.

311   'the police must not fire at the crowds': Ibid.

311   Kalyan Singh estimated that there were 300,00 gathered in Ayodhya that day: Ibid.

311   'By asking the police not to fire, I saved the lives of thousands of Ram bhakts, though I was not able to save the dhancha': Ibid.

311   Kalyan Singh, too, said he felt 'let down': Ibid.

311   They should have warned him if they intended to demolish the structure: Sharma, *Yuddha Mein Ayodhya*.

311   Though he was the CM, it was the Vishwa Hindu Parishad—and Vinay Katiyar: Ibid.

312   Mandir movement in the 1990s: Kalyan Singh had acquired 2.77 acres of land around the mosque three months after he took over. In May 1992, he demolished the buildings and shops that stood on the land and started levelling the ground. This led to a flurry of petitions in the Allahabad High Court to restrain him. The High Court stayed the construction activity on the 2.77 acres taken over by the government. The Supreme Court also came into the picture and ruled that no permanent structure should be constructed there.

312   On the evening of 5 December, the day before demolition, Kalyan Singh had begun to feel uneasy: Kalyan Singh to author, 3 September 2018, Lucknow.

312   'Please ensure that everything goes smoothly with the kar seva today': Ibid.

312   'This was the first time in history that a government was overthrown which did not exist in the first place': Ibid.

312   The atmosphere in the meeting room was 'despondent': Godbole, *Unfinished Innings*, p. 384; M. L. Fotedar to author.

312   'What is this cabinet (meeting) for?': M. L. Fotedar to author, 1 January 2005, Gurgaon.

313   According to Fotedar, everyone looked surprised: Ibid.

313   'The PM asked the Cabinet Secretary': Fotedar, *Chinar Leaves*.

313 'Shankar Dayal Sharma was genuinely in tears': M. L. Fotedar to author, 1 January 2005, Gurgaon.
313 'It was a very strong letter (in which) he held the prime minister responsible for the demolition': Shahid Siddiqui to author, 2019.
313 'I told him to go on the air (and address the nation)': M. L. Fotedar to author.
313 'Mr prime minister, this CM has resigned and thrown this illegitimate child (the government) in the Hazrat Mahal park': Ibid.
313 Others remember Fotedar shouting at the PM: Sitapati, *Half Lion*, p. 248.
313 At one point, Fotedar 'started to cry': Singh, *A Grain of Sand in The Hourglass of Time*.
313 An upset C. K. Jaffer Sharief warned that the country would have to pay a heavy price: C. K. Jaffer Sharief to author, in Parliament, New Delhi; Singh, *A Grain of Sand in The Hourglass of Time*.
313 During the day they had tried to contact Rao and Chavan but were told they 'were resting': Shahid Siddiqui to author.
314 'Usse bhi zyada,' Rao said. 'Sab kuch gir gaya, sab kuch gir gaya. Leken mein banaoonga doobara. Sab kuch banaoonga': Ibid.
314 'Aap banwa deejeye': Ibid.
314 Siddiqui was referring to the meeting of the National Integration Council on 23 November 1992: Shahid Siddiqui to author, 2019; Madhav Godbole, 'Intelligence Bureau could've saved Babri Masjid by alerting PM Rao to demolition conspiracy', *The Print*, 8 September 2019; 'Basu and Deshpande appear before Liberhan', *Milli Gazette*.
314 'Hindu ki toh koi aukaat hi nahi hai iss desh mein, aapki party mein': Shahid Siddiqui, 25 March 2019, New Delhi.
314 '(Today) there is neither a masjid nor a mandir there. Please don't change that status quo': Ibid.
315 'The government will see to it that it is rebuilt': Prime Minister P. V. Narasimha Rao's statement in parliament, 7 December 1992, cited as annexure XII, in Rao, *Ayodhya*, p. 257.
315 Fotedar was the sharpest in his criticism of Rao: Singh, *A Grain of Sand*, p. 278.
315 they could always 'restore the assembly' afterwards: M. L. Fotedar to author.
315 Each time the PM would make the same promise—that he would 'save the mosque at any cost': Ibid.
315 'I did not think it proper to enter into an open confrontation': Singh, *A Grain of Sand in The Hourglass of Time*, p. 279.
315 'I kept beseeching them to resign': Anil Bali to author, 7 March 2018, New Delhi.
316 'Hum aapko bhi dekh lenge': Ved Pratap Vaidik to author, 14 September 2018, Gurgaon.
316 'Agar main raajneeti karne laga hota, toh main aapko Delhi nahi aane deta': Ibid.
316 'He immediately accepted this suggestion,' Singh stated: Singh, *A Grain of Sand in The Hourglass of Time*, p. 279.
317 Godbole had already prepared a shortlist of advisors: Godbole, *Unfinished Innings*, pp. 385–86.
317 After talking to the PM, Rajgopal chose Ashok Chandra and B. K. Goswami as advisers: Ibid.
317 It was another matter they had to return because of bad weather that night, and go the next day: Ibid., p. 386.
317 'Rao sahib has high fever': Ved Pratap Vaidik to author, 14 September 2018, Gurgaon.
317 Rao told Pilot to go ahead with his 'dome' plan. 'Rajesh Pilot and I knuckled down to this': Shahid Siddiqui to author; M. L. Fotedar to author.
318 'The order (not to do it) has come from the top': Shahid Siddiqui to author, 25 March 2019.
318 They were accused of a criminal conspiracy and incitement: TNN, 'Babri demolition case: A tale of two FIRs'.
318 Advani, who had called 6 December 'the saddest day of my life " but also dubbed it as 'a day of Hindu awakening': Sudheendra Kulkarni, 'In Fact, Advani Asked Mobs To Stop Tearing Down Babri Masjid', *NDTV*, 20 April 2017.
318 The tribunal felt that the government had failed to prepare a comprehensive case: V. Venkatesan, 'Beyond a ban', *Frontline*, 22 January 2000.
318 the commission found that the demolition was 'preplanned', carried out with 'painstaking preparation': 'Babri Masjid demolition | Key conclusions by Liberhan Commission', *The Hindu*, 30 September 2020.
318 which left 1,200 dead and 4,000 injured: Bob Drogin, 'India Takes Over 3 States Run by Fundamentalists', *Los Angeles Times*, 16 December 1992.
319 Its report stated that there was a structure beneath the disputed structure, which included temple walls and pillars: V. Venkatesan, 'The excavation order', *The Hindu*, 30 September 2010.
319 The Supreme Court stayed the Allahabad High Court's judgment on 9 August 2011: Virag Gupta (ed.), *Ayodhya's Ram Temple in Courts: Judgment and Review*, 3rd edn, CASC, 2019.
319 On 5 August 2020 the foundation stone of the Ram Janmabhoomi temple was laid by Prime Minister Narendra Modi: ANI, 'Ayodhya: CM Yogi lays foundation stone of Ram Mandir's "Garbha Griha"', *The Print*, 1 June 2022.
320 In a ruling which came in for criticism, the court held in its 2,000-page judgment: PTI, 'Special court verdict in Babri case runs counter to SC judgement: Congress', *Livemint*, 30 September 2020.
320 'I was called (to) the PM's residence': 'Was not ready to come back as Maharashtra CM in 1993: Pawar', *Outlook*, 30 December 2021.
320 Less than a week later, on 12 March, a series of twelve bomb blasts: 'How the 1993 blasts changed Mumbai forever', *The BBC*, 30 July 2015.
320 'I want you to take over as home secretary from 8 a.m. tomorrow': N. N. Vohra to author, 24 November 2021, New Delhi.

320   'I want you to look into how three and a half tonnes of explosive material came into a metro city': Ibid.
320   'But I finished it in eighty-five days': Ibid.
321   'It was so deep seated that it was not going to go away easily': Ibid.
321   In the months that followed, the government gave assurances 'thirteen times': Ibid.
321   'I left a handwritten note': Ibid.
321   'Narasimha Raoji jahaan Ram Lallaji virajman hai, waheen Mandir banaana chahte thae': Kishore Kunal to author.
322   'We can fight the BJP, but how can we fight Lord Ram?': P. V. R. K. Prasad, *Wheels Behind the Veil: PMs, CMs and Beyond*, Vijayawada: Emesco Books, 2010.
322   'Our aim should be to achieve both, not through the courts nor through the politicians': Ibid.
322   He tasked a surprised Prasad to create 'a representative and apolitical committee': Ibid., p. 169.
322   And that, according to Prasad 'was the end of the story': Ibid.
322   'where we cannot take on the BJP successfully': Naresh Chandra to author, 31 March 2017, New Delhi.
322   He considered going in for a nuclear test, but ruled it out when information about it leaked to the Americans: PTI, 'US detected Indian nuclear test buildup at Pokhran in 1995', *Times of India*, 23 February 2013.
322   'hawala' scam in which many of his own party colleagues were involved: Zafar Agha, 'Jain hawala case: Narasimha Rao remained evasive despite being aware of every CBI move', *India Today*, 29 February 1996; Shekhar Gupta,' Narasimha Rao felt betrayed over Babri, he avenged it by trapping Advani in hawala scandal', *The Print*, 6 December 2017.
323   people would walk out his meetings when Rao would start to speak: The author was at one such meeting in Guntur, Andhra Pradesh, April 1996.
324   V. P. Singh had made this suggestion to him at the end of November 1992: Som Pal to author, 12 September 2021, Gurgaon.
324   But all Rao did, by his own admission, was 'alert' the army: Rao, *Ayodhya*, p. 253.
324   'Along with the Babri Masjid, it was me whom they were trying to demolish': Ibid., p. 181.
325   Cases were initiated against him for corruption: Amitabh Tiwari, '5 controversies that marred Narasimha Rao's political legacy', *DailyO*, 28 June 2016.
325   His desperate daughter Vani Devi sent word to the Congress leadership asking them to help: Shivraj Patil to author.
325   Ahmed Patel picked up a glass of water and asked him to drink it: Ibid.
325   'why should I be blamed for something I have not done?': Sitapati, *Half Lion*, p. 300.
325   'Did I speak more than I should have?': Ibid.
325   The flower bedecked cortege was not allowed entry: The author was present at 24 Akbar Road, New Delhi, on 24 December 2004. See also Rasheed Kidwai, 'PV Narasimha Rao: From packing his bags to India's "accidental" prime minister', *India Today*, 28 June 2021.

CHAPTER 5: THE PEACEABLE PRIME MINISTER WHO ROARED: A. B. VAJPAYEE AUTHORIZES THE TESTING OF TACTICAL NUCLEAR DEVICES

328   Joint Intelligence Committee of the government: The Joint Intelligence Committee was tasked with analysing the intelligence data from the Intelligence Bureau, RAW, and all military intelligence and had its secretariat in the Cabinet Secretariat of the government of India; see irp.fas.org.
328   'In 1979, I produced a report that Pakistan was going in for nuclear weapons': K. Subrahmanyam to author, Vasant Kunj, New Delhi, 21 November 2004.
328   'Don't allow any of the other secretaries to come in either': Ibid.
328   They were the specially invited Atomic Energy Commission chairman: Ibid.
328   this would have meant going against the PM's anti-nuclear position and his policy of reaching out to Islamabad: Yogesh Joshi, 'Hubris, Biases, and Overlearning: A Historical Analysis of How India Missed Pakistan's Nuclear Coup', Observer Research Foundation, ORF Issue Brief No. 513, January 2022.
328   'was that we should proceed with our efforts': K. Subrahmanyam to author, Vasant Kunj, New Delhi, 21 November 2004.
329   'Was it Charan Singh?': Ibid.
329   And, he also knew that Vajpayee's parent party, the Bharatiya Jan Sangh: 'India's Nuclear Weapons Program: On to Weapons Development: 1960-1967', 30 March 2001, available at <nuclearweaponarchive. org/India/IndiaWDevelop.html>.
329   'No, it was Vajpayee': K. Subrahmanyam to author, Vasant Kunj, New Delhi, 21 November 2004.
329   'Morarji and Vajpayee were opposed to going ahead': K. Subrahmanyam to author, New Delhi, 13 February 2005. He told this to other journalists as well. See Shivanand Kanavi, 'How Indian PMs reacted to nuclear ambitions', *Rediff.com*, 10 February 2011; 'Vajpayee Opposed Nuclear Option In 79', *Financial Express*, 20 January 2004.
329   'They (Pakistan) had got new centrifuge technology': K. Subrahmanyam to author, 21 March 2004, New Delhi. An earlier form of technology to enrich uranium was gas diffusion; this was mothballed with the advent of centrifuge technology; the latest way in which uranium is enriched is through laser technology (former chairman of Atomic Energy Commission Dr Anil Kakodkar to author, 2 April 2022, video call).
329   The scientists were particularly worried because 'in 1979 we (also) had new evidence about A. Q. Khan': Ibid.

329 It was in September 1974, four months after Indira Gandhi had tested India's 'peaceful nuclear device': Michael Laufer, 'A. Q. Khan Nuclear Chronology', Carnegie Endowment for International Peace, 7 September 2005.

329 Khan focussed on developing Pakistan's indigenous uranium enrichment capability in Kahuta: Ibid.

329 It was much later that Khan was to go rogue: Ibid.

329 'I exposed Pakistan's programme (back in 1976)': K. Santhanam to author, New Delhi, 1 December 2004.

330 began to take a serious note of what Santhanam had been saying: Ibid.

330 Pakistan laid the foundations of its nuclear programme after India divided the country: C. Raja Mohan to author, 3 April 2022, video call.

330 Over the years it was to provide 'significant assistance' to Pakistan's nuclear weapons programme: Charlie Gao, 'China Helped Build Pakistan's Military With These Five Weapons', *National Interest*, 24 January 2022. *Janes Defence Weekly*, the respected defence journal, was to reveal that Pakistan's nuclear arsenal was essentially of Chinese design (Shakti Sinha, *Vajpayee: The Years That Changed India*, New Delhi: Vintage, p. 120).

330 '(Z. A.) Bhutto (had) convened a meeting of nuclear scientists': C. Raja Mohan to author, 3 April 2022, video call.

330 'No, no, now the most important thing is to stop Pakistan from making the bomb': K. Subrahmanyam to author, 21 May 2004, New Delhi.

330 China had detonated a 16-kiloton bomb in its first nuclear test: Manas Tiwari, 'The story of Pokhran: Tests that established India as nuclear power, became cornerstone of Atal Bihari Vajpayee's tenure as PM', *Financial Express*, 17 August 2018.

330 'The only answer to an atom bomb is an atom bomb, nothing else': K. Subrahmanyam to author.

330 introduced a motion in the Lok Sabha on 27 November 1964: 'India's Nuclear Weapons Program: On to Weapons Development: 1960-1967'.

331 Desai had pledged that India would not 'manufacture or acquire nuclear weapons': George Perkovich, *India's Nuclear Bomb: The Impact on Global Proliferation*, Berkeley, Los Angeles, London: University of California Press, 2001, p. 211.

331 'Hiroshima ki Peeda': The poem is undated, but is believed to have been written in the 1950s. For after 1957, when he was elected to the Lok Sabha from Balrampur, Vajpayee referred to the agony of Hiroshima in several of his parliament speeches (Sagarika Ghose, author of *Atal Bihari Vajpayee*, to author, 6 April 2022).

331 killed around 210,000 people: 'Hiroshima and Nagasaki bombings', ICAN, available at <icanw.org/hiroshima_and_nagasaki_bombings#:~:text=The%20two%20atomic%20bombs%20dropped,a%20further%2074%2C000%20in%20Nagasaki.>.

331 Sometimes at night: Atal Bihari Vajpayee, *21 Poems*, tr. Pavan Verma, New Delhi: Penguin Books, 2001. The poem on Hiroshima was also found amongst Vajpayee's papers, published as *Kuchh Lekh Kuchh Bhaashan*, New Delhi: Kitabghar Prakashan, 1999.

332 This vote was not minuted: Krishan Kant to author, 25 December 1995, Hyderabad; Rashmi Kant to author, 2002, confirmed in 2021. Rashmi Kant had heard of it from his father and directly from K. Subrahmanyam several times.

332 Morarji Desai had exercised his 'casting vote': Krishan Kant to author, 25 December 1995, Hyderabad. Reconfirmed by Rashmi Kant to author, 3 April 2018, New Delhi. Both had been told this by K. Subrahmanyam many times.

332 'discontinued the nuclear programme started by the Congress Government': 'Vajpayee Opposed Nuclear Option In 79'.

332 Subrahmanyam told me he wrote out the minutes 'in my (own) hand': K. Subrahmanyam to author, 21 May 2004, New Delhi.

332 'I took a Xerox copy of the minutes': Ibid.

332 'As long as I am prime minister, I will never permit an experiment': Raj Chengappa, *Weapons of Peace: The Secret Story of India's Quest to be a Nuclear Power*, Delhi: HarperCollins India, 2000, p. 220.

332 However, it was clear that it would be far short of a bomb: Ibid., p. 221. Refining the design and reducing the weight is the next step after testing a device to preparing a bomb which is compact enough to be delivered by an appropriate delivery mechanism, like a missile or a plane.

333 The PM, who was known for his self-righteousness, stated this 'vigorously' and 'emotionally': Rezaul H. Laskar, 'Morarji Desai told US: Not sure if 1974 nuclear test was necessary', *Hindustan Times* 10 August 2019.

333 if India had to live in peace with its neighbours, it was necessary to have a credible nuclear deterrent: Sinha, *Vajpayee*, p. 100.

333 'I am the longest prime minister in waiting': A. B. Vajpayee to Krishan Kant, Rashmi Kant to author, March 2021.

333 He did it to enable Vajpayee: Sinha, *Vajpayee*, p. 3.

333 'This is our future prime minister': Shivraj Patil to author, 21 February 2021, telephonic interview. Patil was told this story by Vajpayee himself.

333 he once instructed an Indian ambassador posted in the US to 'introduce' Vajpayee to people 'who mattered': Shivraj Patil to author, 3 November 2022, New Delhi, telephonic interview.

334 'Jisko vote dena hai toh doh, nahin dena toh mat doh': Shivraj Patil to author, 21 February 2021, telephonic interview. Patil was told this story by Vajpayee himself during a conference.

334 'Was it you who invited him to speak at the rally or was it his party?': Shivraj Patil to author, 3 November 2022, New Delhi, telephonic interview.

334 The Vajpayee family were originally from UP: Sagarika Ghose, *Atal Bihari Vajpayee*, Delhi: Juggernaut Books, 2021, p. 46.

335 he suddenly forgot his lines and became tongue-tied: Ibid., p. 48.

335 'These lines may not be upto the mark as poetry': Shakti Sinha to author.

335 'Toote hue sapno ki, kaun sune siski': Atal Bihari Vajpayee, *Meri Ikyavan Kavitayen*, New Delhi: Kitabghar Prakashan, 1995.

335 'Kal agar kaal aakar mere dwar par dastak de': Ibid.

336 'I didn't know he had cancer': Yashwant Sinha to author, 11 June 2019, New Delhi.

336 After the treatment he underwent, the disease did not reappear: Shakti Sinha to author, 11 April 2021, telephonic interview.

336 'The two, kidney and cancer, were interrelated': Ibid.

336 'Meri kavita jang ka elan hai, parajaya ki prastavana nahin': Ghose, *Atal Bihari Vajpayee*.

336 'I would use the opportunity to get the treatment I needed': Ullekh N. P., *The Untold Vajpayee: Politician and Paradox*, New Delhi: Penguin Books, 2018, quoted in Prabhash K. Dutta, 'When Rajiv Gandhi saved Atal Bihari Vajpayee's life', *India Today*, 6 May 2019.

336 'I went to New York and that is one reason I am alive today': Ibid.

336 Apart from attending the UN session, his yearly visit to New York would enable him to get his annual check-ups: Bhuvnesh Chaturvedi to author, 21 March 2000, New Delhi.

336 He had once instructed Brajesh Mishra to inform journalist Rajdeep Sardesai where he would get the best steak in New York!: Ghose, *Atal Bihari Vajpayee*, p. 354.

336 He was particularly fond of Mexican food, according to friend Mukund Modi: Saba Naqvi Bhaumik, 'Vajpayee separates public life from the private successfully', *India Today*, 20 April 1998.

337 he liked the 'high end politics' at the UN, and 'the comings and goings of leaders from around the world': Shakti Sinha to author, 11 April 2021, telephonic interview.

337 Vajpayee 'hoped one day to marry her': Ghose, *Atal Bihari Vajpayee*.

337 The meeting 'rekindled the flame' between Vajpayee and Rajkumari: Vinay Sitapati, 'In Nehru's Shadow (1951–67)', *Jugalbandi: The BJP Before Modi*, New Delhi: Penguin Random House, 2020.

337 remembered her as a 'remarkable woman': Karan Singh to author, 16 March 2023, New Delhi.

337 Much as the RSS dispproved of Vajpayee's 'romancing, whisky drinking, meat-eating ways': Ghose, *Atal Bihari Vajpayee*, p. 114.

337 'The heart of the relationship between Rajkumari and Vajpayee': Sitapati, 'In Nehru's Shadow (1951–67)', *Jugalbandi*.

337 'Rajkumari arguing with Vajpayee on politics': Ibid.

338 became a vistarak (preacher) in 1946: Ghose, *Atal Bihari Vajpayee*, Juggernaut, p. 50.

338 On their part, the RSS pracharaks were enthused by his oratory: Ghose, *Atal Bihari Vajpayee*, p. 54.

338 'the chaat we would go and have at Delhi's Bengali Market': L. K. Advani to author, 11 May 1998, New Delhi.

339 'Hindu Rashtra it means the Indian nation which included non-Hindus as members': 'August 3, 1979, Forty Years Ago: Vajpayee On RSS', *Indian Express*, 3 August 2019.

339 Vajpayee chose 'Gandhian Socialism' as his mantra for the newbie BJP: Sitapati, Radical Hindus, Moderate Vajpayee (1980–84), *Jugalbandi*.

339 it was a model based on 'the values of sanatan dharma', of culture and nationalism: *GK Today*, 13 Nov 2015.

339 the *New York Times* considered the local election significant enough to write about it: William K. Stevens, 'Gandhi party wins big victory in New Delhi', Special to the *New York Times*, 7 February 1983. The Congress had won 34 out of the 56 Council seats and 57 out of the 100 corporation seats, while the BJP got only 19 Council seats and 38 corporation seats in its citadel of Delhi. (Coomi Kapoor, 'Delhi Civic polls: Congress(I) fights back, wins an impressive victory', *India Today*, 28 February 1983.

339 'Advani will never be prime minister as long as Atalji is there': Govindacharya to author at the BJP headquarters, 11 Ashoka Road, New Delhi, 1 December 1989.

339 'I never realized that religiosity was so deep rooted in the lives of Indian people': Advani, *My Country, My Life*, p. 377.

340 he had even called himself a 'champion of non-alignment' in one of his speeches in parliament: Ghose, *Atal Bihari Vajpayee*, p. 137.

340 he came to be seen as more 'moderate': Sagarika Ghose to author, 6 April 2022, telephonic conversation.

341 'Yahi to dikkat hai, baniye hi baniye hain. Aur koi nahi': Sources close to Chaudhary Radhakrishan to author, 3 April 2018, New Delhi.

341 Vajpayee the party's 'mukhota' (mask): Neena Vyas, 'Vajpayee the "Mukhota", Once and Always a Sangh Loyalist', *The Wire*, 17 August 2018.

341 they were not given the chance to speak in parliament: Ghose, *Atal Bihari Vajpayee*, p. 105.

342 Mookerji was arrested by Sheikh Abdullah: Vajpayee was to allege years later in 2004 that Mookerji had died because of a conspiracy to eliminate him. (Shashank Bhardwaj, 'From cover up to conspiracy to murder: Some unanswered questions about Dr Syama Prasad Mookerjee's death in Kashmir', *OpIndia*, 23 June 2021.)

342 Vajpayee went to Pakistan in February 1978 on a visit he called 'historic': 'February 8, 1978, Forty Years Ago: Vajpayee in Pakistan', *Indian Express*, 8 February 2018.

342 'Vajpayee was a clever careerist': Sagarika Ghose to author, 6 April 2022, telephonic interview.

342 Vajpayee spoke in two voices: Siddharth Varadarajan, 'Atal's Temple Talk: Flip Flop big flop', *Times of India*, 4 August 2003.

342 In April 1991, he said a temple was necessary: Ibid.
342 In May 1996, he almost justified the demolition: Ibid.
343 'You have a long innings in politics ahead of you': Som Pal to author, 17 March 2023, Gurgaon.
343 'What she is saying is not right': Ibid. Som Pal said Vajpayee had told him this on 16 May 2004, a day after Sonia Gandhi had been elected leader of the Congress Parliamentary Party.
344 'Yeh toh nahi chalega, yeh toh nahin chalega': Jaswant Singh to author, 15 January 2005, New Delhi.
344 'It's a bloody game you are getting into': One of those trainees present at the meeting to author; he became Indian ambassador to Austria, 29 March 2021, New Delhi.
344 'No one sees these papers, not even the staff knows about it': Inder Kumar Gujral to author.
345 V. P. Singh said he was not briefed by Rajiv Gandhi: V. P. Singh to author, 29 May 2002, New Delhi.
345 Chandra Shekhar complained he was not briefed by V. P. Singh: Chandra Shekhar to author, 15 February 2000, New Delhi.
345 Narasimha Rao sent Naresh Chandra and A. P. J. Abdul Kalam to brief H. D. Deve Gowda: Naresh Chandra to author, 5 February 2004, New Delhi.
345 Gujral did brief Vajpayee in 1998 but he had anyway been brought up to date: H. D. Deve Gowda to author, 30 October 2003, New Delhi.
345 Even Desai, who was the least enthusiastic about weaponization, kept the R&D and small table top experiments going: Anil Kakodkar to author, 15 March 2023.
345 'Despite political differences, no prime minister acted in a manner which was less than responsible': I. K. Gujral to author, 6 October 2003, New Delhi.
345 Nehru was not totally against India building its infrastructure to exercise the nuclear option: Chengappa, *Weapons of Peace*, pp. 83–84.
345 Nehru was 'against outlawing atomic weapons': quoted in Ibid., p. 83.
345 'because we can't completely abjure from it': Ibid.
345 He even wanted Nehru to amend the Constitution: Kanavi, 'How Indian PMs reacted to nuclear ambitions'.
345 'No, no,' Nehru told him. 'Don't go that far': Chengappa, *Weapons of Peace*, p. 83.
346 'they could form a powerful third force': Ibid., p. 84.
346 He sanctioned plans for Bhabha to set up the infrastructure capable of making nuclear weapons: Ibid., p. 83. The AEC was set up by Nehru in August 1948, to supervise all activities related to atomic energy and also to promote a scientific temper in the country. Homi Bhabha was its first chair. Then there was the Bhabha Atomic Research Centre, a premier institution founded by Homi Jehangir Bhabha in 1954, to do advanced research needed for India's nuclear programme. It was located in Trombay in Mumbai, and Bhabha was able to get adequate funds for the programme. It was in 1958 that the other big institution, to have a bearing on the nuclear programme, the DRDO (Defence Research and Development Organisation) was founded. Placed under the Defence Ministry, it was tasked with research on defence technologies and systems needed by the Indian armed forces.
346 Accordingly, a plutonium reprocessing plant was started in 1965 in Trombay: 'India's Nuclear Weapons Program: On to Weapons Development: 1960-1967'.
346 On 5 April 1965, he sanctioned the setting up of a nuclear design group: Ibid.
346 'Peaceful Nuclear Explosion' (PNE): A PNE is a nuclear explosion meant for non-military purposes which can be used for excavation of canals or harbours or purposes such as driving spacecraft.) But Shastri died soon thereafter—on 11 January 1966. It was left to Indira Gandhi, who succeeded him, to initiate a PNE eight years later.
347 'Ramanna had told me this himself (later) in 1978': K. Subrahmanyam to author, 21 May 2004, New Delhi.
347 The government described the device as a 'peaceful nuclear explosive': 'Nuclear Programme Of India', available at <indiragandhi.in/en/milestones/index/nuclear-program>.
348 she hoped to take advantage of a provision in the international Non-Proliferation Treaty (NPT): The NPT was a treaty spearheaded by a group of countries who were among the first to develop nuclear weapons. It came into force in 1970 and was intended to curb the spread of nuclear arms. It has never been accepted by India, Israel, and Pakistan who find it discriminatory.
348 The Nuclear Suppliers Group (NSG), which was formed soon after India's test: The Nuclear Suppliers Group came into existence in May 1974, soon after the explosion by India. It comprised countries which possessed nuclear technology and raw materials and aimed to control nuclear proliferation by curbing the export of nuclear material and technology and by improving existing safeguards.
348 The sanctions came as a huge 'setback' to India's nuclear programme, particularly 'for building power reactors': K. Santhanam to author, 1 December 2004, New Delhi.
348 essentially a private treaty between the signatory nations: Senior diplomat Saurabh Kumar to author, 29 March 2021, telephonic conversation from Bangalore.
348 They did not want India's influence to grow in the region—and came out in support of Pakistan: C. Raja Mohan to author, 3 April 2022.
349 He immediately suggested that India test the two weapon designs: Haresh Pandy, 'Raja Ramanna', *The Guardian*, 1 October 2004.
349 By mid-1982, the shafts in which the explosion would take place, had been dug and readied: Chengappa, *Weapons of Peace*, p. 256.
349 According to R. Venkataraman, who was defence minister at the time, she changed her mind: Venkataraman, *My Presidential Years*.

349 Rasgotra had gone to meet him in Washington DC in May 1982: Chengappa, *Weapons of Peace*, p. 256.
349 'Don't do it again. This time we will destroy you': Chengappa, *Weapons of Peace*, p. 204.
349 Within hours of giving the go-ahead, she asked 'RV' to call up V. S. Arunachalam: Perkovich, *India's Nuclear Bomb*, p. 243.
349 'We don't want our skulls to be broken': K. Subrahmanyam to author, 21 May 2004. Subrahmanyam had heard this from Raja Ramanna. Also in Chengappa, *Weapons of Peace*, p. 260.
349 Rajiv Gandhi was the first prime minister to specifically authorize the assembly of nuclear weapons in 1989: C. Raja Mohan to author, 3 April 2022, video interview.
349 'The PNE in 1974 was only a device. A weapon on the other hand is optimized for vector delivery': K. Santhanam to author, 1 December 2004, New Delhi.
350 'Rajiv was persuaded by evidence that Pakistan was doing naughty things': Ibid.
350 'he did not scrimp on money': K. Subrahmanyam to author, 13 February 2005, New Delhi.
351 'Pakistanis will say "India has become afraid and is doing it out of fear"': Ibid.
351 'You can't go on postponing a decision on this': Ibid.
351 'We can't afford it,' he was clear, 'the economy would be ruined': Ibid.
351 'we want the committee to be headed by Sundarji': Ibid.
351 The concept of a 'nuclear deterrent' first surfaced in this report: Ibid.
352 'balanced posture in relation with the United States and the Soviet Union': Bernard Weinraub, 'As Gandhi Arrives, US Sees Better relations', *New York Times*, 12 June 1985.
352 'Pakistan has already made a bomb,' Reagan told Rajiv: Senior diplomat S. K. Singh to author, 15 March 2005, New Delhi.
352 'Don't talk theory, think of your own protection': Ibid.
352 'I was privy to the instructions that Rajiv gave': Ibid.
352 'We had to provide proof to Britain and America': Ibid.
352 'It confirmed what Reagan had told Rajiv': Ibid.
352 'The question for India, then was, what do you do?': C. Raja Mohan to author, 3 April 2022, video interview.
353 Pakistan was in a position to inflict 'unacceptable damage' on India: S. K. Singh to author.
353 Presented with 'incontrovertible evidence' that Pakistan had the bomb in February 1987: Chengappa, *Weapons of Peace*, pp. 330–35.
353 He was anyway disenchanted with his initiative on disarmament: Ibid., p. 331.
353 He gave the orders to Naresh Chandra, his defence secretary: Ibid., p. 334.
353 Naresh Chandra was also at the event, sitting right behind him: Chengappa, *Weapons of Peace*, p. 321.
353 'Yeh aapko karna hai': Naresh Chandra to author, 5 February 2004, New Delhi.
353 'They were not near Delhi and the architectural plans for the underground site were made': S. K. Singh to author.
354 'I was told formally and officially about India's bomb (only) in July 1990': K. Subrahmanyam to author, 13 February 2005, New Delhi.
354 oversee all matters relating to the nuclear bomb 'now that we had got it': K. Subrahmanyam to author, 13 February 2005, New Delhi.
354 'who would then push the button, all that was worked out': Ibid.
354 'The idea was to flesh out the nuclear doctrine, which could be translated into operational details': K. Santhanam to author, 1 December 2004, New Delhi.
354 'Gentlemen, we are here to discuss who will survive us': Ibid.
354 It was only after this that V. P. Singh knew exactly how advanced the country's nuclear programme was: K. Subrahmanyam to author, 13 February 2005, New Delhi.
355 'As PM, an emphasis was laid on...having an operational bomb': V. P. Singh to author, 14 October 1999, Apollo Hospital, New Delhi.
355 'Decisions are not taken in a vacuum': Ibid.
355 'Has no one briefed you?': S. K. Singh to author, 15 March 2005, New Delhi.
355 'No, no one briefed me': Chandra Shekhar to author, 23 February 2000, New Delhi. The Chinese were to complete their command control structure in 2004. The Russians, British, and Americans completed them many years earlier.
355 'Then you and I are in the same boat': S. K. Singh to author, 15 March 2005, New Delhi.
356 'It was Gujral who did it': K. Subrahmanyam to author.
356 'When we went to meet Deve Gowda after he took over as PM, that is Kalam, Chidambaram, and I': K. Santhanam to author, 1 December 2004, New Delhi.
356 'No, no. Not now': Ibid.
356 But Deve Gowda did contemplate going in for a test at the tail end of his premiership: Chengappa, *Weapons of Peace*, p. 402.
356 'It was at that time that Gujral seriously considered whether he should go in for a test': N. N. Vohra to author, 25 November 2004, confirmed in 24 November 2021, New Delhi.
357 'In his programme, I showed a private lunch between 1 and p.m. and a time for rest between 2 and 5 p.m.': Ibid.
357 'Gujral sahib decided to go in for a test': Ibid.
357 I had told him he should not do it, for the process for the elections had started': Ibid. After the announcement of elections, when a model code of conduct kicks in, the government is not supposed to take major policy decisions which can give the ruling party an undue advantage over other political parties.
357 'keen to get a validation of the researches done by his boys': Ibid.

357   'he stopped making those references' to testing a nuclear device: Ibid.
357   'The only way we could do all this': Naresh Chandra to author.
357   'The scientific community is highly reliable, with committed people': Ibid.
358   made the US determined to prevent any other nation from developing nuclear weapons: Saurabh Kumar to author, 29 March 2021, telephonic conversation.
358   This led to the formation of the UN Atomic Energy Commission: United Nations Atomic Energy Commission. The UNAEC was disbanded in 1952.
358   For it could jeopardize the US's security: This has since remained a major part of US diplomacy. The first Resolution ever tabled in the UN General Assembly (by the USA), mandated the Security Council to 'deal with the problems raised by the discovery of atomic energy', and to 'make specific proposals... for the elimination from national armaments of atomic weapons'. Their attempt was, however, ultimately unsuccessful as the former Soviet Union and other nations saw through the business of all nuclear facilities having to be placed under international control.
358   The world's first nuclear weapons states—the US, USSR, UK, France, China—crafted NPT: Even before the NPT came into force in 1970, there had been the Partial Test Ban Treaty (PTBT) in 1963; it had banned tests in the atmosphere and under water but not underground. The PTBT was signed on 5 August 1963 and was a response to the damaging fallout of radioactive debris on environment and health caused by the large number of tests—estimated around 2,000—carried out by the five NWS. See '1. Treaty Banning Nuclear Weapon Tests in the Atmosphere, in Outer Space and Under Water, done at Moscow August 5, 1963', U. S. Department of State, available at <www.state.gov/limited-test-ban-treaty>.
358   The NPT divided the world into nuclear 'haves' (NWS) and 'have-nots' (NNWS) 'legally': Signing the NPT meant that, other than the five nations mentioned above, other members would have to renounce (not develop or acquire) nuclear weapons. There was no such legally binding rule asking the Nuclear Weapon States from doing away with their arsenals.
358   '[A]n international instrument, brazenly discriminatory in design, aimed at disarming the unarmed': Saurabh Kumar to author, 29 March 2021, New Delhi.
359   This would have meant giving up its option to go for nuclear weapons: Theoretically speaking, the treaty provided for an exit clause, enabling a signatory of the NPT to withdraw from the treaty under certain circumstances, but practically, this was easier said than done.
359   The test in 1974 was, in some ways, a delayed response to China's going nuclear in 1964: C. Raja Mohan to author, 3 April 2022, video interview.
359   which were allowed by the NPT (though India had not signed the treaty) provided they were for peaceful uses of nuclear energy: Saurabh Kumar to author, 29 March 2021, telephonic interview. Today, India 'is committed to growing its nuclear power capacity as part of its massive infrastructure development programme'. ('Nuclear Power in India', World Nuclear Association, accessed 31 May 2023, available at <world-nuclear.org/information-library/country-profiles/countries-g-n/india.aspx>.
359   The NPT had been extended periodically: Today, the NPT has become nearly universal, with 191 states joining the Treaty, according to the US State department.
360   'India will not sign this unequal treaty, not now, nor later': Ruhee Neog, 'CTBT at 20: Why India Won't Sign the Treaty', South Asian Voices, 23 September 2016.
360   Three of them—India, Pakistan, and North Korea—did not sign it in the first place: 'Nuclear Weapons: Who Has What at a Glance', Arms Control Association, January 2022, available at <www.armscontrol.org/factsheets/Nuclearweaponswhohaswhat>.
360   'It was in 1994 that PV raised the matter with me first': Naresh Chandra to author.
360   Then he would put off a decision by saying, 'Baat kareinge fursat se': Ibid.
361   'Do you know that they (Pakistan) can strike back in eight hours?': Ibid.
361   'was probably around thirty-six hours': Ibid.
361   'Twice I got...a bulk of money' for the nuclear programme: Ibid.
361   'I took the Concord from New York to Paris': Naresh Chandra to author, 8 May 2004, New Delhi.
361   'I was in the Louvre, hanging around, ostensibly checking on what paintings to buy': Ibid.
362   Rao had promised Clinton that he would not conduct a nuclear test: Strobe Talbott, Engaging India: Diplomacy, Democracy, and the Bomb, Washington D. C.: Brookings Institution Press, 2004, p. 34.
362   It was the indefinite extension of the NPT which convinced him to go ahead: Naresh Chandra to Neerja, 8 May, 2004, New Delhi. Also K. Santhanam to Neerja, 1 December, 2004, New Delhi.
362   India was also riled that the US had introduced the Hank Brown Amendment: Sunil Dasgupta, 'As US Senate allows arms transfer to Pakistan, India slams move', India Today, 31 October 1995.
362   But the message coming through from the US was clear—that time was running out for India: K. Santhanam to author, 1 December 2004, New Delhi.
362   Rao, according to Naresh Chandra, had 'just been procrastinating': Naresh Chandra to author, 8 May 2004, New Delhi.
362   The scientists—A. P. J. Abdul Kalam and R. Chidambaram—had gone to Hyderabad ostensibly for 'work': Ibid.
362   'We briefed PV completely on...the pitch, the likely consequences': Ibid.
362   'he would put things in a way that nobody could allege (afterwards) that he was actively encouraging': Ibid.
362   'I wrote this paper': Ibid.
363   There was only one copy of it and that was with Kalam': Ibid.
363   'By December 1995, he (Rao) had made up his mind to put oxygen into the option': K. Santhanam to author, 1 December 2004.

363 'It cannot be kept a secret for very long after that': Naresh Chandra to author, 25 December 2002, New Delhi.

363 'That was the closest Rao came to testing': Ibid.

363 India held that what was going on was routine maintenance work: BJP leader Jaswant Singh used to say that there was a mole in Rao's PMO who had 363 the information to the Americans. For years afterwards the speculation continued on who the mole was, but nothing authoritative came of the exercise. The Americans, however, based their apprehensions not just on human intelligence. They also relied on satellite photos.

363 'Wisner came to me first': Naresh Chandra to author.

363 was sharp enough to pick up the details on the photos that Wisner showed him: Sources close to the nuclear establishment to author, 2021.

364 'Naresh Chandra...had told my father (Jaswant Singh) stories about how he had got the better of the Americans': Manvendra Singh to author.

364 'We have no such plans': Naresh Chandra to author, 8 May 2004, New Delhi.

364 Verma went 'ballistic' when he learnt about it: Ibid.

364 'Give the PM a statement and the questions and answers that will come': Ibid.

364 thereby keeping his options open: Naresh Chandra to author, 5 February 2001, New Delhi.

364 Clinton 'kept praising India's stand and (kept saying) that he understood': Ibid.

365 'Washington jana thaa': Ibid.

365 'The second conversation was desultory': Ibid.

366 the situation remained 'delicate': Montek Singh Ahluwalia to author, 29 September 2021, video call.

366 'pessimistic': Naresh Chandra to author, 8 May 2004, New Delhi.

367 And that 'the Americans would then back the BJP': Ibid.

367 CBI Chief Vijay Rama Rao pushed the 'hawala line': Ibid.

367 'Hawala was the biggest folly of his life': Ibid.

367 'The best window of opportunity (for testing) was 1994–95': Ibid.

367 'And conducting of tests on the ground was permissible': K. Santhanam to author, 1 December, 2004, New Delhi.

368 'Why didn't you do it when France and China did it in 1994?': Naresh Chandra to author, 8 May 2004, New Delhi.

368 Rao had a better chance of becoming prime minister again only if the Congress was in a minority: Naresh Chandra to author, 8 May 2004, New Delhi; Bhuvnesh Chaturvedi to author, 23 December 1999, New Delhi.

368 Once he realized he had lost the election, he took back his order: Sitapati, Half Lion, p. 291.

368 'PV missed his tryst with destiny': Naresh Chandra to author, 8 May 2004, New Delhi.

368 'We will fight the next election under the leadership of...Atal Bihari Vajpayee': : Advani, My Country My Life, p. 472.

369 'that the BJP will form the next government under Atalji's prime ministership: Ibid.

369 'The BJP will win the election': Ibid., p. 473.

369 'Atalji hi banaenge': Ibid.

369 'Kya aap maante agar humne aap se poocha hota': Ibid.

369 'How could you make such an announcement?': K. N. Govindacharya to author, 3 July 2018, New Delhi.

369 'If I had consulted (others), it would not have happened': L. K. Advani to author.

369 120 Lok Sabha seats in the 1991 elections: 'Statistical Report on General Elections, 1991 to the Tenth Lok Sabha: Volume I'.

369 Many suspected that, in 1995, Advani had made a virtue of a necessity: A source close to Advani confirmed this to the author.

370 'PV helped Vajpayee by pursuing the Hawala case': Bhuvnesh Chaturvedi to author, 23 March 2007, New Delhi.

370 'PV denied it flatly': Ibid.

370 161 Lok Sabha seats, 41 seats more than in 1991: 'Statistical Report on General Elections, 1996 to the 11th Lok Sabha: Volume I', Delhi: Election Commission of India, 1996, available at <eci.gov.in/files/file/4123-general-election-1996-vol-i-ii>.

371 'Vajpayee was himself surprised that he had been called': Bhuvnesh Chaturvedi to author, 21 March 2000, New Delhi.

371 Some suspected that the invitation to Vajpayee to form the government was a khichdi: Ibid.

371 For he was far from sure that he would be able to get the support of other parties: Ibid.

371 Rao had not yet moved out of the PM House: Shakti Sinha to author, 11 April 2021, telephonic interview.

3711 Tasked to look into intelligence failures and 'make recommendations for the future': K. Subrahmanyam to author, 13 February 2005, New Delhi.

372 'Atalji, who took over from me. I had told him everything': Ibid.

372 'Rao told me the bomb was ready. I only exploded it': Vicky Nanjappa, 'The legend of Pokhran: Rao told me bomb was ready, I only exploded it said Vajpayee', One India, 19 August 2018. Although there are no reasons to doubt that Rao briefed Vajpayee on nuclear weapons during their meeting on 18 May 1996, there are several other versions of how PV had conveyed to Vajpayee the message that he should go ahead with the tests. Some said Rao had sent a 'chit' to Vajpayee at his swearing-in ceremony at Rashtrapati Bhavan on 16 May 1996. The chit said 'Saamagri tayyar hai, tum aage badh sakte ho.' (The material is ready, you can now go ahead.) Narasimha Rao later claimed in an interview that he had given a letter

to Vajpayee. But Brajesh Mishra, Vajpayee's closest adviser, was sceptical about the existence of a letter. 'Vajpayee never mentioned the letter to me. I never found anything in his official files.' However, Mishra confirmed that Vajpayee had met Rao to brief him. (Sitapati, *Half Lion*, p. 279; Prabhakar Rao, 'P V Narasimha Rao', Facebook, 17 August 2018, accessed 16 May 2022, available at <www.facebook.com/SirSriPvnarasimhaRaoGaru/photos/1132931390195999>.)

372 'I told Vajpayee to do it': Naresh Chandra to author, 8 May 2004, New Delhi.
In his meeting with Vajpayee on 18 May 1996, Rao appealed to the new prime minister at two levels: Brajesh Mishra to author.

372 'The shafts had been sealed (from) 1983 onwards': K. Santhanam to author, 1 December 2004, New Delhi.

373 many also saw 'a Brahminical bond' between the two: Bhuvnesh Chaturvedi to author, 23 March 2007, New Delhi.

373 He had retained most of Vajpayee's staff: Rao, 'P V Narasimha Rao', Facebook.

373 *'Ranjishe hee sahi dil dukhane ke liye aa, Aa phir se mujhe chorhne ke liye aa'*: Karan Singh to author, 16 March 2023, New Delhi. English translation from Rana Safvi, <ranasafvi.com/ranjish-hi-sahi-explained>.

373 'Atalji mere haal kaal ke guru rahe hain': Sachidanand Murthy, 'Clash of the titans: When Vajpayee, Narasimha Rao locked horns', *The Week*, 4 February 1996.

373 In fact, they would usually address each other as guruji: Rao, 'P V Narasimha Rao', Facebook.

373 'Vajpayee was sitting between PV and me': Bhuvnesh Chaturvedi to author, 23 March 2007, New Delhi.

374 'Dekhte hain, governor se baat karenge': Ibid.

374 'He must not become CM': Ibid.

374 When Rao returned from New York on 26 October 1995, Motilal Vora was waiting for him: Dilip Awasthi, 'The Battle for Uttar Pradesh', *India Today*, 15 November 1995.

375 'Vajpayee helped in getting Narasimha Rao acquitted': Bhuvnesh Chaturvedi to author, 23 March 2007, New Delhi.

375 On 16 March 2002, the Delhi High Court was to acquit Rao and Buta Singh in the JMM bribery case: 'Rao, Buta acquitted in JMM bribery case', *Times of India*, 16 March 2002.

375 'These are political decisions, the rest (the legal aspect) is mere detail that is worked out': Bhuvnesh Chaturvedi to author, 24 December 2008, New Delhi.

375 'it isn't good to have prime ministers and former PMs proceeded against': I. K. Gujral to author, 6 October 2003, New Delhi. Gujral also told this to Bhuvnesh Chaturvedi, who told this to the author.

375 There were voices of protest by some BJP leaders, led by L. K. Advani: Neerja Chowdhury, 'Bribe case to declaring donor, full circle for JMM', *The Indian Express*, 25 April 2021.

375 'Vajpayee never tried to damage PV—and vice versa': Bhuvnesh Chaturvedi to author, 23 March 2007, New Delhi.

375 'Please get Kalam': Shakti Sinha to author, 11 April 2021, New Delhi, telephonic conversation.

376 'The PM wants to meet you': Ibid.

376 'Patakha chorhna hai': K. Santhanam to author, 1 December 2004, New Delhi.

376 'We could have done it in those thirteen days when Vajpayee had made up his mind': Ibid.

376 Some felt it might have generated the kind of euphoria which might have compelled some political parties to change their mind: Naresh Chandra to author, 8 May 2004, New Delhi.

377 Vajpayee personally met Kanshi Ram: Lakhbir Singh, Secretary Kanshi Ram Foundation, also Kanshi Ram's nephew, 13 April 2021, telephonic interview.

377 'I myself made an appointment for George to see PV': Bhuvnesh Chaturvedi to author, 23 March 2007, New Delhi.

377 'It is not as if the Congress is in a position to form the government': Ibid.

377 The US's wariness of him was reflected in some of the emails: Tandon, 'Ashok Tandon: Atal Bihari Vajpayee went against all odds to establish India's nuclear credentials'.

377 It was unusual for an ambassador-designate to call on an Opposition leader before going on a diplomatic assignment: V. G. Vaidya, IB chief, to author, 2018, Mumbai.

377 'Rao had an inkling that the US would be lobbying to deny (the) premiership to Vajpayee': Ashok Tandon, 'Ashok Tandon: Atal Bihari Vajpayee went against all odds to establish India's nuclear credentials', *The Economic Times*, 17 August 2018.

378 'We both knew what he was coming to say': Naresh Chandra to author, 8 May 2004, New Delhi.

378 'that we attach importance to Indo-US relations': Ibid.

378 Wisner, who had met Vajpayee, was convinced from his 'body language'. Declassified E mail from US Embassy India to the State Department, quoted in William Burr, 'The Clinton Administration and the Indian Nuclear Test That Did Not Happen - 1995-1996', NPIHP, Wilson Center, available at <www.wilsoncenter.org/publication/the-clinton-administration-and-the-indian-nuclear-test-did-not-happen-1995-1996>.

378 'that a test would have "devastating consequences" for India–US relations': Naresh Chandra to author, 8 May 2004, New Delhi.

378 'How are things going?': Krishan Kant to author, in 2000, confirmed by his son Rashmi Kant, 24 June 2020, telephonic conversation.

379 the BJP won 182 seats, more than the 161 it had won in 1996: 'Statistical Report on General Elections, 1998 to the 12th Lok Sabha: Volume I', Delhi: Election Commission of India, 1998, available at <eci.gov.in/files/file/4124-general-election-1998-vol-i-ii>.

379 Vajpayee sat at his dining table and dictated a draft of NAG to his secretary Shakti Sinha: Sinha, *Vajpayee*, p. 61.

379   he had the support of 267 MPs in the Lok Sabha: Ibid., p. 62.

379   She wanted economist Subramanian Swamy to be made finance minister: Thakur, *Prime Ministers*, pp. 407–408.

379   The normally accommodative Vajpayee put his foot down on Swamy: Ibid.

379   She had thirty MPs from the AIDMK and its allies: Sinha, *Vajpayee*, p. 65.

379   It was only when Sonia Gandhi declined to stake her claim: 'Vajpayee to be sworn in on Thursday, has to prove majority in ten days', *Rediff.com*, 15 March 1998.

379   'I had myself typed the list': Shakti Sinha to author, 11 April 2021, telephonic interview.

380   Vajpayee's foster son-in-law, who was in the hotel industry, made sure the meal did not have any tomatoes: Ibid.

380   It was rushed to Rashtrapati Bhavan in the early hours of 19 March 1998: Ibid.

380   Vajpayee sat down for breakfast at 7.30 a.m.: Sinha, *Vajpayee*, p. 12.

380   'What will happen if I retain the finance portfolio?': Shakti Sinha to author, 11 April 2021, telephonic interview.

381   Vajpayee should not retain Finance himself, Advani replied: Shakti Sinha to author, 11 April 2021, telephonic interview.

381   Within four hours, Vajpayee had to eat his words: Neerja Chowdhury, 'The loneliness of Atal Behari Vajpayee', *Indian Express*, 27 April 1998.

381   'Vajpayee was not keen on Yashwant Sinha': Shakti Sinha to author, 11 April 2021, telephonic interview.

381   At the time, Yashwant Sinha was seen to be close to the 'swadeshi' lobby in the RSS: Shakti Sinha, 'To understand Vajpayee's economic worldview, look at his first choice for finance minister' *The Print*, 25 December 2020.

381   She even told Vajpayee who to have in his cabinet: Prabhu Chawla, '"Alliance partners want Vajpayee to assert his authority"', *India Today*, 27 April 1998.

381   'No, please serve her coconut water': Shakti Sinha to author.

382   Swamy called Ram Jethmalani, another minister in the government, 'Jhootmalani': K. M. Thomas and K. Govindan Kutty, 'AIADMK chief Jayalalitha's pressure tactics paralyse BJP-led Government', *India Today*, 4 May 1998.

382   it would be better 'to go back to the people': Ibid.

382   By early April, people began to wonder how long the government would last: Chowdhury, 'The loneliness of Atal Behari Vajpayee'.

382   Harkishan Singh Surjeet and Jyoti Basu even dubbed his government as 'anti-national': Prabhu Chawla, '"Alliance partners want Vajpayee to assert his authority"', *India Today*, 27 April 1998.

382   He had been replaced by an unrecognizable figure—'wan, fatigued, dispirited': Mani Shankar Aiyar, 'Pity poor Vajpayee: the next 300 are going to be even worse', *India Today*, 11 May 1998.

382   'At one point things became so bad that he had made himself incommunicado': Shakti Sinha to author, 11 April 2021, telephonic interview.

382   Does Vajpayee have what it takes to rule the country: Chowdhury, 'The loneliness of Atal Behari Vajpayee'.

382   whom the Opposition respected enough to call him the 'right man in the wrong party': Ibid.

382   Commentators urged him to do something 'bold': Ibid.

383   'He wanted to acquire strength': Bhuvnesh Chaturvedi to author, 14 October 1999, New Delhi.

383   Vajpayee had closely followed the global negotiations on the Comprehensive Test Ban Treaty: Sinha, *Vajpayee*, p. 16.

383   'Atalji also had his political considerations for opting for the test at that particular juncture': Brajesh Mishra to author, 30 November 2004, New Delhi.

383   'We cannot go on quarrelling like this': B. Raman, 'Brajesh Mishra (1928- 2012)', *Outlook*, 3 February 2022.

383   'We had many discussions. That brought us closer together': Brajesh Mishra to author, 30 November 2004, New Delhi.

383   'I want you to become my principal secretary': Brajesh Mishra, 16 September 2005, New Delhi.

384   'I want someone I can trust': Ibid.

384   'You cannot say no to a PM': Ibid.

384   The first order Vajpayee signed after taking over as prime minister was to appoint Mishra as his principal secretary: Sinha, *Vajpayee*, p. 15.

384   'His instincts were marvellous': Brajesh Mishra, 16 September 2005, New Delhi.

384   'We will talk about this later': Ibid.

384   'I like Vajpayee. I don't trust Advani': Sonia Gandhi to author, 10, Janpath, New Delhi.

384   Mishra himself described his relationship with the PM as 'symbiotic': Brajesh Mishra, 16 September 2005, New Delhi.

384   'not even a whiff of a scandal should come out of the Prime Minister's Office or the PM House': Rashmi Kant to author. His father, Krishan Kant, had been told this by Brajesh Mishra.

385   On 6 April 1998, at 7.25 a.m., Pakistan test-fired a surface-to-surface missile from Malute: Hasan Akhtar, 'Target hit without error: FO Pakistan test-fires Ghauri missile', *Dawn Wire Service*, 11 April 1998.

385   The missile that was tested had traversed 1,100 kilometres that day: Zahid Hussain and Harinder Baweja, 'Pakistan test-fires its latest missile, Vajpayee government to create consensus to counter growing nexus between Islamabad and Beijing', *India Today*, 20 April 1998.

385   He asked Mishra to call an urgent meeting of the scientists: Chengappa, *Weapons of Peace*, p. 45.

385   'old mindset of confrontation': Baweja, 'Pakistan test-fires its latest missile, Vajpayee government to create consensus to counter growing nexus between Islamabad and Beijing'.

385 'The public utterances of the BJP that India would go nuclear are a source of great concern for us': Ibid.
385 'main purpose of testing Ghauri was to send a signal to Delhi': Ibid.
385 'our understanding is that China is the mother of Ghauri': Manoj Joshi, 'Despite China aiding Pakistan's nuclear programmes, India sees it as a benign power', *India Today*, 27 April 1998.
385 'It is up to the United States to take it up with Pakistan': Chintamani Mahapatra, 'The US, China and the Ghauri Missile', IDSA, available at <www.idsa-india.org/an-jun8-4.html>.
385 it had supplied over fifty M-11 missiles to Pakistan between 1992 and 1994: Joshi, 'Despite China aiding Pakistan's nuclear programmes, India sees it as a benign power'.
386 India soon realized that Washington was trying to 'whitewash' the Chinese connection: Mahapatra, 'The US, China and the Ghauri Missile'.
386 'No nuclear race will be started due to the firing of Ghauri': Ibid.
386 Hours after the Ghauri launch, a concerned Brajesh Mishra, called in security strategist K. Subrahmanyam: Brajesh Mishra to author, 30 November 2004, New Delhi.
386 'It never occurred to me,' Subrahmanyam was to say later, 'that they would go for the test': K. Subrahmanyam to author, 1 June 2004, New Delhi.
386 'We decided on April 8 (1998) to go in for a test': Brajesh Mishra to author, 30 November 2004, New Delhi.
386 Kalam 'made it a point' to keep in touch with politicians: K. Santhanam to author, 7 December 2004, New Delhi.
387 'we were activated by the end of March 1998': Ibid.
387 'The cables were in a very reasonable condition': Ibid.
387 'So you can call it candlelit lay for cables instead of a candlelit dinner': Ibid.
387 'There were three close circuit cameras installed there and the images were conveyed to the control room 2 kilometres away': Ibid.
387 'though the pits were too wet for their comfort': Ibid.
387 'the filling operation (of the shafts) has to be over in one night otherwise the change would be detected': Ibid.
388 'But by the time the Americans found out, the event was over': Ibid.
388 And, of course, there was the pressing need to do something big to give his government credibility: Sinha, *Vajpayee*, p. 100.
388 'I tended to take a long-term view of things': Brajesh Mishra, 30 November 2004, New Delhi.
388 'We have to give a signal to the Americans that they have to take us seriously': Brajesh Mishra to author, 2009.
388 but was 'the real decision-maker' as far as nuclear tests went: K. Subrahmanyam to author.
388 'The credit must be given to him. He complemented Vajpayee': R. Chidamabaram to author, 31 March 2021, telephonic conversation.
388 'Brajesh played a key role in May 1998': Naresh Chandra to author, November 2000.
388 Ironically, it was another bureaucrat, his foreign secretary Jagat Singh Mehta: K. Subrahmanyam to author, 2004.
389 Mehta felt that the future of the subcontinent lay in India making peace with its neighbours: T. P. Sreenivasan, 'A crown of political thorns', *The Hindu*, 2 February 2015.
389 He found Vajpayee 'very receptive' to the idea: Ajay Mehta, Jagat Mehta's son, to author, 24 March 2021.
389 A week after Vajpayee had taken the decision to test, the US ambassador to the UN Bill Richardson: Manoj Joshi, 'High level US delegation visits India to get a measure of Vajpayee government', *India Today*, 27 April 1998.
389 'Absolutely not,' Fernandes replied, poker faced: Talbott, *Engaging India*, p. 47.
389 meet with Jaswant Singh 'offline'—that is, in private: Ibid.
389 'a discreet—and if necessary, secret—channel to Washington': Ibid.
390 It would also prevent any 'leaks' from taking place: Ibid.
390 'Brajesh Mishra called me on 8 May': General V. P. Malik to author, October 2004, reconfirmed 29 March 2021.
390 the time had come 'to call the three chiefs and brief them now': Brajesh Mishra to author.
390 'When we arrived, Brajesh Mishra and Abdul Kalam were already sitting there': General V. P. Malik to author.
390 Besides asking the chiefs about preparedness, the prime minister 'didn't say much': Ibid.
391 'We did not talk with the PM about the possibility of tests by Pakistan': General V. P. Malik to author.
391 'The PM told me that he had told his political colleagues two days before the test': Brajesh Mishra to author, 30 November 2004, New Delhi.
391 'I am not sure whether the PM told them the exact date of the tests': Ibid.
391 'It was attended by the PM, Advani, George Fernandes, and Jaswant Singh': Shakti Sinha to author, 11 April 2021, telephonic interview.
391 'Earlier nuclear weapons were not ruled out, now they are ruled in': Sinha, *Vajpayee*, p. 97.
391 The Chinese reacted to it sharply and called it 'absolutely ridiculous': Ibid.
391 Summoned by the prime minister, he got to Vajpayee's house: Yashwant Sinha to author, 2018, reconfirmed in 11 April 2021.
392 'I kept thinking about the economic consequences, and what we could possibly do': Ibid.
392 That week, on 11 May 1998, *Organiser*, the mouthpiece of the RSS: 'Was RSS informed in advance of n-tests?', *The Hindu*, 13 May 1998.

392 'We cannot afford to forego our nuclear option': John F. Burns, 'Nuclear Anxiety: The Overview; India Carries Out 2 More Atom Tests Despite Sanctions', *New York Times*, 14 May 1998.
393 'Bhaiya, aap zara paanch number aa jaiye': Yashwant Sinha to author 11 April 2021, telephonic interview.
393 Jaswant Singh did not say anything. Besides Sinha, he had also called up George Fernandes: Ibid.
393 Vajpayee had personally called Advani and asked him to come over: Brajesh Mishra to author, New Delhi.
393 'So, the entire Cabinet Committee on Security was there': Yashwant Sinha to author 11 April 2021, telephonic interview.
393 'We were to do it before 8 in the morning': K. Santhanam to author, 7 December 2004, New Delhi.
393 But it was when 'we saw the crater that...the elation occurred': Ibid.
394 'Sir, we have done it': K. Santhanam to author, 1 December 2004, New Delhi; Chengappa, *Weapons of Peace*, p. 432.
394 'God bless you': Chengappa, *Weapons of Peace*, p. 432.
394 They were tears of relief, of a sense of pride, and of 'finally having done it': Sinha, *Vajpayee*, p. 99.
394 Vajpayee had driven to Rashtrapati Bhavan to brief the president: Chengappa, *Weapons of Peace*, p. 5.
394 'so that he could avoid uncomfortable questions (while abroad)': K. Subrahmanyam to author, 13 February 2005, New Delhi.
394 'The first person who told me about it was Krishan Kant': Ibid.
394 'Aap jo chahte rahen hain, woh hum karne jaa rahe hain': Krishan Kant to author in 2000, reconfirmed by Rashmi Kant, 13 June 2020, telephonic conversation.
394 'Just now the PM spoke to me... I have not told anybody this so far': K. Subrahmanyam, 21 May 2004, New Delhi.
395 'The nuclear test included the thermo-nuclear test (aka the hydrogen bomb)': Ibid.
395 'We were supposed to...discuss...how to manage the consequences and how to announce': Yashwant Sinha to author.
395 Brajesh Mishra and Jaswant Singh dictated it to Shakti Sinha: Sinha, *Vajpayee*, p. 100.
395 Very deliberately, he removed the word 'brief' to describe the statement he was to read: Yashwant Sinha to author, 11 April 2021, telephonic interview.
395 'Today, at 15.45 hours, India conducted three underground nuclear tests in the Pokhran range': The author was present at Race Course Road for the press conference that day.
396 A group of Western scientists were later to question India's claim of 5-kiloton yield for the nuclear tests as overestimated: Raj Chengappa, 'Research by western scientists contests India's claims of successfully testing an H-bomb', *India Today*, 12 October 1998.
396 'India is now a nuclear weapon state': Prabhu Chawla, 'Rise of a strong self-confident India: Atal Bihari Vajpayee on May 1998 nuclear tests', *India Today*, 25 May 1998.
396 Vajpayee also ruled out signing either the CTBT or the NPT because they were discriminatory: Ibid.
396 They also wanted to see if there had been any cracks in the houses in the habitations around: K. Santhanam to author, 7 December 2004, New Delhi.
397 'worried that the recent spurt of rain might have led to some contamination of the underground aquifers around the nuclear test site': Kalpana Sharma, 'Reaping the Whirlwind', *The Hindu*, 13 November 1998.
397 But authorities dismissed their complaints as having 'no scientific basis': Shweta Desai, 'Forty years after Pokharan nuclear tests, villagers complain of frequent cancer deaths', *Scroll.in*, 18 May 2014.
397 'I will give you space on the front page': K. Subrahmanyam to author.
397 Subrahmanyam's piece appeared as 'news analysis' on the front page: K. Subrahmanyam, 'India now joins the club of five N-Weapon States', *Times of India*, 12 May 1998.
397 And he urged the government to invite China, Russia, and Pakistan to join in 'a joint no first use declaration': Ibid.
398 But 'it took him four months to declare that India would not use it first': K. Subrahmanyam to author, 21 November 2004, New Delhi.
398 They would now have to discuss the next steps they needed to take: Yashwant Sinha to author, 11 April 2021, telephonic interview.
398 'tell him that it was not Pakistan but China we had in mind for going for nuclear tests': Ibid.
398 'We value our friendship and cooperation with your country': George Perkovich, 'Test and effect', *Indian Express*, 11 May 2018.
398 For the PM had held China publicly responsible for its decision to test: Shakti Sinha, *Vajpayee*, p. 106.
398 He erupted in a 'volcanic fit' when he heard about them: Talbott, *Engaging India*, p. 52.
398 The US president had taken 'a personal initiative' to roll back the nuclear programmes of both India and Pakistan: K. P. Nayar, 'Time to Tell a Prophetic Secret', *The Telegraph* (Calcutta), 24 December 2004.
399 China's reaction, initially subdued, sharpened after Vajpayee named China as the raison d'etre: Sinha, *Vajpayee*, p. 102.
399 if India continued with liberalization and economic engagement with the US, the international community would come around: Montek Singh Ahluwalia to author.
399 that the '1988 decision' by Rajiv Gandhi (to make an adequate number of weapons) had been kept totally under wraps: Sinha, *Vajpayee*, p. 107.
400 Vajpayee was asking them to start an agitation that India should not sign CTBT: B. N. Uniyal to author, 27 February 2021, telephonic interview.
400 'I can't see any signs of it': B. N. Uniyal to author, 4 March 2021, telephonic interview.
400 'If India had not exploded the bomb, Pakistan would not have done so': '28 May 1998- Pakistan Nuclear Tests', CTBTO, <www.ctbto.org/specials/testing-times/28-may-1998-pakistan-nuclear-tests>.

400   The two sides discussed how to improve relations between their countries: Jaswant Singh to author, 15 January 2005, New Delhi.

400   The lunch had been set up a month earlier: Harinder Baweja, 'Mutual suspicion, hardening of political stands likely to mark Vajpayee-Nawaz Sharief meet', *India Today*, 3 August 1998.

401   'We had a one-on-one meeting with Nawaz Sharif in Colombo': Brajesh Mishra to author, 30 November 2004, New Delhi.

401   'Why shouldn't there be a bus from Delhi to Lahore?': Jaswant Singh to author, 15 January 2005, New Delhi.

401   Both prime ministers immediately 'jumped' at the idea of a 'bus' journey: Brajesh Mishra to author, 30 November 2004, New Delhi.

401   'It was to catch the imagination of people': Jaswant Singh to author, 15 January 2005, New Delhi.

401   India and Pakistan were mature enough to take care of their nuclear concerns and settle their issues 'bilaterally': A. K. Verma, 'Atal Bihari's Lahore Yatra: Limitations and Achievements', Institute of Peace and Conflict Studies, 11 March 1999.

401   'Yeh loha aur ispaat ki bus nahi hai. Yeh hamare dono mulko ke awam ke jasbaaton ke baat hai': Jaswant Singh to author, 5 January 2005, New Delhi.

401   Nawaz Sharif said he was unaware of the action, though this has been disputed: Imtiaz Ahmad,' "Nawaz Sharif was unaware of Pakistan army's infiltration of Kargil"', *Hindustan Times*, 2 June 2018.

402   showed a willingness to talk to India seriously about security issues: C. Raja Mohan to author, 3 April 2022, video call.

402   For the Americans, the Indian tests had come as 'a very serious intelligence failure': Talbott, *Engaging India*, p. 50.

402   But there were Indians who suspected that the American failure was 'contrived': Pallav Bagla to author, 21 March 2021, telephonic interview.

403   'best way to drive (home) any message to India: wrap it in two layers': Brahma Chellaney, 'The Clinton visit: Hype and Reality', *Rediff.com*, 28 March 2000.

403   It might not be an exaggeration to say that at least 300 MPs would have shaken hands with Clinton: As surmised by author who was present in parliament on the day.

403   'Many MPs would not have washed their hands for a couple of days to retain the Clinton touch': Ibid.

403   'India's gamble' on nuclear testing had paid off: Chellaney, 'The Clinton visit: Hype and Reality'.

403   though at the time it was limited to 'regulatory and safety issues': Shyam Saran, *How India Sees the World: From Kautilya to Modi: Kautilya to the 21st Century*, New Delhi: Juggernaut Books, 2017.

403   'It is only by (our) going nuclear, (that) the Americans were willing to go along with us': C. Raja Mohan to author, 3 April 2022, New Delhi.

404   Vajpayee had chosen to 'rely on an official': L. K. Advani to author.

405   'When the family were away, Brajesh or I would baby sit him in the evening': Ashok Saikia to author.

405   Advani had wanted Vijai Kapoor: Brajesh Mishra to author, 30 November 2004, New Delhi.

405   'Advani suddenly found...my...strong influence on Vajpayee': Ibid.

405   'Advani didn't like it. Nor did Jaswant Singh': Ibid.

405   'The RSS also intervened': Ibid.

405   'If we have lunch neither he will talk nor I will talk': Ibid.

406   Many felt he had been wronged, brought down by Sonia Gandhi, Jayalalithaa, and Subramaniam Swamy: Based on the author's impression while covering elections.

406   An RSS leader even met Vajpayee and put this proposal to him: Sitapati, 'The Spectre of Narendra Modi (1999–2004)', *Jugalbandi*.

406   Vajpayee urged chief minister Narendra Modi to observe 'raj dharma': Shobhit Sujay, 'Congress rakes up Vajpayee's Rajdharma remark post 2002 Gujarat riots to take on Modi', *Indian Express*, 11 April 2014.

406   A week later he was giving explanations for Modi's actions: Sitapati, 'The Spectre of Narendra Modi (1999–2004)', *Jugalbandi*.

406   In early June 2002, *Time* magazine carried a piece by Alex Perry on Vajpayee: Alex Perry, 'Asleep at The Wheel?', *TIME*, 10 June 2002.

406   the Vajpayee camp saw it as a 'hatchet job' carried out on behalf of Advani: Shakti Sinha to author, 11 April 2021, telephonic interview.

406   It made him look vindictive: Ibid.

407   The prime minister informed the vice president officially that the NDA and the Congress would both support him for president: Rashmi Kant to author, 25 July 2021, New Delhi.

407   'Yeh to Advani ne garbar kar dee thee': Brajesh Mishra to Rashmi Kant, July 2012; Rashmi Kant to author, 25 July 2021, New Delhi.

407   'Tell Kamlaji, I am coming for lunch and will eat Sindhi kadhi': Anonymous source to author.

407   Vajpayee had deferred to the RSS: Brajesh Mishra, 30 November 2004, New Delhi.

407   'The entire party came to me, what do I do?': Ibid.

407   'perhaps things would have been different': Ibid.

407   Though in power for five years, the Congress increased its tally from 145 to 206 seats: Christophe Jaffrelot and Gilles Verniers, 'India's 2009 Elections: The Resilience of Regionalism and Ethnicity', *South Asia Multidisciplinary Academic Journal*, No. 3, 2009.

408   Vajpayee wanted to be remembered more for his attempts to settle the Kashmir problem: Vajpayee told this to author during the course of a conversation on a trip to Trinidad, Tobago, Jamaica, and Morocco, between 6–14 February 1999. His statements were made in an informal chat before the Lahore Yatra, Kargil, and the Agra summit.

408 it was Advani who shot down the final statement that had been hammered out: Murasoli Maran about the Agra Summit to author in a private conversation.

408 that it was through a spirit of 'Kashmiriyat, Insaniyat, Jamooriyat': 'Atal Bihari Vajpayee's "Insaniyat, Jamhuriyat, Kashmiriyat" is the foundation for peace in Kashmir', *Firstpost*, 16 August 2018.

CHAPTER 6: THE UNDERRATED PRIME MINISTER WHO TRIUMPHED: MANMOHAN SINGH AND THE INDO-US CIVIL NUCLEAR DEAL

410 '[It] signaled it was no ordinary evening at the White House': Roxanne Roberts, 'A Bush Dinner As Rare as a Pink Elephant', *Washington Post*, 19 July 2005.

410 The paper described the evening as 'A Bush dinner as rare as a pink elephant': Ibid.

410 The dinner was meant to be 'a nod to India ': Ibid.

411 'If the oil prices go up to $100, it hurts India': 'Prime Minister Dr Manmohan Singh's Interview on Charlie Rose Show', 27 February 2006, Media Center, Ministry of External Affairs, Government of India.

411 'What can I do for you?': M. K. Narayanan to author, 8 August 2022, telephonic conversation, Chennai.

411 Manmohan Singh had first talked about cooperation with the US on civil nuclear energy: 'Interview of Prime Minister Dr Manmohan Singh on Charlie Rose Show', 21 September 2004, Media Center, Ministry of External Affairs, Government of India.

411 'confirm India's status as a full-fledged nuclear-weapon state with all the rights but also the obligations': Shyam Saran, *How India Sees the World: From Kautilya to Modi: Kautilya to the 21st Century*, New Delhi: Juggernaut Books, 2017, p. 204.

411 'I look forward to doing business with you': Raj Chengappa, 27 August 2007, 'How the deal was clinched', *India Today*.

411 'eighth wonder of the world': 'Our History: Gleneagles throughout the years', Gleneagles, available at <gleneagles.com/explore/hotel-grounds/history>.

411 'A solid relationship is based on values as well as (common) interest': 'Prime Minister Dr Manmohan Singh's Interview on Charlie Rose Show', 27 February 2006.

412 'There was a special embossed programme, the guest list was published': Prithviraj Chavan to author.

412 'I now invite the people of America to complete the voyage of that great explorer': Roberts, 'A Bush Dinner As Rare as a Pink Elephant'.

412 After dinner, the guests moved to the East Room where they were joined by 126 others: Montek Singh Ahluwalia to author.

413 a 'genuine American Art treasure': President (2001-2009 : Bush). Calligraphy Office. 1/20/2001-1/20/2009, '07/18/2005 - Performance on the Occasion of the Visit of His Excellency Dr Manmohan Singh, Prime Minister of the Republic on India and Mrs. Gursharan Kaur – Programs', National Archives Catalog, accessed 20 June 2022, available at <catalog.archives.gov/id/148029141>.

413 'thinking in very bold terms': Glenn Kessler, *The Confidante: Condoleezza Rice and the Creation of the Bush Legacy*, New York: St. Martin's Press, 2007, cited in Noorani, 'Condoleezza Rice & the nuclear deal'.

413 'strategic convergence' between the two countries: Saran, *How India Sees the World*, p. 201.

413 India was not a great power yet. But it had the potential to become one: Condoleezza Rice, 'Campaign 2000: Promoting the National Interest', *Foreign Affairs*, January/February 2000.

413 'do not just mind their own business': Condoleezza Rice, 'Promoting the National Interest', *Foreign Affairs*, Vol. 79, No. 1, January–February 2000, pp. 45–62.

413 'conceptually to connect India with Pakistan and to think only of Kashmir or the nuclear competition between the two states': Ibid.

413 With Rice calling for a 'deep dialogue': Saran, *How India Sees the World*.

414 it had started to look at India as a 'balancing factor': Shyam Saran to author, on the phone in New Delhi, 22 October 2020.

414 India too was apprehensive, foreign secretary Shyam Saran was to reveal, that a US on the decline might cede to China: Saran, *How India Sees the World*, p. 195.

414 'Someday the US will need to let India get out of the nuclear netherworld': A. G. Noorani, 'Condoleezza Rice & the nuclear deal', *Frontline*, 18 January 2008.

414 America had gone back on its agreement to supply fuel to the Tarapur reactors: Chengappa, 'How the deal was clinched'.

414 unless it signed the Non-Proliferation Treaty and gave up its nuclear weapons: Ibid.

414 There was no response from the American side at the time: Ibid.

415 induct India into an anti-China formation to counter China's influence in the region: Saran, *How India Sees the World*.

415 Few Indian officials had expected such an 'expansive presentation': Kessler, *The Confidante*, cited in Noorani, 'Condoleezza Rice & the nuclear deal'.

415 India, too, could buy 'advanced weapons': Glenn Kessler, 'India Protests Possible Sale Of Fighter Jets to Pakistan', *Washington Post*, 17 March 2005.

415 She was clear about the 'broader strategic goal' to pursue: Kessler, *The Confidante*, cited in Noorani, 'Condoleezza Rice & the nuclear deal'.

415 It had to move beyond its attitude of 'restraining India': Ibid.

416 Before arriving in Washington DC, Manmohan Singh had already made two strategic decisions: Montek Singh Ahluwalia to author, 29 September 2021.

417 'the constraints the framework agreement would impose on India's strategic (nuclear) programme': Shyam Saran, 22 October 2020.

417 According to Anil Kakodkar, there were twenty-two power generating reactors in the country at the time: Anil Kakodkar to author, 21 December 2022, telephonic interview, Mumbai. Of the these twenty-two nuclear plants, four were in Tarapur in Maharashtra, six were in Rajasthan, two in Kalpakkam, in Tamil Nadu, two in Narora in UP, two in Kakrapar in Gujarat, four in Kaiga in Karnataka, and two in Kudankulam in Tamil Nadu. The first and second units of the plants at Tarapur were built with American help, and were put under safeguards immediately, The remaining two Tarapur units, three and four, were built indigenously. The first two reactors in Rajasthan were built with Canadian assistance. But the other four were indigenously built. So were all the other reactors—except those in Kudankulam which were built with Russian help. In addition, India had three research reactors to meet the requirement of fissile material for India's nuclear weapons, and one 500 mw fast breeder reactor which was under construction. ('Kudankulam Nuclear Power Plant, Tamil Nadu, India', *Power Technology*, 15 March 2023; 'Nuclear Power in India', available at <world-nuclear.org/information-library/country-profiles/countries-g-n/india.aspx>.)

417 responded with 'caution': Anil Kakodkar to author, 25 November 2022, Mumbai.

417 India's plans to develop a 'three stage nuclear fuel cycle' for its nuclear programme: Ibid.

417 'They (inspectors) will look at it with great suspicion, that we are up to some mischief': Ibid.

418 'The strategy of exploiting thorium to the fullest is embedded in the three stage programme': Ibid.

418 'India would be "sacrificing" its "sovereign" right': Ibid.

418 'More work is needed on the draft': Ibid.

418 'ensuring that the principle of separating the civil from the military was fully embedded in the agreement': Ibid. The difference between the civilian and military reactors lay not in their construction but in the use they would be put to, and how they would be treated by the international community and the global regulatory organizations. The civilian ones would be open to IAEA inspection but would also have the benefit from nuclear commerce globally, with the fuel would be used only for peaceful purposes. The military ones would not be open to inspection, and the Government of India would decide how its re actors would be categorized. The differences in the Indian delegation were essentially on where to 'draw the boundary'.

418 'These were political reservations': Shyam Saran to author, 22 October 2020.

418 'I won't be able to sell it back home': Natwar Singh to author.

418 He would not override the reservations of the scientists: Many years later, the then NSA M. K. Narayanan revealed that Manmohan Singh had called off the deal the night of 17 July 2005, because of a 'killer proposal' the Americans had brought. It proposed that the Indian reactors which would to be kept out of international safeguards, be reduced from eight to two. This, Narayanan said, was not acceptable to the PM and went against the understanding that had been reached between the PMO and the US President's Office during the discussions. (PTI, 'Manmohan Singh wanted to call off Nuclear-deal after US' killer proposals: M K Narayanan', *Economic Times*, 14 July 2015.)

418 'I conveyed this (Manmohan Singh's decision) to Nicholas Burns who was very disappointed': Shyam Saran to author.

418 'Singh just can't make it happen': Condoleezza Rice, 'Building a New Relationship with India', *No Higher Honor: A Memoir of My Years in Washington*, New York: Penguin Random House, 2011.

419 'I want to see you,' she said: Natwar Singh to author, 9 November 2020.

419 'I am not letting this go down, I thought': Rice, 'Building a New Relationship with India', *No Higher Honor*.

419 'It must've been around 6.30 a.m., I was still in my dressing gown': Natwar Singh to author.

419 'Woh aa rahi hain': Ibid.

419 'I joined them a little later': Ibid.

419 At the meeting Rice said to the prime minister, 'You tell me what is standing in the way': Natwar Singh to author.

419 'And let's get it done before you see the president': Rice, 'Building a New Relationship with India', *No Higher Honor*.

419 'eventually gave the nod to his people to try again': Ibid.

420 'the autonomy of our three-stage strategic programme should not be restricted': Natwar Singh to author.

420 'Broadly speaking, there is a convergence of views': Ibid.

420 'From our point of view, we did not want any ambiguity in the language': Shyam Saran to author.

420 'Ho gaya hai, that was obvious': Natwar Singh to author.

421 'It's done,' his voice was jubilant: Sanjaya Baru to author.

421 They could 'be relied upon to keep their stories ready': Sanjaya Baru, 'Ending Nuclear Apartheid', *The Accidental Prime Minister: The Making and Unmaking of Manmohan Singh*, New Delhi: Penguin Books, 2014.

421 'we found him being applauded for every minute of speaking time': Baru, *The Accidental Prime Minister*, p. 210.

421 The statement said the US president would 'work to achieve full civil nuclear energy cooperation with India': Elizabeth Roche, 'How the nuclear deal thawed India-US relations', *Mint*, 17 July 2015.

421 The US would 'work with friends and allies to adjust international regimes': Ibid.

421 'expeditious consideration of fuel supplies for safeguarded nuclear reactors at Tarapur': 'Fuelling the deal', *Hindustan Times*, 17 March 2006.

422 'acquire the same benefits and advantages as other leading countries with advanced nuclear technology':

'White House Press Release: Joint Statement by President George W. Bush and Prime Minister Manmohan Singh', Office of the Press Secretary, Washington, DC, 18 July 2005, available at <2001-2009.state.gov/p/sca/rls/pr/2005/49763.htm>.

422 India's responsibilities, the statement said, would 'consist of identifying and separating': Ibid.

422 'I (too) couldn't sleep that whole night. I kept praying': Anil Kakodkar to author.

422 'Natwar, how could *you* of all the people agree to this?': Natwar Singh to author, 2018; Singh, *One Life Is Not Enough*, p. 341.

422 'You know there is an undercurrent in the country regarding American policy': Singh, *One Life Is Not Enough*, p. 341.

422 She 'reprimanded' the government for the 18 July 2005 agreement: Natwar Singh quoted by Zoya Hasan, *Congress after Indira: Policy, Power, Political Change (1984–2009)*, New Delhi: Oxford University Press, 2012.

422 though later Sonia Gandhi was to change her mind: Natwar Singh to author, 2018.

423 'Nuclear bargain may prove costly in long run': Siddharth Varadarajan, 'Nuclear Bargain May Prove Costly in Long Run', *The Hindu*, 20 July 2005.

423 'India Compromised' screamed the headline in *The Pioneer*: Ibid.

423 'historic breakthrough': Seema Sirohi, 'Historic breakthrough for India-US relations', *BBC News*, 19 July 2005.

423 'paradigm shift': R. Ramachandran, 'Behind the bargain', *Frontline*, 12 August 2005.

423 'Separating the civil and military would be very difficult, if not impossible': PTI, 'Vajpayee derides nuclear pacts', *Financial Express*, 20 July 2005.

423 Mishra also rubbished the government's claim that India had been recognized as a NWS: Brajesh Mishra, interview with Sheela Bhatt, 'There is a cap on India's strategic programme', *Rediff.com*, 21 March 2006.

423 'and all our future reactors under safeguards': Ibid.

424 They dubbed the deal as a 'strategic sellout': P. K. Iyengar et al., *Strategic Sellout: Indian–US Nuclear Deal*, New Delhi: Pentagon Press, 2009.

424 'There is no need for India to surrender its indigenous nuclear power programme': A. Gopalakrishnan, cited by T. V. Jayan, 'No Bullying', *Down to Earth*, 28 February 2006.

424 'We only want money, not their expertise, technology or science': Ibid.

424 'The CPI(M) expects the government not to undertake unilateral measures which may compromise national interests': 'Indo-US joint statement', 21 July 2005, available at <www.cpim.org/content/indo-us-joint-statement-0>.

425 Again, these negotiations 'went down to the wire': Anil Kakodkar to author.

425 'I have promised our parliament that I will do nothing which will hurt India's strategic programme': 'Prime Minister Dr Manmohan Singh's Interview on Charlie Rose Show', 27 February 2006.

425 'convinced that we were about to sell the store to the Americans': Saran, *How India Sees the World*.

425 India put its civilian reactors under safeguards 'permanently': Saran, *How India Sees the World*.

425 Finally, there was a breakthrough—and it came after Bush intervened personally: Ibid.

425 On 3 March 2006, the two leaders announced the joint agreement on civil nuclear cooperation: PTI, 'Chronology of the Indo-US nuclear deal', *Economic Times*, 9 October 2008.

425 'new romance with this one billion strong democracy': The Associated Press, 'Bush: India a jobs opportunity, not an obstacle', *NBC News*, 3 March 2006.

425 'The people of India deeply love you': 'The People Of India Deeply Love You', *Outlook*, 3 February 2022.

426 First there was the passage of the Hyde Act, which amended the US Atomic Energy Act, 1954: Saran, *How India Sees the World*.

426 But 'extraneous' provisions were thrown in the Hyde Act to satisfy the different lobbies: Ibid, p. 216.

426 Senator Jo Biden, also to become president some years down the line, was 'supportive': Ibid., p. 215.

427 'India had insisted that the safeguards should be India-specific': Shyam Saran to author.

428 'expanded India's foreign policy options': Ibid.

428 'post Cold War India was born': Shekhar Gupta, 'How one big India-US deal gave us six big gains to cheer — including decimation of Left', *The Print*, 22 February 2020.

428 'I want to make him the finance minister of India': P. V. Rao to B. M. Bhama to author.

428 'Manmohan Singh wanted Rao to help regularize his appointment: Ibid.

428 'I know you are going to become PM': B. M. Bhama to author. Bhama was at Rao's residence on the day and was told by this by the latter.

428 'I can say that the idea of (making) Manmohan Singh finance minister was mine': R. Venkataraman to author, 22 August 2022, Delhi; confirmed by Bhuvnesh Chaturvedi to author.

429 He replied quickly, 'It will be a technocrat': Congress leader Harikesh Bahadur to author. Satish Sharma had related the incident to Bahadur.

429 Alexander met Singh at 5 a.m. on 21 June 1991: Alexander, *Through the Corridors of Power*, p. 409.

429 P. V. Narasimha Rao was sworn in as prime minister: Sitapati, *Half-Lion*, p. 103.

429 The rate of growth had declined: The rate of growth had come down to 5 per cent (1990–91) of the GDP, (it collapsed to zero percent in 1991–92); rate of inflation had gone up to 10 per cent in 1990–2001 and rose further to 14 per cent in 1991–92, fiscal deficit was 11.9 per cent of the GDP, for the centre plus states. (Arun Kumar, *Indian Economy since Independence: Persisting Colonial Disruption*, New Delhi: Vision Books, 2013, p. 214.

429 'We now need to obtain foreign exchange by pledging gold': Gayatri Nayak, 'When 47 tonnes of gold was in the middle of road', Economic Times, 5 July 2017; C. Rangarajan, 'How Chandra Shekhar govt and RBI hatched a plan to pledge India's gold in 1991', 26 November 2022.

430   'Why do I have to sign it?': Deepak Nayyar to author, 9 September 2001, New Delhi. Nayyar was chief economic advisor at the time.
430   'on the state of the economy, on our choices, our chances': Ibid.
430   'But I did not know it is such a mess': Ibid.
430   'Once Manmohan Singh heard that PV had signed it, he came running': Ibid.
430   Between 4 and 18 July 1991, the RBI pledged 46.91 tonnes of gold: Shaji Vikraman, 'In fact: How govts pledged gold to pull economy back from the brink', *Indian Express*, 5 April 2017.
430   'Well, that's it. We do it,' he would say: Deepak Nayyar to author, 9 September 2001, New Delhi.
431   'Manmohan Singh...told me that if it was done in several lots': R. Venkataraman to author.
431   'If you have to devalue by Rs 5, why don't you devalue 25 paise a day for twenty days': Ibid.
431   'We told the prime minister that it would be unmitigated disaster if we did what RV wanted': Deepak Nayyar to author, 9 September 2001, New Delhi.
431   'The first step of devaluation was done to test the waters': Shaji Vikraman, '25 years on, Manmohan Singh has a regret: In crisis, we act. When it's over, back to status quo', *The Indian Express*, 24 July 2016.
431   The devaluation had already been carried out by 9 a.m.: Jairam Ramesh, *To the Brink and Back, India's 1991 story*, New Delhi: Rupa Publications, 2015.
431   Was Manmohan Singh the 'real star' of the second stage of devaluation: BS Reporter, 'Who was the real star of 2-stage rupee devaluation in 1991', *Business Standard*, 31 August 2015.
432   He was to change his opinion when he became finance minister—his turnaround was criticized: George Fernandes, 'A Statement on Industrial Policy', *Lokayan Bulletin*, November–December 1991,Vol. 9.6, 1991, p. 24.
432   Chandra Shekhar, under whom he had served as chief economic advisor, accused him of withholding from him: Chandra Shekhar speaking during the Budget debate in Parliament, July 1991.
432   'We must not apportion blame': Deepak Nayyar to author, 9 September 2001, New Delhi.
432   'He used to touch Rao's feet': Bhuvnesh Chaturvedi to author.
433   'system of scholarships' for poor students that existed in India at the time: 'Interview of Prime Minister Dr Manmohan Singh on Charlie Rose Show', 21 September 2004, Media Center, Ministry of External Affairs, Government of India.
433   'I could never have afforded to go to Oxford or Cambridge on the basis of resources at my disposal': Ibid.
433   'I do believe that capitalism has shown a great deal of dynamism': Ibid.
433   'he has been a winner all his life': Ritu Sarin, 'Mrs Singh opens her heart and their album', *The Indian Express*, 20 May 2004.
434   'It is not true that I am politically naive': 'Interview of Prime Minister Dr Manmohan Singh on Charlie Rose Show', 21 September 2004.
434   She used to say that when she was tense, she would blink more frequently: Sonia Gandhi to author during a conversation, 2004.
434   The Congress tally was 145 seats, 7 more than that of the BJP: 'Statistical Report on General Elections, 2004 to the 14th Lok Sabha: Volume I', Delhi: Election Commission of India, 2004, available at <eci.gov.in/files/file/4126-general-election-2004-vol-i-ii-iii>.
435   'We have done it,' she said: Rasheed Kidwai, *Sonia: A Biography*, New Delhi: Penguin Books, 2011.
435   Along with its pre-poll allies, the Congress had garnered 222 seats: E. Sridharan, 'Electoral Coalitions in 2004 General Elections: Theory and Evidence', *Economic and Political Weekly*, Vol. 39, No. 51, 2004, p. 5419.
435   The four Left parties—CPI (M), CPI, RSP, and Forward Bloc—had surprisingly totted up 59 seats: 'Statistical Report on General Elections, 2004 to the 14th Lok Sabha: Volume I'.
435   With UP accounting for 15 per cent of the seats in the Lok Sabha, the SP hoped to emerge as the kingmaker in Delhi: Sunita Aron, Akhilesh Yadav: Winds of Change, Tranquebar, 2013, p. 312. Also 'India: Smaller parties hope to play critical role in elections—2004-04-13', voanews.com, 29 October 2009.
435   Within hours of the results, the top brass of the CPI (M) and CPI were huddled together at A. K. Gopalan Bhavan: Zee News, 14 May 2004.
435   The Left had decided even before the elections to support a secular government: Prakash Karat to author, December 2020.
435   support it from 'outside': Support from 'outside' is backing given to a government by a party or a group of parties without joining the ministry and becoming responsible for its actions.
436   She appointed Manmohan Singh to head the group to formulate the CMP: 'CMP to be drafted under Manmohan Singh: Pawar', *Zee News*, 14 May 2004.
436   He moved through journalist Santosh Bhartia, who was close to Singh: Santosh Bhartia, *VP Singh, Chandra Shekhar, Sonia Gandhi aur Main*, Warriors Victory, 2021, pp. 460–62.
436   He spoke at length about why Sonia Gandhi was the best choice for prime minister: Sheela Bhatt, 'The Case for Sonia Gandhi', *Rediff.com*, 14 May 2004.
436   'the oldest Congress member in the Parliament' and yet 'one of the newest members in the Lok Sabha': Pranab Mukherjee, *The Coalition Years: 1996–2012*, Delhi: Rupa Publications, 2017, p. 68.
436   It was a vote to create an 'inclusive, secular and united' India: Randeep Ramesh, 'Sonia Gandhi promises "secular" rule', *The Guardian*, 16 May 2004.
437   They were the Rashtriya Janata Dal (with 24 MPs): 'Statistical Report on General Elections, 2004 to the 14th Lok Sabha: Volume I'.
437   Patel okayed Amar Singh's entry: Ambika Soni to author.
437   But Sonia Gandhi did not even look at Amar Singh that evening, as he sat down: Vinod Sharma, 'How Amar shared dinner table with Sonia, *Hindustan Times*, 18 May 2004.

437   Sonia Gandhi was unusually reclusive at the dinner that evening: A. B. Baradhan to author.
437   it was he who had prevailed upon Ram Vilas Paswan to join the government: Sonia Gandhi to author, 2004.
438   'Kuch tajjub toh hua ki kaise hogaya yeh': Ritu Sarin, 'Manmohan returned my call past 11 pm, he praised my work, said he will carry it forward', *Indian Express*, 21 May 2004.
438   'I will only wear white, sleep on the bare floor and eat only roasted chana (gram)': 'When Sushma Swaraj threatened to shave off her head', *India Today*, 7 August 2019.
438   'If after 60 years of independence we coronate another foreigner for the top': Ibid.
438   A foreigner will be 'privy to all the defence secrets': PTI, 'Swaraj meets President to protest Gandhi becoming PM', *The Tribune*, 18 May 2004.
438   Uma Bharati, resigned as chief minister of Madhya Pradesh 'to uphold the dignity and honour of 100 crore Indians': Ashok Damodran, 'Opposition plays foreign-origin card to stop PM-elect Sonia Gandhi from taking office', *India Today*, 31 May 2004.
438   scores of women in Delhi held knives to their wrists to draw out their own blood: Ibid.
438   'It must have been around 2 p.m.': Natwar Singh to author, 21 June 2018, New Delhi.
439   'In six months, you will be killed': Ibid.
439   'He gave Sonia 24 hours to decide': Singh, *One Life Is Not Enough*, p. 319.
439   'Sonia was visibly agitated and in tears': Ibid; Natwar Singh to author, 21 June 2018, reconfirmed 29 May 2022.
439   'What could you say? It was a very difficult fifteen to twenty minutes': Ibid., reconfirmed in 2020. Also discussed in Singh, *One Life Is Not Enough*, p. 319.
439   'Priyanka did say something like "Rahul is against it"': Natwar Singh to author 21 June 2018, reconfirmed in 2022.
439   'We asked Sonia to go inside': Ibid.
439   'Basically her son made the decision for her': Ibid.
439   'As a mother it was impossible for her to ignore Rahul': Singh, *One Life Is Not Enough*.
439   Sonia Gandhi had called up Vajpayee and sought his 'ashirwad': K. Subrahmanyam to author, 13 February 2005, New Delhi.
439   'You will divide the country and could end up straining the loyalty of the civil services': Ibid.
439   He was touched by her gesture—and many saw it as a sign that 'India's democracy was safe': Ibid.
440   Seven members of the family ruled or wielded power and influence of an unprecedented kind over a large country for over a century: Natwar Singh to author, 29 May 2022, New Delhi.
440   'I have requested Dr Manmohan Singh to take over as prime minister': Natwar Singh to author, 21 June 2018, reconfirmed in 2022, New Delhi.
440   'Manmohan Singhji has no right to say "No"': Ibid.
440   'I got dirty looks from Pranab Mukherjee': Ibid.
441   'You must do it in a way that it is remembered by posterity': Ambika Soni to author.
441   'You should formulate something which will strike an emotional chord with people': Ambika Soni to author.
441   'Her children did not want her to become prime minister, they feared for her life': V. P. Singh to author.
441   'what can we do if her children feared for her life and did not want her to become PM?': Somnath Chatterjee to author.
442   'Why did you not tell us earlier? We have learnt about it from TV': Natwar Singh to author, 21 June 2018, reconfirmed in 2022, New Delhi.
442   they had given their support to Sonia Gandhi, not to someone else: Singh, *One Life Is Not Enough*, pp. 330–31.
442   West Bengal chief minister Jyoti Basu, who was in Delhi that day, expressed 'disappointment (with her decision)': Prakash Karat to author, 4 December 2020.
442   'It was a fait accompli presented to her party, the UPA and the supporting Left parties': Ibid.
442   They discussed 'the most difficult decision of their lives': Sheela Bhatt, 'Ahmed Patel had a sense of Congress' history, and future challenge', *Indian Express*, 26 November 2020.
442   'I will meet the president again tomorrow to complete the negotiations': Author was part of media present outside Rashtrapati Bhavan that day.
442   'Mrs Gandhi came to Rashtrapati Bhavan along with Dr Manmohan Singh': A. P. J. Abdul Kalam, *Turning Points: A Journey Through Challenges*, New Delhi: HarperCollins, 2011.
443   'This was definitely a surprise to me and the Rashtrapati Bhavan secretariat had to rework the letter': Ibid.
443   'If she had made any claim for herself, I would have had no option but to appoint her': Ibid.
443   'I was always certain that if ever I found myself in the position that I am in today': '"My Own Inner Voice"', *Outlook*, 3 February 2022.
443   'Sonia had seized the moral "high ground"': 'Stunning Political Sacrifice', *The Hindu*, 19 May 2004.
443   *The Nation* of Pakistan called it an 'astute' move: Rajeev Sharma, 'World Press salutes Sonia', *The Tribune*, 19 May 2004.
443   *India Today* described it as 'strategic renunciation': Prabhu Chawla, 'Sonia Gandhi declines PM post, anoints Manmohan Singh to head govt', *India Today*, 31 May 2004.
443   'well-calculated assessment of the political forces lined up against her': 'The lady vanishes', *The Times*, 19 May 2004.
444   only person in Indian history to have turned down prime ministership 'not once but twice': 'Editorial', *Hindustan Times*, 19 May 2004, quoted in 'The Editor Press Review India': *The Guardian*, 20 May 2004. Although Sonia was the only politician to have turned down the offer of the prime ministership twice,

in the history of Indian politics there were others who had refused it as well—Jyoti Basu had done so in 1996 as had V. P. Singh in the same year when the United Front, in a position to form a government, had requested both of them, one after the other, to helm the government; both refused.

444   The Congress managers went into overdrive to laud her 'sacrifice': M. L. Fotedar to author.

444   A simple Punjabi meal was cooking in the Singh household that day: Sarin, 'Mrs Singh opens her heart and their album'.

444   'If I was your daughter would you advise me to come into politics?': P. V. Rao to author, informal conversation.

445   But even during those dark years, she did not rule out a political role for herself: Fotedar, *The Chinar Leaves*, p. 296.

445   'It is upto them to decide': Sonia Gandhi to author, in conversations in 2003, New Delhi.

445   both of which she headed after Rajiv's death: Kidwai, *Sonia*.

445   she expressed her unhappiness over the tardy progress made in the Rajiv Gandhi assassination probe: Bhuvnesh Chaturvedi to author.

445   'I am not Nehru's daughter': Sonia Gandhi to author. Also quoted in Neerja Chowdhury, 'Third Man', *The Caravan*, 1 April 2014.

446   'She would read the speech aloud and I would time it': Singh, *One Life Is Not Enough*, p. 312.

446   'I don't talk much. It is she who talked': Sonia Gandhi to author. The infamous 'guest house' incident in Lucknow in 1995, when Samajwadi Party goons surrounded a guest house, forcing Mayawati to lock herself in a room. She alleged they would have killed her, if she had not been rescued. The episode had traumatized her for years. (Ravish Tiwari, 'The story of the Guest House', *Indian Express*, 16 January 2019.)

446   reversing the Congress's 'go-solo' policy of 6 September 1998: : The Congress's go solo policy adopted at the party session in Pachmari was abandoned in July 2003 at its meeting in Shimla. But many felt that joining coalitions for power had led to the Congress's decline. (Sidharth Mishra, 'Why Congress should look at Pachmarhi and Shimla to boast its electoral chances', *Firstpost*, 11 May 2022.)

447   Her coterie made no secret of the fact that the PM would get on with 'governance': Ahmed Patel to author.

447   'the decision of who (was) going to be in his cabinet was not (going to be) his alone': Montek Singh Ahluwalia to author, 29 September 2021, reconfirmed 2022. Also see Montek Singh Ahluwalia, *Backstage: The Story Behind India's High Growth Years*, New Delhi: Rupa Publications, 2020.

447   They did not want to come across as being too deferential: Shiv Kumar to author.

448   'It was a no brainer that it would come up for discussion at the first meeting of the NAC': Anonymous NAC member to author.

448   'The prime minister will see us at 4 p.m. today': Ibid.

448   'Sonia Gandhi was seen like a god, at the time': Ibid.

449   'Even if he had not been FM or RBI governor, how could a PM be asking such a question': Ibid.

449   It aimed at enhancing the 'livelihood security of the households in rural areas': Ministry of Law and Justice, 'The National Rural Employment Guarantee Act, 2005', *The Gazette of India*, 7 September 2005, accessed 23 June 2022, available at <rural.nic.in/sites/default/files/nrega/Library/Books/1_MGNREGA_Act.pdf>.

449   On 5 September 2005, the president gave his assent to it: Ibid. It was later, in February 2008, that Sonia Gandhi's son Rahul Gandhi, an MP, was to step up pressure on the government to make NREGA applicable all over the country. He called on the prime minister with a group of younger MPs on 29 February 2008 and asked that the programme be universalized. The prime minister could not say 'no' to Rahul, which, in this author's opinion, likely had Sonia's approval.

450   She would often write to ministers as NAC chairperson: Anonymous NAC member to author.

450   The BJP took swipes at Sonia Gandhi and called her a 'Super Prime Minister': PTI, 'NAC unconstitutional, Sonia super PM: BJP', Times of India, 18 July 2004.

450   Critics dubbed the NAC as an 'alternative...cabinet': Rasheed Kidwai, *24 Akbar Road: A Short History of the People behind the Fall and Rise of the Congress*, Delhi: Hachette, 2011.

450   NAC was 'disparagingly' referred to as 'Sonia's jholawalla crowd': Priya Sehgal, 'Sonia Gandhi resigns as NAC chief, government leaves 11 member body headless', *India Today*, 17 April 2006,

450   'The NAC is useful only if Soniaji is heading it. Otherwise it has no meaning': Ibid.

450   'Economic growth created an opening and Mrs Gandhi stepped in, with her commitment to social policy': Jean Drèze to author, 9 November 2020.

451   'So be it': Manini Chatterjee '"Anguished" PM to Left: If you want to withdraw, so be it', *The Telegraph*, 11 August 2007.

451   'Who is Doctor sahib to decide about alliances, that is the job of the party': Ahmed Patel to author.

451   'How can the PM be so irresponsible?': Ibid.

452   'I was told to come to his office in Parliament House at 12': Manini Chatterjee to author.

452   Baru okayed what she had noted down: Sanjaya Baru to author.

452   'I told them (the Left) it is not possible to renegotiate the deal': Chatterjee '"Anguished" PM to Left: If you want to withdraw, so be it'.

452   'I had been sitting with him (PM) the previous evening': Sanjaya Baru to author, 25 September 2020.

452   'As far as the approach to the government is concerned, we will take our own counsel.' 'Prakash Karat on PM's statement', 11 August 2007, available at <www.cpim.org/content/prakash-karat-pms-statement >.

452   to go to the IAEA for an 'India specific safeguard agreement', and then to the NSG for a 'waiver': 'PM looks at mid-July deadline for saying 123', *Economic Times*, 23 June 2008.

452   'We should be prepared...to try and thwart the deal,' the CPM's apex body resolved, 'even to withdraw

support': CPM press conference, 19 June 2008.

453 As he and the PM watched Karat's press conference, Baru recalled, 'I could see the PM turn red': Sanjaya Baru to author.

453 He planned it only with his media advisor, Sanjaya Baru: Ibid.

453 'No stop, no rewind...the coalition manages to pause for breath': Smita Gupta, 'Blinkmanship', *Outlook*, 10 September 2007.

454 'For us, it all started when Pranab Mukherjee went to Washington in June 2005': Prakash Karat to author, 4 December 2020.

454 'You had told us it was an exploratory visit': Ibid.

454 'The nuclear deal was a quid pro quo': Ibid.

454 Congress leadership asked nuclear scientist Raja Ramanna: Ibid.

455 Manmohan Singh had wanted Montek Singh Ahluwalia as finance minister: Anonymous sources in the Congress.

455 'offered me tea and biscuits': Ahluwalia, *Backstage*, p. 236.

455 'Sardar to Sardar' bonhomie which had swung the appointment: Anonymous sources in the Congress.

455 in person he was gentle—and a thorough gentleman: D. P. Tripathi to author; Kishore Chandra Deo to author.

455 about 'not moving into the American orbit': Prakash Karat to author.

455 'a strategic partnership with the US': Indo-Asian News Service, 21 May 2008

455 'We cut that sentence out': Prakash Karat to author, 4 December 2020.

456 'He knew the Left, and understood it': Ibid.

456 'The preamble of the Hyde Act made it clear that we will work to isolate Iran': Ibid.

456 In response to the Left's criticism, the prime minister told parliament that the Hyde Act was not binding: A. B. Bardhan, 'Why The Stand-Off?', *Mainstream*, Vol XLV, No.37, 4 September 2007.

456 The Left's opposition to the nuclear deal, he heard Sonia Gandhi say on television, was 'not unreasonable': Varghese K George, 'Sonia was initially against nuclear deal, says book', *Hindustan Times*, 20 October 2012.

456 The government, she promised, would work for a 'consensus': '"Confrontation is not coalition dharma"', *Hindustan Times*, 12 October 2007.

456 And if the nuclear deal did not go through, he added, 'it will not be the end of life': PTI, 'N-deal failure would not be the end of life: PM', *Times of India*, 12 October 2007.

456 'It is a suggestion for action': Ibid.

457 'I completely agreed with her': Montek Singh Ahluwalia to author, 29 September 2021.

457 'We had been opposed to the government going to the IAEA': Prakash Karat to author.

458 'That's where they betrayed us.... (What) happened between November 2007 and June 2008 is the real story': Ibid.

458 The prime minister became assertive again in February and March 2008: Ibid.

458 Biden and his colleagues alerted Manmohan Singh that unless he pressed the accelerator: Sanjaya Baru to author.

458 'We were aware of the (tight) timetable': Montek Singh Ahluwalia to author, 29 September 2021.

458 'We believe the Americans put their foot down': Prakash Karat to author.

459 'The PM fell for it hook line and sinker': Anonymous senior Congress leader to author.

459 'I told Amar Singh, if you help Manmohan Singh, you will go down in history': M. K. Narayanan to author, 8 August 2022, telephonic conversation, Chennai.

459 'Getting MK Narayanan on board..."not tangentially but centrally".... was a very important strategic decision': Montek Singh Ahluwalia to author, 29 September 2021.

459 'I knew where all the pieces were on the chessboard': Ibid.

459 'In 2004, I had suggested his name to Sonia Gandhi, drawing her attention to his proximity to the Gandhi family': Natwar Singh to author.

459 'doing an elaborate namaste to her': Sanjaya Baru to author.

460 An upset Saran met the prime minister; he wanted to know why he had been pushed out: Saran, *How India Sees the World*.

460 'convinced that we were about to sell the store to the Americans': Saran, *How India Sees the World*.

460 'Narayanan made himself the principal interlocutor at a certain stage': Montek Singh Ahluwalia to author, 29 September 2021.

460 'If I wanted them to make a change, they'd trust me.': M. K. Narayanan to author, 8 August 2022, telephonic conversation, Chennai.

460 'I want that deal.': Baru, *The Accidental Prime Minister*, p. 217.

460 'he has communion with God almighty every day': M. K. Narayanan to author, 8 August 2022, telephonic conversation, Chennai.

460 'deal could not be repeated without George Bush and Manmohan Singh': Ibid.

460 'I am committed to him. Help him out': Ibid.

460 'But...the PM and the President were on the same wave length, (and) it became easier to deal with (a difficult) situation': Ibid.

461 'Oh, the PM and his nuclear deal': Anonymous senior Congress leader to author.

462 the BJP had dubbed Manmohan Singh a 'lame duck': PTI, 'PM a lame duck, allies opportunistic, says BJP', *Rediff.com*, 22 May 2008.

462 possibility of Rahul Gandhi 'taking over as prime minister soon': Anonymous senior Congress leader to author.

462 '[But] time tells how effective is his leadership': PTI, 'Sonia praises PM at UPA dinner', *Rediff.com*, 22 May 2008.

462 'But Dr Manmohan Singh never uttered one word against her': Top Congress leader who chose to remain anonymous to author.

462 'We will go soon,' he told them: SP MP who chose to remain anonymous to author.

463 But they had 'underestimated Manmohan Singh's wiliness': Manini Chatterjee to author.

463 'Amar Singh used to keep us informed about what was going on': Prakash Karat to author.

463 The PM had tried to convince him that 'the nuclear deal was in the national interest': Ibid.

463 'And he hinted that they might move off': Ibid.

464 'Let me tell you it was George Bush and Amar Singh': Sanjaya Baru to author, 25 September 2020.

464 'you have to think of what you can give them, not what you can get from them': Amar Singh to Harikesh Bahadur, who shared this with the author.

465 'I first took him to meet Chandra Shekhar': Harikesh Bahadur to author.

465 Amar Singh would later persuade Chandra Shekhar to withdraw the cases against Amitabh Bachchan: Vir Sanghvi, 'The Rise And Fall Of Amar Singh', *Hindustan Times*, 5 August 2020. For years afterwards, Amar Singh would tell the story of how he personally carried the government file relating to a case against the Bachchans around till Chandra Shekhar agreed to sign it and close the case.

465 'Brokering will then start in the party': B. M. Bhama to author.

465 On one occasion, Amar Singh was trying to help Amitabh Bachchan: Prasad, *Wheels behind the Veil*.

465 Senior SP leaders—Azam Khan, Raj Babbar, Shahid Siddiqui—left the party because of him: 'Mulayam's bid to regain Muslim support', *Milli Gazette*, 4 Dec 2012.

466 like 'bade bhaiya' taking care of 'chote bhaiya': Jaya Bachchan to author.

466 Amar Singh had telephoned Prakash Karat, and told him that he was going to invite Bill Clinton to dinner: Prakash Karat to author.

466 'It was quite hilarious': Ibid.

466 'It was a sit-down dinner in the open': Peter Schweizer, *Clinton Cash: The Untold Story of How and Why Foreign Governments and Businesses Helped Make Bill and Hillary Rich*, New York: HarperCollins, 2015.

466 'where he was introduced to an obscure member of Indian Parliament named Amar Singh': Ibid.

466 'brushing the confetti off her jacket': Arati R. Jerath, 'Amar Singh dreams big', *DNA*, 19 November 2013.

466 Amar Singh would go on to rescue the Manmohan Government in the 'cash for vote case': Amar Singh was arrested in 2011 for alleged of payment of huge sums of money to bribe the MPs to vote for the government.

466 it was the UPA government that was tainted: Amar Singh to author, February 2020, telephonic conversation, Singapore.

467 'You know, I could have acted my own role better in that film than the person who you had': Sanjaya Baru to author.

467 the wedding reception of his daughter Sarika: Sarika was a name suggested by Indira Gandhi, after the Gandhi family's 'kuldevi' in Kashmir. Mrs Gandhi wanted to name her granddaughter Sarika but Rajiv and Sonia had decided on Priyanka for her. (B. M. Bhama, now in the BJP, to author. He was once very close to R. K. Dhawan and later to Captain Satish Sharma. Also confirmed by Anil Bali to author.)

468 'I happened to be in the room at the time': B. M. Bhama to author, 17 October 2020, telephonic conversation.

468 The PM must have known that there were photographers: PMO sources to author.

468 he had CBI cases against him in India: 'How CBI gave clean chit to Chatwal', *Governance Now*, 30 January 2010.

468 he attended the wedding of the hotelier's son, Vikram, in Delhi: Deborah Schoeneman, 'Vikram's Big Fat Sikh Wedding', *New York*, 2 March 2006.

468 But the prime minister did not pay any heed to the advice: Anonymous sources close to Manmohan Singh.

468 'There were few well-known Sikhs the prime minister did not give an appointment': Anonymous senior Congress leader to author, also Sanjaya Baru to author.

469 The Indian government would go on to drop the legal cases against Sant Chatwal: 'How CBI gave clean chit to Chatwal'.

469 would even be awarded one of the country's highest civilian honours, the Padma Bhushan: Vir Sanghvi, 'How did this man get a Padma?', *Hindustan Times*, 31 January 2010.

469 The prestigious civilian award was given to Sant Chatwal at the instance of the prime minister: TNN, 'PMO defends Padma for Sant Chatwal', *Economic Times*, 28 Jan 2010.

469 'No tainted person should be given this award': Congress voices opposition to Chatwal's Padma Award, *Hindustan Times*, 27 January 2010.

469 'it would not be appropriate to bestow a Padma award on Mr Chatwal': Siddharth Varadarajan, 'Don't honour Chatwal, Indian envoy told PMO', *The Hindu*, 1 February 2010.

469 He expressed his 'sincere appreciation' to Chatwal for his 'personal efforts': PTI, 'Over 300 letters of support to Chatwal submitted to US court', *Times of India*, 27 October 2014.

469 'to raise awareness about the Indo–US nuclear deal': Sarah Jacob, 'I am proud of what I have done: Chatwal to NDTV', *NDTV.com*, 13 February 2010.

470 'It has become untenable for me to continue': Baru, 'Singh Is King', *The Accidental Prime Minister*.

470 'What the Left wants is not possible': Ibid.

470 'because the position he is taking is very reasonable': Montek Singh Ahluwalia, 29 September 2021.

470 'Either I get this done, or I don't get this done': Ibid.

470 'After that, we will see,' he told them: Prakash Karat to author.

470   'We cannot make him (Manmohan Singh) change his mind': Ibid.

470   '(What you are witnessing) is the fury of a silent man': Ibid.

470   'Resignation' was a weapon Manmohan Singh had deployed several times in the past: 'From PM To Simply Dr Singh Again?', *Outlook*, 29 October 2007.

471   Rajiv Gandhi, then PM, had called the Planning Commission members 'a bunch of jokers': Shivani Singh, 'Not really a 'bunch of jokers', *Times of India*, 18 July 2004.

471   As PM, he had threatened to resign when the Left tried to block Indo-US military exercises: 'From PM To Simply Dr Singh Again?'.

471   The voice on the other end of the phone said he was a 'friend' of Amar Singh: Sanjaya Baru to author. Baru was not prepared to say more about the identity of the 'friend'.

471   the caller could have been Amar Singh himself: B. M. Bhama to author.

471   the PM might want to speak to Amar Singh and wish him a 'speedy recovery': Sanjaya Baru to author.

471   'I can't say anything till Amar Singh comes back from the US': Prakash Karat to author.

471   When Amar Singh came back from the US, he told the media that the situation called for all the 'secular forces' to unite: Baru, 'Singh Is King', *The Accidental Prime Minister*.

471   'briefed them on the nuclear deal': Ibid.

472   It was M. K. Narayanan's idea to get former president A. P. J. Abdul Kalam to issue a statement in favour of the deal: Anonymous Congress leader to author.

472   He hurried into Sanjaya Baru's room and handed him a statement which had to be issued immediately to the media: Baru, *The Accidental Prime Minister*.

472   'I told Joydeep Sarkar (the PM's secretary) that the Left parties will now withdraw their support': Manini Chatterjee to author.

473   In other words, they would back Mulayam Singh Yadav as prime minister: Jaswant Singh to author.

473   Ahmed Patel, B. S. Hooda, R. K. Dhawan, and Satish Sharma handled the operation: B. M. Bhama to author.

473   Wikileaks cables leaked in 2011 were to reveal that massive sums of money: 'US embassy cables: Indian MPs "paid off by Congress party" ahead of nuclear vote', *The Guardian*, 18 March 2011; 'Full text of WikiLeaks cable on trust vote controversy', *NDTV.com*, 17 March 2011.

473   The sting, it was said at the time, was the brainchild of Arun Jaitley: Shantanu Guha Ray, 'Cash-for-votes scam: The deadly secrets of sting Singh', *India Today*, 15 August 2011.

473   Mulayam Singh Yadav had put forth two conditions for the SP's support: Sanjaya Baru to author, 25 September 2020.

473   would 'not be pursued': Anonymous PMO sources to author.

473   'I was standing there and saw them as they got into their big white Mercedes': Sanjaya Baru to author, 25 September 2020.

474   Of the factors working in India's favour, the most important was Mohamed ElBaradei: Anonymous PMO sources to author.

474   The smaller European countries saw themselves as the 'Ayatollahs of non-proliferation': Montek Singh Ahluwalia to author.

475   The delegation would meet in the Indian Embassy during the day: Shivshankar Menon to author, 10 October 2021.

475   The Chinese had previously objected to India getting parity of status with Nuclear Weapon States without signing the NPT: Vijay Gokhale, '123 Deal: The Big Turnabout', *The Long Game: How the Chinese Negotiate with India*, New Delhi: Penguin Random House, 2011.

475   'It was treated at par with a state visit': Anonymous Congress sources to author.

475   'fundamental concerns' about the Indo-US deal: Gokhale, *The Long Game*, p. 100.

475   As the night of 5 September 2008 wore on, the Indian ambassador to Austria had biryani cooked and packed at the embassy: Anonymous sources in the Indian Embassy in Vienna to author.

476   'You should speak to Hu Jintao directly,' Bush advised him: MEA sources in the know to author.

476   The Chinese side was 'cold' to the idea. The PMO tried once again: Ibid.

476   'Back in July 2008, the Chinese had told me—I had gone there—we will not be the last ones standing (against the waiver) if others drop off': Shivshankar Menon to author, 10 October 2021.

476   Bush then called up Hu Jintao personally: Montek Singh Ahluwalia to author.

476   'it would affect the overall India–China relations': Gokhale, '123 Deal: The Big Turnabout', *The Long Game*.

477   'Congratulations,' he said. 'We have done it': Shivshankar Menon to author, 10 October 2021.

477   'did not include or exclude anything': Ibid.

477   'We negotiated separately with each country': Anil Kakodkar to author.

477   'strengthen' its guidelines and make the transfer of ENR technologies contingent on the signing of the NPT: Siddharth Varadarajan, 'NSG ends India's "clean" waiver', *The Hindu*, 24 June 2011.

477   He and President George W. Bush hoped to ink the nuclear deal while Dr Singh was in the US: Shyam Saran to author, 22 October 2020.

478   'This has taken a lot of work on both our parts': Office of the Press Secretary, 'President Bush Meets with Prime Minister Singh of India', The White House, 25 September 2008, accessed 26 June 2022, available at <georgewbush-whitehouse.archives.gov/news/releases/2008/09/20080925-11.html>.

478   The meeting was followed by dinner at the Old Family Dining Room: PTI, 'Bush hosts dinner for Manmohan Singh', *India Today*, 26 September 2008.

478   'You are a calming influence on me': Montek Singh Ahluwalia to author, 29 September 2021; Shyam Saran to author, 22 October 2020.

478   'Mr Prime Minister, we have done some heavy lifting (for you) to get this deal through': Shyam Saran to

author, 22 October 2020; Saran, *How India Sees the World*, p. 239.

478   'This is above selling reactors. This is about the relationship between our two countries': Ibid.

478   He said, "This man is my friend. You take good care of him"': Ibid.

479   Signing the Act, Bush said, 'This is a—it's a big deal': Office of the Press Secretary, 'President Bush Signs H.R. 7081, the United States-India Nuclear Cooperation Approval and Nonproliferation Enhancement Act', The White House, 8 October 2008, accessed 24 June 2022, available at <georgewbush-whitehouse. archives.gov/news/releases/2008/10/20081008-4.html>.

479   Manmohan Singh saw the deal as one of the most important decisions of his tenure: Montek Singh Ahluwalia to author, 29 September 2021.

479   In the 2009 elections, the Congress Party came back to power with an increased majority: 'Performance of National Parties', Delhi: Election Commission of India, 2009, available at <eci.gov.in/files/file/2881-performance-of-national-parties>.

479   'technological apartheid' which had kicked into place as a result of sanctions: Montek Singh Ahluwalia to author, 29 September 2021.

479   Since 2008, India has also acquired four nuclear reactors from Russia: Anil Kakodkar to author, 14 October 2021.

480   Other countries began to look at India differently: : Shivshankar Menon to author, 10 October 2021.

EPILOGUE

482   'he will never admit this but he would like to be another Nehru and to surpass him': Karan Singh to author, 16 March 2023, New Delhi.

482   architecture of a 'civilizational state': 'PM Modi: Pioneering the rise of India as a Civilizational State', *India Narrative*, 12 December 2021.

483   Often, they were informed by the PMO about the decisions they should take: Madhuparna Das, 'Modi PMO tends to control everything, ministers seek nod for press meets too, says Anil Swarup', *The Print*, 30 May 2022.

483   Opposition was single-minded in its focus to defeat him, even 'bury' him in a 'kabr': *Hindustan Times*, '"Modi Ki Kabr...": PM rips Cong as credit war over Bengaluru-Mysuru Expressway rages on | Watch', YouTube, 12 March 2023, available at <www.youtube.com/watch?v=e2JsLTTexqI>.

483   'Ek akela kitno par bhari pada': AajTak HD, PM Modi Speech in parliament: '"Desh Dekh Raha Ek Akela Kitno Par Bhari Hai", Jab Seena Thokkar Bole PM Modi', YouTube, 9 February 2023, available at <www. youtube.com/watch?v=NqMSagf3Qmo>.

484   reshaping his 'new BJP': Walter Andersen, Walter Andersen writes: How Narendra Modi reshaped the BJP,, *Indian Express*, 23 July 2022.

484   by way of PR companies and lobbyists to cultify his leadership and magnify his message: Binoy Prabhakar, 'How an American lobbying company Apco Worldwide markets Narendra Modi to the world', *Economic Times*, 9 July 2012; Mitul Thakkar and Binoy Prabhakar, 'Narendra Modi to hire a Delhi-based PR agency with an eye on general elections 2014', *Economic Times*, 4 July 2013.

485   'Whatever you do,' he told the official, 'it has to be bhavya': Anonymous source to author.

485   'Narendra's forte is political marketing': K. N. Govindacharya quoted in Prashant Jha, *How BJP Wins: Inside India's Greatest Election Machine*, Delhi: Juggernaut, 2017.

485   'And therefore politics revolves around images, messages, and signalling': Ibid.

489   'and both will pull together': Gandhi had chosen Nehru over Sardar Patel—for several reasons. While Patel was a skilled negotiator and a better organizer, Nehru, Gandhi felt, would be better able to handle the problems of transition from British rule to Independence. He had been educated at Harrow, Cambridge and London, used the English language with felicity, had a high comfort level with the British, and understood international relations better than Patel. Nehru was also more popular amongst the people, and had a better rapport with the Muslims. Significantly, Gandhi knew that 'Jawahar will never take second place.' (Durga Das, *India from Curzon to Nehru and After*, London: Collins, 1969, p. 230, quoted in Rajmohan Gandhi, *Patel: A Life*, Ahmedabad: Navajivan Publishing House, 1991.)
      Patel's biographer Rajmohan Gandhi noted that 12 out of 15 state Congress Committees had preferred Patel as party president. No PCC had proposed Nehru's name for President. However, D. P. Mishra, Patel's staunchest supporter, who was a member of the Mahakoshal PCC revealed that 'we had no intention of depriving Nehru of future Premiership'. (D. P. Mishra, *Living an Era*, Vol. 2, New Delhi: Vikas, 1978, quoted in Gandhi, *Patel: A Life*.)

489   Gandhi told Patel calmly that his presence in the cabinet—and that of Nehru—was 'indispensable': Gandhi, *Patel: A Life*, p. 467.

489   Within minutes, Patel and his daughter Maniben were back at Birla House: Ibid.

489   'Then he put his grieving head in the Sardar's lap': Ibid., p. 468.

489   That night, on 30 January 1948, they addressed the nation together: Ibid.

489   as he would be depriving the country of the joint leadership (by Nehru and Patel) that was Gandhi's wish: Ibid., p. 469.

489   'I can assure you that you will have that from me': Ibid., p. 470.

490   'I am fully resolved to approach my responsibilities...in this spirit': Ibid.

490   displaced 15 million people on the subcontinent: Shivani Singh, 'Capital gains: How 1947 gave birth to a new identity, a new ambition, a new Delhi', *Hindustan Times*, 24 April 2018.

490   'I never forget a friend and never forgive an enemy': Inder Malhotra, 'A first principles disagreement', *Indian Express*, 3 April 2009.
490   Nehru believed it was a fascist organization: Aditya Mukherjee, Mridula Mukherjee, and Sucheta Mahajan, *RSS, School Texts and The Murder of Mahatma Gandhi: The Hindu Communal Project*, Delhi: Sage, 2008, pp. 69–70.
490   Patel saw it as patriotic but misguided: Neerja Singh, 'Sardar Vallabhai Patel aur Rashtriya Swayam Sevak Sangh (RSS): Ek Vivechan', *Samajik Vimarsh*, Vol. 3, No. 2, 2020, p. 149.
490   banned it for a year and half after Gandhi's assassination: 'The RSS and Sardar Patel: A curious case of the BJP's selective blindness', *The Telegraph*, 31 October 2018.

BIBLIOGRAPHY

Alam, Jawaid (ed.), *Kashmir and Beyond 1966-84: Select Correspondence between Indira Gandhi & Karan Singh*, New Delhi: Penguin India, 2011.

Anand, Eshwar V., and Jayathi, K. (eds.), *A Handbook of Journalism: Media in the Information Age*, New Delhi: Sage Publications, 2018.

Andersen, Walter and Shridhar D. Damle, *The Brotherhood in Saffron: The Rashtriya Swayamsevak Sangh and Hindu Revivalism*, New Delhi: Penguin Random House India, 2019.

Baru, Sanjaya, *1991: How P. V. Narasimha Rao Made History*, New Delhi: Aleph Book Company, 2016.

———*The Accidental Prime Minister: The Making and Unmaking of Manmohan Singh*, New Delhi: Penguin Books, 2014.

Bose, Sumatra, *Transforming India: Challenges to the World's Largest Democracy*, Cambridge, Massachusetts, and London, England: Harvard University Press, 2013.

Carras, Mary C., *Indira Gandhi: In the Crucible of Leadership*, Mumbai: Jaico Publishing House, 1980.

Chandra, Bipan, Mukherjee, Mridula, and Mukherjee, Aditya, *India Since Independence: Revised and Updated*, Delhi: India Penguin, 2008.

Chandra, Bipan, *In the Name of Democracy: JP Movement and the Emergency*, New Delhi: India Penguin, 2017.

Chengappa, Raj, *Weapons of Peace: The Secret Story of India's Quest to be a Nuclear Power*, New Delhi: Harper Collins India, 2000.

Das, Durga, *India from Curzon to Nehru and After*, New York: John Day Publications, 1970.

Dayal, John and Bose, Ajoy, *For Reasons of State: Delhi Under Emergency*, New Delhi: Penguin Random House, 2018.

Dhar, P. N., *Indira Gandhi, the 'Emergency', and Indian Democracy*, New Delhi: Oxford University Press, 2000.

Dutt, Ravi Bajpai and Harivansh, *Chandra Shekhar—The Last Icon of Ideological Politics*, New Delhi: Rupa Publications, 2019.

Falk, Bertil, *Feroze Gandhi: The Forgotten Gandhi*, New Delhi: Roli Books, 2016.

Frank, Katherine, *Indira: The Life of Indira Nehru Gandhi*, New York: Harper Perennial, 2005.

Friedman, Thomas L., *The Lexus and the Olive Tree*, New York: Farrar, Straus, and Giroux, 1999.

Gandhi, Rajmohan, *Patel: A Life*, Ahmedabad: Navajivan Publishing House, 1991.

Genovese, Michael A., and Steckenrider, Janie S. (eds.), *Women as Political Leaders: Studies in Gender and Governing*, New Delhi: Routledge, 2013.

Ghose, Sagarika, *Indira: India's Most Powerful Prime Minister*. New Delhi: Juggernaut, 2018.

Guha, Ramachandra (ed.), *Makers of Modern Asia*, Cambridge, Massachusetts and London, England: The Belknap Press of Harvard University Press, 2014.

Guha, Ramachandra, *India After Gandhi: The History of the World's Largest Democracy*, New York: Harper Perennial, 2008.

Gupta, Virag (ed.), *Ayodhya's Ram Temple in Courts: Judgment and Review*, 3rd edn, New Delhi: Centre for Accountability and Systematic Change, 2019.

Habibullah, Wajahat, *My Years with Rajiv: Triumph and Tragedy*, Delhi: Westland, 2020.

Hangen, Welles, *After Nehru, Who?*, London: Rupert Hart-Davis, 1973.

Henderson, Michael, *Experiment with Untruth: India under Emergency*, Delhi, Bombay, Calcutta, Madras: The Macmillan Company of India, 1977.

Jaffrelot, Christopher, *The Hindu Nationalist Movement in India*, New York: Columbia University Press, 1998.

Jayakar, Pupul, *Indira Gandhi: A Biography*, New Delhi: Penguin Books, 1995.

Jha, Krishna and Jha, Dhirendra K., *Ayodhya: The Dark Night: The Secret History of Rama's Appearance in Babri Masjid*, New Delhi: Harper Collins Publishers India, 2016.

Johnson, Richard L., and Gandhi, Mohandas Karamchand, *Gandhi's Experiments with Truth: Essential Writings by and About Mahatma Gandhi*, Lanham, MD: Lexington Books, 2006.

Kalam, A. P. J. Abdul, *Turning Points*, New Delhi: Harper Collins Publishers India, 2014.

Kalhan, Promilla, *Kamala Nehru: An Intimate Biography*, New Delhi: Vikas Publishing House, 1973.

Kar, Dev, *India: Still a Shackled Giant*, New Delhi: Penguin Portfolio, 2019.

Kasipathi, Kapila, *Tryst with Destiny*, Hyderabad: K.V. Rao, 1970.

Kaul, T. N., *My Years through Raj to Swaraj*, New Delhi: Vikas Publishing House, 1995.

Khurshid, Salman, *Sunrise Over Ayodhya: Nationhood in Our Times*, New Delhi: Vintage Books, 2021.

Kidwai, Rasheed, *24 Akbar Road: A Short History of the People behind the Fall and Rise of the Congress*, New Delhi: Hachette, 2011.

———*Sonia: A Biography*, New India: Viking (Penguin Books India), 2009.

Malhotra, Inder, *Indira Gandhi: A Personal and Political Biography*, New Delhi: Hay House, 2014.

Malkani, K. R., *The Politics of Ayodhya & Hindu-Muslim Relations*, Faizabad: Har Anand Publications, 1993.

Mehta, Vinod, *The Sanjay Story: From Anand Bhavan To Amethi*, New Delhi: HarperCollins, 2012.

Mukherjee, Pranab, *The Dramatic Decade: The Indira Gandhi Years*, New Delhi: Rupa Publications, 2015.

———*The Coalition Years: 1996–2012*, New Delhi: Rupa Publications, 2017.

———*The Turbulent Years: 1980–1996*, New Delhi: Rupa Publications, 2016.

Mukerji, Debashish, *The Disruptor: How Vishwanath Pratap Singh Shook India*, New Delhi: Harper Collins India, 2021.

Mukhopadhyay, Nilanjan, *The RSS: Icons of the Indian Right*, New Delhi: Tranquebar Press, 2019.

Nag, Kingshuk, *Atal Bihari Vajpayee: A Man For All Seasons*, New Delhi: Rupa Publication, 2017.

Nayar, Kuldip, *The Judgement: Inside the Story of the Emergency in India*, New Delhi: Vikas Publishing, 1977.

Nehru, Jawaharlal, *An Autobiography*, London: Bodley Head, 1936.

Noorani, A.G., *The Muslims of India: A Documentary Record*, New Delhi: Oxford University Press, 2003.

Pande, BD, *In the Service of Free India: Memoir of a Civil Servant*, New Delhi: Speaking Tiger, 2021.

Prasad, P. V. R. K., *Wheels Behind the Veil: PMs, CMs and Beyond*, Vijayawada: Emesco Books, 2010.

Ramesh, Jairam, *Intertwined Lives: P. N. Haksar and Indira Gandhi*, New Delhi: Simon & Schuster, 2018.

Rao, P. V. Narasimha, *Ayodhya: 6 December 1992*, New Delhi: India Penguin, 2019.

Rice, Condoleezza, *No Higher Honor: A Memoir of My Years in Washington*, New York: Penguin Random House, 2011.

Sahgal, Nayantara, *Indira Gandhi—Tryst with Power*, New Delhi: India Penguin, 2012.

Sanghvi, Vir, *A Rude Life: The Memoir*, New Delhi: India Viking, 2021.

Saran, Shyam, *How India Sees the World: Kautilya to the 21st Century*, New Delhi: Juggernaut, 2017.

Sharma, Chandrika Prasad, *Poet Politician Atal Bihari Vajpayee: A Biography*, New Delhi: Kitab Ghar Prakashan, 1998.

Singh, Kumar Suresh, *People of India Volume 6: The India's Communities (N-Z)*, New Delhi: Oxford University Press, 1998.

Singh, Valay, *Ayodhya: City of Faith, City of Discord*, New Delhi: Aleph Book Company, 2018.

Sinha, Shakti, *Vajpayee: The Years That Changed India*, New Delhi: Vintage Books, 2020.

Sitapati, Vinay, *Half-Lion: How P. V. Narasimha Rao Transformed India*, New Delhi: India Viking, 2016.

———*Jugalbandi: The BJP before Modi*, New Delhi: Penguin Random House India, 2020.

Srivastava, C. P., *Lal Bahadur Shastri: A Life of Truth in Politics*, New Delhi: Oxford University Press, 1995.

Srivastava, Sushil, *The Disputed Mosque: A Historical Inquiry*, New Delhi: Vistaar Publications, 1992.

Talbott, Strobe, *Engaging India: Diplomacy, Democracy, and the Bomb*, Washington D. C.: Brookings Institution Press, 2004.

Thakur, Janardan, *All the Prime Minister's Men*, New Delhi: Vikas Publishing House, 1977.

———*Prime Ministers: Nehru to Vajpayee*, Mumbai: Eshwar, 1999.

Tharoor, Shashi, *The Paradoxical Prime Minister: Narendra Modi and His India*, New Delhi: Aleph Book Company, 2018.

Ullekh, N. P., *The Untold Vajpayee: Politician and Paradox*. New Delhi: Penguin Random House India, 2018.

Vaishnav, Milan, *When Crime Pays: Money and Muscle in Indian Politics*, New Delhi: Harper Collins Publishers, 2017.

INDEX